SXSW SCRAPBOOK

People And Things That Went Before

★ THE AUSTIN ★
CHRONICLE

South By Southwest
c/o **The Austin Chronicle**
P.O. Box 49066
Austin, Texas 78765

Dear Friend,

Letters announcing South by Southwest: A Regional Music and Media Conference have been sent throughout this area, and already response has exceeded expectations. The conference, projected as a way for everyone from musicians to publishers to writers to booking agents to get together and examine mutual problems and possibilities, will coincide with the Fifth Annual Austin Music Awards Show presented by **The Austin Chronicle.** Several other papers--the **Dallas Observer,** San Antonio's **Current,** Galveston's **In Between, The Times of Acadiana** of Lafayette, La., Denver's **Westword** and New Orleans' **Wavelength**--have already agreed to participate. Requests for registration are arriving regularly. It seems as if everyone agrees that a regional convention where music and media professionals can discuss common concerns, issues and goals is a good idea.

Here's the tentative conference schedule:

Friday, March 13:
        Day: Registration
        Evening: Austin Music Awards show at the Austin Opera House.
            (Registration includes Awards Show ticket)
Saturday, March 14:
        Morning: Meeting featuring opening speaker Huey Meaux,
            Keynote speaker Carl Grasso (IRS RECORDS),
            followed by a panel discussion on: Breaking Out; How a
            local act makes it nationally: the Timbuk 3 story.
        Afternoon: Workshops and Trade Show
        Evening: Cocktail Hour, followed by a Club Crawl
            featuring showcase gigs by local & regional bands.

Sunday, March 15:
        Morning: Final conference meeting
        Afternoon: Softball and barbeque.

For more information you can call Louis Black or Roland Swenson at **The Austin Chronicle** at (512) 473-8200, or write to PO Box 49066, Austin TX 78765.

SXSW SCRAPBOOK

People And Things That Went Before

Edited by Peter Blackstock, Jason Cohen and Andy Smith

ESSEX PRESS

Austin

"We are deployed in the service of one of the greatest healing forces in the world."
■ Rosanne Cash, from her 1991 keynote address

Requests for permission to reproduce material from this work should be sent to:
Essex Press
P.O. Box 4183
Austin, Texas 78765

⊗The paper used in this book meets the minimum requirements of ANSI/NISO Z39.48-1992 (R1997) (Permanence of Paper).

Library of Congress Cataloging-in-Publication Data available online

ISBN: 978-0-292-72675-8
Library of Congress Control Number: 2011921788

Designed by Brad Grulke — emgusa.com

Contents

Acknowledgments

The editors and designer would like to thank SXSW managing director Roland Swenson, who provided invaluable historical background and insight from start to finish; and Scott Schinder and Luke Torn, who helped to gather and proofread the content, respectively.

Also, the many members of the SXSW staff (past and present) who assisted in the research and collection of documents for this book — especially Elizabeth Derczo, Jamie Miller, and Linda Park, as well as Louis Black, Matt Dentler, Andy Flynn, Hugh Forrest, Brent Grulke, Jeff McCord, Janet Pierson, Ron Suman, Ed Ward, and Leah Wilkes.

Many others assisted in various aspects of the process, including Greg Beets, Brian Berger, Stuart Berman, Scott Booker, Andrew Bujalski and Eric Masunaga, Cathy Casey, Richard Dorsett, Yvonne Garrett, Randy Haecker, Ian Johnsen, Gil Kaufman, Andy Langer, Jennifer LaSuprema and Susan LaInferiora, Alison Macor, David Menconi, Rob Moore, Joe Nick Patoski, Chris Riemenschneider, Elizabeth Schmidt and Marie Moore, Ken Weinstein, and Luann Williams.

Members of the University of Texas Press staff also helped to realize this project, particularly Allison Faust and Dave Hamrick.

We're indebted to the spouses of the editors and designer, and of SXSW's co-founders, for their patience and assistance: Susan Shepard (who buried her nose in old program books to help out with the Stats chapters), Lisa Whittington, Jenny Smith, Laura Grulke, Roseana Auten, and Susan Moffat.

And, most importantly, our thanks to the countless SXSW attendees who shared their perspectives and experiences of the past quarter-century with us, and thereby brought these pages to life.

ABOUT THE AUTHORS Peter Blackstock served as SXSW's archivist from 1989 to 1997. After stints with daily newspapers in Austin and Seattle, he co-founded *No Depression* magazine in 1995 and was co-editor and co-publisher until it ceased printing in 2008. Raised in Austin, he has lived in the Seattle and NC Triangle areas since 1991.

An associate panels coordinator for SXSW from 1992-94, Jason Cohen is a longtime freelancer (*The Austin Chronicle*, *Austin American-Statesman*, *Rolling Stone*, *SPIN*) and the author of *Generation Ecch!* and *Zamboni Rodeo*. In February 2011, he moved back to Austin, where he is senior staff writer at TexasMonthly.com.

Andy Smith has been editor of *SXSWORLD* magazine since its inception in 2006. Prior to that, he was associate editor of *Pop Culture Press* magazine and once taught high school journalism. He has lived in Austin off and on since 1991, not coincidentally the same year he first attended SXSW. ∎

Introduction

MY FIRST CAR was a '64 Barracuda my friends dubbed "Old Smokey" because it burned so much oil. Driving home from high school one day I listened to a local top 40 AM station (FM radios in cars were a luxury then) and heard a track by Jerry Jeff Walker, the great Guy Clark song "L.A. Freeway." As the song ended, the announcer said "that was recorded right here in Austin, Texas." I was stunned. In my mind, music on the radio always came from someplace far away, like Hollywood or England. The idea that bands living here and playing in the clubs could also record music in Austin that got played on the radio had never occurred to me.

For the rest of my high school days, and at the University of Texas, I dove head-first into the Austin club scene. I saw countless shows at now-defunct venues such as Castle Creek, the Split Rail, Soap Creek Saloon, the One Knite, Mother Earth and, of course, the Armadillo World Headquarters.

One Sunday in January 1978, I picked up the Austin newspaper and read that the Sex Pistols would be appearing that night at Randy's Rodeo in San Antonio. Tickets $4. Without hesitation, I rounded up my roommates, and we drove down to see the show. My strongest memory from observing the spectacle was thinking, "Nothing will ever be the same again."

The fallout from this show would have a lasting impact, far beyond it being the Sex Pistols' penultimate show. Dozens of kids from Austin, like us, had made the same trek. By that summer, we would find each other again at a UT campus-area bar called Raul's Club. At Raul's I met writers Nick Barbaro and Louis Black, who had been at Randy's Rodeo and would go on to launch *The Austin Chronicle*. I became the manager of the Standing Waves, a popular Austin band who played Raul's every Monday night for a $1 cover.

I spent the next six years of my life traveling around America, learning about the underbelly of the music industry. I experienced a vibrant New York club scene, introduced to venues like the Mudd Club, Hurrah and CBGBs in their heyday. Back in Austin, I met Louis Jay Meyers, who had played banjo in bands I saw when I was a high school student during the Cosmic Cowboy era.

Eventually, I teamed with Louis, Nick and Louis Jay to launch SXSW, an event based on the distillation of all we had learned about music and media and popular culture. It was a big gamble. At times we were afraid. Many others would join us and make a lasting impression on the shape of SXSW.

Our story has a (mostly) happy ending. As I write this, we're working on the 25th edition of SXSW. This book will tell a fraction of the story. ■ Roland Swenson

14,712 That's the final tally in our comprehensive database containing every single musical act that has performed at South By Southwest since 1987. From a couple hundred in those earliest years to the annual counts of more than a thousand in the present day, that massive number provides some sort of qualitative handle on just how many musicians have helped make SXSW what it has been in the past quarter-century. But more meaningful than numbers are the names – and so, in a Quixotic stab at all-inclusiveness, we present to you, within these pages, a complete listing of all 14,712 of those performers. Thousands of them have made multiple appearances. A fair percentage, naturally, were locals from the Austin area, but in the end, they have come from everywhere: What began as regional gradually became global. The one thing they shared, for a few days in March each year, was their destination. For all those who gathered in Austin with them, it was first and foremost these thousands of performers who drew them there. (Our apologies in advance if we've missed a few names; that's probably inevitable with a list this long.) ■

10:21
11:11
7
27
77
100
127
512
1349
1986
1997
6240
#1 Family Mover
Shit and $hine (Smog)
...music video?
//TENSE//
:papercutz
[DARYL]
{{{ SUNSET }}}
¡Viva Malpache!
+/-
... and you will know us by the trail of dead
10 Speed
100 Monkeys
1001 Nights Orchestra
12 Rods
12 Step Rebels
12 Volt Sex
120 Days
12AX7
12th Planet
13 Engines
13ghosts
14K
14KT
15 Minutes
16 Horsepower
16 Tons of Monkeys
16 Volt
17 Hippies
18 Visions
18th Dye
2 Doors Down
2 Nice Girls
2 Skinnee J's
20 Eyed Dragon
20/20
2020Soundsystem
22 Brides
22-20s
22-Pistepirkko
24-7 Cpyz
25 Suaves
28Costumes
2AM Club
2Mex
2Mex & LifeRexall are $martyr

3 Balls of Fire
3 Colors
3 Inches of Blood
3 MG's
3 on a Hill
30 Amp Fuse
303 Infinity
31Knots
33Hz
35 Summers
3D Stereo
3-Day Wheely
3lb. Thrill
3oh!3
3rd Person
400 Blows
40th Day
43 Songs About 43 Presidencies
44 Long
4ize
4th Avenue Jones
50 Foot Wave
50 Mission Crush
50/50
54 Seconds
5th Cliff
6 String Drag
60 Channels a.k.a. The Angel
60 Second Crush
60 Tigres
60 Watt Kid
65daysofstatic
7 Deadly 5
7 Mary 3
7 Shot Screamers
7% Solution
764-HERO
7EVE
7th Annual Guided By Voices Hoot with (8pm) Cocker Spaniels, Hellweg, Leprechaun, Boy, Dr. Dog, Magnapop, Rogers Sisters, The M's, The Lashes, Moonlight Towers, Silos, The Tinys, Robbers on High St., Will Johnson, Carrie Clark, Subset, Bloom,Calexico, Apollo Sunshine, Oranges Band, Bedbug, Jon Auer, Sally Crewe and the Sudden Moves, Adem, Steve Wynn, Jason Faulkner, Swearing at Motorists, Prescott Curlywolf, Fivehead
8 1/2 Souvenirs
8 Foot Sativa

8 or 9 Feet
86ed with Mike Hall, Jon Dee Graham, Alejandro Escovedo, Kathy McCarty, Steve Collier, Kim Longacre & Randy Franklin
88-Keys
8Ball & MJG
90 Day Men
99 pounds
9dw (Nine Days Wonder)

A

A Armada
A Brand
A Classic Education
A Covert Operation
A Cursive Memory
A Day to Remember
a don piper situation
A Don Walser Tribute with The Pure Texas Band plus Slaid Cleaves, Libby Bosworth & Roger Wallace
A Faulty Chromosome
A Fine Frenzy
A Flock of Seagulls
A Frames
A Good Fight
A Gun Called Tension
A Hawk and A Hacksaw
A Loose Affiliation of Saints and Sinners
A Loose Affiliation of Saints and Sinners, Part II
A Murder of Crows
A Night of Reckoning w/ Kevin Welch, Kieran Kane, Mike Henderson, Harry Stinson, Tammy Rogers & Fats Kaplan
A Northern Chorus
A Pink Cloud
A Place to Bury Strangers
A Roman Scandal
A Shoreline Dream
A Skylit Drive
A Sunny Day in Glasgow
A Thousand Knives Of Fire
A Tiger Named Lovesick
A Weather
A. Graham and the Moment Band

A.A. Bondy
a.armada
A.C. Gonzalez
a.i.
A.J. Croce
A.M Interstate
A.U.M.
A3
Aa
AA Sound System
A-Alikes
Aaora
Aaron Blount
Aaron Booth
Aaron Lacrate
Aaron Pfenning
Aaron Robinson
Aaron Thomas
Aarora
Abalone Dots
Abby Travis Foundation
Abe the Assassin
Abe Vigoda
Aberdeen
Aberdeen City
Aberfeldy
Abi Tapia
Abigail Hopkins
Abigail und Hansel
Abigail Warchild
Abigail Washburn
Abigail Washburn & the Sparrow Quartet with Bela Fleck
ABK
About
About 9 Times
Abra Joy Moore
Abra Moore
Abraham Smith
Abram Wilson
Absinthe
Absinthe Minds
Absorption
Abstract Rude
Abstraq The Grindologist
ABSU
Abuse
AC Slater
Acapelicans
Acceptance
Accumen
Ace Ford
Acephale DJs
Acetone
Acetylene
Aceyalone and the Good Brothers
Acid Girls

Acid King
Acid Mothers Temple
Acid Mothers Temple & The Melting Paraiso UFO
Acoustic Junction
Acrylics
Act Of Congress
Act of Faith
Action Action
Actionslacks
Activator
Active Child
Active Radio
Ad Astra Per Aspera
Adam Carroll
Adam Franklin (of Swervedriver) & Bolts of Melody
Adam Franklin from Swervedriver
Adam Green
Adam Heldring
Adam Kesher
Adam Parfrey
Adam Richman
Adam Snyder
Adam Stephens (of Two Gallants)
Adam Tensta
Addicted & Abducted
Adem
Adept
Admiral Radley
Adolfo's Reversal
Adonis Puentes
Adrian Romero
Adrianne
Adrienne Pierce
Adrienne Young & Little Sadie
Adult Rodeo
Adventure
Adventures Of Jet
ADZ
Aequo Animo
Aero Wave
Aerodrone
Aesop Rock
Aesop Rock w/ Rob Sonic & DJ Big Wiz
Aesop Rock with special guest El-P
Afenginn
Afghan Raiders
Afrirampo
Afro Classics
Afrobots
Afrodite
After Forever
After Shock
After The Fall
Afterglow
Afterhours
Afternoons
Against All Authority
Against Me!
Agent 51
Agent Fury
Agent Orange
Agents of Good Roots
Agnes Gooch
Agony Column
Ahleuchatistas
AIDS Wolf
Aimee Mann
Air Tight Alibi
Air Traffic
Air Traffic Control
Air Waves
Air*Head
Airbourne
Airlane (Gary Numan Tribute)
AJ Croce
Akala
AkashA
Akimbo
Akina Adderley & The Vintage Playboys
Ako
Akron/Family
Akwasi Evans
Akwid
Al & The Transamericans
Al Anderson
Al Kapone
Al Letson
Al Perry & Dan Stuart
Alabama Thunderpussy
Alabama3 (acoustic)
A-Laget
Alamo Choir
Alamo Race Track
Alan Munde & Country Gazette
Alan Rhody
Alana Swidler Band
Alash

Alkaline Trio (2004)

Alaska in Winter
Alaska!
Albert & Gage
Albert Collins
Albert Hammond, Jr.
Alberta Cross
Album
Albuquerque Poetry Experiment
Alchemysts
Alcohol Funnycar
Alecia Nugent
Alejandro Escovedo
Alela Diane
Alesana
Alessi's Ark
Alex Ballard & Sugarfoot
Alex Chilton
Alex Cuba
Alex Khoury
Alex Koll
Alex Marquez
Alex Skolnick Trio
Alex Smoke
Alex Woodard
Alexandre Grooves
Alexi Murdoch
Alexia Bomtempo
Alexisonfire
Alfred Flores & Zarabande
Ali Eskandarian
Ali Harter
Alias
Alice & Albert
Alice Donut
Alice Russell
Alice Stuart
Alien Canopy
Alien Crime Syndicate
Alien Love Child
Alien Time Ensemble
Alih Jey
Alina Simone
Alisa Fineman
Alison Rogers
Alkaline Trio
All
All Access
All Else Failed
All Get Out
All In The Golden Afternoon
All Is Well
All Leather
All Natural
All Night
All Night Radio
All Smiles
All Systems Go
All the Saints
All Time Low
All Tiny Creatures
Allen Brown & the Cadillac Dirt Band
Allen Toussaint
Alligator Gun
Allison
Allison Moorer
Allister
Allo Darlin
Allrise
Almighty HiFi
Almost Blue
Aloha
ALOKE
Alpha Rev
Alphabeat
Alsace Lorraine
Altamont
Altan
Alternative Champs
Alvarez Kings
Alvi B. & Positive Attitude
Alvin Crow
Alvin Youngblood Hart
Alyssa Suede
AM
AM Syndicate
AM/FM
Amanda Blank
Amanda Diva
Amanda Palmer
Amanda Shaw and the Cute Guys
Amanda Thorpe
Amandla Poets
Amaral
Amazing Baby
Amberjack Rice
Amber Pacific
Amber Rubarth
Amber Smith
Amber Sunshower
Ambulance Ltd
Ambulette (aka Bella Lea)
Amelia Curran
America Is Waiting
American Analog Set
American Babies
American Bang
American Eyes
American Flamewhip
American Hi-Fi
American Horse
American Mars
American Minor
American Music Club
American Paint
American Princes

American Steel
American Vodka
Amie & Sangeet Millennium
Amigas y su Grupo Ritmo
Amilia K. Spicer
aMiniature
Amir
Amon Tobin
AMOR
Amor Belhom Duo
Amos Garrett
Amos Lee
Amplified Heat
AmpLive
AMPOP
Amstrong
Amy & the Bullets
Amy Allison
Amy Allison & the Maudlins
Amy Annelle
Amy Brackman
Amy Cook
Amy Correia
Amy Farris
Amy Lavere
Amy Millan
Amy Ray
Amy Ray with the Butchies
Amy Rigby
Amy Rohan
Amy Smith
Amy Wadge
Amy Walsh
Amy Winehouse
An Albatross
An Angle
An Horse
Ana Egge
Ana Laan
Ana Silvera
Anadivine
Anais Mitchell
Analogue II
Anamanaguchi
Anathallo
ANAVAN
Anberlin
Ancestors
Anchondo
Anchorsong
And So I Watch You From Afar
And You Will Know Us By The Trail Of Dead
Anders Parker
Andi Hoffmann & B-Goes
Andi Smith
Andre Matthews
Andre Williams
Andrea Echeverri
Andreas & Jag
Andrew
Andrew Bird
Andrew Bird's Bowl of Fire
Andrew Collberg
Andrew Dorff
Andrew Dyken
Andrew "Jr. Boy" Jones
Andrew Kenny (American Analog Set)
Andrew W.K.
Andrew Winton Duo
Andy
Andy Bull
Andy Carlson
Andy Clockwise
Andy Jackson (Hot Rod Circuit)
Andy Kindler
Andy M Stewart with Gerry O' Beirne
Andy Palacio
Andy Pratt
Andy Ritchie
Andy Schneider
Andy Stochansky
Andy Van Dyke Band
Andy White
Andy Wilkinson
Ane Brun
Angel Dean & Sue Garner
Angel Deradoorian
Angel Rot
Angel Tech
Angela McCluskey
Angela Strehli
Angelic Rage
Angelo Spencer
Anger Mgmt
Angie Aparo
Angie Mattson
Angkor Wat
Angry Amputees
Angry Angles
Angry Vs The Bear
Angus & Julia Stone
Angus Adair aka The Svelt Ms Spelt
Ani Difranco
Animal Alpha
Animal Bag
Animal Collective
Animals of the Bible
Anime Winds
Anita Tijoux
Ann Armstrong & Steve Hughes
Ann Armstrong

Ann Beretta
Ann Dejarnett
Ann Powell & Child Bearing Hips
Ann Vriend
Anna Domino
Anna Fermin's Trigger Gospel
Anna Nalick
Anna Rose
Anne Heaton
Anne McCue
Anne Summers
Anneke
Annette Zilinskas
Anni Rossi
Annie
Annie Hayden
Annie Stela
Annihilation Time
Annuals
Annyland
Anodyne
Another Blue Door
Another White Male
Ansia
Anson Funderburgh & The Rockets
Ant Farmers
Ant Man Bee
Antenna
Antennas Up
Anthony Crawford
Anthony Green
Anthony Hamilton
Anthony Mazella
Anthony Snape
Antibalas
Anticon
Antietam
Antigone Rising
Anti-Heros
Antimc
Antipop Consortium
Antiseen
Antler
Anton Bjorkenvall
Antonio Dionisio & MMR
Anuhea
Anya Marina
Anyone
aonami
Apache
Apache Beat
Apaches of Paris
Apathy
Apex
Aphrodite
Apocalyptica
Apollo Sunshine
Apoptygma Berzerk
Apostle of Hustle
Apothecary Hymns
Appeal To Ignorance
Appleseed Cast
Appogee
Appreciation
April Barrows
April Smith and the Great Picture Show
April Verch Band
Apsci
Apulanta
Aqualeo
Aqualung
Aqueduct
Aqui
Arab on Radar
Arab Strap
Arabrot
Arborea
Arbouretum
Arcane
Archer
Archers of Loaf
Archibald Schaffer
Archie Bell
Archie Bronson Outfit
Archie Bunker
Archie Lee
Archie Roach
Architecture in Helsinki
Arctectonics
Arctic Monkeys
Areola 51
Argyles
Ari Hest
Ari Shine
Ariel Abshire
Ariel Pink
Arkells
Arkham
Arling & Cameron
Arlo
Arlo Guthrie
Arm
Armageddon
Armchair Martian
Armor for Sleep
Arms
Arms & Legs
Arms Akimbo
Arms and Sleepers
Army Navy
Army of Freshmen
Army of Me
Army of Ponch
Arno

Arnold Dreyblatt Ensemble
Arp
Arson
Arson Garden
Arson Optics
Art Alexakis
Art Brut
Art in Manila
Art Marvel
Artefacts For Space Travel
Arthur Dodge & the Horsefeathers
Arthur Yoria
ArthurKill
Artifact Shore
Arts the Beatdoctor
Arturo Tappin
As Tall As Lions
Asa
Asakusa Jinta
Asbestos
A-Set
Asexuals
ASG
Ash
Ash Grunwald
Asher Roth
Ashley Cleveland
Ashley Park
Ashtar Command
Ashtray Babyhead
Ashu
Asian Dub Foundation
Asian Mushroom
Asking Alexandria
Asleep At The Wheel
Asleep in the Sea
Aslyn
Asobi Seksu
Asop
Assacre
Asteroid #4
Astra Heights
Astrid
Astrid Swan
Astrograss
Astronautalis
astroPuppees
Astrosoniq
Asylum Street Spankers
At A Loss
At All Cost
at the drive-in
At Versaris
Atari Teenage Riot
Atash
Aterciopelados
Athena
Athlete
Atlas Sound
Atmosphere
Atom and His Package
Atombombpocketknife
Atomic 61
Atomic Deluxe
A-Trak
Attack Attack!
Attack in Black
Attack! Attack! (UK)
Attention
Attic Ted
Attractive and Popular
ATX Records Clique
Au Revoir Simone
Aubrey Dunham
Audacity
Audio 3
Audio Explorations
Audion
Auditrons of Kemetic Suns
Audra
Audra Mae
Audrye Sessions
Augie Meyers
Augustana
Auktyon
Aun
Aunt Beanie's 1st Prize Beets
Aunt Bettys
Aurora
Aurora Plastics Company
Auschwitz 46
Austerity Program
Austin Cunningham
Austin Hartley-Leonard
Austin Theremonic Orchestra
Austin TV
Autolux
Automusik
Autons (TX)
Autumn
Autumn Owls
Aux Raus
AV Okubo
Avail
Avatar
Avenged Sevenfold
Avengers in Sci-Fi
Aveo
Avey Tare
Avi Buffalo
Avotor
Awareness Art Ensemble
Awen
Awesome Color
Awesome Cool Dudes
AwkQuarius
Awkward I

Awol One
Axel K Soundsystem
Ayah
Aynee Osborn & The Steady Band
AYO
Aytobach Kreisor
AZA
Azeda Booth
AZITA
Aziz Ansari
AzTex
Azz Izz Band

B

BLACKIE
B T
B. Dolan
B. Joe
B.J. Porter
B.o.B.
B+
B-1
Baba Yaga
Babe the Blue Ox
Baboon
Baby Chaos
Baby Fox
Baby Gopal
Baby Lemonade
Baby Robots
Baby Teeth
Baby Woodrose
Babydick
Bacchus
Bachelorette
Bacilos
Back Door Slam
Back Drop Bomb
Back in Spades
Back Porch Mary
Back Porch Vipers
Black Stabbath
Back Ted N-Ted
Backseat Goodbye
Backsliders
Backstreet Girls
Backyard Babies
Backyard Tire Fire
Bad Chopper
Bad Girls Upset by the Truth
Bad Livers
Bad Mutha Goose
Bad Rabbits
Bad Rodeo
Bad Sports
Bad Veins
Bad Wizard
Badly Drawn Boy
Baghdad Jones
Baghouse
Bagual
Bahamadia
Bahrain
Bajofondo
Bakelite
Balaclavas
Balance
Balbora
Baldwin Brothers
Bali Girls
Balistica
Balkan Beat Box
Ball Peen
Ballad Shambles
Ballistix
Balloon Guy
Balloonatic
Balmorhea
Bam Bam
Bambi Lee Conway
Bambi Lee Savage
Bamboo Crisis
Band from Hell
Band Marino
Band of Horses
Band of Skulls
Band of Susans
Band of Thieves
Banda de Turistas
Banda Desenhada
Bandit
Bandit Queen
Bandit Teeth
Bane
Bang Bang Bang
Bang Gang
Bang! Bang! Eche!
Bangs
Banjo Or Freakout
Bankroll Jones
Banner Pilot
Baptist Generals
Barandua
Barb Donovan
Barbara Clark
Barbara K
Barbara Lynn
Barbara Manning
Barbara Mason
Barbez
Barcelona
Bardo
Bardo Pond

Bare Jr.
Bare Naked Ladies
Bare Wires
Barely Broke Family
Barely Broke Family featuring Redd
Barfield
Bargain Music
Various MFS Artists
Bar-Kays
Barking Tribe
The Barn Burners
Barn Owl
Barnyard Slut
Baroness
Barr
Barry & Holly Tashian
Barry McBride's Snake Farm
Barry Saunders
Barry Sobel
Bart Davenport
Bart Ramsey & Neti Vaan
Bas Clas
Basbombing Soundz
Baseball Furies
Baseboard Heaters
Basia Bulat
Basically Speaking
Baskery
Bass Drum Of Death
Bass Odyssey
Bass Odyssey DJ's
Bassnectar
Basswood Lane
Bastard Child Death Cult
Bastard Sons of Johnny Cash
Basya Schechter / Pharaoh's Daughter
Bat For Lashes
Bat Makumba
Baths
Battershell
Battery Acid
Battle
Battle Hymns
Battles
Bauer
Baumer
Bavu Blakes
Bavu Blakes & the Extra Plairs
Bay of Pigs
Bayside
Bazaar Royale
BC Camplight
BCR
BE
Be Your Own Pet
Beach
Beach Fossils
Beach House
Beaches
Beachwood Sparks
Beangrowers
Beans
Beans Barton & the Bi-Peds
Beans on Toast
Bear Hands
Bear in Heaven
Bear Vs Shark
Bearsuit
BEAST
Beasts and Superbeasts
Beat Angels
Beat Meters
Beat Temple
Beat the Devil
Beat Union
Beatnuts
Beat-O-Sonics
Beats Antique
Beau Jocque & the Zydeco Hi-Rollers
Beau Kiss
Beau Sia
BeauSoleil
BeauSoleil avec Michael Doucet
Beautiful Supermachines
Beaver Nelson
Beaver Nelson Band
Becca
Bechtol & McBride's Metal Cow
Beck
Becky Sharp
Becky Thompson
bedbug
Bedhead
Bedlam
Bedouin Soundclash
Bedroom Walls
Bedtime for Toys
Bedwetter
Beecher
Beep Beep
Beer and Rap
bees are black
BeeSwamp
Beets Brothers
Beggar Weeds
Beirut
Bela Fleck & the Flecktones
Belaire
Belem-Horizonte Banda
Belhome
BeLL

Bell X1
Bell, Book, and Candle
Bella
Belladonna
Bellafea
Bellaparker
Bellatrix
Belle & Sebastian
Bellicose
Belloluna
Bellrays
Bells of Joy
Belong
Beltline
Beme Seed
Ben
Ben + Vesper
Ben Atkins
Ben Etchells
Ben Folds Five
Ben Harper
Ben Harper & RELENTLESS7
Ben Jelen
Ben Kronberg
Ben Lee
Ben Mallott
Ben Nichols
Ben Rector
Ben Sollee
Ben Taylor
Ben vaughan
Ben Weaver
Benevento/Russo Duo
Benjamin Rose Band
Benjy Ferree
Benko
Benna Cohen
Benny & The Jags
Benny Gallagher
Ben's Brother
Bent
Benzos
Berkley Hart
Bermuda Triangle
Bernard Fowler
Bernie Leadon Band
Bernie Worrell & the Woo Warriors
Berri Txarrak
Best Coast
Best Friends Forever
Best Fwends
Betchadupa
Beth Freeman
Beth Lisick
Beth Nielsen Chapman
Beth Orton
Beth Ullman
Beth Williams
Beto and the Fairlanes
Beto Lara y sus Muchachas
Beto y Los Fairlanes
Bett Butler
Better than Ezra
Bettie Serveert
Betty Blowtorch
Betty Elders
Betty Lynn Cade & Navasota
BettySoo
Between the Buried and Me
Beulah
Beverly Bond
Bevis Frond
Bexar Bexar
Beyond The Embrace
Beyond Zebra
Beyondo
BFS & the Crappy All-Stars Karaoke w/Special Guests
Bible of the Devil
Bic Runga
Bicasso
Bido & Toe
Biffy Clyro
Big AL
Big Back Forty
Big Bad Voodoo Daddy
Big Balls
Big Bam Boo
Big Bang
Big Bear
Big Ben
Big Block
Big Blue Hearts
Big Boi
Big Business
Big Car
Big Chief
Big Chris Gates & Gatesville
Big Circo
Big City Rock
Big Collapse
Big Don
Big Drag
Big Faith
Big Fish
Big Fish Ensemble
Big Foot Chester
Big Game Hunter
Big Guitars from Memphis
Big Hat
Big Head Todd And the Monsters
Big Holiday
Big House
Big Jack Johnson & Kim Wilson
Big Jerk

continued on page 20

SXSW SCRAPBOOK

People And Things That Went Before

‹ Frank Carter of Gallows at Emo's (2009)

SXSW directors Louis Jay Meyers, Brent Grulke, Roland Swenson (1990)

1987 – 1991

Inspiration, Skepticism, And The Grey Ghost

By Peter Blackstock

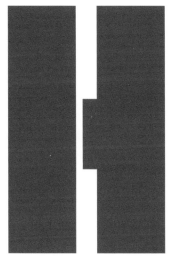

ow in the world are you going to make this happen? You've never done anything like this."

Such were the well-meaning words of caution offered by Austin Convention & Visitors Council president David Lord in the fall of 1986, when a few of his cohorts on the Chamber of Commerce's recently convened Music Advisory Committee suggested launching an industry conference in Austin the following spring.

That advisory committee included Roland Swenson, an *Austin Chronicle* employee who had managed bands and promoted shows primarily in the punk and alternative community, and Louis Jay Meyers, a promoter, booker and manager who had relationships with a variety of local clubs and regional bands. Maybe they hadn't done anything quite like this — but in many respects, they were well-prepared for the journey.

In the summer of '86, Swenson and Meyers, along with Lord and journalist Ed Ward (who'd recently completed a rock history book for *Rolling Stone*), had attended the New Music Seminar, a major music industry convention in New York, to promote Austin music at a Chamber of Commerce-sponsored booth. They caught the attention of NMS honchos Mark Josephson and Joel Webber, who subsequently visited Austin to discuss the possibility of a regional offshoot in Texas. Ultimately NMS opted not to pursue it, leaving the door open for Swenson, Meyers and their allies.

Lord remembers how they answered his concern that this was unlike anything they'd ever done. "They were quiet for a minute. And then they said, 'Well, that's true, but we know the audience really well, and we know we can get the word out to the audience through the alternative press. And we'll learn the rest of it as we go."

The alternative press was in fact the next vital component. Swenson and Meyers took their notion to Louis Black and Nick Barbaro, editor and publisher of *The Austin Chronicle*. "Initially, Nick was noncommittal and Louis thought it was a crazy idea, but they were willing to talk about it," Swenson wrote in a retrospective piece published by the *Chronicle* in 2001. "We began arguing the merits and risks of putting on an event of this nature. For the sake of the argument, Louis took the position that it wasn't a bad idea, but if we failed it could take the *Chronicle* down with it. I took the position that pulling it off would be difficult, but we could do it. I also argued that like every other institution in Austin, the *Chronicle* would be taken for granted unless it could demonstrate it had clout outside of town.

"Louis was winning the argument, which went on for weeks. His point was that we didn't really have the major connections needed to bring the music industry here en masse from L.A. and New York in the way the Seminar could. During one session, in a moment of inspiration, I said, 'We don't have to get those people. We can just invite some bands and music people from the area — Dallas, New Orleans, Houston. Get some other alternative papers like the *Dallas Observer* to sponsor it. Have a day or so of sessions and showcases, and then conclude with a big Sunday barbecue and softball game.' Nick looked up with a smile on his face, interested for the first time in days. Louis cursed me, knowing that I had found his Achilles' heel. There was no way Nick was going to turn down a good excuse for barbecue and softball."

The name – South By Southwest – came from Black, an ardent film buff. Riffing off of Hitchcock's classic film *North By Northwest*, he uttered the regional reconfiguration of that title, "and we all seized upon it," Swenson recalled. "I quickly sketched the 'SXSW' abbreviation in all caps on a piece of paper and held it up for all to see."

Weeks of discussions followed in the evening hours, with cohorts such as Ward, Jungle Records' Bruce Sheehan, *Chronicle* staffer Jeff Whittington and others sitting in with Swenson, Meyers, Barbaro and Black. On December 9, 1986, an official announcement was made: The first South By Southwest Music & Media Conference would take place March 12-15 in Austin. The long meetings and detailed planning continued. As Louis Black wrote in a 2008 *Chronicle* reminiscence: "The constant between November 1986 and March 1987 was the four of us in an office, sitting, lying on the floor or on desks, standing, walking, shuffling, and talking, constantly talking. Regularly, we returned to the central scenario of an individual landing at the airport, renting a car, driving to the hotel, and then registering at SXSW. Operating from that point of view, we tried to anticipate every detail."

Meyers, meanwhile, worked on putting together the lineup of performers, and of venues. "Louis was trying to get clubs to let us produce shows in their venues for free, keep the door if any, and they could keep the bar. For an event where we had no idea how many people would attend," Ward explained. "But Sixth Street turned out to be the best place not only because of its concentration of venues, but also because it already had an association of business owners in existence. They could look at total revenues and see that there was this huge slump during Spring Break. So why not: If we didn't bring in any business, well, that was business as usual."

As for what acts would perform: While SXSW office routines in future years were marked by the daily processing of countless cassettes (and, later, discs) sent in by bands hoping to play the event, Meyers noted that "the first year we did not do submissions. We created a target list of several hundred acts and then got on the phone and invited them. There was a great deal of explaining what we were trying to do. Those that had been to NMS understood what we were doing. Some thought we were crazy. Most asked why they should play for us for free, but many trusted us enough to take a chance."

The majority of the acts that first year were local — Lou Ann Barton, Glass Eye, the Killer Bees, the Wagoneers, Dino Lee — though some came from neighboring cities and states: Shallow Reign (Dallas), Defenestration (Oklahoma City), Dash Rip Rock (New Orleans), the Lonesome Strangers (Los Angeles). Some of those bands were sponsored by the regional publications that Swenson and the *Chronicle* directors had brought on board. Denver alt-weekly *Westword* selected Boulder band Electric Third Rail. Gil Asakawa, the paper's music editor at the time, explained why he was compelled to take part: "My road trip to the first South By Southwest was based on an abstract idea: that a local music scene can have national impact. Up until then, the accepted music hubs were New York, Detroit, Nashville and L.A. Prince put Minneapolis on the map, and the Northwest scene would explode in a few years. Local scenes were where talent incubated and then moved on to one of those national hubs to make their mark, or fail."

Ward, who was officially listed as a co-director that first year in the handout distributed to registrants, went about putting together a plan for the daytime discussions at the hotel. "The early panels were very basic," he recalled. "Nobody knew shit, and that's what SXSW was for: to teach them. The panels had names like A&R, Publishing, Distribution, Retailing, Touring, Publicity. We were conducting basic informational seminars: How to get signed, how to tour, how to get a publishing deal set up.

"And boy, nobody wanted to do it. Nobody. 'Why should I go down there when the NMS is right here in New York? There's music in Texas? Besides ZZ Top? Who knew! If you want to do a clone of the NMS, why don't you do it right here in L.A., where the industry is? Is this a country music seminar? Because we don't do country.'"

Still, the Austin locale did provide some advantages. "The weather was a good worm to dangle in front of them," Ward recalls. "I'd say, 'Man, have you ever been in Texas in the spring, before it gets all hot? You haven't? You should see Austin in March, man. It's great.' And the guy'd be sitting in his office in New York looking at the sleet and thinking, hmmm. The L.A. guys were easier: They were always looking for new ways to spend expense money. So bit by bit we got the panels filled up. And, of course, people dropped out, making for moments of panic."

Some important last-minute confirmations came via the assistance of Mark Josephson, the New Music Seminar exec who'd helped get the ball rolling the previous year. "A few days before the event, Mark flew into town," Ward recalls. "We were operating out of a couple of rooms in the offices of the *Chronicle*, and Mark stormed into the room, said, 'Get me a telephone,' and sat down at the desk he was shown to. 'Now. I want three chicken tacos from the Tamale House. With guacamole! I'm not going to do a thing til I get them.' Someone scurried out the door. The tacos were produced, and I remember Roland and me standing there and Mark said, 'OK. What are the problems?' 'Well, this person is still not confirmed and we really need him.' Mark whips out a book and starts dialing. Bam: the guy's confirmed. 'What next?'"

In the wee hours before the first SXSW commenced on March 12, 1987, Swenson was on edge. "I had dreams that night of crowds chasing me through the hotel screaming, 'There he is. He's the one who got us to travel here for this stupid thing. Get him!'"

As it turned out, Swenson was the one doing the shouting at the hotel, which was the Marriott on 11th Street (now the Sheraton). SXSW had been allotted "only half the ballroom space, which was barely enough room," he remembers. "We spilled over into the lobby, and on the first day of registration, they tried to tell me that our people could only stand in the lobby in front of our half of the ballroom. It was then that I pitched the first of many screaming fits I would have in front of hotel people, convention center reps, or anybody standing in the way of what had to be done for SXSW over the next 25 years."

And yet there was also magic taking place in that hotel lobby. Bill Bentley, a former Austinite who'd moved to L.A. for a job with Warner Bros., remembers an eightysomething barrelhouse blues legend named Roosevelt Williams, a.k.a. the Grey Ghost, taking a seat at a baby grand piano and creating a moment that still lingers a quarter-century later.

"Ghost had been off the circuit a few decades, driving a school bus before retiring in the early '70s," Bentley said. "But folklorist Tary Owens had found him living on the Eastside, and was determined to show the world what a wonder lived right under their noses. When the notes started flowing out of the piano in the lobby, it was like a savior had arrived to deliver the blessings. Grey Ghost then started singing and silence took over the room. Everyone there knew they were in the presence of greatness, and allowed the moment to spread over them with an ethereal aura. When he finished, the musician stood up quietly, slowly walked out the front door, and disappeared into the sunshine. He never looked back, but it felt like the man had christened SXSW for all the years to come."

The keynote speaker that first year was Huey Meaux, the Louisiana producer whose resume included hits with the Sir Douglas Quintet in the '60s and Freddy Fender in the '70s. Writer Joe Nick Patoski, who helped bring Meaux aboard, explained that "Huey was about as high-profile person as could be gotten in the immediate area, and he had been around the block a few times in the music business, which was the goal of the conference — to link the artists not in New York or L.A. or

Huey Meaux, Doug Sahm (late 1980s)

Nashville to the business. Huey had been doing that for years." (A decade later, Meaux landed in prison after charges of sexual encounters with minors.)

Subsequent keynotes drew notable names in journalism (*Spin* magazine publisher Bob Guccione Jr. in 1988, renowned Village Voice critic Robert Christgau in 1989) and songwriting (Jewish cowboy humorist Kinky Friedman in 1990, adventurous country chart-topper Rosanne Cash in 1991). Many years later, Friedman launched an ill-fated gubernatorial campaign. But it was the sitting Texas governor, Ann Richards, who brought extra attention to the '91 keynote with welcoming remarks preceding Cash's speech. "We spent a lot of time worrying about security for Gov. Richards," Swenson said. "The

Department of Public Safety troopers showed up beforehand and scoped the place out. We had an escort plan in place for weeks to bring her in the room. Then while we were waiting at the appointed spot, she walked in the front door of the Hyatt by herself, walked down the center aisle and got up onstage."

The Hyatt, on the south bank of Town Lake, was where SXSW landed in 1990; it remained there until the move to the new Austin Convention Center in 1993. The Hyatt provided some much-needed stability after the first three years saw SXSW move from the Marriott near the Capitol in '87, to the Austin Crest (now the Radisson) on the north shore of Town Lake in '88, and then back to the Marriott in '89.

Another revolving element during the first five years was where to work the Austin Music Awards Show into the mix. Presented by *The Austin Chronicle* since the early '80s, the show initially was perceived as an anchor for SXSW. For the first two years, the Awards was the only music event on the Friday night schedule, with showcases taking place on Thursday, Saturday and Sunday. In 1989, the Awards Show moved to Thursday, with showcases the next three nights. Finally in 1990, it settled into the Wednesday-night slot it has held ever since. (It remained free of any showcase competition until 1997, the first year that the showcases began running Wednesday through Sunday.) There were also constant changes of venue for the Awards Show in those early years: It bounced between the Austin Opera House, Palmer Auditorium and City Coliseum until finally settling at the Austin Music Hall in 1997.

Simple details evolved in the early stretch as well. For the non-badge-wearing public (you didn't need a stinkin' badge to attend SXSW, though it made things easier), a paper ticket got you in to the participating clubs the first couple of years, before the admission-granting wristbands became an annual fashion ritual. Starting in 1989, registrants received a program guide that provided details about the panels and shows (an upgrade from the handful of photocopied handouts from the first two years).

Another first in '89, for the SXSW staff, was a walkie-talkie system — a big development in pre-cell-phone days. "For the first two SXSWs, the staff was able to go to the shows at night and remain blissfully unaware of any of the horrific problems that always attend putting on a festival, unless they stumbled across them live and in person," Swenson recalled. Now everyone was on-call to come to the rescue. "We later learned that ham radio buffs around town were listening in on our conversations and found our turmoil quite amusing. Legend holds that someone recorded an evening of our communications and used it as part of a performance art installation."

Perhaps the most significant new development on the horizon in 1989, though, was the dawning of the notion that SXSW could reach well beyond the South by Southwest region, and even across the pond. "That year also featured one of our first bands from Europe," Swenson recalls. "The act was Cliff Barnes & the Fear of Winning from Berlin. I had attended my first international music event, MIDEM in Cannes, for the first time in January of '89. Of course, SXSW was completely unknown, but I was undeterred and walked around and spoke to anyone who would listen about the event.

"A number of kind people took the time to carefully explain to me why there would never be a reason for Europeans to attend SXSW. I would nod politely and move on to the next person. Fortunately, I met the publisher for the Cliff Barnes act, who were big fans of the TV show *Dallas* and were anxious for any reason to travel to Texas. This was one of the first things that helped create a close relationship between SXSW and Berlin, including an event that was modeled on SXSW called Berlin Independence Days (BID)."

Those two festivals bonded in part over shared interests in a genre of music that Texas was especially known for. "We always went after the roots-friendly international community," Meyers pointed out. "That is what made BID so good for us. Wolfgang Doebeling, their director, had a label that released a very cool live Townes Van Zandt LP and a bunch of other stuff. He was the main roots music DJ in Germany at that time. So there was an immediate effect on SXSW."

Meanwhile, Swenson continued to sow the international seeds at other overseas events. "I traveled to Glasgow in October of 1990 to speak at a music conference on a panel titled 'Are Music Conferences Good for Business (Or Just An Excuse to Party?)'," he recalled. "My fellow panelists included Wolfgang from Berlin Independence Days, Una Johnston from the New Music Seminar, and the irascible Tony Wilson, founder of Factory Records. When we went for the pre-panel meeting in the green room, Wilson was at his vicious best, skewering us all for being parasites, and even worse in his opinion, for being on the sidelines of the record industry instead of in the battle.

"By the time we went out to speak to the audience, we were all totally in defensive mode, but Wilson had become a pussycat, not saying a disagreeable word and letting us trip all over ourselves defending our events. The audience was pretty feisty too, and a recurring theme was the bitterness by the Scots over needing to go to London to make their career. Finally, I said something like, 'Hey, I live in Texas and we have to travel over a thousand miles to L.A. or New York to get noticed. What's the big deal? Even Jesus had to go to Jerusalem.' One of the Scots in the audience stood up and starting screaming at me with a burr in his accent so strong that I didn't understand anything he said past, 'How dare you come over here and tell us...?'

"Of course, Tony Wilson went on to found the first major music conference/festival in the U.K., In The City, held in Manchester, which he compared to SXSW whenever he could. But I emerged from the fire as a fast friend of Una's and Wolfgang's, and even Tony's. I also became friendly with one of Wolfgang's crew attending the Glasgow event, Mirko Whitfield, who had joined the BID staff and was Wolfgang's specialist on Eastern European countries still behind the crumbling Iron Curtain. Mirko would become SXSW's first 'European Manager,' and we labored over the next four years to bring European bands and registrants to Texas."

The long-term result of all that groundwork? "One in five SXSW registrants lives outside the United States," Swenson noted of the present-day numbers. "Through it all, Ed Ward has acted our Senior Consultant for international, first while living in Berlin, and now in Montpelier, France."

Back in 1987, though, the vast majority of the acts who performed at SXSW were from the state of Texas. Brad First, who presented showcases at his venue the Cave Club in '87 and later worked for SXSW in various capacities, remembers one that caught his attention. "They set their amps up at the edge of the stage, bass on one side, guitar on the other, facing at each other across the stage, not out to the audience. They said it was because they played loud and most club PAs couldn't handle the volume.

"There were maybe 20-30 people, at most, in the club, which looked kind of bad as the Cave could hold 500-plus. They proceeded to just blast this really loud, but really great hard rock (nearly metal) music that blew me away. The singer was black and the guitar player and drummer were white, and they hailed from Houston. I had never heard of them. They were called King's X. They got signed to their record deal [with Megaforce Records] from that showcase."

Such label deals were a sort of fabled brass ring that didn't really happen very often—and when they did, they could be nearly impossible to predict. In 1988, there was "a young band from out of state that got booked into Joe's Generic Bar on Sixth Street," recalls Louis Black. Joe's Generic was one of the smallest and lowest-profile venues on the SXSW roster. "Even Louis Meyers felt sorry for them. Until about two weeks later, when Souled American called to say that they had been signed by Rough Trade U.S. out of that showcase."

The band also became good friends that night with some fellow Midwesterners who were playing across the street at the Coyote Club — an up-and-coming Minneapolis group called the Jayhawks. "By accident, we walked into a bar and found a band from Chicago playing called Souled American," remembers Jayhawks co-leader Mark Olson. "We became friends with them and they stayed with us in Minneapolis afterward when we did some co-bills."

A showcase success story the following year involved Wisconsin father-son band the Spanic Boys. "There was a guy from Rounder, Ken Irwin, who'd always ask me for recommendations," Ed Ward remembered, "and I told him these guys were a little rocky for Rounder, but they were great. So I wasn't utterly surprised to see him at the Continental, where the Spanics blew the walls off with an absolutely incendiary set which they ended by tearing the strings off their guitars in one coordinated motion. Ken bounded backstage and offered them a deal."

Inevitably, some showcases were disasters, such as A Flock Of Seagulls' 1989 appearance at The World, a club on Fifth Street. "There were a few things that the band didn't realize," Swenson recounted. "First, they didn't know they were on the downward side of their career. Second, they had no idea this wasn't just another gig, that it was a festival showcase. They were traveling with the standard complement of surly British roadies, who terrorized the other bands and our volunteers. It was kind of like the old game 'King of the Hill': Once they finally pushed all the other bands and their equipment offstage, they held the stage for the rest of the night and wouldn't budge."

And then there was the night that the owner of Mercado Caribe "pulled out a gun during a showcase," remembers Brad First. "We had to clear the club fast, the police came, and we ended up having to find another venue overnight."

Such challenges were par for the course during the years that SXSW was finding its way. "What was exciting in those days was you never knew what kind of problems may pop up, and you had to be creative to solve them," said Bruce Sheehan, who was listed as a co-director the first year and served as production coordinator in year two. "The level of organization of SXSW was nowhere nearly as sophisticated as it is now; you were pretty much on your own, flying by the seat of your pants, winging it. That's what made it so much fun."

By and large, South By Southwest was a runaway success in its first five years. From a roster of 177 acts playing at 15 clubs over three nights of showcases in 1987, SXSW had ballooned to 512 acts at 27 clubs over four nights of showcases in 1991. From a mostly local lineup spiced by a sampling of regional acts that first year, the conference had expanded to attract artists from all over the country as well as a growing international contingent. During those first five years, you could catch up on buzz bands of the moment (Blake Babies, Vulgar Boatmen, Poi Dog Pondering), hear highly respected established artists (Townes Van Zandt, Alex Chilton, Exene Cervenka), and get an early glimpse of future stars (Wilco forerunner Uncle Tupelo, pre-Natalie Maines Dixie Chicks, Detroit's Goober & the Peas with a young Jack White on drums).

For all the dreams of record contracts or publishing deals, sometimes the rewards of SXSW were less tangible, yet more lasting. Jon Dee Graham, who had spent the 1980s playing guitar in various high-profile Austin bands before moving to Los Angeles at the end of the decade, returned for a showcase at Cactus Cafe in 1991 and found inspiration for a solo career in the response he received.

"After spending most of my adult life as a working musician, and already being a writer getting a few songs covered by other artists, I was still safely far behind the front lines," Graham said. "Being 'In Front' is a very different job than being 'Beside,' with a whole different set of demands and obligations, and requiring an entirely different skill set.

"Not only was I unsure if I wanted to take that on, I wasn't completely convinced I could DO it, either. SXSW provided me the opportunity and the venue to TRY, at the exact intersection of Time and Talent where it might work.

"And it did. It was 35 minutes of magic...a magic that I have been trying to recapture for almost 20 years. Without that night at the Cactus, it's hard to see where I'd be now." ∎

continued from page 20

Big Jim Slade
Big Kenny
Big Leaves
Big Leg
Big Light
Big Loud Dog
Big Mello
Big Nee & Lil Squeeze
Big Pokey
Big Poppa E
Big Red Rooster
Big Richard
Big Rude Jake
Big Sam's Funky Nation
Big Sandy & the Fly-Rite Boys
Bigshot Allstar
Big Shoulders
Big Sid
Big Sister
Big Smith
Big Star
Big Star- A Tribute to Alex Chilton
Big Sugar
Big Sun
Big Tuck of DSR
Big Wheel
Big Wooden Radio
Bigbang
Bigelf
Bigg Jus
Bigga Rhythm
Biirdie
Bikini Atoll
Bildmeister
Bill
Bill and Kim Davis
Bill Baker
Bill Callahan
Bill Carter & the Blame
Bill Colbert
Bill Janovitz (of Buffalo Tom)
Bill Kirchen
Bill Kirchen & Too Much Fun
Bill Kirkpatrick
Bill Lloyd
Bill Morrissey
Bill Perry
Bill Ricchini
Bill Rice Band
Bill Swicegood & Fear of Flying
Bill White Acre
Billy Adams
Billy Bacon and the Forbidden Pigs
Billy Bob Thornton
Billy Bob Thornton and The Boxmasters
Billy Bragg
Billy Burnette
Billy Cook
Billy Faier
Billy Franks
Billy Goat
Billy Harvey
Billy Idol
Billy Joe Shaver
Billy Joe Winghead
Billy Paul Band
Billy Ray Cyrus
Billy Reese Peters
Billy the Kid
Billy White
Billy White
Billygoat
Bim Sherman
Binary Audio Misfits
Binary Star
Bing Ji Ling
Bingo
Bio Ritmo
Biomechanical
Bionic
Bird
Bird by Bird
Bird featuring Mark Burgess of the Chameleons
Bird of Youth
Bird Peterson
Bird3
Birdbrain
birddog
Birdmonster
Birds of Avalon
Birds Of Tokyo
Birds of Wales
Birdy
Birdy Nam Nam
Birthday Suits
Bis
Bisc1
Bisco Smith
Biscuit Brothers
Bishi
Bishop Allen

Band from Hell (1988)

Bishop Fred A Jones and The Jones Family Singers
Bison BC
Bit Shifter
Bitsy Rats
Bitter Bitter Weeks
Bitter End
Bjorn Svin
Bjorn Torske
BK One
Black Acid
Black Before Red
Black Cat Music
Black Cherry
Black Cobra
Black Cock
Black Cracker
Black Diamond Bay (formerly Krief)
Black Diamond Heavies
Black Dynamite Sound Orchestra
Black Earth
Black Eyed Dog
Black Eyed Peas
Black-Eyed Snakes
Black Feelings
Black Fiction
Black Furies
Black Gold
Black Happy
Black Heart Procession
Black Helicopter
Black Joe Lewis
Black Joe Lewis & The Honeybears
Black Kali Ma
Black Kold Madina
Black Latin
Black Lips
Black Lipstick
Black Market Flowers
Black Math Horseman
Black Mike
Black Mike and Kemistry
Black Milk
Black Monks
Black Moses
Black Moth Super Rainbow
Black Mountain
Black Pearl
Black Prairie
Black Rebel Motorcycle Club
Black Rose Band
Black Sand Hand
Black Sheep (DRES)
Black Skies
Black Spring
Black Sun Ensemble
Black Tide
Black Tie Dynasty
Black Tie Revue
Black Top Demon
Black Tusk
Black Umfolosi
Black Water Junction
Blackalicious
Blackbud
Blackfire
Blackfire Revelation
Blackgirls
Blackhearted Force
Blackholicus
Blackie and the Rodeo Kings
Blacklist
Blacklisted Individuals
Blackloud
Blackmail
Blackmale
Blackmarket
Blackpool Lights
Blaggards
Blair
Blair Hansen
Blair Lundstedt
Blaise Pascal
Blakasaurus Mex
Blake Babies
Blaksunz
Blanche
Blanche Davidian
Blank Blue
Blank Dogs
Blaqstarr
BLAZE
Bleach
Bleach (Japan)
BLEACH03
Blectum from Blechdom
Bleeding Through
Blessid Union of Souls
Blessure Grave
Bletzung
Bleu
Bleubird
Blevin Blectum and Lesser
Blind Boys of Alabama
Blind Date
Blind Otis & The Lost Highway
Blind Pilot
Blind Willie's Johnson
Blindspott
Blink
Blink-182
Blinker The Star
Bliss 66
Blister

Blitzen Trapper
BLK JKS
Bloc Party
Block
Blockhead
Blofly
Blohazard
Blonde Redhead
Blood On The Wall
Blood Oranges
Blood Test
Bloodgroup
Bloodhag
Bloodline
Bloodsucking Go-Devils
Bloodthirsty Lovers
Bloody Hollies
Bloody L
Bloom
Blowfly
Blowhole
Blowing Trees
Blu
Blu Sanders
Blubinos
Blue Angel
Blue Beat Cartel
Blue Bloods
Blue Canoe
Blue Cheer
Blue Diamond Shine
Blue Giant
Blue Guitars
Blue Hawaiians
Blue King Brown
Blue Matter
Blue Meanies
Blue Meridian
Blue Merle
Blue Mist
Blue Moon Ghetto
Blue Mountain
Blue Noise Band
Blue October
Blue Orphans
Blue Plate Poets
Blue Rodeo
Blue Rodeo & Friends
Blue Runners
Blue Scholars
Blue Sky Roadster
Blue Star
Blue States
Bluebird
Bluebonnets
Bluebottle Kiss
Blue-Eyed Son
BlueGround UnderGrass
Blueline Medic
Bluerunners
Blues Boy Hubbard & the Jets
Blues Brother Castro
Blues Condition
Blues Control
Blues Patrol
Blues Traveler
Blunt
Blunt Force Trauma
Blunt Mechanic
Blur
Blurt
BM LINX
Bo Bice
bo bud greene
Bo Garza
Bo Pepper
Boas
BOAT
Boats
Bob Collum
Bob Lind
Bob Livingston
Bob Log III
Bob Lowery
Bob Mould
Bob Neuwirth
Bob Perry
Bob Perry Band
Bob Rising and Scenario
Bob Schneider
Bob Schneider and Lonelyland w/ The Fireants
Bob Snider
Bob Wiseman
Bob Woodruff
Bobby Bare
Bobby Bare Jr
Bobby Bare Jr & The Young Criminals Starvation League
Bobby Bare Jr w/ David Vandervelde
Bobby Bare Jr.
Bobby Bridger
Bobby Conn
Bobby Conn and the Glass Gypsies
Bobby Flores
Bobby Lee Springfield
Bobby Long
Bobby Lounge
Bobby Mack & Night Train
Bobby Patterson
Bobby Pharelle
Bobby Pulido
Bobby Rush
Bobby Whitlock & CoCo Carmel with David Grissom, Stephen Bruton and Brannen Temple

Bobgoblin
Bobo in White Wooden Houses
Bobo Meets Rhettmatic
Boca Abajo
Bocephus King
BoDeans
Bodhisattva
Bodies of Water
Body Electric
Body Language
Body of War with Kimya Dawson, Serj Tankian, Tom Morello, Brett Dennen, Brendan James, RX Bandits, Ben Harper, Billy Bragg, and Special Guests
Body Politik
Bogart & the Addictives
Boggs
Bohemian Holiday
Bohiems
Bojones
Bo-Keys
Bomani Armah & Project Mayhem
Bomani Armah with The Five One
Bomba Estereo
Bon Iver
Bon Savants
Bon Terra
Bonde do Role
Bone Box
Bonepony
Bonfire Madigan
Bongo Hate
Bongzilla
Bonjay
Bonjour Brumaire
Bonk
Bonkin' Clapper
Bonnie Bramlett
Bonnie Pink
Bonny Holmes
Bontempi Brothers
Boog Brown
Boogie Waters
Book of Black Earth
Booka Shade
Boom Bap Project
Boom Boom Satellites
Boom Hank
Boom Pam
Boom Shake
Boombox ATX
Boondogs
BoonDox
Bootfare
Bop Street
BO-PEEP
Border Radio
BORIS
Born in the Flood
Born Ruffians
Born To Lose
Borne
Bornu Empire
Bosco & Jorge
Bosque Brown
Boss Hogg Outlawz
Boss Martians
Boston Chinks
Boston Slam Team
Botanica
Botellita de Jerez
Botello
Bottle
Bottle Rockets
Bottled Og
Bottom
Bottom of the Hudson
Bottomless Pit
Boubacar Diebate
Bouffant Jellyfish
Boulder
Boulder Acoustic Society
Bound Stems
Bourne & MacLeod
Bow Brannon
Bow Brannon Band
Bowerbirds
Bowling For Soup
Box Elders
Box Set
Box the Walls
Boxcar Satan
Boxcars
Boxing Gandhis
Boxstep
Boy
Boy Crisis
Boy From Brazil
Boy Genius
Boy Hits Car
Boy Kill Boy
Boy Wonder
Boys in a Band
Boys Noize
BoySkout
Boyz
Boyz Noize
Bozaque
Br. Danielson
BR5-49
Brad Anthony Moore
Brad Barr
Bradford Reed and His Amazing Pencilina

BRAHMS
Braille
Brain Failure
Brainiac
BrainStorm
Brakes
BRAL
Bran Van 3000
Brand New Sin
Brandi Carlile
Brandi Shearer
Brandon Jenkins
Brandon Rhyder
Brandtson
Brannen Temple Trio
Brannen Temple's Temple Underground
Brasilian Pizza Mafia
Brasstronaut
Brassy
Brave Combo
Brave New World
Brave Radar
Bravo Silva
Braxton Hicks
Brazil
Brazilian Girls
Brazos
Brazz Tree
Break of Reality
Break the Silence
Breakestra
Breaking Benjamin
Breakup Breakdown
Breathe Carolina
Breather Resist
Breed77
Breedlove
Brenda Dickey
Brenda Kahn
Brenda Kahn Band
Brendan Benson and the Incidentals
Brendan James
Brendon Walsh
Brenmar
Brennen Leigh
Brennen Leigh Band
Brent Best
Brent Mitchell & the Urban Coyote Band
Brent Palmer
Brett Dennen
Brett Johnson
Brett Koshkin
Brewtality, INC.
Brian Andrew Lee
Brian Borcherdt
Brian Cutean
Brian Glaze
Brian Glaze featuring Joe Haener of the Gris Gris
Brian Houser
Brian Jonestown Massacre
Brian Keane
Brian Marshall and his Tex-Slavik Playboys
Brian Posehn
Brian Trainor Trio
Brian Vander Ark
Brian Wright and the Waco Tragedies
Brick Bandits
Brick Chair
Bridget Storm
Bright Eyes
Bright Light Fever
Brightblack Morning Light
Brighton, MA
Brigitte DeMeyer
Brilliant Fools
Brilliant Trees
Brimstone Howl
Bring Me The Horizon
Brisa Roché
Brissa
British Sea Power
Britt Daniel
Brizz
Broadcast 2000
Broadfield Marchers
Broadway Calls
Broadway Elks
Brobdingnagian Bards
Broken Bells
Broken Glass
Broken Records
Broken Social Scene
Broken Teeth
Broken Vessels
Broken Water
Bromheads Jacket
Brooke Waggoner
Brooklyn
Brooklyn Browngrass
Brooks Williams
Brotha K
Brotha Miles
Brother Ali
Brother Eyo
Brother JT
Brother K
Brother Reade
Brother Red
Brother Sal
Brothers and Sisters
Brothers from Another Planet
Brothers Past
Brown Betty
Brown Whornet

Brownout!
Bruce Hampton & the Aqarium Rescue Unit
Bruce Henderson
Bruce Lamont of Yakuza
Bruce Middleton
Bruce Newman
Bruce Newman and Washtub Jerry
Bruce Peninsula
Bruce Piephoff
Bruce Robinson
Bruce Robison
Brutal Juice
Brute Force & Daughter of Force
Bryan Gutmann
Bryan Scary & The Shredding Tears
Bryndle
B-sides
B-Side Players
Bubble
Bubbz
Bubonic Plague
Buchanan
Buck 65
Buck Diaz
Buck Jones
Buck-O-Nine
Buck Pets
Bucket Number Six
Buckfast Superbee
Buckshot
Bucktooth Johnson
Buckwheat Zydeco
bud
Bud Melvin
Buddy
Buddy & Julie Miller
Buddy Guy
Buddy Miller
Buddy Mondlock
Buff1
Buffalo Daughter
Buffalo Killers
Buffalo Nickel (MS)
Buffalo Stance
Buffalo Tom
Bug
Buick MacKane
Built By Snow
Built Like Alaska
Built to Spill
Bukka Allen
Bukue One
Bullfrog featuring Kid Koala
Bumblebeez 81
Bun B
Bun B & UGK Present MDDL FNGZ
Bunker Hill
Bunky
Burd Early
Burden Brothers
Burn Disco Burn
Burn Steady
Burn Unit
Burning Blue
Burning Brides
Burning Bright
Burning Sky
Burning Star Core
Burnt By The Sun
Burrito Deluxe
Burrito Deluxe (featuring Garth Hudson of The Band and Sneaky Pete Kleinow)
Bury Tomorrow
Busdriver
Bush
Bush League All-Stars
Bushwalla
Bushwick Bill
Buster & the Crabs
Busty Duck
Busy Signals
Butch Hancock
Butch Hancock & Jimmie Gilmore
Butch Walker
Butcher Bear & Charlie
Buttercup
Butterfly Explosion
Butterscotch Tuna
Buttless Chaps
Buzz Zeemer
Buzzcocks
Buzzcrusher
Buzzkill
By Any Means Necessary
By Divine Right
By the End of Tonight

C

C Rayz Walz + Kosha Dillz
C.C. Adcock
C.J. Chenier & the Red Hot Louisiana Band
Cable
Cache Cache
Cactus Nerve Thang
Cactus's
Cadaques
Cadence Weapon

Cadillac
Cadillac Angels
Cadillac Moon
Cadillac Tramps
Cadillac Voodoo Choir
Cady Groves
Caesar
Café Funque
Café Noir
Cafe R & B
Cage
Cage the Elephant
Cairo Pythian
Caitlin Cary
Caitlin Cary and Thad Cockrell
Caitlin Crosby
Cake
Cale Parks
Caleb Engstrom
Caleb Klauder
Calexico
Calhoun
Cali Zack & N/A
Calico
Califone
California featuring Berline, Hickman, Crary
California Oranges
Call And Response
Call Me Lightning
Call Me Poupee
Calla
Callers
Callisto
CALLmeKAT
Calvin Johnson
Calvin Krime
Calvin Owens Blues Orchestra
Calvin Russell
Calvin Russell Band
Camaro Hair
Camber
Camera Obscura
Cameron Dye
Cameron McGill
Cameron Meshell
Camisama
Camp Lo
Camp X-Ray
Camper Van Beethoven
Canabis Tribe
Canada
Canadians
Cancer Bats
Chancho en Piedra
Candiria
Candy 500
Candy 66
Candy Butchers
Candye Kane
cane141
Canja Rave
Canoe
Canopy
Canseco
Canvas
Cap D
Capgun Coup
Capitol Years
Caps & Jones
Capsize 7
Capsula
Captain
Captain Ahab
Captain Audio
Captain Danger
Car Stereo (Wars)
Cara Luft
Caracol
Carbon/Silicon
Carbonas
Cardinal Woolsey
Cardinale
Care Bears on Fire
Career Criminal
Carey Ott
Cargo Cult
Carina Round
Carissa's Wierd
Carl Brouse
Carl Clarke
Carl Clarke (Urban DK)
Carl Craig
Carl Keating
Carl Perkins
Carl Sonny Leyland & His Boogie Woogie Trip
Carla Olson
Carlene Carter
Carlene Jones
Carlis Star
Carlo Nuccio
Carlos Villarreal
Carlotta
Carly Binding
Carmaig de Forest
Carmen Consoli
Carmen Rizzo (of Niyaz)
Carmon Rodgers & Geno Young
Carmina Piranha
Carney
Carnival Art
Carnival Beats
Carnival Beats Presents Nac, Swift, Salih Williams, Natasha and the Mo' Drama Project

Carol & Gary Feist
Carol Feist
Carolina Chocolate Drops
Carolina of Texas
Caroline
Caroline Aiken
Caroline Herring
Caroline Keating
Caroline's Spine
Carolyn Hester
Carolyn Mark
Carolyn Mark & Her Roommates
Carolyn Wonderland
Carolyn Wonderland & the Imperial Monkeys
Carrie Elkin
Carrie Newcomer
Carrie Rodriguez
Carsick Cars
Cartel de Santa
Carter Tanton
Carter/Carter/Moore
Carusella
Cary Brothers
Cary Swinney, Richard Bowdon, Michael O'Conner
Caryl P. Weiss
Casey Dienel
Casey Lynn Hosack
Cash Audio
Cash Cash
Casino
Casino & Gutta Gang
Casino Family
Casiokids
Casiotone for the Painfully Alone
Casket Salesmen
Casper Brötzman Massaker
Caspian
Cass King
Cass McCombs
Cassette Kids
Cassettes Won't Listen
Cassim & Barbária
Cassius Khan
Cast Spells
Castanets
Castle Project
Castle Siege
Castledoor
CastleSiege
Casual T's
Casxio
Cat Power
Cat Scientist
Catatonia
Catch 22
Catch Betty
Catchdubs
Cate Le Bon
Catfish Haven
Cath Carroll
Catherine Feeny
Catherine Irwin
Catherine MacLellan
Catherine Tran
Cathy Croce
Cathy Davey
Cathy Fink and Marcy Marxer
Cathy Winter
Catie Curtis
Catscratch
Cattleguard
Caucus
Caulk
Caural
Cause Co-Motion!
Cause for Applause
Caustic Resin
Cavalier King
Cave In
Cavedogs
Cavedweller
Caviar
Cayto
CD & the Modern Guys
Dick Price
Ceci Bastida
Cecil Otter
Cecilia Saint
Cedell Davis
Cedric Burnside & Lightnin' Malcolm
Ceeplus Bad Knives
Celebration
Cella Blue & The Loose 24
Centaur
Centazontale
Centro-matic
Cephalic Carnage
Cerberus Shoal
Cerebral Ballzy
Cerronato
Cerys Matthews
Cesar Rosas
Cex
Chacon
Chad Hudson
Chad Jasmine
Chad VanGaalen
Chaindrive
Chainsaw Kittens
Chairlift
Chalie Boy

continued on page 40

1987

SXSW **STATS** March 12 – 15

Nick Barbaro
AUSTIN CHRONICLE
SXSW Co-Director

SXSW

BY THE NUMBERS

177 showcasing artists

15 panels, workshops & sessions

15 venues & stages

700 registrants

$35-55 registration

$10 festival pass
Paper ticket, not wristband

0 pages in program guide
No formal program guide; a half-dozen photocopied pages of skeletal details

EVENT HEADQUARTERS
Marriott Hotel, 701 E. 11th St.

AUSTIN MUSIC AWARDS
Friday, March 13, at Austin Opera House
   Performers Asleep at the Wheel, Will & the Kill, Eric Johnson, Zeitgeist, Ronnie Lane Band; MC Paul Ray

SXSW SHOWCASE VENUES
Alley Oop's, Antone's, Back Room, Baxter's Jazz, Cave Club, Continental Club, Flying Circus, Hole in the Wall, Liberty Lunch, Raven's Garage, Ritz Theatre, State Theatre, Steamboat, Texas Tavern, Thistles

CO-SPONSORING PUBLICATIONS
Austin Chronicle, Dallas Observer, Gambit (New Orleans), *In Between* (Galveston), *K.C. Pitch* (Kansas City), *New Times* (Phoenix), *Nightflying* (Little Rock), *Oklahoma Gazette* (Oklahoma City), *Public News* (Houston), *Route Sixty-Six* (Albuquerque), *San Antonio Current, Times of Acadiana* (Lafayette), *Upstate* (Shreveport, LA), *Wavelength* (New Orleans), *Westword* (Denver)

KEYNOTE SPEAKER
Huey Meaux Joe Nick Patoski remembers introducing Meaux "as an experienced music business veteran whose entire career was based on working with outsiders and connecting them to the insiders.

south by southwest

SXSW

music and media conference

AUSTIN, TEXAS

MARCH 13-15, 1987

An opportunity for people in the music business and alternative media in this region and nationally to meet and share ideas about mutual interests

THURSDAY, MARCH 12:
■ 8pm-2am: music showcases

FRIDAY, MARCH 13:
2pm: registration check-in begins
8pm: the Austin Chronicle's 5th annual
Austin Music Awards show

SATURDAY, MARCH 14:
9am-6pm: trade show
10am: opening speaker & panel discussion

Once he had the podium, it was Huey's usual rap, in his thick Cajun accent (his comments on the Chicano music segment of the Latin Music USA series that recently aired again on PBS had to be subtitled, even though he was speaking

in English). I'm sure Huey talked in his speech about payola and promo — he loved telling the story about taking twenty and hundred dollar bills, crumpling them up and tossing them into the trashcan when he visited radio stations, then saying, 'I don't think a janitor cleaning up ever found one of those,' to make the point how promo was done, and how the business operated on a 'favor for a favor' basis."

MEMORABLE PANELS

There were just 15 total — 10 Workshops and 5 meetings dubbed the Professional Caucus Series, which included the stern warning: "Attendance is limited to professionals in these fields." (It's unclear whether someone stood at the door to verify the requisite level of professionalism required to participate.)

Panel titles included:

"Band 101" How to get a group started — booking, promotion, getting press coverage, etc.

"Music Industry Business Practices" Business and accounting practices and issues unique to the music field

"Whither Rock?" Music writers talk about where we're headed

NOTABLE PANELISTS

Jim Dickinson, legendary producer and musician, on the "Record Production" panel

Kevin Wommack, future manager of Los Lonely Boys and others, on the "Music Industry Contacts" panel

Jody Denberg, founding program director of

KGSR (but with KLBJ at that time), on the "Alternatiave Radio" panel

Joe Nick Patoski, renowned author and band manager, on the "Band 101" panel

Kim Buie, longtime A&R exec (at that time with Island Records), on the "Dealing With The Majors" panel

Mark Josephson, co-founder of the New Music Seminar, on the "Dealing With Independent Labels" panel

Brownlee Ferguson, head of Bluewater Music, on the "Songwriters' Workshop" panel

Beverly Griffith, of what was then Interfirst Bank, on the "Music Industry Business Practices" panel

Ernie Gammage, then-president of the Texas Music Association, on the "Regional Music Industry Development" panel

Jeff Whittington, early-days music editor of *The Austin Chronicle,* on the "Whither Rock" panel

MEMORABLE SHOWCASES

> A Saturday night bill at Antone's featured the LeRoi Brothers, who at that time were on the downside of their reign as the kings of Austin roots-rock but still were a first-rate bar band, and the blues chanteuses Lou Ann Barton and Angela Strehli, who not long thereafter teamed up with Marcia Ball for a high-profile trio album that helped establish the Antone's record label.

> Steamboat, then the flagship music venue on Sixth Street, featured a bill that included the Eliza Gilkyson Band, well before her return to Austin from Los Angeles and her resurrection as one of the city's most revered singer-songwriters. The hot names on the bill were probably local upstarts Zulu Time and Alamo Choir, but neither ended up becoming more than a passing phase.

> Liberty Lunch's Saturday night lineup cast a light on the venue's renowned musical diversity, with acts such as rising reggae stars the Killer Bees and hot hip-hop/funk acts Bad Mutha Goose and Do Dat.

> Nearly everyone on Thursday night's bill at the Continental Club made waves in the country-folk realm not long after appearing on this show: the Jimmie Gilmore Band, the Darden Smith Band,

the David Halley Band, and Hal Michael Ketchum. (Only opener Greg Schilling, frontman for 1987 Austin Music Awards "Best New Band" winner Hell's Cafe, never got a record out.)

NOTABLE ACTS

Hal Michael Ketchum In an early slot on that Thursday showcase at the Continental, the future country star still billed himself with his middle name at the time. Ketchum had yet to release his indie debut record *Threadbare Alibis*, and his Curb Records breakthrough *Past The Point of Rescue* was still four years away.

Butch Hancock & Jimmie Gilmore Whereas Ketchum was using his middle name, Gilmore was NOT using his at that point; his HighTone debut appeared under the name Jimmie Dale Gilmore the following year. He and his longtime Flatlanders cohort Hancock co-hosted a songwriters showcase on Saturday at the State Theatre.

Reverend Horton Heat The psychobilly sensation-to-be wouldn't see their national Sub Pop breakthrough for another five years, but were quickly becoming a regional favorite on the Texas club scene. They played a Saturday night showcase at the Cave Club featuring almost all Dallas bands.

Dash Rip Rock Up-and-comers on Mammoth Records at the time, the New Orleans trio played Saturday night at the Continental Club. Drummer Fred LeBlanc later went on to form Cowboy Mouth, who had a string of indie and major-label records.

King's X A progressive metal band from Houston that ended up signing with Megaforce Records as a result of their Sunday night showcase at the Cave Club. A young Jeff Ament spoke highly of the group in the early days of Pearl Jam's rise to stardom.

Little Joe y la Familia One of the premier bands in Latin music, Little Joe Hernandez's crew was just starting to hit their peak when they played the first SXSW, on a Sunday night bill at Liberty Lunch. Their first Grammy nomination came a year later; they won one in 1991.

Lonesome Strangers The Los Angeles band, led by Everlys-esque frontmen Randy Weeks and Jeff

Rymes, played Sunday night at the Continental Club. Shortly thereafter, they turned up as backing vocalists on a Dwight Yoakam record, and released a self-titled album on HighTone.

Walter Hyatt The longtime frontman for Austin acoustic institution Uncle Walt's Band was the first act of the evening on Gilmore & Hancock's songwriters showcase. Hyatt had solo albums on MCA and Sugar Hill in the early '90s, but was killed in 1996 on the ValuJet crash in Florida's Everglades.

Wagoneers Drummer Tom Lewis says the young country outfit's Saturday night showcase at Hole in the Wall didn't really play a role in their signing with A&M Records shortly thereafter, but he did have one very distinct if unusual memory of the show: "A few songs into the set I noticed an ex-girlfriend dancing on the small dance floor in front of the band. By the end of the song she

> "At the first producers panel, I asked Jim Dickinson if he thought alcohol was a positive or a negative in the studio. Part of his response was a story about the Replacements: "So after we'd finished cutting the record, one of the maintenance guys asked me how the vomit got so high on the studio walls. I told him, 'Well, man, they were puking into their hands and throwing it at each other.' That's just how it was, man." ■ Steve Chaney, longtime SXSW staffer

screamed and grabbed her face with both hands. She pointed down to the floor and there I saw an almost perfectly round pool of what appeared to be blood. She ran out the front door screaming hysterically. Before I knew it an older woman burst through the crowd and ran up on stage and stood before me and shook a long finger at me, saying, 'You stay away from my daughter!' This was all in the middle of our set. I later found out my ex had concocted a plan to stage her miscarriage complete with fake blood that she poured out of a bottle. This explains the perfect pool of blood I saw on the dance floor."

SOME OF THE REGIONAL ACTS
Buck Pets (Dallas); Daylights (Dallas); Shallow Reign (Dallas); Augie Meyers (San Antonio); Code Red (Houston); Arms Akimbo (Atlanta, GA);

Defenestration (Oklahoma City, OK); Electric Third Rail (Boulder, CO); Soul Merchants (Denver, CO); Jubilee Dive (Little Rock, AR); The Muttz (Albuquerque, NM); Mamou (Mamou, LA)

SOME OF THE AUSTIN ACTS

Beto y los Fairlanes; Bad Mutha Goose; Dino Lee; Glass Eye; Go Dog Go; Mitch Watkins Group; Nice Strong Arm; Ponty Bone & the Squeezetones; Tail Gators; Texas Instruments; W.C. Clark

> "I think everyone who attended got something out of the conference, and most importantly, I think the event went beyond affirming Austin's status as a music center (no great surprise there) and planted the potential in other cities for their own 'scenes.' To that end, SXSW truly was a regional music and media conference." ■ Gil Asakawa of Denver's *Westword*, after attending the first SXSW

WHATEVER HAPPENED TO...

Dan Del Santo The unofficial mayor of world music in Austin, Del Santo played Friday at Liberty Lunch. Legal troubles eventually led him to leave the country; his death in Mexico in 2001 was a sad occasion for the Austin music community.

Supernatural Family Band A father figure of the left-field Lubbock music scene, Tommy Hancock and his daughters, along with other family and friends and occasional guest members, played Thursday night at Raven's Garage (now the site of Emo's). Tommy appeared in the documentary film *Lubbock Lights*; the daughters formed the Texana Dames. Once in a very blue moon, there are reunion shows.

Hickoids The self-proclaimed "children of the corn nuts" were waaaay ahead of the alt-country curve when they played the first SXSW on Sunday night at the Continental Club. Its members later were involved in running the Hole in the Wall, and have performed with the band Gay Sportscasters.

Hundredth Monkey The short-lived but engaging Austin band, which included frontwoman Kris McKay and songwriters James Dodds and Patrice Sullivan, played Saturday night at the Ritz. McKay went on to record solo albums for the Arista and Shanachie labels.

Alison Rogers An Austin coffeehouse regular in the mid-'80s, Rogers eventually married and raised a family with the legendary country-folk singer-songwriter Willis Alan Ramsey.

SOFTBALL TOURNEY

"We don't need paperwork, we're musicians!" The first tournament got off to a rocky start when someone (OK, Louis Meyers) forgot the field rental agreement, leading to a confrontation with neighborhood players who didn't see why they should forfeit their regular Sunday pickup game for a bunch of pallid music types. Barbecue legend C.B. "Stubbs" Stubblefield, hired to cater the event, showed up without serving utensils, leaving diners to scoop food with bare hands and beer cups. At least one registrant was benched with severe food poisoning, but a tradition was born. The Mixed Media team won the first championship game with a 16-3 victory over the Record Companies. ■

1988

SXSW **STATS** March 10 - 13

BY THE NUMBERS

415 showcasing artists

32 panels, workshops & sessions

27 venues & stages

1,200 registrants

$45-75 registration

$10 festival pass
Paper ticket, not wristband

0 pages in program guide
No formal program guide; 18 pages of stapled together photocopies

42 trade show exhibitors

EVENT HEADQUARTERS

Austin Crest Hotel, 111 E. 1st St.

AUSTIN MUSIC AWARDS

Friday, March 11, at Austin Opera House
  Performers Timbuk 3, Joe Ely, Wagoneers, Killer Bees, Darden Smith, True Believers, Grey Ghost; MC Paul Ray

SXSW SHOWCASE VENUES

Anchovies, Antone's, Austin Opera House, Back Room, Big Mamou, Birraporetti's, Cactus Cafe, Chicago House, Colorado Street Cafe, Continental Club, Coyote Club, Driskill Hotel Ballroom, Esther's Pool, Hole in the Wall, Joe's Generic Bar, Hut's, Liberty Lunch, The Loft, Maceo's, Raven's, Ritz, Steamboat, Shuck Finn's, Texas Tavern, Toulouse, Wylie's, 111 Club (at Austin Crest)

CO-SPONSORING PUBLICATIONS

Austin Chronicle, Creative Loafing (Atlanta), *Dallas Observer, Gris-Gris* (Baton Rouge), *In Between* (Galveston), *K.C. Pitch* (Kansas City), *New Times* (Phoenix), *Nightflying* (Little Rock), *Oklahoma Gazette* (Oklahoma City), *Public News* (Houston), *Route Sixty-Six* (Albuquerque), *San Antonio Current, Times of Acadiana* (Lafayette), *Washington Media Ear* (Alexandria, VA), *Wavelength* (New Orleans), *Westword* (Denver)

NICK BARBARO
SXSW CO-DIRECTOR
AUSTIN CHRONICLE
Austin, TX

KEYNOTE SPEAKER

Bob Guccione Jr., publisher of *Spin* magazine. Music critic Michael Corcoran, at the time a columnist for *The Austin Chronicle* and a regular contributor to *Spin*, helped arrange for Guccione's appearance. "I don't remember much about his speech, but he definitely had a good time at SXSW," SXSW director Roland Swenson recalled. "He was omnipresent, hitting all the hot shows, and like his dad, he had an eye for the ladies. We called him 'the Gooch' and he liked it."

MEMORABLE PANELS

For the first couple of years, panels remained quite fundamental and simple. The 1988 batch featured such nondescript names as **"Indie Labels," "Publicity," "Management," "Booking,"** and **"In The Studio."** A bigger challenge was getting the public address system to behave in the conference rooms of the Austin Crest; at times, the voices of the panelists in one room got piped into the speakers in an adjacent panel room, and vice versa.

"Logistically, the conference was about as smooth as the Elephant Man's ass, with slow registration lines, various sound problems, showcase snafus and on and on. But damned if I didn't have the greatest time since the night at Club Hubba Hubba in Honolulu when that stripper snatched enough $5 bills off my nose to put herself through medical school." ■ Michael Corcoran in *The Austin Chronicle*, March 25, 1988

NOTABLE PANELISTS

Frank Riley (Venture Booking), Terry Lickona (Austin City Limits), Mark Williams (Virgin Records), Dave Margulies (CMJ), Jefferson Holt (R.E.M. manager), Pete Anderson (Dwight Yoakam producer), Cary Baker (IRS Records publicist), Joe McEwen (CBS Records), Joel Webber (Island Records)

MEMORABLE SHOWCASES

> The Back Room operated 2 showcase stages that year, perhaps a bit of a stretch given that the club was tucked away in a strip mall on the south side of the river more than 2 miles from the conference hotel. Still, it handled some of the bigger bills of the weekend, including a Saturday night lineup on its main stage that included New Orleans' Dash Rip Rock, Boston's Scruffy the Cat and Austin's Wild Seeds. On the club's second stage that night were — six bands from Tallahassee, Florida?!

> Liberty Lunch's Saturday night lineup featured an improbable 16 Texas acts, billed as a "reggae/rap/funk" showcase. Houston act Sir Rap A Lot didn't quite end up going down in history like the similarly named Seattle artist.

> Antone's could always be counted on to throw a Chicago ringer into the mix, and so Saturday's headliner was the legendary Albert Collins. The opener was a then little-known recent arrival to town named Chris Thomas (later known as Chris Thomas King).

> Raven's Garage, which later became Emo's, had a solid Saturday lineup of Americana talent including Texas songwriting great Billy Joe Shaver, rising honky-tonker Jim Lauderdale (with guitarist/producer Pete Anderson in tow), and Austin fiddle fixture Champ Hood.

> Sunday was a far busier night back in the early days; 20 clubs had Sunday showcases in '88. (This was largely because Friday night was still almost entirely devoted to the Austin Music Awards.) The vast majority of Sunday shows were Austin acts (for obvious reasons, since most out-of-towners were gone by then). The hidden jewel among them was Tex Thomas & the Danglin' Wranglers at Hut's, which featured unsung local hero Harvey Young backed by some of the city's finest players. *Spin* publisher Bob Guccione Jr. was among those who raved about the Hut's show after the fest.

NOTABLE ACTS

Kelly Willis The 19-year-old singer, backed by her band the Fireballs (and listed in the schedule as being from Washington, D.C.), played the opening slot at Antone's on Thursday night. Soon she'd relocate to Austin and issue a series of records on MCA.

American Music Club The San Fransico band was relatively well-established on the underground

circuit by 1988. Their appearance at the Austin Opera House on Saturday night was one of the first showcases at SXSW by a nationally-known indie buzz-band.

Billy Ray Cyrus Among the little-known acts who appeared on Thursday night's showcase at the un-hip Italian restaurant Birraporetti's was a Nashville singer who was listed in the official SXSW lineup as "Billy Ray Cyris."

Poi Dog Pondering The previous spring, the Hawaiian band had stopped in Austin while crossing the mainland playing gigs on the street. They liked the town so much that they settled there after their trek was over, and by March 1988 had become enough of a draw to warrant a Saturday headlining slot at Texas Tavern on the UT campus. They signed with Columbia Records a year later.

Material Issue The power-pop trio was a rising star on the Chicago scene when they played Thursday night at the Coyote Club. They released several major-label albums in the early-mid '90s before meeting a sad end when frontman Jim Ellison committed suicide in 1996.

Jayhawks Do you remember Cleveland's Hyka? D.C.'s The Baltek? NYC's Invisible Pedestrians? Doubtful...but you're probably familiar with Minneapolis band the Jayhawks, who shared a bill with those other bands on Saturday night at the Coyote Club. Soon they'd sign with their hometown label Twin/Tone for a 1989 album before a series of major-label efforts over the next couple of decades.

Ten Hands An all-Dallas lineup at The Loft on Thursday night included this high-energy outfit, whose lineup included drummer Matt Chamberlain. A couple of years later, Chamberlain was the touring drummer for an upstart Seattle group called Pearl Jam just before their debut album was released. He later joined the *Saturday Night Live* band and became one of rock's top session drummers.

Dangerous Toys The young Austin metal band led by Jason McMaster headlined Sunday on the Back Room's main stage and a year later had a record out on Columbia.

Robert Earl Keen A young talent with a lot of promise and a deal with Sugar Hill Records, Keen played a Saturday songwriters lineup at Cactus Cafe on the UT campus. Over the next decade he became one of the most accomplished Texas troubadours since Townes Van Zandt and Jerry Jeff Walker.

"At 2:15 in the morning, with maybe 400-500 people left, the True Believers with Richard Lloyd on guitar truly cleansed my soul and I felt washed in the blood of the lamb. Not that the entire bill wasn't spectacular, but at that moment I could finally relax, and did."
■ SXSW co-director Louis Black, on the 1988 Austin Music Awards show

Barnburners Sunday night's headliner at Colorado Street Cafe was this short-lived Austin bluegrass-folk trio. They never put out an album but all three made their mark on Americana music in the years to come: banjo player Danny Barnes starred with the Bad Livers, guitarist

Rich Brotherton became an ace in Robert Earl Keen's band, and bassist J.D. Foster toured with the likes of Lucinda Williams and Patty Griffin while producing albums for many artists including Richard Buckner and Marc Ribot.

Picket Line Coyotes This ragtag rock band hailed from Shreveport, La., when they played at Joe's Generic Bar on Thursday night. Eventually they moved to Dallas and then Austin, where leader Kevin Russell ended up as a key player in the Gourds, one of the city's most beloved and enduring bands of the past two decades.

Scott Garber A Thursday-night songwriters bill at Colorado Street Cafe featured this Tucson musician, who decided to move to Austin shortly thereafter. A former bassist for noted Tucson band Giant Sand, Garber ended up playing with many well-known Austin acts over the next decade, including Alejandro Escovedo.

SOME OF THE REGIONAL ACTS

3 on a Hill (Dallas); Brave Combo (Denton); Fab Motion (Houston); Song Dogs (New Orleans, LA); Wayne Toups & Zyedcajun (Crowley, LA); Fortunetellers (Oklahoma City, OK); Bill White Acre (Denver, CO); Gunbunnies (Little Rock, AR); River Roses (Tucson, AZ); The Strand (Phoenix, AZ); Michelle Malone (Atlanta, GA)

SOME OF THE AUSTIN ACTS

Bill Carter & the Blame, Do Dat, Evan Johns & the H-Bombs, Grains of Faith, Kris McKay, Lee Roy Parnell, Miracle Room, Shoulders, Steve Fromholz, Two Hoots & a Holler, Two Nice Girls, Van Wilks, Will & the Kill, Zulu Time, Zydeco Ranch

WHATEVER HAPPENED TO...

Donny Ray Ford A forefather of sorts to the Dallas alternative-country scene, Ford (who played on Saturday night at the Continental Club) wrote a song called "Cowboy Boots" that achieved cult-classic status in the '90s through a version recorded by North Carolina band the Backsliders.

Will T. Massey Still in his teens when he played a Saturday songwriter showcase at Chicago House, the Texas songwriter released an album three years later on MCA that was produced by Springsteen keyboardist Roy Bittan, but it took the better part of two decades for his next disc to surface.

Public Bulletin The opening band on Saturday's showcase at the Texas Tavern consisted of high school friends from San Marcos. Lineup and name changes (Hey Zeus, Black Irish) marked the next few years; bassist/songwriter Rob Thomas eventually ended up in Los Angeles and created the cult-favorite TV shows *Veronica Mars* and *Party Down*.

SOFTBALL TOURNEY

The second softball tournament was held at Walnut Creek Park's Havins Fields in far north Austin (or what seemed like "far north" at the time). With plummeting temperatures, no umpires, and an interminable dispute on a game-ending appeal play, the 1988 tournament ended hours late in freezing darkness, with the Record Companies avenging last year's title-game loss by edging Mixed Media 9-8. A disgruntled park concessionaire menaced softball commissioner Susan Moffat with a tire iron, but in the end it was no harm, no foul. ■

SXSW II

SCHEDULE OF EVENTS

THURSDAY MARCH 10
1:00pm- 9:00pm Registration at Waller Creek Plaza (500 N. I-35)
6:00pm- 9:00pm Opening Party
9:00pm- 2:00am South by Southwest Music Festival

FRIDAY, MARCH 11
8:00am   SXSW Trade Show Set Up
9:00am- 7:00pm Registration at Waller Creek Plaza
9:00am- 6:00pm SXSW Trade Show
11:00am-12:30pm Opening Remarks
1:30pm- 5:30pm Workshops & Panels
2:00pm- 8:00pm Registration at Austin Opera House (200 Academy)
8:00pm- 2:00am Austin Music Awards (Austin Opera House)
            'til 4amAfter Hours Party

SATURDAY, MARCH 12
9:00am- 5:30pm SXSW Trade Show
11:00am- 5:30pm Workshops & Panels
6:00pm- 8:00pm Cocktail Party
8:00pm- 4:00am SXSW Music Festival

SUNDAY, MARCH 13
11:00am-12:30pm Closing Meeting and Gospel Music
2:00pm- 8:00pm SXSW Softball Tournament & Bar-B-Q
2:00pm- 2:00am SXSW Music Festival

MAKE RESERVATIONS NOW!
SXSW II will be held at the Waller Creek Plaza Hotel in the heart of Austin's club scene, East Sixth Street
Rates: $55 single   In Texas: 1-800-235-8181
$65 dbl. to quad   National: 1-800-327-8181
        Prices good till 2-26-88
Waller Creek Plaza
500 N. I-35
Austin, TX 78701

REGISTRATION GETS YOU ALL THIS

• **WORKSHOPS AND PANELS** — two days, twenty different topics featuring industry leaders sharing their expertise plus an opportunity to learn and teach with your peers.

• **SOUTH BY SOUTHWEST MUSIC FESTIVAL** Last year 170 bands from all over the country played in fifteen different clubs during the conference. Your registration gets you in for all of it.

• **AUSTIN MUSIC AWARDS** — Every year Austin's music community gathers to honor its own at the party of the year. A chance to hear Austin music at its best.

• **SXSW SOFTBALL TOURNAMENT & BAR-B-Q** Record companies team up against bands, newspapers take on radio stations and everybody eats barbecue. How can you lose?

• **INSERTS** Advertise your business in the SXSW registrants packet for $100. (You provide 1200 8½x11 printed sheets of paper to us.)

• **SXSW TRADE SHOW** Meet with labels, newspapers, music associations, promotion companies and more at the trade show. Rent your own table for $150. Good for two days, includes 2 exhibition-only passes, (gets you in the trade show and the music festival, but not the music awards, panels/workshops or BBQ).

REGISTRATION FORM

Name _____
Company _____
Title _____
Address _____
City _____ State _____
Zip _____ Country _____
Phone _____ Telex _____
Play Softball? _____
Bring a Glove? _____

QUESTIONS? CALL 512/473-8995

☐ Please add me to your mailing list
☐ I enclose
    ☐ $45 (prior to July 30, 1987)
    ☐ $55 (prior to December 31, 1987)
    ☐ $65 (prior to February 26, 1988, walkup $75)

per registration for ____ persons	$
less 20% group discount for four or more registrants	-
REGISTRATION SUBTOTAL	$
EXTRAS	
Trade Show Table $150 (2 days, includes 3x6 table, 2 chairs, 2 exhibition only passes)	$
Inserts in registration packet $100 (you provide 1200 8½x11 sheets)	$
Extra Austin Music Award Tickets ($7)	$
Extra SXSW Music Festival Passes ($10)	$
TOTAL ENCLOSED	$

MAKE CHECKS PAYABLE TO: SOUTH BY SOUTHWEST P.O. BOX 49066 AUSTIN, TEXAS 78765

SXSW **STATS** March 16 - 19

BY THE NUMBERS

349 showcasing artists

39 panels, workshops & sessions

26 venues & stages

1,632 registrants

$55-100 registration

$10 festival pass
Paper ticket, not wristband

54 pages in program guide

42 trade show exhibitors

EVENT HEADQUARTERS

Marriott Hotel, 701 E. 11th St.

AUSTIN MUSIC AWARDS

Thursday, March 16, at Austin Opera House.

Performers Omar & the Howlers; Lou Ann Barton, Marcia Ball & Angela Strehli backed by Doug Sahm & the West Side Horns; Two Nice Girls with special guest Lucinda Williams; Butch Hancock & the Sunspots with special guest Jimmie Dale Gilmore; MC Paul Ray

SXSW SHOWCASE VENUES

Anchovies, Antone's, Apollo's, Back Room, Blue Bayou, Broken Spoke, Chicago House, Club Cairo, Club Sandwich, Colorado Street Cafe, Continental Club, Crest Hotel Ballroom, Driskill Hotel Ballrooom, Esther's Follies, Green Mesquite, Hole in the Wall, Hut's, Liberty Lunch, Mercado Caribe, Planetarium, Raven's, Ritz, Santi's Live, Steamboat, The World, Wylie's

CO-SPONSORING PUBLICATIONS

Austin Chronicle, Creative Loafing (Atlanta/Charlotte/Tampa), *Current* (San Antonio), *Dallas Observer, Maryland Musician* (Baltimore), *Memphis Star, Metro* (Nashville), *New Times* (Phoenix), *Nightflying* (Little Rock), *The Note* (Lawrence), *Oklahoma Gazette* (Oklahoma City), *Public News* (Houston), *Spectrum* (Little Rock), *Times of Acadiana* (Lafayette), *Tucson Weekly, Wavelength* (New Orleans), *Westword* (Denver)

KEYNOTE SPEAKER

Robert Christgau, longtime *Village Voice* rock critic. "He gave an articulate keynote, correctly tracing the origins of rock and roll to our general area, which I appreciated," remembers SXSW director Roland Swenson. "We had expected Christgau to be a little stiff (and we weren't disappointed), so we decided to add a second speaker, Mojo Nixon, to the bill. Borrowing a term from my church background, we called it the 'Invocation.' Nixon got up and said that he had been thinking and thinking about what to say to all of us, and had finally figured it out after staying up all night. And

"I personally feel a sense of pride in having played a part in encouraging BMI to get involved in SXSW from the get-go. Today, when people ask me for advice or counsel about the music industry, I say, 'I don't do that anymore and don't miss it.' Well, that's not exactly true. Of all the things I did while I was with BMI, helping nurture, encourage and grow Texas music was the one thing I am most proud of."
■ Roger Sovine, BMI (retired)

what he had to say was, 'FUCK YOU!' He ranted on for awhile about people who were screwing up the music business. It was pretty funny."

MEMORABLE PANELS

While the panels remained fairly basic in subject matter — **"Publishing Deals," "Do It Yourself," "Radio Promotion"** — there was an increased presence of experienced industry veterans from Los Angeles, New York and Nashville who were taking part. Also of note was a panel titled **"International Concerns,"** which featured representatives from Germany, England, Spain, Denmark and Canada, and hinted at the soon-to-be-expanding international scope of SXSW.

NOTABLE PANELISTS

Larry Hamby (CBS Nashville), Jay Boberg (IRS Records), Guy Clark (Texas songwriting legend), Ken Irwin (Rounder Records founder), Elliott Mazer (Neil Young producer), Rosemary Carroll (Kurt Cobain & Courtney Love attorney), John Kunz (Waterloo Records owner), Mark Proct (Fabulous

Thunderbirds manager), Bill Wyman (Chicago Reader journalist), Glenn Morrow (Bar/None Records), Wolfgang Doebeling (Berlin Independence Days), Geoff Travis (Rough Trade Records)

MEMORABLE SHOWCASES

> The Continental Club's Friday night bill featured Ronnie Lane, who'd relocated to Austin a few years earlier and was backed by several of the city's top musicians, as well as Dallas band Killbilly, a country-punk outfit that influenced several significant acts which arose in their wake (including Bad Livers and Old 97's).
> A Rough Trade Records showcase on Friday night at the Ritz included singer-songwriter Lucinda Williams, whose then-new self-titled album featured songs soon to be covered by Mary Chapin Carpenter, Patty Loveless and Tom Petty; and Chicago band Souled American, who'd been signed as the result of a showcase at SXSW the previous year.
> A songwriters showcase at the classic downtown coffeehouse venue Chicago House included two solo acts who would establish themselves in the '90s with alternative-pop and alternative-country bands, respectively: Austin's Miles Zuniga (later of Fastball) and Dallas' Rhett Miller (later of the Old 97's).
> Mojo Nixon & Skid Roper headlined a blockbuster bill at Liberty Lunch that also featured established Austin act Timbuk 3 (then signed to IRS Records) and rising Atlanta rockers Michelle Malone & Drag the River.
> A Jimmie Dale Gilmore showcase at the Driskill Hotel Ballroom hinted at SXSW's soon-to-be-blooming international element with West German acts Tracy Santa and Justice Hahn sharing the bill.
> A reggae/world-music lineup at Liberty Lunch featured an international draw, England's Pato Banton, as well as Austin's reigning reggae kings Michael E. Johnson & the Killer Bees and the inimitable Dan Del Santo's World Beat.
> Steamboat featured a surprisingly strong bill for a Sunday night, with New York band the Fleshtones and New Orleans' Dash Rip Rock

joined by local roots-scene favorites Jesse Taylor, Two Hoots & A Holler and High Noon.

NOTABLE ACTS

Doug Sahm Antone's on Saturday night was the slot for Sahm's first appearance at SXSW. The historic blues club was an ideal venue for Sahm at the time, as he issued an album on the Antone's record label that year.

Alex Chilton More than two decades before a memorial show in the wake of his sudden passing became an all-time SXSW highlight in 2010, the reclusive rock legend headlined a Saturday showcase on the downstairs stage at Club Cairo.

Alejandro Escovedo Not long after his band True Believers had split up, Escovedo made his first SXSW appearance under his own name on a Saturday night showcase at Hole in the Wall.

Gin Blossoms The pride of Scottsdale, Arizona, was still relatively young and unknown when they played the upstairs stage at Club Cairo on Saturday night. By the early '90s, they'd signed to A&M and had a big hit on modern rock radio with "Hey Jealousy."

Toni Price Opening the Friday night show at Antone's was this young blues-folk-country singer from Nashville. She'd moved to Austin by the end of the year; her Tuesday-night happy-hour gig at the Continental Club became a hallmark of Austin music in the 1990s.

Giant Sand The heralded Tucson underground-rock band, playing just as a duo with Howe Gelb and John Convertino, made the first of many fondly remembered SXSW appearances on a Sunday night bill upstairs at Club Cairo.

Sara Hickman The Dallas singer-songwriter, who played Saturday at Club Cairo, went on to release a string of major-label albums in the early '90s. She eventually moved to Austin in the mid-'90s.

Walter Hyatt & Champ Hood As members of Uncle Walt's Band, Hyatt and Hood had been integral cogs in the Austin acoustic-music community for more than a decade. They reunited for a duo show Saturday at Blue Bayou; their appearances together had become less frequent since Hyatt's move to Nashville, where he put out albums

on MCA and Sugar Hill before his death in the ValuJet Everglades crash in 1996.

REGIONAL ACTS

Decadent Dub Team (Dallas), the Judys (Houston), Chickasaw Mudd Puppies (Athens, GA), Sidewinders (Tucson, AZ), Bluerunners (Lafayette, LA), Spanic Boys (Milwaukee, WI), Sin City Disciples (Kansas City, MO), Black Girls (Raleigh, NC), Wednesday Week (Los Angeles), Dumptruck (Boston), Tiny Lights (Hoboken, NJ), Mauschovonian Love Beat (Stillwater, OK)

AUSTIN ACTS

Angela Strehli, Austin Lounge Lizards, Erbie Bowser & T.D. Bell, Hand of Glory, I-Tex, Jimmy Carl Black & the Grandmothers, Marcia Ball Band, Neptunes, Ray Wylie Hubbard, Reivers, Tish Hinojosa, Water the Dog

WHATEVER HAPPENED TO...

Chris Wall A recent transplant to Austin from Jackson Hole, Wyoming, Wall was a rising country talent when he played a Friday night showcase at the Broken Spoke. He never quite hit the big time as a performer, but one of his songs did when Confederate Railroad had a country smash with "Trashy Women" in 1993.

> "If SXSW showed anything, it was that performers and business people alike have to get out there and let people know they exist, and they can't be shy about it."
> ■ Ed Ward in *The Austin Chronicle,* **March 31, 1989**

John Thomas Griffith — The New Orleans musician was on his way down from a previous tenure with the hitmaking Red Rockers when he played a Saturday showcase at Santi's Live under his own name. He was on the way back up a year later, teaming with Fred LeBlanc of Dash Rip Rock in a new outfit called Cowboy Mouth.

Prezence The San Antonio metal band, part of a Friday night showcase at the Back Room, featured Doug Sahm's son Shawn, who co-produced the 2010 tribute to his dad *Keep Your Soul* and currently performs with the Tex Mex Experience.

SOFTBALL TOURNEY

The Sunday tournament and barbecue moved to its permanent home at the Krieg Complex on Pleasant Valley Road just south of Town Lake in East Austin. Learning from the previous year's controversy, SXSW employs real umpires on the field for the first time, and the games run on schedule. The umps quickly adapt to SXSW rule tweaks: profanity and alternative footwear allowed. Thank journalist Chris Morris for the latter: "I hadn't packed any appropriate shoes,

so I played in my cowboy boots." Just Morris' luck that his Print Media team got all the way to the championship match before losing 10-6 to the Talent Buyers. "I wound up playing three games in those damn boots," he agonized. "I couldn't walk for three days." Meanwhile, back in the bleachers, *Jersey Beat* editor Jim Testa remembers attending with Rabid Cat Records honcho Laura Croteau, who brought along her toddler son: "The little boy wandered off. Laura and I searched for him frantically and finally found him at the beer keg, where Gibby Haynes was giving the lad his first sip of Shiner Bock." ■

South By Southwest co-directors and proselytizers Nick Barbaro, Roland Swenson, Louis Jay Meyers, and Louis Black (from left): "First and foremost," says Swenson, "what we want to do is increase the internal communication in our region."

Beyond Austin's city limits

By John T. Davis

AUSTIN–It was a Friday morning, and the office housing the South By Southwest Music and Media Conference was as quiet as it was ever going to be. The telephones, for a moment, were mercifully silent. Big chalkboards, covering two of the walls, were smudged and scrawled with names: names of bands, names of workshops, names of nightclubs, names of panelists. Another wall housed some makeshift shelving to contain a fraction of the approximately 800 demo tapes sent by regional bands thirsting to be featured on one of the SXSW music showcases. A blizzard of message slips, Post-Em notes, and scraps of paper scrawled with ballpoint heiroglyphics piled up in drifts among the chair and table legs. It was enough to make the editor of *Architectural Digest* open a vein.

But what the hell. Out of chaos, as Pancho Nietzsche said, comes an order of nachos. SXSW89 was emerging from the cups of cold coffee and tooth-marked pencil stubs like a phoenix.

On March 16, some 1,500 registrants and 300 acts converge in Austin to breathe life into the third annual installment of an event which is still very much in the process of defining itself. "The recognition factor is a *lot* higher this year," Roland Swenson was saying. Swenson labors as the director of special projects for *The Austin Chronicle*. It's a title which, fo- about half the year, translates as "director of South By Southwest."

"The first year, nobody knew who we were, obviously, because we hadn't done it yet," says Swenson. "Last year, we still had to do a lot of explaining. But this year, almost everybody we've talked to has heard of the conference, or knows someone who has."

That's hardly surprising. Swenson and the SXSW co-directors spent much of last year proselytizing for the affair at industry functions

> "We're not saying a band is going to get signed. All we say is that we will get the people here who can help a band move up the ladder. It's not often a band gets to invite 20 A&R people to see them play without having to fly them down, put them up, and get them drunk."
>
> —Louis Jay Meyers
> SXSW Music Festival organizer

like New York's New Music Seminar, the Berlin Independence Day convention, the College Music Journal (CMJ) convention, and the MIDEM market in Cannes, France. In its infancy, SXSW was bad. Now it's nationwide.

But the vision that propelled the conference's genesis remains the same, Swenson says. "First and foremost, what we want to do is increase the internal communication in our region. I used to be able to find out what was going on in, say, New Orleans only by reading about it in the na-

tional press. And the same was true in New Orleans; they were only hearing about Austin through the mass media."

To increase the volume of communication, SXSW89 is, like its predecessors, being co-sponsored by the *Chronicle* and other regional newspapers (like *Dallas Observer*) and magazines, representing regions from Atlanta to Phoenix to Denver. "I think the *Chronicle* has done a lot better job of reporting on regional

a regional musical forum. After last year's conference, over 15 showcasing performers received offers or signed deals with companies such as PolyGram (Louisiana's Wayne Toups), Arista (Austin's Kris McKay), Hightone (Austin's Jimmie Dale Gilmore), and Rough Trade (Chicago's Souled American, Austin's Two Nice Girls). SXSW signees from previous years include Darden Smith (CBS) and The Wagoneers (A&M), both from Austin. It would be disingenuous to suggest that the conference is solely responsible for these acts' good fortune, but the timing is difficult to disregard.

"What I'm happy with this year," Meyers says, "is that we have quite a few 'maybe' acts on the major labels—that is, acts that haven't broken [nationally] yet. The labels are trying to get them in front of the buyers and in front of the press, and get a buzz happening."

This year, the showcase bills are split almost exactly between Austin performers and out-of-town acts: some from way out of town. Meyers received submissions from Europe, the Caribbean, even the Soviet Union.

Upstairs, Louis Black is, unaccountably, a happy man. You wouldn't think a guy who had to put out a weekly newspaper (Black is editor of the *Chronicle*), coordinate an awards show, and trouble-shoot at warp speed could look so lighthearted. But Black is all smiles.

"I'm so damn happy with the way it's gone that I would just like to see more of the same," he says. "I mean, I never would have believed the number of groups that have gotten the kind of regional and national attention they've gotten out of the conference. I'd like to see more of that. We've certainly helped raise the recognition of Austin, and of the regional music industries as well."

Black, along with Swenson, Meyers, and *Chronicle* publisher Nick Barbaro, is one of the founding fathers of SXSW. The first year, he recalls, "the four of us decided everything, from the size of the paper clips to how sharp the pen-

cils had to [...]
ger and bigg[...]
have grown [...]
It wasn't lik[...]
dream that [...]
year has exc[...]
of lean back[...]
can do."

Another c[...]
central offic[...]
smoke hang[...]
jangles inc[...]
senior staf[...]
Everything [...]
dinating bl[...]
conference [...]

The roo[...]
and cough[...]
havoc with [...]
Swenson m[...]
schedule, r[...]
recruits thr[...]
Not all of t[...]
their missi[...]
with coffee [...]
through a [...]

"I'd just [...]
out ...."[...]
staffers. A [...]
veteran VI[...]
Showcase [...]
ecutive fro[...]
that, yes, I [...]
Panel. Th[...]

For Sou[...]
ly to appe[...]
animals th[...]
ty limits. I[...]
out and t[...]
dulgence [...]
Southwest[...]
the small l[...]
on. ■

*The 1989 [...]
is March 16[...]
SXSW and [...]
for regiona[...]*

bands since we started the conference," says Swenson, "and I think that's true of the co-sponsoring papers as well.

"Second," he continues, "we've gotten a lot of key people in the music business and the media to come down because they want to know what's going on in Austin. And this is one weekend where they can get a crash course on everything going on outside of L.A., New York, and Nashville."

That seems a fair assessment of SXSW's growing clout. South By Southwest is the sum of a number of components: there is the series of panels and workshops dealing with aspects of the industry, from booking and management to college radio and hip-hop; there's the SXSW Music Festival, which will showcase almost 300 acts in various Austin nightclubs over the course of three nights (March 17-19); there's the Austin Music Awards, the March 16 blow-out which celebrates the winners of the *Chronicle*'s annual readers' poll; and there are attendant events like the SXSW Videofest, a trade show, and an open house involving many of the city's music-related businesses.

"The whole sum of the convention is availability and accessibility," says Louis Jay Meyers, cigarette smoke wreathing his head. Meyers, who runs Austin's booking/talent agency E.Z. Money Productions, is largely responsible for coordinating and booking the *Observer*/Club Clearview Dallas showcase March 18 at The Planetarium at 705 Red River (which features Ten Hands, About 9 Times, Last Rites, Sedition, and Princess Tex).

"We're not saying a band is going to get signed," Meyers says. "All we say is that we will get the people here who can help a band move up the ladder. It's not often a band gets to invite 20 A&R people to see them play without having to fly them down, put them up, and get them drunk."

Meyers has some basis for optimism when he regards the potential of South By Southwest as

*Denton's Last Rites is one of approximately 300 c[...]
SXSW89. The band performs on a Dallas bill at [...]*

1990

SXSW STATS March 14 - 18

BY THE NUMBERS

424 showcasing artists
of 1,200 submissions

66 panels, workshops & sessions

23 venues & stages

2,162 registrants

$95-150 registration

$15 wristband

90 pages in program guide

46 trade show exhibitors

EVENT HEADQUARTERS

Hyatt Regency, 208 Barton Springs Rd.

AUSTIN MUSIC AWARDS

Wednesday, March 14, at Palmer Auditorium
Performers Nanci Griffith; James McMurtry; Poi Dog Pondering; Daniel Johnston; Townes Van Zandt; David Halley with Alejandro Escovedo, Michael Hall & Kris McKay; MC Paul Ray

SXSW SHOWCASE VENUES

Antone's, Austin Opera House, Austin Outhouse, Back Room, Blue Bayou, B-Tex Showbar, Cannibal Club, Chicago House, Colorado Street Cafe, Continental Club, Crest Hotel Ballroom, Hole in the Wall, Hut's, Hyatt Hotel Ballroom, Liberty Lunch, Mercado Caribe, Raven's, Raven's Outdoors, Ritz, Steamboat, Studio 6-A, Top Of The Marc, Tunnel Club

CO-SPONSORING PUBLICATIONS

Austin Chronicle, Creative Loafing (Atlanta/Tampa), *Dallas Observer, Maryland Musician* (Baltimore), *Memphis Flyer, The Metro* (Nashville), *New Times* (Phoenix), *Nightflying* (Little Rock), *The Note* (Lawrence, KS), *Oklahoma Gazette* (Oklahoma City), *Pacific News & Review* (Anaheim, CA), *Philadelphia City Paper, The Pitch* (Kansas City, MO), *Public News* (Houston), *The Rocket* (Seattle), *San Antonio Current, Spectator* (Raleigh, NC), *Spectrum* (Little Rock, AR), *Times of Acadiana* (Lafayette), *Tucson Weekly, Wavelength* (New Orleans), *Westword* (Denver)

KEYNOTE SPEAKER

Kinky Friedman, songwriter, novelist and future gubernatorial candidate. "Kinky gave a long, rambling keynote, punctuated with wisecracks about homosexuals and Jews," SXSW director Roland Swenson recalled. "Some people were offended, but after all, one of his most famous songs is 'They Ain't Makin' Jews Like Jesus Anymore,' so what did they expect?" Friedman's keynote was preceded by an invocation from Exene Cervenka of the punk band X.

MEMORABLE PANELS

The move to the Hyatt allowed for an expanded panels roster, which led to them being broken down into **"Panel Discussions," "Intensive Sessions"** and **"Workshops."** There were the usual **"Booking"** and **"Marketing"** and **"Management"** staples, but now a few curveballs began to be worked into the rotation:

"Trailblazers of the Music Industry" was tagged with the description, "Artists, producers and others who were there at the beginning recall the

"You've gotta be kidding. It's Tuesday morning and there's still visiting band members crashed in my living room!" ■ **Ken Lieck** in *The Austin Chronicle,* **March 23, 1990**

birth and growth of rock and roll and the record industry's reaction to it." Bob Johnston, who produced several of Bob Dylan's classic albums, moderated.

A series of workshops focused on regional scenes, with names such as **"Meet New Orleans"** and **"Meet Nashville"** and **"Meet St. Louis"**...and, in acknowledgment of SXSW's continued openness to the international community, **"Meet London"** and **"Meet Berlin."**

"Dead Van in the Middle of the Road" sought to help musicians learn how to perform basic repairs on their touring vehicles. "We had a mechanic (Steve McGuire) and a van he'd purposely fucked up in the parking lot, which he proceeded to diagnose and repair," explained Ed Ward, co-panels coordinator

in those years. "That went over great with everyone but the hotel, as I remember."

And then there were a couple of sessions labeled **"Band 101,"** which were suspiciously listed as being hosted by Bobbi Fleckman and Artie Fufkin of Polymer Records. "After people were seated in the room," director Roland Swenson recounts, "we would turn on a TV set and VCR and screen *Spinal Tap.* Some were amused, but not as much as we were."

NOTABLE PANELISTS

Tony Brown (MCA Records), Robert Palmer (*The New York Times*), Jonathan Poneman (Sub Pop Records), Jack Emerson (Jason & the Scorchers manager), Buck Williams (FBI Booking), Nigel Grainge (Ensign Records), Radney Foster & Bill Lloyd (hit country songwriters), George Gimarc (KDGE-Dallas), Paige Levy (Warner Bros. Nashville), Clifford Antone (Antone's), Robbie Robb (Tribe After Tribe), Carol Schutzbank (B-Side magazine)

MEMORABLE SHOWCASES

> Liberty Lunch's Thursday-night bill offered an intriguing contrast of veteran '80s artists who'd had moments in the sun (Athens band Pylon, Austin's own Reivers) and burgeoning acts whose heyday was just past the horizon (Kelly Willis, the Jayhawks).

> Studio 6-A, the UT campus room where *Austin City Limits* is filmed, appeared in the SXSW venue lineup for a bill of mostly local talent, including new Arista signee Kris McKay and a young band just catching fire called Twang Twang Shock-A-Boom.

> Raven's, in previous years a country venue, took on a very different tone for its Thursday-night outdoor-stage showcase, which consisted of a dozen rap and hip-hop acts including New York's Ultramagnetic MC's and Houston's Def IV.

> The Tunnel Club, a new Sixth Street venue with two stages, was busy on Thursday night with Boston garage-rockers Scruffy the Cat paired with Austin alt-bands Ed Hall and the Wannabes on one stage, and a bill full of Dallas

bands including Course of Empire and Killbilly on the other.

> The Sunday-night lineup at Antone's featured old-school Austin blues acts associated with Catfish Records, including the Grey Ghost, the East Side Band, and Blues Boy Hubbard & the Jets.

> Though it's perhaps a stretch to call it a "showcase," it's worth noting that the Austin Music Awards finally moved to its permanent Wednesday-night placement in the schedule with 1990's show. It was a particularly noteworthy songwriter-oriented lineup — almost certainly the only time that Townes Van Zandt and Daniel Johnston ever appeared on the same bill.

> Also not officially part of the "showcase" lineup was another gig that helped to spark a continuing tradition. "That year marked the first SXSW 'after-hours' show, which was the Joe Ely Band playing the ballroom of the Crest Hotel on Saturday night," director Swenson recalls. "When (codirector) Louis Black and I arrived at the show, we immediately noticed that none of the security people we had engaged had shown up, and the two of us spent most of the night on the staircase, trying fruitlessly to stop the crowds from swarming into the ballroom. The ceiling was low, and so was the stage, so you couldn't see the band unless you were right up front. Ely's manager was furious with us, until later when MCA president (and former Elvis Presley pianist) Tony Brown signed Ely to MCA after seeing him at the show."

NOTABLE ACTS

Joe "King" Carrasco Somehow it took four years for one of Austin's most recognizable acts of the '80s to make his SXSW debut, headlining a bill at the Austin Opera House.

Vic Chesnutt The late Athens, Ga., songwriter had recently released his Michael Stipe-produced debut album *Little* when he played a Thursday showcase at Hole in the Wall.

Del-Lords The New York outfit, which played Saturday at the Austin Opera House, included Scott Kempner, formerly of the Dictators, and Eric Ambel, who later became Steve Earle's guitarist.

Big Head Todd & the Monsters The Denver trio made its second straight SXSW appearance with a Saturday showcase at the Ritz; a major-label deal and a modest radio hit ("Bittersweet") followed three years later.

Let's Active North Carolina's Mitch Easter was known as much for his production (including R.E.M.'s *Murmur*) as for his quirky pop band, which played on Friday night at the Hyatt Ballroom.

"SXSW has grown. Clubs were more crowded. Breathing space was at a premium. The increased number of registrants meant more black leather jackets in the Hyatt than empty office spaces in downtown Austin." ■ Luke Torn in *The Austin Chronicle*, March 23, 1990

Trip Shakespeare Signed to Twin/Tone, the Minneapolis band, which played Friday night at the Ritz, included brothers Matt and Dan Wilson, the latter of whom had major pop success in the mid-'90s as leader of the band Semisonic (and later co-wrote songs with the Dixie Chicks).

Jon Ims A veteran songwriter from Denver who played an acoustic showcase at Chicago House on Thursday night, Ims would hit the top of the country charts the following year via Trisha Yearwood's version of his tune "She's In Love With The Boy."

Blake Babies The Boston band, which played Saturday at the Ritz, helped launch Juliana Hatfield to solo success in the '90s, while other members continued under the name Antenna.

SOME OF THE REGIONAL ACTS

Fever In The Funkhouse (Dallas), Pariah (San Antonio), Chainsaw Kittens (Oklahoma City, OK), the Jody Grind (Atlanta, GA), Charlie Burton & the Hiccups (Lincoln, NE), X-Tal (San Francisco, CA), Ranch Romance (Seattle, WA), Dumptruck (Boston, MA), Snatches of Pink (Chapel Hill, NC), Janis Eighteen (Norman, OK), Shot Down In Ecuador Jr. (New Orleans, LA), Forbidden Pigs (San Diego, CA)

SOME OF THE AUSTIN ACTS

Alamo Choir, Barb Donovan, Bouffant Jellyfish, Chaparral, Christine Albert, David Rodriguez, Ethyl & Methyl, Herman The German, Jimmy LaFave, Malachi, Pocket FishRmen, Stick People, Wayouts

SOME OF THE INTERNATIONAL ACTS

Mano Negra (Paris, France), Julian Dawson (London, England), Amos Garrett (Calgary, Canada), David Lindholm & White Midnight (Finland), Shuffle Demons (Toronto, Canada)

SOFTBALL GAME

For the second straight year, the Talent Buyers beat Print Media in the championship game, this time in a high-scoring 15-10 affair. One of the two teams of Bands scored a then-record 27 runs in a first-round game, obliterating the Record Companies squad. That must've felt good. ■

SXSW Music Festival Audience Tenders Political Correctness Primer In every situation, always keep in mind that your job is only to try to help people who are trying to get in to see a show, not to try to stop them from getting inside. You are not there to break up fights or throw people out, that is in every circumstance the responsibility of the club. Your only job is to let people know which line they should be in, if we are letting people in or not, what kind of passes are being let in, and how fast the line is or isn't moving. You might also recommend other shows in the area that may have room. Any individuals who might want to engage you in an argument about how unfair it is that they can't get in the show should be reminded that you are a volunteer and you are only there to try to help.

TWO IMPORTANT RULES
1. Be polite and never touch or put your hands on people in line. Do not attempt to argue with angry customers.
2. Never give the appearance that you have the ability to let people cut in line or to let people inside when admission has been cut off (You don't!). You cannot let your friends into sold-out shows. Appearing to have this kind of authority can cause intense resentment from people on line.

Frequently Asked Questions:
The following is some general information and advice on how to deal with some of the more difficult situations that may arise. The questions are ones we hear every year and the answers are suggestions of how you may want to deal with them, but you are not required to say anything you don't want to say.

Why do badges get in before wristbands? Who are these people?
"The bands that come to SXSW, come to play for the people who wear the badges. Without them, the bands wouldn't be here." *If that doesn't work, you could say that badges cost $195-$395 and wristbands cost $40-$51. If they say they can't afford a badge then you could suggest that they volunteer, like you did.*

Why can't I get in to this show? I bought a wristband.
"Your wristband says 'Many shows will fill up. Entry subject to venue capacity'."

Did you oversell wristbands?
"I'm a volunteer, I didn't sell any wristbands. But,there's enough room for everybody with a wristband or a badge a lot of other places, but not here right now. "

I am really pissed off about. . . (insert problem). Who do I talk to?
"You can call SXSW at 512-467-7979."

Once a club has reached its capacity, the SXSW cashier will tell club security to stop letting people in. At this point, dividing people who are walking up into seperate badge and wristband lines becomes very important. As people leave the venue, the venue will begin to allow badges in the same number to enter. (Two out, two in, etc.). Once the badge line is empty, the venue will begin letting wristbands in the same way. Part of your job will be to pay attention to how quickly (or slowly) the line is moving, in order to help people at the back of the line who have just walked up know what is going on. Once people are leaving steadily, you can help by counting people in and directing them to the cashier as someone else counts them out. There may be times when it might be a good idea to tell people not to waste their time waiting in line for a show that no one is leaving for and offer information about other shows.

1991

SXSW **STATS** March 16 - 19

Ron Suman
KTXT 88.1 FM
Lubbock, TX

SXSW 91

BY THE NUMBERS

512 showcasing artists
of 2,000 submissions

84 panels, workshops & sessions

27 venues & stages

2,833 registrants

$95-175 registration

$25-30 wristband

112 pages in program guide

44 trade show exhibitors

EVENT HEADQUARTERS
Hyatt Regency, 208 Barton Springs Rd.

AUSTIN MUSIC AWARDS
Wednesday, March 20, at Palmer Auditorium
  Performers Dangerous Toys, Texas Tornados, Arc Angels, E.R. Shorts; MC Paul Ray

SXSW SHOWCASE VENUES
311 Club, Abratto's, Antone's, Back Room, Broken Spoke, Cactus Cafe, Cannibal Club, Chances, Chicago House, City Coliseum, Continental Club, Hole in the Wall, Hut's, Hyatt Hotel Ballroom, La Zona Rosa, Liberty Lunch, Mercado Caribe, Piranha, Red River Saloon, Ritz, Sanitarium, Saxon Pub, Steamboat, Texas Tavern, Texas Union Ballroom, Thundercloud, Top of the Marc

CO-SPONSORING PUBLICATIONS
Austin Chronicle, Cleveland Scene, Creative Loafing (Atlanta), *Dallas Observer, Flagpole* (Athens, GA), *Goodtimes Magazine* (Long Island, NY, & Savannah, GA), *Maryland Musician* (Baltimore), *Memphis Star, The Metro* (Nashville), *New Times* (Phoenix), *Nightflying* (Little Rock), *The Note* (Lawrence), *Oklahoma Gazette* (Oklahoma City), *Pacific News & Review* (Anaheim, CA), *Philadelphia City Paper, The Pitch* (Kansas City, MO), *Public News* (Houston), *Riverfront Times* (St. Louis, MO), *The Rocket* (Seattle, WA), *San Antonio Current, Spectator* (Raleigh, NC),

SXSW organizers ponder: How big is too big?

Spectrum (Little Rock, AR), *Times of Acadiana* (Lafayette), *Tucson Weekly, Wavelength* (New Orleans), *Westword* (Denver)

KEYNOTE SPEAKER

Rosanne Cash, chart-topping country artist. Welcoming remarks by Texas Governor Ann Richards. Both speakers had a bearing on near-future keynotes as well: Richards returned to give the primary address in 1993, and Cash's father Johnny

> "The Mama Cass Award for the best mixing of food and rock and roll belongs to the singer of Billygoat, who stripped to the bare and covered his genitals with various comestibles, then allowed members of the audience to come up for a tasting." ■ Ken Lieck in *The Austin Chronicle,* March 29, 1991

delivered 1994's keynote. Of Richards' remarks, Casey Monahan, director of the Governor's Office-affiliated Texas Music Office, recalls, "I drafted the speech, but she went extemporaneous many, many times." Monahan, a former music reviewer for the *Austin American-Statesman*, added that "drafting a speech for a politician was not as hard as reviewing Rich Minus playing a happy hour gig at the Continental."

MEMORABLE PANELS

The titles of 1991's major panels all were posed in the form of a question. Among them:

"Is Metal Still Surging Or Has It Reached Its Peak?"...Ah, but aren't we still pondering this same notion today?

"Is 'Alternative' A Musical Movement Or A Marketing System?"...Or, to put it another way, "floor wax or dessert topping?"

"What Is Tejano Music And How Does It Fit Into The Larger Industry?"...A worthwhile effort to acknowledge a genre that had been underrepresented at SXSW, with authorities on the subject including Juan Tejeda, Ramiro Burr and Ruben Ramos.

"What's Country?"...Perhaps because it was still a few years too early to ask, "What's Alternative Country?"

"Who killed JFK?"...A whopper of a music-convention detour, which eventually routed SXSW through Dallas' Dealey Plaza later that year

when it presented the first Assassination Symposium on Kennedy (ASK).

NOTABLE PANELISTS

Mike Greene (NARAS), David Bither (Elektra Records), David Fricke (*Rolling Stone*), Bill Bentley (Warner Bros. Records), Rufus Thomas (pioneering Memphis artist), Moira McCormick (*Billboard*), Barry Poss (Sugar Hill Records), Dennis Constantine (KBCO-Boulder), Mirko Whitfield (Deutsche Schallplatten), Shannon Vale (Benson/Vale Management), Hugo Burnham (Imago Records), Sims Ellison (metal band Pariah)

MEMORABLE SHOWCASES

> Saturday's blockbuster showcase at Liberty Lunch included a young band from Belleville, IL, named Uncle Tupelo, whose leaders went on to form Wilco and Son Volt. Atlanta rockers Drivin' N' Cryin and North Carolina pop duo Peter Holsapple & Chris Stamey (with Marshall Crenshaw sitting in) also were on the bill.

> Thursday night's lineup at the Cannibal Club included a couple of artists who became well-known and then died tragically in the ensuing decade. Mark Sandman, singer for Boston band Treat Her Right, went on to great success with Morphine in the early-'90s before dying of a heart attack onstage in Italy in 1999. Josh Clayton-Felt was lead singer for Los Angeles pop band School of Fish, who released a couple of records on Capitol; he died of cancer in 2000.

> An all-international showcase on Friday night at the 311 Club included bands from England (The Rise), Finland (Hearthill), the Netherlands (Miners of Muzo), and France (Les Garcons Bouchers, Roadrunners, Happy Drivers). Saturday's lineup at the club featured all Canadian bands, most notably the Barenaked Ladies from Toronto.

> The large-capacity City Coliseum (which was torn down a decade later) was used for the first time as an official SXSW venue, hosting showcases on Friday and Saturday that catered mainly to the metal crowd. Saturday's bill was bookended by bands featuring Doug Sahm's sons: Pariah (with Shandon) and Prezence (with Shawn).

> Symphony Square got into the SXSW act for the first time, hosting a daytime showcase of children's music that included the likes of Houston's Trout Fishing in America, Austin's Joe McDermott and New Orleans' Washboard Leo.

NOTABLE ACTS

Dixie Chicks The opening slot on a *Dallas Observer* showcase on Saturday at Abratto's was filled by this relatively new country-bluegrass outfit featuring sisters Emily and Martie Seidel. A few years later they brought singer Natalie Maines into the fold and, well, you know the rest.

Bob Mould The former leader of '80s underground icons Husker Du had gone solo a couple years prior to his Friday showcase at the Cannibal Club. Not long thereafter, Mould decided to move to Austin, spending a fair chunk of the mid-'90s as a resident.

David Ball Along with Walter Hyatt and Champ Hood, Ball was a member of the quintessential Austin trio Uncle Walt's Band in the 1970s. By the time of this Thursday night showcase at the Broken Spoke, he was seeking greener pastures in Nashville; he found them a few years later with the mainstream country radio hit "Thinkin' Problem."

Matt "Guitar" Murphy The blues guitar great, who headlined a Saturday showcase at Antone's, was immortalized in the movie *The Blues Brothers* as a member of John Belushi & Dan Aykroyd's fictional band.

Robin & Linda Williams This husband-wife folk duo from Virginia, which played a Thursday showcase at the Hyatt Hotel Ballroom, was (and still is) a favorite musical guest on Garrison Keillor's *A Prairie Home Companion* radio show.

Spanic Boys The Milwaukee father-son roots-rock band, who'd come to the attention of Rounder Records after a Continental Club showcase the previous year, returned to the Continental for a Saturday headlining slot with an album for Rounder under their belts.

South By Southwest Catchy name this outfit had, eh? The 1991 program guide listing for their Saturday night showcase at the Hyatt Hotel Ballroom stated that the band "records for the Track America label and denies rumors that it is soon changing its name to New Music Seminar."

SOME OF THE REGIONAL/NATIONAL ACTS

Cinco Dudes (Houston), Peglegasus (Houston), Jim Suhler & the Homewreckers (Dallas), C.J. Chenier (Lafayette, LA), Red Dirt Rangers (Oklahoma City, OK), Flat Duo Jets (Chapel Hill, NC), Judybats (Knoxville, TN), Jux County (Denver, CO), the Skeletons (Springfield, MO), Mike Martt (Los Angeles, CA), Kevin Welch (Nashville, TN), Marlee MacLeod (Tuscaloosa, AL), Dead Hot Workshop (Tempe, AZ), Hillbilly Frankenstein (Athens, GA)

SOME OF THE AUSTIN ACTS

Big Car, Calvin Russell, Cornell Hurd Band, Cotton Mather, Happy Family, Ian Moore, Jack Officers, Junior Medlow & Tornado Alley, Loose Diamonds, Michael Fracasso, Omar & the Howlers, Project Crew, Sue Foley, Wammo's Organic Rubber Machine

SOME OF THE INTERNATIONAL ACTS

Kolumbus Kris (Estonia, USSR), Gert Jonkers (Amsterdam, Netherlands), Spirits & Trains (Vancouver, Canada), Tommy Sands (Northern Ireland), Sky High (Falun, Sweden), Doobie Twisters (Tampere, Finland), Killer Tumbleweeds (Calgary, Canada)

SOFTBALL TOURNEY

The Talent Buyers squad — renamed "Clubs/Buyers" in this year — won their third straight championship game, clubbing the Record Companies team 29-12 and setting a new scoring record in the process. ∎

"I remember Julian Cope was supposed to play in 1991. I know Skellington [Daniel's pre-Spoon band, named after one of Cope's albums] existed at that point. I saw him walk in and then I saw him up above the stage area where they were gonna play in the atrium of the Hyatt, so I walked up there and stood next to him, and I was trying to think of something to say to him, and then I looked back over and he was gone. And I never saw him again. Next thing I knew somebody came out and said he wasn't gonna play." ∎ Britt Daniel, Spoon

continued from page 40

Chalk Circle
Chamber 36
Chamberlain
Chamillionaire
Chamillionaire & The Color Changin' Click
Champ Hood
Champ Hood & Walter Hyatt
Champ Hood Band
Champ Hood Tribute
Champagne Champagne
Champion
Chance
Chandler Travis
Chanel Campbell
Change of Heart
Change!
Chango Jackson
Chango Malo
Channel 3
Channel One
Chantal Kreviazuk
Chaparral
Char Busse
Charades
Charalambides
Charanga Cakewalk
Charlemagne
Charlene
Charles Bissell/ The Wrens
Charles Curtis
Charles Gayle
Charles Hamilton
Charles Jenkins
Charles Wright and the 103rd St. Rhythm Band
Charlie Beaver Band
Charlie Burton & the Hiccups
Charlie Burton & The Texas Twelve Steppers
Charlie Chesterman's Harmony Rockets
Charlie Day
Charlie Hunter Trio
Charlie Louvin
Charlie Mars
Charlie Musselwhite
Charlie Musselwhite & Charlie Sexton
Charlie Parr
Charlie Robison
Charlie Robison & the Millionaire Playboys
Charlie Sexton
Charlie Sexton Sextet
Charlie's Holy Happy Hour
Charlotte Martin
Chas. Mtn.
Chase Coy
Chase da Roy.G.Biv
Chase Pagan
Chatham County Line
Chatmonchy
Chatterton
Chavez
Chavy Boys
Che Arthur
Cheap Trick
Cheater Slicks
Cheer-Accident
Cheerleadr
Cheeseburger
Chelsea Peretti
Cher U.K.
Cheri Knight
Cherine Anderson
Cherokee Rose
Cherry 2000
Cherry Poppin' Daddies
Cherubs
Cheryl Beattie
Chester French
Chet
Chevelle
Cheveu
Chew Lips
Chickasaw Mudd Puppies
Chickenhawk
Chicks on Speed
Chicksaw Mudpuppies
Chico Mann
Chiddy Bang
Chief
Chikinki
Chikita Violenta
Child Abuse
Child Bearing
Child Bite
Children
Children Collide
Children In Heat
Children of Bodom
Chill Factor
Chilly Gonzales
Chimeras
Chin

Child Bearing Hips (1988)

Chin Chin
Chin Up Chin Up
China Drum
Chingo Bling
Chingo Bling feat. Stunta, Lucky Luciano, Coast & Jezufavio
Chiodos
Chip Dolan
Chip Pope
Chip Robinson
Chip Taylor
Chip Taylor & Carrie Rodriguez
Chip Taylor & Carrie Rodriguez and Friends
Chip Taylor & The Train Wreck Revue
Chip Taylor with John Platania
Chris Chandler
Chris Smither
Chis Whitley
Chiwoniso
CHLLNGR
Chloe Madison
Chloe Temtchine
Chlorine
CHO Sister-Brother
Choc Quib Town
ChocQuibTown
Choir of Young Believers
Chokebore
Choking Ahogo
Choklate
Chomsky
Choo Choo
Chopper One
Chops
Chore
Choreboy
Chris & Aurore
Chris and Thomas
Chris Anderson
Chris Armstrong
Chris Bathgate
Chris Bell
Chris Bergson
Chris Black
Chris Black and The Holy Ghost
Chris Brokaw
Chris Burroughs
Chris Cacavas & Junkyard Love
Chris Chandler
Chris Colepaugh and the Cosmic Crew
Chris Combette
Chris Crawford
Chris Duarte
Chris Duarte Group
Chris Edmonds Group
Chris Fairbanks
Chris Fertitta
Chris Fortier
Chris Gaffney
Chris Gaffney & the Cold Hard Facts
Chris Garneau
Chris Gerniottis
Chris Hicks
Chris Hillman
Chris Holtzhaus
Chris Knight
Chris Kowanko
Chris Lee
Chris Letcher
Chris Merola Group
Chris Mills
Chris O'Connell & Mary Ann Price
Chris Perez
Chris Pickering
Chris Pierce
Chris Pureka
Chris Shiflett
Chris Smither
Chris Smither
Chris Specht
Chris Stamey
Chris Stamey and Anton Fier
Chris Stamey & Mitch Easter
Chris Stills
Chris Thomas
Chris Trew
Chris Trope
Chris T-T
Chris Von Sneidern
Chris Wall
Chris Whitley
Chris Wilson
Chris Young
Chrissy Flatt
Christian Kiefer
Christian Scott
Christiansen
Christina Bell
Christina Carter & Shawn David McMillen
Christina Courtin
Christina Rosenvinge w/ Two Dollar Guitar
Christine Albert
Christine Albert Band
Christine Fellows
Christof Dienz
Christopher and The Souls

Christopher B McCarty & Papa Mali
Christopher Denny
Christopher O'Riley
Christopher Rees
Christopher Willits
Chromatics
Chrome Addicts
Chrome Flies
Chrome Yellow
Chromeo
Chronics
Chubby Carrier & the Bayou Swamp Band
Chuck & Quince
Chuck D
Chuck E Weiss
Chuck Mead
Chuck Prophet
Chuck Prophet & The Mission Express
Chuck Ragan
Chuck Treece Feat. Dubtronic
Chune
Churn
Cibo Matto
Ciegossordomudos
Cinco
Cinco Dudes
Cinderleaf
Cinders
Cindy Bullens
Cindy Church
Cindy Cruse
Cindy Horstman
Cindy Lee Berryhill
Cindy Symington
Cinema West
Cinematic Orchestra
Circa Survive
Circle
Circle Jerks
Circle Takes The Square
Circo
Cirrus
Citay
Cities
Citizen Bird
Citizen Cope
Citizen Jane
Citizen King
Citizens' Utilities
City and Colour
City Center
City Folk
City of Lindas
City Riots
City Terrace Dukes
Civil Rite
Cla
Clan Destine
Clandestine
CLANG
Clap Your Hands Say Yeah
Clara Bell
Clare & The Reasons
Clare Burson
Clarence "Gatemouth" Brown
Clarence Bucaro
Clarence Hollman & Carol Fran
Clarissa
Clas Yngstrom & Sky High
Class Actress
Class of '78 with Larry Seaman, Jesse Sublett, Randy "Biscuit" Turner, Stephen Marsh, Ty Gavin, Randy Franklin, Terri Lord
Classic Case
Classie Ballou
Classified
Classixx
Classixx (DJs For The Night)
Classy D
Claude Morgan & the Blast
Claude9
Claudia Scott
Claudia Williams & the Voices of Christ
Claudine Kielson
Clay Blaker & the Texas Honky-Tonk Band
Clay Davidson
Clearlake
Clebo Rainey
Clem Snide
Clemits
Clever Jeff
Cliff Barnes & Fear of Winning
Cliff Brown Jr
Cliff Eberhardt
Clifford Scott & the Secret Weapons
Cling
Clinging To The Trees of a Forest Fire
Clinic
Clinton Sparks
Clipd Beaks
Clipse
Clockcleaner
Clockhammer
Clorox Girls
Closure In Moscow

Cloud Cult
Cloudberry Jam
Clouded
Clouds
Clouseaux
CloverStreet
Clovis
Clowns For Progress
CLP
Clue to Kalo
Clumsy
Clutch
Clutch Cargo
Clyde's Ride
CMA
C-Mon & Kypski
CNC
C-Note & Botany Boys
Coach Said Not To
Coachwhips
Coal
Coast
Coax
Coaxial
Cobra Krames
Cobra Skulls
Cobra Verde
Cocco
Coccoon Pit
Cockeyed Ghost
Cocktail Gurlz
Cocktail Slippers
Coco Candissi
Coco Solid
Coconut Coolouts
Coconuts
Cocoon
CocoRosie
Code Blue
Code Red
Codebreaker
Codeine Velvet Club
Codeseven
Codie Prevost
Cody ChesnuTT
Coexist
Coffee Sergeants
Coffinworm
Coheed and Cambria
Coin-Op
Col. Lion & Soldiers of Peace
Colbie Caillat
Cold War Kids
Coldwater Army
Colin Blades
Colin Boyd
Colin Brooks
Colin Gilmore
Colin MacIntyre (aka Mull Historical Society)
Colin Moore
Colin Munroe
COLISEUM
Collections of Colonies of Bees
Collin Herring
Collin Wade Monk
Color
Color Filter
Colored Shadows
Colorsound
Colossal Yes
Colossus
Colour Revolt
Colourmusic
Coltrane Wreck
Coma in Algiers
Comanechi
Combine
Come
Come Down
Come On Gang!
Comeback Kid
Eugene Mirman
Comes With The Fall
Comet
Comet Gain
Comets on Fire
Comfort
Common Loon
Common Market
Communiqué
Comp 1
Company
Company Flow
Complete
Complete Control (TX)
Compound Red
Compromise Band
Computer Club
Con Rumba Son
Concerto Grosso
Concombre Zombi
Concrete Blonde
Concrucio
Condor44
Confuzatron
Congo Norvell
Congorock
Conil
Conquest
Conscious
Conscious Man
Consonant
Conspiracion Alfa 5
Constance
Constantines
Constructive Rukus

Continental Drifters
Contra Coup
Contramano
Control Machete
controller.controller
Controlling the Famous
Convoy
Cooder Graw
Cool Calm Pete
Cool Joe & the Funky Soul Symbols
Cool Nutz
Cooler
Coolhand Band
Cooly Girls
Cooly Nation
Cooper
Cooper's Uncle
Coota Bang
Cop Shoot Cop
Copacabana Club
Copeland
Copernicus
Coprolingus
Copter
Corb Lund
Corb Lund Band
Cordalene
Cordelia's Dad
Cordero
Cordray
Cordrazine
Cords
Core of Soul
Corey Cokes
Corey Glover
Corey Harris
Coreysan
Cori Brewster
Corinne Bailey Rae
Corn Mo
Corn Mo and the .357 Lover
Cornelius
Cornell Hurd Band
Cornerstone
Correatown
Correo Aereo
Corruption is King
Cortney Tidwell
Corto Maltese
Cory Branan
Cory Branan & Ben Nichols
Cory Morrow
Cory Morrow Band
Cosmic Boogie Tribe
Cosmic Chimp
Cosmic Crew
Cosmic Rough Riders
Cosmo Baker
Cosmo Jarvis
Cosmopolitan
Costumbre
Consummatum Est
Cotton Jones
Cotton Mather
Cottonmouth
Cottonmouth, TX
Cougar Den
Coughee Brothaz/14K/Rob Quest of the Odd Squad
Countdowns
Country Joe McDonald
Coupe De Ville
Courage Brothers
Course of Empire
Course of Ruin
Court Yard Hounds
Courtney Audain & FUZE
Cousin
Cousin Cole
Coverage
Coward
Cowbillys
Cowboy Jack Clement
Cowboy Mouth
Cowboys & Indians
Cows
Coy West
Coyote Dreams
CPC Gangbangs
CQ
Cracker
Cracks in the Sidewalk
Cradle
Craig Arnold
Craig Calvert
Craig Gore
Craig Marshall
Craig May
Craig Owens
Craig Ross
Craig Wallace & the Out
Cranebuilders
Crank County Daredevils
Crap Shoot
Crash Four
Crash Gallery
Crash Kelly
Crash Kings
Cravo Carbono
Crawdaddy-O Brass Band
Crawling with Kings
Crayon Fields
C-Rayz Walz
Craze
Crazy Adulterous Giants (featuring Jon Langford)
Crazy Town

Crazy World of Arthur Brown
Creative Opportunity Orchestra
Creature
Creeper Lagoon
Cresta
Crew
Crew54
Crime Mob
Crimson Sweet
Chris Crawford
Crisis
Crisp Arson
Cristin O'Keefe Aptowicz
Criteria
Crocodile
Crooked Fingers
Crooks
Crooner
Crosstide
Crow
Crown City Rockers
Crown Heights
Crown Royale
Crud
Cruelest Month
Cruiserweight
Crumb
Crumbox
Crunc Tesla
Crush
Crushed Stars
Crust
Cry Blood Apache
Crybaby
Cryptacize
Crystal Antlers
Crystal Blu
Crystal Castles
Crystal Fighters
Crystal Skulls
Crystal Stilts
Cuba Libra
Cubanismo! (featuring Jesus Alemany)
Cubic Feet
Cubic Zirconia
Cubiky
Cubismo Grafico Five
Cuca
Cue
Cuff the Duke
Cul de Sac
Cula du Café
Culprit One
Cult Figures
Cultifaderz
Culture Shock
Cunninghams
CunninLynguists
Cupcakes
Curly
Curren$y
Curse Of Blefuscu
Cursed
Cursive
Curt Kirkwood
Curtis Vodka
Curumin
Cut Chemist
Cut Copy
Cut La Roc
Cut Off Your Hands
Cutthroat
Cutthroats 9
CX Kidtronik
CY
Cyann & Ben
Cybortronik World Media
Cymbals Eat Guitars
CYNE
Cypress Hill
Cyrus
Czech Melody Masters

D

D Black
D Braxton Harris
D Folmer
D of Carnival Beats
D Powers 'The Ghetto Rockstar'
D.B. Harris
D.D. Wallace
D.D.T.
D.J. Fontana
D.O.
D.O.A.
D.O.S.
D.R.U.M.
D.S.R.
d.u.s.t.
D:Fuse
D'Zyne
DA C.O.D
Da Mex Connect aka Lil J
Da Ryno
Daara J
Dabrye
DADDY (Will Kimbrough & Tommy Womack)
Daddy A Go-Go
Daddy Longhead
Dadja Petrick

Daedelus
Daemien Frost
Dag för Dag
Dagashi-Kashi
DaHeBeGeBees
Dahli Llama
Dah-Veed
Daisychain
Daisyhaze
Dale Watson
Dalek
Dallas Austin
Dallas Crane
Dallas Slam Team
Dallas Wayne
Dalton Grant
Damage
Damaged Good$
Damero
damesviolet
DâM-FunK
Damhnait Doyle
Damian Green
Damian Lazarus
Damien Binder
Damien Dempsey
Damien Jurado
Damnations
Damon & Naomi
Damon Aaron
Damon Bramblett
Damon Bramblett Band
Damon McMahon
Damon Williams
Damone
Dan Auerbach
Dan Bern
Dan Bern & the IJBC
Dan Black
Dan Boulger
Dan Boulger, Donald Glover, Pete Holmes, Moshe Kasher, Ben Kronberg and Special Guest
Dan Brodie and the Broken Arrows
Dan Bryk
Dan Colehour
Dan Colehour & the Camaros
Dan Crary
Dan Darrah
Dan Deacon
Dan Deacon + Jimmy Joe Roche's Ultimate Reality
Dan Del Santo
Dan Del Santo's World Beat
DAN dYER
Dan Greenpeace
Dan Harrell
Dan Israel
Dan Kahuna
Dan le Sac vs Scroobius Pip
Dan Mangan
Dan McCoy
Dan Melchior Und Das Menace
Dan Sartain
Dan Stuart
Dan Wilson
Dana & Karen Kletter
Dana Cooper
Dana Falconberry
Danananananaykroyd
Danava
Dance Gavin Dance
Dances With White Girls
Dancing Bear
Dancyr
Dandi Wind
Danger Radio
Dangerous
Dangerous Toys
Dangtrippers
Dani Siciliano
Daniel Balthasar
Daniel Davis III
Daniel Francis Doyle
Daniel Jackson
Daniel Janisch
Daniel Johnston
Daniel Lanois
Daniel Link
Daniel Martin Moore
Daniel Martin Moore/Ben Sollee
Daniella Cotton
Danielle Howle & The Tantrums
Danielle Martineau & Rockabayou
Danielle's Mouth
Danielson
Danko Jones
Danny & The Hurricanes
Danny and the Nightmares featuring Daniel Johnston
Danny Barnes
Danny Flowers
Danny Frankel
Danny Levin
Danny Malone
Danny Saul
Danny Schmidt
Danny Solis
Danny Tate
Dao Strom
Don't Mean Maybe
Daphne Gottlieb

Daphne Loves Derby
Daphne Willis and Co.
Dappled Cities
Dappled Cities Fly
DaPuntoBeat
Dar Williams
Darcie Deaville
Darcie Deaville & Taller Dog
Darcie Deaville Band
Darden Smith
Darden Smith Band
Darediablo
Darin
Darin Murphy
Dario y su ComboRican
Darius
Dark Castle
Dark Fog
Dark Holler
Dark Meat
Dark Room Notes
Darker Florida
Darker My Love
Darkest Hour
Darlings of Chelsea
Carol Howell Band
Darondo
Darrell Brown Band
Darren Hanlon
Daryl Hall
Daryll-Ann
Das Boot
Das Psycho Rangers
Das Racist
Das Weeth Experience
DASH
Dash Rip Rock
Dashboard Confessional
Dat Boy Mikee
DATAROCK
Daughter Judy
Daughters
Dave Alvin
Dave Alvin & the Guilty Men featuring Tom Russell & Chris Gaffney
Dave Alvin with Special Guests: A Tribute To Chris Gaffney
Dave Biller and Les Niglos
Dave Derby
Dave Dondero
Dave Fischoff
Dave Gonzalez and The Stone River Boys
Dave Gunning
Dave Lindhome & White Midnight
Dave Melillo
Dave Merenda
Dave Perkoff & Little Big Band
Dave Rave
Dave Schramm
Dave Shidel & Stan Smith
Dave Wakeling
Dave Wilkins Band
Davediggaz
David & The Citizens
David & the Immatures
David Andrews
David Baerwald and the New Folk Underground
David Ball
David Banner
David Bavas and the Down Comforter
David Bazan
David Bean & the Judy's
David Berkeley
David Braza
David Bridie
DAVID BROWN with C.L.A.S.S.
David Broza
David Byrne
David Chenu Ensemble
David Clement
David Cross
David Dallas
David Fonseca
David Ford
David Francey
David Garza
David Garza & the Love Beads
David Gogo
David Gray
David Halley
David Halley Band
David Hildalgo
David Holt
David Hopkins
David Houston Madewell
David Israel
David Jack
David Jewell
David K Wilcox
David Karsten Daniels
David Kersh
David Kirton
David Kitt
David Lee Garza y los Musicales
David Lewis
David Madison
David Martel
David Mead

continued on page 54

The Long Road From Year 1 To Year 25

From 1984-88, I had the best job in the record business at the time – head of publicity at I.R.S. Records. In addition to breaking R.E.M., the Fleshtones and English Beat, I.R.S. also produced a monthly alternative-music variety program for MTV called *The Cutting Edge*. Once a month we'd hold screenings on the A&M lot on LaBrea Avenue in Hollywood, to which we'd

SXSW MEMORIES

invite the press. Venerable journalist Ed Ward happened to be in town and I invited him to a screening of the episode featuring North Carolina. "This ain't a scene," he sniffed at the screening's conclusion. "You want a music scene, come to Austin." So we did, in the summer of 1985. While there, we signed Timbuk 3.

A short while later, they said, "Come to South by Southwest." Come to what?

Cut to March 15, 1987. I arrive in Austin and beeline for the conference hotel. I register for SXSW along with a few hundred other music industry folks. I call Timbuk 3's Barbara K and say, "I registered. Now what?"

"Walk down to East 6th Street," she said. "You'll know when you hit it." I walked the six blocks south and wandered

aimlessly into more bars than I'd ever seen in a square half-mile. Ray Wylie Hubbard was playing for a tip jar at one non-SXSW dive. I was reminded by the best that I was in Texas.

SXSW was small and focused, unlike the sprawling behemoth New Music Seminar in New York. You could drive (and park, free or cheaply) from showcase to showcase – from Liberty Lunch to Sixth Street to the Continental and back to La Zona Rosa. I'd never seen a club like Liberty Lunch – half inside, half outside, with a giant mural for a wall and a makeshift roof, it wouldn't have passed building code in my hometowns of Los Angeles and Chicago. I was instantly in love with Austin. This is before the city was formally articulated as "weird," and then anything weird proceeded to fall to the wrecking ball.

There were no day parties in 1987 – just panels and official showcases. So at 5pm, a bunch of us – Bob Guccione Jr. from *Spin* magazine in the back seat – headed to the Salt

Built On The Talent Of Austin Musicians

Since I transferred from Minneapolis to Austin in high school – actually St. Paul to Round Rock, but that sounds less cool – I knew enough about the Jayhawks to see their SXSW gig at Liberty Lunch in 1990. I had no idea what SXSW was, nor that high school kids would be shut out of it in future decades until Satan invented something called a music blog. Also on the bill that night were the Reivers, Austin newbie Kelly Willis and some long-gone killer band I can't remember. That's when I got turned on to the music scene in my adopted hometown. I haven't missed a South by Southwest since, but even after seeing Johnny Cash and Tom Waits and interviewing Isaac Hayes and Neil Young during the fest, I haven't lost sight of the fact that the thing is still built on the talent and bounced rent checks of Austin musicians. I always tell SXSW virgins who ask about attending: It's a blast for music lovers, but so is any week out of the year in Austin. ■ **Chris Riemenschneider,** *Minneapolis Star Tribune*

Lick. We got lost (and there were no cell phones nor GPS units to guide us). But eventually we found our way and enjoyed a leisurely sit-down dinner, getting back to Sixth Street in time for a 9pm showcase.

Another feature of days gone by was the nearly mandatory Austin Music Awards show (which initially had its own night set apart from all of the showcases). You'd greet your friends and meet the locals. You could spot the Austin folks – they were dressed to the nines. And the rest of us, far from it. The Awards were the first place I heard Daniel Johnston, the Wild Seeds, Jimmie Dale Gilmore, Joe Ely and so many more. And Margaret Moser, then as now, was fabulously in charge.

There's no bringing the old days back. Liberty Lunch is long ago razed, its footprint now that of an office building. A high rise spookily looks up from the exit of La Zona Rosa. Those formerly free parking lots now cost $20 a pop, and are usually full – if you can even traverse the clunky network of one-way streets downtown with all the gridlock. Major artists now play massive townie shows along Auditorium Shores. I sorely miss Las Manitas – criminally still a vacant lot. And I may never get used to the spring break kids. But there's no putting the genie back in the bottle.

I still go to SXSW 24 years later. If you'd told me in 1987 that I'd be doing this in 2010, I'd have thought you were crazy. My revised conventional wisdom is, "If you don't see me at SXSW, I've left the music business. Or there was a death in the family."

I still see Roland Swenson, Louis Black and Brent Grulke scoping out the scene, yelling into walkie talkies, still having fun. I still manage to find my people, albeit needles in a haystack. I still manage to have at least one major musical epiphany and rediscover some old favorites. It's still fun. But it sure ain't as easy to recover from as it was when I started coming, about a quarter-century ago. ■ **Cary Baker, publicist, Conqueroo**

Still Remembering The Beginning

In year one, I had no expectations other than more acts to deal with at a show than usual. I was the stage manager and sound engineer at the Continental Club, which has always been one of the best places in Austin (or the world, for that matter) to see and hear music. So I shouldn't have been surprised to find the venue full, but I was, at least a bit.

The show was proceeding apace, going well, on schedule. I was running back and forth from the sound mixer's position to the stage, positioning microphones and setting the stage, doing line checks, getting the monitor levels right for a fairly well-known Austin artist. She broke a guitar string. Her "manager" yelled at me, "Hey, change that string! Do your job!" or something to that effect.

I was completely taken aback, and froze. Since when does the house engineer/stage manager change a performer's strings? Plus she has a "manager" standing next to the stage? Why doesn't HE change the string?

I jumped to, and started changing her string quickly while the increasingly hostile artist's minder yelled at me to hurry up. Not only was I pissed, I was embarrassed. Maybe the manager knew something I didn't, and Big Name acts always count on the house to tend to their gear? This didn't seem right, and I'd worked a few years doing sound and stage management at this point, but he did seem awfully sure of himself...

Did I make a mistake? I wondered, and steamed, how should I have responded? Should I have yelled something back at him? Doesn't he know it's a mistake to berate the guy mixing your sound?

While I was still stewing, David Halley, who was one of the headliners that night and had witnessed all of this, approached me. I'd never met David before. He bent close and whispered, "Hey, man. Ignore him. Everyone knows he's an asshole. You're doing a great job."

It was just what I needed, and I went back to work. Ever since, I've loved David, and shared how I feel about him with others. The other artist? I remember her, too. And she's still working... ■ **Brent Grulke, SXSW creative director**

Never Mind The Panels, Where's The Beef?

Craig Marks and I shared a room at SXSW in 1991. We stayed at the Hyatt where the convention itself was held. I think this was the only time I ever actually attended any panels!

Besides seeing bands and partying with friends, we had a particular mission in mind: Eating, with an emphasis on Texas barbecue. I believe the very first place we went was the original Elgin Southside Market to try their brisket but especially their 'hot guts' (sausage).

The place was so real; if I remember correctly, it was a small room fluorescent-lit with a few square tables. I believe there was a meat case in that room as well. The shop itself seemed to be in a tiny time-warp of a town. We sat and ate these terrific sausages. There were whiskey bottles of sauce on the tables and I swear an older gentleman that could have been LBJ. I felt like I had stepped back in time 35 years. Craig and I went on to experience further great tastes at Kreuz (in Lockhart) and Louie Mueller's (in Taylor). ■ **Chris Lombardi, Matador Records**

Sleeping Together To Get Ahead

In the early days we would go to NYC to promote SXSW at trade shows like New Music Seminar and CMJ. One of the first times we stayed in New York, we got to the hotel and I had to guarantee the hotel with my credit card as no one else could do it. We stayed four or five in a room to keep it cheap, sleeping anywhere you could. Ya know, if I remember right, Roland snores. ■ Bruce Sheehan, proto-SXSW co-conspirator

Harsh Words For The Critic

South by Southwest brings out the best in people, but it also brings out the worst. Things that don't normally mean too much the other 361 days of the year bring out bulging neck veins when the music industry visits Austin every March.

This all became apparent to me in the very first year, when two managers and a band had it out with me over some innocuous stuff I had written in my *Austin Chronicle* gossip column "Don't You Start Me Talking."

First was the night before it started, when there was a party for keynote speaker Huey P. Meaux, the record producer. I approached my old pal Joe Nick Patoski, who was managing True Believers at the time. "Get out of my face," said the normally mild-mannered Joe Nick, who kind of brushed me aside and kept walking. "I'm not talking to you." I had absolutely no idea

what was wrong until a couple hours later when one of the True Believers scolded me for writing that the band was looking for a new drummer. Apparently everyone in town knew that except the old drummer.

The next morning I was on a rock critics panel, called "Whither Rock?" (after the speech the pompous Jeff Goldblum character in *Between The Lines* had given to a class of teenaged girls). Louis Black and Nick Barbaro were so obsessed with that movie about an alternative newspaper it became the inspiration for *The Austin Chronicle*.

There were about 11 critics on the panel, because back then critics were just about the only industry people who came to SXSW. Every time I thought of something to say, someone else would beat me to the mike I shared with two others. So after about an hour I hadn't said a single thing.

Finally, someone stood up in the audience and said, "I have a question for Michael Corcoran," and I was relieved to finally get a chance to break the ice. The question: "I'd like to ask him if he knows anything at all about journalistic ethics." It was Daniel Johnston's manager, Jeff Tartakov. He was hopping mad because in my column that came out the week of SXSW, I had mentioned that Daniel had been admitted to the state hospital for a couple days of observation. It was true, but I didn't go to Tartakov for verification or comment. I found out later that a couple of labels were interested in signing Johnston, but when the news from my column got around they were hesitant.

I just sat there speechless. I didn't know how to answer that question. Everybody was staring at me and I could feel my face burning. That was the last time I was ever on a panel at SXSW. ■ **Michael Corcoran, former *Austin Chronicle* columnist, now with the *Austin American-Statesman***

From Regional Origins To International Horizons

I think I helped instigate the international thing when Lucinda Williams, who was in Los Angeles, sent a fan of hers, this German girl who was going coast-to-coast via Greyhound, to me as someone she could hang out with in Austin. We clicked right away, and I wasn't quite as sorry to see her go as I might have been, because she was eventually headed to New York to the New Music Seminar to help a friend of hers, Wolfgang Doebeling, promote the first Berlin Independence Days, a music conference he was doing mostly on government money. This was 1988. So I made sure Wolfgang and Roland got to talking.

Since Wolfgang had money in almost unlimited amounts – promoting West Berlin was a priority for the German government, and it was also an EU Culture Capital that year – he offered to fly anyone who wanted to come over to Berlin. Louis Jay Meyers was particularly interested: He was managing the Killer Bees at the time, and Wolfgang offered him a showcase, to be broadcast live on the radio and recorded professionally, after which the tape would be Louis' to keep. (This became their *Live In Berlin* album.) So Roland agreed to let Louis Jay and me go, and to have a little SXSW booth in the BID trade show.

We came back babbling about what a great conference it was (hard to fail when you've got that much money), and although Roland probably discounted a lot of mine as being filtered through my girlfriend, he listened to Louis, and agreed to let Wolfgang have a booth in the SXSW trade fair. Roland went to BID in 1989, and that would have been when he offered the deal: SXSW would rep BID for the States, and BID could rep SXSW for Europe.

Louis Black, I remember, was dead set against all of this, saying it was a waste of time and money, but Roland and Wolfgang's assistant Tracey Bigelow assiduously courted the national export agencies in Europe, because they had money and would send bands over with grants.

The Austin-Berlin Connection

In the early days of SXSW, Roland Swenson, Ed Ward, Louis Meyers and Linda Park would come over to West Berlin to take part in the 'Berlin Independence Days.' This was the first international music festival/conference/trade show ever to be held in Germany, and was organized by an old friend of ours, Wolfgang Doebeling.

Wolfgang had a radio show on one of the local Berlin stations and was an aficionado of American Roots Music, which everyone now terms Americana. In the late '80s and early '90s, he brought over a number of Austin and Texas legends to BID, including Townes Van Zandt, Butch Hancock, Jimmie Dale Gilmore, Joe Ely, Guy Clark, etc. Similarly, it was Wolfgang who introduced me to SXSW and Austin.

That was 1989, and Austin was a different city then – no high-rise buildings, and much more laid-back than it is today. It was also a city of incredible characters, including a certain Mr. Roosevelt Thomas Williams, who performed under the stage name of Grey Ghost and was one of the last of Texas' old-time barrelhouse piano players. I had the pleasure of seeing him play in a cafe somewhere off Congress Avenue. He was 85 years old and was still pumping out syncopated ragtime, jazz, and rhythm & blues like there was no tomorrow. The one moment that really stuck in my memory was when he said, "Well, I wrote this next song in the 1930s. It's called 'Hitler's Blues'." It was a glimpse into a forgotten era. ■ **Mirko Whitfield, SXSW international coordinator**

Mojo's Mushroom Maniac

The fifth year of SXSW I spent an entire day trying to track down Eric "Roscoe" Ambel, who was playing guitar for Mojo Nixon. Roscoe has been sober for years, but he wasn't back then. Mojo used to have leg wrestling contests up in his hotel room, and whenever Mojo was around there would always be someone showing up with psychedelic mushrooms, because he had this song called "Mushroom Maniac."

So one night this guy I knew from around Austin knocked on the door, holding a Hefty bag full of mushrooms. It was about 4 a.m., so most people just grabbed a handful and put them in their pockets or an envelope or something. But one guy there just wolfed 'em down. The next day the word was out that the mushrooms were poisonous. The guy who took them at 4 a.m. had been taken by ambulance to the hospital and had his stomach pumped out. So I was thinking about who else I had seen grab the mushrooms. Roscoe!

So I'm running around asking everybody if they've seen Roscoe. I had to warn him. Mojo was playing at Liberty Lunch that night, and that's when I finally found his guitar player, blissfully tripping. He had heard I was trying to warn him, but he took the mushrooms hours ago and had no ill effects. "But some guy had his stomach pumped," I told him. Roscoe just smiled and said, "That guy's a pussy." ■ Michael Corcoran, *Austin American-Statesman*

And, starting with the Finns and the French, eventually this began to pay off big-time. We'd go to MIDEM (in France) in January, and BID in October, and I'd make contact with people who could talk on panels at SXSW. I became the "International Coordinator," I believe, and I also put the housing program into effect, which was wildly successful: Austinites letting bands stay with them. Lots of longtime friendships occurred, not to mention getting some Americans to see another part of the world when they went over to visit their friends. I'd host a dinner for the international people when they came over, usually at a Mexican joint, and that was always a blast. ■ Ed Ward, journalist and longtime SXSW associate

Riding With The King

March 1990. A new decade and I was a year into a new job as talent editor of *Billboard* magazine, assigned to cover the fourth annual South by Southwest Music and Media Conference. SXSW in 1990 drew 2,162 delegates – a 25% increase over the previous year – with more than 300 bands showcasing in some 20-odd venues. 300 bands! How to see as many as possible?

My answer: Hitch a ride with Roland. I began my own SXSW tradition, riding shotgun in director Roland Swenson's car as he made the rounds from the Hyatt Hotel (the host venue for the first time in 1990) to Liberty Lunch, Antone's, Sixth Street and elsewhere. Trusty notebook in hand, I gathered wit and wisdom from Roland to report in *Billboard*.

Looking back now, I am astonished to realize I attended SXSW for only three years, from 1990 to 1992. It is as if the event offers more music and memories than you can absorb in a lifetime. From my scrapbook: The brilliant Stevie Ray Vaughan earns honors as musician of the decade at the Austin Music Awards on March 14, 1990. By that August, he is gone, killed in a helicopter crash....An emcee at Steamboat remarks: "I see more record company weasels walking in every minute."...In the back room of Cisco's Mexican eatery, a young Will T. Massey straps on a black acoustic guitar and enthralls the room with his performance....New England singer-songwriter Bill Morrissey earns a standing ovation at the Cactus Cafe with his intense and literate songs....The Skeletons from Springfield, MO, play exquisite power-pop at the Continental Club.... The fire marshal shows up when Miracle Legion plays the Jelly Club....Apaches of Paris busk beautifully on 5th Street.

In January 1993, I fled the country. Well, not exactly. The late *Billboard* editor Timothy White offered me a new job as the magazine's Los Angeles bureau chief. I asked him if, instead, he would send me 3,000 miles in the opposite direction, to work in the London office. Thus began my years as a SXSW delegate-in-exile. Mirko Whitfield, longtime international rep for SXSW, befriended me and always seemed to be on hand for a beer, in New York, London or Hong Kong. Each January, I caught up with Roland at MIDEM in Cannes. But the French Riviera can't hold a candle to Sixth Street.

I'm now back in New York, and my role today at *Billboard* no longer includes an annual trip to SXSW. (But I never miss the New York preview party.) In 2010, nearly 2,000 bands played the conference. Others report there for *Billboard*: writing, blogging, tweeting, creating video feeds and more. But I expect when I do get back to Austin, Roland will offer me a ride. ■ Thom Duffy, *Billboard*

Of Bock And Bluebonnets

There was a time when SXSW's future was not assured – when it bore little resemblance to the multi-tentacled beast that now sprawls across Austin every March. Back then, the money being added to Austin's economy could be counted in the

thousands. South Congress had yet to morph into SoCo. And cheap hamburgers at Hut's at the end of the night, not to mention a peck on the cheek from Lou Ann Barton, were de rigueur. That was back when the clubs and streets were so empty you could rip up Guadalupe to the old Antone's for Doug Sahm, stop by the Hole in the Wall for Alejandro Escovedo, and end up in the glorious ruins of the then falling down Ritz Theater for the Reivers, all within an hour.

It all runs together after awhile, but several flashes from the first years remain vivid to this day. Hearing the crowd sing every word of "London Homesick Blues" at Raven's Garage while its composer, Gary P. Nunn, stood back and smiled. Walking into the panelists' breakfast room after being up all night and finding it empty except for Jim Dickinson, who regaled me with tales of the Replacements making *Pleased To Meet Me* as a trio after firing Bob Stinson. Watching as a furious Lucinda Williams went onstage two hours after they'd stopped selling beer, and absolutely killing the material on her epochal 1988 album. Smelling the magical elixir of warm, rank Shiner Bock wafting across a hotel room, just as the sun rose and the zombies began to stir. The bluebonnets never had a chance. ■ **Robert Baird,** *Stereophile*

'Did You Ever Think SXSW Would Get This Big?'

I first experienced the SXSW music festival in 1988. I was just a consumer, and even then it blew my mind! My $15 red paper ticket was a passport to one of the most fantastic experiences I'd ever had seeing live music. I still smile when I remember that Saturday night at the Back Room, with the Wild Seeds, Dash Rip Rock, and Scruffy the Cat on the bill. Wow, I thought, what a cool thing this is, and how lucky we are here in Austin to have it. By the next year, however, I was dating the man I'd eventually marry, Roland Swenson, and my SXSW has never been from the outside ever again.

While I've had my share of fun since that first SXSW, my experience is tempered by the fact that I'm always aware of the time, talent, and sheer stubbornness it takes to launch it. I am always very proud of what Roland and the staff accomplish every year, very proud that our event has become so important to so many people. So, when people ask me, "Did you ever think SXSW would get this big?" I say, Yes! Because even back in the days of the red paper ticket, I could plainly see what happened when a couple thousand people who love what they do, and want to share their work with the world, get together in this one, special city of ours. They make something special happen. ■ **Roseana Auten, music fan and wife of SXSW director Roland Swenson**

From Minnesota To Texas

There was nobody walking down Sixth Street the night we played in 1988; very quiet, very dark....There was a big after-party in the ballroom. A Cajun band was playing; we tried to find someone to dance with and stayed up real late. I'd been wearing the same sweater for a month, and in the morning the band tried to burn it outside in the parking lot. We drove to Houston the next day and played in front of a couple of people, and then drove all night and day home to Minneapolis. It started to rain, and our soundman cranked up Led Zeppelin in order to stay awake. We had all been up for 40 hours and I was feeling uneasy. When we finally hit town, Gary [Louris] and I went to Palmer's on the west bank and congratulated ourselves on making it home, all the way down and back on I-35W. ■ **Mark Olson, The Jayhawks**

Softball Diamonds Are Forever

Like many things that first year, the original SXSW Softball Tournament & Barbecue was born of love and fear. As plans progressed, Louis Black fretted that partner Nick Barbaro was losing interest. Largely to make sure Barbaro showed up, they decided to add two of his big loves to the conference mix: softball and barbecue.

At the last minute, Black also recruited *Chronicle* contributing editor Susan Moffat to oversee player registration for the tournament, sparking what soon became another big love for Barbaro. By the next year, Moffat was the SXSW Softball Commissioner and the pair had moved in together. They'll celebrate their 20th wedding anniversary this May. ■ **Susan Moffat, SXSW softball commissioner**

SXSW: The Next Generation

In March 1988 at the second SXSW, I signed a deal with Sony from Nashville in a Hyatt hotel room, with Larry Hamby and Jim Zumwalt from Nashville in attendance. I was hugely pregnant with my son Troupe, who was born April 20 that year. Last year, 22 years later, Troupe's band SPEAK won Best New Band at the Austin Music Awards. I had a gig that night, so the family sent me video of it as it happened and I watched it on my iPhone. Times have changed and a SXSW generation comes of age! (By the way, the child worked out much better than the record deal!) ■ **Christine Albert, musician**

True Believers' Alejandro Escovedo, Javier Escovedo, Jon Dee Graham
at the Austin Music Awards (1988)

Robert Christgau's keynote (1989)

Mojo Nixon's pre-keynote "invocation" (1989)

Daniel Johnston at the Austin Music Awards (1990) >

Miles Zuniga, Bill David, Mojo Nixon, Ricky Gelb (1989)

Sarah Brown, Marcia Ball, Clifford Antone, Lou Ann Barton, Angela Strehli >
at the Austin Music Awards (1989)

South by Southwest Managers,

You're a bunch of puss-fags, cock-sucking, discriminating mother-fuckers. I hope you burn & die in Hell. Half the bands on your list are not even from the South. You are disgrace to the Austin Music Scene. FUCK YOU

Concerned Musician

Circulation Advisor
John L. Ross, Jr.

Circulation
David Fox, Gary Goethe,
Lieck, Mike McGeary, Keith Sharp

Contributors
Banks, Bud, John Carrico, Steve
imino, Al L. Ears, David Erwin,
icole Hollander, David Johndrow,
a Kirkpatrick, Gary Larson, Jane
t, Tom & Ray Magliozzi, Kathleen
ts, Marc Savlov, Chuck Shepherd,
Patrick Taggart, Robb Walsh,
Chris Walters

Cover Photo
h Life, directed by Ken Harrison
Rub-a-dub-dub
Ken Lieck

le is published by the Austin Chronicle
O. Box 49066, 78765, 512/473-8995.
by the Austin Chronicle Corporation.
All rights reserved.
tions: $55 bulk mail; $120 first class.
iptions: $30 bulk mail; $65 first class.
a week or more to arrive; if you want the
ings, you need 1st class.) Please allow

XW

Dear *Austin Chronicle*:

Shame on the South by Southwest organizers for raising the price of wristbands $25 this year! What a blatant, outrageous ploy to take advantage of Austin's faithful music fans. How hypocritical of them to try to pass this off as a bargain, which they are trying hard to do!

The thing is, the organizers are counting on the fact that people will not remember the prices they charged for wristbands at previous SXSWs. And, admittedly, with good reason. We do not remember precisely ourselves, though we do know that last year they cost $15. In 1989, they were perhaps $8. But most people we have talked to do not remember. The SXSW desk at the Hyatt Regency claimed that they had "always" been $15, and that this year they had gone up by "25 percent" to $25! Imagine that, two false claims in one sentence!

And what does this $25 really get the faithful music fan? Let's see: the chance to dash between the several venues. The chance to just maybe get in to see a few mostly small-time bands looking for ex-

pets   po   y
cats who are br
know: I walk
beds, one on e
creek beds attra
wooden traps o
in the area who
irony is it will
apartments. Th
think the unive
are breaking th
the area.

Unless Y

Dear *Chronic*
I would like
quote of the
Flashback...
"The '90s a
'50s.''

Rosanne Cash and Gov. Ann Richards at the keynote (1991)

‹ Love letters (circa 1990)

continued from page 40

David Moore
David Morrison
David Munyon
David Olney
David Poe
David Rice
David Rodriguez
David Ruthstrom
David Ryan Harris
David Singer & The Sweet Science
David Spann
David Tamaoka
David Thomas Broughton
David Thompson
David Vandervelde
Davin James
Davis Raines
Davis Redford Triad
Davy Jones
Dawes
Dawn Gabriel
Dawn Kinnard
Dawn Landes
Dawn of the Replicants
Dax Riggs
Day By the River
Day For Night
Dayna Kurtz
Dayna Kurtz with Tarantula
Dayroom
Days of the New
Dayta
Dayvid Figler
Dazzling King Solomon Band
DBR
DC Bellamy
DC Snipers
dc Talk
DC-9
DD/MM/YYYY
De Dijk
De los Muertos
de Schmog
Deacon Brody
Dead and Gone
Dead Child
Dead Confederate
Dead End Cruisers
Dead Horse
Dead Hot Workshop
Dead Kennedys (featuring East Bay Ray, Klaus Flouride, D. H. Peligro and Brandon Cruz)
Dead Low Tide
Dead Luke
Dead Meadow
Dead Milkmen
Dead Moon
Dead Prez
Dead Sexy Inc
Dead to Fall
Dead To Me
Dead Whale Tide
Deadboy & the Elephantmen
Deadly Dragon Sound
Deadman
Deadmau5
Deadstring Brothers
Deaf In The Family
Dean Miller
Dean Owens [The Felsons]
Deana Carter
Deanna Varagona
Deanne Bogart
Dear and the Headlights
Deastro
Death
Death at Sea
Death Cab for Cutie
Death From Above 1979
Death In The Park
Death Is Not A Joyride
Death On Two Wheels
Death Sentence: Panda!
Death Ships
Death Valley
Death Vessel
Deathly Fighter
Deathray
Deb Talan and Steve Tannen
Debate
Debayres
Debbie Patino
Deborah Conway
Deborah Giles
Deborah Patino
Debra Peters & the Love Saints
Debris Inc.
dÉbruit
Debutante
Deb Pasternak
Decadent Dub Team
Decahedron
December's Child
Decibully

Don Walser (1993)

Decoder Ring
Dee & La Franz
Dee Dee
Deege
DeeJayBird
Deep
Deep Down Trauma Hounds
Deep Sombreros
Deep South Coalition
Deepdown
Deer Tick
Deerhoof
Deerhunter
Def Four
Def MC's
Def Squad
Defcon
Defenestration
Defryme
deishovida
Deja Voodoo
Dekadens
Del Castillo
Del Rey and the Blues Gators
Del the Funky Homosapien
Delaney Bramlett
Delbert McClinton
Delco
Dele Mandeyah
Delecho
Delegate
DeLeon
Deleted Waveform Gatherings
Delhi 2 Dublin
Delicious
Delicious Food
Delorean
Delorentos
Delta Spirit
Deluka
Delux
Dem 2 Live Dudes
Demi Semi Quaver
Demolished Thoughts
Demolition Doll Rods
Demonio
Demons
Demon's Claws
Denali
Denez Prigent
Dengue Fever
Deni Bonet
Denia Ridley & the Marc Devine Trio
Denice Franke
Denim
Denis Jones
Denise LaSalle
Denison Witmer
Denitia Odigie
Dennis Coffey
Denny Freeman
Dent May & His Magnificent Ukulele
Department of Eagles
Departure Lounge
Deportees
Derby
Derral Gleason
Derrick Brown
Deryl Dodd
Des Ark
Desafinado
deSANGRE
Descartes a Kant
Desert City Soundtrack
Designer Drugs
deSoL
Desolation Wilderness
Desole
Despistado
Dessert Junkys
Destroy All Monsters
Destroyer
Detachment Kit
Detholz!
Detroit Cobras
detroit7
dEUS
Dev/Null
Devendra Banhart
Devics
Devil in a Woodpile
Devil's Island
Devin Davis
Devin the Dude
Devin the Dude & the Coughee Brothaz
Devin the Dude and the Odd Squad
DEVO
Devon Williams
DeVotchKa
Dewato
Dewey Defeats Truman
Dex Romweber Duo
Dexter Freebish
D-Flame with DJ Stylewarz
Diabologum
Diagonals
DIAL-7
DIAMOND
Diamond District
Diamond Nights
Diamond Rings
Diamond Smugglers
Diana Ah Naid

Diana Cantu
Diana Darby
Diana Jones
Diancandor
Diane Birch
Diane Fleming
Diane Izzo
Dick Price
Dick Siegel
Dickie Lee Erwin
Dickie Lee Erwin & The Altered Boys
Didly
Die Art
Die Kreuzen
Die Mannequin
Die Princess Die
Die Slo Entertainment
Die Trying
Die! Die! Die!
Diecast
Dierdre
Dierks Bentley
Dieselboy
Dieselhed
Dig
Dig Mandrakes
Digger
Digital Leather
Digitalism
Dignan
Dikes of Holland
Dillinger Escape Plan
Dillinger Four
Dillinja
Dillon Fence
Dimmer
Dinner is Ruined
Dino Lee
Dino Lee & His Luv Johnson
Dino Martinis
Dinosaur Bones
Dinosaur Feathers
Dinosaur Jr.
Dionne Farris
Dionysos
Dios
Dios Malos
Diplo
Diplomats of Solid Sound
Dir En grey
Dirk Hamilton
George Hamilton V & the NashVegas Nomads
Dirt Bike Annie
Dirt Merchants
Dirt Poets
Dirt Track Brawlers
Dirtblonde
Dirtclodfight
Dirty Americans
Dirty Dialect Click (DDC)
Dirty Epics
Dirty Fuzz
Dirty Heads
Dirty Lucy
Dirty Old Men
Dirty on Purpose
Dirty Pretty Things
Dirty Sweet
Dirty Three
Dirty Wormz
Disappear Fear
Disappears
Disaster Action Team
Disaster Us
Disco Ensemble
disENCHANTed HAZe
Disengage
Disgruntled Seeds
DiskJokke
Dislike
Dissemination Network
Distrito 14
Disturbance
Ditch Witch
Ditty Bops
Divahn
Dive
Diverse
Division Day
Division Minuscula
Division Of Laura Lee
Divit
Dixie Chicks
Dixie Witch
Diz Gibran
Dizzee Rascal
Dizzy Pilot
DJ A.M.
DJ Alex Knight
DJ Amtrack
DJ Angelique
DJ Assault
DJ Atlas
DJ Ayres & Nick Catchdubs
DJ Balance
DJ Big Baby
DJ Bizz
DJ Blondie
DJ Bounz
DJ Car Stereo (Wars)
DJ Carbo
DJ Carpark
DJ Ceeplus
Dj Ceeplus & the House of Bad Knives
DJ CFCF

DJ Chicken George
DJ Chill
DJ Chill Presents Young Samm, Short Texas, Kenika, Lil Boom, 2 Deep
DJ Class
DJ Colette
DJ Coolmann with DJ Mirko Machine & DJ Stylewarz
DJ Crash
DJ Craze
DJ Damon
DJ Dance Party
DJ Dave P
DJ Domo & Good Grief of the Coughee Brothaz
DJ Drop
DJ Dus
DJ Eddie Deville
DJ Eleven
DJ Enferno
DJ Ese
DJ Evil Dee
DJ Fausto
DJ Firewheel
DJ Frances Jaye
DJ Franki Chan
DJ Grip
DJ Hella Yella
DJ Herb
DJ Icewater
DJ Icey
DJ Jacqueline
DJ Jason Hammel (of Mates of State)
DJ Jason Smith
DJ Jester
DJ Jester the Filipino Fist
DJ Jester the Filipino Fist & DJ Klassen
DJ Jester the Filipino Fist and QuadRod
DJ Jon Doe
DJ Josh Wink
DJ Jou-See
DJ Jubilee
DJ Juniper
DJ Kevin Cole
DJ K-Hole
DJ King TUtt
DJ Kip
DJ Knowledge
DJ Kola
DJ Kurupt
DJ Lebowitz
DJ Liquid Todd
DJ Logic
DJ Lt. Dan
DJ Luna
DJ Massive
DJ Me DJ You
DJ Mel
DJ Merritt
DJ Michael 5000 Watts
DJ Micro
DJ MK Ultra
DJ Mum's the Word
DJ Muppetfucker
DJ Notion
DJ Nuts
DJ OBaH
DJ Pajaro
DJ Panko
DJ Paparazzi
DJ Pasta
DJ Pozsi
DJ Primo
DJ Probus
DJ PS1
DJ Pube$
DJ Quik
DJ Radar
DJ Rapid Ric
DJ Rapid Ric & The Whut it Dew Family feat. Magno, Chalie Boy, Da Ryno, Mr. Blakes
DJ Ras Kwame
DJ Reflex
DJ Rekha
DJ Remy Mac (Voxtrot)
DJ Renegade
DJ Reverand Kathy Russell
DJ Rhettmatic
DJ Richard Fearless
DJ Scotch Egg
DJ Shadow
DJ Skeet Skeet
DJ Skeez
DJ Sodapop
DJ SOS
DJ Spaghetti
DJ Spettro
Dj Spinner T and Dj Crop Diggie of the Superstardjs
DJ Spooky
DJ Spooky & The Golden Hornet Project
DJ Spooky That Subliminal Kid
DJ Stef
DJ Stereofaith
DJ Steve Aoki Kid Millionare
DJ Stratus
DJ Strife
DJ Stroke (Rebel Crew)
DJ Sun
DJ Tameil
DJ Taryn Manning
DJ Tats

DJ Tim Skinner
DJ Toy (Control Machete)/ Tarek & Luis Saviour
DJ Tyger Dhula - VELVET
DJ U.N.T.
DJ Wax - VELVET
DJ Wild Hairr
DJ Wood - VELVET
DJ Wrecka
DJ Z-Trip
DJ? Acucrack
Django Walker
Djate
DJ-RJ
DJs On Strike
D-Liar
Dlugokecki
DM Stith
D-Madness
D-Madness/Trio D'Force
D-MAUB
DMBQ
Dmitry Fyodorov
Dmonstrations
DNA Doll
Do Dat
Do Make Say Think
Doc Martin
Doctor Krapula
Doctor Mix and the Remix
Doctorolive
Doctor's Mob
Doe Montoya
Doe Nuts
Does It Offend You, Yeah?
Dog & Pony Show
Dog Fashion Disco
Doghouse Family Jam
Dogs
Dogs Die In Hot Cars
Dogwood Speaks
Dok Holiday
Dok Holiday & Set 4 Life
Dokkebi Q
Doll and The Kicks
Dollar Store
Dollaz N Since - DJ Grip, DJ Spinna, DJ Since
Dollaz N Since
Dollface
Dolly
Dolly Varden
Dolomites
Dolorean
Dolour
domingoSiete
Dominique A
Dominique Leone
Don Bajema
Don Caballero
Don Leady y Los Cadillos
Don McCalister Jr.
Don Mescall
Don Rimini
Don Sanders
Don Schlitz
Don Teschner
Don Tetto
Don Walser
Don Walser & Pure Texas
Don Yojan & La Frescura
Donal Hinely
Donal Scannell
Donald Glover
Doneski
Donkey
Donna the Buffalo
Donnie Davies
Donnie Ray Ford
Donnis
Donnisulana
Donny Hue and the Colors
Donny Ray Ford & the Honky Tonkers
Donnybrook
Donovan
Don't Mean Maybe
Don't Tell Sophie
Doo Rag
Doobie Twisters
Doomsday
Doomtree
Dooney Da Priest
Doosu
Dorian
Doris Henson
Dorothy
Dorothy Wallace
Dorrough
Dos Cojones
Dosastro
dosh
Dot kom
Do-The-Undo
Double D Nose
Double O Go-Go
Double Portion
Doubleman
Double-O-GoGo
Doublewide
Doug Benson
Doug Burr
Doug E. Fresh
Doug Gillard
Doug Hall Trio
Doug Hoekstra
Doug Hoekstra Combo
Doug Kershaw
Doug Sahm

Doug Sahm Tribute feat. Shawn Sahm, Gourds, Dave Alvin, Jimmie Vaughan, Sarah Borges, and more
Doug Sahm Tribute featuring The Texas Mavericks, Joe King Carasco, Angela Strehli, Augie Meyers, The West Side Horns, and many special guests
Doug Sahm, Kim Wilson, Angela Strehli & LouAnn Barton
Doug Wamble
Doug Wamble Quartet
Douglas Armour
Douglas Ferguson
Douglas September
Doujah Raze
Doveman
Dover
Doves
Downy Mildew
Downpilot
Downset
Downsiders
Downthesun
Doyle Bramhall
Doyle Bramhall II
Doyle Lawson & Quicksilver
DP
DQE
Dr. Didg
Dr. Know Featuring Brandon Cruz
Dr. Krelm
Dr. Patterson Barrett & the Associates
Dr. Delay
Dr. Demento
Dr. Dog
Dr. Loco's Rockin' Jalapeno Band
Dr. Mic Livingston
Dr. Miller
Dr. Pepper Family
Dr. Spock
Dr. Strangelove
Dracula Sucks
Drag
Dragmatic
Dragmules
Dragons of Zynth
Drake Bell
Dramarama
Drawlings
Dre Murray
DreadBass Soundsystem
Dream Poppies
Dreamend
Dreaming in English
Dreams So Real
dred skott
Dredg
Dremnt the End
Dressy Bessy
Drew Andrews
Drew Evans
Drew Smith and His Band
Drew Smith's Lonely Choir
Drifter
Drill Team
Drink Up Buttercup
Drippin' Honey
Drive like Maria
Driveblind
Drive-By Truckers
Driver Six
Driver X
Drivin' n' Cryin'
Driving Blind
Driving By Night
Droids Attack
Drojo
Drop
Drop Dead Gorgeous
Drop the Gun
Drop the Lime
Drop Trio
Dropping Daylight
Drowningman
Drug Free Disco Family
Drug Rug
Drumcorps
Drums & Tuba
Drunk Horse
Drunkdriver
Dry Rot
Dry Spells
DSR Featuring Big Tuck & Tum Tum
Duane Andrews
Duane Jarvis
Dub Factor
Dub Is A Weapon
Dub Island Soundsystem
Dub Trio
Dubb Sicks
Dubtex
Duchess Says
Duck Soup
Duke Tumatoe & the Power Trio
Ducktails
Duels
Duff McKagan's Loaded
Duffy
Dujeous
Duke Jupiter

Duke McVinnie
Duke Special
DUKE! The Golden Arm Trio Plays Ellington
Dum Dum Girls
Dumpster
Dumpster Juice
Dumptruck
Duncan Sheik
Dunderhead
Dungen
Duo Zikr
Duquette Johnston
Dust & Blood
Dust Congress
Dustin Kensrue
Dustin O'Halloran
Dustin Welch
Dusty 45's
Dusty Rhodes and the River Band
Dutch Masters
duVergne Gaines
Dwayne Dopsie & the Zydeco Hellraisers
Dwight Baker
Dwight Twilley
Dwight Yoakam
Dyana
Dykehouse
Dylan Hicks
Dylan LeBlanc
Dyme Def
dynah
Dynamic Syncopation
Dynamite Boy
Dynasty Handbag
Dysrhythmia
Dyzack

E

E.C.F.A.
E.S.G.
E>K>U>K
Eagle Claw
Eagle Seagull
Eagle Twin
Eagle Winged Palace
Eagles of Death Metal
Ear Pwr
Earl C. Whitehead & the Grievous Angels
Earl Greyhound
Earl Harvin Trio
Earles and Jensen
Earlimart
Early Day Miners
Early Man
Earshot
Earth
Earth Crisis
Earth The Californian Love Dream
Earthless
earthlings?
Earthpig
Earthpig & Fire
Earthride
East Ash
East L.A. Sabor Factory
East of Eden
East Side Band
East Side Suicides
Eastern Conference Champions
Eastmountainsouth
Eastside Suicides
Easy Action
Easy Star All-Stars
Eat Skull
Eau-1
Ebony Bones
Echo & The Bunnymen
ECHO 7
Echo Base Soundsystem
Echoset
E-Class
Ecstasy of St Theresa
Ecstatic Sunshine
Ed Burleson
Ed Hall
Ed Harcourt
Ed Miller
Ed Vallance
Ed Ward
Edan
Eddie Adcock Band
Eddie Gonzalez
Eddie Richards
Eddie Spaghetti & Friends
Eddie Spaghetti (Supersuckers)
Eddie Whalen
Eden A.K.A.
Edgewater
Edie Sedgwick
Edison Glass
Edison Shine
Edith Frost
Editors
Edsel
Edward Sharpe and the Magnetic Zeros
Edwyn Collins

Eels
Efterklang
Egg Yolk Jubilee Music Band
Eggbo
Eggplant
Egon
Egypt
Eight Frozen Modules
Eighteen Visions
Eileen Ivers
Eileen McGann
Eileen Rose
Eilen Jewell
Eirean Bradley
Eirik Ott a.k.a. Big Poppa E.
Eisley
Eitan Kadosh
Five-Eight
EJ's Reggae Gospel Review
Ekimi
Ekova
Eksi Ekso
el Axel
El Buho
El Caco
El Diablo
El Flaco
El Fudge
El Gato
El Gavachillo y Su Banda Lluvia de Estrellas
El Gran Silencio
El Guincho
El Jesus de Magico
El Magnifico
El Michels Affair
El Nino
El Pus
El Remolon
El Ten Eleven
El Tri
El Tule
El Vez
Elaine Summers
Elana James and Her Hot Hot Trio
Elana James and the Continental Two
Elastica
Elmer Food Beat
Elbow
Eldar
Eleanor Plunge
Electrelane
Electric Airlines
Electric Apricot featuring Les Claypool
Electric Bonsai Band
Electric Eel Shock
Electric Electric
Electric Frankenstein
Electric Pilgrims
Electric President
Electric Six
Electric Third Rail
Electric Touch
Electric Turn To Me
Electric Wizard
Electrico
Electrocute
Electrolightz
Elefant
Elektrolux
Elemeno P
Eleni Mandell
Elephant Parade
Elephone
Elevaters
Elevator Action
Elevator Fight
Eleven Hundred Springs
Eleventh Dream Day
ELEW
Elf Power
Eli "Paperboy" Reed
Eli "Paperboy" Reed & The True Loves
Eli Smith
Eli Young Band
Elias Haslanger
Elijah Bellyfish - VELVET
Eliot Lipp
Eliot Morris
Eliot Partridge
Elisa Nicolas
Elisabeth Belile
Eliza
Eliza Carthy
Eliza Gilkyson
Eliza Gilkyson Band
Eliza Wren
Elizabeth & The Catapult
Elizabeth Cook
Elizabeth Einstein
Elizabeth Hunnicutt
Elizabeth McQueen
Elizabeth McQueen and the Firebrands
Elizabeth Wills
Elk City
Elkland
Ellay Khule the Rifleman
Elle Bandita
Ellegarden
Ellen James Society
Elliott Brood
Elliott Murphy
Elliott Smith

continued on page 64

SXSW SPOTLIGHT

The Giant Truck Of Beer, The Tunnel Of Doom, And The Biscuit Toss

By Roland Swenson

fter five years of putting on SXSW, we were still figuring out how to handle sponsorships. We thought that beer companies were a good prospect, but so far they only wanted to give us beer, not money.

We'd worked with a local beer distributor for a few years, and they gave us enough beer for our parties and the softball game. We held out for a better deal. We wanted more, enough to give all the bands free beer. Finally they said, "How about a LOT of beer?" We said "OK," but we were surprised when we came to work a few days before the fest started, and there was a big green trailer full of beer parked in our office lot.

People were stopping by to admire it, and you could spot the serious beer drinkers by the gleam in their eyes. My thought was, "What are we going to do with all this beer?" I was assured I didn't need to worry, it would take care of itself.

A transportation system was devised to empty what quickly became known as the "giant truck of beer." Cases were dropped off at all the venues for the bands. This was totally illegal, but we didn't know, and the bars didn't argue over getting numerous cases of free beer.

Though the giant truck of beer provided a lot of solace, the Festival staff was worried. Louis Jay Meyers had just added white-hot L7 to an already overbooked bill headlined by red-hot Helmet, with strong local support from Crust and Ed Hall. And it was in an untested new venue on Fifth Street called the Main Event. Louis eventually came around to the idea that the show wouldn't fit in the relatively tiny space, so the solution was to add a tent and a stage and a fence in the gravel beer garden next to the club, which we dubbed the Main Event Forum.

The show was booked for Saturday night, which meant it would come after we had been getting our butts kicked for a couple of nights already. Everyone was still a little jumpy, since this was the first SXSW after our office had been torched by an arsonist the year before. As a spry 36-year-old, I'd heard L7 and Helmet, but it took the twentysomethings on the staff to gin up my fear and dread.

In the wake of the arson, we'd appointed the redoubtable Steve Chaney to fulfill the new title of "Showcase Security." Steve's a big guy, the kind of person you'd want on your side in a bar brawl. He's the type who can stop a fight, though he'd probably never start one. On the Saturday of the show, I decided I'd stick close to him.

I picked up Steve that afternoon and we went over to take a look at the Main Event Forum. When we got there, we knew we were in for trouble. There was already a line of kids outside, and they were surly, worried they wouldn't get in since they didn't have badges or wristbands.

It was not a big tent. It was not a big stage. We went in the club to meet the owner, who turned out to be a kickboxing

champion from Nigeria who had invested his prize money to open the bar. He was complaining because he hadn't seen much business so far that weekend. We assured him that was about to change. One our way out, Steve and I agreed he was feisty.

The bands' road crews were loading into the venue. They looked pissed off as they saw the venue for the first time. We quickly ducked out without being spotted. I went back to the Hyatt and tried to take a nap.

When I turned on my walkie-talkie around 6pm, I could hear the fear in voices calling out for help from venues all over town. But the most insistent cries came from the Main Event.

I got there as fast as I could, and found Steve. The hair on the back of my neck rose as I surveyed the scene. Big production trucks had parked on the curb in front of the club, creating a narrow passage between the fence and the trucks. It seemed as if hundreds of bodies were packed inside what we came to call the "tunnel of doom." Some people were trying to scale the fence to escape the crush. There was screaming, not from pain, but from fury.

I pulled the brick-sized cell phone (this was '92, after all) from my back pocket and dialed 911: "Hello. We're having a riot at 505 East Fifth Street. Please send help! Yes, a riot. Thank you."

Eventually, two policemen wandered up on foot. Steve and I ran over to them, pleading for their help in clearing the "tunnel of doom." They looked over at the crowd and said, "We're not going in there." After pleading a little longer, I asked, "Are you willing to just walk around and let everyone see you?" The cops looked at each other and said "Yeah, we can do that."

Miraculously, the crowd did calm down when the policemen passed by. During this time, Steve was arguing with the Nigerian kickboxing bouncers for the club, insisting that it was indeed a good idea to open the doors early to start letting people inside.

After we started letting people in the gate, things calmed down considerably, and there was even enough room for most of the people waiting in line. I left to respond to radio calls from other venues, and Steve stayed on the scene.

I hadn't been gone long when my radio erupted with more calls for anyone and everyone to report to the Main Event. I rushed back, and the "tunnel of doom" was full once again. Steve was at the head of the line, holding onto the gate with one hand and the fence with the other, literally holding back a hundred people trying to bum-rush the door.

Eventually, the gate was closed with the help of the bouncers, and Steve and I found ourselves out on the street watching it all unfold. We tried walking up and down the line urging everyone to keep calm, that they were going to be able to hear the show just fine where they were. There was a drunken girl who kept yelling, "Get them!" (As in us.) "There are more of us than there are of them!"

We continued walking the entire line trying to calm the crowd. As we got to the alley, we looked up and could see dozens of kids who had climbed on the roof next door, and were taking running leaps across the alley onto the roof of the club. Steve and I stood there, mouths open, watching in awe. Finally, I said, "Can we stop that?" Steve said, "Nah. No way."

After that, a bunch of kids tried to tear down the fence. They must have eventually realized that even if they got inside, they wouldn't be any closer to the stage than where they were standing in line. L7 started playing, and things more or less calmed down.

Steve and I left to respond to emergency calls from a venue on Red River called the Sanitarium, where there had been a last-minute booking of a Butthole Surfers side-project called The Jackofficers. There was a surly group of kids who were determined to force their way inside, and Steve and I along with a handful of staffers made the mistake of getting caught with our backs against the wall of the club, with no way to escape.

Suddenly the girl from the Main Event was there too, and yelling, "Get them! There are more of us than there are of them." I yelled at her, "Don't you have any other material?" Curiously, the crowd did not find this amusing, so without an escape route we went inside the club and held the door closed.

Once inside, we could see that the show consisted of pre-recorded music, a light show, lots of fog, and the naked chick from the Surfers dancing onstage wearing a necktie around her waist. The club manager told me that he had just left Gibby Haynes, who was drinking at the Ritz. Gibby's explanation was that "The Jackofficers" was what they called it when they just sent their sound and light system out for a show without the band. Word of this spread to the crowd outside, and they dispersed.

Steve and I screwed up our courage and went back to the Main Event. First, we dealt with the Nigerian kickboxer owner, who was upset that people were mad at him. Then we spoke to L7's manager, who was totally bent out of shape. We discovered the club had run out of toilet paper after the first night, and the owner hadn't bothered to buy any more. This was especially offensive to the ladies of L7. Then the manager ripped into us about our crew being drunk. I rose to their defense, but the manager said, "Look over there." I turned to see our stage crew, barely able to stand up next to a mountain of empty green beer cans which had originated at the "giant truck of beer." We left as the manager swore L7 would never play SXSW again. At least not until they did a few years later.

That night, at the staff after-party in the Hyatt, we all shared our war stories, which by then had transformed from being horrific to being hilarious, the telling of them fueled by the "giant truck of beer."

A local restaurant had sent us a lot of their leftover food for the party, including many dozens of biscuits. The biscuits had failed to rise, and they were very heavy. Brent Grulke had organized a contest on the balcony to see how far we could throw them into Town Lake. It took many throws to perfect our form, but we became quite adept.

The next morning, I walked by the lake next to the Hyatt. Ducks had eaten the biscuits, and there was duck shit all over the Hyatt patio. ■ **Roland Swenson is co-founder and managing director of SXSW.**

Johnny Cash, Beck at Emo's with Mark Kates, left (1994)

Burnt Ends And New Beginnings

By Peter Blackstock

he first five years of South By Southwest had barely been in the books for 24 hours when the next five years kicked off at a full blaze. Literally.

"It was the Monday night after SXSW and an impromptu, semi-True Believers reunion was taking place at the Hole in the Wall," remembers Michael Corcoran, writer for the *Austin American-Statesman* and former music columnist for *The Austin Chronicle*. "It was about 1:30 a.m., and Alejandro [Escovedo, True Believers' frontman] announced that they were just going to lock the doors at 2 a.m. and play for hours. I had some mushrooms in my pocket, so I figured I'd take them since the party was going to go on all night. But after about 20 minutes it was all over. Last call, all hopped up and no more booze to help me come down.

"I was walking with Debbie Pastor to her house, I think, just looking for a place to hang out the next few hours. When we passed the *Chronicle*/SXSW office [at Nueces and 28th streets, just a few blocks from Hole in the Wall], we saw fire trucks arriving and a fire in the back part of the building. I told the firemen that I was an employee (I wasn't really at the time), and went to the part of the office not on fire and called Louis Black [*Chronicle* editor]. He went back to sleep, so I called Roland [Swenson, SXSW director], and about half an hour later he came screeching up."

Swenson picked up the story from there, in an account published in 2001 by *The Austin Chronicle* on the occasion of the paper's 20th anniversary: "When I got to the office, it was like a scene from a movie. The entire area was bathed in an eerie color with white spotlights and red flashers. The parking lot was filled with fire trucks, and firemen were dragging hoses everywhere. Relieved that I'd shown up instead of going back to bed, Corcoran took me to see the lieutenant in charge of arson investigations. The lieutenant looked like Steve McQueen in *The Towering Inferno*, his face smudged with smoke, wearing his fire hat and gear. He leaned close and fixed his gaze on me, asking in a solemn tone: *"Do you have any enemies?"*

You can't grow a music conference from scratch to the cusp of world renown without accumulating a few enemies along the way. One legendary handwritten note from a "Concerned Musician" that arrived in the mail around this time began with the greeting, "You're a bunch of puss-fags, cock-sucking discriminatory mother-fuckers," and went downhill from there. The 1991 event had been especially revealing of SXSW's growing pains: It was the first and only time the event was *not* held during the University of Texas' spring break, and clubs overflowed as a result, leading to long lines and fire-code closures.

It was clear that the major challenge the next five years would be managing SXSW's growth. From 1992 to 1996, South By Southwest not only moved its office of daily operations, but also transitioned the event's headquarters from the Hyatt Regency hotel to the brand new Austin Convention Center. Conference attendance increased dramatically amid a booming age for both the music industry and the American economy. The quantity of performers surged from about 400 to nearly 700 (a detail I recall quite vividly, given that I was responsible for writing a few words about every single act for the increasingly catalogue-size program guide). SXSW began to experiment with satellite regional festivals in different areas of the country; and in Austin, the main event's purview began expanding beyond music, first with a film fest and then an interactive element. Though regional in name, South By Southwest was growing more international in spirit, with significant contingents from Europe and beyond making the annual trek to Austin in March.

By the time New York's New Music Seminar — the confab upon which the first SXSW had loosely been modeled back in 1987 — met its demise in the mid-'90s, South By Southwest had emerged as the biggest event of its kind in the country, and perhaps the world.

The first step, in the summer of 1991, was finding a new place to do business after the fire. "The whole building had been filled with smoke, and there was a layer of soot over everything in the office," Swenson recounted. "Not having anywhere else to go, we cleaned up as best we could and went back to work. Who knows how long we would have stayed there smelling the fire damage every day, and going home with our clothes stinking from the smoke? But we got an eviction notice from the landlord, who was going to remodel the building with the insurance proceeds. The *Chronicle* was getting booted out as well, so the hunt was on for a new office.

"After looking around at some pretty odd choices, Nick [Barbaro, *Chronicle* publisher] settled on buying the old Butler Brick Company building in Hyde Park on East 40th street for the *Chronicle*. It included a tract of land with five lots, and on the last one was a model home built by Butler Brick in 1940. So SXSW moved into the three-bedroom, one-bath, 1200-square-foot house, and after the fire, we were happy to be in a place built out of brick. Out back was a ramshackle detached two car garage, which [SXSW co-director] Louis Jay Meyers remodeled and turned into the Music Festival office."

The response to the overflow spring-break crowds of 1991 was, initially, to scale things back a little bit. "Last year, the biggest complaint we heard was just too many bands and crowding in the clubs," reads the '92 program guide's "Welcome to SXSW" message, which went on to reveal that there were actually 100 fewer bands on the showcase schedule. Needless to say, this trend did not last, though it may have made for a kinder, gentler SXSW in George H.W. Bush's last year as president.

The ups and downs of the SXSW experience (or in this case, the downs and ups) were neatly encapsulated within the full stretch of 1992's opening day. It began with disaster, when Willie Nelson's bus failed to make it back to Austin from a distant gig in time for the 10:30 a.m. keynote address he was scheduled to deliver.

Swenson fielded the bad-news phone call at 8 a.m. that morning. "I tried hard not to panic, and decided to keep the information to myself," he admitted. Plan B was to let Michelle Shocked, who was booked to give the opening remarks before Willie's keynote, speak for a little longer. "I chatted with Michelle for a few minutes, and asked her how long she planned to speak, and managed to not show any surprise when she said, 'Oh, I guess about 45 minutes.' I thought, 'Great, this buys me some time to figure out what to do!'"

Shocked's speech is best remembered by those who were there as meandering and interminable. Swenson recalls that it had been written by her boyfriend, "a rock critic who had profound confidence in his brilliance. It seemed to be a running leap at describing the development of American music

starting with black-face minstrel shows, carrying it forward to the new folk music. The audience was growing restless, and after playing a few tunes with her mandolin, Michelle finally left the stage."

All the while, Swenson had managed to wrangle a surprise appearance by Willie at a Columbia Records showcase on Auditorium Shores that evening, one of the first such large outdoor shows SXSW had staged. The bill featured up-and-coming Austinites Darden Smith and James McMurtry, the Midas-touch producer-songwriter T Bone Burnett, and headliner Poi Dog Pondering, at the time the biggest band to come out of Austin in years.

Nelson ended up providing the crowning touch to the evening. "Willie went out by himself and did a short great set of songs as the sun was setting, including a favorite of mine, 'Crazy,'" Swenson recalls. All's well that ends well at SXSW, sometimes.

Of course, the rest of the weekend would bring other trials — most memorably a Friday night show by Little Village (a supergroup consisting of John Hiatt, Nick Lowe, Ry Cooder and Jim Keltner) at the 1,500-plus-capacity Terrace. "They were the hottest band in our segment of the music business that year," SXSW co-director Louis Black recalled. "Everyone I spoke to talked about the one show they knew they were going to attend was the Little Village show. I was freaking about capacity, worried about turn-away crowds." Apparently nearly everyone else was worried about that too, and most of them made other plans. So Little Village ended up playing to about a half-capacity crowd.

Meanwhile, back at the Hyatt, some strange left-turns were taking shape in the panel schedules. Out of left field in 1991 had been a forum titled, "Who Killed JFK?" — which had nothing to do with the music industry, but nevertheless had proven popular enough to warrant a follow-up panel in '92 (fueled by the release of Oliver Stone's JFK film). SXSW even went so far as to put on a JFK symposium in Dallas, though it proved a short-lived diversion.

But other satellite events — ones that actually had something to do with music — were also on the horizon. The first, in 1993, was the Mississippi River Music Festival (MRMF), in St. Louis; two years later came North By Northeast (NXNE) in Toronto, and North By Northwest (NXNW) in Portland, Oregon. NXNE, which is still held every year in June, was not run by SXSW, but there were tangential ties between the two festivals, indicative of SXSW's increasing inclinations toward international involvement.

The biggest change for the conference in 1993 was the relocation from the Hyatt, where SXSW had found some stability from 1990-92 after hotel-hopping in its first three years, to the newly built Austin Convention Center. "Holding an event in a convention center is a profoundly different proposition than in a hotel, and we had to rethink how we did the entire daytime event," Swenson reflected. "Our attendees, as usual, longed for the earlier, simpler days of SXSW, and missed the Hyatt, as did we. Still, it allowed for a significantly larger trade show, and even more panels and speakers. For the first time, lack of space was not an issue; figuring out how to use more space than we really needed was the challenge."

In the clubs, another challenge was on the rise, as satellite shows that were not officially affiliated with SXSW began to proliferate. The most notable in 1993 was a Jimmie Dale Gilmore-centered showcase at the Broken Spoke that featured his Elektra labelmate Arthur Alexander, a legendary pop-soul artist and early influence on the Beatles and Stones who was in the midst of a career resurgence. Sadly, it was short-lived; Alexander died of a heart attack less than two months later. His last days were happy ones, playing to greatly appreciative crowds such as the one at the Spoke that night. "During one of their extended ovations," Gilmore remembered, "I glanced over and noticed the giant Arthur with the giant gleaming smile was wiping tears from his eyes."

Over the next couple of years, such unofficial showcases became increasingly prevalent during the daytime, as labels and agents and publications and the like began staging promotional parties in

restaurants, art galleries, parking lots, and just about anywhere a P.A. could be set up. There were official South by Southwest music presentations during the daytime hours, too: Though an initial attempt at afternoon lobby performances had gotten off to a rocky start when Julian Cope got the heebie-jeebies and backed out of a scheduled performance at the Hyatt Atrium in 1991, perseverance led to an established and enjoyable daytime-stage routine. The move to the Convention Center helped, as there was plenty of room for a decent-sized stage in the trade show hall. Artists such as Peter Holsapple, the Mavericks, Lisa Loeb, Flaco Jimenez, and Geno Delafose & the Eunice Playboys played the Day Stage; a special all-afternoon presentation on the stage in 1996 turned the spotlight on the musicians' health assistance program Sweet Relief, with performances by Golden Smog, Giant Sand, Kristin Hersh, Joe Henry and Vic Chesnutt.

The 1994 and '95 editions of the conference also witnessed the sprouting of non-musical branches to the SXSW tree; first a film festival, then an interactive event. The film element had been hinted at since the beginning, with a series of cable-access video music programs curated by Tim Hamblin and Kent Benjamin that were dubbed "SXSW Videofest" in early program-guide listings. Furthermore, many of the prime movers from *The Austin Chronicle*, most notably SXSW co-founders Louis Black and Nick Barbaro, had been active in film organizations since their days at *The Daily Texan* while attending the University of Texas.

"By 1993, SXSW was well established and thriving enough that we began to get serious about doing something with film," recounts co-director Louis Black, who was well-connected to the Austin film industry. "We figured it would be a small focused boutique film festival, both to complement SXSW Music and let us all indulge in our love for film. Early on, to differentiate it from music, there was an attempt to call it the South by Southwest Film and Media Conference, SFMC for short, but that never took hold."

The "FMC" part of the acronym also underscores that the 1994 expansion was actually an attempt to combine the film fest with what would eventually become the interactive conference. "The event gained immediate traction, and the technology track was stronger than we would have guessed," Swenson recalled. "We made the decision to divide the new event into separate events for 1995 — SXSW Film and SXSW Multimedia. We also decided that the two new events would be totally overshadowed if we held them concurrently with SXSW Music, so we moved them to the weekend before, and SXSW became a 10-day event."

Black cited the hiring of Nancy Schafer, now the executive director of New York's TriBeCa Film Festival, to produce the event as a key factor: "Schafer provided just the right sensibility to bring us all together in creating and crafting the event." Another vital figure who emerged during this phase was the man who would become the guiding force of the multimedia and interactive ventures. "Early on we all responded enthusiastically when Dewey Winburne, an acquaintance of ours, approached us about adding an interactive/new media program track to the event," Black recalled. "We agreed, refocusing the event to include multimedia."

Swenson vividly remembers his first meeting with the colorful and energetic Winburne. "He started talking at about 300 words a minute about how SXSW was missing out on all this great new media stuff being done around town, and that we needed to jump on the bandwagon as soon as we could, and how he had an idea for a new event that he could do for us. I told him, 'Stop right there, don't say another word, because I've already thought of this, and we don't necessarily need you to do it.'

"As it turned out, I was wrong about that. Dewey was a force that would not be denied. He kept on talking. He was really hard to get rid of, and I'm usually pretty good at that sort of thing. After a little while, he captured my interest and we ended up talking for an hour or two. And he turned out to be the catalyst for launching the SXSW Interactive Festival."

As new faces were coming into the SXSW orbit, a major figure was departing. Co-founder and music director Louis Jay Meyers left in 1994 to pursue other avenues but kept his ties to the event through the SXSW golf tournament he'd created as a sort of opening bookend to the closing softball tourney. "I was completely burned out," Meyers explained. "There was no doubt in my mind that I had given it everything I had and it was time for me to step aside in order for it to achieve its full potential, whatever that was meant to be. For me, the whole reason we created SXSW was to support a community that we felt was ignored by everyone else in the world. Once we outgrew that ability, my interest was diminished."

But mostly, everyone still remembers 1994 for one presence: Johnny Cash. The Man in Black, newly signed to Rick Rubin's American Recordings at the time, delivered the keynote address, which included quite a few songs performed solo acoustic. "Cash came out alone with his guitar," Swenson remembers, "and held the audience transfixed for half an hour, sharing new songs from the album and telling stories about his life. He concluded by calling us all his 'Grandchildren.'" Later that night, Cash played a showcase at Emo's with the Tennessee Two that has become legendary. ("The chair he sat on is somewhere up in the club's rafters still, I believe," noted *Chicago Tribune* rock critic Greg Kot, who attended.)

Louis Black remembers that Emo's show as the very rare occasion when SXSW employees skirted a fundamental edict. He recalled that at meetings, ringleader Swenson "would remind us several times, 'Remember, SXSW is not for you.' Translated, it means your job and responsibilities come first by a long shot; don't take a break and disappear because there is some band you want to see. Staff had been called on the carpet for this. Except this year Johnny Cash was playing Emo's. This is the only time that I remember seeing most of the staff breaking the rule by showing up for a set. Good thing that Roland was there, as well."

SXSW continued to grow through the mid-'90s, with high-profile moments including Todd Rundgren's keynote address at 1995's inaugural interactive conference; a jam-packed show by Soul Asylum at the peak of their career at the Terrace in '95; an outdoor stage show on Sixth Street in '96 headlined by Iggy Pop; an alternative-country showcase at the Split Rail in '96 that helped young acts Whiskeytown and the Old 97's get major-label record deals; and the addition of the new Austin Music Hall as another large-capacity venue.

Still, some things stayed the same — especially on Sundays, when the fever pitch of the weekend revelry gave way to a sweet and wistful denouement as SXSW drew to a close. In the daytime, the softball tournament remained a huge hit, beloved for its barbecue smorgasbord and for the championship-game calls of colorful guest-announcing duos such as Mojo Nixon & Country Dick Montana and Joe Nick Patoski & Doug Sahm. And at night, a tradition had developed at La Zona Rosa, where hundreds of SXSWers gathered to hear Alejandro Escovedo — that same musician who was holding court at the Hole in the Wall on the night the original South By Southwest office caught fire in 1991. His La Zona Rosa "orchestra" performances featured around 15 musicians, including strings, percussion, horns and steel guitar.

Erik Flannigan, who assembled the Escovedo live album *More Miles Than Money* from his recordings of several shows during the '90s (including the SXSW performances), had a simple take on what those shows meant to South By Southwest. "Alejandro's Sunday night sets at La Zona Rosa marked both the official and spiritual end of the festival — a show for the die-hards, the locals, the staff, the hung-overs, and anyone else who just wasn't ready to let South By go for another year."

Soon enough, the next year would arrive. ■

continued from page 54

Ellis Hooks
Ellis Paul
Ellyn Maybe
Elm
Elouise Burrell's New Mix
El-P
Eltro
Eluvium
Elvis Costello and the Imposters
Elvis Perkins
Elvis Perkins In Dearland
Elwood Galiger
Ely Guerra
Elysian Fields
Elyssia Marie y Senal
Embodyment
Embrace
Emcee
Emer Kenny
Emergency Broadcast Network
emergency music
Emerson Hart
Emery
EMG
Emilio
Emily Grace and Matthew Gardner
Emily Kaitz
Emily Rodgers
Emily Sparks
Emily Wells
Emma Gibbs Band
Emma Lee
Emma Pollock
Emma Tricca
Emmy the Great
Empire Isis
Empire State
Empirion
Employer, Employee
Empyr
Emynd & Bo Bliz
End of Fashion
End of the West
Endless Boogie
Endo
Endochine
Enduro
ENE
Enemymine
Engine 88
Enigma
Enon
Ensimi
Enslaved
Enter Shikari
Entrance
Envelopes
Envy On The Coast
Eol Trio
Epatomed
Ephraim Owens
Ephraim Owens Quartet
Ephraim Owens Quintet
Epic
Epileptinomicon
epo-555
Epoch Of Unlight
Epperley
Eprom
Epstein's Mother
Erase Errata
Erbie Bowser & T.D. Bell
Eric Bachmann
Eric Bibb
Eric Blakely
Eric Coleman
Eric Hanke
Eric Heatherly
Eric Hisaw
Eric Hofbauer
Eric Hutchinson
Eric Jerardi Band
Eric Johnson and Alien Love Child
Eric Krug
Eric Lewis & Andy Ratliff
Eric Mingus
Eric Moll
Eric Moore and Resonate
Eric Philips
Eric Taylor
Erica Nicole
Eric's Trip
Erik Friedlander
Erik Hokkanen
Erik Hokkanen & his Snow Wolves
Erik Moll
Erik Voeks
Erika Machado
Erin Ivey
Erin McCarley
Erin McKeown
Erin Roberts
Erin Roberts/Porlolo
Eris
Erja Lyytinen
Ernest Gonzales
Ernie C Ernst
Ernie Kline
Ernst Langhout
Errol Blackwood
Errol Ranville
Errors
Erule
Ervin Charles
Ervin Charles & the Nite Riders
Erykah Badu
Esbjörn Svensson Trio
ESG
Eskmo
Essence
Esser
Essie Jain
Estelle
ester drang
Estradasphere
Estrojet
Eszter Balint
Et Ret
ETC
Eternal Tapestry
Eternia
Ethan Azarian
Ethan Rose
Ethel-Ann
Esther's Follies
Ethyl & Methyl
Ethyl Ann Powell
Etienne Charry
Etienne DeRocher
Eugene Francis Jnr & The Juniors
Eugene McGuinness
Eugene Mirman
Eulogies
Euripides Pants
Eva & The Heartmaker
Eva Ybarra y Su Conjunto
Evaline
Evamore
Evan and Jaron
Evan Dando
Evan Johns & Ivan Brown
Evan Johns & the H-Bombs
Evan Johns/Ed Cute/Ivan Brown
Evan Seleven
Evangelicals
Evangeline
Evangelista
Eve and the Exiles
Eve Monsees
Eve Stern
Even
Evening
Ever We Fall
Everclear
Everest
Evergreen
Evergreen Terrace
Everlovely Lightningheart
Evermore
Everthus the Deadbeats
Every Move a Picture
Everybody Else
Everybody Was In The French Resistance...Now!
Everything Everything
Evidence of Dilated Peoples
Evidence with DJ Babu
Evil Beaver
Evil Bebos
Evil Mothers
Evil Nine
Evol
Evol Intent DJ
Evren Goknar
Ewa Braun
Ex Cocaine
Ex-Boyfriends
Excess Bleeding Heart
Excess Lettuce
Excision & Datsik
Exene Cervenka
Exene Cervenka and the Original Sinners
eX-Girl
Exit Clov
Exit the King
Expansion Union
Expatriate
Experimental Aircraft
Explode Into Colors
Explosions in the Sky
Explosive
Extra Fancy
Extra Glenns
ExtraVery
Extreme Animals
Extreme Heat
Eyedea & Abilities
Eyeris
EZ T
Ezio
Ezra Charles
Ezra Charles & The Works
Ezra Furman & The Harpoons
Ezra Reich
Ezra Thomas

F

F for Fake
F.O.C.
F.O.S.
F.O.S./Fusion Of Syllables
F.S.K.
Fab Motion
Faboo
Fabric
Fabu
Fabulous Disaster
Face Down
Face of Concern
Facedowninshit
Faceless Werewolves
Facing New York
Factums
Faculty
Failsafe
Fair to Midland
Fair Verona
Fairchild
Faith and the Muse
Faith Kleppinger
Fake Problems
Fakers
Faktion
Fall From Grace
Fall Out Boy
Fallguy
False Virgins
Fama
Fambooey
Family of the Year
Famous
Fanfarlo
Fang Island
Fangs
Fannius III
Fantastic Plastic Machine
Fantasy Mirrors
Fantasy's Core
Fanzine
Far-Less
Farm Boys
Farmer not so John
Gary Negbaur
Fashawn
Fashion Disaster
Fashion Flesh
Fast Forward
Fastbacks
Fastball
Fastbuck
Fat Amy
Fat Man Waving
Fat Mike (Cokie The Clown)
Fat Paw
Fat Pimp
Fat Tony & D ee R ai L
Fat Tuesday
Fatal Flying Guilloteens
Fatboy Slim
Fate Brothers
Fatso Jetson
Faun Fables
Faust & Shortee
Faux Fox
Favourite Sons
FCS North
Feable Weiner
Fear Factory
Feathermerchants
Fedel
FEED
Feeding 5000
Felix Cartal
Felt Nun
Femurs
Fenech-Soler
Fenway Park
Ferdinand
Fergus & Geronimo
Fern
Fernando
Ferraby Lionheart
Ferras
Ferras/Katy Perry
Fetish
Feufollet
Fever in the Funkhouse
Fiasco
Fiat Lux
Fiction Plane
Field Music
Fielding
Fields Of Gaffney
Fierro
5th Ward Juvenilez
Fig Dish
Fight Bite
Fight Like Apes
Fighting Brothers McCarthy
Fighting With Wire
FIGO
Figurines
Filé
Film School
Film Star
fiN
Final Flash
Final Solutions
Finale
Finally Punk
Finde
Findlay Brown
Fine China
Fingathing
Finger
Fingerprints
Fink
Finn McCool
Finn Riggins
Finn's Motel
Fionn O Lochlainn
Fionn Regan
Fire Marshals of Bethlehem
Fire Zuave
Fireball Ministry
Fireballs of Freedom
Firekills
Fires
Fires Were Shot
Firewater
Fireworks Go Up!
First Aid Kit
First Class Fresh
First Light
First Nation
First Session
First-Eight
Fish Hospital
Fish Karma
Fishboy
Fishtank Ensemble
Fitz and The Tantrums
Fitz of Depression
Five Chinese Brothers
Five Eight
Five Fingers of Funk
Five For Fighting
Five Horse Johnson
Five Mile Mule
Five O'Clock Heroes
Five Pointe O
Five Times August
Fivehead
Fivehundred
Fiver
Fl. Oz.
Flaco Jimenez
Flair
Flametrick Subs
Flametrick Subs w/ Satan's Cheerleaders
Flaming Arrows Mardi Gras Indians
Flaming Arrows Mardi Gras Indians with special guest Big Chief Roddy of the Black Eagles
Flaming Fire
Flaming June
Flare
Flash Burns
Flash to Bang Time
Flat Duo Jets
Flatirons
Flavormaus
Fleet Foxes
Fleming & John
Flesh Assembly
Fleshies
Fleshtones
Flexxx & Bass Parade
Flick
Flickerstick
Flies on Fire
Flight of the Conchords
FLiP
Flip Grater
Fliponya
Flipside
Flo Mob
Flo Motion
Floating Action
Flogging Molly
Flophouse
Flor Alicia Hernandez
Flor de Mal
Florence and the Machine
Florian Horwath
Florida Slim
Flosstradamus
Flowchart
Flower Travellin' Band
Flowerhead
Flowers
Flowers Forever
Floyd Dakil Combo
Floyd Domino
Fluf
Fluffer
Fluffy
Fluokids
Flux Information Sciences
Fly Gypsy
Flybanger
Flying Lotus
Flying Luttenbachers
Flying Saucers
Flyleaf
Flynn D
FM Belfast
FM Campers
FM3
FNU Ronnies
Foals
Fobia
Focus
FOE
Fol Chen
Fold Zandura
Follow For Now
Follow That Bird!
Follow The Train
Followed By Static
Fonda
Fono
Food for Feet
Fooled By April
Fool's Gold
Foot Foot
Foot Patrol
Foot Village
Footnotes
For Squirrels
For Stars
For Those Who Know
Forbidden Pigs
Ford Turrell
Foreign Born
Foreign Islands
Foreign Legion
Foreskin 500
Forest City Lovers
Forever Changes
Forever Goldrush
Forever The Sickest Kids
Forget the Name
Formosa
Forro in the Dark
Fortune Tellers
Forty Second Scandals
Forward
Forward Russia
Foscoe Jones
Fouled Out
FOUND
Four Hams on Rye
Four Letter Lie
Four Piece Suit
Fourcolorzack & Pretty Titty
Four Hundred
Fourkiller Flats
Foursight
Foxy Foxy
Foxy Shazam
Foy Vance
Fozlur
Frances
Frances Ann Kyle
Francis
Francis and The Lights
Francis Dunnery
Franck Amsallem
Francoiz Breut
Frank Bango
Frank Fairfield
Frank Jordan
Frank N Dank
Frank Robinson
Frank Smith
Frank Turner
Franki Chan
Frankie Lee
Frankie Lee & Auggie Meyers
Frankie Machine
Frankie Rose And The Outs
Franklin Bruno
Franz Ferdinand
Freakwater
Freaky Age
Fred Argir
Fred Eaglesmith
Fred Koller
Fred LeBlanc
Fred Mitchim
Fred O. Knipe
Fred Sanders
Fred Schneider
Fred Walser
Fred Wilson
Fredalba
Freddie Gibbs
Freddie Steady & the Shakin' Apostles
Freddie Steady's Wild Country
Freddie Stevenson
Freddie White
Freddy Fender
Free Agents
Free Blood
Free Energy
Free Radicals
FREE SOL
Free The Robots
Freebooters
Freedom Fighters
Freedom Sold
Freedy Johnston
Freekbass
Freelance Whales
Freeland
Freeloader
Freestyle Open Stage featuring DJ Jester
Freestylers
Freeway
Freeway & Jake One
Freezepop
French Horn Rebellion
French Kicks
French Miami
Frente!
Freshkills
Frida Hyvönen
Friday
Friday After Dark
Friends Electric
Friends Of Dean Martinez
Friends Of Lizzy
Frigg A-Go-Go
Frightened Rabbit
Frikstailers
Frisbie
Frodus
Frog Eyes
Frogpond
From Ashes Rise
From Bubblegum To Sky
Front Row for the Meltdown
Frontier
Frontier Ruckus
Frontier Theory
Frontline
Frontside
Frosted
Fruet & Os Cozinheiros
Fruit
Fu Manchu
Fuck
Fuck Buttons
Fucked Up
FuckEmos
Fuckshovel
Fuckzilla
Fudge Factory Inc.
Fujiya & Miyagi
Fulflej
Full Flava Kings
Full House
Full White Drag
Fuller
Function
Functional Blackouts
Funeral Diner
Funeral Party
Funky C
Funky Nashville
Funland
Fur Dixon & Blow Up
Fur Packed Action
Furious IV
Furry Things
Furside
Furthest Drive Home
Fur Trappers
Futomomo Satisfaction
Future Blondes
Future Clouds & Radar
Future Future
Future Of The Left
Future Virgins
Futurebirds
Futurecop!
Fuzz Club
Fuzz Club featuring DJ Sue
Fuzzbubble
Fuzzy
Fuzzy Control
Fuzzy Doodah
Fydolla Ho
Fyfe Dangerfield

G

G.G. Elvis
G.T. Block Bleedaz feat. Lil Buck
Gabbie Nolen
Gabriel Mann
Gabriel Minnikin
Gabriel Prokofiev
Gabriel Yacoub
Gabriella Cilmi
Gabrielle Bouliane
Gadarene
GAGAKIRISE
Gage_Inc.
Gahdzilla Motor Company
Gail Davies
Galactic Cowboys
Galactic w/ Lyrics Born, Gift of Gab & Boots Riley
Galen Herod
Gallows
Gals Panic
Game Rebellion
Gammacide
Gandhi in Vegas
GangGreen
Gangrene (Alchemist & Oh No)
Garageland
Garden Variety
Gardenia Benros
Garine
Garland Jeffreys
Garlic
Garmarna
Garotas Suecas
Garrison
Garrison Starr
Gary Burke
Gary Clark Jr.
Gary Graves
Gary Gulman
Gary Heffern
Gary Higgins
Gary Jules
Gary Louris & Mark Olson
Gary Lucas

Goober & the Peas (1995)

Gary Lucas & Gods and Monsters
Gary Mex Glazner
Gary Nichols
Gary P. Nunn
Gary Primich
Gary Stewart
Gary Stier
Gary Stier & Buffalo Nickel
Gary U.S. Bonds
Gary War
Gary Wayne Claxton
Gas Huffer
Gasoline
Gasoline Cowboy
Gator Mayne
Gaunt
Gavin Castleton
Gavin DeGraw
Gavin Holland
Gavin Lance
Gavin Stephens
Gay Witch Abortion
Gaybomb
Gaza Strippers
Gear Daddies
Gecko Turner
Geeks
Geezer Lake
Geggy Tah
Gelbison
Geller
Gem
Gemma Hayes
Gemma Ray
Gena Rowlands Band
Genders
Gene Summers
Gene Williams
General Elektriks
General Fiasco
Generationals
Genevieve Van Cleve
Genghis Tron
Genitallica
Geno Delafose & French Rockin' Boogie
Geno Delafose & the Eunice Playboys
Gentle Readers
Gentleman Auction House
Gentleman Jesse
Gentleman Reg
Geoff Reacher
George Bedard & the Kingpins
George Bugatti
George Byrne
George Carver
George Clinton & the P Funk All Stars featuring Parliament & Funkadelic
George DeVore
George Devore and the Roam
George DeVore Four
George Ensle
George Gilmore & the Powers That Be
George Hamilton V
George Highfill
George Huntley
George Stanford
George Williams
Georgia Barretto
Georgie James
Gerald Bair
Gerald Collier
Gerald Duncan
Gerald G
Geraldine
Gerard McHugh
Gerbils
Geronimo
Gerry Devine
Gersey
Gert Jonkers
Get Busy Committee
Get Cape. Wear Cape. Fly
Geyer Street Sheiks
gfire
Ghandaia
Ghetto Blaster
Ghislain Poirier
Ghost of an American Airman
Ghostface
Ghosthustler
Ghostknife
Ghostland Observatory
Ghostwriters
Ghosty
Ghoti Hook
Giant Ant Farm
Giant Cloud
Giant Drag
Giant Metal Insects
Giant Sand
Giant Squid
Giant Steps
Gib Wharton
Gideon D'Arcangelo
Gifted Da Flamethrowa
Gifthorse
Gifts From Enola
Gigamesh
Gigantics
Gigolo Aunts
Gil Mantera's Party Dream
Gila Bend
Gillian Welch with David Rawlings
Gilly Elkin
Gin Blossoms
Gin Palace
Gin Wigmore
Gina Fobia
Gina Lee
Ginger
Ginger Mackenzie
Gingerbread Patriots
Gingersol
Gino Sitson
Girl in a Coma
Girl Talk
Girls
Girls Against Boys
Girls Guns and Glory
Girls in Hawaii
Girls in The Nose
Girls in Trouble
Git
Gito Gito Hustler
Givers
Glacier Hiking
Gladhands
Glambilly
Glamourpuss
Glass Eye
Glass Intrepid
Glasvegas
Glazed Body
GLC
Glee Club
Glen Clark
Glen David Andrews & The Lazy Six
Glen Hansard of The Frames
Glen Phillips
Glen Reynolds
Glenn Tilbrook
Glide
Glint
Gliss
Global Soul
Global Village
Gloria Cycles
Glossary
Glosso Babel
Glue
GlueBoy
Gluecifer
Glueleg
Glyn Styler
Gnappy
Gnome
Gnomes of Zurich
Go Betty Go
Go Chic
Go Dog Go
Go Gettas Entertainment Feat. Abstraq the Grindologist
Go Kart
Go Metric USA
Go To Blazes
GO!GO!7188
Goat The Head
Goatsnake
Gob
Goblin Cock
God Bullies
God Drives A Galaxy
God Fires Man
God Forbid
God Street Wine
Godheadsilo
Godplow
Gods and Monsters
God's Temple of Family Deliverance
Godzik Pink
Godzilla Motor Company
Goes Cube
Gogogo Airheart
Gogol Bordello
Going Home
Gold Cash Gold
Gold Chains
Gold Chains & Sue Cie
Gold Sparkle Band
Golden Arm Orchestra (playing to F.W. Murnau's "Faust")
Golden Arm Symphony Orchestra
Golden Arm Trio
Golden Bear
Golden Boots
Golden Boys
Golden Delicious
Golden Echoes
Golden Hornet Project
Golden Hornet Project / Golden Arm Trio
Golden Rough
Golden Shoulders
Golden Smog
Golden Triangle
Goldenboy
Goldfinger
Goldfrapp
Goldie Lookin Chain
GoldieLocks
Goldrush
Goldspot
Golem
Gomez

continued on page 85

1992

SXSW **STATS** March 11 – 15

SXSW 92
Ron Suman
KTXT/Native Noise
Lubbock, TX

BY THE NUMBERS

400 showcasing artists
of 2,400 submissions

82 panels, workshops & sessions

24 venues & stages

3,000 registrants

$135-195 registration

$25 wristband

128 pages in program guide

43 trade show exhibitors

EVENT HEADQUARTERS

Hyatt Regency, 208 Barton Springs Rd.

AUSTIN MUSIC AWARDS

Wednesday, March 11, City Coliseum

Performers Michael E. Johnson, Lucinda Williams, Joe Ely, Ruben Ramos, Lou Ann Barton, W.C. Clark, Angela Strehli, Marcia Ball, T.D. Bell & Erbie Bowser, Kelly Willis, Monte Warden, Bad Livers, Tish Hinojosa, Laurie Freelove; MC (and performer) Paul Ray

SXSW SHOWCASE VENUES

311 Club, Antone's, Back Room, Cactus Cafe, Chances, Chicago House, Continental Club, Emo's, Hole in the Wall, Hondo's, Hyatt Ballroom, Jelly Club, La Zona Rosa, Liberty Lunch, Main Event, Main Event Forum, Mercado Caribe, Ritz, Sanitarium, Saxon Pub, Steamboat, Terrace, Top of the Marc, Trinity

KEYNOTE SPEAKER

Michelle Shocked In what was essentially keynote-by-default, Shocked (who had been scheduled to give brief opening remarks) filled in for Willie Nelson when Willie's bus didn't make it back from an out-of-town gig in time. "This was the scenario I'd always feared: a keynote speaker dropping out at the last minute," Roland Swenson recalled. To her credit, Shocked said she could do 45 minutes, which initially seemed like

a good idea. But by the end of her extended ramble (based partly on writings by her boyfriend, journalist Bart Bull) about seeing the band

> ## "SXSW is largely a feast of the Great Unsigned and Stubbornly Uncategorizable, a high-profile forum for rugged, low-paying individualism."
> ◼ *Rolling Stone*, 1992

Fishbone and connecting the dots to blackface minstrelsy, the audience felt as if they'd suffered through a really long joke that had a really empty punchline at the end. Willie never did show up at the Hyatt, but he made it back in time to join the bill at Auditorium Shores that evening for a surprise solo set.

CO-SPONSORING PUBLICATIONS

Austin Chronicle, Cleveland Scene, Creative Loafing (Atlanta), *Dallas Observer, Flagpole*

(Athens, GA), *Goodtimes Magazine* (Long Island, NY, & Savannah, GA), *Maryland Musician* (Baltimore), *Memphis Flyer, Miami New Times, Nashville Scene, New Times* (Phoenix), *Nightflying* (Little Rock), *The Note* (Lawrence), *Offbeat/The Grapevine* (New Orleans), *Oklahoma Gazette* (Oklahoma City), *Pacific News & Review* (Anaheim, CA), *Philadelphia City Paper, The Pitch* (Kansas City, MO), *Private Eye* (Midvale, UT), *Public News* (Houston), *Riverfront Times* (St. Louis, MO), *The Rocket* (Seattle, WA), *San Antonio Current, Spectrum* (Little Rock, AR), *Tucson Weekly, Westword* (Denver)

MEMORABLE PANELS

"Lester Is More: Rock Criticism After Bangs" featured moderator Bill Wyman of the Chicago Reader, eventual George W. Bush biographer Robert Draper, Rhino Records' Jim Fouratt and others in a discussion about how the profession was changed by the writings of Lester Bangs (who lived in Austin for a brief time shortly before his death in 1982).

"Women Rock Writers" focused on that all-too-rare commodity, female music critics, with moderator Gina Arnold and panelists Karen Schoemer, Claudia Perry, Sue Cummings, and Margaret Moser.

"Slacker" was all about the little-movie-that-could which had suddenly made Austin an indie-film buzz-town during the past year. The panel, which foreshadowed the nascent SXSW Film Festival looming on the horizon, included director Richard Linklater (listed as "Rick" in the program guide) and SXSW co-director Louis Black (who had a small role in the film).

"New Music Seminar" was all about the big-dog conference in New York, with executive director Mark Josephson as moderator. That summer's NMS found the event still booming right along, but everything unraveled within the next couple of years.

"Reality Check" featured a panel-description that sounds amusingly Chicken-Little in retrospect, given the era: "Budgets are getting slashed, companies are merging, and while the wheels are

turning, some people will be getting crushed." If that's how it looked in 1992, when Pearl Jam could sell a million records in one week, it's hard to imagine what might have been said about, say, 2008.

NOTABLE PANELISTS

Henry Root (attorney), Casey Monahan (Texas Music Office), Gary Stewart (Rhino Records), Charles Shaar Murray (English journalist), Bernie Leadon (Eagles), Greg Ginn (SST Records), Ken Levitan (Vector Management), Rick Gershon (A&M Records), Gary Smith (Pollstar), Gibby Haynes (Butthole Surfers)

MEMORABLE SHOWCASES & EVENTS

> Though Willie Nelson's unannounced appearance thrilled the crowd at Thursday's early-evening show on Auditorium Shores, the Columbia Records bill already featured a high-quality lineup, with Austin band-of-the-moment Poi Dog Pondering supplemented by rising local singer-songwriters Darden Smith and James McMurtry, plus a ringer of a Fort Worth native in T Bone Burnett (long after his Rolling Thunder Revue days but well before his *O Brother* game-changer).

> The way-past-capacity crowd of young fans that showed up for Saturday's bill with Helmet and L7 at the Main Event Forum (read: tent in parking lot) demonstrated quite vividly that the long-bubbling-under alternative-rock wave had finally boiled over, in a major way.

> 311 Club, which had made its debut the previous year, solidified its standing as the primary place to catch international acts, with a Friday-night lineup that included acts from Russia (Limpopo), Latvia (Jauns Maness), Finland (Piirpauke), Czechoslovakia (Isabelle), Canada (Errol Ranville), and Germany (John Kennedy...who may also have been booked at SXSW's JFK symposium in Dallas that year, we're not quite sure).

> Saturday's all-Austin roots-music showcase at the Continental Club was bookended by a couple of up-and-coming brothers who had moved to Austin a couple of years earlier from nearby Bandera —

Bruce Robison (who eventually married Kelly Willis and wrote a song that the Dixie Chicks took to #1) and Charlie Robison (who married one of those Dixie Chicks, coincidentally enough).

NOTABLE ACTS

Vulgar Boatmen The band that played Saturday at Hole in the Wall was either from Indiana or Florida — supposedly there were different "branches" of the band in both states — but they had become a big hit in Chicago when WXRT took a liking to their song "Drive Somewhere" and played it incessantly.

Tiny Lights The impossible-to-categorize band from Hoboken, NJ, that issued records on Bar/None and Doctor Dream, delivered its folk-rock-funk-guitars-strings-horns cacophonic symphony as a headliner at Chances on Friday night.

Delaney Bramlett The male half of Delaney & Bonnie played Thursday night at Antone's and was a guest presenter at Wednesday's Austin Music Awards.

> "The recurring dream I had when I worked for SXSW as production manager was that I was tied to the railroad tracks in such a way that I could see my watch and I knew what time the train was scheduled to come, and when it would come, everything would slow down like a Sam Peckinpah movie."
> ◼ Roy Taylor, 1990s SXSW staff

Shadowy Men On A Shadowy Planet The Toronto band brought its surf-rock instrumental grandeur to the Main Event on Friday night.

Paw Hailing from Lawrence, Kansas, this hard-rockin' band played Friday at the Back Room and soon inked a deal with A&M Records for what ended up as a relatively short tenure.

Beat Farmers Country Dick Montana, that rare combination of drummer and frontman, was in fine form when the band headlined Saturday's bill at Liberty Lunch. Little did anyone know he had just three more years in him at that point.

Cracker Recently arisen from the ashes of Camper Van Beethoven, David Lowery's new band played Saturday night at Emo's, shortly before their debut record was released.

Also Ranch Romance, Cavedogs, New Riddim, Snooky Pryor, Bluerunners, Cadillac Tramps, Paul K., Dave Alvin, Roger Manning, World Famous Blue Jays

SOME OF THE AUSTIN ACTS

Arc Angels, Ed Hall, Monte Warden, Julie Burrell, Coffee Sergeants, Sarah Elizabeth Campbell, House In Orbit, Girls In The Nose, Sue Foley, Michele Solberg, Flowerhead, Beaver Nelson Band, Monikker

SOME OF THE INTERNATIONAL ACTS

Verlaines (New Zealand), Mack MacKenzie (Canada), Robbi Robb (South Africa), F.S.K. (Germany), Blue Ice Band (Iceland), Fish Hospital (Netherlands), Pigalle (France), East Of Eden (Siberia)

WHATEVER HAPPENED TO...

Gear Daddies At the time of their Thursday-night Continental Club showcase, they seemed as promising an act from the Minneapolis scene as Soul Asylum, with a couple of fine albums on Poly-Gram to their credit; but despite playing a memorable show that night, the band called it quits shortly thereafter. A hidden track on one of those records, "I Wanna Drive The Zamboni," became a staple at hockey arenas in the years to come.

Wylie & the Wild West Show Hailing from eastern Washington, Wylie Gustafson and his cohorts, who played Thursday at the Ritz, made minor waves and became known mostly for his yodeling prowess. Eventually nearly everyone had heard his throaty call, as the voice of those ubiquitous mid-late '90s "Yahooooo!" ads.

SOFTBALL TOURNEY

The Record Companies won their first championship since 1988, beating Mixed Media in the title game by a Cowboys-over-Dolphins-Super-Bowl-like score of 24-3....Given that Gibby Haynes was on a panel and the Beat Farmers played a showcase, this may well have been the year that the championship game announcing team was Gibby Haynes and Country Dick Montana. Everyone seems to remember that it happened, but no one seems to remember which year it was. OK then, we'll say, oh, 1992, sure, that sounds good. ∎

1993

SXSW **STATS** March 17 - 21

BY THE NUMBERS

468 showcasing artists
of 2,500 submissions

81 panels, workshops & sessions

25 venues & stages

3,800 registrants

$175-250 registration

$30 wristband

144 pages in program guide

95 trade show exhibitors

EVENT HEADQUARTERS
Austin Convention Center, 500 E. 1st St.; this has remained the permanent site for SXSW since 1993.

AUSTIN MUSIC AWARDS
Wednesday, March 17, Palmer Auditorium
Performers P, Roky Erickson, Soul Hat, Jo Carol Pierce & Loose Diamonds with Michael Hall, Alejandro Escovedo, Grey Ghost, Michele Solberg, David Rodriguez; MC Paul Ray

SXSW SHOWCASE VENUES
2nd & Colorado, 311 Club, 5th Street Station, Acropolis, Antone's, Austin Convention Center, Back Room/Black Doom, Catfish Station, Chances, Chicago House/Chicago House Upstage, Continental Club, Emo's, Hole in the Wall, Hondo's, Jelly Club, La Zona Rosa, Liberty Lunch, Mercado Caribe, The Place, Ritz, Saxon Pub, Steamboat, Trinity

KEYNOTE SPEAKER
Gov. Ann Richards Technically it was billed as just "Welcome & Opening Remarks," but this year Richards was the main attraction, as opposed to 1991 when her words were a prelude to Rosanne Cash's keynote. "Following her speech, and after shaking hands with executives from SXSW and the *Chronicle*," remembers journalist Jim Testa, "Gov. Richards was introduced to the gaggle of rock critics and music reporters waiting to meet

her. 'And who are these people?' she asked her aide. 'These are all music critics,' the aide answered. 'Oh really?' replied the Governor. And then looking at us, she asked sweetly, 'And you people can actually make a living doing that?'"

CO-SPONSORING PUBLICATIONS

Austin Chronicle, Boston Rock, Cleveland Scene, Creative Loafing (Atlanta), *Dallas Observer, Flagpole* (Athens, GA), *Goodtimes Magazine* (Long Island, NY, & Savannah, GA), *Los Angeles Weekly, Maryland Musician* (Baltimore), *Memphis Flyer, Metro Times* (Detroit), *Miami New Times, Nashville Scene/Riff, New Times* (Phoenix), *Nightflying* (Little Rock), *The Note* (Lawrence), *Now* (Toronto), *Offbeat/The Grapevine* (New Orleans), *Oklahoma Gazette* (Oklahoma City), *The Pitch* (Kansas City, MO), *Private Eye* (Midvale, UT), *Public News* (Houston), *Riverfront Times* (St. Louis, MO), *San Antonio Current, Spectrum* (Little Rock, AR), *Tucson Weekly, Westword* (Denver)

MEMORABLE PANELS

"The Little Town With The Big Guest List" The panel name was coined by Michael Corcoran during his '80s tenure with *The Austin Chronicle*, but it was *Austin American-Statesman* critic Don McLeese who served as moderator here. There was much discussion about the notion of Austin as a "velvet rut" in which musicians were too comfortable to be ambitious. Singer Toni Price's classic reply was, "If you're gonna be in a rut, it might as well be velvet!"

"Elvis v. Colonel Tom" was a role-playing fictional-roundtable discussion between Elvis Presley (played by producer/musician Jim Dickinson) and Colonel Tom Parker (author/journalist Joe Nick Patoski) and their respective attorneys (Austin's Shannon Vale representing Presley, Memphis' Herb O'Mell representing Parker). A memorable quote, from Patoski/Colonel Tom: "When they stopped allowing guns in boardrooms, everything went to hell."

"Stevie Ray Vaughan: Biography Or Necrophilia?" featured Bill Crawford and Keri Leigh, both of whom were working on SRV books at the time (Crawford's was co-authored by the aforementioned Joe Nick Patoski), discussing whether it was too soon after Vaughan's death to be telling his life story.

"What Is Recoupable? You Get What You Don't Pay For" featured attorneys Mike Goldsmith and Adam Ritholz on some of the hidden traps in record deals.

"Rock Books" The description read, "Agents, packagers, editors and authors talk about getting a deal, writing and promoting the book, and whether, after all that, the writer makes any money." (We'll let you know once *SXSW Scrapbook* is actually out there on the shelves...)

"The very growth of SXSW is a testament to the viability of so much of what the industry neglects. In the best Austin tradition, the conference suggests that if you can't find a musical category where you fit, make your own. If you can't find a home within the music industry, develop an industry for yourself outside of it. In fact, that is what the folks responsible for SXSW have done, creating an institution that attracts the music industry on Austin's own terms." ■ Don McLeese, *Austin American-Statesman*, March 22, 1993

NOTABLE PANELISTS

Tony Brown (MCA Records), Joe Boyd (Hannibal/Ryko), Frank Riley (Monterey Peninsula Artists), Lisa Shively (The Press Network), Keith Moerer (*Request* magazine), Exene Cervenka (X), Jon Kertzer (Microsoft), Ruben Ramos (Tejano musician), Elliot Cahn (manager), Faith Henschel (Elektra Records), Donald Passman (attorney), Stephen Bruton (producer)

MEMORABLE SHOWCASES

> In what probably was an all-time record number of acts on a single showcase, Thursday's "An Evening of Spoken Word" at the Ritz paid notice to a rising element of the "music" industry (there was a spoken word panel in '93 as well). Robyn Hitchcock and Exene Cervenka were the big music-world crossover draws.

> The two names atop the bill at Chicago Upstage (an upstairs room at the much-missed downtown acoustic venue Chicago House) stand out especially: inventive Tucson guitarist Rainer, who died of a brain tumor in 1997 but was honored before his death by a tribute album co-produced by Robert Plant and Giant Sand's Howe Gelb; and Lisa Loeb, who had a #1 pop hit a year later when her song "Stay" landed on the *Reality Bites* soundtrack.

> Friday's singer-songwriter showcase at the Ritz Theatre included such veteran performers as Chris Smither, Iain Matthews and Elliott Murphy, but was most notable for kicking off at 7pm with a two-hour production of Austin songwriter Jo Carol Pierce's musical-theater piece "Bad Girls Upset By The Truth."

> La Zona Rosa's Friday-night lineup was all over the map, ranging from the Chicano world-music of Dr. Loco's Rockin' Jalapeno Band (from San Francisco) to the Tex-Mex rock of Sergio Arau (from Mexico City) to the folk-country-Cajun stylings of Danielle Martineau & Rockabayou (from Montreal, Canada).

> You couldn't get more hip-rock-centric than Friday's blockbuster bill at Acropolis, which featured not only Arizona indie heavyweights the Meat Puppets and Giant Sand but also rising Dallas act the Buck Pets and Austin metal heroes Pariah.

NOTABLE ACTS

P It's not often that a band playing its first gig ever gets booked onto the Austin Music Awards show, but you can get away with that if your lineup includes Johnny Depp and Gibby Haynes. (Not to mention the fine Austin blues-rock songwriter Bill Carter, and...uh...remind us who Sal Jenco was again?)

Blue Rodeo The Toronto roots-country-rock band's Saturday-night headlining slot at Antone's "has become legend in Canada, where they are a multiplatinum act," director Roland Swenson noted. "SXSW attendees were surprised to see actors Eugene Levy and Catherine O'Hara in attendance, while they were in the area shooting *Waiting For Guffman*."

Freedy Johnston The NYC-by-way-of-Kansas pop songwriter, who played Friday at Chances, had won a sizable audience with his Bar/None album *Can You Fly* the previous year. He was on his way up to Elektra, which released his next record.

R.L. Burnside The Mississippi guitarist was one of the unsung legends of the blues when he headlined a Thursday-night showcase at Antone's, and gained a whole new following in the mid-late '90s after collaborating with hip rocker Jon Spencer.

"It's a joy ride that veers across the center line, sometimes careening onto the shoulder before it reaches its final destination: honest art." ■ *San Jose Mercury News, 1993*

Grant Lee Buffalo The Los Angeles rock band had just released its debut album *Fuzzy* on Slash Records when they played a Thursday show at Hole in the Wall; leader Grant-Lee Phillips had modest success on his own after the group split up a few years later.

Also Chris Whitley, Everclear, Pete Droge, Love Battery, Kevin Welch, Cindy Bullens, Paul Cebar & the Milwaukeeans, Vigilantes Of Love, The Fluid, Band Of Susans, Barbara Manning

Rolling Stone

1290 Avenue of the Americas. New York. NY 10104 (212)484-1616

24 February, 1993

Stuart Lodge
Panels Coordinator
SXSW '93
Box 4999
Austin, TX 78765

VIA FAX

Dear Stuart,

I'm pleased to accept your invitation to be a panelist for the Rock Books session of SXSW '93. Let me know if I need to send you my CV, recent Rolling Stone Press books I've edited, or anything else.

I need to get from you the conference package ASAP, so I can get a hotel room before they're all booked up (any help on your end would be most appreciated); I also need info about my panel, other panelists, topics of discussion, etc. If you could possibly send me the stuff overnight, that would be great.

I'm looking forward to meeting you -- and participating in SXSW '93 (please tell Ed Ward hello -- I was involved in his Rock of Ages book, as well as The Rolling Stone Illustrated History of Rock & Roll, to which he contributed several chapters.

Hope to hear from you soon.

All best,

Holly George-Warren
Editor
Rolling Stone Press

SOME OF THE AUSTIN ACTS

Kim Wilson, Don Walser & the Pure Texas Band, Storyville, Kris McKay, Hamilton Pool, Pocket FishRmen, Cornell Hurd Band, Slaid Cleaves, Flying Saucers, Cherubs, Golden Echoes, Emily Kaitz

SOME OF THE INTERNATIONAL ACTS

Laika & the Cosmonauts (Finland), Archie Roach (Australia), Huevos Rancheros (Canada), Hex (Slovakia), Something Happens (Ireland), Flor De Mal (Italy), Baba Yaga (Hungary), Insignia (Mexico), Sheep On Drugs (England)

WHATEVER HAPPENED TO...

Queen Sarah Saturday An alt-rock band from North Carolina that played the "Black Doom" (a second stage at the Back Room), QSS didn't last long, but drummer Zeke Hutchins ended up

playing with singer-songwriter Tift Merritt (and marrying her), while guitarist Johnny Irion found his own music and marrying partner in Sarah Lee Guthrie (Arlo's daughter).

Duke McVinnie An inspired and inventive musician and songwriter from Los Angeles, McVinnie never really made a dent under his own name, but turned up in the '90s as a member of the band Shivaree and as a touring guitarist with Joan Baez.

Scott Miller Booked as a solo act on a Friday acoustic bill at Chicago Upstage, the sharp-witted Knoxville, Tennessee, songwriter soon became frontman for the V-Roys, who released a couple of pop-leaning alt-country albums on E-Squared before Miller returned to the solo ranks with a Sugar Hill deal.

SOFTBALL TOURNEY

The Record Companies won their second straight title, with a 16-7 victory over the Agents/Managers team in the championship game. Among the first-round scores was Red Bands 17, Green Bands 4; about the only way a Bands team ever won in those days was by facing another Bands team. ■

1994

SXSW **STATS** March 11 - 20

BY THE NUMBERS

482 showcasing artists
of 2,683 submissions

67 panels, workshops & sessions

30 venues & stages

4,258 registrants

$250-295 registration

$30 wristband

160 pages in program guide

98 trade show exhibitors

300 SFMC (film/multimedia) registrants

AUSTIN MUSIC AWARDS

Wednesday, March 16, Palmer Auditorium

Performers Pariah, Doug Sahm & Sons of Sahm, Little Sister, Angela Strehli Blues Revue, Jimmy La-Fave, Junior Brown & Tanya Rae, True Believers, Los Pinkys y Isidro Samilpa, Don Walser's Pure Texas Band

KEYNOTE SPEAKER

Johnny Cash The Man in Black, on the verge of a career resurgence with the dawn of his *American Recordings* albums produced by Rick Rubin, delivered what remains perhaps the most fondly remembered SXSW keynote address of them all.

"When his guitar tech showed up early with Cash's guitar and began a soundcheck in the ballroom, I realized for the first time that he was going to perform songs during his keynote," SXSW director Roland Swenson recalled. "Cash came out alone with his guitar and held the audience transfixed for half an hour, sharing new songs from the album and telling stories about his life."

Toronto journalist Paul Cantin was among those in the packed Convention Center hall. "I arrived late and squeezed into a spot on the floor directly in front of the stage, which Johnny commanded with electromagnetic charisma....'The joy of learning, of doing something new and doing something the way it feels right here' — he told the hushed crowd, holding his hand to his heart — 'and here' — hand to head — 'it has got nothing to do with age, grandchildren.'"

MEMORABLE PANELS

A curious theme ran through several of 1994's panels: Similarity of format to popular television shows. This was almost certainly unintentional, given that two of the three show-formats had not actually begun proliferating on the airwaves yet. Hmmm, could SXSW have influenced the next generation of network programming? Doubtful, but check out these three sessions:

"Austin's SXSW is a teeming open-air bazaar for music talent...a bellwether event, an indicator of trends that will ripple through the record racks in the months ahead." ■ *The Philadelphia Inquirer,* 1994

"Don't Believe The Hype" A cast of publicists (including Epic's Julie Farman, Shore Fire's Mark Satlof, and MCA's Paula Batson) took turns making pitches to a cast of music journalists (including Claudia Perry of the *Houston Post,* Jim DeRogatis of the *Chicago Sun-Times,* and Grant Alden of *The Rocket*), who acted as judges. *American Publicist Idol,* anyone?

"Band Make-Over" In this less-intense precursor to *Extreme Makover,* the members of Austin post-punk band the Wannabes — who typically dressed, shall we say, a bit shambolically — threw themselves at the mercy of local fashionistas Jenna Radke and Katie Hammet. As the thumbnail description put it, "Can some fashion experts take a scruffy bunch of rockers and polish them up without erasing their souls in the process?"

"Musical Jeopardy" OK, this one was a blatant rip-off, of course, but a fun idea. Jim Fouratt, veteran of the industry and of SXSW, asked questions of Mudhoney's Mark Arm, PLG publicist Regina Joskow, self-described "freelance punk terrorist" Tim Stegall and others. The graphic presentation (transparencies on an overhead projector, if we remember correctly) was a little short of what probably could be rigged up by the Interactive folks today.

Other panels of note included:

"Junkie In The Band" This Joe Nick Patoski-moderated panel discussed the dilemma of drugs' potential affect on musicians' lives and careers, with contributions from David Fricke of *Rolling Stone,* Gerald Cosloy of Matador Records, and manager Mike Lembo.

"Views From The Wobbly Edge" A first-ever Wednesday panel helped to bridge the nascent Film & Media Conference, which included Multimedia components that branched into a separate event the following year. Dewey Winburne of the American Institute for Learning headed up a discussion that was described in the program guide with remarkable prescience, in retrospect: "We are at the brink of something incredible with the emergence of multimedia."

NOTABLE PANELISTS

Teresa Ensenat (A&M Records), Jackson Haring (manager), Bushwick Bill (Geto Boys), Jello Biafra (Alternative Tentacles), Tom Zutaut (Geffen Records), Steve Berlin (Los Lobos/producer), Liz Garo (Restless Records), Kid Leo (Columbia Records), Ben Vaughn (musician/producer), Erik Flannigan (*ICE* Newsletter), Bill Narum (graphic artist), Wiley Wiggins (actor)

MEMORABLE SHOWCASES & EVENTS

> A new outdoor stage made its debut right in the thick of things, at the intersection of Sixth and Brazos streets. The early-evening shows, which ran from 6-8pm, featured Rodney Crowell and the Mavericks on Thursday; Ben Harper, Sam Phillips and Cracker on Friday; and Flaco Jimenez, Radney Foster and Lee Roy Parnell on Saturday.

> Mostly 1994's showcases are remembered for Johnny Cash's unbilled appearance with the Tennessee Two at Emo's on Thursday, but playing a couple hours later on that showcase was Beck, whose single "Loser" was just starting to get significant airplay.

> The Terrace (formerly the Austin Opera House) hosted a strong Tejano showcase on Thursday featuring Ruben Ramos, Johnny Hernandez, and Los Pinkys (who had played the Austin Music Awards the night before).

> '80s Austin favorite the True Believers, led by Alejandro Escovedo, reunited for a Rykodisc showcase on Friday at the Terrace that also featured the hot Boston "low-rock" trio Morphine plus England's high-powered folk-rockers the Oyster Band.

> La Zona Rosa's Saturday night lineup was impressive enough with the likes of Lucinda Williams and Syd Straw in the headlining spots. But it was the club's official SXSW after-party that became the real highlight, with New Orleans' venerable Continental Drifters taking the stage just past 2am and not leaving it until 4:45am, with many guests sitting in along the way.

> An unusual addition to the SXSW venue lineup was the Backyard, a large-capacity part-outdoor amphitheater a half-hour's drive from downtown Austin. Artists including Timbuk 3, the Bad Livers, the Subdudes and the Doug Dillard Band played Friday and Saturday shows there.

NOTABLE ACTS

Veruca Salt The Chicago alternative-rock band fronted by Louise Post and Nina Gordon was on fire at the time of their Friday showcase at the Electric Lounge; by the end of the year, they'd jumped from the indie Minty Fresh to the Geffen-affiliated major DGC.

Mojo Nixon & the Toadliquors with Jello Biafra A regular at SXSW, Nixon threw a curve into his act for Friday night's showcase at Liberty Lunch by inviting former Dead Kennedys frontman Jello Biafra, who'd been part of a spoken word showcase on Thursday, to join in the Mojo mayhem.

"After the keynote, Johnny was very happy and relaxed as he greeted well wishers in the backstage hallway. My sister Dottie, who was 8 months pregnant with her first son, was in the hall with my mother. As he passed by he spotted my sister, said 'Hello, darling' in his deep, mellifluous voice, and kissed her cheek. My sister, who has a quick wit, called out as he walked away, 'It's his baby!' Everyone laughed, including Cash." ■ Roland Swenson, SXSW managing director

Spinanes Singer-guitarist Rebecca Gates had made the unusual transition from band manager (for Oregon band the Dharma Bums) to bandleader in this duo with drummer Scott Plouf; their debut album had recently been released by Sub Pop when they played Saturday night at Blind Alley.

Also Supersuckers, Charlie Hunter Trio, Cher UK, Verve Pipe, Duane Jarvis, Blazers, Dolly Varden, Mother Hips, House Of Large Sizes. Babe The Blue Ox, Rex Daisy

SOME OF THE MEDIA-SPONSORED ACTS

Bedhead (*Dallas Observer*), Coyote Dreams (*San Antonio Current*), Concussion Ensemble (*Boston Rock*), Woggles (*Flagpole*, Athens, GA), Bill Lloyd (*Nashville Scene*), Lowest Of The Low (*NOW*, Toronto), Seam (*New City*, Chicago), Glen Phillips Band (*Creative Loafing*, Atlanta), Slack Jaw (*Cleveland Scene*), Stephen George (*Tucson Weekly*), Earl C. Whitehead & the Grievous Angels (*New Times*, Phoenix), Techno-Squid Eats Parliament (*Nightflying*, Little Rock, AR)

SOME OF THE AUSTIN ACTS

Charlie Sexton, Sincola, Abra Moore, Pork, Ugly Americans, Lisa Mednick, Apaches Of Paris, Malachi, Gay Sportscasters with Evan Johns, Vanguards, Bo Bud Greene, Seth & Amy Tiven

SOME OF THE INTERNATIONAL ACTS

Blue Shadows (Canada), Frente! (Australia), Guillotina (Mexico), EJ's Reggae Gospel Review (Nigeria), Excess Bleeding Heart (Denmark), Julian Dawson (England), Space Cowboys (Germany), Hubert Von Goisern & Die Original Alpinkatzen (Austria)

"The Emo's stage may have rocked harder at any number of shows, but never with a more magical energy that saw the audience and performer so pleased to be feeding each other's musical fever. And when Cash ended his first encore number, 'A Boy Named Sue,' with the line, 'If I ever have another boy, I'll name him Emo,' it became the Emo's show to end all others."
■ Raoul Hernandez in *The Austin Chronicle*, March 25, 1994

SOFTBALL TOURNEY

A dynasty was cemented when Record Companies won their third straight title, trouncing Clubs/Buyers in the championship game. As SXSW's crack sports staff reported in the following year's program guide, the Record Company team "rolled up a big lead in the middle innings, then coasted to a win so comfortable that no one can quite remember the game's final score."

Meanwhile, out in the bleachers, the notorious self-promoting music-biz veteran Kim Fowley was making the rounds. "He approached me with three young brothers," remembers SXSW co-founder Louis Black. "When he got them to start singing a cappella, I ran."

One guy who didn't run was Christopher Sabec, an attorney from Virginia who represented Dave Matthews at the time. "People were smiling at them cutely, and laughing when they walked away. I don't think anybody really listened to their singing," he told the *Austin American-Statesman* later. "I didn't really know a lot of people, so I was kind of just making small talk, killing time. Maybe that's why I was so attentive when they came up to me. I think it was Taylor who said, 'Um, excuse me sir, but can we sing for you?' I was awestruck. The first thing I said was, 'Hey guys, where are your parents? I need to talk to your parents.'"

The song these boys named Hanson were singing was "Mmmbop." Three years later, it was the #1 song in America.

SFMC (SXSW Film & Media Conference)

World Premieres *Doc's Full Service* (D: Eagle Pennell); *Cultivating Charlie* (D: Alex George)

Special Events "Retrospective: A Celebration of Texas Independents," with Bill Wittliff, Richard Linklater, Michael Nesmith, Hector Galan, Bud Shrake, Ken Harrison, Andy Anderson and Tobe Hooper

Memorable Films *Fear Of A Black Hat*, *High Lonesome*, *Floundering*, *Fun*, *Meet The Feebles*, *The Making Of...And God Spoke*, *Totally F***ed Up*

Multimedia Keynote Richard Garriott, co-founder of Austin company Origin Systems

What's In A Name "To differentiate it from music, there was an attempt to call it the South by Southwest Film and Media Conference, SFMC for short," explains SXSW co-founder Louis Black; indeed, that's how the event is listed in the 1994 program guide. "But that never took hold." ■

SXSW **STATS** March 10 - 19

BY THE NUMBERS

467 showcasing artists
of 3,431 submissions

68 panels, workshops & sessions

35 venues & stages

5,000 registrants

$250-350 registration

$35-40 wristband

176 pages in program guide

105 trade show exhibitors

825 film registrants

1,010 multimedia registrants

AUSTIN MUSIC AWARDS

Wednesday, March 15, Palmer Auditorium

Performers Ed Hall, Sincola, Storyville, Toni Price, Charlie Sexton Sextet, Kathy McCarty, Flaco Jimenez, Robert Earl Keen, Mary Cutrufello, Hamell On Trial, Martin Banks; MC Paul Ray

KEYNOTE SPEAKER

Bob Mould The leader of iconic '80s Twin Cities trio Husker Du had relocated to Austin a year or two earlier; after a couple of solo albums, he'd formed the band Sugar, but would return to the solo route shortly after this keynote. It's remembered most for Mould's journey out into the audience, where he asked various SXSWers, "Why are you here?" As *Entertainment Weekly* reported, "the answers — to party, hand out business cards, and hear a few good unsigned bands inbetween — were fairly obvious." Austin gospel group Malachi played a brief set before Mould's remarks; such "preludes" became a frequent feature at future keynotes.

MEMORABLE PANELS

"No Reward: Performance Rights On The New Frontier" Though this panel was primarily aimed at performer vs. songwriter rights of broadcast material, some of the sub-language hinted at a much bigger kettle o' fish on the horizon: "But the rise of new technologies such as computer networks and fiber optic cable transmission

opens areas for musical exploitation that aren't covered by current copyright laws." Ya think?

"Why Radio Hates You" SXSW director Roland Swenson explained that more industry factions were flocking to Austin in '95 in the wake of the New Music Seminar's 1994 implosion. "One particularly significant group was a loose collection of radio programmers who worked in the genre of Post Modern," he noted. "It was the programmers from these stations that helped usher in acts like Nirvana, Pearl Jam, Alice In Chains and others from the fringe to the mainstream of rock music. They were organized by

> "Jazz has been a longtime major component of the Austin music scene, and this year, SXSW seemed to finally discover and present it with proper respect. Several impressive national-level SXSW jazz showcase bookings provided the official acknowledgment..." ■ Michael Point in the *Austin American-Statesman*, March 21, 1995

radio consultant Mike Jacobs, a wily and sometimes abrasive fellow, who made no excuses for his hijacking of the airwaves. Mike put together a panel for us titled 'Why Radio Hates You,' brought his gang to SXSW '95, and things were never the same again."

"SXSW: A User's Guide" A South by Southwest panel about...South by Southwest? "Hear from professionals who have made the most of their SXSW experience, and learn how they did," the program guide stated.

"Koresh And The Waco Disaster: What Really Happened At Mt. Carmel?" The Branch Davidian episode was two years past by the time of this panel, another classic left-field presentation moderated by Joe Nick Patoski. But it had struck a chord with SXSWers, some of whom had made side-trips to Waco when the standoff was still in-progress in March 1993. Rumors that David Koresh had once been rejected for a showcase at SXSW were unconfirmed.

NOTABLE PANELISTS

Ian Copeland (Frontier Booking), Susan Silver (manager), Al Kooper (musician), Bill Holdship (BAM Magazine), Brett Gurewitz (Epitaph Records), Rob Bleetstein (Gavin Report), Matthew Sweet (musician), Frank Callari (manager), Michael Gallelli (Private Music), Michael Morales (musician), Peter Jenner (manager)

MEMORABLE SHOWCASES & EVENTS

> In a rare occurrence, two of the most memorable SXSW shows were on Sunday night. At the brand-new Austin Music Hall, the Indigo Girls and members of Big Fish Ensemble and other Atlanta-area bands staged their massive production of *Jesus Christ Superstar*, with Amy Ray and Emily Saliers as Jesus and Mary Magdalene, respectively. Meanwhile, a couple blocks away at La Zona Rosa, the annual Alejandro Escovedo Orchestra show had a ringer of a special guest in recent R.E.M. recruit Scott McCaughey, who was a very late add when R.E.M.'s European tour went on hiatus after drummer Bill Berry suffered an aneurysm onstage in Switzerland

March 1. McCaughey performed with friends from his hometown of Seattle — Chris & Carla from the Walkabouts — and Austin (the Wannabes served as his backing band).

> The second year of outdoor stage shows at Sixth and Brazos was highlighted by Saturday's Rounder Records celebration of its 25th anniversary, with a Mardi Gras-style costume parade followed by performances from the Rebirth Brass Band, Johnny Adams, Beau Jocque & the Zydeco Hi Rollers, and Irma Thomas.

> Whoever wrote the program-guide blurb for Saturday night's showcase at Waterloo Brewing Company with the Bottle Rockets, Eric Ambel, Terry Anderson, Go To Blazes, the Schramms and others apparently used it as an attempt to enter the phrase "No Depression" into the vernacular as a tag for the swelling tide of alternative-country music among indie ranks. A new magazine debuted later that year.

NOTABLE ACTS

Soul Asylum They were kinda big at that point, enough to where the program guide entry for their Thursday show at the Terrace read, simply, "Soul Asylum. You know who they are." At that point, they were still coasting from the breakthrough of 1992's *Grave Dancers Union*, but the follow-up, *Let Your Dim Light Shine*, which came out three months after their SXSW appearance, didn't quite keep the momentum going, and things went downhill from there.

Wilco Alt-country torchbearers Uncle Tupelo had splintered less than a year earlier, but everyone except Jay Farrar continued on in the new Jeff Tweedy-led Wilco, whose debut disc *A.M.* came out 10 days after they previewed its material on Saturday night at Liberty Lunch.

The Presidents Of The United States Of America The Seattle trio, which included Beck/Mark Sandman collaborator Chris Ballew, quickly became a quirky pop sensation in the wake of their Friday show at Steamboat, graduating from indie PopLlama to major Columbia and going platinum.

Squirrel Nut Zippers The hot swing-jazz big-band from Chapel Hill, NC, had just made its debut album for Mammoth Records when they opened a Thursday showcase at the Continental Club. By their next one the following year, they'd been picked up by Hollywood Records.

Victoria Williams After fellow musicians rallied to her aid by recording the platinum-selling *Sweet Relief* tribute to her songs upon learning she'd been diagnosed with multiple sclerosis, Williams took her own recording career to new heights, and was touring behind the well-received Atlantic disc *Loose* when she played Friday at the Texas Union Ballroom.

Little Milton The legendary Chicago bluesman headlined a Thursday showcase at, where else, Antone's, the home of the blues.

Dar Williams A promising New England folkie who performed Thursday at Chicago House, Williams had recently been picked up by Razor & Tie after an initial independent release of her debut CD *The Honesty Room*.

Heads & Dreads Among the members of this hip-hop group from Dallas that played Friday night at Catfish Station was a young singer named Erica Wright. Soon after, she began billing herself as Erykah Badu, and in 1997 her debut solo album went to #2 on the Billboard charts.

"Wednesday night excursions to the Salt Lick, Thursday night dinners at Vespaio, and a last cocktail of the week at the Continental....I can't single out specific shows that struck me because that would take pages to accomplish!" ■ Chris Porter, One Reel/Bumbershoot Festival

Ronnie Dawson The Dallas rockabilly great was on the comeback trail with a new album, *Monkey Beat*, when he played the Continental Club on Friday.

Also Guided By Voices, Junior Kimbrough, Cake, Billy Joe Shaver, Blues Traveler, Graham

Parker, Joe Lovano, Yo La Tengo, Lisa Germano, Shabazz 3, Toadies, Marshall Crenshaw, Picketts, Seaweed, Marvin Etzioni, Kevin Salem, Chris Chandler

SOME OF THE MEDIA-SPONSORED ACTS

Cafe Noir (*Dallas Observer*), 16 Horsepower (*Westword*, Denver), Handsome Family (*New City*, Chicago), Los Straitjackets (*Nashville Scene*), Coltrane Wreck (*Cleveland Scene*), Ottoman Empire with Wreckless Eric (*Creative Loafing*, Atlanta), SkeeterHawks (*Nightflying*, Little Rock, AR), June (*Independent Weekly*, NC Triangle), Roundhead (*Everybody's News*, Cincinnati), Change Of Heart (*NOW*, Toronto), Naked Prey (*Tucson Weekly*)

SOME OF THE AUSTIN ACTS

Kathy McCarty The former member of Glass Eye, a key member of the SXSW Music staff during the event's first few years, had made a big impression in 1994 with *Dead Dog's Eyeball*, an album of songs written by her good friend Daniel Johnston. She headlined a Saturday showcase at Cactus Cafe.

Ian McLagan & Monkeyjump The former Faces keyboardist had recently relocated to Austin and formed a first-rate band with local aces Don Harvey on drums, Sarah Brown on bass, and Scrappy Jud Newcomb on guitar.

1995 Music Big Bag art courtesy of Mike Judge

Kevin Russell, Jimmy Smith & Claude Bernard Billed as a trio for an acoustic showcase at Chicago House Upstage on Saturday night, they would soon add a couple of members and coalesce into the Gourds.

Also Bush, Wayne "The Train" Hancock, Asylum Street Spankers, Damon Bramblett, Sixteen Deluxe, 8½ Souvenirs, Ray Wylie Hubbard, Elias Haslanger, Pushmonkey, Hamell On Trial, Jake "Guitar" Andrews

SOME OF THE INTERNATIONAL ACTS

Grant McLennan (Australia), Ned's Atomic Dustbin (U.K.), Bettie Serveert (Netherlands), Garmarna (Sweden), Sexepil (Hungary), Victor Essiet & the Mandators (Nigeria), Mario Grigorov (Bulgaria), Nemo (Belgium), Weeping Tile (Canada), Dirty Three (Australia)

SOFTBALL TOURNEY

Clubs/Talent Buyers stopped the Record Companies' three-year winning streak with a 17-14 victory in the championship game. The tournament was best remembered for the color-commentary game-announcing of the Beat Farmers' Country Dick Montana. When Country Dick died onstage in Canada later that year, the decision was made to commission a new SXSW softball trophy to be christened the Country Dick Montana Cup.

FILM / MULTIMEDIA

World Premiere Films *The Return Of The Texas Chainsaw Massacre, A More Perfect Union, The Man With The Perfect Swing, The Underneath*

Memorable Films *The Basketball Diaries, The Buddy Factor, Tigrero: A Film That Was Never Made, The Incredibly True Adventures Of Two Girls In Love, Little Odessa, Songs Of The Homeland*

Notable Film Panelists John Sayles (director), Robert Rodriguez (director), Maggie Renzi (actress/producer), John Pierson (producer's rep), Richard Linklater (director)

Multimedia Keynote Todd Rundgren

Notable Multimedia Panelists Bruce Sterling (science fiction writer), George "Fatman" Sanger (computer music composer), Phil Hood (*NewMedia*), Peter Lewis (*The New York Times*), Bob "Dr. Macintosh" Levitus ■

1996

SXSW **STATS** March 8 - 17

BY THE NUMBERS

664 showcasing artists
of 4,495 submissions

60 panels, workshops & sessions

41 venues & stages

5,531 registrants

$195-395 registration

$35-45 wristband

192 pages in program guide

114 trade show exhibitors

1,036 film registrants

1,356 multimedia registrants

AUSTIN MUSIC AWARDS

Wednesday, March 13, Palmer Auditorium

Performers Sixteen Deluxe, Ian Moore Band, Don Walser's Pure Texas Band, Asylum Street Spankers, Kris McKay, Kelly Willis, Abra Moore, Sara Hickman, Dale Watson, Miss Lavelle White, Wayne "The Train" Hancock, Gerry Van King; MC Paul Ray

KEYNOTE SPEAKER

Krist Novoselic The former Nirvana bassist had become interested in socio-political issues since the death of Kurt Cobain, though apparently not everyone found his activism-oriented address motivating. "Novoselic opened the conference like a hangover, droning on and on about the necessity of galvanizing and politicizing the rock audience to protect us from the right-wing movement," wrote Robert Wilonsky of the *Dallas Observer*. "He discussed the apathy of the American voters, he preached the sins of ignorance, he demanded freedom under the Constitution. 'Who would have thought the music industry would be called upon to protect the First Amendment?' he wondered." Austin jazz group the Elias Haslanger Quartet provided the prelude.

MEMORABLE PANELS

"Selena: Murder, Hype And Tejano's Aftermath" Author Joe Nick Patoski, who was at work on a biography of the Corpus Christi singer a year after her

death, moderated a panel with Latino members of the Texas media that discussed Selena's significance to the popularity of Tejano music.

"Celebrity Interview: Randy Newman" A new and instantly popular panel motif was introduced with this session, which was a simple sit-down Q&A between Microsoft's Jon Kertzer and the revered American songwriter and composer of film-soundtrack music.

> "...one of the best things to happen to American music, period." ■ *Rolling Stone*, 1996

"Were The Grateful Dead Really Any Good?" And, a follow-up question, was SXSW obsessed with panels on recently deceased musicians in '96? Probably it was just coincidence that the passings of both Jerry Garcia and Selena were addressed at the same event. The Dead panel "drew an SRO crowd, and a lot of yelling," Roland Swenson remembered.

"Mark Rubin's Naked Lunch: How To Keep Band Members From Tearing Each Other Into Small Bits" The loquacious bassist for the Bad Livers was in his third year of hosting a Saturday morning panel that was largely a forum for his ruminations (accompanied by the serving of hot bagels). The title of this one hinted at a particularly lively discussion.

"Charles Whitman: How And Why Did It Happen?" If you're going to do panels on JFK and David Koresh, eventually you're going to get around to this one. Author (and *Slacker* actor) John Slate served as moderator.

"Industry Dodgeball: An Interactive Panel" Wisely placed in the final time slot on the last day of panels. Duck!

NOTABLE PANELISTS

Allen Toussaint (musician/producer), Anthony DeCurtis (VH1), Arthur Brown (musician), Brendan O'Brien (producer), Vic Chesnutt (musician), Paul Williams (*Crawdaddy*), Greg Sowders (Sweet Relief), Craig Stewart (Trance Syndicate), Chris Willman (*Entertainment Weekly*), Grant Alden (*No Depression*), Eddie Gomez (Bug Music), Kim Fowley (producer)

MEMORABLE SHOWCASES & EVENTS

> Topping off the slate of outdoor stage shows at Sixth & Brazos was Thursday's performance by Iggy Pop, with openers the Geraldine Fibbers (which included future Wilco guitarist Nels Cline). Joan Osborne, riding high on her hit "One Of Us," headlined Friday's show at the intersection.

> Thursday's lineup at the Austin Music Hall featured not only roots-pop supergroup Golden Smog, Austin hero Alejandro Escovedo and Boston alterna-faves Throwing Muses, but also the legendary piano-playing songwriter Randy Newman in the first timeslot on the bill.

> The Austin Music Hall boasted a blockbuster lineup of top-of-the-line Americana acts on Friday, with Austinites Junior Brown and Kelly Willis, Grammy-winning songwriter Lucinda Williams, and the young band Son Volt, featuring two members of the original Uncle Tupelo lineup.

> Meanwhile, Saturday's Split Rail showcase highlighted young Americana upstarts on the

verge of bigger breakthroughs, most notably Whiskeytown, the Old 97's and Blue Mountain (plus Mekons leader Jon Langford's new insurgent-country band the Waco Brothers).

> Liberty Lunch's Friday-night showcase was an indie-rock smorgasbord, featuring heavyweight champions Guided By Voices and rising contenders Spoon on either end of the bill and the delectable Liz Phair sandwiched in the middle.

> Toronto rock band The Pursuit Of Happiness, huge stars in their homeland, headlined an all-Canadian bill at Tropical Isle that also included acclaimed singer-songwriter Ron Sexsmith and alt-rock stalwarts 13 Engines.

> Sunday's primary showcase was a benefit at Steamboat for the new SIMS Foundation (Services Invested in Musician Support), which was created to help musicians with mental health problems after Sims Ellison of the Austin metal band Pariah took his life the previous year. The foundation continues to help musicians in need today.

NOTABLE ACTS

Fugees A late add to the Friday-night lineup at a new large outdoor venue called Stubb's, the hip-hop sensation (whose just-released album *The Score* eventually would go multi-platinum) was beset by a major downpour just as their set began. They stuck it out, though, and played once the storm had passed an hour or so later.

Gillian Welch & David Rawlings A month before Welch's debut album surfaced on Almo, she and Rawlings played the Crystal Ballroom of the Driskill Hotel; soon enough they'd be accustomed to playing large halls and giant festivals as one of the top-drawing acoustic acts of the past 15 years.

Wayne Kramer The former member of the MC5 was touting a new album on Epitaph Records, *The Hard Stuff*, at his Thursday night Liberty Lunch showcase.

Plimsouls Saturday's reunion show at Waterloo Brewing Company by the Los Angeles early '80s greats was the second of the conference for leader Peter Case, who also did a solo set Thursday at Maggie Mae's West.

Ben Folds Five The buzz had begun in earnest for the Chapel Hill trio (not quintet) when they

played on Thursday night at Scholz Garten, though it was the following year's "Brick" that provided their big breakthrough.

Yayhoos Dan Baird of the Georgia Satellites teamed up with guitarist Eric Ambel, bassist Keith Christopher and drummer Terry Anderson to make up the rambunctious rock band that headlined Waterloo Brewing Company on Thursday night.

Blink-182 The Southern California punk-pop band was a relatively new upstart on Cargo Records when they played Friday night at Emo's. Multi-million-selling success followed in the ensuing few years.

"SXSW director Roland Swenson was standing in the midst of a human swarm a block from Sixth Street Friday night, just after Joan Osborne had finished playing, when some young man in a pickup pulled to the corner where Swenson stood. 'Hey dude,' the guy called out. 'Can you tell me where South by Southwest is?'"
■ Michael Corcoran in the *Austin American-Statesman*, March 19, 1996

1996 Music Big Bag art courtesy of Linda Barry

George Clinton & the P-Funk All Stars The one-of-a-kind kingpins of funk music brought their full-on dance-party assault to the Austin Music Hall for an extended headlining set.

Mark Eitzel The former frontman for San Francisco band American Music Club had just released his solo debut when he opened Saturday night's showcase at Maggie Mae's West.

Also Low, Joe Henry, Bob Neuwirth, Girls Against Boys, Jason & the Scorchers, Corey Harris, Arlo Guthrie, Little Texas, Posies, Brave

"This is how you know you're at the right showcase performance during South by Southwest: *Rolling Stone's* David Fricke is there, the leather-jacket-clad Joey Ramone-look-alike taking notes and doing the palsied white-rock-critic shuffle-dance that inflicts so many members of this so-called profession."
■ Robert Wilonsky in the *Dallas Observer,* March 21, 1996

Combo, Fred Schneider, Pond, Jules Shear, Bill Kirchen, Meatmen, Imperial Teen, Tom Freund, Red Red Meat, Michael Hurley

SOME OF THE MEDIA-SPONSORED ACTS

Slobberbone (*Dallas Observer*), Sons Of Hercules (*San Antonio Current*), BR5-49 (*Nashville Scene*), Dolly Varden (*New City*, Chicago), Blister (*Weekly Alibi*, Albuquerque), Super Deluxe (*Willamette Week*, Portland, OR), Elizabeth Einstein (*Riverfront Times*, St. Louis), Shame Idols (*Black & White*, Birmingham, AL), Stuntman (*Boise Weekly*), Starbilly (*Louisville Eccentric Observer*), Shovelhead (*The Reader*, Omaha, NE)

SOME OF THE AUSTIN ACTS

Michael Hall The former leader of the Wild Seeds, now an editor at *Texas Monthly,* used his 40-minute showcase slot on Saturday at the Ritz to play one song, the marathon "Frank Slade's 29th Dream," in its entirety.

Fastball The tuneful Austin trio featuring Tony Scalzo, Miles Zuniga and Joey Shuffield had a deal with Hollywood Records when they headlined Steamboat on Friday night, but were still two years away from pop stardom with "The Way."

Also Derailers, Vallejo, Horsies, Gourds, Paul Glasse, Jon Dee Graham, Little Sister, Billy White, Drums & Tuba, Libbi Bosworth, SlackHappy, Superego, Leeann Atherton, Euripides Pants

SOME OF THE INTERNATIONAL ACTS

Jet Black Joe (Iceland), Lolita No. 18 (Japan), Mike Peters (U.K.), Moxy Fruvous (Canada), Killawajachi (Peru), Welcome To Julian (France), Bagual (Uruguay), Jackie Leven (Scotland), Uz Jsme Doma (Czech Republic), Gary Heffern (Finland)

SOFTBALL TOURNEY

The Record Companies team avenged last year's championship-game loss to Clubs/Talent Buyers with a vengeance, winning the title rematch 15-0. The inaugural Film/Multimedia team debuted with an embarrassing loss to the lowly Musicians squad, resulting in them being replaced in the bracket by a team from Finland the following year.

FILM / MULTIMEDIA

Memorable Films *Hype!, The Last Supper, 100 Proof, Paradise Lost: Child Murders At Robin Hood Hills, Drop Dead Rock, Shady Grove, The High Road*

Notable Film Panelists Michael Barker (Sony Pictures Classics), Christine Vachon (producer), Richard Linklater (director)

Multimedia Keynotes Bruce Sterling (science fiction writer), Hal Josephson (MediaSense)

Notable Multimedia Panelists Andrew Rasiej (Apple New York Music Festival), Tim Nye (Sunshine Interactive Network), Ted Cohen (Philips Multimedia Music), Marcos Novak (virtual reality expert) ■

continued from page 64

Gone With the Ghosts
GONEBLIND
Gong Li
Gong Myoung
Goober & the Peas
Good
Good Company
Good Old War
Good Times Crisis Band
Goodfoot
goodkungfu
Goodness
Goodshirt
Goons Of Doom
Goran Gora
Gorch Fock
Gordie Sampson
Gordie Tentrees
Gordon
Gordon Gano and The Ryan Brothers
Gordon Voidwell
Gore Gore Girls
Gorky's Zygotic Mynci
Gosling
Gossip
Goudie
Gouge
Gov't Mule
Govinda
Gown
Gowns
Grab the Lizard
Grabass Charlestons
Grace Braun
Grace Potter and the Nocturnals
Graceland
Gracer
Grade
Grady
Grafton
Graham Coxon
Graham Parker
Graham Parker (w/Tom Freund)
Grain USA
Grains of Faith
Gram Rabbit
Grammatics
Grampall Jookabox
Grand Analog
Grand Archives
Grand Atlantic
Grand Buffet
Grand Champeen
Grand Drive
Grand Hallway
Grand Island
Grand Mal
Grand National
Grand Ole Party
Grand Street Cryers
Grand Ulena
Grand Wizard Theodore
Grandaddy
Grandchildren
Grande
Grandmothers
Grandpa's Ghost
Grandpa's Goodtime Fandango
Grandson Demus
Grandsons of the Pioneers
Grant Hart
Grant Lee Buffalo
Grant McLennon
Grant Stevens
Grant-Lee Phillips
Grapefruit
Grapevine
Grass Widow
Gratitude
Grave Babies
Graves At Sea
Graves of Valor
Graveyard
Gravity Jacket
Gravy Boat
Gravy Train!!!!
Grayskul
Grayson Manor
Great Big Everything
Great Big Planes
Great Guns
Great Lake Swimmers
Great Lakes
Great Lakes Myth Society
Great Northern
Great Southern Railroad
Great Western Orchestra
Greater Good
Greazy Meal
Grecco Buratto
Green & Wood
Green Apple Quick Step
Green Carnation
Green Day

Guided by Voices (1996)

Green Magnet School
Green Milk From The Planet Orange
Green River Ordinance
Green Scene
Green Shape
Greencards & Cluan
Greenella
GreenFuz
Greenhouse
Greenstreet
Greg Ashley
Greg Ashley and the Medicine Fuck Dream Road Show
Greg Camp
Greg Cox & Frank Kammerdiener
Greg Ericson
Greg Forrest
Greg Harris Vibe Quintet
Greg Hosterman
Greg Koons
Greg Laswell
Greg Oblivian & Reigning Sound
Greg Schilling
Greg Trooper
Greg Whitfield
Greg Wood
Gregory Page
Gregory Shiff
Greta
Greta Gaines
Gretchen Peters
Gretchen Phillips
Grey Daturas
Grey DeLisle
Grey Ghost
Greyhound Soul
Greyhounds
Grieves with Budo
Grievous Angels
Griffin House
Grifter City
Grimm
Grimy Styles
Grind Orchestra
Grindstone
Gringo Star
Gris Gris
Grit Boys
Grither
Grizzly Bear
Grommit
Grooms
Groop Dogdrill
Groove Thangs
Groovenics
GrooveSession
Groovie Ghoulies
Groovin Ground
Grotus
Grouch & Eligh
Ground Components
Ground Zero
Grouper/Inca Ore
Grover
Gruel
Gruff Rhys
Grumpyhead
Grupo Bandanna de K-Town
Grupo Batacha
Grupo Cenzontle
Grupo Control
Grupo Fantasma
Grupo Limite
Grupo Vida
Grupo Zazhil
GryN
Grynch
Guadalupe Plata
Guafa Trio
Guano Apes
Guardez Lou
Gudrid Hansdottir
Guided by Voices
Guido
Guillamino
Guillemots
Guillotina
Guilty Simpson
Guinea Worms
Guitar Hero Metallica Madness Competition
Guitar Nakisisa
Guitar Shorty
Guitar Wolf
Guitar Women w/ Cindy Cashdollar and Sue Foley
Guitars a Go Go: 3 Balls of Fire, Tomsco & Cole, Boom Chica Boom Girls
Gulf Coast Playboys
Gum
Gun Outfit
Gunbunnies
Gunfighter
Gunga Din
Guns 'N' Bombs/Aaron Lacrate
Gunslingers
Gurf Morlix
Guru
Gus Black
GusGus
Gustavo Alberto
Gustavo Galindo

Guy Clark
Guy Davis
Guy Forsyth
Guy Forsyth Band
Gwenmars
Gwil Owen
Gwil Owen and The Thieves
Gypsy Rogue
Gyroscope
GZA

H

H.I.S.D. (Hueston Independent Spit District)
H.R. Band
Ha Ha Tonka
Haale
Habitual Sex Offenders
Hacienda
Hacienda Brothers
Hackensaw Boys
Hadacol
Hafdis Huld
Hagfish
Haggis
Hai Karate
Hair of the Dog
Hairy Apes BMX
Hal
Hal Ketchum
Haley Bonar
Half Cousin
Half Japanese
Half Way Home
Half-handed Cloud
Halfwatt
Halfway To Gone
Halifax
Hall
Hallelujah The Hills
Halley
Hallo Venray
Halou
Halves
Hamell on Trial
Hamilton
Hamilton Pool
Hammer No More The Fingers
Hammerhead
Hammerlock
Hammers of Misfortune
Hand of Glory
Hand Over Fist
Handsome 3some
Handsome Boy Modeling School and Head Automatica Sound System
Handsome Furs
Hang on the Box
Hangar 18
Hanging Francis
Hank & Patsy
Hank Dogs
Hank Flamingo
Hank IV
Hank Riddle
Hank Williams III
Hannah Cranna
Hanne Hukkelberg
Hannibal Buress
Hans Olson
Hans Ter Burg
Hanson
Hanuman
Hapa
Happily Ever After
Happy Apple
Happy As Hell
Happy Birthday
Happy Bunny
Happy Drivers
Happy Family
Happy Fingers Institute
Happy Flowers
Happy World
Happylife
Har Mar Superstar
Harvey Mandel
Hard Core
Hard 'N Phirm
Hard Place
Hardcop
Hardcore Country All-Stars
Hardcore Superstar
Hard-Fi
Hardknowledge
Hari Kondabolu
Hari Kondabolu and Lucas Molandez
Hari Kondabolu, Rob Delaney, Jimmie Roulette and Special Guest
Hari Leigh
Harlan T Bobo
Harlem
Harlem Shakes
Harlem Slim, Delta Blues
Harley Poe
Harold Garret
Harold Ray Live in Concert
Harper Simon
Harris Newman
Harris Tweed

Harrisons
Harry Shearer's "Le Show Live" with Judith Owen, Henry Butler and Special Guests
Hart-Rouge
Harvard Bass
Harvester
Harvey Brooks
Harvey Danger
Harvey Milk
Harvey Scales
Harvey Sid Fisher
Hash Palace
Haste
Hatcham Social
Hate Fuck Trio
Hatebreed
Hatred Surge
Haunted George
Hauschka
Havalina Rail Co.
Hawk
Hawksley Workman
Hawnay Troof
Hawthorne Heights
Haydn Vitera
Hayes Carll
Hayley Hutchinson
Haymarket Riot
Hayseed
Hayseed Dixie
Haze
Hazeldine
He Is Legend
He Said She Said
Head
Head Automatica
Head First
Head of Femur
Headdress
Headhunters
Headkrack
Headlights
Headphones
Headrush
Heads & Dreads
HEALTH (CA)
Health and Happiness Show
Healthy White Baby
Heart Bazaar
Heartbeats Rhythm Quartet
Heartless Bastards
Hearts & Minds
Hearts of Animals
Hearts of Darknesses
HEARTSREVOLUTION
Heather
Heather Bennett Trio
Heather Eatman
Heather McCullough
Heather Myles
Heathill
HEAVy
Heavy Vegetable
Hecuba
HeeND
Hege V.
Heideroosjes
Heidi Spencer & the Rare Birds
Heinous Bienfäng
Heiruspecs
HeKill Three
Helen Boulding
Helene
Helga Pictures
Helios Creed/Chrome
Helium
Hell City Glamours
Hell Mach 4
Hell On Wheels
Hella
Hellafied Funk Crew
Hello Seahorse!
HelloGoodbye
Hellworms
Helmet
Helms Alee
Heloise & the Savoir Faire
Helstar
Hemoptysis
Henhouse
Henning Kvitnes
Henning Staerk
Henri Dikongué
Henry Brun and The Latin Playerz
Henry Butler
Henry Chow
Henry Ghost
Her Majesty the Baby
Her Space Holiday
Hera
Herb Agapetus
Herb Remington
Herb Steiner & Melissa Miller
Herbert Huncke
Here Holy Spain
Here We Go Magic
Here We Go Magic feat. Luke Temple
Herman Dune
Herman Hitson
Herman the German & Das Cowboy
Heroine Sheiks

Herschel Berry
Hesta Prynn
Hesta Prynn in Civil Shepherd
Hex
Hey Besala
Hey Champ
Hey Marseilles
Hey Monday
Hey Negrita
Hey Ocean
Hey Rosetta!
Hey Willpower
Hey Zeus
Heybale!
Hezeleo
hHead
Hickoids
Hi-Fi Drowning
Hifiklub
High City Miles
High Class Elite
High Cotton
High Llamas
High Noon
High Noon
High on Fire
High Places
High Speed Scene
High Tension Wires
High Water Marks
Hijos Del Sol
Hilary Sloan & Aunt Erma's Fillin' Station
Hilary York
Hildegard
Hill Country Revue
Hillbilly Cafe
Hillbilly Frankenstein
Hillbilly Idol
Hillbilly Werewolf
Hillstomp
Hint Hint
Hip By Association
Hip Hop Humpday
Hip Hop Humpday featuring: Bavu Blakes, Element, D-Madness, DJ Massive, DJ Phyfteen, Bruce James, Brian Mendes, Tee-Double, Traygod
Hippiehaus
Hiromi
His & Her Vanities
His Boy Elroy
His Name is Alive
Hitch
Hitchhike
Hive
Ho-Hum
Hoarse
Hobble
Hobex
Hobo Jim
Hobotalk
Hockey
Hockey Night
Hog Molly
Hogni
Hogpig
John Rey Reed
Hoi Polloi
Holden
Hole
Hole In The Wall Gang with Paul Minor, Jane Bond, Beaver Nelson, Troy Campbell, Scrappy Jud Newcomb, Tony Scalzo, Miles Zuniga, Darin Murphy, Ted Roddy, Andrew Duplantis, Matt Hubbard, Jeff Johnston, Barbara K and Larry Seaman
Holger
Holiday Flyer
Holiday Ranch
Hollerado
Hollowbody
Hollowmen
Hollowpoints
Holly Cole
Holly Cole Trio
Holly Conlan
Holly Golightly
Holly Golightly and the Brokeoffs
Holly McNarland
Holly Miranda
Holly Throsby
Holly Williams
Hollyfaith
Hollywood Holt
Holocaustic Mindfrme
Hologram
Holopaw
Holsapple & Stamey
Holy Bulls
Holy Cows
Holy Fuck
Holy Ghost!
Holy Hail
Holy Moellers
Holy Rolling Empire
Holy Shit!
Holy Water
Home

Home Blitz
Home Video
Homeboy Sandman
Homer Henderson One Man Band
Homestead Greys
Honey Claws
Honey Ryder
Honey Sac
Honey Well
Honeychild Coleman
Honeycut
Honeydove
HoneyHoney
Honeypot
Honk If Yer Horny
Honky
Honky Tonk Chateau
Hoodoo Club
Hoodoo Gurus
Hookah Brown
Hooker
Hoot Night Fever: An all-star tribute to the '70s Disco Era
Hootenanny (with Ramblin' Jack Elliott, Billy Bragg, Jolie Holland, Tim Fite, Joe Henry, Busdriver, and special guests)
Hoots and Hellmouth
Hopewell
Harmonious Wail
HorrorPops
Horse + Donkey
Horse Feathers
Horseshoe
Hosea Hargrove
Hospital Bombers
Hosstyle
Hostile Union
Hot Buttered Rum String Band
Hot Chip
Hot Club De Paris
Hot Club of Cowtown
Hot Head Swing Band
Hot Hot Heat
Hot IQs
Hot Lava
Hot Leg
Hot Little Rocket
Hot Live Guys
Hot Panda
Hot Pink DeLorean
Hot Rod Circuit
Hot Sauce Johnson
Hot Springs
Hot Young Priest
Hotel Hotel
Hotel Hunger
Hotel Lights
Hotrod Moses
Hotwheels Jr
Houndog
Houndstooth
Hours of Worship
House in Orbit
House Levelers
House of Broken Promises
House of Cards
House Of Doc
House Of Fools
House of Hoi Polloi
House of Large Sizes
House Shoes
Household Names
Housewife
Housewives' Choice
Houston Marchman
Houston Tiilltotson Community Choir
Houston's Nawf Side All Stars - Magno, Big Tike, Lester Roy, Lil Mario, Big Pic, Blyndcyde
How I Became The Bomb
How to Kiss
Howard Eliott Payne
Howard Hello
Howard Iceberg & the Titanics
Howard Kremer
Howard Kremer, Tig Notaro, Kevin Avery and Special Guest
Howe Gelb
Howe Gelb and the Band of Gypsies
Howie Beck
HOWL
Howlies
Howlin' Rain
Howling Diablos
Howling Guitar
How's Your News?
HSE
HSGF
Hub Moore
Hub Moore and the Great Outdoors
Hubert Sumlin
Hubert von Goisern & die Original Alpinkatzen
Hudson & Franke
Hudson Bell
Hudson Mohawke
Hudson River School

Huecco
Huelyn Duvall
Huevos Rancheros
Hug
Huggs
Hugh
Hugh Campbell
Hugh Cornwell
Hugh Moffat
Hull
Human
Human Alert
Human Eye
Human Giant
Human Highway
Human Television
Human Touch
Humbert
Humble Bums
Hummer
Hummersqueal
Hundred Reasons
Hundreth Monkey
Hungry Hill
Huntingtons
Huntress
Hunx and His Punx
Hurra Torpedo
Hurray for the Riff Raff
Hurricane Bells
Hurts to Purr
Hush
HUSH (Detroit)
Hush Scarlett
Husking Bee
Husky Rescue
Hussle Club
Huver
HY
Hyakkei
Hydroponic Sound System
Hyka
Hymns
Hypatia Lake
Hyperbubble
Hypernova
Hyperpotamus
Hypnogaja
Hypnotic Clambake
Hysterics
Hystoic Vein

I

I Against I
I Am August
I Am David Sparkle
I AM EMPIRE
I Am Kloot
I Am Spoonbender
I am the World Trade Center
I Can Lick Any Sonofabitch in the House
I Confess
I Don't Know
I Love Math
I Love You But I've Chosen Darkness
I Mother Earth
I See Hawks in LA
I See Stars
I Self Devine
I Speak Jive
I-Tex
I Walk The Line
I Was A Cub Scout
ISIS
Iain Archer
Iain Matthews
I Am X
Ian Britt
Ian Hunter
Ian McLagan
Ian McLagan & MonkeyJump
Ian McLagan & The Bump Band
Ian Moore
Ian Moore Action Company
Ian Wadley
IB3
Ice Cube
Icecream Hands
Icelandic
Icy Demons
Ida
Idaho
i-dep
Idgy Vaughn
Idiot Flesh
Idiot Pilot
Idiots
Idle Warship
Idletime
Idlewild
Iggy Pop
Iglu & Hartly
Ignacio Pena
Ignitor
Ignorance Park
IGT
Iguanamen de Galapagos
Iguanas
Igudesman & Joo
Ikara Colt

Ike Reilly
iLiKETRAiNS
Ill Ease
Ill Lit
Ill Tactics
Illa J
Illegal Artists
Iller Than Theirs (Nuclear Family)
Illinois
iLL-Literacy
Illo '77 with DJ Mixwell and DJ Mad
IMA
Imaad Wasif
Imaginary Icons
Imagine Dragons
Iman
Imani Coppola
i-Men
Immaculate Machine
Immortal Lee County Killers
Immortal Soldierz
Immortal Technique
Imperial Teen
Impossible Shapes
In Case Of Fire
In Extremo
In Fear of Roses
In Stereo (perCeptie & Kapabel)
In The Nursery
Inara George
Incense
Inch
Inch Chua
Incognito
Indian Jewelry
Indigenous
Indigo Swing
Indigos
Infantree
Infidels
Infusion
Ingrid Karklins
Ingrid Karklins & Backbone
Ingrid Michaelson
Inhabit
Initialization String
INK
Inka Inka
Inlets
Inner
Inner Visions
Innercity Pirates
Innerpartysystem
Innocent Bystanders
Insect Fear
Insect Sex Act
Insect Surfers
Insignia
Insite
Inspectah Deck
Inspecter 7
Inspector
Instant Karma
Institute for the Criminally Insane
Instituto Mexicano de Sonido
Instruction
Instrumenti
Instruments
International Thief Thief
Interphase
Interpol
Intimate Stranger
Intrinzik
Intuitive Music Orchestra
Invincible
Invisible Pedestrians
Invisibleman's deathbed
Inward Eye
Io Echo
Iodine
Iota
Ipso Facto
IQU
Iran
Irie Jane
Irie Vibrations
Irina Bjorklund & Peter Fox
Iris Anvil
Iris Berry
Iris DeMent
Irma Thomas
Iron & Wine
Iron Age
Iron Man
Ironweed
IrRAdio
Irving
Isaac Green & The Skalars
Isaac Russell
Isabelle
Ise Lyfe
Ishmael & the Peacemakers
Ishues
ISIS
Islands
Ismael y La Banda Belem
Isobel Campbell
Itch
Ithica Gin
Itoura Moussongo
It's Casual
It's Not Not
It's True!
IV Thieves

continued on page 108

Beyond The Buzz, Epiphanies Await...

South by Southwest is like a knight's quest for music writers. We run around like we're looking for the musical Holy Grail, but the real point is to test our own mettle. Do I have the survival skills to turn down that fourth free margarita? Can I defy the laws of time and space and make it from Emo's to La Zona Rosa in less than ten minutes? Am I virtuous enough to turn away from inappropriate flirting with that cute publicist, yet kind enough to let an overeager undergrad blogger bend my ear? Most of all: Do I have the strength to reject what's hyped in honor of what my heart truly wants to hear?

SXSW MEMORIES

That last question forces the music scribe to face the dragon, the sirens' call, the bewildering labyrinth. It's hard enough for music journalists, a highly insecure and socially tragic lot, to avoid the comfort of the hive mind during the regular year. SXSW's carnival atmosphere emboldens us, but it also encourages rash behavior – including the abandonment of personal taste under the enchantment of others' opinions.

The feeling that You Will Be Nobody if you don't catch [annually interchangeable heatseeker] at [venue you can't get into anyway] can infect the most intrepid independent thinker, leading to much frantic texting of said hot publicist, bribery of list-keepers, and kicking of less fancy Tumblr keepers to the curb. *May I be strong enough*, I pray every year, kissing the scapular adorned with Alex Chilton's sainted face and treading boldly into the mass of humanity on Sixth Street. May I turn away from the serpentine line extending from Antone's, wipe my schedule clean of afternoon shopping at the Fader Fort, and actually go hear the music I want to hear. Music that no more than 75 other people might find worthy, but which offers the biggest possibility of revelation.

Once I fight my way through the buzz-thick forest and enter a space where someone less fashionable is performing, I find that the light falls differently there. The room may or may not be full, but the people present are listening. The musicians are playing for fun. They don't seem scared, or exhausted. Sometimes they'll entertain requests. Sometimes they do what Donovan said that time, and slowly blow my little mind.

I have a few treasured memories of such illuminating sets. Early on, they often involved one or several members of the Flatlanders, house band of my 1990s SXSW. I recall

Sir Doug & The Surfer

I've been attending South by Southwest since 1990, and there are more highlights than I can count: Seeing Alejandro Escovedo with his "orchestra"; hanging out with Jimmie Dale Gilmore at his house in the country and having him play me some new songs at his kitchen table; getting a chance to witness Johnny Cash play solo acoustic at Emo's (the chair he sat on is somewhere up in the club's rafters still, I believe); watching Roky Erickson evolve from a frightened recluse to a commanding artist once more; drinking Lone Stars with Ice-T and his journalistic alter-ego, Claudia Perry. But the most hilarious moment was listening to Doug Sahm and Gibby Haynes serve as broadcasters for the annual conference-closing softball tournament one year. I swung by the field to grab some ribs and a little sunshine before heading home, and ended up staying for a couple hours just to listen to the best sports broadcast comedy duo this side of Harry Caray and Jimmy Piersall.

▪ **Greg Kot,** *Chicago Tribune* **and "Sound Opinions"**

sitting in a hard chair at Butch Hancock's Lubbock Or Leave It art space, witnessing a community unfold before my eyes. Butch's corny jokes, Joe Ely's road dog wandering eye, Jimmie Dale Gilmore's unassuming profundity. This was lived music, unconcerned with being more than it naturally *was*.

Sometimes I found excitement by straying into the parallel universe of SXSW shows not deemed interesting enough by the music-bizzy oligarchy. Twice in 2001: Amy Ray of the Indigo Girls debuted music from her sexy and raw solo debut *Stag* at the feminist-friendly Gaby & Mo's Cafe, rocking a crowd of on-fire riot grrrls and leather-clad womyn with the Butchies backing her up. And at the spectrum's opposite end, grunge Romantics the Toadies absolutely slayed a sweaty, packed crowd at Stubb's – a crowd of rock-made, utterly engaged kids, mostly college students I guess, with me the only professional music nerd in sight.

I loved Ray and the Toadies before I ventured off the hipster map, but there have been other times when I've just stumbled into something utterly surprising. I can't remember the exact year, or the corner bar, where I saw a crazy heavy metal band from China melt walls as part of a generally unnoticed cultural exchange program. I do know that it was just last year when, throwing up my hands at the 45-minute wait to get into a different tent, I stumbled into a little den of joy ruled over by the Codeine Velvet Club, a retro-dorable party band from Scotland whose good cheer set the mood for my whole

weekend. And I was glad when I turned down a schmoozy day party in favor of pausing to catch some gorgeousness from the singer-songwriter Matt Morris, a slight crush of mine when I entered the venue where he was singing but a full-fledged favorite by the time I left.

Just call me girl Galahad. I'll be out there again this year, looking for a sign and a miracle in the thick of things.
■ Ann Powers, *Los Angeles Times*

Welcome to the Working Week

My best memories of SXSW are encompassed in the simple weirdness of some of the things we did. We didn't work in a conventional "work environment." We had office hours that started at 10am and went until the work was done (often well into the wee hours). The barriers of what constituted "music" were vague, and as a result, some of the best events took place with musicians doing everything BUT making music. Wayne Coyne's Parking Lot Experiment (1997) is the most obvious: 30 cars and their cassette players, a parking ramp, a bullhorn and several thousand fans to create the world's largest stereo. Or the Mexican Wrestling Match (NXNW, 1997) in Portland with a bunch of old punk-rock musicians from San Francisco: a regulation wrestling ring, a referee, and a club full of belligerent teenagers. It ended up ugly, but it seemed like such a good idea at the start.

The others were the brilliant musical moments that will stay with me forever. Johnny Cash leaning off the stage at Emo's, shaking hands and thanking people for coming. That took so much class and showed me that humility is one of the best qualities in someone you admire. Or being backstage at the Austin Music Hall, hauling gear and food for George Clinton & the P-Funk All-Stars to take back to their hotel. I got stopped by a sax player who said, "What are you doing, girl? Put that down and dance!" I did. Man, did I dance.

Perhaps the most memorable part of working for SXSW is that feeling of reward. We have all worked jobs (or do now!) where you work day in and day out without a sense of what you are accomplishing. The joy of SXSW (and NXNE, NXNW and MRMF) was that at the end, you had a big, beautiful, loud, shining jewel to show for your sweat, tears, anxiety, excitement and disappointment. It felt so good to see the doors of the convention center flung open on Wednesday morning and you would say, "OK, here we go." I always looked forward to it, and I still miss it. ■ **Leah Wilkes, SXSW Music staff, 1990s**

Austin's Audience For Film

When I started at SXSW, I did not fully appreciate Louis, Nick and Roland's prescience. Over the next decade, film festivals of all shapes and sizes would sprout up all over the country, but no other event would begin to mimic the spirit and camaraderie of their 10-day film, music and technology extravaganza.

What I remember from the first year of SXSW film: meeting Bud Shrake, Bill Wittliff, Eagle Pennell, Rick Linklater, Robert Rodriguez…and realizing that not only had Austin always been a magnet for creativity, but that it would continue to be for generations to come. What I learned over the next few years of working there is that good films deserve an audience, and Austin has a great one, eager to take a chance on what SXSW has to show them.

It also surprises me now that many of those filmmakers we showed in the early days are still making films today. I was pleased to see SXSW is showing Greg Mottola's new film this year, and we premiered *The Daytrippers* in the mid-'90s! I also learned that through all the growing pains we had in those first years, nothing gets you through it like smart colleagues. I have tried to surround myself with the same high level of competence at TriBeCa. I consider myself lucky to do what I do now – running the TriBeCa Film Festival and our distribution business, Tribeca Film – and I know I owe a lot to my decade in Austin. Happy 25 years everyone; have a great festival! ■ **Nancy Schafer, TriBeCa Film Festival**

"The Austin Vortex"

For many of the years I lived in New Orleans (1992-2002) and was a member of the Continental Drifters, we would pack our gear into my Ford Explorer and head for Austin for SXSW. This became an annual ritual for us, right between Mardi Gras and JazzFest. Often we would stay with our friend Patrice, who owned a lovely old farmhouse on the outskirts of town. There were horses to ride, a fridge full of organic carrots to juice, a houseful of musicians and artists, and a hot tub, if one was so inclined. It felt like a place from another time, or several other times, and a world away from the Austin hotels, with their noisy lobbies teeming with badges and wristbands.

Making the short drive into town each day, I discovered the Austin Vortex: that mysterious, disorienting energy that surrounds the city during SXSW. I wasn't alone in this; Peter Holsapple, my bandmate and the Drifters' other designated driver, experienced it as well. I generally have a good, solid sense of direction, but for some reason I would hit I-35 and

unfailingly head in the wrong direction. It was funny the first couple of times. Then I'd try and outsmart my internal GPS and travel the *opposite* way from my inclination, only to find that, once again, I was going the wrong way. Yes, we had maps. But really, why would we need a map? It's *one road*. It has to be this way. Peter did it, too. We finally surrendered to the Vortex and became very familiar with those peculiar turnabouts, which I'm sure were included in the city planning just for people like us.

My friend and fellow Drifter Susan Cowsill and I also occasionally performed and recorded as the Psycho Sisters, and SXSW became a time to indulge our dual roles. In typical Psycho fashion, this idea was very often spur-of-the-moment: One of us would place a last-minute call to [SXSW music director] Brent Grulke, who would sigh, laugh, and find us a spot to play. I don't know why he put up with us, but I'm so glad that he did, because my absolute favorite SXSW visits were the years when Susan and I were Psychoing as well as Driftering. We'd finish a set with the Continental Drifters, jump offstage and into a cab, and zoom off to another club to do a set of our own. Often our friends Giant Sand were playing somewhere, so of course we had to go sing with them as well. And if Jules Shear, with whom we'd also recorded, was in town, well, we couldn't miss that. One memory is of Susan and me stowing our guitars and racing across town on foot, trying to figure out where we were going ("Where's the Church?") and having 12 minutes to get to the gig. We arrived just in time, out of breath and laughing.

There was one spectacularly humiliating SXSW experience for me. I'd been asked, again at the last minute, to fill in as moderator on a panel called "Shit Happens." This was to be about all the things that could go wrong in the process of making and marketing music. A good idea for a panel, I thought – but a bad choice of a moderator. I was in a particularly unfocused place in my life and had *no* idea how to go about preparing for this task. Peter could not have been more helpful, giving me background on my panelists (an eclectic but hardly obscure group) and encouraging me to just relax, it'd be fine. It wasn't. I flubbed the introduction of my fellow panelists ("This is Al Kooper. You know him from...well...lots of things...uh..."), and after telling my own shit-happens story about the Bangles being sabotaged by a famous '80s headliner I wouldn't name, I was informed that I was "too nice" to be a moderator. True, perhaps, but embarrassing. I should have handed over my gavel to Peter before we ever sat down, but instead this became my new SXSW "shit happens" story.

I've heard many complaints about SXSW, but I've always come away with something tangible and valuable. Sure, there were band fights, trips to the hospital, accordions left in the trunks of cabs. But there were also new friends made, new musicians discovered, and, once I figured out which way was east, new memories to take with me back to New Orleans. ■ **Vicki Peterson, Bangles/Continental Drifters**

...And An Army Of Volunteers

I came on board for SXSW #3 (1989), as volunteer coordinator, my title through the 10th anniversary at least. I had worked at the Center for Battered Women, where we relied to volunteers to staff our hotlines overnight and weekends throughout the year. Then there was the Kerrville Folk Festival, where the best crew there (highest participation and esprit d'corps) was the crew that cleaned the toilets. Both examples that you could get volunteers to do anything if you just trained them well and gave them real responsibility.

I "volunteered" my daughter Erin that first year to be my extra legs; she was not yet "legal" at that point, but ended up doing 20 years with SXSW. I think we ended up with at least 60 volunteers that first year, and I called and negotiated shifts with each one. Needed them all and more. By the time I left (to become operations director), we were up to 600 or so. I believe that last year Tammy Stout had nearly 2,000; about the time I moved on was when we had become three events.

One of the original 20, Greg Sells, has been a volunteer in one form or another since the beginning. Amanda Bowman was a volunteer who started with me and then served in Registration for 20 years. The Volunteer Coordinator after me, Peggy Ellithorpe, started as a volunteer. I believe Angela Lee was a volunteer before Film hired her, as was Matt Dentler.

As a staffer, particularly as volunteer coordinator, I could never get to performances. Rarely got to see all of a keynote even. The first few years, I did have one of the newest cars on staff, so when we needed someone to pick up Rosanne Cash (as our keynote speaker), I got asked to do the duty, which I loved. Along those lines, when SXSW scheduled an interview with Joan Baez, I asked for Erin and I to be the ones to escort her from the hotel to the Convention Center, as we had all demonstrated together in Washington, D.C., for better day care support when Erin was 3 years old. Joan remembered the occasion: Women and children circled the Capitol, led by Baez and Bella Abzug. ■ **Eve McArthur, longtime SXSW staff & director**

SXSW Film: In The Beginning

A significant number of the extended family that would first start publishing *The Austin Chronicle* and then later start South by Southwest were students in the Radio-Television-Film department at the University of Texas. The group included both graduate and undergraduate students

(Nick Barbaro and I were the former). Raul's, the punk/new-wave music club on Gudalupe, and *The Daily Texan*, UT's student newspaper, were two other backgrounds most had in common.

All of us shared a passion for both film and music, so SXSW starting out as a music conference and festival fit right in with our interests. Still, from early on there were discussions among all the SXSW partners about adding some kind of film event. It was decided that along with SXSW Music in 1994 we would launch a film event.

Having been involved with film programming for years, we were well aware that events did as much to shape themselves as we might do to consciously mold it. In that context, we were extremely lucky to hire Nancy Schafer to be the hands-on producer. Schafer, who's now executive director and chief programmer of the Tribeca Film Festival, provided just the right sensibility to bring us all together in creating and crafting the event.

Austin was already a home to a number of legendary and important screenwriters. These included famed maverick talents Bill Wittliff and Bud Shrake, who were the best known at the time, but Bill Broyles was already beginning to establish his reputation. There had already been a couple of generations of Texas filmmakers who had achieved some success (Tobe Hooper, Eagle Pennell), although traditionally they had decamped for Los Angeles. By 1994, however, there was an even newer generation of creative talents who were not just making great films but also staying in Texas, most notably Richard Linklater.

The highlight of that first year's festival was a program we had long talked about doing, one that focused on these native film talents. "A Celebration of Texas Independents" included films by Hooper, Pennell, Andy Anderson, documentary filmmaker Hector Galan, Ken Harrison, and Linklater. There were also films representing the work of screenwriting legends Wittliff and Shrake, and a retrospective honoring the work of Texas native and music legend Michael Nesmith (producer of *Repo Man*).

Mockingly, *Austin American-Statesman* film critic Michael MacCambridge said the event should be called the Friends of Louis Black Film Festival. Still, though that was clearly meant derisively, it was not that far from our original ambitions for the event. Given that even by 1994 there were hundreds of American film festivals, our expectations were low.

Early on, we all responded enthusiastically when Dewey Winburne, an acquaintance of ours, approached us about adding an interactive/new media program track to the event. We agreed, refocusing the event to include multimedia, and 1995 saw the second SXSW Film Festival and the first SXSW Multimedia event.

As mentioned, Texas and Austin had both long nurtured film talents. We hadn't really thought through the symbiotic relationship between the community and our event. Rick Linklater stayed after *Slacker*. Producer Elizabeth Avellán and director Robert Rodriguez moved back to town, as did Mike Judge. Paul Stekler was hired by the University of Texas and started recruiting an army of documentary filmmakers. Harry Knowles started *Ain't It Cool News*. The growth of Austin as a unique film community directly influenced the growth of SXSW Film. ■ **Louis Black, SXSW co-founder & senior director**

Diary Of A Mod SXSWer

Some SXSW memories: Musicians I'd played with lots of times. Musicians I'd met minutes before the gig, who dispersed seconds after the show to go play other shows. The band I was in the first time I went (the Shams in 1993), who spent more time thrift-shopping than schmoozing.

Hotels paid for by record labels and pull-out sofas supplied by friends. A motel on the outskirts of town where the taxi never came and the stage manager asked a member of the audience to drive over and pick me up – how was he to know that the guy who volunteered was the guy who'd been stalking me for two years? Motels so far out of town that I wasn't actually in Austin anymore. Or the Driskill or the round Holiday Inn or the Hyatt or a Motel 6. A house made of hay bales.

Gigs in an Irish pub and a daiquiri factory, a speakeasy and a Tandoori restaurant. A parking lot. Lubbock Or Leave It, the Cactus Cafe and Yard Dog. Another parking lot.

A parenting panel, a songwriting panel, a touring panel, an in-the-round with Jules Shear, playing "You're Just What I Needed" with Elliot Easton and Utensil. Meeting Doug Sahm. The Continental Drifters backing me up and my false eyelashes falling off. Eating with friends at Magnolia Grill at 4am after my show. Eating alone at Magnolia Grill at 4am after my show. Feeling happy either way.

Seeing my name in a list of "here at SXSW every year, why do they bother?" in the paper and wondering how the person who wrote that knew, unless they were there every year too. Being told "Wow, you look better at night" at 10am on the Sunday morning after. Congratulations some years. Looks of concern other years.

The audience, the audience, the audience. I don't know who they were or where they came from, but they always made it worthwhile.
■ **Amy Rigby, musician**

SXSW 'N 'Q

Way back in the early days of SXSW, when I was a panels coordinator, somebody had the inspired notion that I should moderate a barbecue panel at the beginning of the first day of the conference. The idea was that since so many of our registrants had heard of Texas barbecue but knew nothing about it, we could discuss the best places in the area for them to sample, and what to look for. I eagerly put together a group consisting of myself; Austinite Richard Zelade, who'd done anthropological research into the varying ethnic styles of Texas barbecue; Los Angeles record collector Dick Blackburn, who traveled the land in search of transcendent barbecue joints, and with whom I'd shared many a platter of the smoked meats; and local writer/cook/BBQ fanatic Jim Shahin, who, among other achievements, had taught me how to barbecue brisket, the Texas staple. We divided up several topics amongst ourselves and ate little except barbecue for the next several weeks to prepare.

No More Watching Basketball

One of the downsides of holding SXSW in March is that staff generally misses out on one of the year's premier sporting events, the first two rounds of the NCAA basketball tournament. Strangely, one of the most vivid memories I have from the mid-90s was Biff Parker and myself sneaking back to our hotel room early in the evening to watch (what was then known as) the Running Horns. I think it was a Thursday night during the Music Fest and I think we caught about 15 minutes of the first half on TV before SXSW creative director Brent Grulke tracked us down via walkie talkie. There was some kind of crisis happening at one of the clubs and our immediate attention was needed. The message that went over the system was something stern like this: "Tell Hugh and Biff that they need to get to such-and-such venue right now. Right now, not when the game is over. No more watching basketball for Hugh and Biff." Those words remain true 15 years later – there is no more March Madness (of the roundball variety, at least) during SXSWeek. Not that it matters too much with so much amazing live music filling the city. And, as I recall, Texas won the game that night, even without the benefit of the SXSW viewership. ■ Hugh Forrest, SXSW interactive director

Things didn't come off quite as planned. Our panel date was moved back, meaning attendees could no longer take advantage of our benign expertise before SXSW got into full swing. Still new to the panels racket, I developed stage fright and, without realizing it, finished my own talking points and then rambled into Jim's. That left him nothing specific to talk about and he had to wing it, which fortunately he does knowingly and vociferously when the subject is barbecue, which is one good reason why he is my BFF. So it was a darn good panel, if I do say so myself, and to our surprise the room was close to SRO. After we finished our prepared remarks, we took questions. A gentleman from Oklahoma asked why we hadn't discussed chicken, to which Shahin, an avowed red meat advocate, offered up what's still the best answer I've ever heard at a SXSW panel. "Fuck chicken," he snorted with a dismissive wave of the hand. *Pithy*, like "Jesus wept," the shortest verse in the Bible.

Today – with the rise of food TV programs, America's deification of regional comfort foods, the high SXSW recidivism rate and the like – nearly everyone coming to town knows all about barbecue except perhaps some of the vegetarians. When Joe Nick Patoski organized a barbecue panel in 2009, he steered us toward finer points of the subject, such as the use of electric vs. non-electric (acoustic?) knives to cut meat. And every year during SXSW, for as far back as I can remember, I always take a carload, or lead a caravan, of out-of-towners on the 45-minute pilgrimage out to Lockhart, which credibly claims to be the state's barbecue capital. I do this at least once, and sometimes two or three days, during the week, and we always go to Kreuz Market, because everybody, even the most uninformed visitor, knows that Kreuz is the best in town. And, likewise, everybody knows that Kreuz doesn't serve chicken. ■ John Morthland, author & journalist

Helter Skelter In A Spring Swelter

In 1994 I was asked to moderate a panel on the enduring (and perplexing) fascination among rock stars with mass-murderer Charles Manson. At the time, I was the editor of *Option*, an influential small magazine that covered indie rock, hip-hop, world music, jazz and all manner of the avant-garde. You'd think I would have been asked to do a fairly mundane panel on the state of independent music or the recent explosion of alternative rock. But no – I got Charles Manson.

That year, a fledgling shock-rocker from Florida, Marilyn Manson, put out his debut album featuring a reworked song the notorious mass murderer had written in the late '60s. Trent Reznor recorded much of Nine Inch Nails' now-classic *The Downward Spiral* in the infamous Sharon Tate house, where the Manson clan's bloodiest massacre occurred. The previous

year, Guns N' Roses had caused a stir when they included "Look At Your Game Girl," another song Charles Manson had written, on the their covers album *The Spaghetti Incident*. And a tiny indie label reissued the bootleg *LIE: The Love & Terror Cult*, a collection of songs Manson had recorded (in retrospect, meta-coincidentally) on September 11, 1967.

Those were just the most recent Manson-related rock happenings. The mass murderer's puzzling appeal stretched back to the Beach Boys, who recorded Manson's "Cease To Exist" (renamed "Never Learned Not To Love") for their 1969 album *20-20*, released seven months before the killings. And the appeal continued, with bands from Sonic Youth to the Lemonheads recording Manson-penned or Manson-related songs.

I began making calls for panel participants, first to the big guns: Would Axl Rose like to be on my panel? No. Trent Reznor? No. A member of Sonic Youth? No. How about a Beach Boy? No. Would Charles Manson like to sit in? No, he's, er, locked into another engagement for that date.

No problem. The crazy cast of characters I was able to round up was just fine. Marilyn Manson, who needed the exposure, agreed. So did Phil Kaufman, the zany road manager for Emmylou Harris, who not only was involved in stealing the late Gram Parsons' corpse and burning it in the desert, but also served time in prison with Manson (pre-murders). Rounding things out was my fellow rock scribe Gina Arnold, who was always good for an intelligent – or at least a humorously cynical – comment or two.

The room was packed with about a hundred curious audience members either intrigued or outraged that we were having such a discussion. Some of the more perceptive comments came from Marilyn Manson, who claimed his appropriation of the mass murderer's name was "more about the exploitation of my generation and my exposure to serial killers being elevated to celebrity status" than about shock value. (I said he was perceptive, not believable.) Manson had recorded at the Tate house, too, because he "wanted to see if there was some kind of vibe there."

Lots More Watching Basketball

It's the same story every year. An overhyped group of stars fall right on their face, with everybody watching. Spine-tingling thrills are delivered by a scruffy bunch of no-names who become the next big thing, however fleetingly. And if you're lucky, an old favorite whom you'd grown accustomed to dismissing steps up and surprises.

It's the NCAA basketball tournament – for some people, an annual SXSW tradition. One good thing about the festival showcases in non-rock hangouts is those venues have TVs, and lots of 'em. Thus it's possible to catch a band, then a score, then a few songs from another band, then those crucial last five minutes of a West Coast game.

But the truth is, attempting to do both SXSW and March Madness is like doing neither. Both events require an almost Clockwork Orangesque immersion, as you suspend all ordinary rituals of work, sleep and food for overstimulation and unreality, whether that means seeing 10 bands in 11 hours (between the daytime parties and the evening shows) or 32 games in 36. When you think about what the two events have to offer, it's really a toss-up – Nolan Richardson's ranting or Courtney Love's? The NCAA, or the RIAA? Dick Vitale, or Beatle Bob?

In 1995, the University of Texas hosted the first and second rounds at the Erwin Center. Hotel rooms were especially scarce. The only afternoon music I remember is the University of Memphis band, marching from the Hyatt lobby to the parking lot. I managed to catch four games out of six in person that weekend, which is probably why a quick glance through the '95 program book reveals few shows I actually remember. ■ Jason Cohen, *SXSW Scrapbook* co-editor

Kaufman, in biker attire with a bushy, David Crosby-style mustache, was the most entertaining panelist, reeling off wild stories about hanging with Manson and producing the *LIE* sessions. "I thought he had a good voice. I thought he sounded like a young Frankie Laine," Kaufman said, to nervous laughter. Kaufman claimed he later became a Manson target, and was spared death only because the killer got confused and ended up at the home of Leno and Rosemary LaBianca. (A similar rumor had Manson missing the home of record producer Terry Melcher and ending up at the Tate house.) When someone from the audience suggested Kaufman was merely exploiting Manson's horrific crimes to sell a book, Kaufman lashed back, "You say I'm exploiting him? He tried to kill me four times."

The best moment of black humor came from Marilyn Manson, concerned at the time that Interscope Records was wary of distributing his debut album, *Portrait Of An American Family*. "There is a ray of hope," he told the audience. "I didn't get a bunch of my girlfriends together to kill the record executive."

Interscope obviously did release *Portrait Of An American Family*, and Marilyn Manson became a superstar. Kaufman's book was adapted into a movie starring Johnny Knoxville, *Grand Theft Parsons*. Gina has since left the music-journalism racket. And I'm still sitting here writing.

Oh, and Charles Manson? He remains locked into that other engagement. ■ Mark Kemp, author & journalist

Creamed By Johnny Cash

In 1994, I was in a band called Some Kind Of Cream. We were from Laramie, WY. We sent our shitty cassette tape, titled *Eggnog For Invalids*, to the South by Southwest folks and were amazed that we got accepted to play. So, we skipped a week of classes at the University of Wyoming and hopped in our van and headed south. If I remember right, the SXSW folks described our music as an Allen/Farrow-esqe marriage of Janis Joplin and Sonic Youth. It doesn't sound good, right?

Anyway, we had the first slot at Emo's on Thursday. We drove all the way to Austin from Laramie with only a few hours of sleep in a motel that was also a halfway house, just outside of Amarillo. We literally barricaded the door to our room because we were terrified of all the pit bulls in the parking lot, people screaming at each other in adjoining rooms, and the ample supply of cocaine residue and cockroaches inside our room.

We got to Austin a day early, I think. So we hit up some random head shops. Everyone was amazed because every head shop was also a sex shop (and vice versa). It seemed like wherever we went there were X-rated comics, bongs and strap-on dildos. Needless to say, spirits were high.

Anyway, after talking to random perverts and stoners all over Austin, we started to realize that Emos was THE place to play. In fact, we were going to be playing in the first slot on opening night of SXSW. What's more, later on that evening, Beck was going to be playing on the same stage. So, in our minds, we were now *opening* for BECK!

I'll cut to the disappointment. We arrive at Emo's and get our shit set up on stage. There were loads of people in the joint. Then, moments before we start our set, it's announced that Johnny Cash will be playing a set on the outside stage at Emo's....RIGHT NOW! Instantly the crowd vanishes. We played our hearts out, but who can compete with Johnny Freaking Cash? Between us we broke at least 3-4 guitar strings, and the screw that held the strap on my bass popped out. So, it was a nightmare.

While loading up our gear, we kept saying, "Well, that sucked. But at least we get to see Beck." So, we load up our gear, grab a gyro from around the corner and head back to Emo's. The club is now at capacity and everyone at the door is looking at us like they have no idea who we are. Which, of course, they didn't. So, no Beck for us.

We moped around Sixth Street with our coveted SXSW passes and proceed to be kicked out of every club we attempted to enter. You see, only one of us was 21. We finally managed to gain entry to a sleazy dive bar and we watched a Doors cover band for an hour, while we cried into our beers. ■ **Shane Hickey, now of the Missoula, MT, band Volumen**

Velvets Guitarist Bashes Cash Over Pork

My favorite part of the night Pork played on the bill with Johnny Cash and Beck [Emo's, 1994] involved Sterling Morrison. Pork was his favorite band, and when Johnny Cash was added to the bill on short notice, Sterling was concerned. Shortly after the show started, he began complaining that "Johnny Cash is cutting into Pork's time." He told Mary from Pork that he was cutting into Pork's time and repeated it several times. Since he towered above most people, heads were turning. *"He's cutting into Pork's time!"*

Incidentally, because of the length of the show, he decided to step out for a bite to eat and come back for Pork. When he returned, he was among those who couldn't get back in. ■ Jeff Tartakov, manager of various Austin artists

Cashing In With Sterling

In 1994 I was writing for *The Austin Chronicle*, mostly about music and working at Waterloo Records which paid the rent. One of the benefits of both jobs was free admission to nearly any of the dozens of shows that came to town each year. Being on the *Chronicle* staff enabled me to get a badge for SXSW, and sometimes I was able to score an extra wristband or two.

But this year I was up against the wall. Johnny Cash was coming to promote his new *American Recordings* CD. Seeing Johnny Cash in concert was one of my unrealized dreams. The show wasn't officially part of SXSW, but was an industry-only-by-invitation event at Emo's. (The actual showcases later at Emo's that night included performances by my friends Dana, Edith and Mary of the band Pork, and some new kid named Beck.) That meant my badge wouldn't get me in. I was beside myself with anxiety.

It was a good thing that my friends Sterling Morrison and Gail Gant were driving up from Houston to stay with us (my roommate Dean Studeny and I) during SXSW. Sterling, of course, was the guitar player in the Velvet Underground. VU had reunited a year earlier and toured Europe, but Sterling and Gail weren't coming in any official capacity, just to see a bunch of shows and visit friends.

What to do? I was desperate, so I resorted to lies and deceit to get in to see Johnny Cash. At Waterloo Records I was able to contact the American Recordings label representative. I conveyed the message that Mr. Sterling Morrison of the Velvet Underground was coming to Austin and wanted to see Johnny Cash. And he was bringing friends.

In less than a day I got back confirmation that Sterling Morrison and party were added to the guest list. OK, that was done.

Now I really started getting scared.

Anyone who knew Sterling can attest to how intimidating he could be. Sterling was extremely intelligent and articulate, and he had no problem expressing a controversial idea or notion, especially if it was going to generate heated debate. I saw him play devil's advocate many times, but I never saw him once lose his temper. He had a very forceful, almost aggressive manner, and I suspected that his temper was probably pretty ferocious. I was afraid I was going to find out for sure.

So the day of the show, Gail and Sterling arrived, and I set them up in my bedroom where they would be sleeping. I waited until Sterling had a few Coronas in him before I fessed up. I was truly embarrassed and remorseful for what I'd done. I realized that I'd taken advantage of our friendship, but there are good ways to take advantage of something as rare as becoming friends with somebody famous, right? I mean, no one was getting hurt or anything, but if he saw it as some sort of betrayal or was hurt or mad, I would totally understand. Over the years Sterling and I had discussed my interviewing him or writing something about him. I had been approached several times by different publishers and editors, but ultimately decided that it might mess with the friendship. Sterling was willing to do it, I was not. I was, however, willing to involve him in my web of lies and deceit to get what I wanted. I felt like a total jerk.

I wasn't going to cry or anything, but I was very nervous. I just blurted out what I'd done. At first he didn't say anything...and then he said quietly, "Why would I want to see Johnny Cash?"

Last Stand At The Hotel

By 1994, South by Southwest was a going concern, and so was our young son Zeke. In those pre-Convention Center days, the conference was headquartered at the Hyatt Regency, where the core staff stayed for the run of the event. Zeke was a strapping almost-2-year-old with mad climbing skills, but at least he hadn't figured out how to open doors – or so I thought.

It was an unseasonably warm March afternoon and Zeke and I had returned to our room after a short break in the hotel pool. I'd just stripped us both out of our wet swimsuits and was standing naked at the bathroom sink when I heard the unmistakable click of a door latch opening behind me. Turning, I was just in time to see Zeke's bare butt tearing out the door onto the 14th floor of the Hyatt.

If you've ever stayed in a Hyatt, you know all rooms open onto an atrium – basically a giant abyss with a lobby at the bottom. The only thing between you and thin air is a flimsy, waist-high railing, easily scalable by the same monkey-child I'd recently found atop our dining room table leaping for the ceiling fan. No time to think, let alone dress. In a nanosecond, I was sprinting after him, stark naked in broad daylight, in full view of the entire Hyatt lobby.

Zeke was already six doors down and hustling like a racehorse when I snagged him. With his chubby wrist in a death grip, I turned back, only to see our room door with its automatic lock...slowly...swinging...closed. Hanging on to Zeke, I launched a flying goalie lunge toward our room, wedging the tip of one finger into the gap just before the lock clicked. As I pulled the door shut, I took one last peek around the lobby. Silence.

We've never stayed at the hotel again. ■ Susan Moffat, longtime SXSW staff & wife of co-founder Nick Barbaro

My response was, "Who cares if you want to see him. I want to see him." I wasn't quite sure what to expect, but I didn't expect him to start laughing. He was incredulous. He didn't seem to fully comprehend that his name had cachet. That his fame could be used to gain privileges...to get things done. This was a guy who'd been part of Andy Warhol's legendary Factory scene. It surprised me that even though he'd been close to the some of the biggest attention-whores ever – and I'm not just talking about Lou Reed – none of it had rubbed off on him.

So we all showed up at Emo's and the streets were packed with people hoping to get in. After a while I pushed past the lines and went up to the door. I told them that I was there with Sterling. The doorman acted like he didn't believe me. "Oh, right. So where is he?" I motioned everyone over and watched the doorman's eyes light up. "Right this way!" he said, opening a passage in the crowd for us to get in. "Goddamn," I said to Sterling, "do you get treated this way everywhere?" (knowing full well that he didn't). "I don't think so," was his response.

The show was very exciting. At first I was a little disappointed because Johnny Cash had mostly lost his voice and sounded terrible. But it didn't matter anyway because Sterling had met up with a friend, David Fricke, the music editor of

Rolling Stone, and they were yammering up a storm like two long-lost girlfriends trying to catch up. They were yakking so loudly that I couldn't hear much anyway. That was fine. I was just enjoying the whole circus all around. I was happy to be in the same room with Johnny Cash.

As they were leaving to drive back to Houston, Sterling told me, "Feel free to use my name anytime you need to." "Thanks, Sterling!" I told him, but of course I never did...not until now, at least. ■ **Stewart Wise, writer**

Alejandro Escovedo at La Zona Rosa

The first couple of years I attended SXSW in the early '90s, I was often asked, "Are you staying to see Alejandro on Sunday night?" As I grew to become a deeper and deeper fan of Escovedo's work, the question turned to, "Why aren't you staying to see Al at La Zona Rosa?" My answer, about needing to return to work, normal life, sobriety, et al., eventually gave way to, "Wouldn't miss it for the world."

Alejandro's Sunday night sets at La Zona Rosa marked both the official and spiritual end of the festival, a show for the die-hards, the locals, the staff, the hung-overs and anyone else who just wasn't ready to let South By go for another year. The Sunday performances began in 1991, the year before the release of Escovedo's first solo masterpiece, *Gravity*, and continued through 1999, skipping only 1996 when a "proper" showcase at the Austin Music Hall took its place in support of his third solo album, *With These Hands*. While the tradition continued into the next century with gigs at the Continental Club, his '90s run was musically unforgettable.

On these special nights, Alejandro would augment his core band of the moment with string and horn sections, second drummers and percussionists, hired guns, friends, even strangers, to become the mighty Alejandro Escovedo Orchestra, pushing the stage to around 15 musicians in any given year. "Bill McCullough on the pedal steel," Alejandro says in the band introductions on a tape of the 1997 show. "Just met Bill the other day."

The One And Only Doug The Slug

Over the years, I found myself in situations, numerous times, when people (or groups of people) were threatening to beat me up. I'd known Doug since he had been a bouncer at the Cave Club on Red River, and I'd watched him win some pretty ugly fights. That's how he got his nickname. So when he volunteered one year, I recruited him to watch my back.

Doug (real name: Charles Gunning) had landed a memorable part in the movie *Slacker* and had moved to Hollywood, where he picked up parts (usually as a thug) playing everything from a gunsel in *Miller's Crossing* to an alien thug in *Star Trek: The Next Generation*. Since his acting career was less than full-time, he'd come home to work on SXSW.

A lot of what we did at night in the early days was go around to clubs to help sort out long lines, and help get our people into the clubs. One night we were on Sixth Street and we'd been talking to one of our cashiers, a cute girl who Doug was flirting with, as was his nature. We were about to leave when a drunken street kid that the cashier had just turned away suddenly threw a full can of beer at her head, barely missing her.

Doug leapt into action without hesitation (one of the reasons I kept him with me) and grabbed the kid in a headlock. While patiently explaining to the kid why he was in trouble and why he needed to learn to behave, Doug was ramming the kid's head into an iron fence repeatedly. Finally, the kid turned his head and looked up at Doug and said in an awe-filled voice: "Wow, man, you're the dude from *Slacker!*"

Doug and I laughed so hard, the kid squirmed out of Doug's grip and ran away. Doug passed away in 2002. ■ **Roland Swenson, SXSW co-founder & managing director**

The resulting scope of his musical assemblage was nothing short of epic, as *No Depression* co-founder Peter Blackstock reflected in an interview with the blog Purple State of Mind: "[Alejandro's] emotional expressiveness and his direction of the sonic maelstrom...put him in a league with the great bandleaders of that century."

Sets such as the one on March 16, 1997, spanned the utterly delicate "Thirteen Years Theme," plinked by the string section, to the cacophonous din of The Stooges' "I Wanna Be Your Dog," a visceral highlight at every show in the run. Covers like "Dog" were cornerstones of the Sunday night sets: Over the course of the decade, the Orchestra assayed Neil Young's "Like A Hurricane" (in 1995 with guests Howe Gelb and Scott McCaughey), the Velvet Underground's "Foggy Notion" and "Pale Blue Eyes," Lou Reed's "Street Hassle," Mick Jagger's "Evening Gown" and John Cale's "Amsterdam," among others.

Escovedo also used the shows as an opportunity to revisit a musical past that is inextricably tied to Austin, going back to True Believers material such as "Rebel Kind," "Hard Road" and "The Rain Won't Help You When Its Over." A reunited Buick MacKane (introduced by Escovedo as "the most hated band in Austin, Texas") even took the encore spotlight in 1997, opening with a killer cover of David Bowie/Mott The Hoople's "All The Young Dudes."

My own personal highlight came on March 22, 1998, when Alejandro name-checked my partner Bob Whitfield and me for our work on his live album, *More Miles Than Money*, released just a few weeks earlier. That particular performance ended well into Monday morning with an elegiac version of a cover song featured on *Miles*, the Rolling Stones' "Sway," which closed more than a few of the shows. Each musician took their bow and exited the stage while the rest of the band kept playing until all that was left was the string section – the Alejandro Escovedo Orchestra built up for one night every year, then taken back apart piece by piece, musician by musician, until next time.

■ Erik Flannigan, Comedy Central

Standing In The Blue Shadows

I'm standing in front of the Santa Fe club in Austin in 1994. It is warm and humid, at least to my Canadian expectations for how warm March should be. Standing next to me is Dave Chesney, and because of my proximity to him, I find myself momentarily at the eye of a music business hurricane. Hands are reaching out of Sixth Street's dimness, either pressing business cards toward Chesney or grasping with open hands, attempting to pry from him a promo copy of *On The Floor of Heaven*, the debut album by the act Chesney manages, the Blue Shadows. Just a few moments before, the group had performed an expertly executed set. On the sidewalk, on this night, Shadowmania has erupted.

The group formed in Vancouver with '60s teen heartthrob Billy Cowsill (you may remember him from the Cowsills' bubblegum anthem "The Rain, The Park & Other Things"), veteran Canadian roots rocker Jeffrey Hatcher, drummer J.B. Johnson and bassist Barry Muir. Their sound was like newly unearthed Beatles sessions recorded in

From SXSW To NXNE

As a club booker in Toronto, I had developed a love of the Austin music scene and all the cool music that was coming out of that area – Alejandro Escovedo, W.C. Clark, Chris Duarte to name a few. Through them, I had heard about this really cool festival in Austin, and decided to go to it in 1992. I have only missed one year since then.

A little while later, more and more people from Toronto were beginning to discover the festival, including Michael Hollett and Andy McLean. Michael and I had a conversation about how cool it would be to start something like that in Canada. Louis, Roland and Nick came to Toronto to meet with Michael, Andy and me. We took them to the Queen Street strip to let them see that the club setup was similar, only on a much smaller scale, to Austin's Sixth Street. They were excited about the prospect right away. We launched North by Northeast in 1995; now in its 17th year, it's the little sister to SXSW.

Some of the things that stand out to me from early days of SXSW: Seeing Doug Sahm in all his cowboy finery at the Broken Spoke… Steamboat, where I went to see Charlie Sexton and Doyle Bramhall's new band, the Arc Angels. At the end of his set, Charlie threw his guitar toward my direction, and just missed my head – that's rock 'n' roll, baby!…Seeing Welsh band Catatonia, with Cerys Matthews singing while pouring beer down her throat, neck and front while reeling about quite sloshed…Being at the packed show by Stereophonics, who were at that time the biggest band in the U.K., at Maggie Mae's; they took up half their set time to set up their stage, therefore getting the chop when they were only halfway through their set. The drummer (now deceased) threw his drumsticks and swore a lot at the stage manager!

The crowds have now multiplied massively at SXSW, and it still shocks me to think how it's grown in the last 6-10 years. In the early days, I rarely saw anyone I knew from Toronto, and now every other person seems to be someone I know – everyone giddy with excitement at being there. It's the holy grail of live music. ■ Yvonne Matsell, NXNE Director

Bradley's Barn. Hatcher and Cowsill harmonized like the Everlys, and as writers, they shed great songs like a dog sheds hair. The Blue Shadows raised some dust in Canada, despite radio's fixation on line dancing, Garth Brooks and Shania Twain. Nashville had already passed (said one label exec to Chesney: "I love this band, but they scare me"). In the weeks leading to SXSW, the sense in the Blue Shadows camp was that Austin would get it. And, with the band still onstage breaking down gear, all evidence here on the sidewalk in front of the club seemed to suggest that on a night where everyone was on the lookout for that breakthrough buzzband moment…*something* had just happened: that often-sought convergence of musical accomplishment, commercial opportunity and hipster zeitgeist.

Across the city and across the week, I had the opportunity to see some impressive performances. After sitting next to Sam Phillips and T Bone Burnett at Miguel's, I watched her play an open-air set. I heard the Mavericks, the Continental Drifters (featuring Cowsill's sister Susan), and Junior Brown at the Continental. I saw Roky Erickson shopping for guitars. Kelly Willis, with Lucinda Williams watching offstage, told the crowd she'd just been dumped by her label. Still, it's that giddy swarm of industry insiders outside the club on Sixth Street, besieging Chesney and beseeching his attention, that lingers in my memory.

History would prove SXSW was not a turning point for the Blue Shadows. They released one more album in Canada, then broke up. Cowsill, 58, passed away in Calgary in 2006. After being out of print for more than a decade, *On The Floor Of Heaven* was reissued in 2010 to broader acclaim than it received the first time around. ■ **Paul Cantin, journalist, Toronto**

Watching The Wheels Go Round And Round

SXSW first appeared in my life in 1993. The landscape was different then: There were ashtrays everywhere, but very few cell phones. There were also many more record deals around. A&M Records (which had been by swallowed by Polygram, but was still visibly writhing in its belly) flew me down to Austin on a jet plane, with ashtrays, to stay in the Four Seasons for four days while I hung out with some of the R.E.M. camp, read the sleevenotes to my forthcoming album aloud in a coffee shop, and visited Jody Denberg on-air at KGSR. Brunch was always at Las Manitas on Congress, where you could watch the tattoos and baseball caps on the *SPIN* writers and A&R people as you absorbed high quality huevos rancheros. This pattern mutated over the years, but remained as different elements swelled or dwindled.

In 1993, Mike Mills and I played a very crowded in-store at Waterloo Records, performing some R.E.M. songs, some of mine, and "Mrs. Robinson" with Jules Shear. *Automatic For The People* was still on the charts, and R.E.M. were at their zenith. My records never troubled *Billboard*, but the "core demographic" of our listeners overlapped: if you liked my songs, you probably liked R.E.M.'s, and vice versa. The other social pillar of R.E.M., their then-manager, Jefferson Holt, was also in town, and took me along to see Ringo, a British act newly signed to his Doggone label. Neither Doggone nor Ringo lasted for long, but their frontman, Tim Keegan, became a dear friend and musical accomplice. Tim and I played at SXSW in 1998 when Jonathan Demme's *Storefront Hitchcock* premiered at SXSW Film.

You Never Know What You're Gonna Get

The best thing about SXSW is simply walking down the street and seeing people you consider friends but whom you only see, and look forward to seeing, year after year at SXSW. You might bump into them elsewhere (a sticky dressing room, a service station), but you know you're going to see them in Austin. You've known them for 20 or so years at this point; they're good friends by default. And I don't even consider myself a veteran of the SXSW scene. There had been a few of them before I even got to America.

The best night I ever had, gig-wise, was a lovely show with Graham Parker, Marshall Crenshaw, Robyn Hitchcock and David Lewis at the Union Ballroom at the University of Texas in 1995; everything just seemed to flow seamlessly from one thing into the other. But the gigs aren't normally like that; that happened to be the right venue for the right show. The other best gig was also the right venue for the right show, but only by chance: with Robyn and Ken Stringfellow at a Mexican restaurant in the middle of the afternoon.

And between those two winners are all the other gigs and guest appearances, planned and otherwise, rehearsed and otherwise, invited or otherwise. The funniest thing last time was playing Radiohead songs with Amanda Palmer to the waiting line, while Quincy Jones went overtime in the hall we were waiting to do our panel in. It made the national news for some reason. And that's SXSW in a nutshell.

If you want the true SXSW experience, just walk down the street with Eugene Mirman, who enjoys a level of fame in Austin at that particular time of year that is truly mind-boggling and unreplicatable anywhere else in the world at any other time. And the other real SXSW experience in recent years was Dag Juhlin, who wasn't even there, sending fake tweets from Woodstock, Illinois. I saved these somewhere. They're genius. Look them up. *[Editors' note: You'll find a bunch of them on page 241.]* ■ John Wesley Harding, musician

Waterloo Records is still there, thankfully, like our red phoneboxes (they have one outside the store) – a vestige of a different age: in this case, the age of record sales. Jefferson left R.E.M. in 1996. Mike is still with them, and we groove together whenever we can, unto senility. KGSR has moved house, winding up on an immaculately hard-to-reach portion of I-35. Jody departed in 2009, but can now be found back inside the city, on-air at KUT. He's an empathic interviewer, and we've had some truly emerald sessions over years, even without reverb. Which they do have at KUT. He is another dear friend and Beatle person, who faithfully clues me in on his front-line encounters with McCartney, Yoko, and Sean Lennon.

In terms of swelling and dwindling, SXSW – or "South-By" to its habitués – has swelled unto bursting. In 1993, a leisurely trail of post-'80s "alternative" music people, mostly between 25 and 40, meandered like relaxed ants through the Texan spring. Las Manitas could accomodate them all for breakfast. By 2007 (my most recent visit), there was a solid mass of groovers from 20 to 60, wedged into Sixth Street and beyond, queuing for shows from Stubb's to La Zona Rosa, and Las

Manitas was closing down. This gradual overloading of humanity is becoming a problem: More often than not when I pop the question "Going to SXSW next year?", the person to whom this question is popped replies that it's getting just too darned crowded. Or are we just getting too darned old?

I've had many roles at SXSW, from being The Man Who Played Every Night to designing the give-away bag to officiating at the wedding of Jason Cohen and Susan Shepard. At last, I'm a minister of The Church Of The Universal Mind in Arizona. I've watched the ashtrays vanish, and the cell phones multiply. I've seen rock music become history-driven. What I've enjoyed most about SXSW is just schmoozing; every year you can meet the same person and get to know them a little better. Maybe after 10 years or so you'll actually seek them out, or meet them on their home territory. Or you can pull away gently if you feel they're not for you. In the hypnotic wheel of human traffic, South by Southwest so rules.

And special thanks to Holly Everett. ■ **Robyn Hitchcock, musician**

How SXSW 1996 And Imperial Teen Saved My Life

Like so many self-absorbed artists, I've spent countless hours contemplating death. Not the ordinary questions, like is there an afterlife. I'm talking important topics, like who goes where on the graveside seating chart, and which ABBA ballad will open the maximum number of tear ducts as a recessional.

I haven't actually reached any concrete conclusions. Like so many self-absorbed artists, I let process trump product. There is no envelope containing neatly typed funeral instructions tucked under my desk blotter. My family will bury me in an ill-fitting navy blue suit, and turn away Michael Musto. This failure is all too real at the moment, because right now, midair between DFW and JFK airports, I am having a coronary.

I cannot catch my breath, and the constriction in my chest grows tighter with each passing moment. When Kelly Marie cooed "my heart it beats like a drum" on her 1980 disco hit "Feels Like I'm In Love," she sounded so exuberant. Trust me, Kelly, palpitations like these are nothing to sing about. Especially on a Sunday afternoon, when you're crammed into a middle seat on a 747 at full capacity.

What a rotten way to wrap up South by Southwest.

I'm not really dying, of course, and a small part of me knows that. The hysterical teenager that governs my frontal lobe, the one responsible for the tenor of most of my published prose, may be convinced that my demise is imminent, but a calm, quiet voice further in back keeps repeating the truth: This is only a panic attack. I'm not a case study in early onset heart disease. I just don't want to step off this plane and be back in New York City.

Damn it, the past few days have been splendid. I saw Mark Eitzel and Girls Against Boys, and apple-cheeked Mary Lou Lord busking for change in front of a bank. A cute guy from Warner Bros. gave me his home phone number. My Manhattan non-music clique can't fathom why I travel to Texas to engage in the same pastimes I do in New York – watching bands, drinking too much, flirting – but this is spring break for my industry. There are more bands, an endless flow of beer and tequila, outdoor pools. People come from all over the world to participate. SXSW 1996 has reminded me, once again, that my shabby little life can be pretty sweet. It can't end now. Not like this. Not in coach.

Internal hostage negotiations commence. I can't ask the pilot to turn the plane around – hell, I'm too freaked out to buzz the flight attendant for a cup of water – so I do the next best thing, and cut myself a deal: If I just relax and resume normal breathing, when I get back to my apartment, I will investigate options for leaving New York permanently.

A week ago, such an idea would've been heresy. New York is the center of the universe. Yet for the second year in a row, South by Southwest has showed me otherwise. Not that I'm planning to relocate to Austin. As thrilling as daily Mexican food for breakfast may sound, I know even the most liberal town in Texas isn't the right place to settle down year-round. But at the parties, shows and panels of South by Southwest, I have bonded with colleagues from Cleveland, Milwaukee and Minneapolis. There are good bands who call Phoenix home. SXSW teems with proof that it is possible to be part of this business without living in a fourth-floor East Village walk-up.

Frankly, that sounds mighty appealing. I'm a few weeks shy of my 29th birthday, and do not wish to be sleeping on a dingy futon when I'm 30. I have managed to carve out a full-time freelance writing career, but it seems increasingly unsustainable in New York. I grow weary of copying my imaginary lawyer on past-due invoices, drawing cash advances

against credit cards to make rent. If I must keep deluding myself that an adult can earn a living cranking out endless front-of-book items on Lotion, Kittywinder, and the latest Grand Royal side projects, let me at least do it someplace where decent water pressure is a right, not a privilege.

Besides, I have a new favorite band. I refuse to entertain the notion of dying until their debut album hits stores. I want my friends in New York to hear them before I leave.

Like this midair meltdown, Imperial Teen completely blindsided me, even though an advance cassette of their debut album, *Seasick*, was mailed to me weeks ago. I took one look at the press release, saw something about the lineup including a member of Faith No More, cursed whomever at MTV's *120 Minutes* was responsible for programming "We Care A Lot" during valuable airtime that could've been allotted to Wolfgang Press, and tossed it aside. Nevertheless, I'm fond of the band's publicist, a diminutive Goth with a penchant for vintage party dresses. There is a very strong likelihood that she will be laid off from her job soon, a victim of label mergers, and I want to show her my support. So when Imperial Teen takes the stage at the annual "Hacks & Flacks" pre-conference kickoff party for journalists and PR folks, I actually pay attention.

They have a boy-girl-boy-girl lineup, a classic pop archetype that gets me every time. Their set opens with a seething, slow-burner called "Imperial Teen" (same as the band's name). By the final chorus, it has bumped Boyce & Hart's "The Monkees" to #2 on my list of all-time favorite theme songs. They switch instruments, drummer Lynn Perko stepping up to the front for "Balloon" while guitarist Roddy Bottum keeps time. Everyone shares vocal duties. When Roddy casually tosses off the lyric "you kiss me like a man, boy" at the climax of "You're One," my inner teenager starts going berserk. The next morning, I call one of my editors back in New York and beg her to let me write a story. Fuck the Matador party; where is the next Imperial Teen gig? I see them three times that week, and chat up the band members every chance I get.

When we sit down in the lobby of the Austin Hyatt to conduct our interview, Roddy is wearing mirrored sunglasses and a tight white T-shirt emblazoned with the word "Master." The band is seated at a long conference table. In this formal setting, they seem strangely reserved. It takes a few minutes to realize they simply haven't done much press; they're still aware of how artificial this situation is, fielding questions about their music from someone they barely know. But once the ice is broken, it's clear I've chosen my new favorite band well.

"I think things in popular music tend to get a little self-conscious, and a little too prefabricated," says Roddy, apropos of where he sees Imperial Teen in a landscape lousy with cookie-cutter alt-rock bands. "I'd like to think that we act sort of impulsively – and naively – and jump into things without thinking about them too much."

"There just doesn't seem to be much vulnerability out there," adds Will Schwartz. "I think making yourself vulnerable exudes a kind of danger."

These comments rush back to me as I slowly regain composure and my plane touches down at JFK. It is time to act impulsively, to make myself vulnerable. The next day, I call Imperial Teen's publicist in Los Angeles, ostensibly to ask about artwork for the story. As anticipated, she has returned home to a pink slip. Unlike me, my friend has an escape plan. She has already laid the seeds to relocate to Seattle and go indie. Do I want to join her?

Almost everyone is dumbfounded when I announce that I'm moving across the country, to a city I've only visited once, to share a house with a woman I know primarily from two visits to SXSW. But that summer, as I drive across the nation in a yellow Ryder rental truck, enjoying the hospitality of editors and writers in the "flyover states" at every stop along the way, I know I've made a smart decision.

"Everything we're doing, we're doing as beginners, and I'd like to keep that perspective on it," concluded Roddy at the end of that first Imperial Teen chat. "Without our sense of naïveté and freshness, we could be like any other band. That's what separates us from a lot of people. We're doing stuff for the learning adventure."

My best friend from New York insists on accompanying me on my cross-country odyssey. After subjecting her to one too many drum-and-bass mix tapes on day two, she makes a new rule that we can only listen to music that one or both of us can sing along with. By the time we pull into the driveway of my new Seattle home, we have both committed *Seasick* to memory. Fifteen years later, it's still my favorite Imperial Teen album. Please play it at my funeral. ■ **Kurt B. Reighley, journalist**

Tary Owens with the Grey Ghost at the keynote prelude (1992)

Texas Monthly (1995) ❯

The maestro of new **Music**

Roland Swenson

LONG BEFORE THE FIRST NOTE was played, Roland Swenson knew that this year's South by Southwest Music and Media Conference (SXSW) would be different. It wasn't the 4,700 registrants or the more than 20,000 anticipated clubgoers that impressed SXSW's 39-year-old managing director. Nor was it the number of bands playing: an astounding 550 acts crammed into dozens of Austin venues over four nights. Nor was it SXSW's roster of corporate sponsors, which included *Entertainment Weekly* magazine and high-tech giant Microsoft. To Swenson, the real sign that the event had taken on a

life of its own came when University of Texas athletic director DeLoss Dodds announced that the school might not bid to host the regionals of the 1996 NCAA basketball tournament, which fall on the same weekend, for fear that SXSW will hog all the hotel rooms between Waco and San Antonio. "I think he wanted us to move out of the way," Swenson says with a shrug.

Pretty cool for a guy who can't play a lick of guitar, has no rhythm, and wears the squarest clothes ever to grace a back-

Each spring, the founder of Austin's South by Southwest brings together 25,000 of the world's coolest people for a rock and roll fantasy camp.

by Joe Nick Patoski

stage dressing room—but not that surprising, considering the past success of SXSW. Indeed, in the eight years since Swenson founded the music festival–convention–trade show, it has grown into an alternative rite of spring. During the second week of March, record company executives, talent scouts, and other tastemakers spend their days playing golf and softball, consuming copious amounts of Mexican food and barbecue, and drinking gallons of beer and margaritas while schmoozing, making deals, and participating in panel discussions with titles like "Touring the Modern World" and "Why Radio Hates You." Musicians and fans, meanwhile, hang out at a sort of rock and roll fantasy camp where no one seems to have a day job and jamming is a way of life. At night, these groups converge to sweat and shake together at concerts by hip bands like Soul Asylum, Veruca Salt, and Blues Traveler; living legends like Johnny Cash, Flaco Jimenez, and Little Milton; and hundreds of hopefuls from Austin, from elsewhere in Texas, from other states, and from Russia, Germany, the Netherlands, [CONTINUED ON PAGE 190]

Joining the club: After eight years, Swenson is a true impresario.

TEXAS MONTHLY **117**

© 1992 R.Eud Beggf

SXSW panel in the Hyatt Ballroom (1992)

Roky Erickson at the Austin Music Awards (1993)

Johnny Cash at the keynote (1994) >

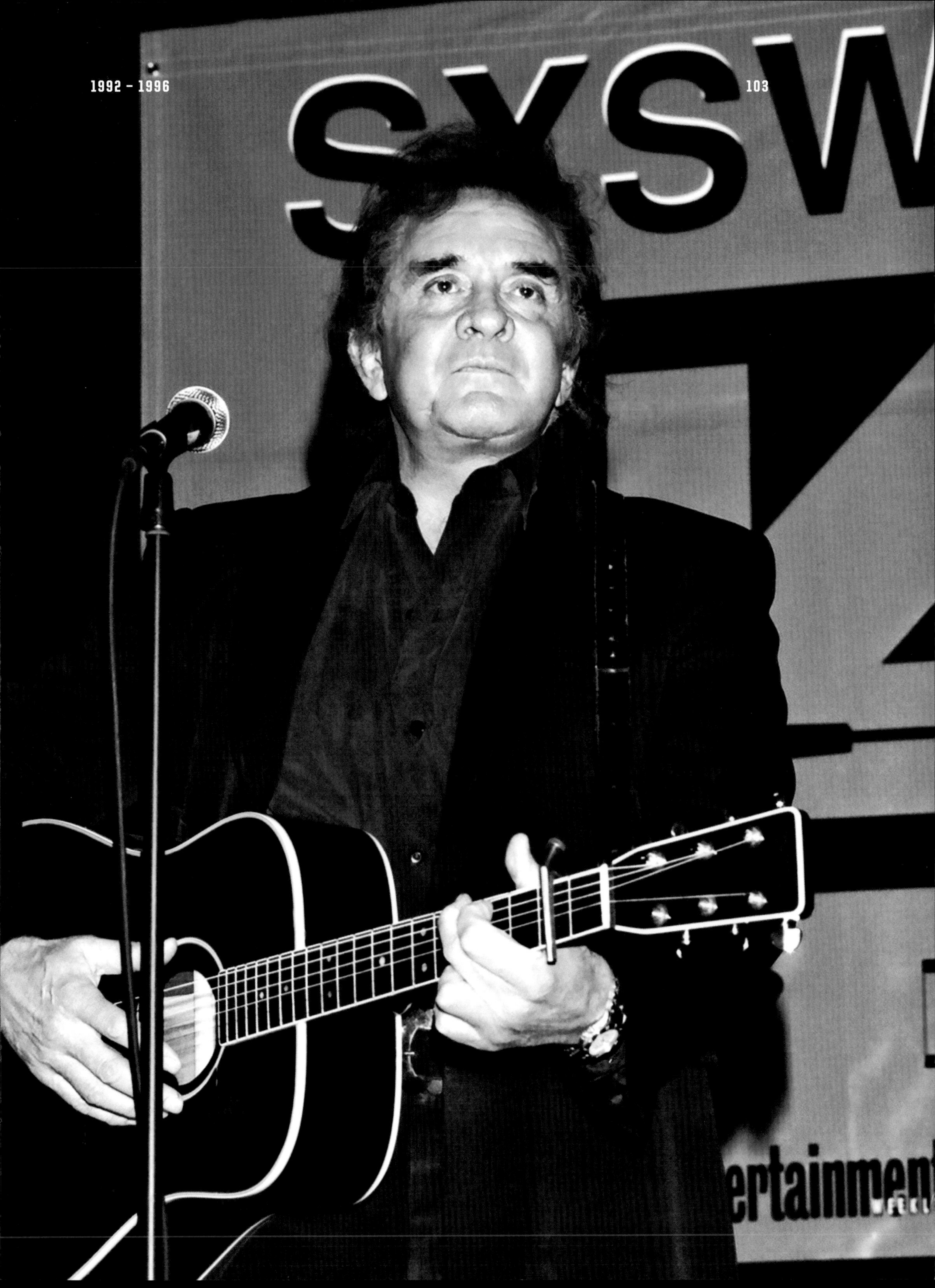
SXSW
ertainment

SXSW staff (1994)

R.E.M./ATHENS, LTD.
30601
POST OFFICE BOX 8010
ATHENS, GEORGIA 30603
TELEPHONE (706) 353-8899

March
Twenty-Fifth
1993

Roland Swenson
South By Southwest
P.O. Box 4999
Austin, Texas 78765

Dear Roland,

    Just wanted to drop you a note thanking you for all of the
help you gave Mike, Brooke, Rachel, Jennifer and me.

    This year's SXSW was the best one yet and everyone I have
spoken to has agreed. The new location was cool and I am already
looking forward to next year's.

    Thanks again, Roland, and best regards.

                                    Sincerely,

                                    W. Jefferson Holt
                                    W. Jefferson Holt

WJH/mw

SXSW staffers Mike Shea, Jo Rae DiMenno
with Johnny Cash (1994)

Beck at Emo's (1994)

Little Village at the Terrace
(1992)
Russia's Limpopo at Saxon Pub
(1994)
Hanson at the softball game
(1994)
Arlo Guthrie at the State Theatre
(1996)

continued from page 85

IV Thieves (Nic Armstrong)
Ivan & Alyosha
Ivan Neville's Dumpstaphunk
Ivan Pedersen
Izrael

J

J Church
J Davey
J Elliott
J Kapone
J Mascis
J Mascis and The Fog
J Rocc
J Roddy Walston And The Business
J.
J. Capone
J. Cole
JJ Fresh
J. Matthew Gerken
J. Pounders
J. Tillman
J.A.M.O.N.
J.B
J.C. Hopkins
J.D. Foster
J.R. Castillo
J.W. Roy & the One Night Band
Jaakko & Jay
Jabarvy
Jabbering Trout
Jabe
Jack
Jack Beats
Jack Brothers
Jack Drag
Jack Harris
Jack Ingram
Jack L.
Jack Oblivian and the Tennessee Tearjerkers
Jack Officers
Jack Penate
Jack Rose
Jack Savoretti
Jack Tempchin
Jack West & Curvature
Jack Wiseman Affair
Jackass
Jackie Bristow
Jackie Greene
Jackie Leven
Jackie Oates
Jackie Ono
Jack-O-Pierce
Jackpot
Jackrabbit King
Jack's Mannequin
Jaco
Jacob Fred Jazz Odyssey
Jacob Golden
Jacob Steele
Jacob's Ladder
Jacque "Jaxon" Patterson
Jacqueline Specht
Jacques and the Shakey Boys
Jacques Renault & Justin Miller
Jad Fair & Jason Willett
Jad Fair & Lumberob
Jad Fair and Special Guest
Jad Fair with Phono-comb
Jade
Jade Day
Jade McNelis
Jaewon
Jaguar Love
Jah Sun
Jah Warrior Shelter Hi-Fi
Jahcoozi
Jahdan Blakkamoore
Jai Alai
Jai Uttal & the Pagan Love Orchestra
Jail Guitar Doors featuring Wayne Kramer, Billy Bragg, Tom Morello, Chris Shiflett and others tba
Jail Weddings
Jaill
Jaime Y Los Chamacos
Jake Andrews
Jake Andrews Band
Jake Brennan
Jake Brennan and the Confidence Men
Jake One
Jakob
Jakob Dylan and Three Legs (Featuring Neko Case and Kelly Hogan)

Joan Jett (2004)

Jakobinarina
Jam Pain Society
Jam Session
Jamalski
Jambo
James Blunt
James Cotton w/Jimmie Vaughan & Lou Ann Barton
James Hall
James Hand
James Hand & Band
James Harries
James Husband
James Hyland & South Austin Jug Band
James Intveld
James Keelaghan
James Kinney
James McMurtry
James Orr Complex
James Polk
James Polk Trio
James T. Slater
James Talley
James Yuill
Jamie Cullum
Jamie Hartford
Jamie Kennedy
Jamie T
JamisonParker
Jammer
Jamtron
Jan Matney
Jana Hunter
Janah
Jandek
Jane & Julia
Jane Begley
Jane Bond
Jane Gillman/Darcie Deaville
Jane Jensen
Jane Kelly Williams
Janeane Garofalo
Janelle Monae
Janet Lynn
Janet Lynn Band
Janice Giovanetti
Janie & the Little Darlings
Janis Eighteen
Janis Figure
Janis Ian
Janne Haavisto & the Farangs
Japancakes
Japandroids
Japanic
Japanther
Jape
Jarboe
Jared Paul
Jarvis Cocker
Jasmine Solano
Jasmine Star
Jason & Alison
Jason & the Scorchers
Jason Allen
Jason Bentley
Jason Carney & Tara Sheth
Jason Collett
Jason Dunne
Jason Eady
Jason Eklund
Jason Falkner
Jason Feddy
Jason Forrest
Jason Isbell
Jason Isbell and the 400 Unit
Jason Luckett
Jason Lytle
Jason Moran
Jason Morphew
Jason Mraz with Raul Midon
Jason Reeves
Jason Scott
Jason Simon
Jason Walker & the Last Drinks
Jason Woliner
Jason Yates
Jasper Stone
Jauns M ness
Javelin
Javelin Boot
Javelins
Javier Escovedo
Javier Galvan Y Fama
Jawbone
Jay Aaron
Jay Bennett
Jay Chevalier and the Haunted Hearts
Jay Electronica
Jay Eric
Jay Farrar
Jay Jay Pistolet
Jay Nash
Jay Reatard
Jay Rock
Jay Semko
Jaymay
Jazz One
Jazz Passengers (featuring Deborah Harry)
Jazz Pharaohs
Jazz PR
Jazzy Jay

Jazzie Redd
JBM
J-Boogie
JC & Co.
JD Natasha
Je Suis France
Jean Caffeine
Jean Caffeine's All-Nite Truckstop
Jean Grae
Jean-Louis Mahjun
Jeanne-Marie Houston
Jeb Loy Nichols
Jedd Hughes
Jedi Mind Tricks
Jeff
Jeff Anderson
Jeff Beck
Jeff Black
Jeff Finlin
Jeff Graham
Jeff Hanson
Jeff Hughes & Chaparral
Jeff Klein
Jeff Krebs
Jeff Lang
Jeff McDaniel
Jeff Meyers
Jeff Plankenhorn
Jeff Romeo
JEFF The Brotherhood
Jeff Trott
Jeff2
Jefferson Pitcher
Jeffrey Foucault
Jeffrey Lewis
Jeffrey Lewis & The Jitters
Jeffrey Steele
Jehova Waitress
Jello Biafra
Jello Biafra (spoken word)
Jen Foster
Jen Lane
Jen Wood
Jenai
Jenifer Jackson
Jenn Grant
Jennifer Cook
Jennifer Gentle
Jennifer Glass
Jennifer Howe
Jennifer Knapp
Jennifer O'Connor
Jennifer Y Los Jetz
Jenny Hoyston
Jenny Hoyston's Paradise Island
Jenny Owen Youngs
Jenny Reynolds
Jenny Toomey
Jenny Whiteley
Jennyanykind
Jens Lekman
Jerel
Jeremy Fisher
Jeremy Jay
Jeremy Larson
Jeremy Messersmith
Jeremy Neal
Jeremy Toback
Jeremy Warmsley
Jerkuleez
Jern Eye
Jerome Cox
Jerry Alfred & the Medicine Beat
Jerry Cantrell
Jerry Douglas
Jerry Giddens
Jerry Jeff Walker
Jerry Joseph & the Jackmorons
Jerry Lightfoot & the Essentials with Jerry Lacroix
Jerry Sires
Jerry Sires and the Stallions
Jerry Sires Band
Jesca Hoop
Jess Klein
Jess Lee & the Honky Tonk Men
Jesse Dangerously
Jesse Dayton
Jesse Dayton as Captain Clegg
Jesse DeNatale
Jesse 'Guitar' Taylor & John 'X' Reed
Jesse Harris
Jesse Harris & The Ferdinandos
Jesse Malin
Jesse Sublett
Jesse Sykes & the Sweet Hereafter
Jesse Taylor
Jesse Taylor & Junior Medlow
Jesse Woods
Jessi Alexander
Jessi Colter
Jessica 6
Jessica Fichot
Jessica Lea Mayfield
Jessica Lurie
Jessie and Layla
Jessie Baylin
Jessie Frye

Jessy Moss
Jessy Serrata & the New Wave Band
Jester
JESU
Jesus Christ Superfly
Jesus Christ Superstar
Jesus Chrysler Supercar
Jesus Makes the Shotgun Sound
Jet Black Joe
Jet By Day
Jet Fugu
Jet Horns
Jet Lag
Jet Lag Gemini
Jetpack
Jets Overhead
Jets To Brazil
Jetscreamer
JFJ
Jibe
Jill Barber
Jill Sobule
Jim and Jennie and the Pinetops
Jim Bianco
Jim Boggia
Jim Bryson
Jim Campilongo & the 10 Gallon Cats
Jim Campilongo Trio
Jim Cuddy
Jim Dewan
Jim Dickinson
Jim Dickinson and Delta X
Jim Greer
Jim Guthrie
Jim Heald
Jim Infantino
Jim James
Jim Lauderdale
Jim Lauderdale & Pete Anderson
Jim Lauderdale, Radney Foster and Jeff Black in the Round
Jim Montgomery
Jim Moray
Jim Noir
Jim Roll
Jim Stringer
Jim Suhler and Monkey Beat
Jim Volk
Jim Weider
Jim White
Jim Yoshii Pile-Up
Jimbo Mathus Knock Down Society
Jimi Dyson Blues Band
Jimmie Dale Gilmore
Jimmie Dale Gilmore & the Continental Drifters w/ Katy Moffatt
Jimmie Gilmore Band
Jimmie Roulette
Jimmie Vaughan
Jimmie Wood & the Immortals
Jimmy Carl Black
Jimmy Carl Black & the Grandmothers
Jimmy Chamberlin Complex
Jimmy Davis
Jimmy Eat World
Jimmy Elledge Band
Jimmy Gnecco
Jimmy LaFave
Jimmy LaFave & Night Tribe
Jimmy LaFave Band
Jimmy Rankin
Jimmy Rogers
Jimmy Ryan
Jimmy Tittle
Jimmy Walsh
Jimmy Webb
Jimmy Webb And The Webb Brothers
JinnyOops!
Jinx Crossing
jj
JJ Grey and MOFRO
JJ Paradise Players Club
JL Stiles
Jo Carol Pierce
Jo Mango
Joan as Police Woman
Joan Jett and The Blackhearts
Joan of Arc
Joan Osborne
Joanna Carter
Joanna Connor
Joanna Cotten
Joanna Newsom
Joaquin Diaz
Joaquina
Jody Hughes
Jody Lazo
Joe B.
Joe Bidewell & Blake Travis
Joe Butcher
Joe Christmas
Joe Doucet
Joe Ely
Joe Ely & Friends
Joe Ely and Joel Guzman w/ Special Guests

Joe Ely, Joel Guzman, Ruben Ramos & Rick Treviño of Los Super Seven
Joe Forlini
Joe Henry
Joe Jack Talcum
Joe Jackson Band
Joe Jonas
Joe King Carrasco
Joe Lean & The Jing Jang Jong
Joe Lovano
Joe Mande
Joe Manning
Joe McDermott
Joe McDermott and the Smart Little Creatures
Joe Miranda & Texas Hurricanes
Joe Nadeau
Joe Popp
Joe Pug
Joe Purdy
Joe Rockhead
Joe Stark
Joel Cage
Joel Rafael Band
Joel RL Phelps & The Downer Trio
Jo-El Sonnier
Joep Pelt
Joey Keithley
Joey Ryan
Joey Skidmore Band
Johan
Johan Asherton
John & Mary
John Arthur Martinez
John B. Spencer
John Biz
John Boutte
John Bunzow
John Butler Trio
John Cale
John Cale & Alejandro Escovedo
John Casey
John Cheatham
John Cruz
John David Souther
John Dear Mowing Club
John Doe
John Doe Thing
John DuBois
John Eddie
John Egan
John Ellison
John Fairhurst
John Fannon
John Flynn
John Forte
John Freeman
John Fremgen & Jeff Hellmer
John Galt
John Gorka
John Grant
John Hammond
John Hiatt
John Kennedy
John Kruth
John Matthias & Nick Ryan
John Maus
John Mills
John Nitzinger
John P. Strohm
John Paul Jones
John Paul Keith & The One Four Fives
John Popper Project
John Price
John Ralston
John Ramberg
John Ramsey
John Rey Reed
John Roderick
John Schooley and his One Man Band
John Sinclair
John Smith
John Southworth
John Staehely
John Stewart
John Thomas Griffith
John Thomas Griffith Band
John Trudell & the Graffiti Band
John Vanderslice
John Watts
John Wesley Harding
John Wesley Harding and Eugene Mirman's Cabinet of Wonders w/ special guests
John Wilkes Booze
John William Gordon
Johnathan Pace
Johnathan Rice
Johnboy
Johnette Napolitano
Johngomi
Johnny A.
Johnny Adams
Johnny and "New" Sensations
Johnny Bush
Johnny Cooper
Johnny Dee & the Rocket 88s

Johnny Degollado y su Conjunto
Johnny Dilks & the Visitacion Valley Boys
Johnny Dowd
Johnny Dowd Band
Johnny Favourite Swing Orchestra
Johnny Flamehead
Johnny Flynn
Johnny Flynn & The Sussex Wit
Johnny Foreigner
Johnny Goudie
Johnny Goudie and The Little Champions
Johnny Hernandez & Third Coast
Johnny Hickman of Cracker
Johnny Invisible
Johnny J. & the Hitmen
Johnny Law
Johnny Mears
Johnny Mears & the Texicans
Johnny Monster & the Nightmares
Johnny Nicolas
Johnny O'Neal
Johnny Quest
Johnny Reno
Johnny Reno Band
Johnny Rodriguez
Johnny Schex
Johnny Shoplifter
Johnny Society
Johnny Toxic w/ special guest Nina Whett
Johnny Winter
Johnossi
Joint Chiefs
JoiStaRR
Jokaman
Jokers Of The Scene
Jolie Holland
Jon Allen
Jon Auer
Jon Benjamin
Jon Cleary
Jon Cleary and The Absolute Monster Gentlemen
Jon Dee Graham
Jon Dee Graham w/Eliza Gilkyson
Jon Emery
Jon Emory
Jon Foreman (of Switchfoot)
Jon Glaser
Jon Ims
Jon LaJoie
Jon Langford
Jon Langford & the Sexy
Jon Langford And Skull Orchard
Jon Langford And The Pine Valley Cosmonauts
Jon Langford's Ship & Pilot
Jon McLaughlin
Jon Mueller
Jon Randall
Jon Rauhouse
Jon Rauhouse's Steel Guitar Rodeo (feat. Kelly Hogan & Sally Timms)
Jon Taylor
Jon Todd
Jonah Ray
Jonah Smith
Jonas
Jonathan Fire*Eater
Jonathan Kane's February
Jonathan Tyler & the Northern Lights
Jonell Mosser & Enough Rope
Jones Benally Family
Jones Family Singers
Jonezetta
Jonna Lee
Jonneine Zapata
Jonny Craig
Jonny Lang
Jonny Lives!
Jonny Polonsky
Jono Manson Band
Jont
Jookabox
Jorane
Jorge Palomarez
Jorma Kaukonen
Jose Gonzalez
Joselo
Joseph Arthur
Joseph Israel
Josh Alan
Josh Caldwell & Harmony Tope
Josh Charles
Josh Davis & English Dave
Josh Fadem
Josh Martinez
Josh Martinez & Sleep are the Chicharones
Josh Pyke
Josh Ritter
Josh Rouse
Josh T. Pearson
Josh Tatum
Josh Todd

Joshua James
Joshua Morrison
Joshua Radin
Josiah Wordsworth
Josie
Joss Stone
Jovi Rockwell
Joy
Joy Electric
Joy String
Joy Zipper
Joydrop
JP5
JPP
Jr. Robby
Jr. Medlow & the Bad Boys
Jr. Medlow & Tornado Alley
JT Donaldson
Juan Atkins
Juan Martín
Juan Son
Jubilee
Jubilee Dive
Jucifer
Jud Newcomb
Judah Bauer/20 Miles
Jude
Judge Roughneck
Judith Owen
Judy Bats
Jody Lazo
Juguete
Juiceboxxx
Juiceboxxx/Roxy Cottontail
Jukebox Junkies
Jukebox the Ghost
Jule Brown
Jules Shear
Jules Verdone
Julia Ann Delbridge
Julia Darling
Julia Greenberg
Julia Marcell
Julian Berntzen
Julian Cope
Julian Coryell
Julian Dawson
Juliana Hatfield
Julianna Barwick
Julianne Richards
Julie Burrell
Julie Delpy
Julie Doiron
Julie Feeney
Julie Howard
Julie Neumark
Julie Ritter
Julieann Banks
Julien Jacob
Juliet Turner
Juliette & The New Romantiques
Juliette and the Licks
Juliette Commagere
Juliette Torres
Jully Black
Jumbo
Jump
Jump Back Jake
Jump, Little Children
June
June Panic
Junebug
Jungle Brothers
juni
Junior Brown
Junior Gone Wild
Junior Kimbrough
Junior Medlow
Junior Senior
Junior Varsity
Junius
Junk Science (Nuclear Family)
Junkie XL
Juno
Jupiter and Teardrop
Jupiter One
Jurassic 5
Just Archie
Justice Hahn
Justice Leeg
Justice Yeldham
Justicia
Justin Chin
Justin McRoberts
Justin Nozuka
Justin Paul
Justin Rutledge
Justin Thompson
Justin Townes Earle
Justin Trevino & Johnny Bush
Jux County
JW Roy
Jyrojets
JZ Barrell
JZJ Records

K

K9 Arts
K. McCarty
K.F.O
K. Flay
K.K. Wilde
K/R featuring Rosie Flores and Katy Moffatt
Kacy Crowley
Kaddisfly
Kaiser Cartel
Kaiser Chiefs
Kaisha Vega
KaitO
Kaito UK
Kaki King
Kalas
Kalashnikov
Kam
Kam Franklin
Kam Moye aka Supastition
Kamera
Kamikaze Queens
Kamran Hooshmand
Kamran Hooshmand & 1001 Nights
Kanko
Kante
Kap Bambino
Kapsize
Kara Grainger
Karan Chavis
Karaoke Apocalypse
Karaoke Apocalypse: The Dead Motley Sex Maidens
Karen Anderson
Karen Chavis
Karen Kraft
Karen Pernick
Karen Poston & the Crystal Pistols
Karg Boys
Kari Renee
Karina Nistal
Karkwa
Karl Blau
Karl Wallinger
Karma To Burn
Karnivool
Karon
Karyna McGlynn
Kasabian
Kasey Chambers
Kashmir
Kaskade
kasms
Kaspar
Kostas
Kat Edmonson
Kat Jones
Katahdin's Edge
Katau
Katchafire
Katchie Cartwright/Richard Oppenheim Nonet
Kate Bradley & The Goodbye Horses
Kate Campbell
Kate Earl
Kate Havnevik
Kate Jacobs
Kate MacLeod
Kate McLennan
Kate Miller-Heidke
Kate Tucker and the Sons of Sweden
Kate Voegele
Kate Walsh
Katell Keineg
Katey Red
Katherine Dines
Kathleen Edwards
Kathleen Grace Band (KGB)
Kathleen Haskard
Kathleen Wilhoite
Kathryn Murray
Kathy & the Kilowatts
Kathy Hart and the Bluestars
Kathy Mattea
Kathy McCarty
Kathy Taylor
Kathy Wade
Kathy Ziegler
Katie Moore
Katie Stelmanis
Katie Stuckey
Katy Moffatt
Katy Perry
Katzenjammer
Kava Kava
Kayo Dot
Kaz Murphy
Kaze
KB da Kidnappa
KB da Kidnappa of Street Military
KB the Boo Bonic
KbN
K-Drama
Keaton Simons
Keefrider
Keegan DeWitt
Keelay and The Park with Ragen Fykes
Keelay and Zaire
Keepaway
Keisho Ohno
Keite Young
Keith Gattis
Keith Killgo Jazz
Keith Morris of the Circle Jerks (DJ Set)
Keith Newton

continued on page 118

SXSW SPOTLIGHT

Takin' It To The Streets

By Steve Chaney

ack in 1993, I was in the sad process of closing Nick's Diner, a great restaurant where I'd lost my lease. I got a call from Roland Swenson. It was about three months before SXSW. I'd done a lot of production work for them over the years, but Roland had a different proposition for me.

The directors had decided to stage a three-day series of free shows in the late afternoon on a stretch of Brazos Street between Sixth and Seventh streets. (The present site of the free shows, the very user-friendly Auditorium Shores, was at that time closed to us because of the objections of the South Austin Community Association.) Their dynamic, aggressive new marketing manager, Phyllis Arp, had already sold the shows. The problem was, nobody had figured out how to do a show there, on a busy street with no access to electricity. Roland asked if I'd take the gig as part of a full-time job. Suddenly unemployed with two small kids, well, what the hell?

If you look closely, that block is a perfect amphitheater. A gentle slope that gradually gets steeper from Sixth to Seventh, bounded on either side by beautiful stone buildings – to the east, the Mexican Consulate, and across the street, the Driskill Hotel, which ended up functioning as production office, backstage, caterer, and all-around headquarters. It also featured a beautiful balcony overlooking the concert, with a 600-capacity ballroom immediately behind it. Sponsors do enjoy a good party room.

Only thing was, nobody had actually asked the City of Austin if they'd give us that block, and if so, when. The way it shook out, we got a street closure at 8am, with a 4:30pm showtime. Between SXSW production manager Roy Taylor, Phyllis Arp and me, we managed to book the people it took to pull it off.

This was no Pecan Street Festival setup. We had a 40-foot stage, full Tomcat roof, big Rock Show sound and lights. Back then you had to hand-build a scaffold stage. We had the best hippies money could buy: guys named Dawg and One Arm. Eight hours is pretty short time to build and put on a pro show, but we did it. And it looked great.

The *Austin American-Statesman* ran a front page pic from the top of the crowd on Seventh Street with the beautiful buildings on each side, the bright lights of the stage, and the lights of the city behind. It was gorgeous. The directors were hooked. We had to do it again. Louis Meyers, director of the Music Festival and my immediate boss, congratulated me, said we should never try it again, and left SXSW. Not to say there's a connection.

Years passed. Great shows ensued. Cracker, Rodney Crowell, Matthew Sweet, Charlie Sexton, T Bone Burnett, an incredible Rounder show with Esther Phillips, the Rebirth Brass Band and Beau Jacques...It got bigger and bigger.

I got more and more scared. The crowds were overrunning the space. We were bound on each side by solid buildings, with Brazos closed off on the Sixth Street side by the massive stage. We had developed something of a system in the first

few years, but it still took every minute of the few hours we had to set up the venue for the first day. Soundcheck often consisted of me saying a few words into the vocal mics just minutes before showtime. A good crowd ran around 5,000, which was just about all the makeshift venue could handle, but we pretty much had the run of the Driskill at that point, which was very helpful.

But 1996 was different. Phyllis had booked Iggy Pop for the first day, and for the second, Joan Osborne, who at that point had the #1 record in the country. Each was bound to draw thousands more than we'd ever had, and Iggy's crowd was known to be, well, unusually enthusiastic. Iggy's tour was also known to be very professional, and I didn't look forward to telling them there'd be no soundcheck.

Then we caught a little break. Roy Taylor had managed to book the Lollapalooza tour's "B" stage, which was a 40-foot trailer with two enormous steel flaps and a hydraulic system to lower them into place. After a few anxious minutes maneuvering the trailer into place, the flaps came down and, voila, instant stage. We had sound, light and roof up before noon, and all afternoon to set up Iggy.

At some point while we were setting up gear, a couple of guys ambled onstage. One was Iggy's manager, whom I'd met earlier, and the other, unmistakable even in sweats and a floppy hat, was The Man Himself. He strolled up to me: "You running the show?"

"Uh, yeah, Iggy, my name's Steve."

He said, "Call me Jim," and shook my hand. He walked to the front of the stage, looked over the lip, turned to me and said, "No barricade?" I froze. I had no budget for a barricade, and how was I going to rent one and get it in place in three hours?

Then he said, "Cool, can I talk to the light man?" Turns out he hated barricades. He likes to be able to get right in his fan's faces, to touch them and let them touch him. He wanted to talk to the light man so the first few rows could be lit, and he could see the crowd's faces.

I spent the rest of the afternoon setting up and soundchecking with Iggy's crew. They were a colorful bunch, especially his guitar techs/onstage bouncers, two burly New York Italians who ran a guitar store when not on the road with Iggy. They had some special requirements. For instance, the rider called for four vocal mics, even though nobody sang backup. "That's in case he breaks 'em", it was explained. Also, local crew got some unusual assignments. Mine was to stand onstage next to one of the P.A. speaker stacks. "If he decides to go up, your job is to keep the speakers from falling over." OK.

Meanwhile, the crowd continued to build. The directors hired a few more off-duty cops than usual, for which I was quite grateful. We had already met and discussed security strategy, but events rendered all plans meaningless. There was a fairly large barricaded staging area behind the stage that backed up to Sixth Street. By the beginning of the second band's set, the crowd reached almost up to Seventh Street, totally surrounded the stage, and spilled back behind the staging area and onto Sixth Street to the extent that the police had to close it. Getting Iggy from the front door of the Driskill's corner bar to the backstage area 50 feet away wasn't going to be easy.

I asked his road manager if he'd be OK with a police escort to the stage. "Nah, Jim won't go for that. He sees cops, he crosses the street." So I got on the radio and rounded up the biggest SXSW staffers I could find. After the second band finished, my crew and I headed to Iggy's dressing room, a small converted conference room. I could hear these "clump-clump-clump-BANG! clump-clump-clump-BANG!" sounds coming from inside.

The road manager said, "Jim ain't ready yet. It'll be just a minute." I couldn't resist sticking my head in the door. Iggy was running the length of the room, leaping into the air, and pushing himself back from the wall with his hands, some kind of flying push-up. I quickly retreated. Iggy emerged a minute later, looked at me and asked if it was a good crowd.

"Real good crowd, Jim."

Iggy was wearing tight pants and a star-spangled red-white-and-blue sequined vest I'd seen hanging in the Driskill gift shop earlier that day. He had a towel over his head like a boxer heading into the ring. We went the back way through the kitchen and the bar and formed a box around Iggy before forging out the door and into the crowd. It turned out I had nothing to worry about. The crowd politely parted and we headed for the stage.

Iggy played the prizefighter schtick to the hilt, clutching the towel and bouncing on his toes. When he got into the backstage pen, he went totally nuts. He ran around like a maniac, high-fiving, kissing girls, waving his vest in the air and

generally giving a hell of a show to the backstage crowd that wouldn't be able to see the concert. I made my way to the stage where the band was standing ready, and took my place by the speaker stack.

Iggy bounded onto the other side of the stage like a dervish, spending a solid five minutes whipping the crowd into a frenzy before the band had played a note. I wish I could say I remember what song they played first, but I can't. I did notice that Iggy always sang to one person at a time, whether it was someone onstage with him or a fan in the front rows. I'll never forget the second number, though.

The band went into one of my favorite songs, the Stooges "No Fun." About halfway through, Iggy spun around, charged me, and screamed "NO FUUUUN!" into my face from about two feet. I'd like to say it was one of the great moments of my life, but frankly, it scared the living shit out of me. (Though it was pretty cool in retrospect.)

Iggy spent a good deal of his time on his belly leaning over the lip of the stage half-swallowed by the crowd. When he was up and running, he was joined by a constant stream of fans who generally stayed onstage clowning around for a few seconds before hopping back into the crowd, sometimes with the gentle assistance of the Italians. Occasionally a woman just had to give Iggy a kiss, which he cheerfully accepted. One enterprising young man jumped onstage, slung one arm around Iggy's neck, held a camera in front of them with the other, and snapped a picture. In the middle of "Lust For Life."

My professional composure was beginning to return somewhat, and it came to me that I was in charge of an event that had lapsed into sheer mayhem. The stage was completely surrounded by a crowd crush so intense that someone could have died and not hit the ground for half an hour. Not a cop in sight. I guess I thought I had to "DO SOMETHING!" so I relinquished my speaker-stack position and headed out.

There was no way to fight my way through the crowd, so I headed toward Seventh Street through the bowels of the Driskill. At the top of the street were the cops we had hired, the regular duty officers, and the sergeant in charge of downtown that night, a guy I actually knew pretty well. I was freaking out, but they were all strangely calm.

"Sergeant, this is insane!" I bellowed. "There's no way for anybody to get out of there. Somebody's gonna get killed!"

"Well, Steve, I don't see there's much we can do at this point," he replied. "You got anything in mind?"

"I guess I don't," I answered, "I just feel like we should do *something*."

"You know, Steve," he said, "I think the best way to proceed is wait 'til this is all over, then walk down the street and pick up the bodies."

When the show ended, the crowd dispersed quickly. There were no bodies.

After the show, the band and crew went back to the dressing room. There weren't supposed to be any backstage guests, but Iggy's guitar player Whitey slipped in a couple of strippers, replete with glitter-bedecked cleavage.

I pulled out an 8-by-10 glossy of myself at 24 with 28 stitches in my face and asked Iggy to sign it. He looked confused for a minute, then said, "This happen at one my shows?"

"Yeah, Jim, 1980." He half smiled and signed.

Iggy had a commitment to have a drink with a good friend of his sister's who lived in Austin. She turned up, a very straight looking middle-aged woman, and Iggy got ready to go. Then he remembered something.

"Hey, anybody got a mirror? Somebody told me I messed up my face." One was produced and he took a quick look.

"That ain't too bad," he said. Then he slipped on a sportscoat, pulled his hair back in a ponytail, put on his glasses, and Jim Osterberg walked out the door and into the night. ■ **Steve Chaney has been involved with SXSW in many capacities over the years. By his account: "I was part-time staff from '89-'93, full-time year-round from '94-'99, built the office '97-'99, ran the outdoor stages on Brazos Street and at Waterloo Park, advanced the Portland festivals, worked Toronto, etc. – even played the damned thing in '97 with Shoulders."**

Wayne Coyne of the Flaming Lips conducts the Parking Lot Experiment (1997)

1997 – 2001

Experiments, Expansions, And Explosions

By Jason Cohen

here have been a lot of memorable SXSW venues. Bedrock Austin clubs like Antone's, Emo's, and the Continental. Sorely missed rooms like Liberty Lunch and Steamboat. Somewhat less sorely missed spaces like the Austin Opera House or Upstairs at the Ritz. There are also venues that play no part in the Austin music scene the other 361 days of the year, for better (Buffalo Billiards has hosted many a great showcase) and for worse (the regulars at South Congress dive bar Trophy's brawled amidst a Cher U.K./ Magnolias show in 1997). But the greatest, oddest setting of them all was part of SXSW 1997, otherwise unused before or since: an unassuming little parking ramp at 702 Brazos Street.

This was the setting for the Flaming Lips' Parking Lot Experiment, which was being clinically tested for the first time outside of the band's home base in Oklahoma City. Registrants signed their cars up at the *Cake* magazine trade show booth, though the process skewed a bit toward Austin residents, since we had better stereos than any rental car (says the owner of an after-market Kenwood amp, though I'll be damned if I recall the number that the Lips' Wayne Coyne gave my car).

While Roland Swenson says he barely remembers preparations for the unconventional performance, former Music Festival executive staffer Leah Wilkes says he was skeptical. "Terms such as 'parking ramp,' 'multiple cars' and 'Wayne Coyne' make people nervous," she says. "When he agreed to indulge me, it was with the understanding that there wouldn't be a significant siphoning of SXSW resources: either money or manpower." The trick was finding a location, since so much property in Austin belongs to either the University of Texas or the state. "Trying to explain to various government employees that we needed to use their parking ramp for a rock music experiment was a fiasco," Wilkes says. "One guy hung up on me because he thought it was a prank." Eventually, she was able to sublease one floor of 702 Brazos from *Texas Monthly*, which had its offices across the street, for a whopping $100. (My own memory is no better than Swenson's, as I wrote for the magazine, and apparently middlemanned the whole transaction.)

Wilkes remembers looking at the second floor from street-level and thinking, *please don't let the fire marshal in on this one*. "All I saw were hundreds of people, sitting on the low walls on two sides of the ramp," she says. "When I walked up, there was hardly room to move. Wayne had the cars parked in a flower pattern which he stood in the middle of, with a bullhorn and a bright yellow

raincoat." Coyne handed out 29 cassettes, ornately marked with gold paint, with, "No! No! No!" in big letters on the B sides. Together, they added up to a bizarre symphony of time, space, and sound, with echoes and separation circling the garage. During the second song ("Rotting Vegetables Marching Through Meatville"), car #16 blew a fuse. Unfortunately for Coyne, it was a crucial part. In its absence, he described the piece as "the quietest music heard in this whole conference."

Coyne "was the only person in the garage dissatisfied with the experiment," Jim DeRogatis wrote in his Lips biography *Staring At Sound*. "Listeners gave the band a wildly enthusiastic five-minute ovation. The group had pulled off a show unlike any of the other four hundred ninety-nine during the music conference."

For the Lips, the Parking Lot Experiment laid the foundation for the next 10 years of their career. They returned to South by Southwest for showcases in 1999 and 2006, Coyne's SXSW Interview in 2004, and Bradley Beesley's documentary *The Fearless Freaks* in 2005. The 1999 show in particular was legendary, only the second time (after a warm-up show in Dallas) the band had performed in a new incarnation spurred by the album *The Soft Bulletin*, with no drummer (Steven Drozd having moved to keyboards and guitars), a ton of multimedia, and Coyne's now-familiar props and let-me-entertain-you vibe. Like the Johnny Cash show, it was a case where the biggest "buzz" was not about an unknown band, or someone scoring that big major label deal, but a great artist using SXSW as a platform for reinvention — while also launching a marketing campaign to the assembled media, radio programmers, talent buyers and overseas people, sometimes on purpose, sometimes not. From the the Strokes and the White Stripes to Norah Jones and Arctic Monkeys, this would continue in the years to come — and it was not an accident, in SXSW's view.

"When the signing frenzy became what a lot of the media described as SXSW's main function, that worried me," says Swenson. "We never put together lists of acts who got record deals at SXSW to give the press because I always thought that would bite us on the ass. I'd always say, 'Acts don't get signed because of SXSW. They get signed because they are talented, work hard and are lucky.' I think there were two events that helped us turn the corner on the perception that SXSW was only about getting signed. The first was Johnny Cash. The second was when we hooked up with the postmodern radio promoters and programmers after the New Music Seminar folded. The labels were anxious to get their acts in front of the radio programmers, and all the other possible print and electronic media coverage became more recognized."

In 1997, even as the conference had become more well-known to the general public, SXSW recommitted to the music industry and Austin locals, ending the sale of wristbands to out-of-towners, limiting single-show tickets and increasing its hotel blocks. "There was increased national participation by consumers, but all of our efforts were going into making sure we didn't lose the industry aspect of the event," says Swenson. "The reason we began getting so many label buzz bands was because the industry side of the event became more established in the last half of the '90s."

The last years of the '90s featured many other changes. In 1997 — still a bit shy of the ubiquitous-cell-phone era — the staff was given brand new lightweight walkie-talkies, only to find they shared a frequency with Delta Airlines' ground crew. "We can just have them land the planes here," Roland Swenson told *Austin American Statesman* writer Chris Riemenschneider, pointing to East Cesar Chavez Street from the Convention Center.

It was also the first year there were Wednesday showcases, a year after Lou Reed's Austin Music Hall booking provided competition for the Music Awards. (The Music Hall subsequently became the Awards Show venue, and Reed would come to SXSW 2008 as keynote speaker.) And while day parties were ultimately more of a 21st-century thing, they were already starting to proliferate. The popular

Americana-tinged shows at Yard Dog Gallery began in 1996. In '97, reviewing a set by Masters of Reality at Emo's, Andy Langer of *The Austin Chronicle* proclaimed it "The Year of the Day Party." Little did we know. "A side effect of our making it more difficult for out-of-town consumers to attend SXSW was that eventually we pushed them into the unofficial party side of SXSW," Swenson acknowledges.

1997 was also meant to be the year SXSW moved beyond the little house next to the *Chronicle*, with construction of a new two-story building. By then, remembers Swenson, "film and interactive occupied one of the three bedrooms, somehow managing to office eight people in a 12 x 12 room. Then, spring rains flooded the garage the music fest had occupied for five years, forcing them into the kitchen of the main house."

Alas, the office wasn't finished until the stretch between the 1998 and 1999 events. Swenson told the *Statesman*'s Riemenschneider that the days of working in cramped quarters were "probably the last time I knew everything that was going on at SXSW." And, well, the more things change... former SXSW registrar Rachel McGruder sums up the entire journey: "Oh! The evolution of the offices," she says. "From the original rabbit warren (on 28th Street) to the ranch-style house to the sleek modernist building that was immediately stamped with the...well, the ethos and décor of the original rabbit warren."

The newer building's two-floor spaciousness would help thwart one band's plan to curry favor with the music staff. "I'm kind of stupid, because they said, 'Hey Brent, would you come downstairs, somebody's got something for you," creative director Brent Grulke told the Austin 'zine *Geek Weekly*. That something was a woman, brandishing a bottle of Jack Daniels. "I didn't know she was a stripper. There were all these people gathered around to watch, and I was like, 'Hey, I'm busy, why do I have to come downstairs?' She didn't take her shirt off, and I don't know if she was predisposed to or not, but I wasn't predisposed to have her do it." Grulke also made a point of not learning which band sent her. So for all we know, they did get in.

Grulke had joined founders Swenson, Black and Barbaro as a director in 1997, along with Eve McArthur (operations), Phyllis Arp (marketing), and Hugh Forrest (the fledgling Interactive event). 1997 was also the year Nancy Schafer's four-year-old SXSW Film Festival had something of a coming-out party. The documentary *Full Tilt Boogie*, about the making of Robert Rodriguez's *From Dusk 'Til Dawn*, meant Quentin Tarantino (the film's screenwriter and Razzie-nominated star) made one of his many trips to Austin. Though QT had inititally gone AWOL, he joined locals Rodriguez, Richard Linklater and Mike Judge, as well as Kevin Smith and George Huang, for a panel called "Outside The System Inside The System."

"That was a huge deal," future SXSW Film producer Matt Dentler said in Alison Macor's 2010 book *Chainsaws, Slackers and Spy Kids*. He was in the audience for the panel, and he became a South by Southwest volunteer for the first time soon after. "Great timing. Here are these guys who have been this huge overnight sensation, they do this panel and they all went on to do bigger things." Just as Linklater and Rodriguez proved you could thrive in movies from a place like Austin, Texas — echoing Swenson's original music business raison d'etre — SXSW would also thrive as a film festival.

Interactive's moment was still some years off. It enjoyed a growth spurt from the dot.com boom between 1999 and 2000, but then endured the bust like everybody else. "We would tease Hugh mercilessly that the reason he had so many panels was to keep his numbers up with speaker comps," says Swenson. "I always believed it would turn around, but it was only Hugh's stubbornness and drive that kept it going."

A tragic setback came in February 1999, when Interactive founder Dewey Winburne suddenly passed away. "I told people that Dewey had the perfect mind for dealing with interactive media

because he was nonlinear in his thinking," Swenson wrote on a Winburne memorial web site. "He was one of those people who just burned too bright; who moved too fast for this world.

Johnny Cash's 1994 show would not be the only time that staffers broke the "SXSW is not for you" command. In 1999, Tom Waits played the Paramount Theatre. "I turned off my radio and watched that show, I'll confess," says Grulke. "I was not gonna miss Tom Waits.

"It was a really miraculous show," he continues. "Every year we have a wish list: 'We ought to see if Tom Waits wants to play,' and I said, 'Oh, Tom Waits doesn't have any reason to play SXSW, he doesn't have a record.' Waits' manager called like two weeks out and said, 'Tom wants to play, but he'll only play a theater, blah blah blah. So everybody really worked hard.'"

Including — talk about service! — giving Waits his own personal contact lens valet. "He'd just gotten contact lenses," Grulke told *Geek Weekly*. "I got a call a day or two before the show and [Waits' manager] said, 'Brent, can you get me the name of an optometrist in town who can put Tom's contacts in and take them out?'" Austin physician Ron Byrd, also of the band Prescott Curlywolf, handled the assignment.

Waits was SXSW 1999's tough ticket (the reserved seats were split among badgeholders, wristbands and a same-day general public sale), with fans lining up as early as 4:30 am. "People tried to hide in the theater during the day and we had to chase them out," says Swenson. "One enterprising young woman brought a mop and bucket and tried to pretend she was a janitor." Gil Kaufman of *Addicted To Noise* surveyed the line before the show, spotting Sparklehorse's Mark Linkous and Calexico's Joey Burns hoping to get in with everybody else.

The show's aftermath was not so smooth. Waits' set ran long, with three standing ovations, but the cops working security still left at their appointed time. This allowed a woman to come in the theater and walk right up to the stage, screaming at Waits during his encore that she couldn't buy a ticket. Then, on Sunday at La Zona Rosa, after Alejandro Escovedo's traditional closing-night show, Don Hyde, a San Francisco promoter and friend of Waits, clashed with club security. According to the *Austin American-Statesman*'s Michael Corcoran, Hyde suffered five broken ribs, a broken collarbone and a separated shoulder. "The violence started when La Zona Rosa's bouncers tried to clear the hall after the show," Corcoran wrote. "The 51-year-old Hyde said he and his son needed to go backstage, where they'd been earlier in the evening, to get their things — and when a security guard shoved Hyde, son Sam pushed away the guard's hand and...an all-out melee erupted."

SXSW was ultimately dropped from the subsequent lawsuit, as its venue contract stipulates the club is solely responsible for security. "I had encountered Hyde the night before in line for the Waits show, yelling at anyone listening about how much better things would be if the show was in San Francisco," Swenson says. "I was appalled by how [La Zona Rosa owner] Direct Events' bouncers handled the situation. I don't care what the guy did, he didn't deserve to get beat up. Still, I'm always puzzled when 50-year-old music business guys don't realize that they are about to get beat up by the bouncers. I got beat up by the bouncers at the Armadillo when I was in my early 20s, so I know when to shut up and back off."

In any case, Tom Waits hasn't played Austin since (he finally relented on a vow to not set foot in all of Texas in 2008). The incident also put an end to Escovedo's Sunday SXSW gig. "I won't even drive by La Zona Rosa anymore," he told Corcoran. Escovedo now does a Sunday-night benefit show at the Continental Club; he continued to play SXSW throughout the 2000s at venues ranging from Stubb's to Waterloo Brewing Company to Auditorium Shores.

"The thing to remember is that Alejandro launched the La Zona Rosa Sunday closing event on his own," says Grulke. "It was his event. We eventually worked with him to make it an official

SXSW show, but he was the one that created it. So, understandably, he was pretty proprietary about the show. We always haggled over the details of it, and neither was ever completely happy with the compromises. That night, Al swore he'd never play another Direct Events venue, and except for an Austin Music Awards appearance, and perhaps a benefit or two, I think he's kept that promise. The Sunday La Zona Rosa SXSW Alejandro show was finished.

"I still miss it."

As the aughts approached, what affected SXSW most is what affected everybody, from the music business to the media to grandparents and children: the internet.

In 1996, SXSW had but a single Compuserve e-mail address. "All of our registrations and applications came in by mail or fax," remembers CTO Scott Wilcox. "My day-to-day responsibilities consisted mostly of typing registrations into Filemaker one at a time." Looking back on SXSW 1997 is almost like watching *Mad Men*. "As far as downloading music directly from websites," wrote Greg Beets in *The Austin Chronicle* about one panel, "the consensus was that the hype is still a few steps ahead of the common man's hardware. Slow downloading is the predominant barrier, followed by poor sound quality and the fact that sitting at a desk with your face in a monitor isn't exactly a pleasant way to hear your favorite music."

By 2000, of course, "the Tech Bubble was fully inflated," says Swenson. "The trade show was the biggest ever, taking over two exhibit halls for the first time. My main mental image is flat-screens in every direction." Adds Wilcox, "everywhere you turned there were hordes of dot-com employees running around talking in nonsensical lingo about their new companies. It had become increasingly apparent over the past 18 months that there was no real business model behind many of them, but the venture capital was flowing so freely that they all had money to attend SXSW to market their brands." One prominent trade show hawker would go on to be played by Justin Timberlake in *The Social Network* — yes, Napster was in full force that year.

Easy come, easy go. In 2001, SXSW suffered its first-ever decline in registrations. But it was now a digital event. Panels chief Andy Flynn had started SXSW's online music business newsletter *The Daily Chord*, an early example of aggregation, in 1998. In 2000, Wilcox began using miniDV cameras to shoot bands and red carpet film premieres, and he also posted film trailers and MP3s on SXSW.com. "Many of the bands and filmmakers were initially concerned that they were giving their product away," says Wilcox (hey, who wasn't?). Today, SXSW uses more than 80 volunteers and staffers to film, edit and publish content for the web, mobile and YouTube.

2000 also brought changes to SXSW's non-Austin events. Toronto's NXNE, while still part of the family, had become largely independent, while Portland's NXNW simply ended. This would prove to be fortuitous, as the next edition had been scheduled for September 13, 2001. Swenson says that the inevitable cancellation "might have taken down SXSW," which got hammered by the post-9/11 economic climate anyway (along with the entire music business).

But in the bigger picture, he notes, "our decision to stop trying new out-of-town events, and focus on the three in Austin, really marks the beginning of the serious, steady growth of SXSW from a regional event to an international phenomenon" — as well as a phenomonen where the two "other" festivals got equal billing. Swenson was downright prescient in 1999 when he told the *American-Statesman*'s Riemenschneider, "[Film and Interactive] have always brought in enough money to pay their hard costs. We believe that eventually they'll be truly profitable...and position us to remain vital in terms of whatever entertainment is likely to become in the next 20 years." ∎

continued from page 118

Keith Secola & the Wild Band of Indians
Keller Williams
Kelley Hunt
Kelley James
Kelley Stoltz
Kelly & the Fireballs
Kelly Hogan
Kelly Hogan & Sally Timms
Kelly Hogan and the Pine Valley Cosmonauts
Kelly Joe Phelps
Kelly Kessler and the Wichita Shut-Ins
Kelly Kessler and the Wichita Shut-Ins featuring Lawrence Peters
Kelly Malone
Kelly Pardekooper & the Devil's House Band
Kelly Rains & The Ringos of Soul
Kelly V Queensberry
Kelly Willis
Kelly Willis & Radio Ranch
Kellye Gray
Kellye Gray Band
Kelsey Wild
Kelvynator
Kemetic Suns
Ken Hunt
Ken Stringfellow
Kenan Bell
Kendall Payne
Kendra Ross
Kenn Rodriguez
KENNA
Kenny and the Kasuals
Kenny Cordray
Kenny Wayne Band
Kenny Wayne Shepherd
Kenny Wayne Shepherd w/ Special Guests Pinetop Perkins & Hubert Sumlin
Kent & Jenni Finlay
Kent & Jenni Finlay Show
Kent Cole
Kepi: The Band
Keren Ann
Keri Leigh & the Blue Devils
Kermit Ruffins
Kermit Ruffins and the Barbecue Swingers
Kerretta
Kerry Hansen
Ketchup Mania
Kev Brown
Kev Brown/Oddisee/ Diamond District
Kevin Avery
Kevin Avery, Dan Boulger and Ben Kronberg with Special Guest
Kevin Bowe
Kevin Bowe & the Okemah Prophets
Kevin Brandt
Kevin Brown, Lucky Peterson & Silent Partners
Kevin Burke's Open House
Kevin Carroll
Kevin Connolly
Kevin Deal
Kevin Devine
Kevin Devine & the Goddamn Band
Kevin Doherty
Kevin Fowler
Kevin Gant
Kevin Gilbert & the Skinner Box
Kevin Gordon
Kevin Hearn & Thin Buckle
Kevin Jack
Kevin Johnson
Kevin McKinney
Kevin Russel, Jimmy Smith, Claude Bernard
Kevin Russell
Kevin Salem
Kevin Seconds
Kevin Shields
Kevin Welch
Kevin Welch & the Danes
Kevin Welch and the Overtones
Kevin Welch/Kieran Kane
Kevn Kinney
Kevn Kinney's Sun Tangled Angel Revival
Keys N Krates
Khan
Khanate
Kheanny
Ki and Ky
Kid 606
Kid Beyond
Kid Biscuit & his Famous Biscuit Boys
Kid Congo and the Pink Monkey Birds
Kid Congo Powers
Kid Cudi
Kid Dakota
Kid Fantastic
Kid Icarus
Kid Koala
Kid Sister
Kid Sister & Flosstradamus
Kid Symphony
Kid 606 and Friends
Kidz in the Hall
Kieran Kane
Kieran McGee
Kiernan McMullan
Kiiiiiii
Kila
Kilgore Trout
Kilians
Kill Creek
Kill Hannah
Kill It Kid
Kill Me Tomorrow
Kill Memory Crash
Kill the Client
Kill The Noise
Kill The Vultures
Kill Whitey
Killa Kela
Killbilly
Killer Bees
Killer Mike
Killer Tumbleweeds
Killers for Hire
Killola
Killswitch Engage
Kilowatthours
Kim Beggs
Kim Fontaine
Kim Hiorthoy
Kim Holzer
Kim Lenz and her Jaguars
Kim Loe
Kim Miller
Kim Norlen
Kim Richey
Kim Taylor
Kim Taylor Band
Kim Wilson
Kimarie Lynn
Kimberly M'Carver
Kimbute & the Freedom Tribe
Kimmie Rhodes
Kimmie Rhodes Band
Kimmo Pohjonen
Kimya Dawson
Kincaid
Kinch
Kind
Kind Of Like Spitting
Kindred
Kinesis
King Apparatus
King Black Acid
King Bob
King Britt
King Brothers
King Bub
King Can
King Cartel
King Coya & El Trip Selector
King Dude
King Friday
King Khan & the Shrines
King Louie One Man Band
King Memphis
King Missile III
King of Conspiracy
King of Prussia
King of Spain
King Rat
King Solo
King Soul
King Straggler
King Wilkie
King Zero
Kingdom
Kingman and Jonah
Kings County Queens
Kings Go Forth
Kings In Disguise
Kings of Convenience
Kings of Leon
King's X
Kinky
Kinnie Starr
Kino Eye
Kinship
Kinski
Kiotti
Kips Bay Ceili Band
Kirby Dominant
Kirk Kelly
Kirk Whalum
Kirsten Ketsjer
Kirt Kempter
Kishidan
Kiska
Kiss Kiss
Kiss Me Deadly
Kisschasy
Kissing Chaos
Kissing Tigers
Kissinger
Kissy Sell Out
KIT
Kitchen Radio
Kitten
Kittens Ablaze
Kitty Gordon
Kitty, Daisy & Lewis
KJ Hines
Kleckley Sweet
Klever
Klondike Kat
K'Naan
Kneebody
Knievel
Knife in the Water
Knife Party
Knife Skills
Knife World
Kennedy Rose
Know How
Knuckle Yummy
Knyfe Hyts
Koester
Kokeshi Doll
Kolumbus Kar Kommandos
Kona
Koncrete Law
Koneveljet
Koopa
Kopecky Family Band
Koro Crew
k-os
Kosha Dillz
Kotchy
K-Otix
Kottonmouth
Kottonmouth Jesse
Koufax
Kraak & Smaak
Kramer
Kreamy 'Lectric Santa
Kreisor
Kreyol Syndikat
Kria Brekkan
Krief
Kriminals
K-Rino
K-Rino & The South Park Coalition
Kristin Ross 7 the Rambers
Kris Delmhorst
Kris Gruen
Kris Kristofferson
Kris Kristofferson & Jessi Colter
Kris McKay
Kris McKay/Michael Hall
Krista Muir
Kristeen Young
Kristen Hall
Kristen Schaal
Kristen Schaal & Kurt Braunohler
Kristie Stremel
Kristin Hersh
Kristina Train
Kristofer Astrom
Kristoff Silva
Kristoffer Ragnstam
Kristy Kruger
Kristyna Myles
Krizz Kaliko
Krossfyah
Krum Bums
Krush
Krysis
KT Tunstall
KTB
K-the-I???
KTU (Pohjonen, Gunn, Mastelotto)
Kudu
Kulap Vilaysack
Kunimoto Takeharu
Kuroma
Kurt Braunohler
Kurt Braunoler, Kyle Kinane, Pete Holmes and Special Guest
Kurt Vile
Kurupt
Kush & Jah Bloodfiyah Angels
Kustom Kar Kommandos
Kutt Calhoun
KVLR
Kydd
Kyle Andrews
Kyle Kinane
Kyle Lee
Kyle Riabko
Kylesa
Kylie Burtland
Kylie Harris

L.

L.A.B.
L.A.X
L.D.
L.E. McCullough
L.Stadt
L'Usine
L7
La Conquista
La Diferenzia
La Gusana Ciega
La Habitacion Roja
La Honda
La Mafia
La Makita Soma
La Melodia
La Nueva Movida
La Patère Rose
La Pestilencia
La Pupuna
LA Riots
La Rocca
La Santa Cecilia
La Sinfonia
La Snacks
La Strada
La Touche
La Tribu
La Tropa F
Lab Partners
Labrea Stompers
Lach
Jack Logan & Liquor Cabinet
Lackey
La-Di-Da
Lady Danville
Lady Dottie & the Diamonds
Lady Lux
Lady Sovereign
Ladyfinger (NE)
Ladyfingers
Ladyfuzz
Ladyhawk
Ladyhawke
Laguardia
Lagwagon
Laika & the Cosmonauts
LAKE
Lake Trout
Lakuna
Lalo
L'altra
Lamb of God
Lambretta
Lana Phillips
Lance Cashion
Lance Keltner
Land Of Talk
Landmine Marathon
Landon Pigg
Langhorne Slim
LAPKO
Lara & Reyes
Large Number
Lari White
Larisa Bryski
Larkin Grimm
Larry
Larry Crane Band
Larry John McNally
Larry John McNally
Larry Seaman
Larry Seaman's Paperhouse
Larry Yes
LarryLand
Larrys
Lars Vaular
Las Cruces
Las Palomas de la Frontera
Las Toolitos
Las Ultrasonicas
Last Crack
Last Days Of April
Last Laugh
Last Rites
Late Night Chinese
Late Of The Pier
Latest Flame
Latimer
Latin Breed
Latin Image
Latyrx
Laub
Laundry
Laundry Room Squelchers
Laura Barrett
Laura Cantrell
Laura Critchley
Laura Gibson
Laura Jansen
Laura Mann
Laura Marling
Laura Pellegrino
Laura Smith
Laura Veirs
Lauralei Combs
Laurel Collective
Laurels
Lauren Shera
Lauri Kranz
Laurie Boedee
Laurie Freelove
Laurie Lewis
Laurie Lewis & Tom Rozum
Lava Love
Lavender Diamond
Lay Quiet Awhile
Layton
Lazaro Casanova
Lazarus
Lazarus Clamp
Lazer Sword
LAZRtag
Lazy
Lazy Cowgirls
Lazy K
Lazy Lester

Lyle Lovett (2003)

Lazy Magnet
Lazy Sunday Dream
Lazywall
LCD Soundsystem
LD & Ariano
L-D Section II
Le Baron
Le Castle Vania
Le Chat Lunatique
Le Concorde
Le Le
Le Loup
Le Meu Le Purr
Le Monsieurs Du Rock
Le Roi
Leaderhouse
Leadville
League of XO Gentlemen
League510
Leeann Atherton
Leeann Atherton & Fortunate Sons
Learning From Las Vegas
Leather Uppers
LECHE
Lecrae
Led Zeppelin 2
Lederhosen Lucil
Lee "Scratch" Perry
Lee Ann Womack
Lee Burridge
Lee Feldman
Lee Gibson
Lee Mayjahs?
Lee Milo & Tishan
Lee Person Band
Lee Rocker
Lee Roy Parnell
Leels
Leeroy Stagger
Left Hand Solution
Left Lane Cruiser
Legendary Tiger Man
Leif Inge
Leigh Nash
Leila Bela
Lemon Sun
Lemonade
Lemonator
Lemurians
Lemurs
Leni Stern
Lenine
Lenka
Leo Allen
Leo Stokes
Leon Polar
Leon Russell
Leona Naess
Leonard Eto
Leopold
LeRoi Brothers
Leroy Justice
Leroy Shakespeare & the Ship of Vibes
Les Aus
Les Baton Rouge
Les Breastfeeders
Les Fauves
Les Garçons Bouchers
Les Georges Leningrad
Les Handclaps
Les Huff
Les Huff & the Lonesome Dove Band
Les Moore
Les Psycho Riders
Les Savy Fav
Les Tetines Noires
Lesbian
Lesbians On Ecstasy
Lesley Schatz
Leslie and The Badgers
Leslie Dowdall & Band
Leslie Keffer
Leslie Smith
Less Than Jake
Lesser Gonzalez Alvarez
Lester Swing
Lethal Bizzle
Let's Active
Let's Go Bowling
Let's Go Sailing
Let's Go To War
Let's Wrestle
Letters to Cleo
Letty Guval y Xpresso
Levi Weaver
Leviathan
Levinhurst
Levy
Lex Land
Lexie Mountain Boys
Lil' Brian & the Zydeco Travelers
Liam Finn
Liam Frost
Liar
Liars
Liars Academy
Libbi Bosworth
Libbi Dwyer
Libby Kirkpatrick
Libido
Lick Lick
Lida Husik
LidoLido
Lies In Disguise
Life In A Blender
Life of Crime
Lifestyl
lifeYes
Lift To Experience
Lifter
Light FM
Light Pollution
Lighthouse
Lights
Lightspeed Champion
LIK
LIKEHELL
Lil' Band O' Gold
Lil' Band O' Gold: featuring Classie Ballou, Archie Bell, Eddie Bo, DJ Fontana, Roy Head, Al "Carnival Time" Johnson, Barbara Lynn, Tommy McClain, Lil Buck Sinegal & Warren Storm
Lil' Brian Terry & the Zydeco Travelers
Lil' Cap'n Travis
Lil' Keke
Lil' O
Lil Peace
Lil' Flex
Lili Haydn
Lilitu
Lille Palmer
Lillian Standfield
Lily Afshar
Lily Allen
Lily Electric
Limbeck
Limbo Zamba
Limited Express (has gone?)
Limpopo
Linda Albertano
Linda Hargrove
Linda McLean
Linda McRae
Linden Sherwin
Lindi Ortega
Lindsay Jane
Lindsey
Lindstrom
Linea 77
Link 80
Linus of Hollywood
Lion Fever
Lionheart Brothers
Lions
Lions In The Street
Lions of Tsavo
Lipstick Terror
Liquid Logic - DJ Logic with Liquid Soul
Liquid Soul
Liquidators
Liquits
Liquor Giants
LiR
Lisa Buscani
Lisa Colvin
Lisa Germano
Lisa Hannigan
Lisa J. Cornelio
Lisa Lauren
Lisa Loeb
Lisa Loeb & Nine Stories
Lisa Mednick
Lisa Miller
Lisa Richards
Lisa Scott
Lisa St. Ann
Lisa Taylor
Lisa Tingle
Lise Liddell
Lissie
Lissy Trullie
List Christee
Listener
Lithium X-Mas
Litl. Willie
Littl'ans
Little Big Man
Little Birdy
Little Bit of Texas
Little Black Dress
Little Boots
Little Brazil
Little Champions
Little Claw
Little Freddie King
Little Girls
Little Jack Melody
Little Jack Melody & His Young Turks
Little Jackie
Little Jimmy King
Little Joe Washington
Little Joe y la Familia
Little Louie y la Potencia
Little Man
Little Milton
Little Miss Dangerous
Little Miss Higgins
Little O
Little Red & the Renegades
Little Red Rocket
Little Richard
Little Saints
Little Sister
Little Steven
Little Sue
Little Teeth
Little Texas
Little Thief
Little Village
Liturgy
Live Fast Die
Livewire Down (Ryan Turner)
Living Better Electrically
Living Legends
Living Sacrifice
Living Things
Liz Belile
Liz Durrett
Liz Green
Liz Larin
Liz Lee
Liz Pappademas
Liz Phair
Lizard House
Lizard Music
Lizzy Borden
Llama Farmers
LMFAO
LMNO
Lo Fidelity Allstars
LOAD
Laughing Hyenas
Lo-Ball
Lobi Traoré & Joep Pelt
Local 808
Local H
Local Natives
Local Rabbits
Locale A.M.
Location Location
Loch Lomond
Locksley
Loco Gringos
Locomotives
LoCura
Lodger
Loene Carmen
Loer Velocity
Lo-Fi Champion
lo-Fi-Fnk
Lois
Lokomotiv
Lola Ray
Lolita No. 18
Lollipop
Lone Star Ridaz
LoneLady
Lonely China Day
Lonely Kings
Lonelyland
Lonesome Bob
Lonesome Strangers
Lonesome Val
Loney, Dear
Long Gone Daddy
Long John Hunter
Long John Hunter & The Walking Catfish
Longital
Longview
Longwave
Lonnie Walker
Look See Proof
Looker
Lookout Joe
Looptroop Rockers
Loose Diamonds
LOOT
Lopez
Loquat
L'Orchidee D'Hawai
Lord Douglas Phillips
Lord Fyre
Lord Jeff
Lord Sterling
Lord T & Eloise
Lords (UK)
Lords (US)
Lords Of Altamont
Lori Carson
Lorrie Matheson
Los #2 Dinners
Los #3 Dinners
Los Abandoned
Los Agues
Los Amparito
Los Angeles Solitarios
Los Aventureros de Nueva Rosita
Los Bad Apples
Los Burbanks
Los Campesinos!
Los Claxons
Los Coronas
Los Dynamite
Los Fancy Free
Los Fronterizos de Acuña
Los Fugitivos
Los Gusanos
Los Halos
Los Hombres Calientes: Irvin Mayfield & Bill Summers
Los Infernos
Los Llamarada
Los Lobos
Los Lonely Boys
Los Mismos
Los Mocosos
Los Nativos
Los Odio
Los Palominos
Los Pinkys
Los Pirata
Los Planetas
Los Rock Angels
Los Skarnales
Los Spacers
Los Straitjackets
Los Super Elegantes
Los Super Seven
Los Tailpipes
Los Terribles del Norte
Los Texas Wranglers
Lost & Profound
Lost Bayou Ramblers
Lost Dakotas
Lost Goat
Lost Gonzo Band
Lost In Holland
Lost in the Trees
Lost John Casner
Lost Lonely And Vicious
Lost Luggage
Lost Pilots
Lo-Star
Lou Ann Barton
Lou Barlow
Lou Barlow w/ Imaad Wasif
Lou Dalgleish
Lou Ford
Lou Lou and The Guitarfish
Lou Rhodes
Loud Family
Loud Lucy
Loud Posse
Loud Sistah
Loudermilk
Loudmouf
Loudon Wainwright
Louie Austen
Louis XIV
Louise Attaque
Louise Hoffsten
Louque
Lourdes Perez
Love As Laughter
Love Battery
Love-Cars
Love Gravy
Love is All
Love Love Straw
Love of Diagrams
Love of Everything
Love of Lesbian
Love Psychedelico
Love Riot
Love Tractor
Love You Moon
Love:Fi
Lovedrug
Lovehammers
LoveLikeFire
Lovemakers
Lover!
Lovers
Lovesauce & Soulbones
Lovetones
Lovetron
Lovvers
Low
Low Flying Owls
Low Frequency In Stereo
Low G
Low Line Caller
Low Max
Low Pop Suicide
Low Skies
Low vs Diamond
Lower Class Brats
Lower Life Form
Lowery 66
Lowest of the Low
Lowkey
Lowkey of SouthBound
Lowlights
Loxsly
Lozen
LRJ
LRJ with Desperados
Lubricated Goat
Lucas Hudgins and The First Cousins
Lucas Molandes
Lucero
Lucian Turk
Lucie Silvas
Lucifer Wong
Lucille
Lucinda Williams
Lucky
Lucky 7
Lucky Fonz III
Lucky Guns
Lucky Luke
Lucky Machine
Lucky Pineapple
Lucky Tomblin
Luckyiam
Luckyiam/PSC
Lucy and The Popsonics
Lucy Wainwright Roche
Lucy Walsh
Lucy Woodward
Lucy's Fur Coat
LudaChrist
Luder
Ludicra
Ludo
Lukan
Luke Brodie
Luke Doucet

continued on page 136

1997

SXSW **STATS** March 8 - 16

BY THE NUMBERS

788 showcasing artists
of 4,290 submissions

61 panels, workshops & sessions

40 venues & stages

5,896 registrants

$230-450 registration

$51-60 wristband

204 pages in program guide

108 trade show exhibitors

1,414 film registrants

1,401 interactive registrants

AUSTIN MUSIC AWARDS

Wednesday, March 12, Austin Music Hall

Performers Gerry Van King, 8½ Souvenirs, Texas Tornados with Roy Head, Sexton Brothers Sextet, Jimmie Dale Gilmore's tribute to Townes Van Zandt, Lou Ann Barton with Jimmie Vaughan

SXSW SHOWCASE VENUES

Antone's, Atomic Cafe, Austin Music Hall, B-Side, Babe's, The Backroom, Bob Popular/Headliner's/Upstairs, Cactus Cafe, City Coliseum, Club DeVille, Club Universe, Continental Club, Copper Tank, Driskill Hotel Crystal Ballroom, Electric Lounge/Electric Pavilion, Elephant Room, Emo's/Emo's Jr., Flamingo Cantina, Hang 'Em High Saloon, Hole in the Wall, Katie Bloom's, La Zona Rosa, Liberty Lunch, Maggie Mae's/Maggie's West, Mojo's, Ritz Lounge, Roadhouse Cafe, Ruta Maya Coffee House, Scholz Beer Garten, Speakeasy, Steamboat, Stubbs, Texas Union Ballroom, Trophy's, Tropical Isle, Victory Grill, Waterloo Brewing Company

KEYNOTE SPEAKER

Carl Perkins (preceded by a DJ set from Gus Gus) Perkins, who died the following January, was introduced by an investor/manager who'd backed his latest record. "What's a keynote?" he said Perkins had asked him. "I'm no keynote."

"Once the [investor] got up there, we practically had to use a hook to get him offstage," remembers

Roland Swenson. "After 10 minutes, panels chief Jeff McCord stood at the foot of the stage in full view of the audience, drawing a 'cut' line across his neck." Finally, Perkins came out with his guitar and let loose with a string of stories, testifying church-style about Elvis, the Beatles, booze, cancer and God, while also playing snippets of such songs as "Honey Don't" and "Blue Suede Shoes."

"The best keynote speaker in my five years of watching a variety of folks get up there and fumble to say something smart and inspirational to a bunch of groggy musicians and industry professionals," wrote Raoul Hernandez of *The Austin Chronicle*.

MEMORABLE PANELS

"Who Cares?" Social change and politics with moderator Andy Schwartz and artists Jon Langford and Amy Ray.

"Still Cosmic After All These Years" Outlaw Country (a.k.a. "The Great Progressive Country Scare of the '70s") in the age of *No Depression*, with Joe Nick Patoski, Marcia Ball, Steve Fromholz, Micael Priest, Jan Reid, Rusty Weir and Eddie Wilson.

"The Digital Crapshoot" "How have computers and the Internet changed the way we do business in the music industry?"

"Have It OUR Way: The Wal-Mart Dilemma" The retailers' increasing role in record sales and "clean" versions of lyrically explicit music.

"Can (or Should) the Music Industry Do Anything about Drug Abuse?" A contentious discussion in which journalist Dave Marsh eventually stormed off the panel after clashing with fellow panelists over privacy matters and other issues.

> **"As far as downloading music directly from websites, the panel consensus was that the hype is still a few steps ahead of the common man's hardware. Slow downloading is the predominant barrier, followed by poor sound quality and the fact that sitting at a desk with your face in a monitor isn't exactly a pleasant way to hear your favorite music."**
> ▪ Greg Beets, reviewing the "Why Your Web Site Blows" panel in *The Austin Chronicle*, March 21, 1997

NOTABLE PANELISTS

Tony Bennett ("Celebrity Interview"); Cameron Randle (Arista Records Austin), Jeff Kwatinetz (then at Gallin Morey Associates, but about to found The Firm), George Huang (film director), Matt Pinfield (MTV), Moby (on "New Wave of Electronica" panel), Dr. John Hipple (Texas Center for Music and Medicine, University of North Texas)

MEMORABLE SHOWCASES & EVENTS

"Tejano Concierto y Baile" on Thursday night at City Coliseum featured Letty Guval, Jennifer y los Jetz, Pete Astudillo, Stefani, Eddie Gonzalez, Bobby Pulido, La Diferenzia, Grupo Limite and Fama.

"All The King's Men" on Saturday night at the Austin Music Hall featured legendary Elvis collaborators Scotty Moore and D.J. Fontana joined by Joe Ely, David Hidalgo, Cesar Rosas, Tracy Nelson, Rocky Burnette and Billy Burnette, among others.

"Flaming Lips Parking Lot Experiment #4" involved one downtown garage, 30 car stereos, Wayne Coyne in a yellow raincoat and the Lips' "random, precision, surround-sound inner sound tape deck performance," resulting in one of the most weirdly indelible gigs in SXSW history.

NOTABLE ACTS

Of Montreal Today's wildly theatrical pop fabulists were an unknown quantity when they played a Wednesday showcase at Hole in the Wall, described in the program guide simply as "new to the Bar/None stable."

Jonny Lang The blues guitar-slinger was coming off his self-released debut, newly signed to A&M and still not even 17.

Buddy & Julie Miller Alt-country's first couple had yet to release a duo record when they played together on Thursday at Speakeasy to promote their respective Hightone solo albums.

Also Jimmy Eat World, Jimmy Webb, Archers Of Loaf, Ron Sexsmith, Josh Wink, Swamp Dogg, Peter Wolf, 20/20, Cake, dc Talk

SOME OF THE MEDIA-SPONSORED ACTS

Comet (*Dallas Observer*), Hillbilly Cafe (*Fort Worth Weekly*), Horseshoe (*Houston*

Press), Terri Hendrix (*San Antonio Current*), Rock*A*Teens (*Creative Loafing,* Atlanta), Jennyanykind (*Independent Weekly,* NC Triangle), Skeeterhawks (*Nightflying,* Little Rock, AR), C.C. Adcock (*Offbeat,* Lafayette, LA), Hazeldine (*Weekly Alibi,* Albuquerque), Less Than Jake (*Weekly Planet,* Gainesville, FL)

SOME OF THE AUSTIN ACTS

Omar & the Howlers The Austin blues-rock veterans became the first band to headline at the brand-new Antone's location at 5th and Colorado streets, a lease the club signed just mere days before the conference started.

The Instruments The Austin band that was forever known as Texas Instruments had finally drawn the ire of the computer company before playing their 11th straight (and final) SXSW show. "I think we released [*The Texas Instruments*, 1987] right after the first conference," recalled singer David Woody in '97. "It was exciting because SXSW was brand new and nobody knew what it was going to mean or what could happen. But it actually did a lot of good, because when we went on tour right afterwards, we had a certain amount of journalists and people that had seen us at the conference go to our road gigs. Now, we're lazy and everyone has to come to us...so it works out really well."

Also The Adults, Gary Primich, Gomez, the Hormones, Spoon, Euripides Pants, Vallejo, James Polk

SOME OF THE INTERNATIONAL ACTS

Atari Teenage Riot (Germany), dEUS (Belgium), Ben Lee (Australia), Bis (Scotland), Guitar Wolf (Japan), Catatonia (Wales), Sloan (Canada), Sto Zvirat (Czech Republic), Yat-Kha (Tuva, Siberia), Peter Jefferies (New Zealand)

WHATEVER HAPPENED TO...

Nikka Costa The flame-haired singer, who had been a child star, came to SXSW on the strength of her 1996 Australian release *Butterfly Rocket* but was still four years away from her first U.S. hit.

Radish Fifteen-year-old Ben Kweller's grunge band had signed to Mercury that year; nothing

happened for them, but the Greenville, TX, native ultimately did just fine.

Illbient Ilbiwhat? One of several genres (along with "anti-folk," "post-rock" and, less seriously, "metalipalooza") genres mentioned by the *Village Voice* in their SXSW program guide ad.

SOFTBALL TOURNEY

Rainout! Much like the music festival itself, the softball tournament was all wet. Only a single first-round game was completed, between the Musicians and the Finnish "Mighty Reindeer" team ("whose boundless enthusiasm was offset by a profound lack of understanding of the game," reported the following year's program guide). The historically hapless Musicians enjoyed a rare romp, winning 22-2.

FILM

OPENING NIGHT

Full-Tilt Boogie (D: Sarah Kelly) A documentary about the making of the Robert Rodriguez/Quentin Tarantino collaboration *From Dusk Till Dawn.*

> "Number One on my list dates back to 1997, when I saw Dwight Twilley, with Susan Cowsill on backing vocals, and then walked around the corner to see Swamp Dogg. My mind gets hazy on the details; I'm pretty sure that one of them performed "I'm On Fire" and the other did "Total Destruction To Your Mind," but I can no longer remember who did what." ■ Ira Kaplan, Yo La Tengo

> "*HITS* magazine's ultra-influential 'Wheels and Deals' column traced the weasel race towards two Northwest risers, Absinthe, a pretty-boy Portland outfit, and Harvey Danger, a momma's-boy Seattle outfit and NXNW veteran. The latter signed to Slash/London late last month and dropped off the *HITS* must-see radar, but because Absinthe eat their free meals right up to and during SXSW, their showcase was clearly the hotter ticket. After Absinthe's phenomenally lackluster Friday night performance, however, the free meals should be drying up. Don't believe the hype – unless of course somebody's still pitching Harvey Danger to you. Their Saturday night showcase was everything a set from signed artists should be: tight, straightforward, and representative of the upcoming album they're there to promote....Playing SXSW with a deal intact is far more fun than using it to find one." ■ Andy Langer, *The Austin Chronicle*

"3:45pm, outside the panelists' green room: 'Where is Quentin?' asks Nancy Schafer, the whites of her eyes showing. I grab her cell phone. After fruitless calls to Quentin's hotel room, as well as those of five members of his posse, the other panelists decide to go on without him. We post Quentin-spotters outside the convention center, and, indeed, he arrives, joining the monster panel fashionably late. It was a joy to see these guys (George Huang, Mike Judge, Richard Linklater, Robert Rodriguez, Kevin Smith, and Quentin Tarantino) in one room and hear them rib each other about their diverse experiences with studios. ■ Former Austin Film Society director Elizabeth Peters in *The Austin Chronicle*, March 14, 1997

south by southwest music | media festival | march 12-16, 1997
austin convention center | austin, texas

WORLD PREMIERES

Traveller (D: Jack N. Green) Renowned Clint Eastwood cinematographer Green made his directing debut with this gypsy-themed thriller/drama, starring Bill Paxton, Julianna Margulies and Mark Wahlberg.

Still Breathing (D: James F. Robinson) Starring Brendan Fraser and Joanna Going.

SOIREES

"There are two parties that are beginning to run together in my head: The post-screening party for *Full Tilt Boogie* on Friday night, and the after-*Traveller* party on Saturday night (both at the Speakeasy). The second night, with Lou Ann Barton playing and the sublime Derek O'Brien on guitar, I wandered around the bar watching a crowd that included Bill Paxton, Julianna Margulies, Quentin Tarantino, Robert Rodriguez, Elizabeth Avellán, Mira Sorvino, Richard Linklater, Kevin Smith, Steven Soderbergh, Mike Judge, George Huang and *Full Tilt Boogie* producers Rana Joy Glickman and Sarah Kelly. And that list was honestly just the beginning. It was pretty dazzling." **Louis Black, SXSW co-director**

AWARDS

Narrative Feature Winner *Shooting Lily* (D: Arthur Borman); Honorable Mentions: *Purgatory County* (D: George Ratliff), *Chocolate Babies* (D: Stephen Winter)

Documentary Feature Winner *Letter From Waco* (D: Don Howard); Honorable Mention: *Battle For The Minds* (D: Steve Lipscomb) ■

1998

SXSW **STATS** March 13 - 22

BY THE NUMBERS

834 showcasing artists
of 4,100 submissions

63 panels, workshops & sessions

40 venues & stages

6,500 registrants

$230-450 registration

$60-95 wristband

216 pages in program guide

112 trade show exhibitors

1,649 film registrants

1,252 interactive registrants

AUSTIN MUSIC AWARDS

Wednesday, March 18, at Austin Music Hall

Performers Derailers; MC Overlord & Hot Buttered Rhythm; Kacy Crowley, Ana Egge and Trish Murphy with Jon Dee Graham; Asleep At The Wheel with Leon Rausch, Don Walser, Floyd Tillman and Johnny Gimble; Gourds and Damnations; Malachi

KEYNOTE SPEAKER

Nick Lowe The first live music that SXSW director Roland Swenson and Roseana Auten's newborn daughter Christiane ever heard was Lowe's solo performance at this keynote of "What's So Funny About Peace, Love And Understanding?" It was "a sublime version," says former panels honcho Jeff McCord. "[Lowe] was a total gentleman. He essentially gave a short toast to kick off SXSW. The staff all loved him."

MEMORABLE PANELS

"Who Killed Bobby Fuller?" delved into the mystery of the Texas legend's violent death and what might have been, with Joe Nick Patoski, Marshall Crenshaw, Miriam Linna, and Bobby's brother Randy Fuller.

"What's Next For Electronica?" was pegged thusly: "Aside from Prodigy's success, Techno entered the U.S. mainstream only as an influence."

"Parenting In The Music Business" featured Amy Rigby, Susan Cowsill, Ray Wylie Hubbard, writer

Moira McCormick, and club owner Sue Miller Tweedy.

"Online Groups: Hard News Or Loose Talk?" carried the subtitle, "...vitriol, rumor and lies can be posted just as easily as real news."

"So IS Paul Dead?" presented Michael Azzerad, Vic Chesnutt, Lorraine Ali, Tommy Keene and others discussing whether Paul McCartney should have quit while he was ahead.

"SXSW is spring training for the music business."
■ *Minneapolis Star Tribune*

"Charting Success" was canceled, but that didn't stop future *Saturday Night Live* cast member Fred Armisen from taking over, as seen in his *Fred Armisen's Guide To Music And SXSW* video.

NOTABLE PANELISTS
Dust Brothers (producers), Gary Gersh (Capitol Records), Neil Strauss (*The New York Times*), Lloyd Doggett (U.S. congressman), Jonathan Demme (film director), Tony Wilson (In The City festival)

MEMORABLE SHOWCASES
> A Thursday showcase at the Buffalo Club featured headliners Les Savy Fav and House Of Large Sizes...oh, and a young M.C. squad from Los Angeles called the Black Eyed Peas.
> Native American Night on Saturday at the State Theatre included performances by Keith Secola

"No matter what country they were from and how different their music was, rock bands seemed to be screaming: 'Look at me! We're something different!" They spit fire and set their instruments ablaze (Motor City Devils, Nashville Pussy), wore bizarre or coordinated outfits (Motor City Devils, the Eyeliners, Cornelius, Demi Semi Quaver), played nontraditional rock instruments (Drums and Tuba, for example, were exactly what the name promised) or simply strove for classic pop perfection (the High Llamas, Richard Davies, the Push Stars, and Apples in Stereo), all of these acts a throwback to a time before and a contrarian response to alternative rock." ■ **Neil Strauss,** *The New York Times*

& His Wild Band Of Indians, Ulali, Robert Mirabal, Blackfire, Jerry Alfred & the Medicine Beat, Indigenous, Roxy Gordon, Thon-gya!, Cherokee Rose, Clan/destine, and the Jones Benally Family.
> Siblings Rufus and Martha Wainwright were part of a Friday night bill at La Zona Rosa; their father, Loudon Wainwright III, played on Saturday at the Texas Union Ballroom.

NOTABLE ACTS
Sonic Youth A line wrapped around the block to see their 7pm Thursday performance at La Zona Rosa, which was originally a CDNow private party.

Neko Case & the Sadies Two years before the New Pornographers debuted, Case was credited in the program book as "also drummer for Vancouver pop/punks MAOW."

Also Queens Of The Stone Age, Buddy Guy, Sam Moore, Urinals, Bardo Pond, Olivia Tremor Control, Negro Problem, Todd Snider & the Nervous Wrecks, Handsome Boy Modeling School

SOME OF THE MEDIA-SPONSORED ACTS
Hollisters (*Houston Press*), Jasper Stone (*Fort Worth Weekly*), Homer Henderson One Man Band (*Dallas Observer*), Grace Braun (*Creative Loafing*, Atlanta), Calexico (*Tuscon Weekly*), Get Up Kids (*Pitch Weekly*, Kansas City, MO), Andrew Bird's Bowl Of Fire (*News City*, Chicago), Sunset Valley (*Willamette Week*, Portland, OR), Paul Burch & the WPA Ballclub (*Nashville Scene*)

SOME OF THE AUSTIN ACTS
Molly Ivins The late political humorist's Cactus Cafe show with Austin singer-songwriter Jimmy LaFave failed to win over *Dallas Observer* critic Robert Wilonsky: "Her next book ought to be titled *Molly Ivins Sings Worse Than You*," he wrote.

Also Fastball, Scabs, Monroe Mustang, Gourds, Silver Scooter, Sixpence None The Richer, Golden Arm Trio, Fred Sanders, Reckless Kelly

SOME OF THE INTERNATIONAL ACTS
I Against I (Netherlands), Chantal Kreviazuk (Toronto ON), Arab Strap (Scotland), Cornelius

(Japan), Turbonegro (Norway), Buffalo Daughter (Japan), Plastilina Mosh (Mexico), High Llamas (UK), To Rococo Rot (Germany), Stereophonics (Wales)

WHATEVER HAPPENED TO...

Semisonic was just a couple of months from a Modern Rock #1 with "Closing Time." They released their last album in 2001, and drummer Jacob Slichter wrote a popular memoir, 2005's *So You Wanna Be A Rock And Roll Star.* Frontman Dan Wilson wrote several songs with the Dixie Chicks on their 2006 album *Taking The Long Way.*

Imani Coppola charted with "Legend Of A Cowgirl" in 1997. During Christmas 2010, a song by her group Little Jackie, "Mrs. Claus Ain't Got Nothing On Me," was featured in a Target ad campaign.

A3 had just ceased to be Alabama 3, and would go on to HBO ubiquity when "Woke Up This Morning" was chosen as the title music for a new series, *The Sopranos.*

SOFTBALL TOURNEY

Pitcher Mike Mordecai led the Clubs/Talent Buyers team to their fifth title, beating Print Media 16-12 in extra innings. The feckless rock scribes had already proven they were nowhere near as hung over as DJs, MDs and PDs, trouncing Radio 27-0 in the first round.

FILM
AWARDS

Narrative Feature Winner *Men Cry Bullets* (D: Tamara Hernandez); runner-up: *Bury Me In Kern County* (D: Julien Nitzberg)

Documentary Feature Winner *Letters Not About Love* (D: Jacki Ochs); runner-up: *Baby, It's You* (D: Anne Makepeace)

OPENING NIGHT

The Newton Boys (D: Richard Linklater) World premiere.

NOTABLE FILMS

Storefront Hitchcock (D: Jonathan Demme), *American Cowboy* (D: Kyle Henry), *Dancer* *Texas Pop. 81* (D: Tim McCandless), *Tomororw Night* (D: Louis C.K.), *Antone And The Blues: A Story Of Obsession* (D: Robb Niles)

"The Cannes Film Festival of the music world."
■ *Chicago Sun-Times*

Also The full-length cut of Austinite Paul Stekler's *Vote for Me: Politics In America* and Todd *(Old School, the Hangover)* Phillips' ill-fated *Frat House.*

INTERACTIVE
KEYNOTE SPEAKERS

Howard Rheingold, Steven Johnson, Richard Grimes, Chipp Walters

PANELS

The panels were divided into six tracks: Money And Marketing, Web Publishing, Gaming Trends, Music 2000, Digital Hollywood, and Business-To-Business. ■

"Welcome to the Festival of Broken Dreams; the one event that lets you know where you stand – somewhere in front of Wammo and behind Exene." ■ Jon Dee Graham, Austin musician

1999

SXSW **STATS** March 12 – 21

BY THE NUMBERS

829 showcasing artists
of 4,500 submissions

68 panels, workshops & sessions

46 venues & stages

7,259 registrants

$245-475 registration

$65-95 wristband

208 pages in program guide

107 trade show exhibitors

2,668 film registrants

2,233 interactive registrants

AUSTIN MUSIC AWARDS

Wednesday, March 17, Austin Music Hall

Performers Monte Warden, Kelly Willis, Charlie Robison and Bruce Robison, Reckless Kelly with Joe Ely, Kinky Friedman, the Resentments, Meg Hentges, David Garza

KEYNOTE SPEAKER

Lucinda Williams "Prior to her keynote, Lucinda was a wreck," says then SXSW panels chief Jeff McCord. "Fretting, pacing, saying she wasn't sure she could do it, that people would hate it, on and on like that. Her talk was rambling but very engaging, and she clearly loved the experience. She ran way past her time, but was completely gracious about it — when it became clear we were running very late, I just went up and stood at the side of the stage, she looked over at me, still talking, gave me a knowing smile and wrapped things up."

MEMORABLE PANELS

"Two panel titles sum up 1999," says Roland Swenson. The first: **"Downloading On The Upswing: Trouble For The Music Industry?"** ("Is the status quo in jeopardy as music becomes more readily available?"). The other: **"Writing Online vs. Writing For Print"** ("Can a writer, especially a freelancer still make a living on print alone?")

"What Are Words Worth?" A discussion about whether rock 'n' roll lyrics matter, with Gina Arnold,

Robert Christgau, Jon Langford, Paul Williams, Miriam Linna, Andy Schwartz

"The Rise And Fall Of The MC5" Moderated by Dave Marsh, with Wayne Kramer, John Sinclair, Jaan Uhelzski

"The Fastball Story" Described thusly: "For a band whose first album initially sold less than ten thousand copies, it's been a long road to overnight success. And while it's one thing to get on top, it's another to stay there. Does Fastball have another pitch?"

"The Criminalization Of Dance Culture" A discussion of how to help dance culture flourish in the face of law enforcement opposition

NOTABLE PANELISTS

Joe Boyd (Interviewed by Tom Moon of *The Philadelphia Inquirer*), Greil Marcus ("I Can't Help It If I'm Still In Love With You: Hank Williams"), Juan Atkins ("Is Rock Music Becoming Dance Music?"), Right Said Fred's Richard Fairbrass ("Artists: How We Make Records"), Kramer ("Recording Strategies"), David Byrne and Perry Watts-Russell ("A&R: The Way We Work"), Inspectah Deck ("Getting Heard In Hip-Hop")

MEMORABLE SHOWCASES

> Thursday's blockbuster country-oriented show at Stubb's featured headliners Doug Sahm and Leon Russell, but the worst rainstorm in SXSW history caused the show to be halted for fear of onstage electrocution. Sahm and Russell "played cards with secret guest performer Willie Nelson on his bus while waiting out the storm," says Roland Swenson. "At one point, the three of them decided they would all play a set together if the rain ever stopped. It didn't."

> The free-to-the-public Outdoor Stage shows had moved the previous year from Sixth Street a few blocks north to Waterloo Park. Saturday evening's lineup featured the mighty Guided By Voices plus a triptych of top local talent: Spoon, the Gourds, and Damnations TX.

> The Flaming Lips, Sparklehorse, and Mercury Rev headlined Friday's bill at Liberty Lunch. With the exception of a warm-up show in Dallas, this

was the first time the Lips had performed songs from their soon-to-be released album *The Soft Bulletin*, which was released two months later. Their performance featured the over-the-top multimedia antics that have defined them ever since.

NOTABLE ACTS

Built To Spill The Boise, ID, band played two official showcases, as well as *Spin* magazine's after-hours party with labelmates the Flaming Lips, and "caused perhaps the greatest stir of the weekend," wrote Christopher Hess in *The Austin Chronicle*.

Tom Waits His performance on Saturday at the Paramount Theatre, rarely used for SXSW shows, was one of the most memorable — and

> "And it's South by So What in the City of Austin
> I never been to Texas and I said so
> 40 minutes on stage and back at the hotel
> Somebody tell Sir Doug I said hello"
> ■ Ronny Elliott's "South by So What" from his 1999 album
> *My Nerves Are Bad Tonight* (he played Wednesday at Liberty Lunch)

hardest to get into — shows in SXSW history. "Hundreds of fans, some of whom you might have heard of, lined up outside the ornate old theater on Congress Avenue as early as 4:30 a.m. Saturday hoping to score one of South by Southwest's hottest tickets," wrote Gil Kaufman on the website *Addicted To Noise*. "At the front of the line was 28-year-old Shane Carbonneau, of Austin, who said he had to literally beg, borrow and lie to get in....Waiting behind Carbonneau on the cold concrete was Mark Linkous, frontman of the experimental Virginia rock band Sparklehorse. 'I'm a huge fan of Tom,' Linkous said. 'I'm really looking forward to this.' Linkous did, it should be noted, have more than the usual fan interest in the show. He said he was anxious to meet up with Waits later, hoping to determine that the troubadour had completed recording his part for a song on Sparklehorse's next album."

> "It's like a big summer camp for adults."
> ■ Lucinda Williams, 1999 keynote speaker

Also Bright Eyes, Patty Griffin, Hives, Robert Fripp, Mike Ness, Richard Buckner, DJ Icey, Death Cab For Cutie

SOME OF THE MEDIA-SPONSORED ACTS

Shabazz 3 (*Dallas Observer*), Go Metric USA (*Fort Worth Weekly*), Big Holiday (*Houston Press*), Czars (*Westword*, Denver), Dieselhed (*San Francisco Weekly*), Terry Allen (*Santa Fe Reporter*), Tares (*Nightflying*, Little Rock, AR), Josh Rouse (*Nashville Scene*), Tigerlilies (*Everybody's News*, Cincinnati), Ronny Elliott & the Nationals (*Weekly Planet*, Tampa, FL)

SOME OF THE AUSTIN ACTS

...And You Will Know Us By The Trail of Dead left a trail of destruction at Buffalo Club. "Objects that hit this writer, at close range," noted Christina Rees in the *Dallas Observer*, included: "1. Chunks of ice mixed with beer spat; 2. A Flying V guitar; 3. A very sweaty 140-pound drummer, who, upon destroying his drum kit, lost control of his limbs and flailed off stage. And I wasn't even up front."

Also Knife In The Water, Daniel Johnston, Enduro, Morningwood, Los Pinkys, Prescott Curlywolf, Hot Club Of Cowtown, Lil Cap'n Travis, Alejandro Escovedo Orchestra

SOME OF THE INTERNATIONAL ACTS

Jeff Beck (UK), Lo Fidelity Allstars (UK), ex-Girl (Japan), Bellatrix (Iceland), Guano Apes (Germany), Cubanisomo! (Cuba), Miles Hunt (UK), The Hives (Sweden), Seagull Screaming Kiss Her Kiss Her (Japan), Gluecifer (Norway)

WHATEVER HAPPENED TO...

Liberty Lunch The venerable indoor/outdoor venue closed out a 13-year run as one of SXSW's largest and most beloved venues with a Saturday-night show headlined by the Meat Puppets and the Bottle Rockets. Later that year, it was demolished by the City of Austin to make way for an office building (an all-too-often-repeated story in local music lore).

Tal Bachman The son of Randy Bachman (of Bachman-Turner Overdrive) had a hit with "She's So High" when he played a Thursday show at Pecan Street Ale House. He has occasionally provided political commentary on Canadian television.

SOFTBALL TOURNEY

Clubs/Buyers won over Print Media for the second straight year, 10-3. Sadly, this was the last time Doug Sahm was able to provide his wild color commentary; he died of a heart attack later that year. The tournament would be named in his memory the next year. Softball Commissioner Susan Moffat noted: "After losing two announcers in rapid succession (Country Dick Montana, d. 1995; Doug Sahm, d. 1999), SXSW wisely dropped the 'Announcer for Life' title. Current mic jocks Joe Nick Patoski and Kevin Connor were still standing last we heard."

FILM
AWARDS

Narrative Feature Winner *La Ciudad* (D: David Riker); runner-up: *Drylongso* (D: Cauleen Smith)

Documentary Feature Winner *Wadd: The Life And Times Of John C. Holmes* (D: Cass Paley); runners-up: *Hill Stomp Hollar* (D: Bradley Beesley), *Secret People* (D: John Anderson)

NOTABLE FILMS

Ed TV (opening night; D: Ron Howard, starring Matthew McConaughey), *Radiohead: Meeting People Is Easy* (D: Grant Gee), *Sex: The Annabel Chong Story* (Gough Lewis), *Desert Blue* (Morgan J. Freeman), *A Slipping Down Life* (D: Toni Kalem), *The Living Museum* (D: Jessica Yu), *Splendor* (D: Greg Araki), *A Walk On The Moon* (D: Tony Goldwyn)

INTERACTIVE
KEYNOTE SPEAKERS

Mark Cuban (billed as "co-founder of Broadcast.com"), author Michael Wolff, composer Philip Glass ■

"SXSW is a world-class festival with Southern hospitality." **Bill Paxton**

2000

SXSW **STATS** March 11 - 19

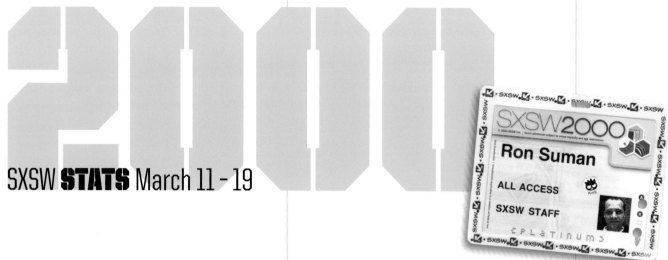

SXSW 2000
© 2000 SXSW Inc. | Event admission subject to venue capacity and age restrictions
Ron Suman
ALL ACCESS
SXSW STAFF
PLATINUM

BY THE NUMBERS

970 showcasing artists
of 4,745 submissions

67 panels, workshops & sessions

47 venues & stages

8,070 registrants

$265-495 registration

$75-95 wristband

266 pages in program guide

145 trade show exhibitors

3,787 film registrants

3,755 interactive registrants

AUSTIN MUSIC AWARDS

Wednesday, March 15, Austin Music Hall

Performers Bob Schneider; Kelly Willis; Doug Sahm Memorial with Shawn Sahm, Augie Meyers and Friends; Texas Trumpets; Terri Hendrix; Ray Wylie Hubbard; Sterling Morrison tribute with Tosca, John Cale and Alejandro Escovedo

KEYNOTE SPEAKER

Steve Earle Much of Earle's speech was about his opposition to the death penalty. "While most of us were checking into our hotels yesterday and picking up our credentials, this state, my home state, was killing a man a couple hundred miles to the northeast, and they were doing it with our money," he said. "A little piece of every dollar we spend here in Austin at South by Southwest will kill someone somewhere down the line."

"He'd been on our most-wanted list for years," says Roland Swenson. "At the end, he anguished over whether some deserving band might be ignored while he played his showcase later that night. A short rainstorm during his set emptied Stubb's, relieving his conscience."

MEMORABLE PANELS

"Secure Digital Music Standards & The Future Of Internet Music"
"No less than 10 panel sessions were devoted to music and the internet that year," recalls Roland Swenson. "On the SXSW Trade Show floor, exhibitor Sean Parker greeted visitors asking about his new company, Napster."

"Consumer Remixing: The Next Mp3?" This prescient panel was a part of SXSW Interactive.

"The Next Shit: Forging New A&R Directions In A Climate Of Soundalikes" a.k.a., "we're really sick of Limp Bizkit and Korn."

"Sterling Morrison: The Velvet Underdog" and **"Made For You And Me: Woody Guthrie's Dust Bowl Legacy"** Tribute panels to two greats, the former with Bill Bentley, John Cale, Mary Hattman (Pork), college professors

"Kiss was never cool. Kiss is not cool now. Kiss is never going to be cool." ■ Steve Earle

Joe Kruppa and Marvin Williams Jr., and writer Stewart Wise; the latter with Dave Marsh, Mary Jo Guthrie Edgmon, Michael Fracasso, writer Greg Johnson, and Jimmy LaFave.

NOTABLE PANELISTS

Patti Smith (interview with Chuck Phillips of the *Los Angeles Times*), JD Souther (Songwriting), Bob Ezrin (Internet Radio), Chuck D (Artist's panel), Elliot Roberts (interview with

"SXSW is an invigorating experience. From the quality of the films and panels to the equally important enthusiasm of the participants, SXSW is a great festival at which to celebrate all things indie." ■ *Moviemaker*

David Fricke of *Rolling Stone*), Thomas Dolby Robertson ("Making Noise on the Net"), John Perry Barlow ("Legal Concerns in the Digital Music Era"), teenage singer-songwriter Shannon Curfman and her mother Mary ("The Kids are Alright"), John Paul Jones (inteview with Jim DeRogatis of the *Chicago Sun-Times*)

MEMORABLE SHOWCASES

> A BMI Showcase on Friday at Austin Music Hall featured a major-league Americana lineup, with Jim Lauderdale, Kim Richey, Whiskeytown, Shelby Lynne, Reckless Kelly and Robert Earl Keen.
> SXSW and Hip Hop Mecca presented five showcases, including "Hip Hop Hump Day"

(on Wednesday, natch) at the Mercury; the two-stage "Four Element And Year Zero Battle" (with P.E.A.C.E, Blackalicious, X-ecutioners and Del Tha Funkee Homosapien) on Thursday at Velvet and Velvet Patio; "Underground Superfest 2000" (hosted by J Smoov and Chuck D) on Friday at the Back Room (with Atmosphere, Rhymesayers Collective and Living Legends); "A Night of Hip-Hop With The Entertainer" on Saturday at Stubb's (featuring Guru, Doug E Fresh, Jungle Brothers and Dead Prez); and a Sunday show at Velvet headlined by the Deep South Coalition.

> The Frogs and Sixteen Deluxe were among the headliners at "Beerland at the Gallery Lombardi Lounge (at the location of the former Electric Lounge)." This convoluted temporary venue name included elements of Austin rock clubs past (Electric Lounge) and future (Beerland, which later opened on Red River) — and the actual patch of real estate became an office building that, as of December 2010, now houses SXSW itself.

> The return of Austin/San Francisco punk legend Gary Floyd (the Dicks, Sister Double Happiness) with his new band Black Kali Ma, as part of an Alternative Tentacles-sponsored showcase at Atomic Cafe on Saturday, was marred by problems with the club's in-house security, as *Austin Chronicle* music editor Raoul Hernandez told the *Austin American-Statesman*:

"I'm up front and start getting into it when I remember the joint a friend of mine had given me that day. Now, I like to indulge as much as the next guy, but I don't carry it around. This night, I just happened to have a joint in my wallet. Without even thinking about it, I whip it out and try to light it. Notice I say 'try.' As I'm fumbling with it, suddenly there's this flashlight in my face, and the next thing I know, I'm being hustled through the front door by a snarling, 6-foot-5, 300-pound security guy. Booted!

"But, but, but...I'm outside pleading with the door guy ('PLEAZZZZZEEEEEE. Do you know who I am?!?'), and I'm not out there two minutes when Mr. Flashlight comes crashing through the same front door manhandling two

skinny kids. He pushes one out onto the side-walk, and literally picks up the other guy, who was in the crook of his arm, and body slams him down on the pavement. Literally at my feet. The guy's out cold, eyes wide open, pupils complete-ly dilated. It's one of those things you lean over the guy hoping he's not dead. Fortunately the poor kid was OK — EMS got there quickly — but it was one of the most brutal things I've ever witnessed. My SXSW ended right there."

NOTABLE ACTS

Tenacious D When his band the Wannabes were scheduled to play at the same time on Saturday night, Austin rock scene gadfly Hunter Darby successfully begged SXSW to reschedule them so he could see Jack Black and Kyle Gass's comedy-metal duo at Austin Music Hall.

Patti Smith The legendary poetic rocker played a free Outdoor Stage show on Friday at Waterloo Park, with local favorite the Alejandro Escovedo Orchestra opening.

Guided By Voices Robert Pollard's heralded rock band went rogue with their *Revolver*-sponsored show. "He apologized to SXSW for 'having this little party without them,' adding, 'Hey, man, you scratch my back, I'll scratch yours,'" wrote Mindy LaBernz in *The Austin Chronicle*. "This sentiment reflected a comment he made at a par-ty the day before, mentioning that SXSW was probably mad at him for not playing the confer-ence, but the money for the *Revolver* party was too good to pass up."

Also Gov't Mule, Elliott Smith, Helio Sequence, South Park Mexican, Modest Mouse, Charles Gayle, John Paul Jones, Ray Price with Hank Williams III, At The Drive-In

SOME OF THE MEDIA-SPONSORED ACTS

Adventures of Jet (*Dallas Observer*), Stumptone (*Fort Worth Weekly*), Japanic (*Houston Press*), Randy Garibay & Cats Don't Sleep (*San Antonio Current*), Tift Merritt & the Carbines (*Independent Weekly*, NC Triangle), Beachwood Sparks (*Los Angeles New Times*), Sarah Harmer (*NOW*, Toronto), Supagroup (*Offbeat*, New

Orleans), ThaMusemeant (*Santa Fe Reporter*), Star Room Boys (*Flagpole*, Athens, GA)

SOME OF THE AUSTIN ACTS

Okkervil River Then a trio that "takes folk music back to Leadbelly and Dock Boggs," per the program-guide description.

Also Adult Rodeo, Spoon, Barbers, Barkers, Kiss-Offs, Rubinchik's Orkestyr, Charlie Burton & the Texas 12 Steppers, Sister 7, 7% Solution, Texacala Jones & the TJ Hookers

SOME OF THE INTERNATIONAL ACTS

Tegan & Sara The 19-year-old twin sisters from Cal-gary, Canada, had just signed to Neil Young's Vapor label.

Glen Hansard of the Frames That's how the future *Once*/Swell Season star from Dublin, Ireland, got billed this time around.

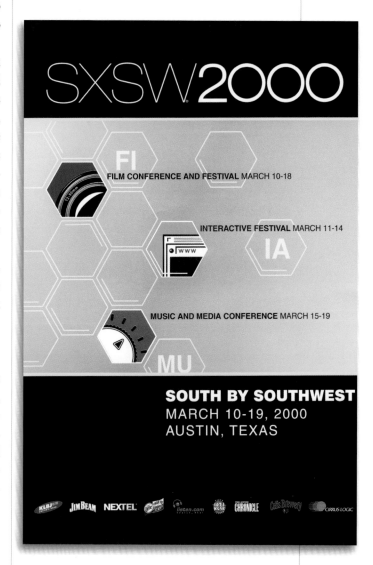

Also David Gray (Wales), Daryl Ann (Netherlands), Astrid (Scotland), Resorte (Mexico), Not From There (Australia), Love Love Straw (Japan), Merrymakers (Sweden)

WHATEVER HAPPENED TO...

Scared of Chaka The New Mexico garage-pop-punk band broke up in 2001, then reunited in 2009; in between, bassist Dave Hernandez was a member of the Shins.

> "One of the coolest and most filmmaker friendly festivals to ever exist...SXSW is...about the making of films, the filmmakers, and the films themselves." ■ *indieWIRE*

Shivaree Highly touted while on Capitol, these Angelenos were last heard from with the 2007 covers album *Tainted Love: Mating Calls & Fight Songs.*

Webnoize The online music trade mag co-presented the "Future Of Internet Music" panel. It was offline by December 2001.

SOFTBALL TOURNEY

A nine-game winning streak and two-year title run for Clubs/Talent Buyers ended as Print Media, the losers in both 1998 and 1999, finally got the better in a 21-4 laugher. The ink-stained wretches — for another year or two at least — were led by "rookie righthander Charlie Sotelo," also a comedian and host of Austin's cable access *Show With No Name.* Also, the Musicians team moved out of last place in the all-time standings for the first time in frachise history, and "about a ton of barbecue was eaten."*

*(this statistic was not fact-checked)

> "(SXSW) has become a staple on the festival circuit...for its ability to launch a film." ■ *Indiemaker*

FILM
AWARDS

Narrative Feature Winners *Rollercoaster* (D: Scott Smith) and *Wildflowers* (D: Melissa Painter)

Documentary Feature Winner *The Target Shoots First* (D: Chris Wilcha); runners-up: *The Ballad Of Ramblin' Jack* (D: Aiyana Elliot) and *Just, Melvin* (D: James Ronald Whitney)

NOTABLE FILMS

Neil Young: Silver and Gold (D: L.A. Johnson), *American Pimp* (D: Allen Hughes, Albert Hughes), *George Wallace: Settin' The Woods On Fire* (D: Daniel McCabe, Paul Stekler), *Grass* (D: Ron Mann), *Live Nude Girls UNITE!* (D: Julia Query, Vicky Funari), *Noriega: God's Favorite* (D: Roger Spottiswoode, written by Lawrence Wright)

Also Retrospectives of D.A. Pennebaker and Monte Hellman films; Todd Phillips' documentary about Phish, *Bittersweet Motel*; the directorial debut of Phish bassist Mike Gordon, *Outside Out*; Bradley Beesley's documentary short *The Flaming Lips Have Landed*

INTERACTIVE
KEYNOTE SPEAKERS

Rob Burgess and Kevin Lynch (Macromedia), Denise Caruso (*New York Times* digital commerce column), Stewart Brand

OTHER FEATURED SPEAKERS

Michael Robertson (MP3.com), Dannie Ashe (Danni's Hard Drive), Tiffany Shlain (Webby Awards), Steven Johnson (Feed), Michael O'Donnell (Salon) ■

2001

SXSW **STATS** March 9 - 18

BY THE NUMBERS

1,012 showcasing artists
of 4,735 submissions

69 panels, workshops & sessions

48 venues & stages

7,067 registrants

$295-500 registration

$85-105 wristband

266 pages in program guide

116 trade show exhibitors

3,293 film registrants

164 films screened

3,155 interactive registrants

AUSTIN MUSIC AWARDS

Wednesday, March 14, Austin Music Hall

Performers Vallejo; Lucinda Williams; Slaid Cleaves; Gourds, "86ed: A Tribute to Austin music in the '80s" featuring Michael Hall, Alejandro Escovedo, Jon Dee Graham, Kim Longacre, Cindy Toth, Randy Franklin, Joey Shuffield, Steve Collier, and Kathy McCarty; Blues Revue featuring James Cotton, Jimmie Vaughan, Lou Ann Barton and Derek O'Brien with George Rains, Roscoe Beck and Riley Osborne; MC Paul Ray

KEYNOTE SPEAKER

Ray Davies The legendary leader of the Kinks "read a very funny, literate speech for his keynote that included his ability to do dead-on impressions of Johnny Rotten and other Brit notables," remembers Roland Swenson. "Later he jumped onstage with the New Pornographers for a song during their set at La Zona Rosa."

"We should just go out and listen to as much music as possible, and enjoy it," Davies said. "It's really why we are here."

MEMORABLE PANELS

"The Real Buddy Holly Story," with Holly's widow Maria Elena Holly, Connie Gibbons of the Buddy Holly Center, and Joe Nick Patoski; and **"The Gram Parsons Legacy"** with Holly George-Warren, Earle Poole Ball, Rhino Records' James Austin, Stanley Booth and Jon Langford

"Pro Tools: Gift Or Curse?" The follow-up question being: "Does Pro Tools level the playing field for underfunded artists or does it degrade the talents of professional engineers?" With Dave McNair, Steve Berlin, Barbara K, Chris Stamey.

"The warm wind outside smells like desert flowers and the taxi drivers all say 'Y'all'. And it's all even better if you're going to the 15th South by Southwest. SXSW is the largest event of its kind in the U.S. outside of New York and L.A., and showcases new and independent music, film and interactive media technologies. There are hundreds of live music gigs, more than 80 films, and various new technology events, industry discussion panels and two seriously large trade shows. There are thousands of delegates and journalists, mostly North American, and frankly it's the best way you can spend 10 culture-filled days in the US. It really is that good." ■ *The Herald*, Scotland

"Almost Famous?" Why are contemporary rock critics less interesting than the gonzo mavericks of the past? Featuring: contemporary rock critics!

"When Will Digital Music Be Legal And Popular?" Described thusly in the program guide: "The notion of the 'Celestial Jukebox,' any song available digitally any time, has great appeal, but has obstacles to overcome before its successful development."

"Boy Howdy! The Creem Story" In which panelists considered the contention: "What the *New Yorker* was to the golden age of theater criticism, *Creem* was to rock 'n' roll literature." With Jim DeRogatis, Ben Edmonds, Bill Holdship, Dave Marsh, John Morthland, Jaan Uhelski, Ed Ward, and Susan Whitall

NOTABLE PANELISTS

David Byrne (interview with Greg Kot), Hal Willner (interview with Erik Flannigan), Sharon Osbourne (interview with David Fricke), Miles Copeland III ("The View From The Helm"), Jello Biafra ("Will Music Be Regulated By Law?"), Jennifer Toomey ("Does Gender Hinder?"), Ike Turner ("Artists: Recording v. Performance"), Glen Phillips ("If I Knew Then What I Know Now"), Jazzy Jay ("Cut Paste And Scratch: Hip-Hop Innovation From DJ Culture")

MEMORABLE SHOWCASES

> VH1 Presented "Bands On The Run" with the Josh Dodes Band, Soulcracker, Harlow, and Flickerstick with special guests Fastball.

> A showcase by booking agency the Billions Corporation featured Idlewild, Saul Williams, Brassy, Preston School of Industry, the New Pornographers, and Atomic Numbers.

> A showcase in conjunction with the movie *Scratch* featured MC Rakaa Iriscience & the Jurassic 5 emcees, Mathmatic Djs, DJ NuMark, DJ Z-Trip, Mix Master Mike, Jazzy Jay, and Grand Wizard Theodore.

NOTABLE ACTS

Strokes Hyped as a return to form for New York rock 'n' roll, they had a good amount of buzz preceding their SXSW showcase from early Rough Trade EP *The Modern Age*.

Soft Boys The cult-favorite band featuring Robyn Hitchcock and Kimberley Rew played together for the first time in two decades to commemorate the Matador reissue of *Underwater Moonlight*.

White Stripes The Detroit two-piece played the Sympathy for the Record Industry showcase just before the release of their breakthrough album, *White Blood Cells*, in June 2001.

Also Deerhoof, Ike Turner, Unwound, ALL, Robert Randolph, Interpol, My Morning Jacket, DJ Assault, Jello Biafra, Black Crowes, DJ Spooky, Dr. Demento, Lazy Lester, Yngwie Malmsteen, Shins

SOME OF THE MEDIA-SPONSORED ACTS

Drive-By Truckers (*Flagpole*, Athens, GA), Japanic (*Houston Press*), Icelandic (*Weekly Alibi*, Albequerque, NM), Epstein's Mother (*Citylife*, Las Vegas), Chomsky (*Dallas Observer*), Standing Wave Phenomenon (*Santa Fe Reporter*), Zach Parrish (*Salt Lake City Weekly*), Kind (*Nightflying*, Fayetteville, AR), Venus Hum (*Nashville Scene*), Anders Osborne (*Offbeat*, New Orleans, LA)

SOME OF THE AUSTIN ACTS

Adult Rodeo, Jeff Klein, Bob Schneider, Explosions in the Sky, Pong, Bukka Allen, American Analog Set, Stephen Bruton, Sangre de Toro, Palaxy Tracks

SOME OF THE INTERNATIONAL ACTS

Elbow (UK), Thomas Mapfumo (Zimbabwe), Mogwai (Scotland), Peaches (Canada/Germany), Cath Carroll (UK), Cosmic Rough Riders (Scotland), King Brothers (Japan), Tahiti 80 (France), Senegal Acoustic (France), Kasey Chambers (Australia)

WHATEVER HAPPENED TO...

Train The San Francisco band, which played Thursday at La Zona Rosa, went on to win two Grammy Awards in 2002 and then more or less faded out...until 2010's "Hey Soul Sister," which was named both the best video (VH1) and worst song (the *Village Voice)* of that year.

Wesley Willis The wildly prolific, mentally ill Chicago artist and punk rocker died of leukemia at age 40 in 2003.

SOFTBALL TOURNEY

Another wet one as the entire tournament was canceled because of bad weather and instead became an afternoon BBQ party at Antone's, with guest DJ Dr. Demento.

FILM
AWARDS

Narrative Feature Winners *Low Self Esteem Girl (D: Blaine Thurier);* an especially thrilling SXSW for Thurier, as the Canadian filmmaker is also in the New Pornographers. Runner-up: The Zero (D: John Ryman).

Documentary Feature Winner *Hybrid* (D: Monteith McCollum); runners-up: *Arnato: A Love Affair With Opera* (D: Stephen Ives); *Okie Noodling* (D: Bradley Beesley).

NOTABLE FILMS

Jerry Wexler: Immaculate Funk (D: Tom Thurman), *Lillith On Top* (D: Lynn Stopkewich), *Pavarotti Of The Plains: Don Walser's Story* (D: T.J. Morehouse), *Southlander* (D: Steve Hanft), *Scratch* (D: Doug Pray), *We Sold Our Souls For Rock 'n' Roll* (D: Penelope Spheeris), sneak peek at *Waking Life* (D: Richard Linklater), *Memento* (D: Christopher Nolan), *Accordion Dreams* (D: Hector Galan), *Supertroopers* (D: Jay Chandrasekhar)

1ST ANNUAL TEXAS FILM HALL OF FAME INDUCTION

Sissy Spacek, Liz Smith, Robert Benton, Mike Simpson, Bill Witliff

INTERACTIVE
KEYNOTE SPEAKERS

John Battelle (The Industry Standard), John Heileman (author of *Pride Before The Fall: The Trials Of Bill Gates And The End Of The Microsoft Era*), Ian Clarke (The Freenet Project), DJ Spooky and Michael Hirschorn (Inside.com)

NOTABLE PANELISTS

Larry Harvey (Burning Man), Scott McCloud (Reinventing Comics), Derek Powazek (Powazek Productions), David Talbot (Salon) ■

2001 Film Big Bag art courtesy of Cartoon Network and the Power Puff Girls

"Steadily growing in stature, the (SXSW) film festival is now a full on event...bringing together young and emerging filmmakers, journalists, and a smattering of celebs and established peers for a surprisingly lively mix." ■ *Film Comment,* May/June 2001

continued from page 118

Luke Doucet and the White Falcon
Luke Doucet and Veal
Luke Pickett
Luke Temple
Luke Zimmerman
Lullaby for the Working Class
Lullabye Arkestra
Lumba
Lumberob and Limber Jad Fair
Lumbre Chicana
Lume
Luminares
Luminous Orange
Lump
Luna
Luna Halo
Lunar Heights
Lunatex
Lusine
Lusk
Lust Murder bOX
Lusting After Mary
Lustre
Lustre King
Lutefisk
Luther Wright & the Wrongs
Lydia Loveless
Lydia Lunch
Lying In States
Lykke Li
Lyle Lovett
Lymbyc Systym
Lynhurst
Lynn Miles
LynnMarie
Lynx Squad
Lyrics Born
LZ Love

M

M-Dot
M. Takara 3
M. Ward
M. Ward (solo)
M.A.N.D.Y.
M.C. Candy
M.I.A.
M.I.R.V.
M.O.T.O.
M1 of dead prez
Mac Arnold & Plate Full O' Blues
Mac Lethal
Mac McAnally
Macavity
Macha
Machinedrum
Machinery Hall
Mack mackenzie
Mack Winston & The Reflections
Mackintosh Braun
Macromantics
Macrowaves with Tom "X" Hancock
Macy Gray
Mad Flava
Mad for the Racket
Mad Hatter
Mad Juana
Mad Scientist
Mad Staring Eyes
Madagascar
Madame Recamier
Madeleine Peyroux
Madelia
Madeline
Madeline Minx
Madi Diaz
Madison
Madlib
Madrugada
Mads Langer
Mae
Mae Day
Maggie Estep
Maggie Horn
Maggie Walters
Magic Arm
Magic Bullets
Magic Christian
Magic Cropdusters
Magic Lantern
Magic Magic
Magic Surprise
Magic Wands
Magik Markers
Magna-Fi
Magnapop
Magnet
Magnet School

Morrissey (2006)

Magneta Lane
Magnifico
Magno aka Magnificent
Magnolia Electric Company
Magnolia Shorty
Magnolia Summer
Magpie
Mahjongg
Mahogany
Maia Sharp
Maimou
Mainline
Majesty Crush
Major Lazer
Major Stars
Majorette
Majority DOG
Make A Rising
Make Believe
Make Believers
Make Model
Make the Girl Dance
Makeshifte
Maki Rinka
Makina
Maktub
Mala Rodriguez
Mala Suerte
Malachai
Malachi
Malacoda
Maladment
Malajube
Malcolm Holcombe
Malcolm Middleton
Maldita Vecindad y Los Hijos del Quinto Patio
Male Bonding
Malente
Malford Milligan
Malford Milligan & Friends
Malford Milligan's Soul Revue
Malkovich
Mall Weirdos
Maluca
Malverde
Mambo Combo
Mammoth Grinder
Mammút
Mammy Namms
Mamou
Man Man
Man or Astro-Man?
Man Ray
Man Scouts of America
Manatee
Manchester Orchestra
Manda
Mandarin
Mandi Perkins
Mandible
Mando Diao
Mando Saenz
Mandy Barnett
Mandy Mercier
Mané Badiane
Maneja Beto
Manhattan Love Suicides
Manhole
Manic
Manic D Press showcase hosted by Jennifer Joseph
Manic Hispanic
Manic Shuffle
Manic Shuttle
Manikin
Manishevitz
Mannequin Men
Mannish Boys
Mano Negra
Manooghi Hi
Mansions
Mantler
Mantles
Mapei
Maplewood
Maps & Atlases
Maquiladora
Marah
Marbles
Marc Berger
Marc Broussard
Marc Maron
Marc Moss
Marc Muller
Marc Olsen
Marc Smith
March
Marchel Ivery
Marching Band
Marching Two-Step
Marcia Ball
Marcia Ball, Lou Ann Barton, Angela Strehli
Marco Benevento Trio
Marco Polo & Torae
Marcus Bonfanti
Marcus Hummon
Marcy Playground
Mare
Maren Parusel
Margaret Cho
Margot & The Nuclear So and So's
Maria Bamford
Maria Fatal
Mariachi El Bronx

Marian Bradfield
Marianas Trench
Marianne Dissard
Marianne Osiel
Marigold
Marilisa
Marilyn Rucker and Goose Gumbo
Marina & The Diamonds
Mario Grigorov
Mario Matteoli
Marion Loguidice Band
Marion Winik
Marissa Nadler
Marit Bergman
Marit Larsen
Maritime
Marjorie Fair
Mark Agee
Mark Bingham
Mark Bragg Band
Mark Curry
Mark D
Mark Daniel Brown
Mark David Ashworth
Mark DeNardo
Mark Deutrom
Mark Eitzel
Mark Erelli
Mark Gardener (RIDE acoustic)
Mark Geary
Mark Halata & Texavia
Mark Kozelek
Mark Lizotte
Mark Luke Daniels
Mark Luna
Mark Mallman
Mark McGrain & Plunge
Mark Morris
Mark Mulholland
Mark of Kane
Mark Pickerel
Mark Pickerel & His Praying Hands
Mark Rubin and his Ridgetop Syncopators featuring musicians from the Newton Boys Soundtrack and many special guest!
Mark Schatz
Mark Selby
Mark Sultan
Mark Tabberner
Marked Men
Marko Ellinger
Markus Nordenstreng
Marla Hansen
Marlee MacLeod
Marlee MacLeod & The Lonesome Choir
Marli
Marlowe
Marmoset
Marnie Stern
Marshall Chapman
Marshall Crenshaw
Marshall Ford Swing Band
Marshall Law
Marshmallow Coast
Marta Gomez
Martha Kelly
Martha Wainwright
Marti Brom
Martin Devaney
Martin Zellar
Martin, Barton, Sweeney
Martina Sorbara
Marty Raybon (of Shenandoah) and Full Circle
Marty Stuart
Marty Stuart and His Fabulous Superlatives
Marty Willson-Piper
Martyn Bennett
Maruosa
Marv Won
Marvin
Marvin Denton/Scott Newberg
Marvin Etzioni
Mary and Mars
Mary Bouc Trio
Mary Coppin
Mary Cutrufello
Mary Gauthier
Mary Jane Lamond
Mary Karlzen
Mary Lee's Corvette
Mary Lorson and Saint Low
Mary Lou Lord
Mary McBride
Mary McCaslin
Mary 'n Tary
Mary on the Dash
Mary Reynolds
Mary Schindler
Mary Timony
Mary Van Note
Mary Weiss
Mary Welch y Nopal Negro
Maryann Price
Maryann Price with the Slim Richey Jazz Band
Maryanne
Marynka and Some Lovely Girls

Maryslim
Mascott
Maserati
Masha Bijlsma Band
Mason Jennings
Mason Ruffner
Masonic
Master Shortie
Mastodon
Mat Kearney
Matador Down
Matchless
Material Issue
Mates of State
Math the Band
Mathematicians
Mathmatic DJ's
Mathmatic Turntable Collective
Matias Aguayo
Matisyahu
Matson Belle
Matt & Kim
Matt Barber
Matt Bearden
Matt Braunger
Matt Braunger, Chelsea Peretti, Scott Aukerman, Joe Mande
Matt Braunger, Howard Kremer, Joe Mande and Andi Smith
Matt Caldwell
Matt Hires
Matt Keating
Matt Keating & Emily Spray
Matt King
Matt Mays & El Torpedo
Matt McCormack
Matt Morris
Matt Murphy
Matt Nathanson
Matt O'Donnell
Matt Pond
Matt Pond PA
Matt Powell
Matt Pryor
Matt Ruby
Matt Sheehy
Matt Shipp and William Parker
Matt Suggs
Matt the Electrician
Matt Walker with Ashley Davis
Matterhorn
Matthew
Matthew and the Arrogant Sea
Matthew Caws (of Nada Surf)
Matthew Dear
Matthew Good
Matthew Good Band
Matthew John Conley
Matthew Mayfield
Matthew Perryman Jones
Matthew Robinson
Matthew Ryan
Matthew Sweet
Mau Mau Chaplains
Maurice Kirya
Mauschovnian Love Beat
Maven
Maverick Sabre
Mavis Staples
Max Cady
Max Julien
Max Stalling
Max Tundra
Maxeen
Maximo Park
Maximum Coherence During Flying
Maxon Blewitt
Maya Azucena
Maybe It's Reno
MayDay
Mayer Hawthorne & The County
Maylin
Mayyors
Mazarin
Mazoni
MC Chris
MC Fatal
MC Frontalot
MC Lars
MC Overload
MC Overlord
MC Rakaa Iriscience / the Jurassic 5 emcees
MC Teddy Lee
MC Trachiotomy
MC Yella
McCarthy Trenching
McKay Brothers
MCKC
McLemore Avenue
McPhD
Mddl Fngz
Me First
Me First and the Gimme Gimmes
Meaghan O'Bryne
Mean Gus
Mean Reds
Measles Mumps Rubella

Mach One
Mectapus
Medeski Martin & Wood
Medi & The Medicine Show
Media Kreeps
Medicine
Medicine Fuck Dream
Mediumwave
Meese
Meg Hentges
Meg Hutchinson
Meg Lee Chin
Megababe
Megafaun
Megan Reilly
Megaphone
MegaRex
Megasoid
MegaZilla
Meiko
Mekons
Mel
Mel Brown & the Silent Partners
Mel Sandico
Melanie Doane
Melee
Meliss FX
Melissa Auf der Maur
Melissa Ferrick
Melissa Javors
Melissa McClelland
Melissa McClelland and the White Falcon
Melissa Miller
Melissa Miller & John Strohm
Melissa St. Pierre
Melissa Young
Mellow
Melodyboy
Melomane
Melonie Cannon
Melys
Mem Shannon
Mem Shannon & The Membership
Memory Dean
Memory Tapes
Men
Men from Earth
Men From Nantucket
Mendoza Line
Meneguar
Menomena
Mensclub
Mental Chaos
Menwhopause
Meow
Meow Meow
Merchants of Venus
Merciana
Mercova
Mercury Rev
Mercy Rule
Mere Mortals
Meredith Bragg
Meredith Bragg and the Terminals
Meredith Louise Miller
Meridian
Meriwether
Mermen
Merrick
Merrick Brown
Meryn Cadell
Merz
Messiah J & The Expert
Mest
Metal Hearts
Metal Urbain
Metalchicks
Metallagher
Meterman
Methods of Dance
Metric
Metro Riots
Metro Stylee
Metronomy
Mew
mewithoutYou
Mexiclan
Mezklah
MF Doom
MG&V
MGMT
Mi Ami
Mia Riddle
Miami Horror
Micachu
Micah Dalton
Micah Gilbert
Micah Green
Micah P. Hinson
Mice Parade
Michael "5000" Watts
Michael Ballew
Michael Ballew, Rusty Wier & Friends
Michael Bellar/the AS-IS Ensemble
Michael Bradford
Michael Dart
Michael de Jong
Michael Denvir
Michael E. Johnson & the Killer Bees
Michael Erhardt

Michael Fath
Michael Feinberg
Michael Fracasso
Michael Glabicki
Michael Haaga
Michael Hall
Michael Hall and the Woodpeckers
Michael Hardie
Michael Holland
Michael Hurley
Michael Hurtt and the Haunted Hearts
Michael J. Martin
Michael James Band
Michael Martin Murphey
Michael McDermott
Michael Michael
Michael Monroe
Michael Penn
Michael Petak
Michael Shelley
Michael Showalter
Michael Smith
Michael Tolcher
Michael Tomlinson
Michael Whitmore
Michael Williams
Michael Zapruder's Rain Of Frogs
Michaelangelo
Michaell Peak
Michal Towber
Michael Elwood
Michele
Michele M. Serros
Michele Solberg
Michelle Anthony
Michelle Biloon
Michelle Malone
Michelle Malone & Drag the River
Michelle Schumann & Austin Chamber Music Center
Michelle Shocked
Michna
Mickey Factz
Micky and The Motorcars
Mico De Noche
Micranots
Micro Mini
Micronaut
Mic T
Middle Class Rut
Middle Finger Salute
Middlefinger
Middleman
Midfield General
Midget Minor
Midiron Blast Shaft
Midlake
Midnight Masses
Midnight Movies
Midnight Peacocks
Midnight Youth
Midnite Snake
Midori
Midori Umi
Midred
Midtown Dickens
Midwest Product
Mieka Pauley
Migas
Miguel Mendez
Miho Wada
Miike Snow
Mika
Mika Miko
Mika Uchizato
Mikaela's Fiend
Mike 2600
Mike and Ike
Mike Badger
Mike Bones
Mike Doughty
Mike Dowling
Mike Errico
Mike Farris
Mike Griffin & the Unknown Blues Band
Mike Hearne
Mike Ireland & Holler
Mike Jones
Mike Keneally
Mike Kindred
Mike Ladd
Mike Landschoot
Mike Martt
Mike Morris
Mike Ness
Mike Nicolai
Mike Peters
Mike Peters / The Alarm
Mike Plume Band
Mike Posner
Mike Relm
Mike Rep
Mike Rosenthal
Mike West & Myshkin
Mike Wexler
Mildred
Miles Dethmuffen
Miles
Miles
Miles Benjamin Anthony Robinson
Miles Hunt
Miles Kurosky (Ex-Beulah)

Miles Zuniga
Militant Babies
Miller's Tale
Million Dead
Million Dollar Marxists
Million Year Dance
Millo Torres y el Tercer Planeta
Milo Binder
Milow
Milton Mapes
Mimi Schnieder
Mind Splinters
Mindcandy
Mindcrime
Mindy Klusmann & Damian Green
Mindy Smith
Mineral
Mingering Mike
Mingo Fishtrap
Mini Crab
Mini Mansions
Miniature Tigers
Minibar
Minibosses
Minipop
Mink
Mink Lungs
Minmae
Minnie Driver
Minor League
MINSK
Mint Royale
Minus Grace
Minus The Bear
Miracle Drug
Miracle Fortress
Miracle Legion
Miracle Room
Mirage
Mirah
Miranda Lee Richards
Misfats
Misha
Mishka
Miss Derringer
Miss Galaxie
Miss Kelley Foster
Miss LaVelle White
Miss Li
Miss Molly & the Passion
Miss Molly & the Whips
Miss Murgatroid
Miss Murgatroid & Petra Haden
Miss Universe
Miss Xanna Don't & the Wanted
Missile Command
Missile Girl Scoot
MissinCat
Mission of Burma
Mission to the Sea
Mississippi Mafia
Missy Higgins
Mistah F.A.B.
Mistletoe
Mistress Stephanie & Her Melodic Cat
Mitch Easter & the Virtuosos
Mitch Watkins
Mitch Watkins Group
Mitch Webb and the Swindles
Mitra
Mittens OK
Mittens on Strings
Mix Master Mike
MixHell
Mixtwitch
Miz Korona
Miz Metro
Mizpah
MJ Torrance
MK Ultra
MNDR
Mo Jamal Rumi Band
Mo Robson
Mo Solid Gold
Móa
Moanin' Michelle Malone and L.B.#1
Mobile
Mobius Band
Mobtown
Moby
Mocean Worker
Mockinpott
Model Engine
Model Rockets
Model/Actress
Modern Farmer
Modern Skirts
Modest Mouse
Modey Lemon
modlang
Moe Green
moe.
Mofro
Mog Stunt Team
Mogue Doyle
Mogwai
Mohair
Mohammed Al Farra
Moi Caprice
Moist
Moist Fist

Mojave 3
Mojo Monkeys
Mojo Nixon
Mojo Nixon & Skid Roper
Mojo Nixon & the Toadliquors
Mojo Nixon & the Toadliquors w/ Special Guest Jello Biafra
MOJOE
Moka Only
Moka Only + Def 3
Moke
Moler
Molly
Molly & the Makers
Molly Ivins, Honkytonk Sweetheart and Friends
Molly McGuire
Molotov
Moly
mom
Moments Notice
Mommy and Daddy
Mon Khmer
Mona De Bo
Monahans
Monarch
Monarchs
Monareta
Mondo Drag
Mondo Generator
Mondo Topless
Mondoz
Moneen
Money
Money Mark
Money Money
Money Waters
Moneybrother
Moneypenny
Monica Giraldo
MonicaBlaire
Monikker
Monk E. Wilson
Monkey Meet
Monkey Paw
Monk's Night Out
Monks of Doom
Mono
MonoBand
Monokino
Monotonix
Monotract
Monroe Mustang
Monsieur Jeffrey Evans
Monster
Monster Magnet
Monster Maker
Monsters Are Waiting
Montag
Montana
Monte Montgomery
Monte Negro
Monte Warden
Monterey Jack
Month of Sundays
Monty Are I
Monty McClinton
Monty Montgomery
Mood Ruff
Moodafaruka
Mook
Mookie Jones
Moon Duo
Mooncoup
Moonlight Towers
Moonman
Moonpools & Caterpillars
Moonraker
Moonrats
Moonshine Willy
Mooseknows Jazz Trio
More Dogs
More Or Les
More Power to Your Elbow
Moreland & Arbuckle
Morgan Murphy
Moriarty
Morning 40 Federation
Morning State
Morning Teleportation
Morningwood
Moros Eros
Morphine
Morrisey, Cleaves, and Hubbard
Morrissey
Mos Generator
Moscas
Moshe Kasher
Mosquitos
Most Precious Blood
Most Wanted
Mostly Bears
Motel Motel
moth wranglers
Moth!Fight!
Mother
Mother Falcon
Mother Hips
Mother Mother
Mother Superior
Mother Tongue
mothercoat
Motor Skills
Motörhead
Motorpsycho

continued on page 158

Mayhem And Music

If I hadn't taken a year off, this would be my 20th SXSW. Some of my favorite music industry moments have taken place during this conference – randomly ending up in an Arquette's hotel room with Robyn Hitchcock, watching Imperial Teen make a splash, making a splash in the Hyatt's hot tub late night with Carol Schutzbank, Rick Gershon and friends, ending

SXSW MEMORIES

the week drinking beer iced in a bathtub and geeking out to someone's iPod at 4am with friends from several continents, throwing an afternoon party that featured some of my favorite musicians, repeatedly and literally

running into Ed Harcourt in strange places, watching Mudhoney mock a very hungover Mark Pickerel, watching my male musician friends be jealous because Rhett Miller hugged me and not them, a mind-blowing Robyn Hitchcock/You Am I/Sloan triple bill, geeking out to Imperial Teen (again) with Regina Joskow, a watergun-fueled "no schmooze cruise," Alejandro Escovedo at La Zona Rosa, Grant Lee Buffalo at Hole in the Wall, an accidentally-caught but mind-blowingly brilliant set

by Dallas Crane, hanging out with pals from all over and watching them become friends, the '04 Posies/Big Star/ Roslyn Recordings/Jon Auer/Ken Stringfellow whirlwind, being dragged to a Bright Eyes set by the Death Cab guys, blue margaritas, insane amounts of laughter and bonding, mischief, mayhem and even more music.

I started going to SXSW when the whole convention was at the Hyatt and you could meet everyone you needed to in the lobby bar or on the back patio. It's all growed up now and I miss those simple, halcyon days – but I continue to keep racking up more great memories (and even crazier stories) every time I go. ■ **Barbara Mitchell, writer/ publicist/manager/label owner**

Ginger Magnolia

Each year's SXSW success was based on how many times I got to order the gingerbread pancakes at Magnolia Cafe…how many breakfasts, how many late-night meals. I

Absolute Debauchery

Lordy, where *do* I begin? Just a few memories in no particular order and just barely scratching the surface:

Penny Herman and I not wanting to miss Bush [Liberty Lunch, 1995] because of maximum capacity inside. So we snuck around back, waited for someone to be inevitably thrown out through the huge back gate and made a bum-rush dash past security when they opened it. We didn't make it. However, we did eventually get in the front door.

Singing at the top of my lungs to the Pretenders at Stubbs.

Absolute debauchery at the Four Seasons.

Dancing onstage with the Impotent Sea Snakes at some last-minute, makeshift basement venue near the convention center.

Driving from club to club and being pulled over twice in the same day, downtown, with a car full of amped-up, drunken degenerates and being let go. Twice.

I love SXSW. ■ **Sam Heineman, Sam Heineman Events**

manipulated all business meetings to further my goal. The last straw for me was sitting in my hotel room, plotting out the time I'd need on a Sunday morning to get pancakes and still make my flight back home. The timing didn't work out quite as well as I had hoped – I got a speeding ticket on my way to the airport, and consequently missed my flight. All in the name of the gingerbread pancakes. I still think it was worth it. ■ **Lori Blumenthal, Former I.R.S. Records Director of Promotion**

Alison Macor's Top Five SXSW Films

The Big One (1998): Arguably not one of Michael Moore's best films, but the experience itself was memorable. A funny, very animated Moore had whipped the Paramount Theatre audience into a good-natured frenzy during the post-screening Q&A. Afterward I went backstage to introduce myself (I was scheduled to interview him the next day for the *Austin American-Statesman*). When I walked through the curtains, there was Moore, sitting quietly on a folding chair on the otherwise empty stage. It reminded me of the scene in *The Wizard Of Oz* when Toto pulls back the curtain on the "wizard." It was both eerie and poignant.

The Life And Times Of Hank Greenberg (1999): Greenberg was a terrific subject – charismatic, interesting, funny – and Aviva Kempner made the most of him and the doc's archival footage and interviews.

Spellbound (2000): I couldn't stop talking about this terrific, well-edited documentary. I'm normally not a "pusher," but I told everyone, even complete strangers, to see this movie.

Dear Pillow and *Metallica: Some Kind Of Monster* (2004): Watching director Bryan Poyser's *Dear Pillow* got me excited all

A&R In The WC

Like a great many rock 'n' roll stories, it all starts in a bathroom – specifically, the bathroom of Antone's during a Neko Case/Calexico showcase at SXSW 2000. Ryan Adams, who'd I met in *another* bathroom at SXSW 1997, cornered me by the sinks and asked if Bloodshot would want to put out his first solo album. Of course we would. We were mutual fans and friends and it was a natural fit. I'll never forget the day we first heard the finished record. Wide-eyed. Breathless. While Ryan's songwriting gifts had been hinted at, on *Heartbreaker* they burst forth with astonishing, brash and gutsy power. It was, as they say, lightning captured in a bottle. With *Heartbreaker*, the stars aligned in the oft fickle and unfair world of popular music: Talent begat praise, praise begat publicity, publicity begat momentum and momentum begat a record, a singular artistic statement that, like any true classic, holds up, exists beyond the time in which it was released. It sounds as fresh and compelling and exciting today as the day I first heard it. All thanks to a line in a men's room at SXSW. ■ **Rob Miller, Chief Executive Oaf, Bloodshot Records**

over again about Austin film. And while I'm not a metalhead by any stretch, Joe Berlinger and Bruce Sinofsky's *Metallica* nearly converted me. It was gripping and over the top.

Neil Young: Heart Of Gold (2006): Jonathan Demme's documentary transformed this screening at the 1,200-seat Paramount into an intimate private concert. Everyone in the theater seemed caught up in the musical performances within the film. ■ **Alison Macor, author of *Chainsaws, Slackers, And Spy Kids: Thirty Years Of Filmmaking In Austin, Texas* (University of Texas Press)**

It Does Not Get Any Better Than This

I'd heard of the SXSW film festival but had never attended until I moved to Austin in 1997. It was a revelation. Great panels, large appreciative audiences, and lots of filmmakers wandering around downtown in what was almost always glorious spring Austin weather. The highlights are almost too many to sort through. Sneaking into the back of a convention center screening venue to what I'd heard was some film about spelling bees and tearing up ten minutes into the wonderful *Spellbound*. Watching a surly Peter Bogdanovich walk off stage for a bathroom break in the middle of his one-on-one and seeing ancient documentary legend Albert Maysles literally bound out of the crowd, sit in his chair, and tell the startled moderator, "Ask me something." Sitting on a panel about politics and film with the late Molly Ivins, and hearing her laugh, "It always rains on losing campaigns." Watching a packed house roar through the world premiere of *Harold And Kumar Escape From Guantanamo Bay*. Listening to almost any of Louis Black's intros to films. And, as a filmmaker, standing onstage at the Paramount and looking out at a thousand people before the start of *George Wallace* and thinking that it does not get any better than this. And it doesn't. SXSW, what a wonderful festival. ■ **Paul Stekler, Filmmaker (*George Wallace: Settin' The Woods On Fire*)**

Mutual Appreciation

I think SXSW was the first film festival I ever attended, as a wide-eyed straight-outta-college movie nerd. For me, it was heaven, skipping from screening to screening and trying to jam in as much as my eyes/ears/cortex could handle. The programming was full of delights – some I saw coming, some which snuck up on me – back then, as it remains today. Ten years later, to have my third film [*Beeswax*] premiering for so many of the Austin cast and crew and friends who supported us up on the big beautiful screen in the mystic palace that is the Paramount was a real dream, the kind of thing to make you scratch your head and think, "How am I supposed to top this?" ■ **Andrew Bujalski, film director**

Interviews With Vampires

The SXSW that lives on in infamy for me is 2000. It was the year that I publicly revealed – twice – exactly how much humiliation I will suffer in pursuit of my chosen profession.

I was on a panel called "War Stories" with the esteemed former *Rolling Stone* editor Ben Fong-Torres, *Fresh Air* contributor Ed Ward, Ann Powers of the *Los Angeles Times*, and, perhaps most impressively, the elegant, sanguine and enormously talented Stanley Booth, best remembered for his Faulkneresque insider's guide into the dark heart of the world's second-best rock 'n' roll band, *The True Adventures of the Rolling Stones*.

Booth spoke about his time with Mick and Keith in his lazy somnolent Georgia drawl. Here was someone who had penetrated the inner sanctum of the Stones and still retained that patina of cool 30 years later; did I have a war story to beat that?

Well, not exactly. Instead, I confessed to the gathered SXSW masses that the only way I could get Jimmy Page, Led Zeppelin's dark lord, was to agree to speak to him through an interpreter – despite the fact that we both spoke English. Yes, really. After suffering an excruciating 15 minutes of stony, awkward silence, Page finally said the only way he would answer my questions was if I would address all my questions to his publicist and then she would relay them to him.

Did I walk out in a cloud of indignity and Chanel No. 5? I did not; I figured I had a lot at stake. The Page interview was my very first cover story for *Creem* magazine, so I endured, a study in compliance, deference, even obsequiousness, but with huge psychic costs.

"What were you trying to achieve with your new album *Presence*?" I asked the publicist, but looking straight at Page.

"She wants to know what you think of the new album," the PR relayed to his Pageness. And so it went for the next 45 minutes – me asking the publicist, she asking Page, Page telling her, she telling me.

Talk about lost in translation. I wanted to scream. While it made for what is probably one of the most awkward hours in my life, it did make for good copy, despite the attendant mortification. "You know, I should have strangled him instead of putting up with the situation." I mused aloud to the SXSW crowd. "Actually," quipped Fong-Torres, "you should have strangled the publicist, and then she should have strangled Jimmy Page!"

Perhaps I should have kept that in mind the very next day when I was summoned, along with several other journalists, to interview Neil Young in his Driskill Hotel suite about his then-new album *Silver & Gold*. Always diffident about the interview process, Young made us wait for a full two hours on the clubby couches that run along the upstairs lobby. We sat like anxious dental patients waiting for our root canals. Who would go first? How much time would we get? Does the other guy have better questions than I do? What if I didn't really understand the narrative arc of the new album? There was a lot to think about as we waited in that drafty lobby.

We were told, on the QT of course, that Neil wasn't even sure he wanted to do any interviews that day – not a real surprise from a guy who once canceled his 1976 tour with Stephen Stills midway through by sending Stills a telegram that said: "Funny how some things that start spontaneously end that way. Eat a Peach, Neil."

Finally, we got the word that Neil would indeed do an interview – but with all of us simultaneously. Not a perfect scenario, but as the saying goes, you have to play it as it lays. As we filed up to his suite, we were confounded even

The Glamour Of International Travel

I was on my way to an event in the U.K. I'd landed at London Heathrow and waited in the long queue, and now I'd been pulled out of line and found myself detained at some length at customs for the usual inexplicable reasons. I hadn't slept on the overnight flight and was tired and getting annoyed, but only a fool conveys annoyance to customs officials. I wasn't going to be that fool that day.

"Where are you staying in the U.K., Mr. Grulke?"

"The Thistle Hotel in Brighton, sir."

"Brighton, England..."

"Yes, sir."

"How long do you plan to stay in the U.K., Mr. Grulke?"

"I'm here until Sunday."

"So that would be four days, correct?"

"Yes, sir."

"So what is your business in the U.K., Mr. Grulke?" he asked, flipping through my passport.

"I'm here to attend a music industry event."

"And what is the nature of your business, Mr. Grulke?"

"I help organize a music industry event held in Austin, Texas, each year."

I reached in my pocket and handed him my business card.

He burst into a grin, ushering me through. "South by Southwest! I've heard all about you on the 'Beeb'! I'd like to come someday. Welcome to the U.K., sir!" ■ Brent Grulke, SXSW creative director

further when we spotted Young waiting for us in the hall, in what was tantamount to a perversion of rock star protocol – I should have been suspicious then and there. But the sight of the great man dressed in an oversized navy great coat that hung almost to his feet, slouching up against the pale lemon-yellow wall of the century-old hotel, was a little unexpected and unnerving.

"I just stepped out of my room and let the door shut behind me. I'm locked out," he said simply. Waiting a beat, he said, "Why don't we just do it out here," he said. Without giving us a choice, he casually parked his long frame square in the middle of a pale brocade divan that just happened to be in the hallway outside his door, sat back and gave us a broad smile.

That in itself should have been a tip-off. Neil Young is never ever jubilant before an interview.

What strikes me as quite odd now is that no one protested, or asked why a bellman didn't bring him up a new key – especially when a hotel staffer brought four uncomfortable metal folding chairs for us.

But this clarity came later – and with it, the realization that this was all probably a setup. At the time, I remember I was trying to figure out how I was going to get the iconic musician to answer my questions, jockeying for time like a member of the Washington press corps grilling the President. And to tell you the truth, that's not a bad analogy. After a brief 20 minutes, Young told us little, worked his austere arboreal charm on us, teased us with scraps of information about his famous cohorts Crazy Horse and CSN, and dangled revelations in front of us, like "I doubt Buffalo Springfield will ever play together again," without explaining why. He then stood up without ceremony, walked over to his hotel door and opened the door to his suite, in what was tantamount to an artful sleight of hand, or a graceful "fuck you," depending on which way you choose to look at it. ■ Jaan Uhelszki, music journalist

It's A Marathon, Not A Sprint

I might be wrong, but I think that my band the Miracle 3 and I may have invented the concept of scattershot SXSW gigging and the Herculean athletics of hitting double digits on the number of shows played during the four days of the convention. When we went down in 2001, I figured I would just ask anyone I knew who was having a party if we could play on the bill. Everyone said yes. And so I said yes as well. Next thing you know, I was diving into the logistics of how to move a band and backline to three or more shows (including radio sessions) a day. The challenge, and the last-minute arrivals, became as much fun as the shows themselves.

Like most musicians, I feel most relaxed and in my own element when I'm actually onstage playing music. So we did it again when we went back in 2003. And again in 2006. For SXSW 2011 I am coming back with two bands, Steve Wynn & the Miracle Three and the Baseball Project – and we'll *each* be doing three or more shows a day. Sure, these marathons might be a little tougher, with the extra years added to our bones. But I wouldn't have it any other way. To borrow from the sports phrase book, I came to play. ■ Steve Wynn, musician

Dressed Up Like Nebraska

I have been to every South By Southwest since number three. My memories of the initial years aren't so much about shows or panels, but of its size. The conference fit into a single hotel and it was easy to walk into every venue to catch any show. I recall sitting on couches drinking in a hotel bar with Guy Clark and Lucinda Williams sometime early on, and shows by Butch Hancock and Joe Ely as particularly memorable.

Over the years, the shows that I've most connected with have been by legends and heroes that I'd either never seen, or not caught so up close and personal. That list is a long one – Johnny Cash and Carl Perkins, the Sonics and the Stooges, Little Richard and Elvis Costello, Ray Davies and Roky Erickson, and, of course, the late, great Sir Doug Sahm. There is nothing to compare to being greeted by Doug in full cosmic cowboy regalia in your hotel lobby with a "Hey man" and then heading out for the night.

I've discovered plenty of bands at SXSW – the Raveonettes, Drive-By Truckers, Marah, the Bottle Rockets pop immediately to mind – and I've seen many more for the first time. Many of the bands never pass through a small market like Lincoln, Nebraska, so SXSW has been invaluable for me on that front. After 22 times, it's still big fun, and I can't imagine trip 23 to Austin will be any different. ■ L. Kent Wolgamott, *Lincoln Journal Star*

For The Love Of The Game

There were a million stories at the 2000 South by Southwest Music Conference, but one story eclipsed them all. For this was the year of the Print Media Softball Team. After 13 years of embarrassing disasters and heartbreaking near-misses, after the Princes of Print had so many times raised their fans' hopes only to cruelly dash them, this time they finally claimed the championship of the SXSW Softball Tournament.

The grueling three-games-in-one-day tournament took place at Krieg Fields on the South Bank of the Colorado River beneath the glazed-porcelain blue Texas sky. Print Media took the field in their black-and-white uniforms—the same crisp colors as their record reviews, so beloved by millions.

They did not look imposing. They had the pale, pasty skin of those who seldom stray from their computers and the skinny arms of those who never lift anything heavier than a pile of promo CDs. But looks can be deceiving. These ink-stained wretches proved as aggressive on the basepaths as they are in getting on guest lists; they exploited every mistake and hesitation of the opposition. On defense, they proved every bit as stingy with runs as they are with praise.

Print Media brushed aside the Radio team in the first round 16-5 and peremptorily dismissed the Record Companies team 18-9 in the second round. This brought about the much-anticipated grudge match with the Clubs & Talent Buyers team.

These same two teams had battled for the crown the previous two years. In 1998 Clubs & Talent squeaked by in extra innings, and they won easily in 1999. The Clubs & Talent pitchers, well practiced in the art of the low-ball offer and the underhanded deal, had baffled the Print Media hitters in the past. But not this year, as the Softball Scribes jumped out to an early 9-1 lead and cruised to a 21-4 victory.

When Clubs & Talent's last pop fly settled into a Print Media glove, pandemonium erupted on the field. Players who had seen the golden ring slip through their fingers so many times leapt into each others' arms. Fans who had invested so many hopes in the Journalists wept openly in the stands. As the Print Media team took a victory lap around the field, hoisting their golden trophies above their heads, an unexpected solar eclipse darkened the skies over Austin, confetti rained down from the upper deck and fireworks exploded behind the centerfield scoreboard. Children scrambled over the fences and past the overwhelmed police; a brass band in the bleachers struck up the old Queen song, and the entire stadium took up the refrain, "We are the champions! We are the champions!"

A number of bands also played at the conference. ■ Geoffrey Himes, Print Media softball team

The Lord Of Sixth & Brazos

"For over a decade, Mary Lou Lord has been charming the punters on Sixth Street with her battered Martin Guitar and amplifier. From indie to major to indie, Mary Lou has always stayed true to her 'busking' roots and is much happier playing guitar on a street corner than in any club."

That's how Mary Lou Lord was described in the 2006 program guide, and it serves as a pretty good summary of the Boston troubadour's indelible presence at SXSW. Lord cut her teeth playing a mix of covers and originals in the subway stations of her home turf, so when she was booked for her first showcase in 1997 it was no surprise that she quickly identified the heavily-trafficked corner of Sixth and Brazos streets as a prime spot for busking.

I didn't catch Lord's official showcase at Club DeVille that night – but a couple hours later, walking back to my car just past 2 a.m. after seeing the Jayhawks at Stubb's, there she was, strumming and singing for tips to a small but appreciative after-hours audience. A tradition had begun. Over the next decade, it would come to exemplify the heart and spirit of South by Southwest.

Between 1997 and 2006, Lord made the mid-March journey to Austin eight times (absent only in 1999, shortly after her daughter was born, and 2001 if my records are correct). Six of those years, she played an official showcase, but it was the DIY street gigs that made her part of the fabric of the event. Typically, she played for hours upon hours, getting started around 8 or 9pm and often continuing well past 3 in the morning. Few who attended SXSW during that ten-year stretch did not hear Lord playing at least a song or two.

When you play such marathon outings, it helps to know a whole lotta songs, so Lord built up a pretty substantial repertoire. Her most avid fans delighted in hearing some of the originals that had populated her '90s releases on Kill Rock Stars and Columbia, from "Jingle Jangle Morning" to "Western Union Desperate" to "Salem '76"; but it was her extensive range of cover tunes that helped draw increasingly flocking throngs to the corner across from the Driskill Hotel.

Reinvention Via Kinko's

I've been going to SXSW for the last 10 years. It's overwhelming and crazy, but very, very fun. The first year I came was because my website was nominated for an Interactive award. I'd always wanted to go to SXSW, but had never really had a chance before that, so I went down with my friend who designed the website. We were just gonna go for Interactive, and then we decided to stay for the music part. But we had no money. We went to Kinko's and made stationery for my website that said it was now a music-reviewing website. My site was made with Flash at the time, so I couldn't change anything, but we eventually adjusted it, and now I do actually write about stuff. But at the time, we literally just took a picture of me at Kinko's and made this letter, and we got press passes and got to stick around.

I also ended up doing stand-up that first year, sort of, because I was walking around and a guy who had an afternoon showcase recognized me and asked me if I would go up and do five minutes during the show.

There was another time that I was gonna stay with friends of friends, and I had the address, but I didn't realize it was an apartment complex. So I showed up after hanging out with friends at 3 in the morning, and I was fairly sure that it's *that* apartment – but not sure enough to go into a stranger's home at 3 in the morning. So I tried to sleep outside on a concrete staircase, and then I took a bus back into town and maxed out my credit card staying at a hotel for one night. ■ Eugene Mirman, comedian

Just to be clear, Lord was hardly one of Sixth Street's infamous human-jukebox cover-bands (I'm looking at you, Duck Soup). She had immaculate taste in the songs she chose to interpret, from Richard Thompson's "1952 Vincent Black Lightning" (before Del McCoury had a bluegrass breakout with it), to the Elliott Smith throwaway "I Figured You Out" (literally: he'd thrown it in a trash can and Lord retrieved it), to Pete Droge's instantly memorable "Sunspot Stopwatch" (which was written on a couch in SXSW music director Brent Grulke's living-room in 1993, as it happens).

She also skewed strongly toward Austin. Possibly her two favorite songwriters to cover were Daniel Johnston – her version of "Speeding Motorcycle" eventually turned up in a Target commercial – and Shawn Colvin, whose "Polaroids" was almost certain to be played if you stuck around Sixth & Brazos for an hour or two. Lord's cover choices were selective and personal enough that when she did reach for a universally-known classic – say, Bruce Springsteen's "Thunder Road" – it connected with the crowd the way *New Times* critic Robert Wilonsky described in 2002: "In that setting, it sounded sad and brand-new – like she'd written it on the spot, for anyone who cared to listen."

I had my own amusing moment with Mary Lou at Sixth & Brazos in 2000. A few years earlier I'd reworked her indie-rock roll-call song "His Indie World" into an alternative-country spinoff titled "His N.D. World" (after *No Depression*, the magazine Grant Alden and I launched in 1995). At some point, I'd passed along a copy of the rewrite to Mary Lou, who enjoyed it enough that she started singing the "N.D." lyrics at her shows. By 2000, both versions were known pretty well to her street-gig devotees. So when I passed by her busking-spot on the way to a show at Buffalo Billiards, I asked if she'd be up for a duet. She played the guitar (thankfully!), and we batted back-and-forth the names of Whiskeytown, Blue Mountain, the Backsliders and the like, just barely but triumphantly getting all the way through it.

My notes show that I heard Mary Lou play on the streets a total of 11 different times from '97 to '06, including both Friday and Saturday at the end of the night in that final year. Problems had arisen – the cops, after years of being cool with it, suddenly started hassling her – and between that and her struggles in recent years with a condition affecting her vocals, she has not returned since then.

If You Love SXSW So Much, Why Don't You…

Before meeting my wife, SXSW was the greatest thing that ever happened to me. And in a lot of ways, I was married to the festival. Through good times and bad, I was always standing side-by-side with the festival. It was a pleasure to find and premiere new films, to celebrate filmmaking legends, and to experience the mesmerizing Music and Interactive festivals when I had a free moment during the event. My time at the festival was an amazing experience, and it taught me so much about the entertainment business, from artists to audiences. We always said that the SXSW staff was like a family, and that's true. I probably took that to an extreme, living in the office and taking the job home with me without any real vacations or breaks. In short, if I could have babies with SXSW, I would. I can't, so I had to move to New York and get married to a human being. ■ Matt Dentler, longtime SXSW Film staff

"So hold my eye, while the rest of the city flies by / And the tips and the tokens you left me today / Are the price of my ride on the subway," Lord sang on the final track of her lone major-label album, in tribute to the busking environs where it all began. That she brought the same unflappable spirit, hard work, and brilliant songs to the streets of South by Southwest for a decade was worth a price that all the badges and wristbands of a quarter-century will never be able to repay. ■ Peter Blackstock, *SXSW Scrapbook* co-editor

How To Not Make It In The Music Biz

When Fred Armisen came to SXSW 1998, he'd been the drummer in Chicago post-punks Trenchmouth for a decade. A few years later, he joined the cast of *Saturday Night Live* (where he's known for playing President Obama, among many other characters). Armisen's week in Austin played a key part in that journey. Partially inspired by U.K. celebrity interview prankster (and Ali G forerunner) "Dennis Pennis" (a.k.a. comedian Paul Kaye), he decided to make satirical sport of SXSW in a video he eventually dubbed *Fred Armisen's Guide to Music and SXSW 1998*.

With his then-wife Sally Timms (of Mekons fame) working the camera, Armisen pretended to conduct a canceled panel ("Chart Success"), befuddled Siouxsie & the Banshees with thickly accented questions that were probably no sillier than the ones real music TV interviewers ask, and suggested to *Rolling Stone* writer David Fricke and then-Capitol Records president Gary Gersh that since their interview was billed as "Face To Face With Gary Gersh," the two men ought to kiss.

Armisen remains a big music fan as well as a committed satirist of indie culture and bohemia, most recently with his IFC show *Portlandia*, co-written by and co-starring former Sleater-Kinney guitarist Carrie Brownstein.

I remember getting in the mail the schedule: it was the first time I'd ever seen what all the different seminars and stuff were. The band that I was in, Trenchmouth, we didn't succeed in a lot of ways. We would tour, we had a good label, we had support, people would come to see us, but we certainly weren't making a ton of money or really sustaining ourselves that well.

So I think I was a little frustrated, and when I got this book, there were all these panels on, y'know, "How to make it in the music biz," and I think from that, that's where I decided, "Oh, I'm just gonna get my video camera and go to these seminars and interrupt them and ask stupid questions."

I don't even know why. I think it was out of boredom, or just wanting to be a part of it. Because even though I'm kind of making fun of it, I do think SXSW is a great thing. Whenever anybody has a problem with something, it really comes down to jealousy or frustration. I had a really good time when I was there, I met great people, and looking back now, I'm like, "God, that was such a great time." There were so many bands, and labels. And also hard copies of vinyl and CDs. That's so gone. But that's OK. That's the nature of things. I don't look back with nostalgia.

Michael Dorf from the Knitting Factory, at first he didn't realize that it wasn't real. But as soon as he found out it was a joke, he gave me his badge. That was a "mentor" session, where you go one-on-one with people, and he just said, you should be me in the next thing. Which I did. The guy I hassled, the one with the shaved head, he was in a band and he wanted to play at the Knitting Factory. He was just trying to get out there. Now I look back and it's like, oh man: I hope I wasn't too harsh. But I think most people knew I wasn't doing it with any malicious ideas. Pretty much like right away, as soon as I had done it, I talked to the guy from Pavement [percussionist Bob Nastanovich]. He was drunk at the time, so he didn't realize it was a joke. Other than that, I kinda sorta knew a lot of those people already. There was a guy from Warner Bros. who I interviewed for like a second [publicist Rick Gershon], and I see him at shows all the time.

So I made the tape and somehow it all came together: It became my first foray into doing comedy. Ironically, for all that I was poking fun at about "how to make it" at SXSW, it actually did become something that led me to another field. I came away from it with a whole new arsenal of things I could be doing. I went down there as a musician, and after that tape, my whole life changed. ▪ **Fred Armisen**

He Left Her Heart In Austin

I remember going to the airport to pick Tony Bennett up [in 1997]. After all the work it took to put his appearance together, I was thrilled I would get to spend some quality time with the man. Well, my friend Tracey drove the car so I could run in and fetch him, and as a consequence he sat in the front seat while I sat in the back with very little opportunity to speak to him. Embarrassing but true: I totally cried afterwards. ▪ Linda Park, longtime SXSW staff

Ray Davies Sits In With The New Pornographers, 2001

Carl Newman (singer/guitarist): "It's not like Ray Davies came up and said, 'I'm blown away by your music, I must perform with you!'"

John Collins (bassist): "I think he just felt like playing. He wanted to play at a certain time of night and basically, we fit the bill. He happened to be sitting with our booking agent."

Carl: "His people knew our people."

Neko Case (vocalist): "We got the call at dinner from our booking agent and we were like, 'Sure!' But also, 'Oh, that's never gonna happen!'"

Carl: "We were like, 'Has he even heard our record?' I think he heard it that morning and thought, 'These guys seem ok. They won't embarass me.'"

Neko: "We had some Kinks CDs at the hotel and picked a song. We asked him if he was cool with doing 'Starstruck' and he said, yeah, but the Kinks had never done that song live before. Carl had to give him a lyric sheet."

John: "It was a pretty inspired choice. That was kind of an astonishing fact: We got to debut it for the whole world. I think I got it right, but I could have been playing a completely different song."

Carl: "There were times when Ray was looking at me and I still don't know if he was angry or just, 'Hey, how's it going pal?' But what was going through my head was, *'You're just like fucking Dave, you prick! I ask you to play one fucking song and you got it wrong!'* Those eyes, they burn in your soul. Those hateful hateful eyes."

Neko: "It was a Twilight Zone experience. We knew logically that it happened, but none of us can remember it. It was way too good for me. I was not worthy." ▪ **The New Pornographers**

Steps Along The Way To Running SXSW Film

I think my favorite memory of SXSW before I moved here in 2004 was the year my husband John and I came down with *How's Your News?* while also working with IFC promoting our cable television series *Split Screen*. IFC made these fabulous little toy RVs to promote it, and built a cool lounge with a pool table at the SXSW Trade Show. What I loved the most personally, though, was that we were put up at the Four Seasons, and we got to spend hours with Matt Stone of *South Park*. We'd met him years earlier when he attended our Cold Spring Film Workshop with *Cannibal! The Musical*, and now he was at SXSW as one of the executive producers of *How's Your News?* with John. He's just amazingly bright and funny, and I have the sweetest memories of hanging with him on our own, and later at group sushi dinner, with the whole crew.

I don't know if it was that year or another – the years all blend together for me – but I also remember one year sneaking away from all my film pals to listen to Stewart Brand talk about the Long Clock. It was all the way on the other side of the Convention Center – it was like entering another land – but I was mesmerized.

Of course, our trips down to SXSW from New York from the earliest days of SXSW Film had everything to do with our moving here in 2004. We already had a relationship with Richard Linklater from *Slacker*. Michael Barker of Sony Pictures Classics introduced us to Marge Baumgarten early on and we became great friends. From there we got to know Louis Black and Matt Dentler, and others in the Austin film community. We loved coming down – and when it was time to move on from New York, Austin, with SXSW at the center, became the obvious choice. It never occurred to me that I'd end up running SXSW Film Festival & Conference, but I couldn't be more grateful and proud. ■ **Janet Pierson, SXSW Film producer & senior programmer**

A History Of Giant Sand, Thru The SXSW Looking Glass

The first time we played SXSW was in 1989. Although Giant Sand had existed since 1980 with other members, John Convertino and I were touring as a two-piece the first time there. My touring credo was always to represent the record we were about to make instead of the one we had just released. It's a jazz thing, not a marketing thing.

Craig Marks, who worked for the label [Homestead] at the time with Gerard Cosloy, had bought us a 1981 Honda Civic for tour support. We were driving it cross country promoting the current record, *The Love Songs*. By the time we reached Austin for the SXSW show, John was having stomach problems. We didn't know it till we reached Los Angeles that his appendix was leaking. He was lucky to survive. The Civic delivered us.

While in Austin, we were invited to a wedding party there at a lake, and Dusty Wakeman approached me about a place he was buying up in Joshua Tree and how it might be perfect for us to record there. That place did become the location of our next record in a red barn there: *Long Stem Rant*. It also became home for me as caretaker to the property. Cabin # 4 at Rimrock Ranch, 5 miles up the road from Pioneertown – the happiest place I've ever lived. My Camelot.

Harvey Danger And Bright Eyes

One of my favorite SXSW memories took place in 1998. My friend Regina Joskow, then a publicist at London Records, begged me to come to the Electric Lounge to check out a new band that was just about to release its first album. The singer was a fellow music journalist, and Regina was sure I would love them. The band turned out to be Harvey Danger, and I did. This was when the Electric Lounge erected tents outside and had bands play there as well as indoors. After Harvey Danger finished, I noticed a forlorn 16-year-old kid with messy hair and a beat-up old acoustic guitar was about to go on next in the same tent. I hung around for his set – the most depressing, angst-ridden, suicidal-teen folk I'd ever heard. I seriously wondered if he'd still be alive in a year. Immediately bought every CD he had for sale. The kid called himself Bright Eyes, although he introduced himself to me as Conor. I wonder what ever happened to him? ■ Jim Testa, *Jersey Beat*

The next few times we played SXSW is a blur. The early '90s were like that. People still hoot over a show we did there at a place called the "Electric something." [Editors' note: 1995, Electric Lounge, Saturday 1am.] Apparently we were stunning. Don't remember, but I recall it being fast and furious because of time restraints and that wonderful careless abandon that

was fueling things then. After that, the SXSW people offered us an entire night to fill with friends and new bands we thought were good that no one else knew about, like Grandaddy or Medeski, Martin & Wood. [1996, State Theatre, Friday.]

And in 1993, we actually got signed. Kate Hyman approached us from a new mid-sized label called Imago. She seemed approachable enough and I enjoyed her sensibility of bands she'd chosen for that label; Henry Rollins, Paula Cole, Pere Ubu,

Aimee Mann. That made sense to me somehow. So we ate some mushrooms and digested the notion.

When we did the Texas Union Ballroom [1997, Friday], we had so many friends with us onstage that night. My best friend from Tucson, who started Giant Sand with me back in 1980, the late great Rainer Ptacek, was with us then. So were the Psycho Sisters (Vickie Peterson from the Bangles and Susan Cowsill from the Cowsills), and Victoria Willams too. That was a blast. When we played at Liberty Lunch in 1994, it harbored a severe missingness in the recent loss of Pappy Allen, the beloved 75-year-old we met up in Pioneertown after that first invitation to record there by Dusty. Pappy was an amazing fellow. We met him on that first drive up to Rimrock to record in 1989, in the middle of a July night, when my hot and tired '66 Barracuda was in need of a rest as much as we were. Glowing there on that dark high desert road in the middle of nowhere was a luminescent oasis: Pappy & Harriet's Pioneertown Palace. We became very good friends, and soon after that, I took him on tour with the band to Europe. Recorded with him too: *Ramp*. [Restless Records, 1992.]

One night at the State Theater, we had the Continental Drifters, Lisa Germano, and our good buddy Vic Chesnutt. [The 1996 "Giant Sand & Friends" show.] I remember something dark beginning to shadow the proceedings then, some looming curtain of doom. The stage was tilted in traditional theater fashion, and was tricky every time I'd lunge for the stomp box, like almost a plunge into the first row. There was also the trick of securing Vic's wheelchair so he wouldn't roll off in midset. Maybe the place was haunted. Maybe just my boots were.

"Z Car!"

A friend was working with Billy Gibbons at the time and I didn't really know him very well at all, particularly not well enough to run around with at SXSW. But our friend wanted to see a band neither of us did, so Billy opted to walk with me to the Electric Lounge for Japanese night. Billy's always been fascinated by all things Japan and I sold him by recommending the Boom Boom Satellites. The walk over was painfully slow – I'd argue that by the nature of the beard, nobody in rock 'n' roll is as instantly recognizable as Billy F. Gibbons. People who've never heard a ZZ Top song still know to shout "that's the guy from ZZ Top" and to want their picture taken. Billy has been famous so long and is so gracious that he deals with it well, giving everyone who asks an autograph and a pose for a picture. Particularly back then, when there were fewer bona fide celebrities making the SXSW rounds, it was a big deal to spot BFG.

When we got the club, Mike Henry let us in and we lingered in the bar area for three minutes or so. At that point, every Japanese band member, road manager, record label exec – anybody there that was Japanese, period – ran into the bar area from the actual stage area and surrounded us. Surrounded. No room to move. They didn't say much except to mimic the exaggerated swooping hand gesture ZZ made famous, photograph, and yell "Z Car!"

Gibbons forgot to mention on the way over that ZZ Top was in the middle of a multimillion-dollar television campaign for the Z Car in Japan. I'm not sure any of them knew his band, but they knew him as the TV pitchman they loved. It was 15 minutes of Beatlemania. And Billy loved it. ■ Andy Langer, journalist

It took a very long time for our set to happen that night. All our friends were playing before us, and we didn't want to cut their time short or hurry them. So it got very late by the time we hit the stage. I still recall that "wiped out" feeling. Someone from the crowd shouted for a guitar lead: "Take it, Howe!" Then instead of blasting it, I recoiled in its reverse psychology, playing as quiet as possible, reflecting the off-kilter slant of the eve.

In those early '90s, I moved back home to Tucson again, like I'd always done after losing myself elsewhere for a spell.

Come the mid-'90s, things went to hell.

First, the new record label folded up at the moment of our new release, *Glum*. [1994, Imago.] Then because of personal problems with my ex, I became a single parent, which severely limited my availability and tour aspects. Finally, most disastrously, Rainer became stricken with brain cancer.

I was slammed.

The rest of my band, way younger than I was, took the opportunity to fill that lag time with what they were forming inside of Giant Sand. This became the Friends Of Dean Martinez, before they reinvented themselves again as Calexico. They had been waiting for the right time to explore their own sound. When we were supposed to sign the Imago contract, they informed me they would not sign the deal. They did not want to be held down to that paperwork. Joey [Burns, Giant Sand's bassist] was beginning to make plans for something else.

So the label agreed that only my name was needed and proceeded. But this held me up for a very long time when the deal went south. And that is the big problem with big labels: It takes forever for their legal team to draw up a release –

forever, compared to how fast I liked to get on to the next album. So I was stuck for a while, and all the while my rhythm section were free to pursue.

The next to last time at SXSW, one morning after migas at Las Manitas, I defended Joe's singing to City Slang's Christof Ellinghouse, who confided in me he would only sign them to his label if Joey wouldn't sing on record. That made no sense.

Meanwhile, Kate Hyman was now at V2 and signed us again – this time based on the label's excitement for an album we'd done with Lisa Germano: *Slush*, with Giant Sand reconfigured as OP8. [Released February 1997.] And then the option record would be a Giant Sand one again. But Rainer had passed away soon after that, and I had a very diffciult time recording the next record, *Chore Of Enchantment*. [Released March 2000.]

The last time at SXSW, the Calexco project was gaining momentum. Joe must've figured it was best not to fill me in on any of their plans, and that began to sprout the eventual end spoink. Though not initially menacing, that hidden agenda within coexistence eventually became severely disruptive for both bands to continue as we had been.

When we arrived that final year (2000) playing as Giant Sand for a Friday night show at the Scottish Rite Theatre, Alejandro Escovedo confirmed that we would headline his annual closing show for SXSW at the Continental Club. [Editors' note: In 2000, Escovedo moved his Sunday-night appearance from an official showcase at La Zona Rosa to a non-SXSW show at the Continental.] When I informed the band of Al's sweet invite is when Joe informed me they would be unavailable for it. They had planned to leave directly after their Calexico show on Saturday night for some work set up by their new label, City Slang.

The next day, I found myself sulking alone at an Alejandro BBQ event. He kept filling my glass with frozen margaritas, unaware of my predicament. Couldn't figure how to tell him either. By the time I had to drive across the river, I was in a walking coma state. Parked the car somewhere I'd never remember and then found myself in the venue where Calexico was playing. [Antone's.] With my band in ashes and Rainer gone, I wondered what the f@ck had happened.

Somehow at that moment, I was taken to symbolize the cold end of the band's demise. John and I had been playing together three years ahead of taking Joey into the band. In my frozen margarita stupor, it made sense to flick ice cubes up on John's cymbals to exemplify the notion of such icy severance. I had shape-shifted badly. It could've been worse, though. Fortunately John Rauhouse was clear-headed enough to deny my request to sit in with them on his pedal steel guitar. This was the right thing to do since I'd never played pedal steel. One way or the other, I could not just let the night slide.

The next night, I was there alone with a capacity crowd at the Continental Club, trying to figure out what the hell to do.

Epilogue: And so I ended up doing the only decent thing one should do after such a clobbering string of incidents: have more babies. My son was born March 16, which relieved me from further SXSW activity. Children might never remember the birthdays their parents were there for, but they will forever never forget the ones they weren't.

So after a dedicated decade of young Luka's birthdays, I accepted the invitation at SXSW in 2009 for a gig presented by our new record company [Yep Roc]. It happened to be at the Continental Club. Kate Hyman was there again too, and so we reminisced. Took in the sad toll of all those that had passed on since we first met there. That very night underscored the tragic loss of our mutual friend, Tarka Cordell, son of the legendary Denny Cordell, a friend and Kate's former publishing partner, who had succumbed to cancer several years prior. But many old friends showed up that night too, Jason Lytle and Matt Ward among them. And so it felt like an end to a healing cycle of sorts.

Then last year again I was requested to return there with my gypsy band. Knew it was badly set up by the contingent from Spain, but relented anyway since playing with those dudes is ridiculously fun for a man my age and severely inspiring. They play like they invented the guitar. (Which they did.) There's talk of returning again this year for the "Blurt" stage and no matter how much I think I won't, it'll probably suck me back in just like that stupid joke from the *The Godfather* movie.

Austin is a stunning town but I never expected to grow gray returning there for "South By." I suppose I still enjoy the challenge of its cluster muck and the impossible notion of improbable juxtapositioning; like asking Sissy Spacek there last year if she wanted to make a record after she got done watching "the karate kids" spurl the night away. (She didn't.)

Conclusion: It's all worth it. The ups. The downs. The tragedies and the triumphs. It's a point of no return in an annual return. I never thought it made any sense, but then again, nothing makes sense on paper in the sonic kingdom.

SXSW is a stunning clot of music-related flim flam. It used to be more fun when it was new, the way everything used to be more fun before too many people figured it out. But it is still a unique and viable wondermint of yippity and probably useful for many young bands and semi-young bands.

Austin is a monumental city. It's a privilege just to be there having a moment like this every March in a city literally overrun by the likes of us and you and your friends. It's like Facebook, except in real life. And real life is absolutely better than Facebook. It's full of adventure and a bizarre amount of coincidence. It'll suck you in and spit you out. It's not unlike a sonic loop-de-loop.

Go, and try to stop going.

It'll serve you right. ■ Howe Gelb

A Collective Effervescence

Thinking about SXSW makes me feel like Methuselah. All my memories run together, a colorful stream of snapshots and anecdotes strung together like proverbial Christmas lights – see, the process even makes me think in clichés. Sixth Street at midnight, Seis Salsas at noon – this what they mean by the phrase "your life flashed before your eyes." Only I'm not about to die, and it wasn't really that long ago.

The whole music industry has changed since then – the industry, and the world. When I first went to SXSW in 1987, I didn't feel like I was part of an old guard: quite the opposite. I thought I was a new breed of music fan, one who had rejected punk and new wave and hippiedom and hip-hop alike. But upon reflection, I wasn't in on the beginning of a movement, I was somewhere near the end of one. That year was only five years after the start of MTV, less than a decade since the Pistols had broken up, and less than two decades since Woodstock. I thought of bands like Black Flag as crusty old punks and bands like the Stranglers as absolutely retro. I'd been rehabilitated into a newfound love of American indie rock by a chance statement I'd overheard Pete Buck utter at my local college radio station, and it had led me to Texas.

That first SXSW convention was really very small. I recall attending the opening remarks in a half-empty ballroom at the hotel and meeting every single person in the room afterward, although I only remember Bob Christgau, Louis Black, and Pat Blashill (why Pat Blashill, I wonder?). I recall seeing the Reivers (who were still Zeitgeist), and Texas Instruments, and Glass Eye. I think I went to Waterloo Records, ate Tex-Mex and swam in Lake Travis; and I know

Ode To SXSW, 1997
.........And I Didn't Want The Night To End

Yellow Rose scent is filling the Austin night air
Grackles in the trees
Like a Hitchcock movie and under
The crescent moon and Arabian stars
It's a Texas Saturday night and we are swinging like bar doors.
Blues is walking the floor at Antone's and Clifford Antone
is shaking like green jelly on a plate and crying
off stage.
It's Austin.........and everyone feels like a friend
and no one wants the night to END
  Riding lonesome
  All the King's pretty Ponies and all the King's Men
  Scotty and D.J.
  are looking for their singer
  but he is long gone
  he knocked down heaven's door.
  But the King's Men rocked just like it was
  Tennessee Saturday Night
  and we were dancing on a sawdust dance floor
  slip sliding in spilled beer, cigarette butts and SIN
  and baby we still didn't want the night to END
 A strange Parisian night
deep in the heart of Texas
Music is all around
Homeboy Joe Henry hushes the crowd
as they call out for more
in the early morning mist
tremolo and steel
grabbing those notes and
making those notes bend
and baby we are behind the moon
and we still don't want the night to END
  Outside the hotel Driskill
  that grand old lady
  outside all that is left in the street
  are paper bags, greasy hot dog wrappers
  and crushed beer cans
  tumbling in the wind
  and on 6th street, Brother Hacker and I
  are digging
  sweet folk music played by
  a reed thin blonde from Beantown
  Bonjour Mary Lou
  and I and I and I don't
  want the night to end.........SXSW, I'm going to stay until it's
  OVER ■ Paul Body, as submitted to scrapbook@sxsw.com

we listened to gospel on Sunday morning and then played softball in a field and ate BBQ. Those actions alone seemed fraught with exoticism. At the time, Reagan had been President for seven years and I hated absolutely everything the mainstream stood for, so being in Austin revived my love of my own culture. That first SXSW changed the way I thought not only about music, but about America.

I went to SXSW faithfully for the next 13 years, and as I said before, the memories now blend together. Raucous meals at La Zona Rosa, the Butthole Surfers at Liberty Lunch, Butch Hancock at the Driskill Ballroom, Green Day at Emo's (I might have dreamed that one). And there were many non-musical events as well. I remember diving into Barton Springs, leading a seminar for Riot Girls, and cutting Al Jourgenson off on the freeway and having him shake Devil Fingers at me. Once I spent an afternoon at the Buttholes' Ranch, watching *Oprah*, which was a new show at the time. And I drove to the David Koresh compound in Waco when it was in full siege mode. At the time, such events seemed weird and anomalous, unique to Texas and offset by set after set of fabulous American music. Little did I know that they were prescient of a new American mindset, presided over by W Bush.

2000 was the first year I didn't attend. That weekend I was in Paris – a fine city in its own right, but it wasn't the same: That March I missed Texas, the sunshine, the salsa, the bluebonnets, terribly. The year after, I was pregnant, and that was all she wrote. It's actually ironic that 2000 was my last year, since that was the year Napster was at its peak: Indeed, by the time SXSW occurred, it had over six million users. People used to say how sharing music with strangers was so bizarre and disorienting, but the first time I logged on to Napster, I downloaded a track by Run Westy Run that had been uploaded by someone I had met at SXSW. No joke.

Peer-to-peer file sharing has irrevocably changed the music business, if not the music itself and its cultural place and value in our mental landscape. It certainly changed rock journalism, the business I was in until 2002. But although I haven't been to the convention in over a decade, I don't think it has touched the meaning of SXSW. SXSW is the embodied version of Napster, a microcosmic internet that includes all the things the internet is missing: human interaction, a sense of community, and what sociologist Emile Durkheim calls "collective effervescence."

These days the only music I listen to is on Radio Disney. But maybe it's time to go back. ▪ **Gina Arnold, former rock journalist**

Buddy Guy at Antone's (1998)

Balbora at Japan Nite at Tropical Isle (1998)

I remember going to the first one. Mammoth was still an idea yet to become a reality. Cool helpful people, great clubs & bands not to mention great eats & the ambience that's Austin. Its gotten a little bigger since then but the basic ingredients still hold. You can get a lot of business done & its a lot of fun. Educational w/out the usual big city attitude of much of the music biz. Oh yeah - we also signed our first artist, the Sidewinders, ~~there~~ off a showcase @ Liberty Lunch my first nite ~~there~~ there.

Jay Faires
President Mammoth

Sean Lennon at Liberty Lunch (1998) >

Volunteer handbook (1998)

sxsw film 98

Saturday, March 14

12:30	**Funding for Documentaries** There are many pockets of funds for documentaries. Lisa Heller (POV), Judith Helfand...	**Introduction to Screenwriting** Michael Hacker	**DGA**	**Mini Meeting** *Mini Meetings are...*

3:30-5:00	**Turning Real Life into Documentary Storytelling** A complicated topic, this will explore what is and isn't ethical in documenting issues, as well as people's real lives and careers. Don Howard (*Letter from Waco*), Ruth Leitman (*Alma*), Todd Phillips (*Frat House*), Paul Stekler*(*Vote for Me*)	**Desktop Filmmaking** How filmmaking is changing with new techniques. Ken Adams (Rose-X Media House), Mark Levine (Puffin Design)	**Non-Linear to Negative** Zahid Ali (Allied), Bruce Hutter (Allied), Drew Mayer-Oakes (Allied)*, Jim Maxwell (Avid)	**Mini Meeting** Robert Hawk

Tuesday, March 17

11:00-12:30	**First Features** Are you ready to make your first feature? Rana Joy Glickman (*God Said Ha*), Geoff Gilmore (Sundance), Robert Hawk (IICI), Mike Judge (*Beavis & Butthead*), Steven Israel (*Swimming with Sharks*)	**Creating a Buzz** How to promote your film. Harry Knowles (*Ain't it Cool News*), Dan Mirvish (*Omaha*), Thomas Pallota (AIVF)*, David Sikich (IRS)		**Mini Meeting** Tony Safford
1:30-3:00	**Self Distribution** With the glut of independent films today, filmmakers find creative alternatives to get their films seen. A how-to on the festival circuit, cable and self-distribution. Peter Baxter (Slamdance), Chris Gore* (*Film Threat*), Michael Hacker (*Destiny of Marty Fine*), Dan Mirvish (*Omaha*), Jonathan Sehring (IFC)	**Insurance** Surry Shafter III.		**Mini Meeting** Bob Berney
3:30-5:00	**Making It in the Film Business** What does it take to make it in the film business? Jed Alpert (Rudolph & Beer), Elizabeth Avellen (*Real Stories of the Donut Men*), John Anderson (*Newsday*), Jason Blum (Miramax), Peter Broderick (Next Wave), Atom Egoyan (*The Sweet Hereafter*)	**Digital Animation Techniques** Kyle Anderson (Codeworks), Mark Meadows (Construct), Sergio Rosas (Codeworks) Bob Sabiston (MTV Animation)	**Critics & Filmmakers** Ann Hornaday*, Robert Byington, Dan Rosen, Marjorie Baumgarten	**Mini Meeting** Jason Blum

(Manager), Lisa Heller (POV), Aimee Patrick (Phaedra), Debra Zimmerman (Women Make Movies), ITVS

Sunday, Mar 15, 1:30-3pm Peter Baxter (Slamdance), Bob Berney (Banner), Jonathan Burkhart (Nantucket), L M Kit Carson (One Way), Michael Hacker, Megan O'Neill (Forefront)

Monday, March 16, 1:30-3pm Cynthia Hargrave (Hurricane Streets) Glen Reynolds (Curb), Rana Joy Glickman (God Said Ha!) Jed Alpert (Rudolph & Beer)

Finland's Kimmo Pohjonen at Electric Lounge (1999)

Jonathan Demme (1997)
Dave Marsh (1997)
Nick Lowe (1998)
Tony Bennett (1997)

Announcers Doug Sahm, Joe Nick Patoski with SXSW's Hugh Forrest at softball game (1998)

Carl Perkins at Austin Music Hall (1997)

continued from page 136

Motorway
Moufs of Da Souf
Mount Carmel
Mount Pilot
Mountain Clyde
Mountain Con
Mountain Man
Mouse and the Traps
Mover
Moving Parts
Moving Units
Moviola
Movits!
Moxine
Moxy Fruvous
Mozelia
MQN
Mr. Brown
Mr. Complex
Mr. Fabulous and Casino Royale
Mr. Rosewater
Mr. Sicc
Mr. Airplane Man
Mr. Blakes
Mr. Blakes of "Smooth"
Mr. C
Mr. Capone-E
Mr. Criminal
MR. DNA
Mr. E.
Mr. Entertainment and the Latter Day Pookiesmackers
Mr. Henry
Mr. Jones
Mr. Len
Mr. Len & the Pity Players
Mr. Lewis & The Funeral 5
Mr. Lif
Mr. Mike
Mr. Mirainga
Mr. Pookie & Mr. Lucci
Mr. Pookie & Mr. Lucci & the Stoney Crook Family
Mr. Ray
Mr. Resistor
Mr. Rocket Baby
Mr. Scruff
Mr. T Experience
Mr.Cree and DJ Spinner T.
MRK1
Mrs. Fun
Ms. Tee
Ms. 45
MSTRKRFT
Mt. St. Helens Vietnam Band
MU 330
MU330
Mucho Macho
Muchos Backflips!
Muchuu
Muck & the Mires
Muckafurgason
Muddy Frankenstein
Muddy World
Mudgirl
Mudhoney
Mugu Guymen
Muleskinners
Multiple Places
Mum (DJ Set)
Mumbleskinny
Mumblin' Jim
Mumford & Sons
Mumiy Troll
Mumm-Ra
Mummy Powder
Mummy the Peepshow
Munch Munch
Mundo
Mundo Aparte
Mundy
Municipal Waste
Munkster
Munly
Murali Coryell
Murcof
Murder
Murder By Death
Murder City Devils
Murdocks
Murdoq
Murs
Mus
Musab
Muscadine
Muscular Christians
Muse
Mushroomhead
Music Man Miles
Must
Mustang Lightning
Mustard Plug
MuteMath
Mutlu
Muttz
MV/EE and The Bummer Road
Mvsclz
Mwangaza Children's Choir
MxPx
My American Heart
My Brightest Diamond
My Brilliant Beast
My Dad is Dead
My Dear Disco
My Disco

My Education
My Epiphany
My Favorite Martian
My Federation
My Friend Steve
My Gold Mask
My Jerusalem
My Latest Novel
My Morning Jacket
My Sad Captains
My Second Surprise
My Sister Jane
My Summer as a Salvation Soldier
My Vitriol
My Way My Love
mylgay!husband!
myballoon
Myka 9
MyNameIsJohnMichael
Myra Manes
Myra Spector
Myracle Brah
Mystery Girls
Mystery Jets
Mystery Palace
Mystery Theatre
Mystik Journeymen
Myth
Mythical Beast

N.A.S.A.
N.E.R.D.
n.f.ect
N.I.L.8
n.Lannon
N.O.T.A.
n0 things
Naam
Nacho Vegas
Nacional
Nad Navillus
Nada Surf
Nadastrom
Nadia Bacon
Nadine
Nadja
Naiomi's Hair
Naked Age
Naked Barbies
Naked Grape
Naked On The Vague
Naked Prey
Naked Raygun
Naked Twister
Naked Vanilla
Nakia
Nakia & His Southern Cousins
Nameless Sound Collection
Nana Grizol
Nanachill
Nananine
Nancy
Nancy "Shaggy" Moore
Nancy Garcia
Nancy Scott
Nappy Roots
Nas & Damian "Jr. Gong" Marley
NASA
Nash Kato
Nashville Bill Wise
Nashville Pussy
Nat Jenkins
Natalia Lafourcade
Natalia Mallo
Natalie & Heartbreak
Natalie Portman's Shaved Head
Natalie Withers
Natalie Zoe
Natasha Leggero
Natasha's Ghost
Natasha®
Natccu
Nate Denver's Neck
Nate James
Nathan
Nathan Crow & the Wedding Band
Niall James Holohan
Nathan Gaunt
Nathan Hamilton
Nathan Hamilton & No Deal
Nathan Wiley
Nathaniel Rateliff
National Anthem
National Eye
National People's Gang
Native
Native Poet
Native Son
Natty Nation
Nautilis
Navel
Navruz
Nawal
Nayrok
NBK
Neal Casal
Neal Coty
Neal Kassanoff
Neal Pollack and Tammy Faye Starlite

Near Dark
Near Miss
NearMiss
neat neat neat
Nebula
Neck
Neckbone
Necropolis
Nectarine
Ned Henry
Ned Massey
Nedelle
Ned's Atomic Dustbin
Need New Body
Neighborhoods
Neighborly
Neil Blumofe
Neil Cleary
Neil Finn
Neil Halstead (of Mojave 3)
Neil Michael Hagerty
Neil Mooney
Neil Thomas
Neilson Hubbard
Neimo
Neko Case
Neko Case & The Sadies
Nekomushi
Nekromanitix
Nell Bryden
Nellie McKay
nelo
Nemesis
Nemo
Neon Angels
Neon Indian
Neon Neon
Neon Trees
Neptune
Nerdie
Nerdy Girl
Nerf Herder
Nero
Nero's Day At Disneyland
Nerves
Nervous Hospital
Nervous Turkey
Nethers
Neurosis
Neutral
Neutral Sisters
Neva Dinova
Never Shout Never
NeverShoutNever!
Neville Brothers
New American Shame
New Amsterdams
New Bloods
New Dealers
New Duncan Imperials
New Fashion
New Grand
New Kingdom
New London Fire
New Marines
New Mastersounds
New Mexican Disaster Squad
New Model Army
New Monsoon
New Opera Theatre Ensemble
New Orleans Klezmer All Stars
New Politics
New Radiant Storm King
New Riddim
New Rob Robbies
New Roman Times
New Sweet Breath
New Texas Swing
New Texicans
New United Monster Show
New Violators
New Wave Hookers
New Wet Kojak
New Wine (Jerry Miller, Don Stevenson and Omar Spence of Moby Grape)
New York Dolls
Newham Generals
News on the March
Newton Faulkner
Next Wave of Jazz
Ngoma
Nic Armstrong
Nic Armstrong & The Thieves
Nic Cosmos
NiCad
Nice Nice
Nice Strong Arm
Nicholas Tremulis
Nicholas Tremulis Orchestra
Nick Butcher
Nick Catchdubs
Nick Kelly

Neko Case (2006)

Nick Lowe
Nick Marsh
Nick Nack
Nick Nack & Enfoe
Nick Thune
Nick Villareal Y Su Conjunto
Nickel Creek
NickNack
NickNack & DJ Tats
Nico Stai
Nico Vega
Nicolai Dunger
Nicole Atkins
Nicole Atkins & the Sea
Nicole Atkins featuring Future Clouds and Radar
Nicole Campbell
Nicole Eitner
Nicole Panter
Nicotine
NID & SANCY
Nieminen & Litmanen
Nigel Richards
Night Horse
Night of Pleasure
Nightingales
Nightmare of You
Nik Freitas
Nikhil Korula Band
Nikka Costa
Nikki Jean
Nikki Meets the Hibachi
Nil Lara
Nils Lofgren
Niña
Niña Dioz
Nina Hynes
Nina Nastasia
Nina Nastasia & Jim White
Nine Black Alps
Nine Parts Devil
Nine Pound Hammer
Nine Stories
Nineteen Forty-Five
Nini Camps
Ninja Bass Squad featuring Manic1 - Mantis
Ninjasonik
Niño Astronauta
Nino Moschella
Niños con Bombas
Ninth Day Underground
Niobe
Nite Jewel
Nive Nielsen
Nixon Pupils
Nizlopi
NMS
Nneka
No Age
No Bounds
No Comply
No-DoZ
No Kids
No Luck Club
No Mas Bodas
No North
No One Is Innocent
No Reason to Hate
No Stangers
No te va gustar
No Weapon
Noah and the Whale
Noahlewis' Mahlon Taits
Noam Weinstein
Nobodys
Noel Jones
Noella Hutton
NOFX
Nogood Boyo
Noisettes
noJazz
Nomo
Non Phixion
Nona Hendryx
Nonie Johns
Nonymous
Noodle
Noodles
Nook
Nora
Nora O'Connor
Norah Jones
Norfolk & Western
Norm Ballinger
Norrin Radd
North Mississippi Allstars
Northampton Wools
Northern State
Nosaj Thing
Nosaprise
Not Daniel Johnston
Not For Sale
Not From There
Notekillers
Nothing Rhymes with Orange
Nothington
NOTORIOUS SHOUT! DJs
Noush Skaugen
Nouveau Riche
Nouvellas
Nov. 9th
Novadriver
November
November Foxtrot Whiskey
Novembers Doom
Novillero
Now It's Overhead

Now On
NOXAGT
NQ Arbuckle
NRA
NRSHA
Ntymydat
N-Type
Nu Vizion
Nudozurdo
Nukes
Nullsleep
Num
Num9
Number Girl
Number One Cup
Numbers
Numbers on the Mast
Numbskulz
Unicorn Magic
Nural
Nurses (SF)
Nuwamba
Nydia Rojas with Campanas de America

O + S
O*N*T*J
O.G. Style with Darque Seed
Oak Ridge Boys
Oakley Hall
Poanjandrum
Obi Best
Obits
Obstruction
Oceansize
Ocelot
Ocote Soul Sounds
Ocote Soul Sounds and Adrian Quesada
Octave One
Odawas
Odd Man Out
Odd Man Out (TX)
Odd Nosdam
Oddisee
O'Death
Odiorne
Of a Mesh
Of Mexican Descent
Of Montreal
of Verona
Ofer
Off With Their Heads
OFF!
Office
OG Ron C's Platinum Sound's Presents Wreckin' Mr. Kaila, Kool Rod, Big Nik, 5050 Twin, Roc 4 Roc, Rasaq (Raw Green), DJ Lil Steve
Oh Juliet
Oh Land
Oh Mercy
Oh My God
Oh No Not Stereo
Oh No Ono
Oh No! Oh My!
Oh Snap!!
Oh Susanna
Oh,Beast!
Ohbijou
Ohmega Watts
Ohtis
Ojala
Ojo Del Sol
ok city ok
OK GO
OK Sweetheart
Okamoto's
Okkervil River
Okkervil River feat. Roky Erickson
Ol' Yeller
Ola Podrida
Old Crow Medicine Show
Old Haunts
Old Man
Old Man River
Old Pike
Old Reliable
Old Time Relijun
Oldominion
Oleg Kireyev and Exotic Band
Oiga
Olin Murrell
Olive
Oliver Future
Oliver Magnum
Olivia Chaney
Olivia Tremor Control
Oliabelle
Olof Arnalds
Olospo
Olympic Lifts
OM
Om Trio
Omar & the Howlers
Omni
Omodaka
On My Side
On Neation

On The Speakers
On Trial
Once Upon A Time
Oncore
One
One Be Lo
One Botti
One Day International
One Fell Swoop
One Foot In The Grave
One Hundred Dollars
One Man Army
One Mississippi
One Nation
One Night Only
One People
One Pin Short
One Right Turn
One Riot, One Ranger
One Step Beyond
One Time Angels
One Umbrella
O'Neal McKnight
Oneida
onelinedrawing
Onili
Onion Creek Crawdaddies
On-Pointe
Onry Ozzborne
Onyxx
Oonceoonce
OP8...Lisa Germano with Giant Sand
Open Hand
Open Mike hosted by Genevieve Van Cleve
Open Mike hosted by Phil West
Open Road
Open Stage featuring DJ Jester
Operahouse
Operator Generator
Opiate For The Masses
Opium Symphony
Oppenheimer
Or, the Whale
Ora Cogan
Orange Jefferson and Tary Owens
Orange Jefferson and Thierry Cognee
Orange Kandy
Orange Mothers
Oranger
Orbit
Orchard Lounge
Orchid and Hound
Ordained in Lyrics
Ordinary Boys
Oren Bloedow
Oreskaband
Orangutang
Orgasm Addicts
Orgone
Oriental Love Ring
Original Love
Original P with members of Parliament and Funkadelic
Original Sinners
Orixa
Oro11
Orphan
Orphaned Land
Orquestra Tradicion
Ortegas
Ortolan
O'Ryan Isand
Oscar Lopez
Oso Closo
Other Lives
OtherStarPeople
Otherwize & the Blak Forest
Otis Gibbs
Otis Taylor
Otto Cruz
Ottoman Empire with Special Guest Wreckless Eric
Ouija Radio
Our Lunar Activities
Our Small Capital
Out From Animals
Outasight
Outer Spacist
Outformation
Outhouse
Outlaw Order
Outrageous Cherry
ova looven
Ovadose
OVENS
Over the Rhine
Overcasters
Overflow
Overlord
OVERTONE
Overwhelming Colorfast
Ovis
Owen
Owen Temple
owkmj
Owsley
Ox (BC)
Ox (Canada)
Ox.Eagle.Lion.Man
Oxbow
Oxe

Oxes
Oxford Collapse
Oxide & Neutrino
Oxy Cottontail
Oy
Oyster Band
Ozo
Ozomatli

P Kellach Waddle
P. W. Long
P.E.A.C.E.
P.E.E.
P.F. Sloan
P.K. 14
P.L.A
P.O.S
P.P.F
P.u.M.a.J.a.W.
P.W. Long
P.W. Long's Reelfoot
Pac Div
Pacer 21
Pachinko
Pack Of Lies
Pack Of Wolves
Paddy Casey
Pagan Saints
Page France
Pagoda
Paik
PAIN
Pain Teens
Paint
Paint it Black
Pal Shazar
Palace of Oranges
Palaxy Tracks
Pale
Pale Divine
Pale Horse and Rider
Pale Soul
Paleface
Palenke Souitribe
Paleo
Palestinian Rapperz
Palm School Choir
Palmyra Delran
Palo Viejo
Paloalto
Palomar
Palomo
Pam Hart Group
Pam Peltz
Pam Tillis
Pam Ward
Pamela Des Barres
Pamela Goodchild
Pamela Hart
Pamela Hart Quartet
Pamela Means
Pancho Kryztal & Hitman
PANDA
Panda & Angel
Panic Cell
Panjea
Panoply Academy Legionnaires
Pansy Division
Panther
Panthers
Panties
Paolo "Apollo" Negri
Paolo Bonfanti
Paolo Nutini
Papa Chuk
Papa Mali
Papa Mali & The Instagators
Papa Roach
Paparazzi
Papas Fritas
Papaya Paranoia
Paper Cranes
Paper Lions
Paper Moon
Paper Rad
Paper Route
Paper Route Records
Papercuts
Papier Tigre
Parachute
Parade
Paradime
Paradise Titty
Paradox
Paramore
Parenthetical Girls
Pariah
Paris Motel
Paris, Texas
Parkas
Parker & Lily
Parlor Frogs
Parlor James
Parlour
Parlour Steps
Parlovr
Parmalee
Parry Gripp
Part Chimp
Particia Smith
Particle
Partners N Crime

Parts & Labor
Pas/Cal
Passenger
Passion Pit
Passion Pit DJs
Past Lives
Pat Boyack and the Prowlers
Pat Dinizio
Pat Green Band
Pat MacDonald
Pat Maloney
Pat McLaughlin
Pat Mears
Pat Thornton
Pat Todd & The Rank Outsiders
Patafunk
Pataphysics
Pato Banton
Pato Machete
Patrice Pike
Patrice Pike & The Black Box Rebellion
Patricia Vonne
Patrick Dodd
Patrick Park
Patrick Phelan
Patrick Stump
Patrick Thomas
Patrick Watson
Pattern Is Movement
Patterson Barrett
Patterson Hood
Patti Dixon
Patti Smith
Patty Booker
Patty David
Patty Griffin
Patty Hurst Shifter
Patty Larkin
Paul "Lil' Buck" Senegal
Paul "Lil' Buck" Senegal and the Buckaroos feat. Stanley "Buckwheat" Dural
Paul Benjamin Band
Paul Body
Paul Buchanan
Paul Burch & The WPA Ballclub
Paul Burlison
Paul Cebar & the Milwaukeeans
Paul Clements
Paul Collins Beat
Paul Couture
Paul Dempsey
Paul Duncan
Paul F. Tompkins
Paul Glasse
Paul Jones
Paul K
Paul K & the Prayers
Paul K & the Weathermen
Paul Kelly
Paul Lippert
Paul Marshall
Paul Melancon
Paul Metsa
Paul Metsa Trio
Paul Metzger
Paul Minor & the Superego All-Stars
Paul Newman
Paul Saucido
Paul Scheer
Paul Taylor
Paul The Girl
Paul Thorn
Paul Tiernan
Paul van Dyk
Paul Wall & Chamillionaire
Paula Cole
Paula Friedrich
Paula Jean Brown
Paula Nelson Band
Pave The Rocket
Pavo
Paw
Pawa Up First
Pawtuckets
PBN
PC Worship
PDHM
Peace Corps
Peacemaker
Peachcake
Peaches
Peanut Butter Wolf
Pearl Harbor
Pearlene
Pearls and Brass
Pearly Gate Music
Pearly Gates
Peasant
Pedal Jets
PEDESTRIAN
Pedro Luz
Pedro Menendez Ensemble
Pedro Menendez JazzTango Ensemble
Pedro Moraes
Pedro the Lion
Pee Shy
Peekaboo Theory
Peel
Peelander-Z
Peenbeets

continued on page 168

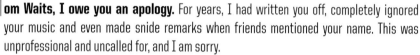

SXSW SPOTLIGHT

About A Girl

By Todd Martens

om Waits, I owe you an apology. For years, I had written you off, completely ignored your music and even made snide remarks when friends mentioned your name. This was unprofessional and uncalled for, and I am sorry.

That doesn't necessarily mean I now love your music, nor does it mean that I no longer believe you're sometimes simply being weird for weird's sake. It's true, you've written some killer love tunes, some I may even want played at my wedding, should a lady ever deem me fit for marriage. All it means is that I have never really listened to you. I've heard you, and I've even seen you, but I've never sat down, with the lights dimmed and a six-pack of heretofore unknown craft beer at the ready.

So supporters of Waits, please, do not turn away and forever disregard my name. I have no ill will toward one of your favorite artists. I do appreciate the fact that he is consistently unpredictable, and rock 'n' roll needs far more of that. If you truly want to know why I have shunned Waits through my entire 20s, I will tell you now. It was because of a girl. More specifically, a girl I took to my first ever South by Southwest.

My disinterest in Waits can be traced back to one lovesick mistake. My error was a relatively simple one, and it's a lesson I stubbornly refuse to admit I have learned. I believed, in 1999, that some grand gesture could win back my high school crush, who was now my college crush. It was largely unrequited through both academic levels, but I persisted for years, and that explains why I didn't get so much as a fourth date with a girl until I was 23.

My grand gesture was the suggestion that we go to South by Southwest. To accomplish said vacation between myself and my ex, who at that time had a boyfriend that she just loved to tell me about, I first had to con my college, the University of Southern California, into believing that sending the music editor of the *Daily Trojan* to Austin for a week was a very fine use of donor money.

To the 19-year-old me, SXSW was something of a myth. I had heard the cliche – the oft-cited "spring break for the music industry" line – and I fully believed in it. Come on, I told USC administrators, we are a cutting-edge (*cutting-edge*, I did say that) student newspaper that needs to stay on top of pop music trends. The only way to do so, I argued, was to attend SXSW. I left out all the stuff about how this trip to Austin was simply an excuse to spend a week with my ex and show her that she had been a fool for leaving me.

To my surprise, someone at USC said sure. The crap about this being an important learning experience for a young music journalist, and the plea to be near some rock crit heroes of mine and meditate with them, or whatever, in order to absorb their knowledge, was, to my astonishment, bought. No way would Nicole keep seeing that other loser now. I was in!

So at this point I feel obligated to say that one should never, ever go to SXSW – or anywhere, for that matter – with an ex, and especially do not go if the sole explicit intent of such trip is to sleep with her. It is not going to work, unless you're in a Nora Ephron film or reading a sappy script that's ultimately meant for John Cusack.

Yet I flew to St. Louis, and she picked me up and we drove to Columbia, Missouri, where she was attending journalism school. Our plan was to drive to Austin the morning after I arrived.

At her place, I got ready for the couch. I wasn't going to push or rush or assume anything, which was all part of my plan. Nicole looked at me and said, "Oh, hey, you can sleep in the bed with me." Really? I can sleep in the bed with her? That meant something. It had to. But don't you have a boyfriend, I asked, as if my intentions were kitten-innocent all along. "Yes," Nicole said, "but you're Todd. Really, I mean, you're Todd. It's not a big deal."

So here's another mistake I made. When a girl says, "But you're [insert your name here]," she is not declaring you as something special. Rather, she is simply saying, 'What? No one could believe I would sleep with you. That's insane. You're [insert your name here]. Sexless.'"

Yet there I went, and just to further set me up for what would eventually be an excruciatingly brutal heartbreak, she cuddled with me. I didn't sleep much. I was too excited. This was already the best vacation ever, and if she's already cuddling with me on Night 1, things are going to be awesome.

About 18 hours later, on the car drive to Austin, it became clear that the next six days of my life were going to be pure misery. I said something, somewhere in the Texas panhandle I believe, along the lines of, "So hey, what's taking you so long to dump this Bryan guy? You're clearly in love with me." If you grew up somewhere in the Midwest or central South, you have become accustomed to the noise of a weather siren, which is something of a blaring, high-pitched bomb-alert sound. Each brief moment of silence is almost immediately answered with another blast of noise. Whatever Nicole said for the remainder of the drive to Austin sounded something like that.

I spent the next few days begging her to forgive me. However, early in the trip we saw, among others, Paul K solo and Lullaby for the Working Class. I won't go into detailed descriptions of the artists, but just know that they are both a sad bastard soundtrack, and I love them for that. It did nothing, however, for my mood. I didn't keep score, but I cried quite a few times over this week.

South by Southwest, I started to believe, was the worst place ever. Here I was, buying Nicole dinner after dinner, taking her to one of the coolest events ever for a music fan, and here was she, just spreading contaminated saliva all over my dreams. I started to blame her for my misery. Why, I said, would you go on vacation with a guy who you know is crazy about you if (A) you have a boyfriend and (B) you don't want to date him. That's just cruel, I yelled.

I don't think I received a satisfactory answer. But if there is one thing I can ace, it's pathetic behavior. I could have a doctorate in being a doormat. Why, just recently I sent a puppy-picture-per-day to a girl who had rejected me seven months prior. She was going through a rough patch, and I floated the idea as a joke, and she accepted. So there I was, staying up till 3 a.m. every night for a couple weeks to crop puppy photos and write detailed histories for each image.

So I simply believed if I was just awesomely nice and overly forgiving, I could erase the last few days of fighting and sulking. If I left the toothpaste on the bathroom counter as opposed to the shelf, I apologized. If I dropped my pen on the floor, I apologized. If my shoe came untied, I apologized. I did this all until she screamed, "STOP APOLOGIZING FOR EVERTHING YOU DO!"

All right, that wasn't going to work.

Word, however, had started to travel through Austin that Tom Waits was going to play a surprise show. I had zero interest in this, despite how rare it is Waits tours. I believe SXSW is a place of discovery, a chance to see artists for the first time or revisit someone who has a marvelous album on the horizon. I did not then, and I do not now, believe it is a place to see superstars (sorry, Muse) or reunion acts (sorry, Devo). I am also a complete hypocrite, as more recently I planned my whole trip around a reunited gig from Chicago's bluesey-rock experimentalists Red Red Meat.

Yet at word of a Waits gig, Nicole's mood changed. She went from I-hate-you-Martens to TOM-WAITS-IS-PLAYING! When she said we had to see him, I said no at first. Look, Waits was the favorite artist of her current boyfriend, Bryan. No way would I sit through a concert in which she spent the night thinking of him.

Unless...perhaps I could use Waits as a way to show how we are meant to be together. That's it, I thought, like some worthless mad scientist. I would take her, I would stand in line at 6 a.m. to get tickets, which were available on a first-come,

first-serve basis, and I would treat her to a nice dinner. Please, I said, you love Tom Waits, and I was wrong to tell you to dump your loser of a boyfriend. Dinner is the least I could do.

About $80 later we were seeing Waits. Before he came on, Nicole was giddy. She was making jokes. She was touching me – SHE WAS TOUCHING ME! – and she was writing out dream setlists for him to play. Perfect, I thought. Now Waits would forever be associated with this happy memory in Austin, and I would be the one attached to it. This would have to work!

It didn't. As soon as the show let out, she pulled out her cell phone, called The Loser and told him all about seeing Waits. She told me to run up ahead, don't wait for her, and hey, she added, thanks for everything. Then she said: "I'm so glad we're best friends again."

I walked ahead. I turned the corner. I sat on a curb, and I cried. This is what us hopeless romantics do. I was no longer mad at her, but simply mad at myself. I wasted a night seeing an artist my ex wanted to see, believing it would somehow persuade her to marry me. I spent the past few days moping and fighting with her, nearly ruining my first-ever SXSW experience.

But I do have the occasional moment of sanity, and I decided, as I was crying on the curb and people were giving me weird looks, that this could not be how I remembered Austin. It couldn't all be about Nicole, and if I stopped being a sap for just a moment I would realize that it wasn't. After all, it was only about 24 hours ago that I was seeing the Flaming Lips, a band Nicole hated, with Mercury Rev and Grandaddy.

The tears were gone by the time Nicole met up with me, and I said little for the next 17 or so hours. Instead, I focused as much as possible on the South by Southwest moments that hadn't been thwarted by an ill-fated crush. The Flaming Lips had offered a hint of what would ultimately become *The Soft Bulletin*, and I was astonished to see what the Oklahoma weirdos had cooked up.

Even now, at 32, I despise older critics who reminisce about great past shows, or the time they saw so-and-so in a club. Whatever, don't care, so I won't get too nostalgic. I will, however, say that when I think of my all-time favorite shows, this is probably at the top of the list. I was unfamiliar with Grandaddy, but I would soon become entranced with the band's mix of sarcasm, romanticism, pop-culture references and effervescent melodies. Mercury Rev was something of a revelation, as La Zona Rosa became awash in various shades of blue. I remember having a giant grin on my face the entire set, and I return to the dream-pop orchestrations of *The Deserter's Songs* on a regular basis.

As for the Flaming Lips, I had dug *Clouds Taste Metallic* and *Transmissions From The Satellite Heart*, but the symphonic grandeur the Lips were now striving for was something rather magnificent. I'm corny, and I may have shed a tear or two. These weren't "hey-this-girl-doesn't-like-me" tears, but more "this-music-stunned-me-and-I-don't-know-how-to-react" tears. Right behind *Yankee Hotel Foxtrot* on my list of desert island albums remains *The Soft Bulletin*, and each listen returns me to the beauty I had witnessed at La Zona Rosa.

My first trip to Austin had been marked by crushed dreams, endless fights and sleepless nights – ones that had nothing to do with partying. Yet I knew I would be returning to South by Southwest. Yes, I would still spend the next few years chasing after Nicole. For the record, I ultimately won, and then was instantly bored. If it wasn't for Facebook I wouldn't even know she was still alive.

If my first trip to Austin had been a bust, I knew this is what I wanted. I wanted to document culture, I wanted to interview those who deserved it, and I wanted to experience art for art's sake. Yes, there are sponsors everywhere, and there are all sorts of crazy day parties interfering with the always-informative industry discussions – but there's music. A ton of music, and if something stinks, it's over in 30 minutes, and surely something awesome is happening next door. Really, seriously awesome, but no one knew about it; and with a new band hyped every day somewhere, be it a newspaper, a blog or the dude in a Misfits shirt at Amoeba Music, South by Southwest somehow has remained an annual rock 'n' roll education series.

Spring break for the music biz? Sure. Still, I like to think of it as a reminder that love, relationships and the like can come and go, but a song stays with you forever. ■ **Todd Martens covers music for the *Los Angeles Times*.**

Neil Young, Jonathan Demme at the keynote (2006)

2002 – 2006

The War, The Web, And Mumblecore

By Jason Cohen

XSW co-founder Roland Swenson didn't *really* prompt Neil Young to make his 2006 protest album *Living With War*. But for a while, it sure seemed that way.

Young was SXSW's keynote that year, in conversation with director Jonathan Demme — part of an extraordinary keynote string of honest-to-god geniuses that even the most jaded lifers in the SXSW office could get moony over. Robert Plant had come the year before, and Pete Townshend would be next. But for Swenson, nobody meant more than Young, his hands-down favorite both before and after punk rock changed his listening habits.

"The chance to introduce one of my heroes was daunting," Swenson says. "I stayed up late writing a long, mildly overwrought speech covering the importance of the song 'Ohio' — how it did so much to crystallize opinion against the war in Vietnam. It had demonstrated to me for the first time just how powerful a force music could be."

Operation Iraqi Freedom had been going on since 2003, so to conclude his introduction, Swenson threw in an aside: "Mr. Young, if you can hear me [backstage], we need another song."

"I was quite surprised by the level of applause from the audience," Swenson says now. "I was pretty pleased with myself, but as I crossed the stage and shook hands with him, I noticed a bit of steel in his eyes. I thought to myself 'Uh-oh.'"

Young's fellow Ontarian Michael Hollett, of NXNE and *NOW* magazine, whispered to Swenson, "Say, you kind of challenged him there." But Young was gracious, saying onstage that he gets "a lot of input, and I just got some more."

Says Swenson, "I felt a sinking sensation as I realized I had not only put my hero on the spot, I had also done one of the worst things you can do to an artist: Compare his early work to what he is or isn't doing right now."

Mere weeks later, Young wrote and recorded *Living With War*, which then received a May 8 rush-release. "My phone started ringing with reporters asking if I thought I had anything to do with it," remembers Swenson. "I did my best to play down that idea. I said that at most, I was like the rooster who crowed before the sun rose — but I sure didn't make the sun rise. Still, stories appeared across the world quoting my introduction to Young's keynote. Finally, Young gave an interview where he credited billionaire Steve Bing for the inspiration of the album, and my fifteen minutes of fame were over."

Politics and war had been on people's minds throughout the festival, and for each of the four years before. When Salon.com writer Andrew O'Hehir contemplated the SXSW 2006 films *Al Franken: When God Spoke* ("forces you to revisit those dark, dark days" of the the 2004 Bush/Kerry election) and the Pixies documentary *loudQUIETloud* ("a story of resistance and rebellion grown old and adapting to changing times"), he concluded SXSW was "in its own unthreatening, vintage-clothes-'n'-cappucino manner...launching one protest after another against the way America is right now, and how it's being run."

On the Saturday of SXSW 2003, an estimated 7,000 anti-war protestors moved from a rally at the Texas state capitol to Congress Avenue, merging with (and in some cases already a part of) the collective Sixth Street masses (though *Chicago Sun-Times* critic Jim DeRogatis wondered why no showcasing musicians formally joined the rally). That year's artists' panel, held just a few days after the Dixie Chicks' Natalie Maines told a London audience that she was ashamed President Bush was from her home state of Texas (and then apologized), was subtitled "Activism And Protest."

Moderator Greg Kot of the *Chicago Tribune* was joined by the Pakistani artist Salman Ahmad, X's John Doe, Woodstock icon Wavy Gravy, the Future of Music Coalition's Jenny Toomey, author Neil Pollack, R.E.M.'s Mike Mills, and poet, revolutionary and MC5 cohort John Sinclair. While Lyle Lovett would speak well of the commander-in-chief in a separate SXSW Interview, Mills referred to him as "non-President Bush," defending Maines and noting that the political climate made people feel that "to protest has been unseemly, like stomping on the graves of the dead."

"It was surreal," Kot says. "Being in the same room with Wavy Gravy and John Sinclair was pretty cool. I thought they would be polar opposites, with Wavy as the west coast merry prankster and Sinclair the midwest hardcore militant. I seated them at opposite ends of the panel because I thought it was somehow symbolic: the bookends of the '60s anti-war movement. I didn't think they knew each other all that well, since they came from such different scenes, but backstage they acted like old pals, cracking jokes in the green room and keeping everyone loose. Mike Mills and John Doe were just in awe of them.

"Things felt heavy," Kot continues. "Folks were just pissed off. Wavy and Sinclair had been there before, obviously. Their hearts had to be breaking to see it happen once more. But they weren't crying about it. They were laughing in its face, and making us laugh too."

One year earlier, of course, SXSW 2002 could not help but be affected by the aftermath of 9/11. Former sales manager Gaylynn Kiser was in Manhattan on the day of the attacks, meeting with clients before the CMJ Music Marathon. "I was staying at a bed & breakfast on the Lower East Side which was run by ladies from Ireland, so there were several Irish bands staying there that had been booked for CMJ," Kiser remembers. "Roland got together the staff in Austin for a group call to me. The 1,500-mile distance never felt so close." Later that evening, the B&B guests ended up in Union Square with instruments, taking in the grief-stricken memorials and missing-persons flyers. "We sang 'Give Peace A Chance,' 'Imagine,' and an impromptu ditty, 'Have No Fear, Drink American Beer,'" Kiser recalls. "But much of that day and the days that followed are still a fog to me."

SXSW 2001 had been a bumpy one financially, but "it seemed like heaven compared to the post-9/11 SXSW '02," says Swenson. (Attendance dropped for the second straight year, though it has risen ever since.) "The major labels were in freefall as illegal downloading seemed to be the primary means of obtaining music for everyone under 40. By March, most record industry people who still had a job saw their travel budgets slashed. A lot of people just didn't want to travel. Some, like Gaylynn and Angela [SXSW film producer Angela Lee, who had been at the Toronto International Film Festival], had been trapped out of town for a week or more."

A saving grace was international participation. "A few lucky internationals had made deals with acts like the Strokes and White Stripes the year before, when they weren't so famous," says Swenson. "So the word of mouth in the U.K. and Europe on SXSW was stronger than ever." That, of course, was always part of Swenson's blueprint. "When I worked for Joe 'King' Carrasco & the Crowns, their first deal was with Stiff Records, and they had their early success overseas when they toured in Europe before signing with MCA," he says. "I was also aware that at one point, the biggest part of Doug Sahm's touring business was in Scandinavia. I saw SXSW as a tool for acts to find alternative ways to build a career, and international outreach is key to that."

That has been a two-way street, with foreign companies and trade associations looking to do more and more each year. "It's one-stop shopping for American contacts," says longtime SXSW international consigliere Ed Ward. "No other event can offer that. With America having a strong technological leadership position, they can check out the state of the art while offering their own products. What's been particularly strong over the years is the presence of the international export agencies, government and quasi-governmental bodies who consider culture to be an exportable product. They're a strong presence in the trade shows and on panels. That's why PopKomm and MIDEM are important events for SXSW: The crew goes there to recruit customers."

2002 also brought a new SXSW tradition in Flatstock. The rock 'n' roll poster art exhibition might never have happened were the industry not slumping: The conference had little to lose, and the MP3 age gave the idea real resonance. "Music was no longer packaged with cover art or visuals to look at, touch, or put on display," says SXSW's Ron Suman, a longtime collector. "The time seemed right for an event that would put rock-related art in the spotlight. Austin already had a legacy of brilliant poster artists dating back to the '60s that included Guy Juke, Micael Priest, Jagmo, Jim Franklin, Lindsey Kuhn, and Frank Kozik. A concert poster exhibition at SXSW, where the love of music and the business of music are so celebrated, made perfect sense." The inaugural Flatstock, which is held two or more times a year, had been held in San Francisco; Flatstocks #2, 4, 6, 8, 12, 16, 20, 24 and 29 have all been at SXSW.

"Doom-and-gloom" was 2002's buzzword — until everybody actually went to see some bands. At the record industry "buzz" level, it was the year of Norah Jones. But it's possible the reduced business action made the showcases more fun. Lifelong SXSW veteran David Menconi of the *Raleigh News & Observer* was especially taken with the Polyphonic Spree, which had started the whole conference on an optimistic note, delivering the invocation before Robbie Robertson's keynote. Menconi chronicled them as "two dozen people in white robes who put on the most riotous live performances I've ever seen," comparing the Dallas band to *Godspell, Jesus Christ Superstar* and *Up With People* on acid. The first song exploded into a chorus that everybody in the house was screaming in testimony by the second time it rolled around: 'You gotta be GOOD/You gotta be STRONG/You gotta be TWO-THOUSAND PLACES AT ONCE!!!'...It's music that has almost nothing to do with the music industry, existing for its own sake.

"Despite all the doom-and-gloom talk," Menconi also wrote, "I heard more jawdropping, unexpected, drop-dead amazing music here this year than any other in recent memory."

On the film side of 2002, there was a world premiere that *Fort Worth Star-Telegram* and *Texas Monthly* critic Christopher Kelly had to see alone. "I couldn't seem to persuade any of my friends to attend *Spellbound* with me," he says. "You want to see a documentary about a spelling bee?," Kelly would ask. "If it was any good, it would have been at Sundance," people replied.

"I carried forth solo, and within minutes was enraptured by this alternately heartbreaking and harrowing movie about a group of kids competing at the Scripps Howard National Spelling Bee," Kelly

continues. "As the closing credits rolled, the audience — most of us in tears — erupted in the most enthusiastic round of applause I've ever heard before or since at the festival. All at once, the film portion of SXSW no longer seemed a poor cousin to Sundance, but a vibrant, scrappy entity entirely its own."

"I think it was the first — but not the last — sleeper hit in SXSW history," says Matt Dentler, then a coordinator under Angela Lee, who had replaced Nancy Schafer in 2000. "We thought *Spellbound* was a good film, but we had no idea it would be that big. The screenings of the film drew larger crowds with each passing day. I remember getting a call that John Sayles, who was attending that year, wanted to reserve seats, because word-of-mouth was so great. When it won the jury prize, I remember thinking, 'This film is a sensation.' Little did we know, it would become an even bigger one." *Spellbound* went on to receive an Oscar nomination for Best Documentary Feature, and it's listed on the the Internet Movie Database's Box Office Mojo site as the 21st highest-grossing documentary of all-time.

In 2004, Dentler succeeded Lee as SXSW Film producer. The roots of his main legacy were planted in 2005, when Andrew Bujalski's *Mutual Appreciation*, Jay and Mark Duplass' *The Puffy Chair*, and Joe Swanberg's *Kissing On The Mouth* all screened. These naturalistic, sometimes improvised small dramas brought to mind the likes of John Cassavetes and Richard Linklater — the umbrella term "Slackavetes" was even proposed by journalist and film director Jamie Stuart.

But another buzzword won the day: mumblecore, as coined by *Mutual Appreciation* sound mixer Eric Masunaga in a bar after one SXSW screening. Bujalski first uttered the word to *indieWIRE* the following August: "Pretty catchy," he said, creating the monster.

"It lay more or less dormant for two years after that, and then somehow exploded," Bujalski says. It probably happened during SXSW 2007, when Bujalski and Mark Duplass both acted in Swanberg's *Hannah Takes The Stairs*, also starring Greta Gerwig. "A dream team film," Dentler called it in *The New York Times*. He also commissioned a series of pre-SXSW screening shorts (filmed on the set of *Hannah*...) involving many of the mumblecore writer/actor/directors. "It was an obnoxious name nobody liked and it was meant to be a joke," said Swanberg to the *Times*. "But we haven't been able to get rid of it."

Actually, Eric Masunaga still stands by the term. "It wasn't an offhand joke by any means," he says. "I'd been battling performances in *Mutual Appreciation* for months that were, well...plain mumbly. The audio was mostly a rescue mission — but the film's uncommon charm and fresh, new-but-familiar facets of human interaction contained within it made it all worth the effort. When Andrew turned to me at SXSW '05, saying, 'they are calling it a movement, it needs a name,' I knew exactly what to say."

The New York Times' Dennis Lim proclaimed that "mumblecore is the sole significant American indie film wave of the last 20 years to have emerged outside the ecosystem of the Sundance Film Festival." To SXSW's Louis Black, that was both good and bad. "People tell me after Sundance, it's Tribeca and then SXSW," he told the website Austin Daze. "And you really see it in the films we get. People say: Well, you're going to be the next Sundance. But I don't want to be the next Sundance. I really don't. When SXSW started, the New Music Seminar was number one and we were number two. And that was great, because everybody hated them and liked us. So Sundance is Sundance. It's about people that don't really care about movies. It's a market. It's see and be seen. In Austin, film is really about film. And music is about music."

Except when music is also about 0s and 1s. Roland Swenson sums up 2002-2006 as "the period when the entertainment and information industries could no longer deny the fundamental changes the internet was causing, and they began to find ways to deal with it, even when, in most cases, their revenue was shrinking. SXSW became positioned as one place to go to learn about ways to deal with the changes."

During SXSW 2006, *The New York Times*' Kelefa Sanneh went even further, suggesting the conference proved that in the age of MP3s, there's still an awful lot of music business left. "When those songs get beamed around the Internet, it's seductive to think that bands and listeners have eliminated the middleman: Music goes straight from the recording studio to your laptop," he wrote. "This conference is a reminder of how many professionals it takes to turn an amateur band into a popular MP3. Here, 'behind the scenes' is the scene: the place is packed with publicists...and managers and booking agents and marketing teams and even a few old-fashioned radio D.J.s. This is a big part of what makes SXSW tick: middlemen as far as the eye can see."

Meanwhile, on March 21, 2006, Jack Dorsey typed the world's first tweet, though Twitter, the service he founded with Biz Stone and Evan Williams, didn't really launch until July, and didn't start to take over the world until it made a much more public splash at SXSW 2007. But Williams had already been to SXSW many times, first with Pyra Labs (which invented Blogger — Williams coined the very term — and was bought by Google in 2003) and then with his podcasting company Odeo (which evolved into the Twitter parent Obvious Corp). 2006 was also the debut of SXSW Screenburn, devoted to the video game industry. Interactive was about to finally arrive: Its registration numbers, which had hovered at 3,000 since the bubble popped, rose from 3,343 people in 2005 to 4,733 in 2006. By 2010, it was over 14,000.

"One of the things we used to ask ourselves was, 'Who is this event for?'" says Swenson. "We knew it was supposed to be for creative people making content. But after all the VC-funded start-ups imploded, not so many of those people had jobs anymore. In my mind, the turning point was when everything returned to a more entrepreneurial, 'start small and build' attitude from bloggers and people doing interesting things with what was then becoming known as social media."

Says Interactive director Hugh Forrest, "There were plenty of times that I wanted to throw in the towel. Because we didn't seem to be growing, and because we seemed so out of sync with everything else at SXSW. But Roland never flinched on his commitment to this event." Shortly after SXSW 2006, Forrest started PanelPicker, which encouraged registrants and the entire public to propose events. "It gave a tangible indication of how much interest the event was generating, and how much more it could generate," he says. "After so many years of shouting into the darkness, people were finally shouting back."

In his 2007 music keynote, Pete Townshend would reflect upon the dying music industry and, by extension, Interactive, saying, "An Austin music festival, SXSW, built on top of a really solid, healthy internet is a very different music festival from one built just on the fact that people in Austin really like to drink beer and listen to live bands."

But SXSW still tries to be both. "I still think of SXSW as a place for local and regional acts," says Swenson. "Over the years, we've just added more and more regions." Responding to the various critics and conspiracy theories that are as much a part of each year's conference as migas and Shiner Bock, Swenson sarcastically reveals "SXSW's hidden agenda. When SXSW started, I worked for *The Austin Chronicle,* which was primarily supported by advertising from live music clubs. We started SXSW as a way to bring in money to the nightclubs to help them stay in business and keep advertising." He also notes that Austin bands still make up the largest portion of the music lineup every year: "When we travel," he says, "the rest of the world complains that we have too many Austin acts."

"If we tried to do this anywhere else it wouldn't work," Louis Black told the Austin Daze website. "If you go to Park City, Utah, the week before or the week after Sundance you would never know that this was a town that had a film festival. You go to Austin any day of the year, and it is exactly the same as SXSW — it's just not as intense. There's great music, great films, tons of great intellectual activity and all kinds of media activity. SXSW *is* Austin." ■

continued from page 158

Peer Pressure
Peer Pressure DJs
Peggy James
Peggy Sue
Peggy Sue & The Pirates
Pegi Young
Peglegasus
Pekka Pohjola
Pela
Pelican
Peligrosa All-Stars
Pendulum
Penelope Houston
Pennie Lane
Penny Dreadfuls
Penny Hewson
Penny Jo Pullus
Penny Long
People
People In Planes
People Under the Stairs
Pepe Deluxe
Pepi Ginsberg
Pepper Morris
Pepsi Generation
Peralta
Percee P
Perceptionists
Perfect
Perforated Head
Perfume Tree
Perla Batalla
PermaFrost
Permagrin
Pernice Bros.
Perry Farrell
Perry Farrell's Satellite Party
Perseph One
Persephone's Bees
Persil
Person 13
Pet Clarke
Pete & Maura Kennedy
Pete & The Pirates
Pete Astudillo
Pete Droge
Pete Holmes
Pete Kennedy
Pete Krebs
Pete Krebs & The Gossamer Wings
Pete Mayes
Pete Molinari
Pete Philly & Perquisite
Pete Robbins & Centric
Pete Rock
Pete Teo
Pete Tong
Pete Wylie and The Mighty Wah!
Pete Yorn
Pete.
Peter Adams And The Nocturnal Collective
Peter and the Wolf
Peter and the Wolf (TX)
Peter Anthony
Peter Bjorn and John
Peter Bradley Adams (of eastmountainsouth)
Peter Broderick
Peter Bruntnell
Peter Case
Peter Elkas
Peter Fitzpatrick
Peter Holsapple
Peter Holsapple & Chris Stamey
Peter Jefferies
Peter Karp
Peter Morén
Peter Mulvey
Peter Murphy
Peter Pan Speedrock
Peter Rosenberg
Peter Rosenberg's Noisemakers w/ Bun B
Peter Rowan
Peter Rowan & Special Guests
Peter Salett
Peter Walker
Peter Walker (CA)
Peter Walker (NY)
Peter Wolf
Peter Wolf Crier
Peter's Songs
Petey
Petrol
Petting Zoo
Petty Booka
pexbaA
Pe'z
PFFR
PFFR videos: Final Flesh
Pfister Sisters
Phantogram
Phantom Helmsman
Phantom Limb
Phantom Limbs
Phantom Planet
Pharoahe Monch
Phaser
Phat J
Phat K.A.T.S.
Phil Alvin
Phil and the Osophers
Phil Broikos
Phil Cody
Phil Lee
Phil 'n' the Blanks
Phil Roy
Phil Tagliere
Philip Marshall Quintet
Phillips & Driver
Philly's Most Wanted
Philo
Phoenix
Phonograph
Phooka
Phosphorescent
Phranc
Phranchyze
Phunk Junkeez
Phylr
Picas o Platicas
Picasso Trigger
Picastro
Piccola Orchestra Avion Travel
Picket Line Coyotes
Pictureplane
Pidgeon
Piebald
Pierced Arrows
Pierre & the Zydeco Dots
Pierre Aderne
Piers Faccini
Pieta Brown
Pig Destroyer
Pig Iron
Pig Out
Pigalle
Pigeon John
Pigeon Religion
PigGie Hat
Pigs in a Blanket
Piirpauke
Pikahsso allen Poe
Pilar Diaz
Pilaseca
Pilate
Pill
Pills
Pilot To Gunner
Pilotdrift
Pilot's Lounge
Pimpadelic
Pimpbot
Pimpin' Pen
Pimpin' Pen of VIP
Pimpstress
Piñata Protest
Pinback
Pinching Judy
PINE*am
Pineal Ventana
Pineforest Crunch
Pinehurst Kids
Pinetop Perkins
Pinetop Seven
Pinetops
Piney Gir
Pinfield
Ping
Pink & Brown
Pink Mountaintops
Pink Nasty
Pink Reason
Pinkeye d'Gekko
Pinkston
Pinstripe
Pinwheel
Piranha Brothers
Pirate Love
Pissed Jeans
Pistol Grip
Pistol Love Family Band
Pistol Valve
Pistolera
Pistoleros
Pistolita
Piston Honda
Pit er Pat
Pitchfork's Closing Night Party
Pitty Sing
Pivot
PJ Harvey & John Parish
PJ Morton
PKT
P-L-A
Place of Skulls
Placebo
Places
Places to Park
Plagues
Plain Ole Bill
Plan B
Planes Mistaken for Stars
Planet Asia
Planningtorock
Plants and Animals
Plaster
Plastic Crimewave Sound
Plastician
Plastilina Mosh
Plastiscene
Play - N - Skillz
Players Club
Playing For Change
Play-N-Skillz
Pleasant Gehman
Pleasant Grove
Please
Please The Trees
Pleasure Club featuring James Hall
Pleasure Forever
Plexiq
Plouen Catximbes
Plow On Boy
Plum
Pluto
PM
Po' Girl
Pocahaunted
Poder Norteno
Podunk
Poet In Process
Poetic Asylum
Poetic Pilgrimage
Poetic Souls
Poi Dog Pondering
Point Blank
Point Blank Revue
Point Blank "the Bull"
Poirier ft MC Zulu
Poison Arrows (GA)
Poisoned Policy
Pokerface
Polak
Polar
Politicians
Polka Madre
Pollen
Pollo Elastico
Polly Mackey & the Pleasure Principle
Polly Paulusma
Polara
Polyphase
Polysics
Polytechnic
Pomegranate
Pomegranates
Pompeii
Poncho Kingz
Pond
Pong
Poni Hoax
Ponikijo
Ponticello
Ponty Bone
Ponty Bone & the Squeezetones
Pony
Pony Up!
Ponytail
Poor Rich Ones
Poorboys
Pop Levi
Pop Unknown
Popdefect
Poper
Poplolly
Popsicko
Popular Damage
Popup
Porcelain Grind
Porcupines
Pork
Porn
Porn (featuring Billy Anderson, Dale Crover & Tim Moss)
Porn (The Men Of)
Pornstore Janitor
Port O'Brien
Portastatic
Porter Hall, TN
Porterdavis
Porterville
Portrait of Poverty
Portugal. The Man
Possum Dixon
Post Stardom Depression
Post War Years
Poster Children
Postman
Potential Frenzy
Poul Krebs
Pow Wow
Powda
Powderfinger
Powell St. John
Power Douglas
Power Pill Fist
Power Squid
Power System Earth
PowerSolo
Powerspace
PPT
Prairie Cats
Praise the Twilight Sparrow
Prairie Oyster
Pre
Precious Blood
Precious Metal
Pree
Prefuse 73
Premium
Prescott Curlywolf
Presence
Press Gang
Preston School of Industry
Pretty & Nice
Pretty Girls Make Graves
Pretty Lights
Pretty the Quick Black Eyes
Prezence
Price
Prick
Pride Tiger
Priestess
Primal Scream
Prime STH
Primm
Primordial
Primordial Undermind
Prince Poetry
Princess Superstar
Princess Tex
Princeton
Priscilla Ahn
Prisonshake
Private Identity
Prizehog
Pro Bro Gold
Profecia
Professor Punn
Professor X
Progress
Project Alpha featuring Nite Owl & Te' Don/DJ Nsane
Project Crew
Project Jenny, Project Jan
Project Kids
Project Trio
Project X
ProjeKct Three (a King Crimson FraKctal)
Projekt Karpaty Magiczne
Prolyphic
Promise
Promise Ring
Propellerheads
Prophets of the Ghetto
Prophit
Prosser
Protokoll
Prototypes
Prozak
PS
Psalm One
Psyched Up Janis
Psychedelic Breakfast
Psychedelic Horseshit
Psychic Ills
Psychic Reality
Psycho Sisters
Psychodelic Zombiez
Psyclone Rangers
Psyko Ward
Pterodactyl
Public Bulletin
Public Enemy
Public Offenders
Public Service
Puddu Varano
Pudge Zeppelin
Puerto Muerto
Puffy
Puffy Areolas
Pugs
Pugs Atomz
Puller
Pulsations
Pumpskully
Punch Havana
punch TV
Punchbox
Punchy
Punish The Atom
Punkinhead
Puny Human
Puppetmastaz
Puppy Love Bomb
Pur
Pure
Pure Laine
Pure Reason Revolution
Pure Rubbish
Purge d.i.
purity
Purly Gates
Puro Slam Showcase
Purple Crush
Purple Ivy Shadows
Push On Junior
Push To Talk
Pusher
Pushmonkey
Pushy
Pustki
Pyeng Threadgill
Pylon
Pyscho Tribe
Pyschodots With Guest Adrian Belew

Q

Q-Burns Abstract Message
QT
Quaff
Qualo
Quango
Quantic
Quantic DJ
quaquaversal
Quarashi
Quarta Agg
Quartz-head 02
Quasi
Quatropaw
Queen Majesty
Queen Sarah Saturday
Queens of the Stone Age
Quest For Fire
Question
Question?
Quetzal
Qui w/ David Yow
Quien es, BOOM!
Quiet Company
Quincy Coleman
Quinimine
Quintaine Americana
Quintron and Miss Pussycat
Quit
Quit Your Day Job
Quitter
Quitters
Quizumba
Quruli
Qwasi Qwa

R

R.B. Morris
R.C.
R.C. Banks
R.E.M.
R.L. Burnside
Ra
Ra Ra Riot
Rabanes
Rabi
Rabid Rabbit
Racebannon
Rachael Cantu
Rachael Yamagata
Rachel Brown
Rachel Fuller
Rachel Goetz
Rachel Goetz & Ghostown
Rachel Goldstar
Rachel Goodrich
Rachel Loy
Rachel Trachtenburg Morning Show
Racoon
Radar Bros.
Radar Brothers
Radar Tanta
Radial Spangle
Radiant
Radio 4
Radio La Chusma
Radio Moscow
Radio Nationals
Radio Radio
Radio Vago
Radioclit
Radiogram
RadioRadio
Radiostar
Radish
Radney Foster
Radsoles
Rafter
Rafter and Friends
Raggamassive
Raging Honkies
Raging Saint
Raging Slab
Raging Speedhorn
Raging Teens
Rahdunes
Rahim
Rail
Railroad Jerk
Rainbow Arabia
Rainbow Bridge
Rainer
Rainer Maria
Rainshine
Raising The Fawn
Rajamani
Rakaa
Raking Bombs
Ralfe Band
Rally Boy
Ralph Camey
Ralph Covert
Ralph Myerz
Ralph Myerz & the Jack Herren Band
Ralph Soul Jackson
Ralph White
Ram Herrera
Ramblin' Jack Elliott
Ramesh Srivastava
Ramin Nazer
Ramin Nazer, Andi Smith, Andy Ritchie and Special Guest
Ramon Ayala (y sus Bravos Del Norte)
Ramsay Midwood
RANA
Rana Santacruz

Randy Newman (1996)

Ranch Romance
Randall Bramblett
Randall J. "Biscuit" Turner
Randi Laubek
Random
Random aka Mega Ran
Randy Beckett's Rebel Train
Randy Erwin
Randy Flines
Randy Franklin
Randy Garibay
Randy Garibay & Cats Don't Sleep
Randy McCullough
Randy Newman
Randy Weeks
Range Hoods
Rankin Scroo And Ginger
Raphael Saadiq
Rapid Ric
Rapid Ric featuring Magno and Chalie Boy
Rapid Ric's Whut it Do Family feat. Magno, Chalie Boy, Bavu Blakes, Black Mike, Gerald G, Rob da Ryno
Rapider Than Horsepower
Rasheed
Rasputina
Ratas del Vaticano
Ratatat
Ratón Pérez
Ratteled Roosters
Rattledown
Rattletree
Rattletree Marimba
Rauberhohle
Raul Malo
Raul Midon with Jason Mraz
Raúl Salinas
Raunch Hands ' Bigg Topp
Rausch
Ravens & Chimes
Raw
Raw'LT
Raxas
Ray Bonneville
Ray Campi
Ray Condo & the Ricochets
Ray Davies
Ray Doyle
Ray McNiece
Ray Price
Ray Reed
Ray Sauls
Ray Sharpe w/Augie Meyers, Charlie Sexton, Mike Buck and Speedy Sparks
Ray Wilko
Ray Wonder
Ray Wylie Hubbard
Raya Yarbrough
Raydibaum
Ray's Music Exchange
Razbone
Razor
Razorlight
Re Winkler
Reach the Sky
Read Yellow
Reading Rainbow
Real Estate
Real Ones
Real Shocks
Real Vocal String Quartet
Realness
Realtyme
Rebecca Cannon
Rebecca Cannon & Thor
Rebecca Gates
Rebecca Gates and the Consortium
Rebekah Higgs
Rebel Diaz
ReBelle
Rebuilding the Rights of Statues
Rec Center
Receptors
Reckless Kelly
Record Hop
Recover
Red Animal War
Red Aunts
Red Autumn Fall
Red Bacteria Vacuum
Red Cortez
Red Delicious
Red Dirt Rangers
Red Dye #4
Red Elvises
Red Fang
Red Herring
Red House Painters
Red Jumpsuit Apparatus
Red Leaves
Red Lightning
Red Meat
Red Planet
Red Platinum
Red Red Meat
Red Riders
Red River
Red River Revue: Black Joe Lewis, Walter Daniels, Chili Cold Blood
Red Sparowes
Red Star Belgrade
Red X Red M
Red Young & Friends w/ Silvie Rider
Red Young Quartet
Red Zone Fam
Redd Volkaert
Redd Volkaert and Cindy Cashdollar
Rediscover
redlightmusic
Redman
Ree Van Vleck
Reef The Lost Cauze
Reel Big Fish
Reelaktz
Reeltime Travelers
Reeve Carney & The Revolving Band
Reeve Oliver
Reflection Eternal
Reflection Eternal (Talib Kweli & Hi-Tek)
Reggae Cowboys
Reggae of Will
Reggie Gaines
Reggie Gibson
Reggie Watts
Regurgitator
Rehasher
Reid Speed
Reigning Sound
Relay
Relief
Relish
Remains of Something Human
Remate & La Loco Band
Reminder
Remy Zero
René
Renee Knauth
Renee Sebastian
Renee Woodward
REO Speedealer
Reppy
Rescue
Resonators
Resorte
Resplandor
Response
Responsible Johnny
Restavrant
Restiform Bodies
Restless
Retardos
Retarted Elf
Retisonic
Reto Burrell
Retribution Gospel Choir
Retrospect
Rev KM Williams & The Amazing Trainreck
Rev. Kathy Russell
Reverb Brothers
Reverberation
Reverend Glasseye
Reverend Horton Heat
Reverend Peyton's Big Damn Band
Revolution Smile
Rewake
Rex
Rex Daisy
Rex Hobart & The Misery Boys
Rey Fresco
Reyez
Reykjavik!
Reynardine
Rezillos
Rezound
Rheostatics
Rhett Miller
Rhonda Coullet
Rhudabega
Rhyme Sayers Collective
Rhymefest
Rhys Chatham "Guitar Army"
Rhythm Kings
Rhythm of Black Lines
Rhythm Rats
Ricaine
Ricardo Lemvo & Makina Loca
Rich Brotherton
Rich Ferguson & the Midwest Creole Ensemble
Rich Ferguson/Fuzzy Doodah
Rich Harney Quartet
Rich Price
Richard Allen
Richard Barone
Richard Bell
Richard Boyce
Richard Buckner
Richard Buckner & friends, including Alejandro Escovedo
Richard Buckner & the Doubters
Richard Davies
Richard Earl
Richard Hawley
Richard Henry
Richard Johnson
Richard Julian
Richard Patureau
Richard Swift
Richard Younger & Blue Horses
Richie Furay
Richie Havens
Richmond Fontaine
Rick Broussard
Rick Margitza
Rick Parker & the Lazy Stars
Rick Ross
Rick Sal
Rick Smith & the Lonesome City Kings
Rick Treviño
Rick Vito & the Mondo Rythmnm Kings
Rickie Lee Jones
Ricky Rasura
Ricky Skaggs and Kentucky Thunder
Rico Bell
Rico Bell and the Snake Handlers
Rico Pabon
Riddim Please
Riddim Saunter
Riddlin' Kids
Ridgetop Syncopators
Riff Random
Right As Rain
Right Away, Great Captain!
Right on Dynamite
Right Or Happy (former Reivers)
Right Said Fred
Righteous Babe Allstars featuring members of Drums & Tuba, Hamell on Trial, Andrew Bird and Special Guests
Rigor Mortis
Rika Shinohara
Ring of Power
Ring Theatre
Ringer
Ringling Sisters
Ringo
Ringo Deathstarr
Ringos of Soul
RinneRadio featuring Wimme
Rint Zykle & the Speed Queens
Rip & Destroy
Ripe
Rise
Rising Lion
Rita Chiarelli
Rita Redshoes
Ritual Device
Rival Schools
Rival Suns
River
River City
River City Rapists
River City Tanlines
River Roses
Rivulets
Riz MC
RJD2
Ro Spit
Road Runners
Roadrunners
Roadsaw
Roam Elsewhere
Roar! Lion
Rob Crow
Rob Delaney
Rob Delaney, Moshe Kasher, Chelsea Peretti, Andy Ritchie and Special Guest
Rob Dickinson
Rob G
Rob Giles
Rob Huebel
Rob Jungklas
Rob Laufer
Rob McColley
Rob Quest
Rob Roy
Rob Sonic
Rob Swift
Robb Roy
Robbers on High Street
Robbi Rob
Robbie Fulks
Robbie Hardkiss
Robbie Lee
Robedoor
Robert Bradley's Blackwater Surprise
Robert Burke Warren
Robert Burke Warren & Turpentine
Robert Earl Keen
Robert Earl Keen Band
Robert Francis
Robert Gomez
Robert Hazard
Robert Jetton
Robert M
Robert Martinez
Robert McEntee
Robert Miller
Robert Minott
Robert Mirabal
Robert Plant and Strange Sensation

continued on page 188

2002

SXSW STATS March 8 - 17

BY THE NUMBERS

1,035 showcasing artists
of 5,100 submissions

63 panels, workshops & sessions

49 venues & stages

6,300 registrants

$325-525 registration

$85-105 wristband

192 pages in program guide

100 trade show exhibitors

3,098 film registrants

187 films screened

3,015 interactive registrants

AUSTIN MUSIC AWARDS

Wednesday, March 13, Austin Music Hall

Performers Salute to Ray Benson with Asleep at the Wheel, Jimmie Vaughan and Johnny Gimble; Sixpence None the Richer; Champ Hood Tribute with Warren Hood, the South Austin Jug Band and Toni Price; Spoon; Snobs; Supergirls with Lord Douglas Phillips, Patrice Pike, Dottie Farrell, Nancy Scott and Kris Patterson; MC Paul Ray

KEYNOTE SPEAKER

Robbie Robertson The guitarist for The Band "had a lot to say, and he took his time," recalled Roland Swenson. (*Austin American-Statesman* writer Michael Corcoran was less diplomatic, calling the keynote "windy"). "After introducing him, I had been called to registration to deal with some problem, and missed most of his speech. Louis Black helped keep me abreast of the proceedings, running in periodically with reports like, 'He's just met Ronnie Hawk.' Then 15 minutes later, 'He's on tour with Dylan in the U.K. getting booed!' Then, much later: 'They're recording...*Big Pink* in Woodstock.'"

MEMORABLE PANELS

"Crash Course" The conference featured Wednesday panels for the first time, including seven nuts-and-bolts sessions under this umbrella title that dealt with distribution, management, contracts,

publishing, touring & booking, publicity & promotion, and "How To Make It In The Music Business" (with Jim Halsey).

"How Do Jam Bands Do It?" How the children of the Grateful Dead succeed without traditional radio, video, or print media exposure.

"Bagels with Mark Rubin" The Bad Livers bassist and all-around local music legend's near-annual forum discussed musicians' health issues.

"O Brother – Anomaly Or Phenomenon?" Panelists addressed the question, "Will the success of the *O Brother, Where Art Thou?* soundtrack lead to lasting exposure for Americana artists?"

"South by Southwest is an annual event that attracts people who love movies. Aside from the music, film and interactive media programming, a major part of its allure is the panel discussions, which are packed with serious audiences interested in conversation about the meaning of the pictures, offering access to filmmakers in such a winningly low-key setting that you can see the panelists slowly, surely falling in love with this city." ■ *The New York Times,* March 12, 2002

Courtney Love Interview (with Chuck Philips of the *Los Angeles Times*) SXSW panels chief Andy Flynn met up with Love the day before their interview, escorting her to Robertson's address. "I've never felt the glare of public scrutiny as strong before or since," he says. "She had people gasping at her presence."

After the panel, Love sat down for an interview with News 8 Austin's Andy Langer. "She didn't like the lighting, so she cut the Convention Center's dividing curtains to use as diffusers, and had SXSW staffers hold them near her face off-camera," Langer says. "She must have been on her hands and knees cutting huge swatches for ten minutes. She said, 'Bad lighting kills careers' at least twice. I'm thinking drugs and ego were far bigger problems."

"The music industry may be reeling, but the musicians are still rocking. That's the message that came out of this year's renewal of South by Southwest, the Austin, Texas-based conference that has become the standard by which popular music conventions are judged." ■ UPI, March 26, 2002

NOTABLE PANELISTS

Hilary Rosen (interview with Tamara Conniff of *Hollywood Reporter*), Miles Copeland III (interview with David Fricke of *Rolling Stone*), Peter Guralnick (interview with Evan Smith of *Texas Monthly*), Gerard Cosloy of Matador Records ("The A&R/Artist Relationship"), Wanda Jackson ("Rockabilly Fillies"), Jason Schwartzman of Phantom Planet ("What To Expect When You're Expecting"), Patty Schemel ("Artists vs. Technology"), Nic Harcourt ("Hey! That's My Song")

MEMORABLE SHOWCASES & EVENTS

> Friday's Swedish Music showcase at the Red Room featured Sahara Hotnights, The Soundtrack Of Our Lives, Citizen Bird, Left Hand Solution and Maryslim.

> The NARAS show on Thursday at Auditorium Shores featured La Mafia, Palomo, Costumbre and Grupo Control.

> In addition to her now famously undersized official showcase at Indian restaurant the Clay Pit, Norah Jones played at the Starbucks on West 24th Street near the University of Texas campus...the beginning of a beautiful relationship with the Seattle coffee giant.

NOTABLE ACTS

Polyphonic Spree The Dallas choir made a huge splash with their prelude/invocation to the keynote, as well as with their nighttime show at Stubb's.

Icarus Line Guitarist Aaron North (who would later join Nine Inch Nails) earned notoriety by smashing a display case at the Hard Rock Cafe to get at one of Stevie Ray Vaughan's guitars. "Some versions of the story have him running down Sixth Street with it before being tackled and pummeled by the bouncers," says Roland Swenson. "Other versions have him being kicked out of the club after trying to plug it in."

Also OK Go, Yeah Yeah Yeahs, T-Model Ford, Prefuse 73, Mastodon, Drive-By Truckers, Freddy Fender, Minus The Bear, They Might Be Giants, Greenhornes

SOME OF THE MEDIA-SPONSORED ACTS

Caitlin Cary (*Independent Weekly*, NC Triangle), Free Radicals (*Houston Press*), Mechanical Walking Robotboy (*San Antonio Current*), Soviet Space (*Fort Worth Weekly*), Supagroup (*Offbeat*, New Orleans), Immortal Lee County Killers (*Black & White*, Auburn, AL), Five Eight (*Flagpole*, Athens GA), Departure Lounge (*Nashville Scene*), George DeVore (*Little Village*, Cedar Falls, IA), Mistletoe (*Weekly Alibi*, Albuquerque)

SOME OF THE AUSTIN ACTS

Shearwater Jonathan Meiburg's sui generis lush-pop band was just about to finish up its second record, the Misra release *Everybody Makes Mistakes*. They now record for Matador.

Also The Gloria Record, Vietnam, Don Walser, Cotton Mather, David Baerwald & the New Folk Underground, Octopus Project, Los Lonely Boys, Grupo Fantasma, Endochine

SOME OF THE INTERNATIONAL ACTS

Ash (U.K.), The Darkness (U.K.), Neil Finn (New Zealand), Kinky (Mexico), Acid Mothers Temple (Japan), Dears (Canada), Big Leaves (Wales), Bigbang (Norway), Cravo Carbono (Brazil), Rock Four (Tel Aviv), John Butler Trio (Australia)

WHATEVER HAPPENED TO...

Starsailor While the *Los Angeles Times* gave the year's hyped U.K. act "next Radiohead" honors, praising their "sweet, dreamy take on Anglo Pop," the *Austin American-Statesman* sneered, "Starsailor are what Matchbox 20 would sound like if they listened to My Bloody Valentine instead of Pearl Jam."

Mr. Scruff Then known for the TV commercial ubiquity of his track "Get A Move On," the U.K. DJ and producer has remained prolific in both music and cartooning, and also has his own line of tea, "Make Us A Brew!"

SOFTBALL TOURNEY

Clubs and Talent Buyers took the trophy back from Print Media, winning its *seventh* title 10-4, after a pair of early laughers (26-3 over Agents/Managers in the first round, and 25-3 over the Volunteers in the semis).

FILM
AWARDS

Narrative Feature Winner *Manito* (D: Eric Eason); runner-up: *The Misanthrope* (D: Allen Colombo).

Documentary Feature Winner *Spellbound* (D: Jeff Blitz); runner-up: *Escuela/School* (D: Hannah Weyer).

Audience Awards *Mai's America* (D: Marlo Poras), documentary feature; *Lifetime Guarantee: Phranc's Adventures in Plastic* (D: Lisa Udelson), documentary first film; *By Hook or by Crook* (D: Harry Dodge, Silas Howard), narrative feature; *Charlotte Sometimes* (D: Eric Byler) and *Made-Up* (D: Tony Shalhoub), narrative first film (tie)

NOTABLE FILMS & EVENTS

Journeys With George (D: Alexandra Pelosi), *CQ* (D: Roman Coppola), *Chelsea Walls* (D: Ethan Hawke), *Gigantic: A Tale Of Two Johns*

"[SXSW] has matured into one of the North American film festivals that filmmakers love to attend and hate to leave." ▪ indieWIRE, March 14, 2002

(They Might Be Giants documentary, D: AJ Schnack), *Y Tu Mama Tambien* (D: Alfonso Cuarón), *Money For Nothing* (D: Sut Jhally); John Sayles, Lloyd Kaufman and Albert Maysles retrospectives; Actors Workshop with Jeffrey Tambor.

INTERACTIVE
KEYNOTE SPEAKERS

Kevin Lynch, Jeff Veen, Simon Assad and David Carson, Cory Doctorow, Bruce Sterling

NOTABLE EVENTS

"Iron webmaster" showdown hosted by Ben Brown and Dana Robinson: Two teams attempted (and failed) to build a web site, live, in front of an audience, in one hour. ▪

2003

SXSW **STATS** March 7 - 16

BY THE NUMBERS

1,100 showcasing artists of 6,200 submissions

72 panels, workshops & sessions

53 venues & stages

6,577 registrants

$325-525 registration

$95-115 wristband

200 pages in program guide

143 trade show exhibitors

3,132 film registrants

150 films screened

3,036 interactive registrants

AUSTIN MUSIC AWARDS

Wednesday, March 12, Austin Music Hall

Performers "The Improbable Return of Redneck Rock" with Steve Fromholz, Rusty Wier, Billy Joe Shaver, Ray Wylie Hubbard, Bob Livingston, Ray Benson, and guests; Tribute to the Hole in the Wall with Paul Minor, Beaver Nelson, Troy Campbell, Scrappy Jud Newcomb, Jane Bond, Tony Scalzo, Miles Zuniga, Darin Murphy, Ted Roddy, Barbara K, Andrew Duplantis, and Matt Hubbard; Chip Taylor and Carrie Rodriguez; Ruthie Foster; MC Paul Ray

KEYNOTE SPEAKER

Daniel Lanois The renowned producer and musician began his talk with an allegorical tale of childhood, often referring to himself in the third person as "Danny." He closed it with a solo pedal steel version of his song "Transmitter." "We've reached a place where we have too much music," he said. "Silence is golden. Enjoy silence, or you might stop loving [music]." During the prelude set, bluesman Cedell Davis was joined onstage by R.E.M.'s Peter Buck (on bass).

MEMORABLE PANELS

"About A Mover: Doug Sahm" With Joe Nick Patoski, Ray Benson, Bill Bentley, Augie Meyers, Shawn Sahm and Speedy Sparks

"Artists Panel: Activism And Protest" Moderated by *Chicago Tribune* writer Greg Kot, with Salman

Ahmad, John Doe, Wavy Gravy, Mike Mills, John Sinclair, Jenny Toomey and Neil Pollack

Lyle Lovett Interview (wth Evan Smith of *Texas Monthly*) "With the war in Iraq escalating, we themed the artists panel toward activism," says Roland Swenson. "Later, Lyle Lovett stunned the crowd by saying he believed Bush was a good guy and was telling the truth about the yet-to-be-discovered WMDs."

"Leave No Musician Behind: The Health Care Emergency" Moderated by Dave Marsh, the panel included various musicians and musicians' health organizations.

"Government And Media Consolidation" A different kind of panelist roster featured longtime U.S. congressman Lloyd Doggett of central Texas plus a couple of political correspondents (Rick Carr of NPR and John Nichols of *The Nation*).

NOTABLE PANELISTS
Anthony Wilson (interview with Jason Cohen), FCC commisioner Jonathan Adelstein (featured speaker), Michael Dorf ("Digital Leaders Going Back To The Basics"), Don Fleming ("Missing In Action"), Scott McCaughey ("Songs And Their Writers"), Jeff "Skunk" Baxter ("Crash Course: Guitar Workshop"), David Ritz ("Creating A Music Biography"), Steve Schnur ("Music In Games")

MEMORABLE SHOWCASES & EVENTS
> There were more people in the Blender Bar at the Ritz on Friday night for the blistering debut of British Sea Power, which filled the stage with greenery and ended with a speaker-climbing/instrument-tossing injury, than there were for fellow U.K. band The Darkness. But everyone who saw The Darkness had their ears assaulted and their jaws dropped to the floor, even if they weren't sure about the band's level of irony (answer: none). SXSW never felt more like Wembley Stadium. "Will soon rule the world," predicted Rollingstone.com. "Is there someplace to buy Freddie Mercury spandex jumpsuits or do you have to have those made?"
> British bands Blur and Simian shared a bill with The Rapture on Thursday at La Zona Rosa. Blur's surprise set (they were billed simply as "special guest" in the program guide) was already going to be their first without departing lead guitarist Graham Coxon, but they also

> "I absolutely trust President Bush's sincerity, and at the same time trust there is more information [yet to come out]," Lovett, an acquaintance of the Bush family and [the Dixie Chicks' Natalie] Maines, said Saturday during an interview session at the Austin Convention Center. "Just because [pop musicians] have the forum to speak out doesn't mean they should." ■ Chris Riemenschneider, *Los Angeles Times*, March 17, 2003

had to play without bassist Alex James, who couldn't get into the country. Rival Schools' Chris Traynor filled in on 24 hours' notice.
> Saturday's free public show at Auditorium Shores ran from 4:30-10pm and featured Concrete Blonde, Presidents Of The United States Of America, Joe Jackson Band, Alejandro Escovedo, and Reckless Kelly.
> Thursday's Austin Music Hall lineup featured the Yardbirds, Jay Farrar, Michael Penn, Daniel Lanois, and Billy Bob Thornton. Bassist Chris Dreja and drummer Jim McCarty have kept the Yardbirds going ever since the band's 1960s heyday; on this night, they were joined by guest guitarists Slash, Skunk Baxter and Steve Vai.
> Flatstock 2, a music poster art show, became part of SXSW for the first time (Flatstock 1 was held in San Francisco in 2002), and it has been returning regularly ever since. The Convention Center exhibit showcased more than four decades of work by 80-plus artists, including Jason Austin, Kerry Awn, Jagmo, Jaxon, Frank Kozik and Delany Gill with Hatch Show Print.

"Every year, for one long weekend in March, Austin is the best rock & roll city in America because nearly every hungry band in the land turns up for the South by Southwest Music Conference." ■ *Rolling Stone*, April 17, 2003

NOTABLE ACTS

Fall Out Boy The future pop-punk hitmakers were still a couple of months away from releasing their first full-length when they played an 8pm set Wednesday at the Emo's Annex.

"If you want to make it big as a musician in the United States, the South by Southwest festival in Austin, TX, is a good place to start."
■ *News of Norway*, 2003

Icarus Line The Los Angeles band played La Zona Rosa on Friday, despite a previous SXSW incident in which their singer had supposedly appropriated a Stevie Ray Vaughan guitar from a museum display during a performance. No hard feelings!

Trachtenburg Family Slideshow Players Fresh off a *Conan O'Brien* appearance, the quirky high-concept outsider-art band filled La Zona Rosa on Friday. "You haven't really lived until you hear a 9-year-old girl drummer say, 'I need more vocals in the monitors,'" wrote Greg Beets in *The Austin Chronicle*.

"The main reason to come to South By is for networking. I've made almost all my lasting contacts at the softball game. It's the most amazing networking opportunity, and most people fly out of town Sunday morning and miss it." ■ Lawyer/manager Steve Easley in the *Austin American-Statesman*, March 17, 2003

Also Decemberists, Black Keys, Visqueen, Stellastarr, Dirtbombs, Pretty Girls Make Graves, Gavin DeGraw, Mountain Goats, Lucero, Pinback, El-P, Avenged Sevenfold, B-52s, James Blunt, Tony Joe White

SOME OF THE MEDIA-SPONSORED ACTS

Iron & Wine (*Miami New Times*), Broken Social Scene (*NOW*, Toronto), Mudhoney (*Seattle Weekly*), Erase Errata (*SF Weekly*, San Francisco), Baboon (*Dallas Observer*), Mechanical Walking Robotboy (*San Antonio Current*),

Clouseaux (*Houston Press*), John Price (*Fort Worth Weekly*), Motorway (*Offbeat*, New Orleans), The Friendly (*Weekly Alibi*, Albuquerque, NM), Ware River Club (*Boston Phoenix*)

SOME OF THE AUSTIN ACTS

Explosions In The Sky, Sound Team, Jane Bond, I Love You But I've Chosen Darkness, Tia Carrera, Guy Forsyth, Li'l Cap'n Travis, Colin Gilmore, Patrice Pike & the Black Box Rebellion, Crack Pipes

SOME OF THE INTERNATIONAL ACTS

Kathleen Edwards (Canada), Sondre Lerche (Norway), Junior Senior (Denmark), Iguana Men of Galapagos (Ecuador), Theory Of A Deadman (Canada), The Raveonettes (Denmark), Scout Niblett (U.K.), Redneck Manifesto (Ireland), Git (Australia), Hot Hot Heat (Canada)

SOFTBALL TOURNEY

And you thought seeing the Lakers or Yankees every year got old? Print Media and Clubs/Talent Buyers faced off for the fifth straight time. The profession with the less-bright future — if you have to ask, you're not a journalist — prevailed on the diamond, 17-11.

FILM
AWARDS

Narrative Feature Winner *Sexless* (D: Alex Holdridge), which was shot and set in Austin. Special Jury Award: *Happy Here And Now* (D: Michael Almereyda)

Documentary Feature Winner *Flag Wars* (D: Linda Goode Bryant and Laura Poitras); Special Jury Award: *Jon E. Edwards Is In Love* (D: Chris Bradley and Kyle La Brache)

Audience Awards *Sexless*, narrative feature; *Melvin Goes To Dinner* (D: Bob Odenkirk), narrative first feature; *Girlhood* (D: Liz Garbus), documentary feature; *The Flute Player* (D: Jocelyn Glatzer), documentary first feature

MEMORABLE FILMS & EVENTS

Spun (D: Jonas Akerlund), *A Mighty Wind* (D: Christopher Guest), *Assassination Tango* (D: Robert Duvall), *Go Further* (D: Ron Mann), *Tom Dowd And The Language Of Music* (D: Mark Moormann), *Lubbock Lights* (D: Amy Maner and George Sledge), *Rise Above: The Tribe 8 Documentary* (D: Tracy Flannigan), *Rebel Without A Pause* (D: Nancy Savoca), *Lilya Forever* (D: Lukas Moodysson), *Phone Booth* (D: Joel Schumacher), *Live From Shiva's Dancefloor* (short, D: Richard Linklater, with Timothy "Speed" Levitch)

The festival's 10th anniversary also included retrospective screenings of *Swimming With Sharks* (D: George Huang), *Dancer Texas Pop. 81* (D: Tim McCandless), *The Life And Times Of Hank Greenberg* (D: Aviva Kempner), *The Target Shoots First* (D: Chris Wilcha), *The Journey* (D: Eric Saperston), *Made-Up* (D: Tony Shalhoub) and *It's Impossible To Learn To Plow By Reading Books* (D: Richard Linklater).

INTERACTIVE
KEYNOTE SPEAKERS

Artificial intelliegence expert Doug Lenat (Cycorp), web designer Joshua Davis, author Richard Florida

NOTABLE PANELISTS & SPEAKERS

Po Bronson (author), Bruce Sterling (author), Frank Casanova (Apple), Cory Doctorow (who'd just published his novel *Down And Out In The Magic Kingdom*), Dan Gillmor (journalist), Philip Kaplan (Fucked Company), Lawrence Lessig (Stanford University), Kevin Warwick (*I Cyborg* author), Web Awards MC John Halcyon Styn (cockybastard.com)

"Sometimes I do too much research. [My SXSW schedule] looks like a big racing form; I'm circling things keeping in mind what's before and after, which clubs are close together, and which clubs are small enough that I'd need to be there an hour early. You can't be everywhere at once; you're always missing something good at this festival. You have to forget about what you're missing and focus on what you're seeing at that time." ■ Beatle Bob in *The Austin Chronicle*, March 14, 2003

MEMORABLE PANELS

"Some Rights Reserved: The Creative Commons Project," "Beyond The Blog: The Future Of Personal Publishing," "Steve Mack's Streaming Media Bible Workshop," "Justin Hall's Geek Out," "How To Counter Attack A Spammer," "User Not Found: Dealing With The Death Of Online Friends," "Adult Webmaster 2003: Hard Problems In A Soft Economy." ■

2004

SXSW **STATS** March 12 - 21

BY THE NUMBERS

1,279 showcasing artists
of 7,000 submissions

70 panels, workshops & sessions

55 venues & stages

7,213 registrants

$325-525 registration

$105-125 wristband

232 pages in program guide

175 trade show exhibitors

3,667 film registrants

180 films screened

3,270 interactive registrants

AUSTIN MUSIC AWARDS

Wednesday, March 17, Austin Music Hall

Performers Los Lonely Boys; Chip Taylor & Carrie Rodriguez; "Class of '78" with Larry Seaman, Stephen Marsh, Randy "Biscuit" Turner, Jesse Sublett, Jon Dee Graham, Randy Franklin, Terri Lord, and Ty Gavin; Tia Carrera; St. Patrick's Day Throwdown with Greencards vs. Cluan; MC Paul Ray

KEYNOTE CONVERSATION

Little Richard (with Dave Marsh) All's well that ends well, as the conference couldn't have obtained a more impressively high-wattage replacement for Antonio "L.A." Reid, whose booking fell apart in the wake of his move from Arista to Def Jam. "Little Richard was everything we could hope for in a keynote: funny and wise," says Roland Swenson. "He gave perhaps the best piece of advice ever given out by a keynote: 'Always sign your own checks.' No doubt that was a bit of wisdom he'd learned the hard way. Backstage he was quite warm and friendly, obviously enjoying having his photograph taken with everyone willing to wait. As we walked down the corridor from the green room to the stage, dozens of workers from the convention center kitchen and janitorial staffs appeared, and he greeted each of them with hugs and greetings, working the crowd like a seasoned politician on a rope line. He was the first keynote we'd had that held any interest for these workers."

MEMORABLE PANELS

"Big Star #1 Panel" discussed the iconic Memphis band's origins and accomplishments, with Andy Hummell, Jody Stephens, Jon Auer, Ken Stringfellow, Terry Manning, and moderator Kent Benjamin

"Alt Weekliess And Other Uses For Wood Pulp" asked "who gets the best hate mail?" of Peter Margasak, Rob Harvilla, Sarah Hepola and other music writers.

"The End Of The Record Store?" covered the new challenges for retail outlets.

"Playing Games With Music" addressed the notion that "music placement in video games gets your tunes into the ears of our youth in a most effective way."

NOTABLE PANELISTS

Interviews with Walter Yetnikoff, Wayne Coyne, Andrew Loog Oldham, Ani DiFranco, and Joan Baez; Simon Raymonde (Bella Union), Charles Attal (Stubb's), Mark Cuban (HDNet/Dallas Mavericks), Nils Bernstein (Matador Records), Megan Jasper (Sub Pop Records), Jim Pitt (*Late Night With Conan O'Brien*), Robyn Hitchcock

MEMORABLE SHOWCASES

> Joss Stone, Kris Kristofferson, and Toots & the Maytals with special guests Rachel Yamagata and Charles Mars played Auditorium Shores on Friday. Saturday's show, headlined by Los Lonely Boys, set a SXSW Auditorium Shores attendance record with some 20,000 people.

> Franz Ferdinand and the Decemberists were booked at Buffalo Billiards on separate nights; both showcases had people lined up all the way across Sixth Street hoping to get in.

> You don't generally think of Dizzee Rascal, Chamillionaire and "beach volleyball" in the same breath, but they and several other hip-hop artists played at Aussie's on Saturday.

> The Ozomatli show at Exodus on Wednesday night became famous after-the-fact when the band's attempt to lead a drumline onto Sixth Street resulted in a clash with police.

NOTABLE ACTS

Killers The Las Vegas band was tucked away at 8pm on Thursday at the Caucus, a few months before their debut album took the charts by storm.

"In 2004, [Andy Hummel] and I did a Big Star panel together at SXSW. That was so much fun – I got to hang out with him. But when he came to the gig that night, Andy showed up with all this camera gear, and they wouldn't let him in. His hotel was 30 minutes away; it wasn't practical for him to take it all the way back and come back to see us in time. So he didn't come to the show. For years, I thought, 'Wow, he just decided not to come to the show, for whatever reason.' That was finally explained to me at this last SXSW, when he came up to do another panel."
■ Big Star's Jody Stephens, to David Fricke in *Rolling Stone*, July 29, 2010

Hold Steady The debut album from singer Craig Finn and his bandmates came out the same week as their Friday-night showcase. "Seeing them at their first SXSW appearance in 2004 had a Saul-to-Damascus quality," Joe Gross reminisced in the *Village Voice* a year later. "Booked into a small goth club called Elysium, Finn flailed around the stage, clapping his hands randomly, hitting his Telecaster now and then, shouting his wildly funny and complicated lyrics off-mic and pushing his glasses up every three seconds. The band churned something that wasn't quite classic rock, but bore no trace of monthly-flavor influences."

Also Big Star, Mindy Smith, Nellie McKay, Dizzee Rascal, N.E.R.D., Scissor Sisters, Joan Jett & the Blackhearts, Modest Mouse, Eugene Mirman, David Cross, Coheed & Cambria, Sufjan Stevens, The National, TV On The Radio, Against Me!, Six Organs Of Admittance, Mission Of Burma, Walkmen, Dirty Projectors, Dresden Dolls, Joanna Newsom, Devendra Banhart, Lost Sounds, Silkworm, Battles

SOME OF THE MEDIA-SPONSORED ACTS

Demolition Doll Rods (*Metro Times*, Detroit, MI), Bobby Bare Jr & the Young Criminals Starvation League (*Nashville Scene*), Comets On Fire (*SF Weekly*), Why? (*East Bay Express*, Oakland, CA), Pleasant Grove (*Dallas Observer*), Collin

Herring (*Fort Worth Weekly*), Walter Clevenger & the Dairy Kings (*Orange County Weekly*), Butchies (*Independent Weekly*, NC Triangle), Slim Cessna's Auto Club (*Westword*, Denver), Blanche Davidian (*Phoenix New Times*)

> "In short, SXSW is the best place in music in the world....If you have been there, you know what I mean, and if you've never been, what are you waiting for?" ■ Jim McGuinn, WPLY, in *Radio & Records*, April 2, 2004

SOME OF THE AUSTIN ACTS

Alvin Crow & the Pleasant Valley Boys, Pretty Please, Shane Bartell, Primordial Undermind, Liz Pappademas, Neal Pollack & Tammy Faye Starlite, What Made Milwaukee Famous, Centro-matic, Milton Mapes, Wideawake

SOME OF THE INTERNATIONAL ACTS

Hives (Sweden), Thrills (Ireland), Razorlight (U.K.), Death From Above (Canada), Julie Delpy (France), Futureheads (U.K.), Singapore

> "The whole of Austin feels like the grown-ups have fled town, leaving the indie-rockers to run things." ■ *NME*, April 3, 2004

Sling (Iceland), Beangrowers (Malta), League Of XO Gentlemen (Netherlands), Carmen Consoli (Italy), Abuse (Czech Republic), Uzbegim Taronasi (Russia), The Church (Australia), The Have (New Zealand), Dr. Pepper Family (Belgium), Petty Booka (Japan), Rock Four (Israel), Electrelane (U.K.)

WHATEVER HAPPENED TO...

Dramarama Why, they were right here at SXSW, lured back together by VH1's *Bands Reunited* program.

SOFTBALL TOURNEY

If you really want to know who played for this year's championship, go back and read any of the previous five yearly roundups. (Oh, OK: Clubs/Talent Buyers 4, Print Media 2.)

FILM
AWARDS

Narrative Feature Winner *Luck* (D: Peter Wellington); Special Jury Award: *Mind The Gap* (D: Eric Schaeffer)

Documentary Feature Winner *A Hard Straight* (D: Goro Toshima); Special Jury Award: *Witches In Exile* (D: Allison Berg)

Audience Awards *Blackballed: The Bobby Dukes Story* (D: Brant Sersen), narrative feature; *A League Of Ordinary Gentlemen* (D: Christopher Browne), documentary feature; *The Naked Feminist* (D: Louisa Achille), "Emerging Visions"; *Mojados: Through The Night* (D: Tommy Davis), "Lone Star States"

MEMORABLE FILMS & EVENTS

Bush's Brain (D: Michael Paradies Shoob and Joseph Mealey), *Last Man Standing* (D: Paul Stekler), *The Agronomist* (D: Jonathan Demme), *The Hunting Of The President* (D: Harry Thomason, Nickolas Perry), *Supersize Me* (D: Morgan Spurlock), *Saved!* (D: Brian Dannelly), *Public Domain* (D: Kris Lefcoe), *Jersey Girl* (D: Kevin Smith), *Male Fantasy* (D: Blaine Thurier), *I Love Your Work* (D: Adam Goldberg), *The United States Of Leland* (D: Matthew Ryan Hoge), *Mail-Order Bride* (D: Huck Botko, Andrew Gurland)

SXSW 2004

GUARANTEES NO COVER • MANY SHOWS WILL FILL UP! • NO REFUNDS • MUST BE WORN ON WRIST
ADMISSION SUBJECT TO LEGAL CAPACITY • MOST VENUES RESTRICT ACCESS TO MINORS

The festival also began its music documentary "24 Beats Per Second" program, which this year featured: *270 Miles From Graceland,* about Bonnnaroo (D: Danny Clinch); *DIG!* (D: Ondi Timoner); the hip-hop history *Five Sides Of A Coin* (D: Paul Kell); *Jandek On Corwood* (D: Chad Friedrichs), *Mayor Of The Sunset Strip* (D: George Hickenlooper); *Metallica: Some Kind Of Monster* (D: Joe Berlinger and Bruce Sinofsky); the experimental Radiohead collage *The Most Gigantic Lying Mouth Of All Time* (D: Chris Bran); *The Portrait Of Billy Joe* (D: Luciana Pedraza), about Billy Joe Shaver; *Radio Revolution: The Rise And Fall Of The Big 8* (D: Michael McNamara), about a legendary Canadian radio station; *A Night Of Ferocious Joy* (D: David Zeiger), about hip-hop anti-war activism; and *Antone's: Home Of The Blues* (D: Dan Karlock).

INTERACTIVE
KEYNOTE SPEAKERS

Zach Exley and Eli Pariser (MoveOn), Howard Rheingold (*Smart Mobs: The Next Social Revolution*), Jonathan Abrams (Friendster founder)

"But what about the 'Friendster Whores' – a term used by SXSW panelist danah boyd, of UC-Berkeley, to describe people who accumulate and post as many friends as possible? Is this sort of public self-endorsement delusional?" ■ Courtney Fitzgerald in *The Austin Chronicle*, March 5, 2004

NOTABLE PANELISTS & SPEAKERS

Francis Preve (laptop composer), Joe Trippi (Howard Dean campaign manager), Craig Newmark (Craigslist), Josh Gabriel (musician), Joi Ito (Neoteny), Marissa Mayer (Google), Virginia Postrel (author); Kevin Werbach, Juan Cole, Matt Welch and Carl Zimmer (bloggers) ■

© 2004 Shepard Fairey - www.obeygiant.com

2004 Music Big Bag art courtesy of Shepard Fairey

2005

SXSW STATS March 11 – 20

BY THE NUMBERS

1,331 showcasing artists
of 7,000 submissions

72 panels, workshops & sessions

56 venues & stages

9,692 registrants

$345-545 registration

$110-150 wristband

264 pages in program guide

191 trade show exhibitors

AUSTIN MUSIC AWARDS

Wednesday, March 16, Austin Music Hall

Performers Pinetop Perkins; Daniel Johnston; John Cale & Alejandro Escovedo; Hardcore Country All-Stars with Alvin Crow, James White, Pete Mitchell, Neil Flanz, Jason Crow, Danny Young, Jon Kemppainen, Earl Poole Ball, Ariel, and Patricia Vonne; the Crickets with Sonny Curtis, J.I. Allison and Joe Mauldin plus special guest Nanci Griffith

KEYNOTE CONVERSATION

Robert Plant (interviewed by Bill Flanagan) Before the keynote began, NARAS president Neil Portnow presented Plant with a Lifetime Achievement Grammy for his work with Led Zeppelin; Plant had not been present to receive it at the Grammy ceremonies a few weeks earlier. ("It meant what it meant when it meant it...there's no going back," Plant said of the band without John Bonham.)

During the talk, he told of meeting Elvis Presley, a tale he repeated to Conan O'Brien six years later. "Plant was at ease, joking about the shallowness of his Led Zeppelin lyrics, his idol worship of American blues artsts, and how 'the blue note' has influenced every aspect of his career," observed *Star Newspapers* reporter John Everson. The prelude was performed by Mavis Staples with Marty Stuart.

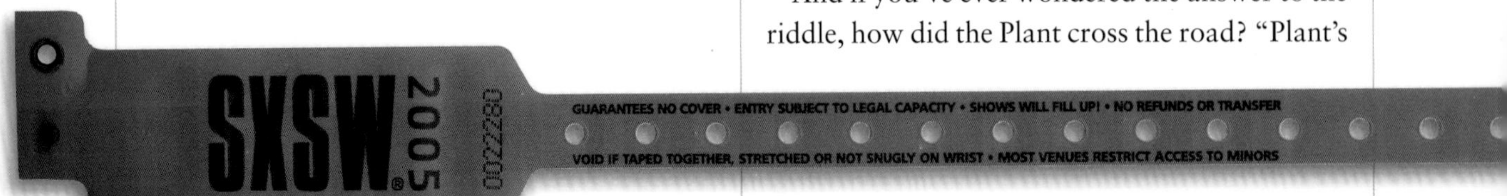

And if you've ever wondered the answer to the riddle, how did the Plant cross the road? "Plant's

security chief spent several hours with us planning the most secure route from the Hilton to the Convention Center — elevator down with no other guests, out the back door, SUV one block to the loading dock," remembers SXSW executive planner Mike Shea. "The next morning, the walkie-talkies were jammed with minute-by-minute updates from two dozen handlers and two SUVs, all deployed to safely deliver Mr. Plant. I was tracking the situation in the Hilton lobby when a smallish Brit with an unmistakable halo of blond locks stepped off an empty elevator, introduced himself, and asked for directions to the Convention Center. I like to think he just crossed the street by himself, but in reality the handlers probably caught up a few minutes later and whisked him away in his SUV."

MEMORABLE PANELS

"Young And Over The Hill: A&R After 30" With David Katznelson, Ron Goudie, Seymour Stein, Jazz Summers. "I started as an A&R intern at Warner Bros. when I was 18 years old, and got my first band signed when I was 20 (the Flaming Lips)," wrote Katznelson in the SXSW program guide. "How does a person's age and industry experience affect the way that person thinks about music and making records?"

"Ringtones as an Income Stream" How bands and collection societies struggle to keep pace with these new sources of revenue.

"Holy Fire: The 13th Floor Elevators' Quest For Enlightenment" Margaret Moser (*The Austin Chronicle*), David Fricke (*Rolling Stone*) and Bill Bentley (Warner Bros.) were joined by Roky Erickson and four of his former bandmates: Ronnie Leatherman, Powell St. John, Benny Thurman and John Ike Walton. "We'd always looked outside of Texas to find great music," Bentley said. "The 13th Floor Elevators completely changed how we thought about ourselves."

"Living With Hep C" Moderated by Harold Owens of Musicares, this panel discussed treatment options and resources for those with Hepatitis C, which has become increasingly common in the rock 'n' roll community.

NOTABLE PANELISTS

Interviews with Jacob Slichter (Semisonic drummer and author), Elvis Costello, Shawn Fanning, Mavis Staples, and Erykah Badu; Brian Wilson and Van Dyke Parks, Mac McCaughan (Merge Records), Ian McLagan, Bob Ludwig (Gateway Mastering & DVD), Marty Diamond (Little Big Man), Michael McDonald (ATO Records/Mick Management), Dan Reed (WXPN/World Cafe)

MEMORABLE SHOWCASES & EVENTS

> SXSW presented 19 Official Day Parties, including shows at Brush Square near the Convention Center with such partners as the State of Louisiana and the City of New Orleans, the Australian Music Collective, and BBC Radio. Bands included Embrace, James Blunt, Kermit Ruffins, Petty Booka and the Grates.

"SXSW has become an increasingly important event for UK acts, and is seen as an essential gateway to the world's biggest market by all levels of the business." ■ *VIP News*, April 4, 2005

> As if playing with John Cale at the Austin Music Awards on Wednesday wasn't enough, Alejandro Escovedo returned to Auditorium Shores on Friday evening as the opening act for another hero, Ian Hunter.
> The 7th Annual Guided By Voices Hoot came to Emo's Main Room, on Thursday, with performances by the likes of Hellweg, Dr. Dog, Magnapop, the Silos, Will Johnson, Calexico, Jon Auer, Salley Crewe & the Sudden Moves, Steve Wynn, Jason Faulkner, and Swearing At Motorists, plus an appearance by Robert Pollard & company themselves.

NOTABLE ACTS

Swishahouse The ensemble featuring Paul Wall, Archie Lee and Cooda Bang headed up Wednesday's hip-hop showcase at the Back Room.

Robyn Hitchcock According to Michael Corcoran of the *Austin American-Statesman*, Hitchcock started off the week by performing the wedding of "a rock critic and an exotic dancer"; he then played an official showcase every night, at Emo's, the Blender Balcony, the Cactus Cafe and La Zona Rosa.

"In 2005, I spent two nights going out with my 15-year-old, and despite the fact the kid had to wake me up after I nodded out in the bleachers of Emo's one night, we turned each other on to loads of music. He led me to the Raveonettes. I convinced him the New York Dolls could rock real hard for old farts. In between, we both dug Fatboy Slim, the Kills, Bloc Party, and Blanche, and we both dismissed the Futureheads and Louis XIV as overrated. Thanks to SXSW, we know we share the same family values." ■ Author/journalist Joe Nick Patoski

Also Amos Lee, John Legend, New York Dolls, Sleater-Kinney, We Are Scientists, Be Your Own Pet, Blowfly, American Music Club, LCD Soundsystem, Chingo Bling, Slim Thug, Erykah Badu, Ariel Pink, Definitive Jux Crew, Jason Moran

SOME OF THE MEDIA-SPONSORED ACTS

Billy Idol (*LA Weekly*), Son Volt (*Riverfront Times*, St. Louis), Lucero (*Memphis Flyer*), Collin Herring (*Fort Worth Weekly*), Sorta (*Dallas Observer*), Buttercup (*San Antonio Current*), Studemont Project (*Houston Press*), William Elliott Whitmore (*Little Village*, Montrose, IA), A Frames (*Seattle Weekly*), Kim Taylor Band *(Cincinnati City Beat)*, World Leader Pretend (*Offbeat*, New Orleans), James Talley (*Urban Tulsa Weekly*)

SOME OF THE AUSTIN ACTS

Beto y los Fairlanes, Jesus Christ Superfly, D:FUSE, Tony Scalzo, ST-37, Kathy McCarty, David Halley, Grand Champeen, Jesse Dayton, Sub Oslo, What Made Milwaukee Famous, This Microwave World, Yuppie Pricks, Jolly Garogers

SOME OF THE INTERNATIONAL ACTS

M.I.A. (U.K.), Seis Pistos (Mexico), Seyi Solagbade & the Blackface Band (Nigeria), Bloc Party (U.K.), Death From Above 1979 (Canada), 22 Pistepirkko (Finland), Missy Higgins (Australia), Fatboy Slim (U.K.), Dead Sexy Inc. (France), Raveonettes (Denmark), Nicolai Dunger (Sweden), Cut Copy (Australia), Daara J (Senegal), Kaiser Chiefs (U.K.)

SOFTBALL TOURNEY

Trailing 9-2 and down to their last out in a semifinal matchup with the Mixed Media team, Print Media proved it's not dead after all with a string of eight straight hits that lifted them to a 10-9 victory. After that, their 14-3 triumph over Clubs/Talent Buyers in the championship game was mere denouement.

FILM BY THE NUMBERS

183 films screened

3,807 registrants

42 panels, workshops & sessions

176 pages in program guide

2005 Film Big Bag art courtesy of Daniel Johnston

"Acting Out" with Marcia Gay Harden and Tim Blake Nelson

"20 Years Of The Austin Film Society" with Marjorie Baumgarten, Richard Linklater and Janet Pierson

"Future Of Digital Filmmaking"

"A Sample Of Style From The Homestar Runner Folks"

"You can't step around vomit anywhere in Austin's Sixth Street entertainment district without noticing the Heartless Bastards. To promote the punk-blues trio's debut album, *Stairs And Elevators*, Fat Possum Records has been papering the streets, boutiques, and lavatories with a plethora of postcards, red and black and glossy on thick stock, with recent critical acclaim emblazoned on a photo of Erika Wennerstrom in mid-wail. "I kept picking them up," Wennerstrom says. "I thought somebody had discarded a bunch. Then I kept on walking and saw there were lots of piles." ■ Jason Cohen, *Cincinnati Magazine*, May 2005

INTERACTIVE BY THE NUMBERS

3,343 registrants

84 panels, workshops & sessions

96 pages in program guide

AWARDS

Narrative Feature Winner *Hooligans* (D: Lexi Alexander); runner-up: *Cavite* (D: Ian Gamazon & Neill Dela Llana)

Documentary Feature Winner *Cowboy Del Amor* (D: Michele Ohayon); runner-up: *The Boys Of Baraka* (D: Heidi Ewing & Rachel Grady)

MEMORABLE FILMS

Opening Night Film: *The Wendell Baker Story* (D: Luke Wilson/Andrew Wilson); *Enron: The Smartest Guys in the Room* (D: Alex Gibney), *Layer Cake* (D: Matthew Vaughn), *Murderball* (D: Harry Alex Rubin/Dana Adam Shapiro), *The Dreams Of Sparrows* (D: Hayder Mousa Daffar), *The Devil And Daniel Johnston* (D: Jeff Feuerzeig), *You're Gonna Miss Me* (D: Keven McAlester), *Hedwig And The Angry Inch* (D: John Cameron Mitchell), *Far From Heaven* (D: Todd Haynes), *Occupation: Dreamland* (D: Garrett Scott/Ian Olds), *The Puffy Chair* (D: Jay Duplass)

MEMORABLE PANELS/EVENTS

Featured conversations with Christine Vachon, Todd Solondz, and Al Franken

"Making Fun Of Filmmaking" with Sarah Silverman and Patton Oswalt

KEYNOTE SPEAKERS

Jeffrey Zeldman (web design standards pioneer), Malcolm Gladwell, Ana Marie Cox (*Wonkette*), Alex Steffen, Bruce Sterling

MEMORABLE PANELS

"Blogging vs. Journalism"; "Spam, Trolls, Stalkers: The Pandora's Box Of Community"; "Web Design 2010: What Will The Web Look Like When It Turns 20?"; "The New New Economy: Is 2005 the Next 2007?"; "Open Source Marketing: The New Unweildy/Unlimited Product Publicity"; "How To Obtain Startup Funding: The Care And Feeding Of Angel Investors" ■

"SXSW has now joined skiing in Aspen as the latest A-list celebrity hangout" ■ *The Times* (London), March 25, 2005

2006

SXSW STATS March 10 - 19

BY THE NUMBERS

1,493 showcasing artists of 8,065 submissions

71 panels, workshops & sessions

64 venues & stages

10,821 registrants

$375-575 registration

$130-175 wristband

280 pages in program guide

192 trade show exhibitors

AUSTIN MUSIC AWARDS

Wednesday, March 15, Austin Music Hall

Performers Roky Erickson & the Explosives with special guest Powell St. John; Kris Kristofferson & Jessi Colter; Jon Dee Graham with Eliza Gilkyson; Guitars A Go Go with 3 Balls Of Fire, George Tomsco, Jerry Cole, and the Boom Chica Boom Girls; Red River Revue with Black Joe Lewis, Walter Daniels, and Chili Cold Blood; MC Paul Ray

KEYNOTE CONVERSATION

Neil Young, with Jonathan Demme (and interviewer Jaan Uhelszki) Demme's documentary *Neil Young: Heart Of Gold* showed at the Film Festival. "Getting Neil Young to keynote was mind-blowing for me," says Roland Swenson. "In my college days, we referred to *On The Beach, Tonight's The Night* and *Zuma* as the holy trinity. Long after seeing the Sex Pistols and the Talking Heads, and moving most of our classic rock to the bottom shelf, Neil Young still had considerable spin on the house turntable." Adds Louis Black: "I don't think we ever asked him before because we didn't think we could get him."

Young commented during the session: "*USA Today* said I was ripping off my audience [with his 2003 tour for the rock opera project *Greendale*] because I didn't give them what they wanted to hear. I thought, 'I must be on to something.' That experience was so scary and rewarding. It's

good to be scared. Re-creating your famous album over and over again — that's death."

SXSW panels chief Andy Flynn remembered, "I met Neil Young in the service corridor of the Convention Center amid his full entourage heading to the ballroom. After a quick greeting, he said (about the keynote), 'I've been nervous about this for months.' To which I replied, 'Then we're even.'"

MEMORABLE PANELS

"Podcasts Invade Earth" How do traditional outlets use the new format, and what are the legal issues involved in licensing music for them?

"Blogs Gone Wild" The jetset lifestyle of the new big influence on the scene, music bloggers! With Jason Gross (Perfect Sound Forever), Brooklyn Vegan, Matthew Perpetua (fluxblog).

"New Orleans Music After Katrina" What will happen to the great musical heritage of New Orleans? With Scott Aiges, Cyril Neville, Harry Shearer, Keith Spera.

NOTABLE PANELISTS

Interviews: Ted Cohen (EMI Music), Beastie Boys, Sam Moore, Morrissey, k.d. lang, Kris Kristofferson, Judy Collins, Pretenders, Billy Bragg, and Matthew Knowles; Hank Shocklee, Steve Earle, Dave Allen (Pampelmoose), Brian Turner (WFMU), Anthony Wilson (In The City), Gary Calamar (music supervisor), U.S. Representive Mary Bono

MEMORABLE SHOWCASES & EVENTS

> Echo and the Bunnymen, Spoon, Blackalicious and Mr. Lif took over Auditorium Shores on Thursday, while Norah Jones' Little Willies opened for 1991 SXSW keynote speaker Rosanne Cash there on Friday.

> The Flaming Lips previewed material from *At War With The Mystics* with a pair of not-so-secret shows at the Fox & Hound and Eternal. The former featured a cover of Black Sabbath's "War Pigs" (performed with Peaches), the latter, Queen's "Bohemian Rhapsody." Frontman Wayne Coyne also wandered Sixth Street in his now-signature hamster bubble.

> Table Of The Elements filled the Central Presbyterian Church with such experimental greats as Zeena Parkins, Tony Conrad, Jonathan Kane's February, and Rhys Chatham's Guitar Army, featuring Thurston Moore, Chris Brokaw (Come), Doug McCombs (Tortoise) and Ernie Brooks (Modern Lovers).

NOTABLE ACTS

Arctic Monkeys The U.K. band came to town on the heels of a *Saturday Night Live* appearance and an early rave in *The New York Times* by

"Although South by Southwest has evolved over the years to include podcasts, videobroadcasts and even text-message updates, the event is built on the idea that the best way to discover new music is face to face." ■ *The New York Times*, March 17, 2006

Kelefa Sanneh, who took note of frontman Alex Turner's Ray Davies-like lyrical gifts, then noted, "If only the music weren't so thrilling, there would probably be a serious backlash afoot." Cue the *Austin American-Statesman*'s Michael Corcoran, who left after seven songs. "Psssssst," he wrote, "that's the sound of deflated expectations." Turner didn't disagree: "This is everything a gig should not be," he blanched onstage from underneath a hoodie.

2006 Music Big Bag art courtesy of Wayne Coyne of the Flaming Lips

Also Chamillionaire, My Brightest Diamond, Brightblack Morning Light, Blowfly, Devin The Dude, Cloud Room, The Gossip, Clap Your

"Over the years, big-name filmmakers have chosen the venue for their premieres (Altman, John Sayles, Christopher Guest and Joel Schumacher among them), and it consistently attracts a quirky and absorbing line-up of features, shorts and documentaries. The festival's programming, as well as the cred of the music conference, has made it one of North America's best and most highly regarded second-tier festivals, a regional gem..." ■ *The Washington Post*, March 18, 2006

Hands Say Yeah, Eagles Of Death Metal, Dr. Dog, Sir Richard Bishop, Sharon Jones & the Dap-Kings, Beirut, Antietam, Princess Superstar, Ariel Pink, Animal Collective, Tapes 'N Tapes, Tilly & the Wall, Spank Rock, Savage Republic, Silversun Pickups, Dresden Dolls, Andy Dick

SOME OF THE MEDIA-SPONSORED ACTS
Elf Power (*Flagpole*, Athens, GA), Moaners (*Independent Weekly*, NC Triangle), Wussy (*Cincinnati CityBeat*), Pieta Brown (*Little Village*, Iowa City, Iowa), Charlemagne (*The Reader*, Omaha, NE), American Princes (*Nightflying*, Little Rock, AR), Magnolia Summer (*Riverfront Times*, St. Louis), Hyperbubble (*San Antonio Current*), Chatterton (*Fort Worth Weekly*), Limbeck (*Orange County Weekly*), Tolchock Trio (*Salt Lake City Weekly*), Die Princess Die (*LA Weekly*)

SOME OF THE AUSTIN ACTS
Black Angels, Voxtrot, Standing Waves, Glass Eye, Helios Creed/Chrome, The Sword, Jad Fair & Lumberob, Awesome Cool Dudes, South Austin Jug Band, Applicators

"But even as it has gotten bigger and more oriented to the indie-film industry, SXSW is still admired for its modesty, its integrity and – this is the only word for it – its niceness." ■ Salon.com, March 12, 2006

SOME OF THE INTERNATIONAL ACTS
Belle & Sebastian (Scotland), Bats (New Zealand), Holy Fuck (Canada), Sia (Australia), Cribs (U.K.), You Say Party! We Say Die! (Canada), Get Cape. Wear Cape. Fly (U.K.), Art Brut (U.K.), Goldfrapp (U.K.), Faith Healers (U.K.), KT Tunstall (U.K.), Serena Maneesh (Norway), Presets (Australia), Wolfmother (Australia), Whitehouse (UK), Flight Of The Conchords (New Zealand), Syd Matters (France), dEUS (Belgium), Circle (Finland)

SOFTBALL TOURNEY
Let's play none! For the third time in tournament history (1997, 2001) rainy weather caused cancellation of the tournament, though barbecue was still served at a super-secret indoor location (where apparently bouts of wiffle ball broke out). Perhaps the break was needed, because ever since that '97 washout, Print Media and Clubs/Talent Buyers had squared off in the championship game. Was that seven-year itch broken the following year? Tune in to the next SXSW Stats chapter.

FILM BY THE NUMBERS
230 films screened
4,939 registrants
50 panels, workshops & sessions
192 pages in program guide

AWARDS
Narrative Feature Winner *Live Free Or Die* (D: Andy Robin & Gregg Kavet); Special Jury Prize, Outstanding Ensemble Cast: *AMERICANese*, (D: Eric Byler); Special Jury Prize, Outstanding Visual Achievement: *Inner Circle Line* (D: Eunhee Cho)

Documentary Feature Winner *Jam* (D: Mark Woollen); Special Jury Award: *Maxed Out* (D: James D. Scurlock)

MEMORABLE FILMS

Opening Night Film: *A Prairie Home Companion* (D: Robert Altman); *The Notorious Bettie Page* (D: Mary Harron), *Hard Candy* (D: David Slade), *Friends With Money* (D: Nicole Holofcener), *Lower City* (Cidade Baixa) (D: Sergio Machado), *Neil Young: Heart Of Gold* (D: Jonathan Demme), *Old Joy* (D: Kelly Reichardt), *L'Enfant* (D: Jean-Pierre Dardenne/Luc Dardenne), *Don't Come Knocking* (D: Win Wenders), *a/k/a Tommy Chong* (D: Josh Gilbert), *Before the Music Dies* (D: Andrew Shapter), *Heavens Fall* (D: Terry Green), *Even Money* (D: Mark Rydell), *Fired!* (D: Chris Bradley/Kyle Labrache)

MEMORABLE PANELS/EVENTS

Featured conversations with Peter Bart and Henry Rollins; "*Lone Star*: 10 Years Later" with John Sayles; "Behind The Social Scenes" featuring Bob Odenkirk and Andy Dick; "The Documentary Beat" featuring Charlize Theron (who had just produced *East Of Havana*, a Cuban hip-hop documentary); "Keep It Short! Filmmaking From Broadcast To Broadband"; "The Future Of Darknets: Can Hollywood See The Light?"

INTERACTIVE BY THE NUMBERS

4,733 registrants

100 panels, workshops & sessions

108 pages in program guide

KEYNOTE SPEAKERS

Jim Coudal & Jason Fried, Heather Armstrong & Jason Kottke, Craig Newmark (Craigslist founder), Burnie Burns

MEMORABLE PANELS

"How to Blog For Money By Learning From Comics"; "Bootstrapping Your Digital Convergence Business"; "Standard Deviation: Hacks And Dirty Tricks For The Web"; "How And Why To Podcast An Event"; "Increasing Women's Visibility On The Web: Whose Butt Should We Be Kicking?"; "Demystifying The Mobile Web" ■

"By the second day, you've stopped fretting about the bands you're missing. By the third day, you've developed museum legs. By the fourth day, you've begun to believe there are bands soundchecking in your hotel room." ■ *The Irish Times*, March 31, 2006

2007 Film Big Bag art courtesy of Ed "Big Daddy" Roth

continued from page 168

Robert Pollard
Robert Randolph
Robert Randolph & The Family Band
Robert Roth
Robert Roth from Truly
Robert Shields
Robert Skoro
Robert Thomas
Robert Trudeau
Robert Trussell
Robert Walter's 20th Congress
Robert Ward
Robin & Linda Williams
Robin Holcomb
Robin Nolan Trio
Robin Plan
Robinella
Robots, Please!
Robyn
Robyn Hitchcock
Robyn Ludwick
Rocco Deluca and the Burden
Roche
Rochelle Terrell
Rochelle, Rochelle
Rock & Plex
Rock Bottom Choir
Rock City Morgue
Rock' n' Roll Soldiers
Rock Plaza Central
Rock-A-Teens
Rockenstein's Freakout featuring members of Friends of Dean Martnez, The Stingers & Stinky Del Negro
Rocker T
Rocket Fuel is the Key
Rocketbaby
Rockets to Mars
RockFour
Rockie Charles
Rockin' Horse
Rockin' Rian Murphy from KROQ
Rockland Eagles
Rockwell Church
Rockwell Knuckles
Rocky Burnette
Rocky Business
Rocky Dawuni
Rocky Swanson
Rocky Votolato
Rod Moag featuring Johnny Gimble
Rod Picott
Rod Thomas
Rodeo Boy
Rodney Crowell
Rodney Fisher
Rodney Hayden
Roesy
roGer
Roger Bonair-Agard
Roger Clyne & the Peacemakers
Roger Dean Young & The Tin Cup
tinez, The Stingers and Stinky del Negro
Roger Joseph Manning, Jr.
Roger Manning
Roger McGuinn
Roger Miller
Roger Miret and the Disasters
Roger Wallace
Rogue Wave
Rokhsan
RokkaTone
Roky & the Explosives w/ Powell St. John
Roky Erickson
Roky Erickson w/The Black Angels
Roky Erickson with Okkervil River
Roll The Tanks
Roller
Rollerball
Rollers Redefined
Rolling Blackouts
Rolling Hayseeds
Rolo Tomassi
Roman Candle
Roman Candles
Romance Fantasy
Romantica
Romeo Poet & Gee
Romeo Touch
Romi Mayes
ROMZ record CREW
Ron Brown
Ron Flynt
Ron Flynt and the Bluehearts
Ron Franklin
Ron Sexsmith
Ron Wilkins
Ron Wilkins Quartet
Ronnie Dawson
Ronnie Day
Ronnie Gene & Lighthouse
Ronnie Lane
Ronnie Montrose
Ronnie Word
Ronny Cox
Ronny Elliott
Ronny Elliott & The Nationals
Roc Nation
Room 101
Roommate
Roosevelt Franklin (Kimani from Masterminds and Mr. Len)
Rooster
Rooster Head
Root 1
Rootbeer
Rootz Underground
Rope
Rory McLeod
Rosalie Sorrels
Rosanne Cash
Rose Elinor Dougall
Rose Hill Drive
Rose Polenzani
Rose Thomas
Rosi Golan
Rosie & The Goldbug
Rosie Flores
Rosie Flores & Ray Campi
Rosie Flores and Katy Moffatt
Rosie Flores and the Long Stems
Rosie Thomas
Ross Hogg
Ross Royce
Rotary Downs
Rotten Apples
Rottin Razkals
roué
Round Table Knights
Round Trip with Glenn Rexach
Roundhead
Roxanne Hale
Roxie
Roxy Cottontail
Roxy Gordon
Roy Head
Roy Head and The Westside Horns
Roy Heinrich & The Pickups
Roy Loney
Royal Bangs
Royal Bliss
Royal City
Royal Crown Revue
Royal Fingerbowl
Royal Forest (formerly Loxsly)
Royal Neanderthal Orchestra
Royal Pain
Royal Space Force
Royal Trux
Royal Wade Kimes
Royden
Royston Langdon
RP Cola
RTX
Rubber Kiss Goodbye
Rubberbullet
RubberHed
Rubberoom
Rube Waddell
Ruben Ramos
Ruben Ramos & Texas Revolution
Ruben Ramos & The Mexican Revolution
Rubicks
Rubik
Rubinchik's Orkestyr
Rubinchik's Orkestyr
Rubinchik's Yiddish Ensemble
Ruby
Ruby Coast
Ruby Collins
Ruby Isle
Ruby Jane
Rudy Vega
Rufio
Rufus Cappadocia
Rufus Wainwright
Ruido Rosa
Rule 62
Rumble
Rumblefish
Rumbullion
Rumpelstiltskin Grinder
Rumspringa
Run C&W
Run Chico Run
Run On
Run Run Run
Runaway
Runaway Planet
Runner & the Thermodynamics
Rupa and The April Fishes
Rusko
Russ Somers
Russell Gunn
Russell Scott & His Red Hots
Russell Taylor
Russian Circles
Rust Farm
Ruste Juxx
Rusted Shut
Rustic Overtones
Rusty
Rusty Rae
Rusty Wier
Ruth
Ruth Huber
Ruth Minnikin
Ruth Moody
Ruthie Foster
Ruthie Foster with Cyd Cassone
Rwake
RX Bandits
Ryan Bingham
Ryan Cabrera
Ryan Jewell
Ryan Kisor
Ryan McPhun and The Ruby Suns
Ryan Scott
Ryan Shupe & the Rubber Band
Rye Coalition
Rye Rye
Rykarda Parasol
Ryno
Ryno & Slim Gutta

S

S
Soulhat
SWITCHhiTTER
S. Alton Dulaney
S.M.U.G.G.L.A.Z.
S.O.M.
S.O.M.B.A.
S.Rock Levinson
Sa
Saafir
Sabaton
Sabrina
Sack
Sacred Hearts
Sacrilicious
Sad Accordions
Sado
Sado
Saffire-The Uppity Blues Women
Saffron
Sage
Sage Francis
Sahara
Sahara Hotnights
Sahara Rain
Sahara Smith
Slaid Cleaves and The Moxies
Sailboats Are White
Saint
Saint Bernadette
Saint Motel
Salaman
Salamander (Velvet Collective)
Salamander Tales
Salaryman
Salem
Salem Tree
Salim Nourallah
Sally Crewe
Sally Crewe & The Sudden Moves
Sally Seltmann
Sally Timms
Salome
Salsa Brava
Salt
Salt & Samovar
Saltine
Salvador Santana Band
Sam & Ruby
Sam Amidon
Sam Ashworth
Sam Baker
Sam Black Church
Sam Brown
Sam Champion
Sam Isaac
Sam Lipman Sextet
Sam Moore
Sam Phillips
Sam Roberts
Sam Roberts Band
Sam Taylor
Sam the Sham
Sam Weis
Samadha
Samantha Crain & the Midnight Shivers
Samantha is The Highway Girl
Samantha Shelton
Samantha Stollenwerck
Samara Lubelski

Santogold (2008)

Samba Ngo & the Ngoma Players
SambaDá
Sambaxe
Samiam
Sammo
Sammy
Samuel
San Agustin
San Andreas
San Antone Roses
San Antonio Slam Team 2000
San Saba County
Sand Rubies
Sandbox
Sandi Thom
Sandra McCracken
Sandwitch
Sanford Arms
Sangre de Toro
Sanguine Piss
Santiago Jimenez Jr.
Santogold
Sara Bareilles
Sara Craig
Sara Evans
Sara Gazarek
Sara Haze
Sara Hickman
Sara Wasserman
Sara Woldridge
Sarabian
Sarah Blasko
Sarah Borges
Sarah Borges & the Broken Singles
Sarah Brown
Sarah Brown Band
Sarah Brown Trio
Sarah Dougher
Sarah Elizabeth Campbell
Sarah Harmer
Sarah Hepburn
Sarah Jaffe
Sarah Jarosz
Sarah K. Wooldridge
Sarah Lee Guthrie & Johnny Irion
Sarah Sharp
Sarah Snyder
Sardina
Sarge
Sarkoma
Sasquatch
Sass Jordan
Satan's Pilgrims
Satelite
Satin Dolls
Saturday Looks Good To Me
Satya
Satyre
Saucer
Saul Williams
Savage Republic
Save Ferris
Saves the Day
Saviours
Savoir Adore
Savvy
Sawed Off
Sawt el Atlas
Saxon Shore
Say Anything
Say Hi
Say Hi (solo)
Say Hi To Your Mom
Say No More
Saybia
Scale The Summit
Scalpel & the Sledgehammer
Scanners
Scared of Chaka
Scarling
Scarlitt
Scars on 45
Scarub
Scary Kids Scaring Kids
Scary Mansion
Scatter The Ashes
Scavone
Scenic
Schaffer the Darklord
Schatzi
Schel Reaux
Schfvilkus
School of Fish
School of Seven Bells
School Trauma Flashback
Schoolyard Heroes
Schrödinger's Cat
Schtum
Sci-Fi Uterus
Sciflyer
Scissor Sisters
Scissors for Lefty
Scorpio Rising
Scorpion Child
Scotland Yard Gospel Choir
Scott Amendola
Scott Aukerman
Scott Aukerman, Ramin Nazer, Jimmie Roulette and Special Guest
Scott Garber
Scott H. Biram
Scott Hoyt
Scott McCaughey & Friends
Scott McGill
Scott Mckenzie & Pam Peltz
Scott Miller
Scott Miller & The Commonwealth
Scott Nolan
Scott O'Reilly
Scott Randon
Scott White
Scottie B
Scotty Barnhart Quartet
Scotty Moore
Scout Niblett
Scouting For Girls
Scouts Honor
Scram
Scrambled Eggs
Scrappy Jud Newcomb
Scrawl
Screamfeeder
Screamin' Cyn Cyn & The Pons
Screaming Tea Party
Screens
Scroat Belly
Scruffy the Cat
Scud Mountain Boys
Scurvy Dog
SDQ2: The Doug Sahm Tribute w/Shawn Sahm and Augie Meyers and Alejandro Escovedo
Sea of Thousand
Sea Ray
Sea Wolf
Seabear
Seabird
Seachange
Seaflea
Seagull Screaming Kiss Her Kiss Her
Seam
Seaman's Quartet
Sean Bones
Sean Carnahan
Sean Costello
Sean Hayes
Sean Holt & High Fidelity
Sean Lennon
Sean McNulty
Sean O'Connor
Sean O'Neal
Sean Patrick
Sean Price
Sean Rowe
Sean Smith
Sean Walters
Sean Wayland
Seana Carmody
Search/Rescue
Season to Risk
Seaweed
Seaworthy
Seba
Sebadoh
Sebastian Campesi
Sebastian Whittaker
Sebastien Grainger
Sebastien Schuller
Second Movement
Secondhand Serenade
Seconds Flat
Secret Chiefs 3
Secret Guest
Secret Lives! of the Freemasons
Secret Room
Secret Shine
Secret Weapons
Secretary Bird
Sedition
Seed
Seed
Seela
Seely
Seen (aka HIM)
sEiS PisToS
Sek LoSo
Seksu Roba
Selby Tigers
Self
Self Against City
Selfish Cunt
Selig
Selma Oxor
Semi Gloss
Semi Precious Weapons
Semiautomatic
Semisonic
Senegal Acoustic
Sense Field
Senser
Seoul Electric Band
Sera Cahoone
Serafin
Serena Maneesh
Serena Ryder
Serene
Serengeti
Seres Ocultos
Serge Lopez
Sergio Arau
Serious Sam Barrett
Serj Tankian
Serman Lee Dillon
Sertified
Services
Servile Sect
Servotron
Set 4 Life
Set Aflame
Seth & Amy Tiven
Seth Kauffman
Seth Lakeman
Seth Walker
Seth Walker and the Mojo Hands
Seth Walker Band
Settie
Setting Sun
Settle For Enemy
Settlefish
Seven Ages
Seven Day Diary
Seventh Day Slumber
Seven Simons
Seven Storey Mountain
Seventeen
Seventh Heaven
Sex Mob
Sex With Strangers
Sex Worker
Sexepil
Sexfresh
Sexto Sol feat. Vernon 'Spot' Barnett
Sexton Bros Sextet
Sexton Sextet
Sexy Finger Champs
SFDK
Sgt Dunbar & the Hobo Banned
Shabazz 3
Shabazz 3 Shabazz
Shad
Shades Of Blue
Shadow Puppets
Shadow Shadow Shade
Shadows Fall
Shadowy Men on a Shadowy Planet
Shag
Shagnastys
Shaï No Shaï
Shake Russell
Shakin' Apostles
Shalini
Shallow Reign
Shallow, North Dakota
Shame Club
Shana Morrison
Shandon Sahm
Shane Bartell
Shane Decker & Vibrolux Cowboys
Shane Henry
Shane Nicholson
Shankin' Pickle
Shannon Bourne
Shannon McNally
Shannon Moore
Shannon Worrell
Shannon Wright
shannonwright
Shapes and Sizes
Shapes Have Fangs
Shappy
Shappy Seasholz
Sharde Thomas and The Rising Star Fife And Drum Band
Shark Chum
Shark Taboo
Sharkey
Sharon Jones & the Dap-Kings
Sharon van Etten
Sharq
Sharron Kraus & Christian Kiefer
Shat
Shatterproof
Shaver
Shawn Amos
Shawn Camp
Shawn Chrystopher
Shawn David McMillen
Shawn Mullins
Shawn Phillips
Shawn Sahm & Friends
Shawn Sahm and the Tex-Mex Experience
Shayna Steele
She and Him
She Keeps Bees
She Rides
She Wants Revenge
Shearwater
Shedding
Sheelah Murthy
Sheep on Drugs
Sheer Threat
Sheila Nicholls
Shelby Bryant's Cloud Wow Music
Shelby Lynne
Shelley King
Shelley Short
Shells
Shellshag
Shelly as DJ Safire
Shelly Bajorek
Shelly Lares
Shepard Fairey
Sheree Thomas
Sheridans
Sherlock's Daughter
Sherry Rich
Shesus
Shibboleth
Shift
Shifter
Shifters
Shikasta
Shilpa Ray and Her Happy Hookers
Shina Rae
Shindig Shop
Shine
Shiner
Shining
Shinola
Shinuk
Shiny Toy Guns
Ship of Fools
Shir Khan
Shit And Shine
Shitdisco
Shitty Carwash
Shivaree
Shoebomb
Sholi
Shonen Knife
Shooter Jennings
Shootin' Pains
Shooting Spires
Short Fuze
Short, Bird Street, Mike Moe & DJ Wrecka of Beltway 8
Shorty Long
Shot Down in Ecuador, Jr.
Shot x Shot
Shotgun Solution
Shoulders
Shout Out Louds
Shout Out Out Out Out
Shovelhead
Show Of Hands
Showbread
Shuffle Demons
Shufflepuck
Shuggie
Shurman
Shuttle
SHV
Shwayze
Shy Child
Shyboy
Shyne Factory
Si*Sé
Sia
Sian Alice Group
Sianspheric
Sick of it All
Sick People
Sick Water
SICKBOY
Sickert
Sid Griffin
Sid Griffin & the Coal Porters
Siddhartha Suns
Sidecar
Sidedoor Johnnies
Sidewalk Poets
Sidewinder
Sidewinders
Sidney Hillman
Sientific American
Sightings
Sign
Signs of Life
Signal Path
Signal To Noise
Signals
Celinda Pink & Cellar Dwellers
Silent Drive
Silicon Valley Poetry Slam Team
Silje Nes
Silk Flowers
Silkenseed
Silkworm
Silo the Huskie
Silver
Silver Apples
Silver Daggers
Silver Pines
Silver Scooter
Silver Starling
Silver Thistle Pipe & Drums
Silversun Pickups
Silvertide
Simian
Simian Mobile Disco
Simon
Simon Bruce
Simon Collins
Simon Dawes
Simon Stokes
Simon Townshend Band
Simona
Simple Kid
SIMPLIFIRES
Sin City Disciples
Sin Ropas
Sinai Beach
Since By Man
Sincola
Sindicato Argentino del Hip Hop
Singapore Sling
Single Frame
Single Frame Ashtray
Singleminded
Singing Spoons
Sing-Sing
SINIS
Sinister Dane
Spiny Norman
Siobhán O'Brien
Sioen
Sir Douglas Quintet
Sir Rap-a-Lot
Sir Richard Bishop
Sir Smith
Sissy Bar
Sissy Wish
Sista Stroke
Sistas In The Pit
Sister "P"
Sister 7
Sister Double Happiness
Sister Machine Gun
Sister Sonny
Sisterhood of Convoluted Thinkers
Sisters Morales
Siva
Six Degrees of Freedom
Six Finger Satellite
Six is Nine
Six Organs of Admittance
Six Volt Sunbeam
SixNationState
Sixpence None The Richer
Sixsouth
Sixteen Deluxe
Sixty Second Quickies
Sixty Watt Shaman
Skaireekanairee
Skankin' Pickle
Skanic
Skapulario
Skatenigs
Skatterman & Snug Brim
Skavenjah
Skavoovie & the Epitones
Ske
Skeleton Key
Skeletons
Skeletons & The Girl-Faced Boys
Skeletonwitch
Skibunny
Skiploader
Skoidats
Skor-Ski
Skratch Bastid
Skrew
Skullening
Skulpey
Skunk D.F.
Skwod X
Sky High
Sky Larkin
Skybox
Skye
Skywriter
Skyzoo
Slack Jaw
SlackHappy
Slaid Cleaves
Slamjammers
Slammin' Watusis
Slanglords
Slapbook
Slaraffenland
Slash Cowboy
Slaves to Gravity
Sleater-Kinney
Sledville
Sleep
Sleep Capsule
Sleep (of Oldominion)
Sleep Station
Sleep Whale
Sleepercar
Sleeping People
Sleepway
Sleepy
Sleepy Sun
Sleepy Vahn
Sleepytime Gorilla Museum
Sleestacks
Sleestak
Slicker
Sliimy
Slim Cessna's Auto Club
Slim Dunlap
Slim Richey's Dream Band
Slim Thug
Slim Twig
Slitheryn
Sloan
Slobberbone
Slo-Mo
Slot
Sloth Scamper
Slough Feg
Slow Club
Slow Coming Day
Slow Roosevelt
Slowburn
Slowpoke
Slowreader
Slowride
Sludge Nation
Slug (of Atmosphere)
Slum City
Slum Village

continued on page 209

The Person Who Learns From The Star

In late 2003, SXSW panels chief Andy Flynn called to tell me that Little Richard was going to be the keynote speaker in 2004. Richard wanted someone to ask him questions, and Andy asked if I'd be interested. I said yes eagerly.

The next morning, I sat up in bed with a shot and waited around nervously all morning. When I finally figured it was

SXSW MEMORIES

business time at the SXSW office in Austin, I called Andy back. "Did you call me last night and ask me to do the Little Richard keynote?" Sure, Andy said. "I said yes, didn't I?"

As far as I'm concerned, Little Richard issued every one of his recorded thunderbolts from a perch on Olympus. His talent is immense: a voice as great as Sam Cooke's, an imagination as twisted as Iggy Pop's, unparalleled mastery of the

put-on, a crafty sense of history (and not only his own). He's everything he ever said he is – a sex bomb gift from God who discovered the Beatles and invented rock 'n' roll, a man of the cloth (I saw him officiate at a wedding). Except "Little"– he's six feet four – but how could you be an artistic genius without any irony at all?

I'd never interviewed him, although we once talked about Elvis on the same national television program. Which is bragging, yes.

The SXSW gig wasn't really an interview, maybe not even a conversation. I understood my role: setup man. I have a reputation for talking a lot – really a lot – but if I'd had my way that day, I'd have said about four sentences. And I pretty much did have my way, by letting Richard have his.

To tell you the truth, setting up Little Richard isn't that difficult. He's not only one of the wildest actors in music history, he's also very smart. He pays attention to what counts and he knows how to take advantage of an opportunity. My job was to open a hole in the line and watch as he romped to the goal line. To listen, not speak.

The night before the keynote, I sat in the lobby of the Four Seasons scribbling. Someone asked me what was up. I said, "I've got 26 questions for Little Richard....I only need four, but they have to be the right four."

It took just about four to launch Richard into an incredible 22-minute soliloquy that ranged from shrewd music business advice ("Sign your own checks!" he

Management And MGMT

I have been to most of the SXSWs, so there are more memories than a book would hold. Meeting Billy Gibbons, Mick Jones, Paul Simonon, Jim Dickinson, and God knows who else; the night Momo's was transformed into Canada by Broken Social Scene and the Stills; avoiding the Four Seasons lobby; not avoiding the Driskill bar; the Beastie Boys interview; UT baseball; the PA going out at Urban Outfitters and MGMT not missing a beat; Liberty Lunch; DJing at Twist.

Other gigs I will never forget include Kris Kristofferson at Auditorium Shores, Alabama 3 with Mick Jones at La Zona Rosa, Blur at the same venue, the return of the Hoodoo Gurus at the Ritz, LCD Soundsystem upstairs somewhere on Sixth Street, and on and on. Also being involved with nights like Beck and Johnny Cash at Emo's, memorable Fenway (and Grand Royal) shows at Club DeVille, and my personal ultimate gig, the Cribs and MGMT at Stubb's.

From a career standpoint, in one night there I became a manager. It happened in 2005 and when the smoke cleared I had two clients, one of whom I still work with. And at a Fenway show the same night at Pecan Street Ale House, I saw the Cribs for the first time. They later became a client and remain one to this day. My favorite thing about the evolution of SXSW is that it has become such an international destination, particularly for promoters and agents who, over the last few years, have done some of the earliest and best A&R out there. But best of all is the warmth and support that any artist I have ever worked with has received there, no matter what their level. ■ Mark Kates, Fenway Recordings

commanded several times) to self-referential comments toward members of his entourage out in the dark. It was a seminar in how to work a room, sure. But it was also a crazily clear assessment of the music industry and how to manage yourself in it – as instructive a summary as anything I've ever heard.

At the end of it, Richard was a little winded so he turned back to me. "Dave!" he shrilled. "You still here?! I bet you want to ask me some more questions."

"I'm just like everybody else," I said. "I'm here to see Little Richard." Then we chatted with the audience.

For most of the hour or so we were on that stage, I just sat back in my wicker chair next to Richard and laughed and exulted along with everybody else. What the hell was there to say, any more than you could find words for any Little Richard performance.

After it was over, Andrew Loog Oldham took me by the shoulders, squared me up, looked straight into my eyes and

said, "Well done!" You could say, therefore, that I got what I wanted and did not lose what I had. It was one of the great experiences of my life, let alone my career.

This is not what SXSW is about.

But after Andrew, a young woman I'd never met came up to me. Tears streamed down her face – a face I'll never forget, though I have no idea who she was or where she went next. "Thank you," she said. "That was everything I came here to learn. I know what I need to do now."

I think about her every year when I go down to Austin for the music version of March madness. Because at its best, that is what SXSW is all about: not just the star, but the person who learns from the star. A chance to listen and learn. ▪ **Dave Marsh, author/journalist/Sirius XM Radio host**

Daniel Johnston Meets His Muse

On March 15, 2005, producer Henry Rosenthal and I were standing onstage at Austin's famed Paramount Theatre as the end credits rolled for the SXSW premiere of our film *The Devil And Daniel Johnston*. We were a bit nervous, not just about

From Uzbekistan With Love

I was behind the registration counter in 2003 when five men, four dressed identically, approached to get their credentials. The guy who dressed differently spoke the best English, maybe 50 words. I could hear them speaking to each other in Russian, so I walked over and greeted them in Russian (I took six semesters at UT). They were Uzbeks who had just arrived, after traveling 12,000 miles thinking they had a gig at SXSW.

It turned out the band, Abbos, had applied for a showcase, and a South by Southwest volunteer, a UT graduate student named David, had spotted their application. David worked with an Uzbek rocket scientist, who had been invited in 1999 to work at UT Austin's Department of Aerospace Engineering and Engineering Mechanics. David knew his co-worker was homesick, and he couldn't wait to tell him that a little bit of his homeland was coming to Austin. They had been accepted some two months earlier, but they never confirmed their visa with SXSW, so the festival hadn't slotted them. Then they just "showed up."

I kind of adopted them when I realized the futility of their situation. Heck, everybody who met them that week adopted them. Over the next four days they played the huge Charles and Charlie party across from Arkie's, got a paying gig at a private party at La Zona Rosa, got an upgraded hotel from longtime SXSW housing honcho Diane Currier, recorded at Tequila Mockingbird with Danny Levin, played live on John Aeilli's show in KUT Studio 1-A, were featured in a *Dallas Observer* article by Robert Wilonsky, and had a kind of master class with Austin drumming legend Barry "Frosty" Smith.

Since that '03 SXSW I've been to Uzbekistan five times. I was adopted by the Uzbek rocket scientist's family, and four other Uzbek bands have traveled to Austin, three performing at SXSW. I have met many, many, many people at SXSW (I am fortunate to have attended every cotton-picking one of them), but no meeting personally affected me more than meeting the Uzbeks that day. Not only do I now know who Jurâ-khân Sultânov and Munadjat Yulchieva are, but I gained a second family. It's a small world. Assalomu Alaykum! ▪ **Casey Monahan, director, Texas Music Office, Governor's Office**

having screened a controversial portrait of one of Austin's hometown heroes, but because moments from now, unbeknownst to Daniel, we were about to make his most fervent wish come true. We hoped.

We had spent the previous four and a half years immersed in Daniel's world – eating, breathing, ruminating and reflecting on all things Daniel. If you're a Daniel Johnston fan, you know that in the mythical universe of his fertile imagination, one person reigns supreme. Bigger than King Kong, Frankenstein, Casper the Friendly Ghost, Polka-Dot Underwear Man, or even Jeremiah the Innocent, the enduring tentacle-eyed frog from the cover of his *Hi, How Are You?* tape that today still adorns the south-facing wall of the former Sound Exchange record store on the Drag. That person is Daniel's muse, Laurie Allen.

In a nutshell, Daniel met Laurie in Art School, he fell hopelessly and hopefully in love with her, his overtures went unrequited, she married the local undertaker, and his heart was broken, thus spawning countless achingly beautiful love songs like the haunting and consoling "True Love Will Find You In The End." So focused was his yearning, and so obsessive his zeal, it's fair to say that without Laurie Allen, there is no Daniel Johnston. In Daniel's mind, she is his one true love, and someday he will win her heart with his psalms and paeans, and they will spend eternity together.

If you've seen *The Devil And Daniel Johnston*, you know that Laurie's only appearance in the film occurs in a single faded Super-8 film that Daniel made of Laurie and her magic boots in the full flower of youth. As we learned in our research, Daniel to this day watches this film loop over and over, drawing inspiration for the countless songs and drawings that his mania has made possible. We made the decision to preserve Laurie in the film exactly as she exists in Daniel's memory.

But in the real world, almost from the time we first met him in 2000, Daniel's one request of us – which he made hundreds of times – was that Henry and I somehow find Laurie and bring her to him. So in 2005, the film having by now made a big splash at the Sundance Film Festival, winning me the prize for Best Documentary Director and selling to Sony Pictures Classics for theatrical distribution, we decided to fly Laurie in for the film's Austin premiere at SXSW as a surprise for Daniel, and to film the moment for our DVD extras (this being the era of the cherished DVD bonus feature).

As the credits finished and the house lights went up, followed by a standing ovation, we announced that we had a very special guest here with us today all the way from Columbus, Ohio. And out walked the lovely and bright...Laurie Allen. As I remember it, there was a collective gasp. There were a lot of hardcore Daniel Johnston fans in the audience that night that had been listening to these songs about her since the early 1980s. A lot of them didn't even believe she was real, but rather

was a figment of Daniel's avid imagination. I'll confess that at one point, I had harbored that belief myself. But now here she was in the flesh. It was otherworldly, like a dream episode of the 1950s TV show *This Is Your Life,* where we had actually harvested characters from the lyrics of his songs.

At the same time, Laurie in the flesh was almost TOO real. As we heard later from many of those in the audience that night (and later in the blogosphere), this was too great a potential shock to Daniel's delicate nervous system. He couldn't take it. Our actions bordered on the irresponsible. And we were more interested in capturing "a moment" with some publicity stunt to market our DVD than in Daniel's well-being. As if to bolster the latter position, when we called Daniel to the stage, there was a hushed silence, but no Daniel. Blinded by the stage lights, we could not see Daniel tearing through the aisles – in the wrong direction – straight out the back of the theater and out onto the street! As we conducted a somewhat awkward Q&A afterward with Laurie, Henry and I kept glancing toward the wings to see if Daniel would materialize, but to no avail. We learned later from those sitting near him that as soon as Laurie came out

Double Anniversaries

The first year I was in Austin I was bowled over by a band from Dallas, a country-punk outfit called Slick 57, and ended up signing them. And after meeting Nan Warshaw from Bloodshot, I licensed albums by Alejandro Escovedo and Split Lip Rayfield. Some years later I saw Dengue Fever and decided my label sooo needed them! I've had five artists' showcases over the years and had some astonishing experiences at SXSW – seeing Alejandro with his full band at a free concert down by Town Lake, the first of many Drive-By Truckers shows, Booker T. & the M.G.'s at Antone's, Marah at the same venue, Big Star at the Austin Music Hall, Lucinda Williams and Ryan Adams & the Pinkhearts on the same bill the first year I attended, an inspired Richmond Fontaine gig, and so many others. Did I mention Joan Jett & the Blackhearts at Stubb's? Or catching up with Jello Biafra for the first time in 20 years on the street outside the Continental? I could go on, you know. And hey, SXSW coincides with my wedding anniversary, so, both of us being huge fans of Guy Clark and his song "Dublin Blues," we always celebrate with a Mad Dog Margarita (or two) at the Texas Chili Parlor. This year will be our 11th anniversary and the 25th SXSW. ■ Stuart Coupe, Laughing Outlaw Records (Australia)

onstage, Daniel loudly muttered that she was an impostor, then took off around the corner to Schlotzsky's Deli for a Coke.

That would have been the end of our SXSW moment, except that two hours later, at our celebration party at a nearby art gallery, as we chatted with Laurie and friends and fans, Daniel Johnston finally arrived. He walked up on the front porch and sat down on a chair all alone. And then moments later, as I saw with my own eyes through the front glass window, Laurie Allen sat down on a chair next to him. For the first time in 25 years, Laurie and Daniel were together, alone, holding hands and having a conversation.

If you want to know the rest of the story and what transpired that night, you'll have to consult the Bonus Section on the DVD. But what I will tell you is that at the end of the evening, after Laurie left to go home, Daniel came up to me and said, "Thank you so much, Jeff F., for bringing Laurie here. She is still so beautiful. This truly is a dream come true. This is the greatest night of my life." ■ **Jeff Feuerzeig, director,** *The Devil and Daniel Johnston*

"This Is A Really Bad Idea. Let's Do That."

Ironically, the idea started in the Second Life Herald hospitality suite on the second floor of Austin's venerable Driskill Hotel. The online newspaper's publisher, University of Michigan professor Peter Ludlow, had come to the 2006 SXSW Interactive Festival to talk about the hugely popular online multiplayer game Second Life, in which thousands of people do almost everything online that they do offline. But that night, interactivity was flowing in the opposite direction, toward what Ludlow

now refers to as a "game instantiation event." Which is another way of saying that instead of taking "real life" online, guests took a computer game out into the world.

In other words, they played Frogger. On a real street. Against real cars. Though not with a real frog.

MAKE magazine editor Phil Torrone was conveniently packing a number of Roomba vacuum cleaners that he had tricked out with Bluetooth remote control technology for some illegal Roomba cockfights in San Diego. After using some of them to play a form of pool, Torrone landed on the idea of Frogger, prompting the by-now-legendary response from Eyebeam fellow Limor Fried: "This is a really bad idea. Let's do that."

After being fitted with a frog costume cut out of a hastily procured green T-shirt, the Roomba was deployed across Austin's Sixth Street, a four-lane one-way running in front of the hotel. Because Torrone's laptop didn't have the Bluetooth range, he went down to street level to operate the Roomba. A crowd of revelers stayed on the balcony upstairs; from there, Ludlow says that "it looked exactly like the angle you see it from in the game."

She's Still With The Band

After his keynote in 2005, Robert Plant and his band were holding a press conference when a woman with bright red hair and lipstick stands up in the middle of the room to ask a question. After a few seconds, it registers with Mr. Plant that it is former rock 'n' roll groupie and author Pamela Des Barres. He jumps up and leaves the stage, and she has to work her way from the middle of the room to where he is. Everyone is watching in surprise at this genuinely happy reunion. They hug and kiss and then things return to normal. It was one of those moments that SXSW is known for — you just never know who you'll encounter. ■ **Elizabeth Derczo, longtime SXSW publicist**

One of those revelers was Kyle Machulis, a self-described teledildonics expert. "We were trying to stay quiet so as not to attract attention," he recalls. "But the second the 'bot hit the street, we were all screaming."

Despite, or perhaps because of, the deranged crowd demanding its destruction, the plucky frogbot managed to cross the street ten or so times, abetted by baffled drivers who slowed down to determine what was crossing their paths. Pedestrian passersby got it immediately, even after hitting the bars on Sixth Street. "[Frogger is] something that's universally recognized no matter how cognition-impaired you are," observes Ludlow.

The Roomba finally met its match in a white Toyota 4Runner and was retired with dignity, but its brief appearance left a strong impression. "There's a certain something about a car running over a Roomba," says Machulis. "It seems very much a prank that could only have happened at this conference."

Torrone concurred via email, writing that "there are only a few examples and opportunities to do an art project like this." ■ **John Ratliff, writer**

Beauty, Eh?: Five Great Canadian SXSW Sets

Once upon time, the term "Canadian music" was, for many Americans, a joke, delivered by Celine Dion, punchlined by Bryan Adams, and wrapped in a Loverboy headband. But like our socialized healthcare system, legal gay marriages, generous artist grants and 6%-alcohol beer, Canada's musical output has become a coveted commodity over the past 10 years, and South by Southwest has played a big part in boosting its market value. Here's a list of five proud Canadian moments at SXSW that made us feel a little less self-conscious about saying "aboot" aloud in Austin.

1. The New Pornographers at La Zona Rosa, 2001: The Vancouver power-pop ensemble's delightful 2000 debut, *Mass Romantic*, had already started to redirect the collective gaze of U.S. critics north of the border, but at their debut SXSW performance, the Pornos got all the validation they needed: an impromptu guest cameo from Ray Davies, the festival's keynote speaker that year. Following an introduction from a visibly awestruck Neko Case, Davies sauntered onstage to perform the Kinks' 1968 nugget "Starstruck," a moment that must've been as humbling for Davies as his younger charges, given that Pornos frontman Carl Newman seemed to know the lyrics better than the man who wrote them.

2. The Constantines at B.D. Riley's, 2002: One of the most hotly tipped live acts in Toronto at the time, the Constantines had harnessed their considerable onstage vigor playing all manner of DIY venues, from basement house parties to Jewish community centers. But the B.D. Riley's stage presented a unique set of challenges, given that its tiny, elevated windowfront area seemed more accustomed to solo-acoustic folksinger acts than five-piece powerhouse rock bands. To make matters more awkward, singer-guitarist Bry Webb's amp crapped out during the first song. But rather than let that setback derail the show, the band

embraced the chaos: Webb dropped his guitar, grabbed the mic and transformed the pub into his pulpit, hurtling himself out of the venue's open street-front window to deliver the Cons' soul-punk salvos to a growing congregation of onlookers on Sixth Street. Shortly thereafter, the band was signed to Sub Pop, laying the foundation for the nascent nu-Springsteen movement.

3. Broken Social Scene at Momo's (2003) and Stubb's (2004): The Momo's show was one of Broken Social Scene's first U.S. dates after a rave review from Pitchfork had introduced the band's 2002 album, *You Forgot It In People*, to the American indie-rock nation at large. So naturally the small, second-floor room was packed with curious journalists and dignitaries, including Creation Records poobah Alan McGee and future BSS collaborator Scott Kannberg of Pavement (though, years later, Kannberg admitted to me in an interview that he had just been dragged to the show by a friend and wasn't really paying attention). If BSS's rapturously received Momo's set sowed the seeds for their U.S. success – earning them their American

publicity team and booking agent – the band's subsequent SXSW visit to a packed Stubb's brought it to fruition. While Broken Social Scene have become synonymous with sprawl – both in terms of their expansive membership and three-hour long concerts – they're arguably at their greatest when forced to focus their energies into a 45-minute showcase. And with *You Forgot It In People* by then firmly ingrained into the psyche of undergraduates everywhere, BSS's triumphant Stubb's stand transformed their imagined anthems into a genuine greatest-hits revue. The next morning, the band made the cover of *The Austin Chronicle*'s SXSW daily edition, effectively confirming the coronation.

4. Feist at Levi's/FADER party (2005): Feist's only SXSW visit to date wasn't even an official one – in 2005, she played two hastily-arranged afternoon shows at the behest of her prospective U.S. benefactors, Cherry Tree/Interscope, the second of which was held at the Levi's house on Sixth Street on a gloomy Saturday afternoon. Though she performed solo with just an electric guitar and loop pedal, Feist was the beneficiary of a special effect no major-label budget could buy: Just as she raised her arms to punctuate a sustained high note on "The Water," a powerful gust of wind shot through the backyard venue and threatened to take the tented stage with it. Her subsequent closing cover of Nina Simone's "Sea-Lion Woman" was then accompanied by a torrential downpour. Needless to say, she passed the audition.

5. Fucked Up at Red 7 (2007): Like the New Pornographers' Ray Davies dalliance six years earlier, this

Her Morning Jacket Was A Good Fit

I'd recently left my job booking the Viper Room in Los Angeles and was coming to the 2002 festival hoping to figure out my next move. I'd always wanted to tour-manage bands, so I thought maybe I could make some inroads, or network, or whatever it is real attendees at SXSW do. A few weeks before, my friend Louie Bandak, who at the time was doing A&R for Capitol, told me about a band he'd seen that he thought I would like: My Morning Jacket. The night of their showcase at Buffalo Billiards, my friend Sean Eden told me he knew the band's manager, so we went over together. Little did I know how huge that hour of my life would end up being.

After 12 years in the music biz I was jaded and cranky, but the band blew me away. They reminded me of all the reasons why I love music. As they played on well past their 2am cutoff, I was mesmerized. Later I had Sean inquire with their manager, Mike Martinovich, about their need for a tour manager but received the reply that they weren't really looking. Fast forward to June, and I met Mike at an in-store the band did at Rhino Records in Westwood. He invited me to travel up to Santa Barbara with them, and as we drove up, he asked if I'd ever thought about tour managing. Two days later I was on a trial run with the guys as they toured up the west coast with Guided By Voices. I got the job, but the happy ending of this story is that I also got the guy: I've been married to Tom [Blankenship, the bassist] for over four years now.

I have SXSW to thank for a 20-plus-year career and two husbands (my first was a volunteer I met in 1993). Director Roland Swenson and his wife Roseana Auten are the only people, besides my mother and brothers, who went to both weddings. ■ Linda Park, longtime SXSW staff

noontime set represented not just a showcase for the Toronto hardcore insurgents, but also a symbolic passing of the torch. For their final song, Fucked Up were joined by ex-Black Flag belter Keith Morris for a blitzkrieg charge through the Flag's 1978 classic "Nervous Breakdown," proving that 12:30 is not too early for a circle pit. Among the moshers was another approving elder statesman: Sloan singer/bassist Chris Murphy, who at least had the good sense to take his glasses off first before diving in. ■ **Stuart Berman, Toronto's** *Eye Weekly* **and author of** *This Book Is Broken: A Broken Social Scene Story*

Free The Ozo Three!

It was St Patrick's day 2004, Ozomatli's second time at SXSW. (Their first was in 1999.) They were headlining the BMI Latin Showcase on Wednesday night at what was then Club Exodus on Sixth Street.

When Everything Goes Right

In the lobby of the Paramount Theatre as an 800-plus audience watched a crystal clear (in picture and audio) screening of my first, and best, feature (so far): *Melvin Goes To Dinner* **(2003), and I'm on my cell phone talking to my wife (who produced but couldn't make it to the fest 'cause our kids were very young still) and trying to share with her how amazing the film looked and sounded and how wonderfully it was playing. Every funny moment landed, every human moment played, it was beautiful, and a fantastic antidote to our other festival screenings which included f'ed up sound (on a movie that is all dialogue – that's death), and poorly handled presentations. It's rewarding to have been there and seen all our hard work presented once with care and given a chance for people to see it in its best light. We won the audience award and I'm told that out of 500-plus comment cards there was only one negative…hey, I had to put in my two cents, didn't I?"** ■ Bob Odenkirk, filmmaker

The club's production was, um…er…subpar. The night ran late as bands struggled with set changeovers. The room was packed beyond capacity, and we were starting to bump up against curfew by the time Ozomatli took the stage.

The fire marshals came in. I went and met with them, and told them we could help them empty the room at 2am. I informed them that the band usually does a drum procession (samba line) off the stage and around the room. We could take the audience outside on to the street; that way they would quickly clear the room without incident. (The band also did this in 1999 at SXSW, and had a kickin' drum circle in the middle of Sixth Street.)

Deal. They loved it.

So, as the band ended their set, they did just that. As they left the building and emptied out on to Sixth Street, the audience following behind them, they bumped into several Austin police offers in front of the club. The officers heard the sounds and saw the crowd and pretty much freaked. They told the band to go back inside and to stop playing, which they did. However, there was only one door, and it was impossible to re-enter the club. Some confusion ensued as the band tried to go back in as people were pouring out.

Next thing we knew, pepper spray was hitting the crowd and Wil-Dog, the bass player, was in handcuffs. Jiro, the smallest guy in the band who carries the biggest drum, put it on top of his head so he wouldn't hit anyone in the melee. He tried to go back in.

Next thing he knew, he heard a cop say, "There he is, get him!" He was like, huh? Who? And then he was cuffed and put against the wall right next to Wil-Dog.

I saw a long-haired dude on the floor getting the shit kicked out of him by several police, pepper-sprayed and in a fetal position. People were yelling, running, flash bulbs popping.

Dog and Jiro got carted off down Sixth Street to the paddy wagon waiting a few blocks away, through throngs of fans booing the cops and shouting words of encouragement to Ozo.

I followed behind with the rest of the band trying to get info on where the two are being taken so we can get them out as quickly as possible. They wouldn't answer the simple questions: Where is the jail, what is it called, where can we go to help our guys?

Wil-Dog and Jiro are thrown into the paddy wagon. They poignantly recall having the local classic rock station blasting into the back as they sat cuffed on the metal benches awaiting what was next. Then, in comes the long-haired guy who was getting pepper-sprayed and beaten. He is a mess, can't see or talk.

I am face to face with a woman cop on the street who shoves me back up on the sidewalk as I persist in trying to get info about why they are being arrested and where I can go bail them out. Once she lays her hands on me, I yell back at her to keep her fucking hands off me, and…I am cuffed too. I'm thrown into the paddy wagon along with Dog and Jiro, who describe the moment as if in cinematic slow motion: Something akin to REO Speedwagon is pumped into the ethers, the doors slowly open, and in comes their manager in handcuffs. We feel for the long-haired dude, who is just mauled.

We head to the jail and are held in a loading dock, at which point Jiro overhears one cop say to another, "That's the guy that hit me." Jiro says, "That's bullshit!"

At this point it's around 3am, and we had caught the 6am flight out of Los Angeles the previous morning. We are going on 24 hours of no sleep, and needless to say are a little impaired of judgment. But we didn't think we would be charged. Didn't think it was a big deal.

They bring us in, book us, take our mug shots, and seat us in a holding area with plastic benches and News 8 Austin on a loop that we must have heard, well, 30 times while we were sitting there for six or so hours. I have Andy Langer's SXSW

coverage permanently ingrained in my brain. As well as the acceptance speech of the drummer from Los Lonely Boys when he won some Austin Music Award.

We make collect calls about every 15 minutes – $360 worth to my husband, to be exact. He became the intermediary who stayed up all night relaying information between the three of us, who were not allowed to talk to each other; our brand spanking new criminal lawyer Bobby Earl Smith, who was retained by BMI; our music lawyer Lisa Socransky; and the media. We began to get updates on our charges from outside, since nobody inside would answer our questions.

Finally Jiro was called first to see the dude who tells you what your charges are. He was told, "Son, you are in a lot of trouble. You are being charged with third degree felony assault of a police officer, which is punishable by up to 10 years in federal prison." WTF??? Jiro gets hauled off to the cell blocks.

I was called next, and was told I was being charged with a Class B misdemeanor – "Interference with Police Procedure" – which meant I was getting sent upstairs to general population as well.

Dog was booked on a Class A misdemeanor – "Violation of a Noise Ordinance" – and was let go at about 9am.

Jiro and I were put into stripes. Jiro was shackled with the other inmates (I was just re-cuffed) and sent upstairs.

Then we were really "in jail." Like in a cell. All day long. With no phone calls. Bologna sandwiches. Steel toilet bowl. Just like on TV. We had no idea what was happening or how long we would be held. No idea what time it was, what the process was for getting us out, what would happen next.

Late that evening we were finally released on our own recognizance. Charges were pending; it took two years and many thousands of dollars to get our records expunged.

As I left the jail, I saw throngs of news cameras. Not knowing they were there for me, I started to walk away and got swarmed with questions. I burst into tears, because at that point I was running on 40 hours of no sleep. My crying unglued face was all over the Austin evening news. Turns out, this had become a major news story; AP, Reuters, etc. picked it up and it traveled around the world. People were turning out in droves to support us. There were "Free The Ozo 3" shirts popping up all over the city. Cabbies and folks from all over were rallying for us, apologizing, having our backs, showing us love.

Invasion Of The Music Snatchers

We moved to Austin full time in summer 2004, so SXSW 2005 was the first time we were in Austin for the whole shebang. It was an amazing year. We were here as subjects of the documentary *Reel Paradise* (director Steve James) which was crazy enough, but it was also the first time we were de facto hosts welcoming our extended filmmaking world to our new home during SXSW. It was a great year, lots of wonderful films. But what particularly stands out in my memory is watching the sea change on Wednesday, the first day of Music. I'd been watching films in the Paramount for days, but all of a sudden, the movie palace and the downtown streets were full of rockers. Undeniable rockers by the dozens and hundreds. The black-T-shirted film and interactive registrants – slightly similar, just a tiny bit different – were replaced by groups of skinny tattooed kids. And when I say kids, I mean kids of all ages. But they couldn't have been mistaken for anything other than musicians. It was just a true phenomenon to see the invasion in every nook and cranny of town. I loved it. ▪ Janet Pierson, SXSW Film producer & senior programmer

This incident had struck quite a nerve in the city of Austin, with the media, with the local government. And while we didn't deign to know the vagaries and nuances of city politics or the Austin public's relationship with the APD, somehow we became the de facto spokespeople for this rift. We were informed to stay out of it as we still had criminal charges pending against us, and APD was refusing to drop them.

However, what we did learn was how much love there is for Ozo by the people of Austin. They were there for us 100%, and still are to this day. People who care about what happens to musicians are alive and well and in full force in the city of Austin. They took up our cause. They rallied for us. They had Ozomatli's back. And we are grateful. We can look back on it and laugh, but sitting in Travis County jail was no laughing matter.

And here's the postcript: Our ground transportation pulls up in front of a hotel by the Nashville Airport to take us to the Bonnaroo Festival site in 2008. We get in and realize there is already another band in the van. They are in the back. Our tour manager is coming unglued, but we tell him its cool, we'll ride down there with whoever.

We pull away and I hear a voice from the back seat:

"I know you!!! I was that guy in jail with you in Austin!!! Holy crap!!! I can't believe this!!!"

We turn around and it's the long-haired dude who was pepper-sprayed and mauled. Turns out it's Aaron Behrens from

Oldies But Goodies

Over my two decades attending SXSW, I've caught countless memorable sets by artists new and old, hyped and unhyped, up-and-coming and on the downward slide. But if forced to name an act that keeps me coming back year after year, I'd have to name a band that's never played an official showcase, yet whose SXSW-week performances consistently embody the festival's music-loving spirit.

The combo of which I speak is the Allen Oldies Band, who in 1999 began making a yearly pilgrimage from their hometown of Houston to perform marathon sets of '50s and '60s pop covers on the sidewalk in front of Rue's Antiques on South Congress on the Friday afternoon of SXSW. Like many future AOB fans, this is how I first experienced the group's gleeful, irony-free embrace of all that is transcendent and liberating about rock 'n' roll, and the uninhibited abandon of frontman Allen Hill.

A tireless dervish sweating through his secondhand tux while shouting himself hoarse beneath the searing Texas sun, Hill preaches the Oldies gospel with the fervor of a true believer, belting out the hits of such AM godheads as Sam the Sham, Tommy Roe, the Standells and the Royal Guardsmen. The band wasn't in Austin to look for a record deal or revive a flagging career; they were there to remind us what we loved about music in the first place.

Hill and company soon began augmenting their SXSW sidewalk gigs with Saturday-morning sets across the street at the Continental Club, and later trod the boards in the Jo's Coffee parking lot. They also found time during various SXSWs to serve as a backup combo for such old-school survivors as Roy Head, Barbara Lynn and Andre Williams.

The band's sidewalk audience originally consisted mainly of unsuspecting passers-by who'd been drawn in by Allen's impassioned reading of "Sugar Shack" or "Secret Agent Man." As the years progressed, many of us began blowing off panels and parties and setting our Friday afternoons aside for the Oldies. Todd Abramson, owner of Maxwell's in Hoboken, NJ, became such a fan that he flew the band up – twice – to perform at his club. The first time, they played for over five hours without a break and never ran out of songs. During their visits, WFMU DJ Joe Belock (who, like Abramson, had discovered the band playing on South Congress) invited them to the station for a couple of live sessions, the first of which became the band's debut CD, *Live And Delirious*. Others who'd witnessed the band's SXSW shenanigans booked the band for subsequent gigs in Chicago, San Francisco and New Orleans. So if you're walking down South Congress and see a manic guy in a tux singing "Double Shot (of My Baby's Love)," pay attention. ■ **Scott Schinder, journalist**

Ghostland Observatory. Before he was in a band, he was a local Austin kid working in a law office. He happened to be walking home, stopped at Exodus to see what was going on, and got caught up in our run-in with the cops. He was beaten and thrown in jail along with us.

Needless to say, it was a wonderful, tearful, hilarious, bizarre reunion: a bizarre ending to a totally bizarre story. 'Cause that's how Ozo rolls. ■ **Amy Blackman is manager of Ozomatli; Jiro Yamaguchi and Wil-Dog are members of the band.**

The Power Of Song

My parents saw Billy Faier sing "Hell-Bound Train" and play his banjo during the winter of 1958-59. Faier was briefly the toast of the small circle of folk aficionados in Berkeley, California, to which they had briefly attached themselves, and "Hell-Bound Train" was one hell of a song. Is one hell of a song.

I was born a few months later, and we moved three days north. Two boys, father's books, and boxes of LPs acquired during the folk boom. Mother played them once a week, while ironing. Sometimes Mozart, sometimes Paul Clayton, often Peggy Seeger and, if I said please, Billy Faier.

The author Michael Perry and I corresponded about the poem Faier set to banjo in the late 1950s. Michael found it in a 1936 book titled *The Best-Loved Poems of the American People*, selected by Hazel Felleman of *The New York Times Book Review*, and Perry notes in his book *Coop* that just the words put him to his knees in the bathroom. I did not touch drink until spring of my 18th year, a very late bloom in the '70s, though I did my best to catch up.

Such is the power of song.

It didn't take long to fall into the world of used record stores and Top Ramen. Every time I found a new one – every time I traveled to a new city – I had the same question, a test, an excuse for being there: Billy Faier?

Not once. Never even the pretense of recognition.

So we started this damn alt-country magazine, and filled a hole in our seventh issue with my plea: Does anybody know anything about Billy Faier? (Today, of course, one would simply Google and learn the whole story from Faier's website. It was AOL's world, then.) The phone rang. "Here's his phone number," said the caller.

I sat down. Slumped. Wrote it down.

Called Woodstock, New York. Billy Faier answered. I fumbled words: "I thought you were as important as Earl Scruggs," mindful that once I'd managed a beginner's impression of the Scruggs roll, but not a patch on a single thing Faier had played.

"What were you doing?" I asked. Now, one can find his discography online, read about the John Sebastian projects, the

1974 LP on John Fahey's Takoma. "Living," he laughed, and he told me I'd missed him in Seattle during the two weeks he played with Townes Van Zandt.

In 2006 Billy Faier relocated to Marathon, Texas, and sought me out online. I convinced him to review a book about folk music; he announced he'd been signed to a new label, Tompkins Square (in the end, he released a single compilation track). And that he would be playing SXSW. I toyed briefly with prevailing upon my partners to book him on the *No Depression* showcase, but saw reason. I made my way up Congress Avenue to the Hideout, a small-scale theatrical venue behind an indifferent coffee shop. And there he was, 47 years later.

White-haired and blind in one eye, with a bottle of aspirin in his banjo case. Long, agile fingers like Gatemouth Brown.

By the end of his half-hour set, the audience had swelled to eight.

Such is the power of song. ■ Grant Alden, *No Depression* co-founder & co-editor

Wanda, Gram, Doug, Sugar Bear, And More

It's been 25 years since SXSW started? No way! My recollections go back as far as 1993 – what a year to become a regular. I had the thrill of meeting Jim and Mary Lindsay Dickinson, there to watch their teenage sons Cody and Luther play with their then-band DDT. If memory serves, Jim (looking his most hippified) joined them onstage for a few songs. I also made the acquaintance of the man who could have been called the Ambassador of SXSW: Doug Sahm. He had more joie de vivre than probably anyone I've ever met. And he loved to turn people on to his favorite Austin places. It would be a highlight every year to see Doug, catch up, find out about his latest obsessions, and of course see him onstage. Watching him reunite with the Sir Douglas Quintet at the old Antone's was a night I'll never forget. A guy named Sugar Bear helped us get our parked-in car out of the tiny parking lot at night's end.

I've always enjoyed being on panels at SXSW (I think about 15 or so!), and some of those really stand out too. The Wanda Jackson panel – which included the Queen of Rockabilly, vocalist Kristi Rose, Bloodshot honcho Rob Miller, and filmmaker Beth Harrington, who directed a fantastic film on female rockabilly artists (*Welcome To The Club*) – was pivotal in Wanda's resurgence, I think. This panel led to a very cool Wanda Jackson tribute album, *Hard-Headed Woman*, released in '04 by Bloodshot, with performances by many SXSW regulars. Wanda was just getting back out there around this time, and now she has a spectacular new album out, *The Party Ain't Over*, produced by Jack White. SXSW helped put Wanda back into the spotlight, and over the years, she's played some amazing gigs during the conference, including one of my favorites in 1999 at the Soho Lounge backed by Henhouse (with Rosie Flores, Cindy Cashdollar, Sarah Brown, Lisa Pankratz and Lisa Mednick).

Another really interesting panel that helped to celebrate the legacy of an influential American artist was on Gram Parsons in 2001; it included Jim Carlton (Gram's high school friend and bandmate from Florida), legendary pianist Earl Poole Ball, Jon Langford, and James Austin, who produced a superb Parsons anthology for Rhino. There were some great stories told at this panel, and if I recall correctly, Jon Langford threw up after it was over...from nerves?

A book I edited with Scott Schinder, *Alt-Rock-A-Rama*, also resulted in a once-in-a-lifetime SXSW event. Many of the book's contributors were attending that year (1996), and we presented a reading at the convention center that was lots of fun and featured riveting performances by Robyn Hitchcock, Wayne Kramer, Peter Holsapple, Steve Wynn, Eric "Roscoe" Ambel, Kristin Hersh and others. What a great venue for a book-release event!

I'm hoping to make it to SXSW for another 25 years – though my son Jack, who first accompanied me to the conference at 7 weeks of age and just turned 13, may have to push me around in a wheelchair! ■ Holly George-Warren, author/journalist/editor

To A Conference

O, Southbysouthwestia,
All-consuming bitch
Who said she'd in the end
Leave me famous and rich
Whose success vows are spoken
With nary a word
Where a consolation token
Is spotting the Langford
When beer becomes food
And barbecue a tonic
Where outlanders consume
Mexican food like the chronic
How I stand in awe
At your thundering host
Their lucre? Our merchants
Dig it the most
Whose Black hand my Swenson
Did place twixt the Grulke
'Midst the unsigned hordes
Odd smelling and sulky
O, Southbysouthwestia,
You love-murmuring stoat
Pour not one more draft
Again down my throat,
Temptress, force me not
To quaff one more free beer
No, never again
Least not 'til next year!

■ Rich Malley, musician (and poet), from 2006

South By Spoon By Southwest

1994 was back when they had those specifically "anti-SXSW" shows. I wouldn't be surprised if we tried to get in, but we didn't. I think we had played at the Blue Flamingo once before. There were probably seven bands on the bill that night, and at least three or four of them had been told that they were playing first, at 10. Which was when I thought we were playing, and that's when I wanted to play, for some reason. I can't remember why. I guess I figured that more people were gonna be there. Maybe (drummer Jim Eno) had to get home early to go to bed.

I was arguing with Toby from the Motards; I somehow won the argument and we did play first. And I was glad we did, because Gerard Cosloy just happened to be there at that particular moment. I didn't know who he was. I was just at that point figuring out what Matador Records was – starting to notice that that label was on the back of a lot of a records that I liked at the time. That ended up being pretty fortuitous.

I didn't meet him that night. The next thing I heard regarding Matador was that they bought some of our 7 inches [for distribution], but I'd still never talked to him. And then when I put out that Drake Tungsten [solo] cassette, I sent him a copy, and that was the first time I heard back from him. Then he invited us to play the next year's SXSW show, even though we weren't on Matador. It was a Matador show at the Austin Opera House, 1995. So that was our first official SXSW show.

It was a momentous night. Not because it was SXSW but because we were playing with Yo La Tengo and Railroad Jerk and Guided By Voices. It was awesome. A huge show for us. It was just a lot of fun. And as soon as we played the Matador showcase, all these labels started coming after us. "We hear Matador was interested in this band, so we should be interested in them too." That was exactly the thinking. But Matador was the label we wanted to go with.

1996 was the first year that we played a SXSW show *and* played a non-SXSW show. You weren't allowed to do that at that time. In order to go around that rule we played at the Blue Flamingo and billed ourselves as Spoon Doggie Dogg. Somehow that got in the paper and then somebody from SXSW called me and was not amused.

1999 was the Waterloo Park show with Guided By Voices. That was before they were doing shows at Auditorium Shores. That felt huge. I felt like we were lucky to get put on the bill, because at that moment, things weren't going that great for us. We had Hunter Darby (of Austin band the Wannabes) on keyboards with us at that show. It might have been the first show where we ever had a keyboard player.

Auditorium Shores, we played that twice. First in 2006 with Echo & the Bunnymen – we played "Don't Make Me A Target" for the first time at that show. And then we played it two years later. We've played a lot of big outdoor settings, but I just remember hearing about Auditorium Shores when I was in my late teens and early 20s and just thinking of it as the place where they had Aqua Fest, a thing where probably Stevie Ray Vaughan played it, or if not him, a lot of people like him. It seemed like something I would never do, and there we were, headlining it. I remember I just happened to be walking through the hotel bar where I was staying later on that night. The TV news was doing a piece on SXSW and they showed a good 15-20 seconds of us playing, which blew my mind. ■ **Britt Daniel, Spoon**

SXSW Film – And How I Perceive It

Anyone who knows me even a little bit knows that sunshine and light is not exactly my thing. Golden optimism is to be feared; those too enthusiastically pleasant are to be avoided. The glass is never half full or half empty but always about to fall and break, spilling everywhere.

In certain ways that has made the whole SXSW experience difficult. There have been so many more good moments than those running very deep in the other direction. Whenever anyone says "I never in my wildest dreams thought that this great tree would spring from that little acorn," I'm always at least suspicious. I want to ask, "Come on, at your kookiest you never imagined Oz, never allowed your imagination to run to the grandiose?" But clearly the growth of SXSW has been extraordinary and the international prestige of SXSW Film has been surprising. I never dreamed it would ever become what it is now. I never came close to dreaming it. Few have been more astonished than I at what has happened over the years.

At this point we have two divergent stories. One is the evolution and role of SXSW Film. The other is how I perceive it.

There is the story of SXSW. Although we weren't exactly sure what kind of film festival we were looking for when we first plunged into the waters, I don't think we could have asked for anything better than what we got – an event that cherishes

films, filmmakers and audiences. The foundation of SXSW is built on our belief in and affection for Austin and what goes on here. Ideally, SXSW mirrors and reflects this large, extensive, diverse but cooperative community.

Business isn't far behind — not as a celebration of business (though not excluding that either) but because by understanding it, creators can control their careers and work. This is the core belief — that media is both art and business. The more creative talents understand the latter, the more flexibility and control they have over the former. This is not to say every creative talent has to be an independent artist. Instead, it is to argue against any single template as being best for all artists.

When I look forward to the future, I banish memory and ignore experience. I expect the worst and more than the worst. Ahead, I see only dense swamp, voracious quicksand and vegetation growing quicker over every surface. Looking back, I can see the thin sliver of a yellow brick road winding through the nightmare. But if things are going too well, then I can't look, because if I did, I'd jinx it. The dichotomy of me & me, of I & I is critical here. If I gave a contemporaneous diary account of the last almost decade of SXSW Film, it would seem a horror tale. I don't look. Sure, the whole SXSW Film Fest experience has had its share of problems causing both ups and downs. But it's still there.

In 2004, Matt Dentler was running the show. And doing a damn brilliant job. Remarkably in 2004 and 2005 our biggest grossing films were political documentaries. SXSW 2005 also had a dazzling collection of music docs: *You're Gonna Miss Me* (directed by Keven McAlester) about the rise, fall and resurrection of the 13th Floor Elevators great Roky Erickson; *The Devil And Daniel Johnston* (directed by Jeff Feuerzeig), about the legendary idiosyncratic songwriter whose work has been covered by so many other artists; *Be Here To Love Me: A Film About Townes Van Zandt* (directed by Margaret Brown), one of the great American songwriters. And the film genre Dentler was to pioneer, Mumblecore, was not to far off in the future. With all our love and gratitude, Dentler left after the 2008 SXSW Film Fest. But when it seemed entirely beyond reason, the creator smiled on us again. Janet Pierson became the head of SXSW Film.

In reality I don't get to see all that many films. The talk, excitement, and explosive creative energy that people leave in streaks behind them is what I'm hooked on. My best memories of SXSW are personal. One morning sometime after 1am standing on the street in front of the Driskill and talking film for a couple of hours with Ron Mann and Jim Jarmusch. Another time we were having dinner at Uchi with Jonathan Demme, Elvis Mitchell, Marge Baumgarten, Robert Wilonsky and Cindy LeMire. Over time, the talk degenerated more and more into pure film geek talk. When the saner folks had left the dinner, we finally and gleefully turned down that unpaved one-way road to hell — discussing guilty pleasures.

Tale Of The Tapes

It's probably not the first or most prominent example, but the curious case of Minneapolis band Tapes 'n Tapes might be the best for summing up the muddying, megalomaniacal effect that music blogs had on South by Southwest in the mid-'00s — when bloggers rose out of suburban bedrooms disguised as Brooklyn or Chicago apartments to become national tastemakers.

Before that virtual crossroads, bands generally didn't come into SXSW with write-ups in *Rolling Stone* and *The New York Times* before they had any kind of substantial press back home. Likewise, bands never landed eight showcases at SXSW when they couldn't even earn the headlining slot at a dive bar back home for their CD-release party. Come to think of it, before that era, bands never played eight SXSW showcases, period.

Tapes 'n Tapes had all that and more with its triumphal arrival in 2006 on the backs of sites such as Pitchfork and Brooklyn Vegan, the latter of which literally declared them that year's winner thanks to their eight-gig bonanza. It included a slot at the then-new Levi's/Fader Fort and parties presented by KEXP, VH1, *Blender* and Le Tigre (the clothing company, not the band). A standout memory from the whirlwind was the sight of Tapes frontman Josh Grier running up Red River Street at full throttle, perhaps the hardest-working man not on the SXSW staff that year.

Of course, the Tapes machinery had run out of hype quicker than you can clap your hands and say yeah. The band's signing to XL Recordings was met with a yawn and vague skepticism after the festival. The feast-to-famine downturn was so great that *Austin Chronicle* critic Christopher Gray wrote before the following year's festival, "Does anybody even remember Tapes 'n Tapes?"

Here's the rub, though: Tapes 'n Tapes has improved from charmingly ramshackle into a sharp, solid live band and made two albums superior in almost every way to their breakout debut. As of this year, though, TnT is no longer signed to a label. The band's albums have garnered only a smattering of press, not much of it favorable. Pitchfork gave their latest one a paltry 5.5 rating. Ironically or not, though, hometown fans and critics have really grown to love them. This year, their CD-release party is even at Minneapolis' big-kahuna club First Avenue -- headlining slot, no less. ■ Chris Riemenschneider, *Minneapolis Star Tribune*

But it is still about movies. In 2004, Richard Linklater graciously allowed us to do a sneak preview of *Before Sunset*. I liked *Before Sunrise* but it was not an all-time favorite. So I wasn't prepared for *Sunset*. Leaving the darkened theater into the light-bursting early afternoon, I was babbling about how great the film was, and found I didn't stop for several days.

That is it! That's the heart of it all that you are searching for. Something greater than just films, filmmakers and friends, but something right out of that as well. ■ **Louis Black, SXSW co-founder & senior director**

Why I Keep Coming Back

My first South by Southwest, in 1991, ended well after midnight on the final evening, in a conference room at the Hyatt Regency on the south shore of Town Lake. There was zero ambience. It still felt like West Texas heaven. For two hours, the Lubbock song brothers, Jimmie Dale Gilmore and Butch Hancock, magnetized a packed congregation with what I called, in my report for *Rolling Stone*, "the spirit of SXSW – music that sells itself." The two men, with the stunning acoustic lead guitar of Jesse Taylor, drew deep from their respective songbooks and a long friendship in and after their mythic early-'70s band, the Flatlanders. That night was my live introduction to Hancock's wide world of prairie-Dylan wit and empty-plains heartbreak – the drinker's masterpiece "Firewater (Seeks Its Own Level)"; the acute earthy loss of "She Never Spoke Spanish To Me." It was also the first time I'd been in the same room with Gilmore's voice, a pilgrim's prayer of haunting sky-high drawl.

In Good Company

It was always so nice to go there year after year. Like a bird on a yearly stopover. First couple times I went, Elliott [Smith] and I both got rejected, but went anyway. Then, 10 years later [2005], I was looking through the booklet thing and there was a page near the index that said, "This year's highlights" – there were four people: Mavis Staples, Brian Wilson, Robert Plant, and...me. I almost shit myself. There was absolutely no reason for them to do that. I wasn't even on a label. I was on a panel with Robyn Hitchcock, Nona Hendryx and John Langford. SXSW tipped the hat to me. Love you guys! ■ **Mary Lou Lord, musician**

That show was, I wrote, "the singular sublime collision of bluesy feeling, rock & roll spirit, alcoholic bonhomie, emotional straight talk and wily wordplay that characterizes great Texas music." And when it was over, I knew I'd come back. And I have – every year since.

SXSW was still small enough in 1991, its fifth year, for the actual conference to fit in that Hyatt. The number of artists performing at the evening festival showcases was in the lower three figures, and there were no lines. The biggest names were local working heroes, like the Texas Tornados – I remember the irrepressible Doug Sahm launching into his '65 hit "She's About A Mover" like it had just crashed into *Billboard's* Top 20 – and the brilliant, ill-fated Arc Angels, an Austin power-blues alliance (future Dylan and Clapton sidekicks; the late Stevie Ray Vaughan's rhythm section), then only six months old and, it turned out, two years from breaking up.

The promo was low-key, even awkward, especially for singers and players hardened by the rigors and small but honest victories of everyday life in one of the country's best and most demanding music cities. I knew singer-songwriter David Halley, another Lubbock cat, by reputation and a 1990 import masterpiece, *Stray Dog Talk*, when I saw him at the old Steamboat, on Sixth Street, in '91. "This next number is from our album," Halley said, laughing and a little embarrassed, as he rolled out perfect unions of '50s dance-party twang, late-'70s Springsteen and West Texas healing. "Too bad you have to take a plane to England to get it." It would have been worth it. (I am still stunned that Halley was never signed by a major U.S. label.)

At that point, SXSW was still a secret just getting out, an opportunity to see living legends in rare, provocative settings – like my '93 sighting of Roky Erickson, the truly psychedelic voice of the 13th Floor Elevators, not yet out of his dark ages but with his third-eye howl intact – and new magic that was not yet nationwide. My closing night, in 1992, was the start of a personal tradition: Alejandro Escovedo – then already a veteran of the great bands and near misses, Rank and File and the True Believers – with the best musicians in town, playing his grand-rock deep-roots songs. That year, he was leading his fabled Alejandro Escovedo Orchestra, "an unorthodox but bewitching blend of jazzy saxes, melancholy strings, explosive guitar and heart-tugging boy-girl harmonies," as I wrote later. It wasn't enough. Over the last two decades, I've spent a part of every SXSW with Escovedo in some form: variations on that big band, his Sensitive Boys, the hoodlum-glam holiday Buick MacKane, and even, in a mighty '94 reunion, the True Believers.

When I started attending SXSW, writers and label folks who attended the small early editions fondly referred to the festival as their "spring break" from the usual business, a holiday from offices and oversight. That changed in 1994, the minute Johnny

Cash walked onstage at the punk club Emo's – alone and in black – to preview the rough-granite soul of his first record with producer Rick Rubin. It was an unforgettable demonstration of absolute integrity in tight close-up – powerful stories (the traditional murder ballad "Delia's Gone") and confession (Cash's own "Redemption") with solitary strum and *that* voice.

A new standard was set, with the help of an industry in its last boom times. SXSW became a destination event for major artists launching new wares and vintage idols working on reignition. It's less like spring break now – more like Times Square at Christmas. Here is a partial list of why I don't mind: the reformed New York Dolls in 2005 mowing down a packed mob at Stubb's in search of a new record deal (they got it); My Morning Jacket previewing their *Evil Urges* album, at full Dixie-Zeppelin strength, in 2008 at the Austin Music Hall; Stone Temple Pilots at the same venue in 2010, back in their peak grunge-era form and showing why so much worthy, 21st-century indie rock never gets further than blog chatter and instant-download appeal (no stage presence). There was also the afternoon in 2007 when I had the dream-come-true honor of announcing, "Ladies and gentlemen, please welcome the Stooges!" before conducting a live SXSW interview with Iggy Pop and Ron and Scott Asheton – then watching Iggy bolt out the front door at Waterloo Records, during the Stooges' manic in-store set there, to shake it for the fans in the parking lot who couldn't get inside.

Okay, I get some inside track. I also stand in line – you meet interesting people and get a few good records that way – and enjoy the chatter and ground-floor commerce at the merch tables. One solid bargain: the dollar I spent on a homemade cassette by Drums & Tuba – "hot post-punk instrumerntals with real oompah-licks," as I put it in the magazine – after the group's street gig outside the Electric Lounge in 1997. I also take serious advice from good ears and the lasting friends I've made along the way. Local heavies Tia Carrera and Amplified Heat; psychedelic torchbearers ST 37 and the Black Angels; the composer-bandleader Graham Reynolds and his many ensembles: Those are a few of the permanent residents in my record collection as a result of wise recommendations and knockout performances. One year, in a tiny back room on Red River, I had my mind split open by Lift To Experience, a holy-fire power trio from Denton, Texas, that finished its act with actual flames. I also remember the night their singer-guitarist, Josh T. Pearson, came up to me at a club and insisted I stay for the four young guys, also from Denton, then setting up their gear onstage. Another friend had already hipped me to the show. They were both right. Explosions In The Sky were sublime indoor fireworks, playing an incandescent modern psychedelia – long, tidal twin-guitar pieces with no vocals and empathic heads-down fury – that made me an instant believer.

I have my SXSW habits. I like making the early-evening sets, when a lot of people are still at happy hour or mopping up the barbecue sauce at dinner. One of the best under-attended SXSW shows I ever saw was a last-minute gig Willie Nelson put on at the Austin Music Hall in 1995, with a truly old-school band of western swingers – fiddler Johnny Gimble had been one of Bob Wills' Texas Playboys. Word, apparently, didn't make it to the lobby bar at the Four Seasons; Nelson played for a full sweet hour to only 200 people. But we were so close to living history that we could literally almost touch it.

Another quirk: I don't spend much time with the band schedule before I get into town. I prefer mixing instinct and accident, often right on the street. I get it a lot, between shows: "Where are you going next?" (A couple of times it's actually been, "Can we follow you?") My usual answer: "I don't know – yet." Like on opening night, 2009. Stuck with an empty hour, nothing specific or potential checked off, I walked into a club on the far end of the Sixth Street strip. Capsula, a trio from Bilbao, Spain, were inside, making a fantastic mayhem I later called "a high-velocity union of the Cramps and the Who, coated in corroded glam." There was a lot more dynamite over the rest of that festival – Metallica at Stubb's; the last date on the first-ever U.S. tour by early-'70s Japanese-metal gods Flower Travellin' Band – but no greater surprise.

SXSW, at 25, is not the festival that seduced me in 1991, that night with Butch Hancock and Jimmie Dale Gilmore. It is much bigger – unfortunately so, some say – in a business of volatile expectations. But some things have never changed. In her 1993 keynote address, Texas governor Ann Richards proudly claimed that music in her state "has become much more than the chicken wire stretched between the band and the patrons." But, I noted in *Rolling Stone*, "the scene still operates according to three essential commandments: Respect the elders; embrace the new; encourage the impractical and improbable, without bias." (The New York DJ Vin Scelsa, a veteran paragon of free-form broadcasting, uses that list at the introduction to his long-running show, "Idiot's Delight." I am deeply flattered.)

The great British singer-songwriter and psychedelic wit Robyn Hitchcock had his own spin on the action, at the 2005 SXSW. "A lot of rock 'n' roll musicians are dead," he noted, during his set on the first night. "But there are still a lot them around. You should see them all this weekend." I tried. I still do. ■ **David Fricke,** *Rolling Stone*

Kris Kristofferson at the Continental Club (2004)

The Yardbirds with Slash at the Austin Music Hall (2003)

Cake at the Austin Music Hall (2004)

< Willie Nelson at the Austin Music Hall (2003)

Daniel Lanois at the keynote (2003)

Little Richard at Austin Music Hall (2004) >

Flight of the Conchords at Red Eyed Fly (2006)

continued from page 188

Slumber Party
Slush
Sluts For Hire
Sluts Of Trust
Slykat
Smackmelon
Smackola
Small Ball Paul
Small Black
Small Factory
Small Sins
Smalltown DJs
Smallwhitelight
Smart
Smash Gordon
Smil N Wessun
Smiles Davis
Smith & Scheidel
Smith Westerns
Smitty
Smoke
Smoke
Smoke Fairies
Smoke or Fire
Smokekiller
Smokey Angle Shades
Smokey Logg
Smokey Logg & the Flamethrowers
Smokey Robinson
Smokey Wilson
Smoking Popes
Smoosh
Smut Peddlers
Snake & Jet's Amazing Bullit Band
SnakeFarm
Snapline
Snatches of Pink
Sneakster
Sniffy
Sniffy 2
Snooky Pryor
Snout
Snow Patrol
Snowbyrd
Snowden
Snowglobe
Snowmen
Snuff Johnson
Snuff Johnson & Amie Deaver
So Cow
So Many Dynamos
So Percussion
So So Human
So So Modern
So Wat
So What
Soak
Socalled
Social Code
Socialistik
SocioPath Left
Sock Puppet
Sockeye
Socratic
Soda
Sodastream
Sodopp
Sofia Talvik
Soft
Soft Boys
Soft Circle
Softy
Soiled Mattress & The Springs
Soko
Sol Okarina
Solace
Solace (KY)
Solange
Solange and the Hadley Street Dreams
Solar Coaster
Solaram
Sole
Sole & The Skyrider Band
Solea
Solex
SOLI Chamber Ensemble
Solid Gold
Solid Gold 40
Solid Senders
Solillaquists of Sound
Some Action
Some By Sea
Some Girls
Some Kind of Cream
Someday I
Someone Still Loves You Boris Yeltsin
Something Fierce
Something for Kate
Something For Rockets
Something Happens
Something With Numbers
Somi
Son Lux
Son Of Dave
Son of Light
Son Volt
Son Y No Son
Son Yuma
Son, Ambulance
Sondre Lerche
Song Dogs
Song Island Revue
SonGodSuns aka 2Mex
Songs For Eleanor
Songs for Moms
Songs: Ohia
Songwriters In The Round
Songwriters in the Round (with special guests)
Sonia Freeman
Sonic Youth
SonicBlonde
Sonidero Nacional
Sóniko
Sonna
Sonny & The Sunsets
Sonny Burgess
Sonny Landreth
Sonodaband
Sonpub
Sons & Daughters
Sons of Albion
Sons of Dada
Sons of Hercules
Sons of the Desert
Sons of William
Sonya Kitchell
sorry-ok-yes
Sort Sol
Sorta
Soul Asylum
Soul Coughing
Soul Food Café
Soul Free
Soul Hitch
Soul Merchants
Soul Position
Soul Position (Blueprint & RJD2)
Soul Rebels
Soul Savivas
Soulcracker
Souled American
Soulhat
Soulico
Soulive
Soul-Junk
Soulsberry
Sound & Fury
Sound Of Stereo
Sound Team
Sounds Under Radio
Soundscape
Sourball
Sourhand
sourvein
South
South Austin Jug Band
South by Southwest
South Filthy
South Park Coalition
South Park Mexican
South San Gabriel
SouthBound
Southeast Engine
Southern Bitch
Southern Culture on the Skids
Southern Intellect
Southside
Soviet
Soviet Space
Soweto Kinch
Space City Gamelan
Space Cowboys
Space Team Electra
Space Twins
Spacehog
SpaceTruck
Spanic Boys
Spank Rock
SparechangeOO
Spark Dawg
Sparkle Motion
Sparklehorse
Sparks The Rescue
Sparkwood
Sparky Lightbourne
Sparrow
Sparta
Sparta Locals
Sparticle
Speak
Speaker Bite Me
Spear of the Nation
Special DJ set by Fischerspooner
SpecialThanks
Spectator Pump
Speech
Speed Queens
Speed Twin
Speedbuggy
Speedbuggy USA
Speedealer
Speedloader
Speedwolf
Speedy West, Jr. Band
Speer
Spektrum
Spells
Spencer Bohren
Spettro
Spider and the Webs
Spider Monkey
Spigga
Spike Blake
Spike Gillespie
Spike Priggen
Spindle (OH)
Spindrift
Spinning Chain
Spinning Grin
Spinout
Spiral Beach
Spiraling
Spirit Animal Sound System
Spirit Creek
Spirit of the West
Spirits & Trains
Spitalfield
SPiTZZ
SPL
Spleen United
Splinter
Splinter & the Straight Shooters
Split Image
Split Lip Rayfield
Spod
Spoke
Sponge
Spookey Ruben
Spoon
Spoozys
Spot
Spot Barnet & The Twentieth Century Orchestra
Spot Barnett
Spot Barnett with O.S. Grant
Spottiswoode & His Enemies
Sprawl
Spree
Sprengjuhollin
Spring Heel Jack
Spring Tigers
Spy vs Spy
Spylab
Spymob
Squad Five-O
Squat Thrust
Squatweiler
Squid Vicious
Squiky
Squincy Jones
Squirrel Nut Zippers
Squirtgun
SSM
S-S-S-Spectres
ST 37
ST 37 Orchestra (playing to Fritz Lang's "Metropolis")
St. Deluxe
St. Thomas
St. Cecilia
St. Vincent
Stabba
Stacey Earle
Staci Russell
Stacy Wilde
StaceyAnn Chin
Staehely's Comet
Stained Glass Man
Stainless Steel
Stainless Steele
Stairwell
Stalkers
Stampede
Stan Martin
Stan Ridgway
Stand
Standard Fare
Standing Wave Phenomenon
Standing Waves
Standstill
Stanford Prison Experiment
Stanley Jordan
Stanton Meadowdale
Star & Micey feat Jody Stephens
Star Eyes
Star Fucking Hipsters
Stara Zagora
Starbilly
Stardeath And White Dwarfs
StarFish
Starflyer 59
Starfucker
Stargazer Lily
Stargunn
Starhustler
Stark Raving Chandler
Starks & Nacey
Starky
Starlight Mints
Starling
Starlite Desperation
Stars
Stars As Eyes
Stars Go Dim
Stars Like Fleas
Stars of the City
Stars of Track and Field
Starsailor
Starsailor (James Walsh Solo)
State of Mind
Statistics
Status Joe
Stavesacre
Stavin' Chain
Stax 50 Revue
Steadman
Steady Freddie's Wild Country
Stealin' Horses
Steaming Wolf Penis
Steamroller
Steed Lord
Steel Panther
Steel Power
Steel Shank
Steel Train
Steep Canyon Rangers
Stefan George
Stefani
Stella
Stella By Starlight
Stella Marie
stellastarr*
Steph Pockets
Stephane Wrembel with David Grisman
Stephanie Dosen
Stephanie McKay
Stephanie Nilles
Stephen Allen Davis
Stephen Brodsky
Stephen Bruton
Stephen Clair
Stephen Doster
Stephen Doster & the Libertines
Stephen Doster & the Sore Losers
Stephen Fretwell
Stephen Jerzak
Stephen Kellogg & The Sixers
Stephen Malkmus
Stephen Malkmus & The Jicks
Stephen Spyrit
Stephen Yerkey
Stereo Pony
Stereo Skyline
StereoHeroes
Stereophonics
Stereotyperider
Sterling Morrison Tribute with John Cale, Alejandro Escovedo and Tosca
Sterling Moss
Steso Songs
Steve Allen
Steve Aoki
Steve Austin
Steve Bernal
Steve Burns (& the Struggle)
Steve Carter
Steve Christopher
Steve Collander
Steve Collier & John Clayton
Steve Conn and Free Advice
Steve Dawson
Steve E Nix & the Cute Lepers
Steve Earle
Steve Forbert
Steve Goldberg & the Arch Enemies
Steve Hudson
Steve J. Dawson
Steve James
Steve James & the Dashboard Saints
Steve Kolander
Steve Loria
Steve McDonald Group
Steve Nagel
Steve Parkess
Steve Parkess & the Sax Maniacs
Steve Poltz
Steve Pryor
Steve Reich
Steve Riley & the Mamou Playboys
Steve Smith
Steve Turner
Steve Weichert
Steve Wynn
Steve Wynn & the Miracle 3
Steve Young
Steven Camden
Steven Fromholz
Steven Moakler
Steven Wray Lobdell
Stevie Tombstone
Stew
Stewart Walker
Stick People
Stickpony
Stickygreen Productions
Stiffed
Stiffs, Inc
Still Flyin'
Still Going
Still Life Still
Still Remains
Still Stanley
StillLife Projector
Stinkbug
Stinking Lizaveta
Stinky del Negro
Stir
Stitch
Sto Zvírat
Stoic Frame
Stoll Vaughan
Stone River Boys
Stone Temple Pilots
Stonekracker
Stones Throw
Stoney
Stop the Truck!
Storm Inc.
Storm Orphans
Storsveit Nix Noltes
Story of The Year
Storyhill
Storyville
Storyville
Stout
Stove Bredsky
Strabismus
Straight Lines
Strait Laces
Stranded at the Drive-In
Strange Boutique
Strange Fruit Project
Strange Parade
Stranglmartin
Stratocruiser
Stratotanker
Stratus
Straylight Run
Street Dogs
Street Drum Corps
Street Sweeper Social Club
Street To Nowhere
Stressface
Stretford
Strike Twice
Stricken City
Stride
Strikeforce Diablo
Strobe Talbot
Stroller
Strong Arm Steady
Stuck Mojo
Studemont Project
Student Rick
Stuka
Stump the Host
Stumptone
Stunta
Stuntman
Stupid Party
Stylofone
Suave Octopus
Sub Oslo
Sub Swara
SubArachnoid Space
subject:defect
Sublime
Subminute:Radio
Subotnik
Sunbrain
Subrosa Union
Subset
Subsonics
Substance
Subtitle
Suburban Terror Project
Subway To Sally
Suckers
Sue Foley
Sue Medley
Suffrajett
Sufjan Stevens
Sugar & Gold
Sugar La-Las
Sugar Plant
Sugar Shack
Sugarbomb
Sugarcult
Sugarsmack
Suicide Kings
SuicideGirls Burlesque Act
SuidAkrA
Suishou no Fune
Suite Jayne
Sukia
Sukpatch
Suli McCullough
Sum 41
Sumack
Summer Cats
Summer Hymns
Summerbirds in the Cellar
Summercamp
Sun 60
Sun Araw
Sun Studio Revue
Sun Vocina
Sunburned Hand Of The Man
Suncatcher
Sunday Driver
Sundowner
Sunflower
Sunflowers
Sunglass
SunnO)))
Sunnshine
Sunny Sweeney
Sunrise Hammers
Suns Owl
Sunset Valley
Sunshine Club
Suntan
Sunwrae
Supa DJ Dimitri
Supafuzz
Supagroup
Super Chron Flight Brothers
Super Creep
Super Dream Pill
Super Girls
Super Human Strength
Super Pal Universe
Super Sonic Festival Projectionists
Super Soul Shakedown DJs
Super XX Man
Super XX Man & Metronome
Supercar
Superchunk
Superdrag
Superego
Supergrass
Superheroes
Superlasciva
Superlitio
Supermodel
Supernatural
Supernatural Family Band
Supernova
Supersonic
Superstar DJs
Superstar Djs
Superstar Djs feat. DJ Spinner T
Superstar Djs featuring DJ Crop Diggie
Supersuckers
Supersystem
Superzero
suplecs
Supreme Court
Surf City
Surfer Blood
Surferosa
Surgery
Surina & the Daves
Surreall
Surrender Dorothy
Surrogat
Surrounded
Susan Alcorn
Susan B. Anthony Somers-Willet
Susan Cagle
Susan Colton
Susan Cowsill
Susan Cowsill and the Midcity Ministers
Susan Enan
Susan Gibson
Susan Gibson and The Moving Parts
Susan Hickman
Susan James
Susan Lindfors
Susan Marshall
Susan Otten
Susan Tedeschi
Susan Toney
Susan Voelz
Susan Werner
Susanna Hoffs & Matthew Sweet
Susanna Sharpe & Samba Police
Susanna Van Tassel
Susie Suh
Suspense Rubberband
Sussie 4
Sutro
Suzanna Choffel
Suzanna Choffel, Ruthie Foster and Carolyn Wonderland
Suzanne Vega
Suzi Stern
Suzi Stern Quintet
Suzi Stern-Luna
Suzy Elkins Band
Svelt
Svengali
Swag
Swamp Boogie Queen
Swamp Dogg
Swamp Dogg and McLemore Avenue
Swamp Zombies
Swampass
Swampmeat
Swan Island
SWARM of ANGELS
Swati
Sway
Sway Machinery
Swearing at Motorists
Sweaty Nipples
Sweep the Leg Johnny
Sweeper and Keeper
Sweet Apple
Sweet Jones
Sweet Revenge
Sweet Trip
Sweet Water
Swell
Swift Haywire
Swimming With Dolphins
Swine King
Swing Set
Swing Team
Swinging Steaks
Swirlies
Swisha House

The Ting Tings (2008)

Swisha House featuring Paul Wall, Archie Lee & Coota Bang
Switchblade Kittens
Switches
SWITCHhITTER
Swizzle Sticks
Swollen Members
Swoon 23
Swords Project
Sxip
Sxip Shirey
SXSW Poetry Slam
SXSW Poetry Slam hosted by Mike Henry
Sybris
Syd Matters
Syd Straw
Sydnee
Sydney Wayser
Syl Johnson
Sylk Smoov
Sylvia Juncosa
Sylvia Patricia
Sylvie
Sylvie Lewis
Symbiosis
SYME
SYRUP
Syrup USA
System Of A Down
Systema Solar

T

T Bird and The Breaks
T Cash
T. C. Kross
T. Tex Edwards
T.D. Bell, Erbie Bowser & the Blues Specialists
T.D. Lind
T.M. Harding
T.R.
T.Solo
Ta Mére
Tab Benoit
TAB the band
Tabi Bonney
Tablet
Tabula Rasa
Tacks, the Boy Disaster
Tahir
Tahiti 80
Tahiti Boy and the Palmtree Family
Tai Burnette
Tail Gators
Takadja
Takashi Kamide
Taking Back Sunday
Takka Takka
Tal Bachman
Tal Ross
Talib Kweli
Talk Is Cheap
Talk Normal
Talk To Angels
Talkdemonic
Tall Dark and Lonesome
Tall Firs
Tall Hands
Tally Hall
Tamaryn
Tamasha Africana
Tammany Hall Machine
Tammy Faye Starlite
Tammy Gomez con la Palabra
Tammy Lynn
Tammy Rogers
Tandy
Tanger
Tangiers
Tangletown
Tanlines
Tanner
Tanworth-in-Arden
Tanya Morgan
Tanya Tagaq
Tanz Waffen
Tao Ravoao & Vincent Bucher
Tape Deck Mountain
Tapes 'N Tapes
Tara Angell
Tara Holt
Tara Jane O'Neil
Tara Key & Antietam
Tara M.A. Sheth
Tara MacLean
TarantisT
Tarantula
Tarantula A D
Tarbox Ramblers
Tartufi
Tarwater
TAT
Tats
Tavana
Tawnya LoRae
Taxi Chain
Taylor Hawkins & The Coattail Riders
Taylor Hollingsworth
Taylor Mali
Taylor McFerrin
T-Balla
Te Vaka
Tea Leaf Green
Teakayo Mission
Team Facelift
Team Robespierre
TeamUSA
Tearaways
Tech N9ne
Techno-Squid Eats Parliament
Tech-Sun
Ted Leo
Ted Leo/Pharmacists
Ted Roddy & the Talltops
Ted Roddy's Tearjoint Troubadors
Tedashii
Teddy and the Talltops
Teddy Morgan
Teddy Morgan & the Sevilles
Teddy Thompson
Tee Double
Teen Angels
Teen Cool
Teenage Bottlerocket
Teeth Mountain
Teeth of the Hydra
Tegan & Sara
Teisco Del Rey
Teitur
Tek 3
Telefon Tel Aviv
Telegraph Canyon
Telekinesis
Telepathe
Telephone Jim Jesus
Telephoned
Telerama
Television Ghost
Temper Temper
Templo Diez
Temposhark
Temptress
Ten Bears
Ten Grand
Ten Hands
Ten Out of Tenn
Ten Percenter
Ten Speed
Ten Ton Swing
Tenacious D
Tenderloin
Tendril
Tenebrous
Tengoku Jack
Tera Melos
Ter'ell Shahid
Terence Blanchard Quartet
Terminal
Terminal 46
Terminal Mind
Terp 2 It
Terra Naomi
Terrance Simien
Terrance Simien & Mallet Playboys
Terrell
Terrell
Terri Binion
Terri Clark
Terri Hendrix
Terri Hendrix with Ray Wylie Hubbard
Terri Hendrix with Lloyd Maines
Terri Lord
Terrible Twos
Terribly Empty Pockets
Terror at 10,000 Ft.
Terror Couple
Terror Pigeon Dance Revolt!
Terry Allen
Terry Anderson
Terry Bowness
Terry Bozzio
Terry Clarke
Terry Garland
Terry Lee Hale
Terry Poison
Terry Radigan
Terry Reid
Tesch
Tess McKenna
Tetuzi Akiyama
Tex Thomas & the Danglin' Wranglers
Texacala Jones & the TJ Hookers
Texana Dames
Texas Belairs w/Ponty Bone and John X Reed
Texas Burlesque Fest Revue
Texas Crude
Texas Eastside Kings
Texas Johnny Brown and the Quality Blues Band
Texas Northside Kings
Texas Redemptors
Texas Sheiks w/ Geoff Muldaur, Jim Kweskin, Bruce Hughes, Cindy Cashdollar, Floyd Domino, and Suzy Thompson, John Nicholas, John Chipman
Texas Terri and the Stiff Ones

continued on page 218

SXSW SPOTLIGHT

Billy Gibbons Saves The Day

By Scott Wilcox

was having an extremely bad day during SXSW 2008. This was the first year we decided to sell music festival wristbands online and have people pick them up at the Convention Center once SXSW Music had started. Part of the system was to track every wristband that was given out to make sure that each was was accounted for, and it was not working very well.

It had been a very difficult show for me so far. We had lost one of our key staff, a person responsible for the technical equipment. We were constantly sending this or that person to this or that store trying to locate all the switches, cables, dongles and webcams that we needed to build out every lounge, every listening station, every odd installation, usually discovering we were lacking them only hours or minutes before they were needed.

Simultaneously, we were still running our own email server for the staff email addresses, and it was getting spam-bombed by servers from China, making it unusable and compromising our staff communications, while the sys-admin worked to keep email up and running. And the Filemaker server which ran our on-site registration had crashed because someone had kicked a switch, creating a spike that corrupted a key database. Registrants stood in line for over an hour without moving, and everyone was really really angry.

So, when the person responsible for making sure all the wristbands added up passed me in the hallway at 9pm and recounted an angry conversation between herself and one of my staff, it was the last thing I wanted to hear. I walked the six blocks back to the Radisson, where I was staying, with the day's events churning in my brain. I felt terrible.

I tried to get some sleep, but my brain would not shut up. Midnight turned to 2am and then to 4. My head was pounding and I felt very ill. It was 6am and I had not slept a wink although I was exhausted. I started to dry-heave. This felt like my darkest hour in my history of working for SXSW.

Finally at 6am I called my wife, just to hear her voice. She answered sleepily and asked, "What's wrong?" I burst into tears and told her I wanted to quit. She gave me the most amazing pep talk of my life and a simple plan for getting through the day: "Keep your head down. Don't talk to anyone you don't need to. If it is not a technical issue, then it is not your problem. It will be all right."

I ordered some room service and somehow managed to get showered and dressed, and walked back to the Convention Center. First thing, I had a staff meeting and gave them a pep talk with similar advice. After checking in on our Tech Room, I was able to delegate some of my responsibilities so that I could go back to the Radisson and try to sleep for an hour or two.

After trying for 45 minutes, I discovered I could not sleep and decided to go try to eat something again at the restaurant downstairs in the lobby. Blissfully, there was no one at the bar, so I could hide. After eating some pasta and drinking a dozen glasses of water, my pounding headache started to abate, although I was still feeling mentally frayed.

Then Billy Gibbons walked in and sat at the bar along with another guy I did not recognize. They ordered some drinks and were joking and laughing. When the bartender asked Gibbons how he was paying for his drinks, he joked about me paying for them. I told her I would. I was buying Billy Gibbons from ZZ Top a drink! Then, Billy Bob Thornton and a few other people walked in and joined at the bar.

About this time, I decided now was a pretty good time to close out my tab and head back to the Convention Center. I went over and introduced myself to Thornton, Gibbons and company. After shaking hands and talking for a bit, Billy Bob and company told Gibbons that they were going to head outside to the patio. To my astonishment, Gibbons said he was going to hang at the bar with me for a while.

So, we sat there for a good 45 minutes talking about life and politics and everything, as he imparted his deliberate brand of Gibbons wisdom. Every 10 minutes or so his phone would ring and alternately he would either answer with a deep and firm "Gibbons here" or with a voice of a frail old lady saying "He's not here right now, I am his housekeeper." He explained that he constantly got spam calls from India and that this helped.

I told him about my sleeping problem and he confessed he had the same issue too. He said to try listening to the old-time radio shows like Roy Rogers westerns or detective mysteries.

After what seemed like hours, my wife called and asked me how and where I was. I told her that I was hanging out with Billy Gibbons. For a minute, I think she may have thought I was losing my mind. After I mentioned that she could come over, I returned to the bar.

Once Rachael was there, we talked for another 10 or 15 minutes. She asked to see his skull ring. He took it off and handed it to her saying that he had carved it himself out of wax and then had it cast. She was impressed. He told her that I was bright, and in a slow , deliberate, deep, quiet voice, he said, "Put babies on the ground."

We all walked outside so that Rachael could also meet Billy Bob Thornton. We took pictures. I felt so proud that I could introduce her to my new friends. An hour after my adventure with Billy Gibbons had started, I found myself talking and laughing alone with Rachael. I was energized for the first time in days. As I tried to compile the many minutes of deep wisdom imparted to me by a true Texas legend, I walked back to the Convention Center, ready to tackle the next five days of SXSW 2008. ■ **Scott Wilcox is SXSW's director of technology.**

Lou Reed at the keynote (2008)

2007 – 2010

Come Together: Music, Film, And Interactive As One

By Andy Smith

ooking back, South by Southwest's 20th anniversary in 2006 seems to belong to a different era. The Music, Film and Interactive conferences, though united under the SXSW banner, were still generally regarded as separate entities, with far less crossover than in the years to come. Changes in technology that would help trigger more convergence among the three spheres were on the immediate horizon but had not fully arrived.

Musically, the four major labels still accounted for more than 80% of all U.S. music sales, though the labels were scrambling to try to figure out how to prevent CD copying and downloading by implementing such features as the dreaded Digital Rights Management (DRM) technology. While artists such as Arctic Monkeys, TV On The Radio, Gnarls Barkley and My Chemical Romance wowed both critics and audiences, annual American sales figures indicated that the general music-buying public was more interested in the likes of *American Idol*, Rascal Flatts and the *High School Musical* soundtrack. At least Justin Timberlake had taken on the noble cause of bringing "Sexy Back."

In film, *Pirates Of The Caribbean: Dead Man's Chest* was the top grossing film of the year, while *The Departed*, *Babel* and *The Last King Of Scotland* made noise on the awards circuit. On the home-viewing front, video-on-demand was still in its infancy, and the first Blu-ray Disc titles were introduced in the summer of 2006.

In the tech world, MySpace was the dominant force in social network sites, though a new site called Facebook was released to the general public in late September. Meanwhile, the heads of Odeo, a San Francisco-based podcasting company, had unveiled a new "micro-blogging" service called Twitter earlier in the summer to little attention. Google purchased YouTube in October, validating the huge growth in user-generated video, and Apple dropped rumors of a new touch-screen mobile phone that would enable pictures and video, leading to Steve Jobs' iPhone announcement at the MacWorld conference in January 2007.

Back at SXSW, the company announced that it was becoming carbon neutral. Though SXSW had undertaken "green" initiatives for years, the new carbon neutral program included offsetting 100% of the carbon emissions arising from SXSW business activities by purchasing Texas wind energy carbon credits. In addition, SXSW made a $5,000 donation to the Austin Parks and Recreation Department for the purchase and maintenance of native trees, set up recycling programs for all waste

generated by outdoor parties and events, and used biodiesel for generators and production vehicles during the conferences.

"Bottom line, our challenge — as a business or as an individual — is to remain ever mindful of our actions and their consequences, and to recognize that doing something, though small, is better than doing nothing," said Eve McArthur, SXSW director of operations, who helped lead sustainability efforts.

SXSW 2007 brought another legendary figure as music keynote. "Following the shock and awe of having Neil Young as keynote," remembers Roland Swenson, "I was back on the floor with my socks knocked off when Andy Flynn confirmed another major figure from my personal pantheon of heroes, Pete Townshend." The legendary rocker's appearance followed the October 2006 release of *Endless Wire*, the first Who record in 24 years. Townshend also was in the midst of a performance project with collaborator Rachel Fuller called Attic Jam, which brought together a number of well-known singer-songwriters for gigs on both sides of the Atlantic.

"Following his keynote, he was very friendly and totally down to earth as he chatted with me and my wife Roseana and posed for photos with us," recalls Swenson. "The next morning I was standing in line for coffee at the Hilton with a dozen other people, when I noticed Townshend by himself, fetching his own coffee, carrying a shoulder bag and newspaper like any other SXSW delegate. I thought, 'This may be taking down to earth too far.' But nobody was bothering him, and it was like that for the rest of the week, as Townshend was everywhere, seeing shows, hopping up onstage with various bands and generally making the most of SXSW. He must have liked Austin, because when he was due to check out of his hotel, he stayed a couple of extra days before rejoining The Who tour in Mexico City."

Elsewhere, SXSW Music was rife with discussion of the music industry downturn, even as the conference hosted more music registrants and artists than ever before. "Although the industry is being increasingly decentralized by technology, person-to-person contact is still king, and one of the best places to get it is at SXSW," stated a report in the *Pittsburgh City Paper*. The showcase roster was as broad and diverse as ever, highlighted by numerous noteworthy acts. Lily Allen was the big opening-night buzz artist, even if she never ascended to the heights her packed showcase at Stubb's seemed to promise. Another London-based, hype-riding female singer named Amy Winehouse made fewer waves at the conference, though she achieved a higher degree of fame afterward, for better or worse.

SXSW Film saw the "mumblecore" films of Joel Swanberg, Andrew Bujalski and the Duplass brothers that the festival had championed begin to be recognized as an innovative new indie film genre. Meanwhile, a fairly unassuming big studio comedy called *Knocked Up* world-premiered at the festival before going on to become a surprise summer hit nationwide.

SXSW Interactive 2007 would come to be known as the year of Twitter. After its soft launch the previous summer, the Twitter team brought attention to its unheralded service in Austin by installing large video screens in the Austin Convention Center hallways where registrants could view live Twitter feeds. Over the course of the conference, the service spread like wildfire as people discovered the ease and intrigue of its 140-character-max posts; the company claimed that its traffic tripled during the event. Twitter's momentum only grew, and other entrepreneurs realized that SXSW was the perfect event for social media.

The following year brought yet another rock legend as music keynote. Lou Reed traveled to Austin to support the release of the Julian Schnabel-directed concert film, *Lou Reed's Berlin*. Interviewed by noted producer Hal Willner, Reed bemoaned the sound quality of the MP3: "It's like if no one knows any better or doesn't care, it's gonna stay on a really, really low level and people who like good sound are gonna be thought of as some kind of strange zoo animal."

More than 1,800 artists performed at SXSW 2008, including R.E.M., a band that had served in the 1980s as a standard-bearer for the kind of regional indie acts that SXSW championed in its early years. Also notable in '08 was an increased presence of international artists, including performers from Brazil, Iran, Malta and Slovenia, as well as packed showcases featuring Mexican acts. "Mexico is our closest neighbor and a principal cultural influence in Texas, so it makes sense in countless ways to reach out to them," explained Brent Grulke, SXSW creative director. "Mexico has been represented at SXSW for over a decade now. Once the Mexicans started attending in large numbers and having success, it became easier to convince the rest of Latin America to see the utility of being at SXSW."

Meanwhile, the British government trade export agency UK Trade & Investment, which had been promoting U.K. acts at SXSW for several years, unveiled the British Embassy at Latitude 30, a dedicated venue where U.K. artists played both day parties and nighttime showcases. This idea would be copied during the next couple of years by Canada and Australia. "SXSW has provided a tremendous platform for UK Trade & Investment and the British Music partnership to help highlight the exciting new talent that U.K. music has produced over the years," said Phil Patterson, UKTI's Sector Specialist for Music.

SXSW Film also featured a number of high-profile speakers, including Billy Bob Thornton, Helen Hunt, and Moby, who was in the midst of offering free music for filmmakers. The festival continued its burgeoning reputation as an outlet for comedies with such films as *Run Fatboy Run, Forgetting Sarah Marshall* and *Harold And Kumar Escape From Guantanamo Bay*. One documentary that gained notice was *Body Of War*, a film about paraplegic Iraq War veteran Tomas Young. A release party at Stubb's featured musical performances by Tom Morello, Serj Tankian of System Of A Down, Ben Harper, Billy Bragg and Kimya Dawson, with Young in attendance.

The interactive festival was remembered for the keynote interview with Facebook founder Mark Zuckerberg, or more specifically how the audience reacted to it. Dissatisfied with the way the interview was conducted, a number of attendees used mobile social media such as Twitter to post instant feedback, which could be seen by others in the room. The result demonstrated how social media enabled the crowd to alter events as they happened, by putting the communication means in the hands of all users.

The idea of user-generated content was instrumental in SXSW Interactive's launch of the PanelPicker in the months prior to SXSW 2007, though this feature really began to show its popularity and influence the following year as users determined the programming for 2008. By giving registrants the means to propose and then vote for which panels should be presented, Interactive looked to the crowd to determine its programming. This feature became so popular that it was extended to the other two conferences.

During the summer of 2008, SXSW Film underwent a big change as festival producer Matt Dentler left for a job in New York City and was replaced by indie film stalwart Janet Pierson. Having had a hand in the making of such landmark films as *She's Gotta Have It, Roger And Me, Slacker* and *Clerks*, as well as creating the show *Split Screen* for the Independent Film Channel, Pierson brought a wealth of experience and a reputation as a champion of independent cinema.

After a long pursuit, SXSW Music was able to procure the iconic Quincy Jones as keynote for 2009. With some six decades of memories to reflect on, Jones kept the audience transfixed for two-plus hours with stories of artists ranging from Dizzy Gillespie to Michael Jackson.

At the conference in general, there seemed to be an increased emphasis on ways musicians could look for career paths outside of the old recording contract model, including film and TV licensing and product branding. "Labels have experienced a steady erosion of their incomes over the past eight years, and consequently, they have ceased playing the traditional role of art patron for up-and-coming musical

artists," explained SonicBids CEO Panos Panay in 2009. "In their place have stepped in major (and niche) consumer brands who have figured out that music can help them sell whatever product they produce."

As for the nearly 2,000 showcasing artists, the buzz bands of the day were in full force, including the Decemberists, Black Lips and Those Darlins, while a slate of acts from Colombia showed attendees why that country is viewed as a key hotbed of Latin American music. The highest-profile show featured Metallica, who performed at Stubb's as the "surprise guest" on the *Guitar Hero Metallica* show. Who knows how long it had been since the band had played a venue with a capacity of fewer than 2,000, but the fans who packed the club got to see one of those "only at SXSW" events.

The film festival opened with *I Love You, Man*, a buddy comedy with Paul Rudd, Jason Segel and Rashida Jones (daughter of Quincy). The conference attracted a number of film luminaries, including directors Henry Selick, Sam Raimi and Todd Haynes, as well as Jan Harlan, who was Stanley Kubrick's longtime producer. Still, the biggest noise echoed nearly a year later, when Kathryn Bigelow's Iraq War drama, *The Hurt Locker*, which had its American premiere at SXSW 2009, won the Academy Award for Best Picture in March 2010.

SXSW Interactive presented keynote speakers with innovative ideas, including Zappos CEO Tony Hsieh, who shared his belief that customer satisfaction is the best form of marketing, and Chris Anderson, editor-in-chief of *Wired*. Anderson, author of *The Long Tail*, came to SXSW in advance of his book *Free: The Future Of A Radical Price*, which discussed how businesses could build customer loyalty and subsequent earnings by giving products away. A new addition to Interactive was SXSW Accelerator, a competition in which entrepreneurs presented their ideas to a panel of venture capitalists in hope of securing funding.

As 2010 arrived and the SXSW Interactive registration numbers eclipsed the SXSW Music numbers for the first time, it became clear that Interactive had become a phenomenon. There had been a noticeable increase in the number of people at its various panels and evening events over the past few years, but in 2010, registrants packed the Austin Convention Center for all nine days of the Interactive, Film and Music conferences. Panels and speaker sessions that once had been held in smaller meeting rooms moved to the large ballrooms.

"To put the growth into context, imagine a city the size of Austin exploding to the size of Mexico City, or becoming as dense as Manila, in the course of a mere 12 years," said design strategist Molly Wright Steenson, who had been attending SXSW Interactive since 1998. "That makes sense, though: The web is no longer a funky little town; it is a megalopolis. Accordingly, everyone who is working with or a fan of the web, mobile or social media makes a pilgrimage to Austin."

The Film Festival continued to earn accolades and prestige, offering a mix of major studio movies such as *Kick-Ass* along with critically acclaimed films including *Winter's Bone* and *Marwencol*. Pierson pointed to the audiences of film lovers at SXSW as a key drawing point for filmmakers, something not always present at Sundance or Cannes. The festival also hosted a number of film stars during the course of the week, including the irrepressible Bill Murray, who delighted patrons and staff at Shangri-La by climbing behind the bar and serving drinks.

SXSW Music hosted Motown luminary Smokey Robinson as its keynote speaker. Interviewed by lifelong fan and fellow Detroit native Dave Marsh, Robinson told stories about his hometown, working with Motown founder Berry Gordy, his new role running his own label, and his love of classical music: "This music is 300 years old, 400 years old, and we're still listening to it!...I want to be Mozart. I want to be Beethoven."

Robinson also performed to a packed crowd at the Austin Music Hall, where his warmth and charm were on full display. "Smokey was incredibly kind and gracious, complete with an equally friendly crew, band and dancers who were quick to make friends with everyone involved in the showcase," remembers Stacey Wilhelm, SXSW Music Festival booker.

The week was colored by tragedy and loss when Alex Chilton, who had been scheduled to appear on a Big Star panel and to perform with his old band, died suddenly at his home in New Orleans just prior to leaving for Austin. Quickly, the panel became a tribute as original Big Star members Jody Stephens and Andy Hummel shared stories about their bandmate. The scheduled concert at Antone's on Saturday turned into a poignant all-star tribute event as artists from John Doe to M. Ward to Chris Stamey joined the rest of Big Star to salute Chilton.

By the time SXSW Music ended, the festival had hosted nearly 2,000 artists on 89 stages. SXSW Film had screened more than 270 films, and SXSW Interactive had hosted 300-plus panels and sessions. Combined, the three conferences contributed an estimated $113 million to the local Austin economy.

As SXSW reaches its 25th anniversary in 2011, it has been firmly established as a force in Austin's local economy and civic identity, as well as an internationally lauded showplace for innovation and discovery. The music industry that SXSW once relied upon has changed dramatically, especially in the past decade. Revenues from CD sales decreased by more than 50% between 1999 and 2009 (according to Forrester Research), and the dominance of major labels as incubators of new artists has waned accordingly. However, performing rights organizations such as BMI and ASCAP are reporting record royalty revenue, while smaller independent labels and booking agents are more visible and arguably more influential than ever before. And the collision of the digital realm with the music business is on annual display at SXSW.

"Until the industry comes to terms with the ISPs, and finds a way to share in the revenue from all the music being downloaded for free, the recording industry will continue to shrink," says Swenson. "Other parts of the music business will adapt and even prosper, but it's all on shifting sand until that piece is in place."

With digital media dominating so much of what used to be the traditional ways of doing business in music and film, the clearly defined lines between the various conferences have blurred, leading to the application of the term "creative industries" as a catch-all. SXSW has responded by introducing cross-conference events that bring together registrants from different conferences. As barriers are broken even further by new technological innovations, this trend is likely to continue. The 2011 introduction of the Exhibition For Creative Industries — an integrated interactive, film and music trade show — points to this trend.

Yet even with the big-name bands, industry executives, film luminaries and tech gurus, the attraction of SXSW is something more organic, and it speaks to what continues to draw registrants despite the sometimes great distance and expense required to attend. "In a word: community," says Swenson. "I've always thought of SXSW as a meeting of the tribes. Everyone gathers, curious to see what people are doing now. Re-connecting with old friends and colleagues. Meeting new people and sharing the SXSW experience, for good or ill. As electronic communication has made the world smaller, and has become an ever-increasing influence on how we live, it's only heightened the need for face-to-face, real world contact."

SXSW has come a long way in 25 years, growing from 700 registrants in 1987 to more than 36,000 in 2010. The event's profile has gone from local and regional to national and global, with Austin's downtown transformed into the center of the creative universe for nine days each March. So what will the future bring?

"SXSW will continue to be a platform for creative people to promote and distribute their work to the rest of the world," Swenson says. "What new technology is going to come along that enhances how that's done is what will keep it interesting." ■

continued from page 209

Texas Tornados
Texas Trumpets
Teye & Belen
Teye & Belen: Flamencobsesionarte
Teye & Viva el Flamenco
Th' Corn Gangg
Th' Faith Healers
th' Losin Streaks
Thad Cockrell
Thad Cockrell and the Starlite Country Band
Thalia Zedek
ThaMuseMeant
Thao With The Get Down Stay Down
That 1 Guy
That Dog
That Ghost
That Petrol Emotion
Thavius Beck
The (International) Noise Conspiracy
The 101
The 144 ELiTE
The 1-4-5s
The 1900s
The 757s
The 88
The A.K.A.s
The Abe Lincoln Story
The A-Bones
The Acorn
The Action Is
The Actual Tigers
The Addictions
The Adored
The Adults
The Aeffect
The Aeroplanes
The Affair (Brooklyn)
The Affair (St Louis)
The After Party
The After School Special
The Age of Electric
The Agenda
The Aggrolites
The Agony Scene
The Aimless Never Miss
The Airborne Toxic Event
The Aislers Set
The Alarm
The Alarm Clocks
The Album Leaf
The Alice Rose
The Alien Project
The Alliance
The Allisons
The Alpha Rhythm
The Always Already
The Amazing Pilots
The Amazing Royal Crowns
The American Analog Set
The American People
The Amps
The And/Ors
The Andy Owens Project
The Angel
The Anix
The Ankles
The Anointed Voicez
The Anonymous
The Answer
The Answering Machine
The Antarcticans
The Antlers
The Anubian Lights
The Apes
The Apples in Stereo
The Appleseed Cast
The Applicators
The Aquabats!
The ARC Angels
The Ark
The Ark Band
The Arlenes
The Arm
The A-Sides
The Asteroid #4
The Asteroids Galaxy Tour
The Ataris
The Atlas Moth
The Atomic Bitchwax
The Atomic Numbers
The Attack Formation
The Audience
The Audition
The Austin Lounge Lizards
The Automatic
The Autumn Defense
The Autumns
The Avett Brothers
The Awful Truth
The Awkward Stage
The B-52's
The Backsliders
The Bad Plus
The Bad Rackets

The Polyphonic Spree (2003)

The Bad Roads
The Bad Trips
The Bad Wizard
The Badlees
The Beltek
The Bamaz
The Band of Brotherz
The Band of Heathens
The Bang Gang Deejays
The Bangers
The Banks
The Baptist Generals
The Barbers
The Barker Band
The Barkers
The Barnburners
The Basals
The Bassturd
The Bastard Sons of Johnny Cash
The Bats
The Batusis
The Bayou Pigs
The Be Good Tanyas
The Beasts Of Bourbon
The Beat Farmers
The Beat Poets
The Beatards
The Beatoes
The Beauties
The Beautiful Authentic Zoo Gods
The Beautiful Mistake
The Beautiful New Born Children
The Beauvilles
The Bees (TN)
The Believers
The Belles
The Belleville Outfit
The BellRays
The Bells
The Bells of Joy
The Belmont Playboys
The Ben Taylor Band
The Berg Sans Nipple
The Besnard Lakes
The Besties
The Beta Sweat
The Beth Lisick Ordeal
The Bewitched Hands on the Top of our Heads
The Big Bang
The Big Six
The Big Sleep
The Big Train
The Bigger Lovers
The Billy Nayer Show
The Billygoats
The Billys
The Billys
The Bingemen
The Bird and the Bee
The Bird Sisters
The Birdwatcher
The Birthday Massacre
The Biscuit Boys
The Biscuit Rollers
The Bishops
The Bitters
The Bizness
The Black
The Black & White Years
The Black Angels
The Black Atlantic
The Black Box Revelation
The Black Crowes
The Black Ghosts
The Black Girls
The Black Halos
The Black Hollies
The Black Keys
The Black Lips
The Black Maria
The Black Rabbits
The Black Swans
The Black Watch
The Blacks
The Blakes
The Blank Theory
The Blazers
The Bled
The Bleu Edmondson Band
The Blind Shake
The Blood Arm
The Blood Lines
The Bloodsugars
The Bloodthirsty Lovers
The Bloody Beetroots
The Bloody Hollies
The Bloody Tears
The Blow
The Blue Aeroplanes
The Blue Ice Band
The Blue Noise Band
The Blue Rags
The Blue Shadows
The Blue Van
The Blue Whale
The BlueBonnets
The Bluerunners
The Blues Specialists
The Blueskins
The B-Movie Rats
The Boat People
The Bob Schneider Big Band
The Bob Schneider Show
The BoDeans

The Boggs
The Bogmen
The Bo-Keys
The Bones
The Boneshakers
The Bootleg Remedy
The Borrowers
The Boss Martians
The Botswanas
The Botticellis
The Bottom Line's "In Their Own Words"
The Boxer Rebellion
The Boxing Lesson
The Boy Least Likely To
The Brakes
The Bramhalls
The Bravery
The Break And Repair Method
The Breakdowns
The Breakers
The Breakup Society
The Breathers
The Brew
The Brian Jonestown Massacre
The Bridges
The Briefs
The Bright Light Social Hour
The Brilliant Mistakes
The Brokedown
The Broken Family Band
The Broken West
The Bronx
The Brooders
The Brother Boys
The Brother Kite
The Brothers
The Brothers Bounce
The Brothers Groove
The Brothers Movement
The Brought Low
The Bruce James Soultet
The Brunettes
The Bubble Boys
The Buddy Blue Band
The Buddy System
The Budos Band
The Budz
The Buicks
The Builders and The Butchers
The Bulemics
The Burning Hotels
The Burnouts
The Business Machines
The Butchies
The Cab
The Cactus Brothers
The Cages
The Cancer Conspiracy
The Candle Thieves
The Candles
The Cannabinoids feat. Erykah Badu
The Cansecos
The Cape May
The Capes
The Capitol Years
The Capstan Shafts
The Caribbean
The Carlsonics
The Carpetbaggers
The Carrots
The Casanovas
The Cash Brothers
The Cassettes
The Casting Out
The Cataracs
The Catch
The Cate Bros.
The Catherines
The Catheters
The Caulfields
The Causey Way
The Cave Singers
The Cavedogs
The Cells
The Chairs of Perception (formerly Urinals)
The Chalets
The Chandeliers
The Changes
The Channel
The Chap
The Chapin Sisters
The Chapman Family
The Chapters
The Charlatans
The Cheek
The Cherry Valence
The Chesterfield Kings
The Chevelles
The Chicharones
The Chicharones featuring Sleep and Josh Martinez
The Children's Hour
The Chinese Stars
The Chocolate Horse
The Choir Practice
The Chris Vestre Group
The Chromatics
The Chumps
The Church
The Churchills
The Cinematics
The Circle G'z

The City Champs
The City Drive
The City Lives
The Classic Crime
The Clements Brothers
The Click Clack Boom
The Cliks
The Cloud Room
The Clowns
The Clutters
The Coal Men
The Coal Porters
The Coal Porters
The Coast
The Coathangers
The Cocker Spaniels
The Cocktail Slippers
The Coctails
The Coffee Sergeants
The Collapse
The Color Bars
The Color Scheme
The Color Turning
The Comas
The Commercials
The Common Faces
The Confusions
The Constantines
The Constellations
The Contradicks
The Contrast
The Converters
The Convocation Of...
The Cool Jerks
The Cool Kids
The Coolies
The Coolness
The Cooper Temple Clause
The Cops
The Cops (WA)
The Coral
The Cornell Hurd Band
The Coronas
The Cost
The Cotton Jones Basket Ride
The Countrypolitans
The Court and Spark
The Cousin Lovers
The Cowsills
The Cowslingers
The Coydogs
The Coz
The Crack Pipes
The Crash
The Crash That Took Me
The Creature Comforts
the Creteens
The Cribs
The Cricket Taylor Band
The Crickets
The Crimea
The Cringe
The Cripples
The Crooked Jades
The Crookes
The Cruel and Unusual
The Crumbs
The Cruxshadows
The Crystal Method
The Cuban Cowboys
The Cubical
The cuf
The Cute Lepers
The Cuts
The Cuts
The Cynics
The Czars
The D4
The Dagons
The Dam' Place
The Damn Personals
The Damnations
The Damnations TX
The Dan Band
The Dancehall Boys
The Dandies
The Dandy Warhols
The Dangerous Summer
The Dansettes
The Darcie Deaville Band
The Darkness
The Dashboard Saviors
The Datson Four
The Datsuns
The Dave & Deke Combo
The David Halley Band
The Dawn Parade
The day after...
The Daylights
The Daylights
The Dead Bodies
The Dead Science
The Deadbeat Poets
The Deadly Snakes
The Deadly Syndrome
The Deaf
The Dears
The Death Set
The Deathray Davies
The Deaths
The Debonairs
The DeBretts
The Decemberists
The Deep Dark Woods
The Deep Season
The Deep Vibration
The Defectors

The Del Lords
The Del McCoury Band
The Delevantes
The Delgados
The Delilahs
The Delphines
The Delta 72
The Delusions
The Demonics
The Dentists
The Depreciation Guild
The Derailers
The Desires
The Details
The Detholz!
The Detroit Grand Pubahs
The Devil & the Dames
The Devil Bat
The Devil Makes Three
The Dexateens
The Dexter Romweber Duo (formerly The Flat Duo Jets)
The Diablo Project
The Diamond Smugglers
The Diaz Brothers
The Dick Nixons
The Dick Price Factor
The Dicks
The Dicks w/ David Yow
The Diffs
The Dillinger Escape Plan
The Dime Store Poets
The Dimes
The Din
The Dingees
The Diplomats of Solid Sound
The Dirt Drifters
The Dirtbombs
The Dirtclods
The Dirty Dozen
The Dirty Dozen Brass Band
The Dirty Hearts
The Dirty Projectors
The Dirty Skirts
The Disco Biscuits
The Dishes
The Dismukes
The Disowned
The Distressed
The Divorce
The Dixons
The D-Madness Project
The Dodos
The Dogs (Detroit)
The Dollyrots
The Dolomites
The Dolomites (Stevhen Iancu)
The Domino Kings
The Donkeys
The Donnas
The Dooms U.K.
The Dorkestra
The Double
The Doug Dillard Band with Ginger Boatwright
The Downbeat 5
The Downtown Fiction
The Draft
The Drag
The Dragons
The Drakes
The Drams
The Drapes
The Drawn Together Movie: The Movie!
The Draymin
The Dresden Dolls
The Drew Sparks Project
The Drift
The Drones
The Dropouts
The Drovers
The Drugstore Cowboy
The Drums
The Dt's
The Duckhills
The Duhks
The Duke Spirit
The Dung Beatles
The D'Urbervilles
The Dusters
The Dutchess & the Duke
The Dwarves
The Dykeenies
The Dylan Group
The Eames Era
The Earlies
The Early Tapes
The Early Years
The Earthtones
The East Side Band
The Edlos
The Effects
The Effigies
The Egg
The Eggmen
The Eh Team DJs
The Eighteenth Day Of May
The Eighties Matchbox B-Line Disaster
The Elected
The Electric City
The Electric Diorama
The Electric Soft Parade
The Electric Windows

The Elements
The Elevator Drops
The Elite
The Elms
The Elysian Quartet
The Emeralds
The End (CANADA)
The End of the World
The Endless Blockade
The Ends
The English Beat
The English Department
The Enright House
The Entrance Band
The Environment
The Envy Corps
The Equators 1
The Escape Frame
The Essex Green
The Etheopeons
The Etiquette
The Ettes
The Euro Boys
The Evangelicals
The Evaporators
The Everyday Visuals
The Everyothers
The Evinrudes
The Excels
The Excentrics
The Ex-Husbands
The Exies
The Exit
The Exotics
The Experimental Tropic Blues Band
The Explorers Club
The Explosives with Peter Lewis and Stu Cook
The Extraordinaires
The Eyeliners
The Fabulous Bowler Boys
The Faceless Werewo!ves
The Fags
The Failures
The Faint
The Faintest Ideas
The Fairline Parkway
The Fairways
The Falcon Project
The Falkon
The Fall Collection
The Fall of Troy
The Falling Wallendas
The Fall-Outs
The Fancy Trolls
The Fashion
The Features
The Federation
The Feds
The Feeling
The Felice Brothers
The Fells
The Femurs
The Fence Cutters
The Fence Sitters
The Ferocious Few
The Fever
The Feverpitch
The Field Guides
The Fiery Furnaces
The Figgs
The Fighting Brothers McCarthy
The Films
The Final Impact Band
The Finches
the finders
The Finns
The Fire Marshals of Bethlehem
The Fire Show
The Fire Theft
The Fireants
The Firebird Band
The Fire Eaters
The Fitsners
The Five Deadly Venoms
The Flairz
The Flametrick Subs
The Flaming Flames of Fire
The Flaming Lips
The Flaming Sideburns
The Flashing Lights
The Flatchested Girls From Maynardville
The Flatlanders
The Flatliners
The Flesh
The Fleshtones
The Floorbirds
The Fluid
The Flying Dutchman
The Flying Fish Sailors
The Fold
The Forecast
The Forms
The Forty-Fives
The Fountains
The Four Corners
The Foxx
The Foxymorons
The Frames
The Frampton Brothers
The Frank and Walters
The Franklin-Devlin Band
The Fratellis
The Frauds

The Freak Accident
The Freight Hoppers
The Fresh & Onlys
The Friendly
The Friggs
The Frogs
The Fruit Bats
The Fuckemos
The Fugees
The Fumes
The Fundamentals
The Funeral Pyre
The Furry Crocodiles
THE FUSE!
The Futureheads
The Futurists
The Fuzz Club (featuring DJ Sue spinning underground music from the 1960's , go-go dancers, a light show, groovy decor, twist contest, plus the beat sounds of the Waistcoats from the Netherlands.
The Gabe Dixon Band
The Gabe Granitz Quartet
The Gadjits
The Galactic Heroes
The Gang
The Ganjas
The Gaskets
The Gaslamp Killer
The Gates Of Slumber
The Gathering
The Gay
The Gay Blades
The Gay Sportscasters
The Gay Sportscasters with Evan Johns
The Gear
The Geezinslaws
The Generators
The Gentle Good
The Gentlemen
The Genitorturers
The George W. Bush Singers
The Geraldine Fibbers
The Get Hustle
The Get Up Kids
The Ghost of a Thousand
The Ghost Songs
The Gift
The Gift
The Gimmicks
The Gin Riots
The Gingbreadmen
The Giraffes
The Girl Robots
The Girls
The Glands
The Glass Family
The Glasspack
The Glitch Mob
The Glitterati
The Globes
The Gloria Record
The Gluey Brothers
The Go
The Go! Team
The Goddamn Gentlemen
The Goin' Along Feelin' Just Fines
The Golden Apples
The Golden Boys
The Golden Dogs
The Golden Echoes
The Golden Filter
The Golden Republic
The Goldentones
The Goldstars
The Good
The Good Guys
The Good Looks
The Good The Bad
The Good, The Bad & The Queen
The Goodnight Loving
The Goods
The Goods with DJ Skratch Bastid
The Goodwill
The Goons
The Goops
The Gospel According To Austin
The Gospel Stars
The Gossip
The Gougers
The Gourds
The Government
The Graduates
The Grandmothers
The Grascals
The Grass
The Grassy Knoll
The Grassy Knoll Boys
The Grates
The Gravel Pit
The Graves Brothers Deluxe
The Gray Kid
The Great Divide
The Great Lines
The Great Nostalgic
The Great Redneck Hope
The Great Spy Experiment
The Green & Yellow TV
The Green Pajamas
The Greencards

The Greenhornes
The Gretchen Phillips Experience
The Grey Ghost
The Grifters
The Grim Northern Social
The Grip Weeds
The Gris Gris
The Groobees
The Grouch & Eligh
The Growlers
The Guggenheim Grotto
The Guilty Party
The Gun & Doll Show
The Gunbunnies
The Gusto
The Hacienda Brothers
The Hackensaw Boys
The Haden Triplets
The Halibuts
The Hal Lovejoy Circus
The Hall Monitors
The Halo Friendlies
The Hamicks
The Hammer Heads
The Handsome Family
The Hang Ups
The Hangdogs
The Hangmen
The Hannibals
The Happy Bullets
The Happy Hollows
The Harcourts
The Hard Feelings
The Hard Lessons
The Harmony Theory
The Harvesters
The Have
The HaveNots
The Havoline Supremes
The Haynes Boys
The Hazey Janes
The Heart Attacks
The Heatseekers
The Heavenly States
The Heavy
The Heavy Blinkers
The Heavy Pets
The Hedrons
The Heights
The Hellecasters
The Helio Sequence
The Hell Caminos
The Hellacopters
The Hells
The Henry Clay People
The Henrys
The Hentchmen
The Hi Fives
The Hicks
The Hidden Cameras
The Hidden Persuaders
The Hi-Fives
The High Class Elite
The High Dials
The High Fidelity
The High Strung
The High Violets
The Higher State
The Highwaymen
The Honkies
The Hint
the Hiss
The Hissyfits
The Hives
The Janglers
The Jinns
The Hold Steady
The Holiday Plan
The Holidays
The Holland Nix Band
The Hollisters
The Holloways
The Holmes Brothers
The Holy Fire
The Holy Ghost
The Holy Kiss
The Homopolice
The Homosexuals
The Honey Brothers
The Honeydogs
The Honeygos
The Honeyrods
The Hong Kong
The Hong Kong Blood Opera
The Honorary Title
The Hood Internet
The Hookers
The Hooks
The Hormonauts
The Hormones
The Horrors
The Horsies
The Host
The Hot Kicks
The Hot Melts
The Hot Puppies
The Hot Shots
The Hot Springs
The Hounds Below
The Hourly Radio
The Hours
The House Band
The Houstons
The Hudsons
The Human Abstract
The Humpers
The Hunches

continued on page 232

2007

SXSW **STATS** March 9 – 18

MUSIC BY THE NUMBERS

1,580 showcasing artists
of 8,200 submissions

74 panels, workshops & sessions

70 venues & stages

11,750 registrants

$425-600 registration

$130-175 wristband

47 countries represented

272 pages in program guide

200 trade show exhibitors

AUSTIN MUSIC AWARDS

Wednesday, March 14, Austin Convention Center
Performers Bobby Whitlock & CoCo Carmel; Barbara Kooyman and Unstrung Heroes of Tex-americana with Carrie Rodriguez and Michelle Shocked; Ian McLagan & the Bump Band doing a tribute to Ronnie Lane (with special guest Pete Townshend); Tex Mex Experience and Texas Tornados with Sam the Sham; Six Strings Down: the Clifford Antone Tribute, with Jimmie Vaughan, Derek O'Brien and Gary Clark Jr.

KEYNOTE CONVERSATION

Pete Townshend (interviewed by Bill Flanagan) In addition to the keynote, Townshend played a number of shows including joining old friend Ian McLagan at the Austin Music Awards, as well as performing alone and with Rachel Fuller at several all-star Attic Jam shows.

MEMORABLE PANELS

Emmylou Harris in conversation with Jonathan Demme
"Why Does Today's Music Sound Like Shit?" with Sandy Pearlman
"Comedy On The Music Circuit" with David Cross, Patton Oswalt and Zach Galifianakis
"Nick Drake Remembered" with Joe Boyd, Robyn Hitchcock and Gabrielle Drake
"Monterey Pop At 40" with Lou Adler, Michelle Phillips and Andrew Loog Oldham

SXSW music 2007

NO RESALE 16876

GUARANTEES NO COVER • MANY VENUES FILL UP • BADGES GET PRIORITY ENTRY • ADMISSION SUBJECT TO LEGAL CAPACITY   US 5,973,600 EP 1012804
VOID IF SEVERED, TAPED, STRETCHED OR NOT SNUG ON WRIST • MOST VENUES RESTRICT MINORS • NO REFUNDS OR TRANSFER   and other U.S. and foreign pate

NOTABLE PANELISTS & SPEAKERS

Gilberto Gil, Tom Anderson (MySpace president), Terry McBride (Nettwerk label founder), Booker T. Jones (interviewed by Jim DeRogatis and Greg Kot), Iggy Pop (interviewed by David Fricke), Rickie Lee Jones, David Byrne, Marc Weinstein (Amoeba Music founder), Richard Gottehrer (The Orchard), Marco Werman (PRI/BBC's *The World*)

MEMORABLE SHOWS

> Ozomatli and Public Enemy drew a huge crowd to Auditorium Shores on Friday evening for a free, public concert that was estimated to be the largest hip-hop show in Austin history.

> Hotel Cafe Night at the Parish on Thursday brought out the celebrity sing-along during Tom Morello's Nightwatchman set, with Slash, Nuno Bettencourt, Wayne Kramer, Les Claypool and Perry Farrell all joining in.

"Our week at SXSW was absolutely overwhelming – there was way too much to take in, just too much to experience. But it was equally enriching for us as a band. The excess of stimulus left us feeling completely incapable of making even simple decisions during the week of the festival. But on our return home, the experiences have been converted into inspiration. We are now even more desperate than ever to get better at what we do, to create beautiful music, to experiment and push boundaries." ■ Harris Tweed, one of the first two South African artists to showcase at SXSW

> The Stooges with Spoon, Kings of Leon and Paolo Nutini at Stubb's. Saturday's show was a tough ticket with lines around the block for the opening bands, but the Stooges still schooled everyone with Iggy Pop inviting dozens of people to join him onstage for the encore.

> Stax 50 Revue at Antone's Thursday evening (before the Astralwerks showcase began). Booker T. & the M.G.'s played a set and then acted as house band, while Isaac Hayes, William Bell and Eddie Floyd all took turns at the mic.

> The Ponderosa Stomp was staged on Friday night in the parking lot behind Opal Divine's Freehouse. Headlined by the great Archie Bell,

the lineup included a number of New Orleans acts (including the Flaming Arrow Mardi Gras Indians) and was a prelude to the Stomp's official return to the Crescent City, post-Hurricane Katrina.

NOTABLE ACTS

Mary Weiss The Shangri-La's singer performed on the Norton Records showcase Thursday at Red 7, backed by Reigning Sound. Also on the eclectic bill were Dexter Romweber and Sam the Sham.

Amy Winehouse Just months before she became a tabloid staple, Winehouse was on the verge of international breakout. Her La Zona Rosa set on Friday was generally described as solid and professional, which would have been hard to believe just a few months later.

Sparklehorse Leader Mark Linkous had just seen the release of *Dreamt For Light Years in the Belly of the Mountain* and come down from his rural Smoky Mountain outpost to headline Thursday night's Astralwerks showcase at Antone's. Linkous committed suicide three years later.

Lily Allen Wednesday night at Stubb's brought Allen's super-hyped performance. Also on the bill was Razorlight, who were huge in the U.K., but their U.S. fortunes were summed up by the half of the crowd leaving after Allen finished. Razorlight singer Jonny Borrell didn't seem to mind as he drove girlfriend Kirsten Dunst around town on a rented motorcycle.

Black Moth Super Rainbow and the Octopus Project The two bands combined for a massive instrumental psych set Saturday night at Elysium. The onstage instruments included two sets of drums, a bass, guitar, sitar, two glowing tambourines, a Theremin and four keyboards.

SOME OF THE MEDIA-SPONSORED ACTS

Chingo Bling (*Houston Press*), Watson Twins (*LA Weekly*), The Whigs (*Flagpole*, Athens, GA), The Clutters (*Nashville Scene*), Postmarks (*Miami New Times*), Menomena (*Portland Mercury*), Colourmusic (*Urban Tulsa Weekly*), Tilly & the Wall (*Omaha Weekly Reader*), Cloud Cult (*Citypages*, Minneapolis)

SOME OF THE INTERNATIONAL ACTS

Lee "Scratch" Perry (Jamaica); Hoodoo Gurus (Australia); the Dears (Canada); Bloc Party (U.K.); Boris (Japan); Rodrigo y Gabriela (Mexico); Peter, Bjorn & John (Sweden); Balkan Beat Box (Israel); Field Music (U.K.); Os Mutantes (Brazil); Turbonegro (Norway); YB (South Korea)

SOME OF THE AUSTIN ACTS

What Made Milwaukee Famous, Moonlight Towers, When Dinosaurs Ruled the Earth, Shearwater, Riverboat Gamblers, Okkervil River, Nervous Hospital, the Service Industry, Jesse Dayton, Those Peabodys, Charanga Cakewalk, Sally Crewe & the Sudden Moves

SOFTBALL TOURNEY

After a rainout year in '06, Print Media and Clubs/Talent Buyers continued their annual battle for supremacy (the two had squared off in the championship game every year since 1998), but this time Print Media administered a 26-0 shellacking, the most lopsided final game in SXSW history.

FILM BY THE NUMBERS

240 films screened

5,816 registrants

59 panels, workshops & sessions

208 pages in program guide

AWARDS

Narrative Feature Winner *Itty Bitty Titty Committee*; Special Jury Awards: *Frownland, Orphans*

Documentary Feature Winner *Billy the Kid*; Special Jury Awards: *Cat Dancers, Audience of One*

MEMORABLE FILMS

The Lookout (opening night film), *Run Granny Run, Hannah Takes the Stairs, King Corn, Monkey Warfare, The Whole Shootin' Match, Knocked Up, Dirty Country, Disturbia*

MEMORABLE PANELS/EVENTS

Featured conversations with Bill Paxton, Morgan Spurlock and Richard Linklater

Suffering Man's Charity world premiere Q&A, with director Alan Cumming, joined by co-stars David Boreanaz and Karen Black

"Sex Scenes Stay Hard" panel featuring John Cameron Mitchell

"Ready For Primetime: TV Comedy Today" panel featuring Seth MacFarlane, Al Jean and Rob Corddry

"Panel Of The Dead: Horror Films Of Today" with Eli Roth and Harry Knowles

INTERACTIVE BY THE NUMBERS

6,843 registrants

186 panels, workshops & sessions

136 pages in program guide

KEYNOTE SPEAKERS

Kathy Sierra (*Lifehacker* blog), Limor Fried and Phil Torrone (*MAKE* Magazine), Dan Rather, Will Wright (*SIMS, Spore* game designer)

MEMORABLE PANELS

"Bruce Sterling's SXSW Rant"

"The Future of the Online Magazine" panel featuring Joan Walsh of *Salon*

"User Generated Content And Original Editorial: Friend Or Foe" with Evan Williams (Twitter CEO)

"Conversation Culture: A Conversation With Henry Jenkins" featuring danah boyd

"Story Behind *Snakes On A Plane*" panel

"Customer Service Is The New Marketing" panel with Tony Hsieh (Zappos CEO) ■

2008

SXSW **STATS** March 7 - 16

MUSIC BY THE NUMBERS

1,809 showcasing artists
of 10,850 submissions

68 panels, workshops & sessions

83 venues & stages

12,651 registrants

$500-650 registration

$139 wristband

42 countries represented

288 pages in program guide

196 trade show exhibitors

AUSTIN MUSIC AWARDS

Wednesday, March 14, at Austin Convention Center

Performers Walter Hyatt Tribute featuring David Ball, Jimmie Dale Gilmore, Colin Gilmore, Warren Hood, Taylor Hyatt, the Belleville Outfit, and Audrey Ball; Roy & Sundance Head with the West Side Horns; the Judy's; Gary Clark Jr.; Okkervil River with Roky Erickson

KEYNOTE CONVERSATION

Lou Reed (interviewed by Hal Willner) Reed's trip to SXSW was in conjunction with the screening of the Julian Schnabel-directed concert film *Lou Reed's Berlin*, and he performed no shows while in town. "People told us that Lou Reed was going to be a handful as keynote, but he turned out to be very professional, and relatively low-maintenance," remembers Roland Swenson. "However, Reed was the only keynote ever to bring his own microphones and demand a soundcheck... just to speak."

MEMORABLE PANELS

Administration of the **"Rhino Musical Aptitude Test,"** hosted by Roky Erickson

"Producers: The Analog-Digital Shift," featuring Alan Parsons

"Vinyl Revival," with Waterloo Records' John Kunz and others discussing the surge in vinyl sales amid the digital age

SXSW MUSIC 2008   NO RESALE   0012469

GUARANTEES NO COVER · ADMISSION SUBJECT TO LEGAL CAPACITY · MANY VENUES FILL UP · BADGES GET PRIORITY ENTRY

VOID IF SEVERED, TAPED, STRETCHED OR NOT SNUG ON WRIST · MOST VENUES RESTRICT MINORS · NO REFUNDS OR TRANSFER

"Pros and Cons of 360 Deals," putting the ballyhooed all-inclusive deal under the microscope

"Through The Lens: Photographers On Musicians," with top music photographers discussing their work and the invasion of the cellphone camera

NOTABLE PANELISTS & SPEAKERS

Steve Reich (interviewed by Thurston Moore), Seymour Stein, Louis Messina (PACE Concerts founder), Danny Goldberg, Sean Moriarty (Ticketmaster CEO), Ice Cube and DJ Pooh (interview by Dave Marsh), Carrie Brownstein, Rob Glaser (RealNetworks founder), Mick Jones and Tony James, Daryl Hall

MEMORABLE SHOWCASES

> Thursday night's NPR Showcase at the Austin Music Hall featured My Morning Jacket, who had made the long trek from regional obscurity to headliner. Yo La Tengo and the Whigs opened.

> Club 115, one of those venues that only seems to exist during SXSW, hosted a Saturday night show featuring four acclaimed Brazilian rock bands, including Debate, who had caused a stir the previous year. The Brazilian presence has continued to grow every year.

> Japan Nite at Elysium was held on both Friday and Saturday. The highlight was Friday's stunning set by detroit7, whose punishing Stooges-style garage-rock left the crowd slackjawed and delighted before Petty Booka pulled out their ukuleles. The exquisitely named Ketchup Mania finished the night.

> The all-Mexico showcase at the Dirty Dog on Friday, sponsored by Gibson Guitars, gave evidence of the popularity of Rock en Espanol just across Texas' southern border.

> Venerable indie radio station, WFMU, celebrated its 50th anniversary with a two-stage showcase at Spiro's which featured 14 eclectic indie acts, including Psychedelic Horseshit and Half Japanese.

> Friday night's ASCAP showcase at the small, intimate Victorian Room at the Driskill Hotel was opened by an acoustic strumming Katy Perry, before her pop tart makeover and chart-topping success.

NOTABLE ACTS

R.E.M. One of the keys to the regional indie band scene of the '80s that helped spawn SXSW, R.E.M. headlined a Stubb's opening-night show, delivering a fiery set mixing rockers from the new *Accelerate* record with old favorites.

"Trying to pick the best moments of the South by Southwest Music Fest is like trying to pick your favourite grain of sand on the beach." ■ *London Free Times* (Canada), March 19, 2008

Darondo Ubiquity Recordings presented a Saturday night show at Club DeVille featuring this retired '70s-era pimp and R&B singer and '80s cable access television host, whose long-forgotten recordings had just been reisssued. In between blasts of greasy funk, the pompadoured Darondo gave detailed and explicit advice for how men could please their special ladies.

Also Van Morrison, Kimya Dawson, Bon Iver, She And Him, Fleet Foxes, Dr. Dog, Earlimart, Supersuckers, Wooden Shjips, Blitzen Trapper, MGMT, Tapes 'n Tapes, Black Keys, Japanther, High On Fire, David Banner, Nada Surf

SOME OF THE INTERNATIONAL ACTS

Afenginn (Denmark), The Soundtrack Of Our Lives (Sweden), Chikita Violenta (Mexico), Mala Rodriguez (Spain), Duffy (U.K.), Volodja Balzalorsky (Slovenia), Carbon/Silicon (U.K.), Constantines (Canada), Jens Lekman (Sweden), Beangrowers (Malta), 127 (Iran)

SOME OF THE AUSTIN ACTS

Lions, Complete Control, Bad Rackets, Amplified Heat, Brazos, Black Angels, Black And White Years, Balmorhea, DJ Rapid Ric, David Garza, Neckbone, Carrie Rodriguez

SOFTBALL TOURNEY

Clubs/Talent Buyers had been waiting to exact revenge for their 26-0 humiliation in the 2007 championship game at the hands of Print Media. But for the first time since 1996 (excluding the two rainout years), Print Media failed to reach the finals, falling 10-9 to Mixed Media in the semifinals. Mixed Media pushed Clubs/Talent Buyers to the limit but fell 17-16.

FILM BY THE NUMBERS

273 films screened

6,675 registrants

62 panels, workshops & sessions

208 pages in program guide

AWARDS

Narrative Feature Winner *Wellness*; Special Jury Awards: *Explicit Ills, Up With Me*

Documentary Feature Winner *They Killed Sister Dorothy*; Special Jury Award: *Full Battle Rattle*

MEMORABLE FILMS

21 (opening night film), *Body Of War, Run Fatboy Run, Forgetting Sarah Marshall, Harold And Kumar Escape From Guantanamo Bay, Battle In Seattle, Young@Heart, The Night James Brown Saved Boston, The Promotion, At The Death House Door, Stop-Loss*

"The festival mirrors the changes the Web has wrought. There's too much music for even the most energetic fan, and bands are playing for exposure rather than money. As sales of recorded music have dried up, the importance of live performance has grown – and SXSW is where you come to show you have what it takes." ■ *The Philadelphia Inquirer*, March 18, 2008

MEMORABLE PANELS/EVENTS

Featured conversations with Billy Bob Thornton, Moby, Helen Hunt, Michael Eisner and Harlan Ellison

"Stanley Nelson: History In The Making" spotlighted the renowned documentarian

"Jeffrey Tambor Acting Workshop" gave attendees hands-on tips

"Deal Or No Deal: The Road To Self-Distribution" talked about the DIY route for filmmakers

"Video Production For The Web And Mobile Devices" looked to the future

INTERACTIVE BY THE NUMBERS

9,052 registrants

220 panels, workshops & sessions

136 pages in program guide

KEYNOTE SPEAKERS

Henry Jenkins (MIT Comparative Media Studies) and Steven Johnson (*Everything Bad is Good For You* author), Mark Zuckerberg (Facebook), Frank Warren (PostSecret project), Jane McGonigal (game designer)

MEMORABLE PANELS

"Worst Website Ever: That's So Crazy, It Just Might Work" featuring seven presenters, each representing a fake web startup, pitching their worst idea to a venture capitalist, with the winner receiving funding on the spot

"True Stories From Social Media Sites" featuring Guy Kawasaki

"Games For Change: Real World Games With Real World Impact," about using video games for social change and political activism

"How Piracy Will Save The Music Industry," one of a slate of Tuesday panels open to SXSW Music registrants

"Building A Worldwide Climate Movement" with renowned environmentalist/author Bill McKibben ■

2009

SXSW **STATS** March 13 - 22

MUSIC BY THE NUMBERS

1,987 showcasing artists
of 10,815 submissions

79 panels, workshops & sessions

88 venues & stages

11,687 registrants

$550-695 registration

$129-165 wristband

49 countries represented

248 pages in program guide

155 trade show exhibitors

AUSTIN MUSIC AWARDS

Wednesday, March 18, at Austin Music Hall

Performers Suzanna Choffel, Ruthie Foster and Carolyn Wonderland; Bob Schneider with the Fireants; the Dicks with David Yow; SDQ2: A Tribute to Doug Sahm, with Shawn Sahm, Augie Meyers and Alejandro Escovedo; Roky Erickson with the Black Angels

KEYNOTE SPEAKER

Quincy Jones The legendary producer discussed a number of topics during his speech, including his childhood, his work in his early '20s with Dizzy Gillespie, and his instinctual ability to spot talent, using Michael Jackson as an example. Jones signed copies of his autobiography and even dropped by the "*Kind Of Blue* at 50" panel to give his personal take on the Miles Davis classic. Later on, he presented pianist Alfredo Rodriguez at the Elephant Room. "Wherever he is, I'm guessing Quincy Jones is having a good time," Roland Swenson figures. "He's had a life populated by some of the most famous, popular and powerful people on the planet, and held his own with them every step of the way."

MEMORABLE PANELS

"Woodstock: Untold Stories" featured Michael Lang (festival producer) and members of Santana, Creedence Clearwater Revival and Sha Na Na.

"Bands, Brands And Fans" talked about the integration of music and consumer branding as sources of revenue for musicians.

"Great Expectations: Artist Development Meets Economic Reality" brought together label execs and managers to discuss the changed music industry landscape.

"Annoying Things That Bands Do" gave booking agents and promoters a chance to "find fault and point out mistakes in a caring fashion."

"History Of British Indies" included Martin Goldschmidt (Cooking Vinyl), Peter Jenner (manager of T. Rex, Pink Floyd, Billy Bragg and others), Seymour Stein, and Geoff Travis (Rough Trade).

NOTABLE PANELISTS & SPEAKERS

Little Steven Van Zandt, Devo, Oak Ridge Boys, Tab Kubler and Craig Finn (Hold Steady), Martin Atkins, Carlene Carter, Michael Ochs (owner of the world's largest collection of rock 'n' roll images), Alexandra Patsavas (music supervisor for TV and film), Rick Rogers (manager of the Specials, the Damned and others), Panos Panay (Sonicbids founder)

MEMORABLE SHOWCASES

> The Decemberists topped the bill at NPR's packed (and nationally broadcast) opening-night showcase at Stubb's with support from the Avett Brothers and Heartless Bastards, but early arrivals got to see the electric Janelle Monae's show-stealing opening set.

> "[Sacramento band] Mayyors' house party show in 2009 was easily one of the craziest gigs I've ever seen. I'm pretty sure I saw someone do a flying leap off a kitchen counter. It was absolutely one of those occasions where I thought, 'You've been going to shows for years and you've never gotten physically injured...and that ends, here.' Ironically, I got my glasses smashed about two hours later when Tyvek played on the Lamar Street pedestrian bridge." ■ Gerard Cosloy, co-president, Matador Records

> The Sounds From Colombia showcase at Speakeasy showed why Colombia is often seen as the cradle of innovative Latin American music. Among others, the bill featured Bomba Estereo and Choc Quib Town, both of whom have since found international success.
> The Scottish Arts Council showcase at La Zona Rosa brought a great mix of Scotland's old guard and new faces, with the likes of We

Were Promised Jetpacks, Camera Obscura, the Proclaimers, and Glasvegas, with a closing set by Primal Scream.

NOTABLE ACTS

Devo The new-wave icons put on one of the week's most anticipated shows on Friday at the Austin Music Hall, churning out their most memorable songs while dressed in their trademark regalia and backed by a huge video screen.

Mayer Hawthorne & the County The Detroit-area soul crooner had little live experience and was unknown to anyone but his label when he and his band played the Scoot Inn on Friday, but the crowd went nuts and Hawthorne's career took off from there.

Sonics The Legendary '60s Seattle garage band made a rare appearance at Emo's on Friday night, and though their menace had been tamed somewhat after 40-plus years, singer Gerry Roslie showed he can still wail like it was 1965.

Gallows The British hardcore band left a path of tattooed mayhem at Emo's on Wednesday. Singer Frank Carter whacked himself in the head with the mic until he bled, and led the crowd in a circle pit. Then, on Friday night at Latitude 30's U.K. Embassy venue, he climbed out the open windows to swing on the shutters and harass unsuspecting passers-by.

Also Metallica, Silversun Pickups, Black Lips, Dillinger Escape Plan, Justin Townes Earle, Andre Williams, Crystal Method, Ra Ra Riot, Gary Louris & Mark Olson, Those Darlins, Kid Cudi, M. Ward, Hold Steady

SOME OF THE INTERNATIONAL ACTS

Futumomo Satisfaction (Japan), Tokyo Sex Destruction (Spain), Datarock (Norway), David Dallas (New Zealand), The Moog (Hungary), Lazywall (Morocco), Tallest Man On Earth (Sweden), Kraak And Smaak (Netherlands), Lenka (Australia), White Shoes & the Couples Company (Indonesia), High Dials (Canada), Echo & the Bunnymen (U.K.), Division Miniscula (Mexico), David Kirton (Barbados)

SOME OF THE AUSTIN ACTS

Daniel Johnston, Babydick, Black Joe Lewis & the Honeybears, Sam Baker, Grupo Fantasma, ...And You Will Know Us By The Trail Of Dead, Pong, Bruce Robison, Patricia Vonne, Harlem, White Denim, Brownout

SOFTBALL TOURNEY

In just its second year of existence (after having made its debut in the 2008 tournament), the SXSW Staff team made it to the championship game, only to have its hopes rudely dashed by Print Media in a 17-6 trouncing. Rumors abounded of retaliatory cuts to media registrations the following year, but we're pretty sure nothing actually happened with that.

FILM BY THE NUMBERS

260 films screened

7,144 registrants

62 panels, workshops & sessions

208 pages in program guide

AWARDS

Narrative Feature Winner *Made In China*; Special Jury Award: *The Way We Get By*

Documentary Feature Winner *45365*; Special Jury Award: *Full Battle Rattle*

MEMORABLE FILMS

I Love You, Man (opening night film), *Anvil! The Story of Anvil*, *Office Space* (10th Anniversary Screening), *Drag Me To Hell*, *Sin Nombre*, *Moon*, *The Hurt Locker*, *Humpday*, *500 Days Of Summer*, *Adventureland*, *Best Worst Movie*, *ExTerminators*, *Winnebago Man*, *Alexander The Last*, *Know Your Mushrooms*, *Neil Young Trunk Show*

MEMORABLE PANELISTS/EVENTS

Featured conversations with Richard Linklater and Todd Haynes, Col Needham (IMDB founder), Henry Selick and Robert Rodriguez, Michael Penn

"A Stanley Kubrick Panel With Jan Harlan" featured Kubrick's longtime producer.

"Smoke And Mirrors: The Art Of Visual FX" discussed integrating graphic design fundamentals into filmmaking.

"Observe And Report: A Case Study – A Man And His Gun" included Seth Rogen and fellow cast members.

"Managing Your Expectations: Indie Film Realities" discussed the importance of marketing and publicity.

"Making The Perfect Trailer: Mark Woollen Workshop"

INTERACTIVE BY THE NUMBERS

10,741 registrants

313 panels, workshops & sessions

208 pages in program guide

KEYNOTE SPEAKERS

Tony Hsieh (Zappos CEO), Nate Silver (FiveThirtyEight.com), James Powderly (artist/engineer), Chris Anderson (*Wired* magazine editor-in-chief and author)

MEMORABLE PANELS

"Help! My iPod Thinks I'm Emo" surveyed music recommendation tools.

"What Do I Do With Myself, Now That The Economy Has Collapsed?" talked about issues and opportunities related to the economic downturn.

"Is Privacy Dead Or Just Very Confused?" discussed the pervasive privacy issues facing internet users.

"Can Social Media End Racism?" explored how increased knowledge and awareness can impact larger issues.

"Rebuilding The World With Free Everything" included keynote speaker Chris Anderson and examined whether "free" could truly be the future of business.

"Video Blogging: Turn Wine Into Gold" with Gary Vaynerchuk ∎

2010

SXSW STATS March 12 - 21

MUSIC BY THE NUMBERS

1,978 showcasing artists
of 10,076 submissions

138 panels, workshops & sessions

89 venues & stages

13,020 registrants

$595-750 registration

$129-165 wristband

49 countries represented

256 pages in program guide

181 trade show exhibitors

AUSTIN MUSIC AWARDS

Saturday, March 20, at Austin Music Hall

Performers Texas Sheiks w/ Geoff Muldaur, Jim Kweskin, Bruce Hughes, Cindy Cashdollar and Johnny Nicholas; Will Sexton and Friends; Sarah Jarosz with special guest; The Explosives with Peter Lewis (Moby Grape) and Stu Cook (Creedence Clearwater Revival); Mother Falcon; All Star Soul Jam starring Black Joe Lewis and the Honeybears

KEYNOTE CONVERSATION

Smokey Robinson (interviewed by Dave Marsh) The genial Robinson shared stories about his life and career, but also dispensed useful advice. "When Dave Marsh asked Smokey to offer advice to the musicians in attendance," remembers Andy Flynn, SXSW Music Panels Coordinator, "He very directly told the crowd to develop a thick skin, and went on to warn of the criticism and hurdles that artists face in finding an audience. For someone who had spent decades at the top of his craft, he connected with the uncertainties of an unknown artist quite directly." Robinson also turned in a masterful performance at the Austin Music Hall, at one point leading the large crowd in a mass sing-along to "Cruisin'."

MEMORABLE PANELS

"Grinding in the New Economy" offered tips for independent hip-hop artists on how to think locally before moving on to broader audiences

"Hidden Stories Shaking Up American Pop Music" discussed U.S. music scenes being influenced by Latin music

"The Library of Congress: Music For Generations" informed listeners about how the library is preserving musicians' recorded legacy for listeners in the future

"Music Publishing: Making Money In Your Sleep" explained the importance of mechanical and performance royalties to musicians seeking a reliable income stream

"CBGB Stories" brought together a number of regular performers from the legendary New York City club's halcyon days including Tina Weymouth and Chris Frantz of the Talkng Heads and Clem Burke of Blondie

NOTABLE PANELISTS & SPEAKERS

Lemmy Kilmister, Cheap Trick (interviewed by Jim DeRogatis and Greg Kot), Derek Sivers (CD Baby founder), Feargal Sharkey (Undertones, UK Music), Mac McCaughan and Laura Ballance (Merge Records), Andrew WK, Lenny Kaye, Hugh Padgham (XTC producer), Dr. Ike Padnos (Ponderosa Stomp founder), Suzanne Vega

MEMORABLE SHOWCASES

> Big Star was scheduled to participate in the "I Never Travel Far Without a Little Big Star" panel and headline a Saturday night show at Antone's, but tragically, Alex Chilton died suddenly on Wednesday just before leaving for Austin. As a result, both events became tributes to Chilton and the beloved and influential Big Star. Drummer Jody Stephens and original bassist Andy Hummel (who would die of cancer in July 2010) were on-hand for both events along with latter day members Ken Stringfellow and Jon Auer. At the celebratory Antone's show, the four were joined by special guests John Doe (X), Curt Kirkwood (Meat Puppets), Mike Mills (REM), M. Ward, Evan Dando (Lemonheads), Chris Stamey (dBs), and Sondre Lerche.

> In a gloriously surreal pairing, Japanese psychedelic masters Acid Mothers Temple and the Melting Paraiso UFO closed Wednesday night

with a packed-to-rafters show at Rusty Spurs, self-described as "Austin's straight-friendly Country & Western Dance bar." Many third-eyes were opened.

> **"SXSW is the annual conference that helped bring about the ascendancy of user-generated content. My first year in attendance, I considered it a mecca for creative technologists. Some call SXSW 'geek spring break.' But amongst all the revelry lies the core value of the event – connection."**
> ■ Stephanie Agresta, digital media specialist

> Spoon, which got its start in Austin in the early '90s, seized the coveted opening night headlining slot on the NPR Music show at Stubb's, fulfilling every aspiring hometown band's dream and cementing its status as one of the biggest indie bands around. Also on the bill were Broken Bells with James Mercer (Shins) and Danger Mouse, Sharon Jones and the Dap-Kings, and The Walkmen.

> Submerged, next to the Austin Convention Center, hosted the sold-out bounce showcase on Saturday night, featuring top purveyors of the homegrown, inner city New Orleans hip-hip style. Flamboyant, self-proclaimed "sissy rappers" such as Big Freedia and Katey Red had the crowd enthralled, helping raise bounce's national profile in the process.

NOTABLE ACTS

Band Of Horses Having turned in an abbreviated set opening for Broken Social Scene at Stubb's on Thursday, the Sub Pop group took to the stage (or altar) at Central Presbyterian Church with a huge buzz. The intimacy of the venue, as well as its great acoustics enhanced the band's melodic grandeur and left the crowd glued to the pews.

"There is no question for me that SXSW has become one of the most vital and exciting festivals for discovering new talent...It is also one of the festivals I have the most fun at."
■ Ryan Werner, IFC Films

Man Or Astro-man? The legendary Alabama surf rock band played a rare comeback show on Thursday, after being on hiatus for the better part of a decade. Dressed in red jumpsuits in front of a capacity crowd at the Club de Ville, the band ended its reverb-drenched show by setting an oversized theremin aflame before bringing a giant Tesla coil on stage to shoot electric striations over the crowd's heads.

"As the music industry struggles to figure out a business model that works in the digital era, musicians increasingly find it's more important to connect with their peers at SXSW than it is to try to land a record deal or find management. Lining up a tour, or connecting with players from a powerful regional music scene, can lay the foundation for building a successful fan base." ■ Wired.com, March 22, 2010

Peelander-Z The New York City-based Japanese "Comic Action Punk Band" had been at SXSW many times, but despite its reputation for crazy onstage antics and props, Saturday night's Headhunters' show topped them all. Bass player Peelander Red ascended to the club's second floor and climbed onto a beam 20 feet above the stage before hanging upside down by his legs while still playing.

Also Wanda Jackson, Death, Mike Posner, Nas and Damien "Jr Gong" Marley, Hole, Lucero, Lou Barlow, Stone Temple Pilots, The Low Anthem, Rogue Wave, Raphael Saadiq, Dengue Fever, We Are Scientists

SOME OF THE INTERNATIONAL ACTS

Plants and Animals (Canada), Bajofondo (Argentina), Miike Snow (Sweden), Nneka (Germany), The xx (U.K.), John Dear Mowing Club (Netherlands), The Pinholes (Singapore), Tiger! Shit! Tiger! Tiger! (Italy), King of Conspiracy (France), Overflow (Croatia), Anita Tijoux (Chile), Maki Rinka (Japan), L. Stadt (Poland), Mumiy Troll (Russia), Grand Atlantic (Australia), Maldita Vecindad y Los Hijos Del Quinto Patio (Mexico)

SOME OF THE AUSTIN ACTS

Hickoids, Sarah Jarosz, Jon Dee Graham, Ocote Soul Sounds, Shearwater, White Ghost Shivers, T. Bird and the Breaks, Dustin Welch, Eagle Claw, Follow That Bird!, BettySoo, Walter T. and the Rated G's, Court Yard Hounds

SOFTBALL TOURNEY

In a reverse of last year's championship game result, the SXSW Staff team earned its first-ever title with a 21-10 victory over Print Media. Also in 2010, Softball Commissioner Susan Moffat passed the tiara to longtime crew chief Nanette Labastida. But with Labastida unexpectedly battling cancer this year, the Commish is back on for 2011 — though she insists this *really* is the last time. Meanwhile, longtime caterer Ruby's BBQ keeps on dishing it out; though owner Luke Zimmerman passed away in 2010, life partner Pat Mares continues to work magic with natural meats and fierce sauce.

FILM BY THE NUMBERS

277 films screened

9,500 registrants

86 panels, workshops & sessions

192 pages in program guide

AWARDS

Narrative Feature Winner *Tiny Furniture*; Special Jury Award (Best Ensemble): *Myth of the American Sleepover*; Special Jury Award (Best Individual Performance): Brian Hasenfus in *Phillip the Fossil*

"It's one of spring's most exhilarating and exhausting rites: The South by Southwest music festival, a five-day continuum of concerts where pop music's sprawling blogosphere is transposed into real life."
■ *Washington Post*, March 22, 2010

Documentary Feature Winner *Marwencol*; Special Jury Award: *War Don Don*

MEMORABLE FILMS

Kick-Ass (opening night film), *Winter's Bone, Four Lions, When I Rise, Micmacs, Cyrus, Get Low, LEMMY, The Thorn in the Heart, Mr. Nice, The Runaways, No Crossover: The Trial of Allen Iverson, American: The Bill Hicks Story, Strummerville, Thunder Soul*

MEMORABLE PANELS/EVENTS

Featured conversations with Michel Gondry, Gilbert Shelton (Fabulous Furry Freak Brothers), Gustavo Santaolalla (Academy Award-winning composer), David Gordon Green

"Directing the Dead: Genre Directors Spill Their Guts" featured Quentin Tarantino, Eli Roth and Matt Reeves

"How to Diffuse a Bomb and Other Life Lessons From the Cast of MacGruber" featured Will Forte, Kristen Wiig, Ryan Phillippe and the filmmakers of *MacGruber*

"Filmmaker War Stories" brought together directors to share their trials and tribulations while making movies

"How to Create A Viral Video" tried to unlock the secret of finding an online video audience

INTERACTIVE BY THE NUMBERS

14,251 registrants

313 panels, workshops & sessions

256 pages in program guide

KEYNOTE SPEAKERS

Daniel Ek (Spotify), Valerie Casey (Designers Accord), Evan Williams (Twitter CEO), danah boyd (social networking expert)

MEMORABLE PANELS

"Pay TV vs the Internet" debate between Avner Ronen (Boxee) and Mark Cuban was interrupted by a fire alarm, though a large number of attendees chose to ignore the alarm and stay in the ballroom

"Ze Frank Conversation: The Creative Lifestyle" featured the noted internet personality

"Negotiating the Parent/Teen Divide Over Social Networking" offered tips and advice for parents over their children's use of social media

"One of the great things about South by Southwest is that you never know who's going to show up, in the audience or sometimes onstage. Some of these surprise appearances are planned...but many are fairly spontaneous, and only seen by a handful of lucky individuals." ■ Metromix.com, New York, March, 2010

"Perfectly Irrational: Who Put the Monkey in the Driver's Seat" featured Dan Ariely, a specialist in studying irrational behavior

Microsoft Bizspark Accelerator gave entrepreneurs a chance to present to a group of venture capitalists with the prize of venture funding on the line

"Program or Be Programmed: Ten Commands for a Digital Age" featured writer and cyberpunk theorist, Douglas Rushkoff ■

continued from page 218

The Hundred Handed
The Hush Sound
The Hylozoists
The Hyperions
The Hypno-twists
The Icarus Line
The Idle Wilds
The Iguanas
The Ike Turner Revue
The Ill Relatives
The Illuminati
The Immediate
The Immortal Plants
The Immortals
The Impossible Shapes
The Improbable Return of Redneck Rock with Steven Fromholz, Ray Wylie Hubbard, Bob Livingston, Rusty Wier, Ray Benson and Billy Joe Shaver
The In Out
The Inbreds
The Incredible Moses Leroy
The Indelicates
The Independents
The Indigo Girls
The Industrial Jazz Group
The Industry
The Infamous D.J.s
The Inklings
The Innerspacemen
The Instruments
The Intelligence
The International Playboys
The Interpreters
The Invincible Czars
The Invisible
The Ironweed Project
The Isles
The J. Davis Trio
The J.J. Paradise Players Club
The J.U.S. Evolution
The Jack Saints
The Jack West & Lalo Vibe
The Jacka
The Jai Alai Savant
The Jane Shermans
The Japanese Motors
The Jason Seed Elixir Ensemble
The Jayhawks
The Jazzus Lizard
The Jealous Sound
The Jeff and Vida Band
The Jellydots
The Jels
The Jerry Lee Phantom
The Jessica Fletchers
The Jigsaw Seen
The Jim Jones Revue
The Jimmies
The Jinkies
The Jody Grind
The Joggers
The John Sparrow
The Jolly Garogers
The Jonbenét
The Jonez
The Joykiller
The Joys
The Juan Maclean
The Jubilettes
The Judy's
The Juggernaut Jug Band
The Juggs
The Juliana Theory
The Junk Monkeys
The Jupiter Affect
The Kabalas
The Keller Brothers
The Kennedys
The Keytones
The KGB
The Kick
The Kickz
The Kid Daytona
The Killdares
The Killer Bees
The Killers
The Kills
The Kin
The Kinetics
The King
The King Of France
The King Valentine Octet
The Kingdom
The Kingsbury Manx
The Kingsnakes (Detroit)
The Kinship
The Kiss Offs
The Kissaway Trail
The Klezmatics
The Knievels
The Knux
The Kodiaks
The Kokessies

The Pretenders (2006)

The Kominas
The Kooks
The Kowalskis
The Krayolas
The Krayolas and The West Side Horns
The Krayolas feat. Augie Meyers
The Krum Bums
The La Donnas
The Lackloves
The Ladies and Gentlemen
The Ladybug Transistor
The Lanedrifters
The Lanternjack
The Larry Stephenson Band
The Lascivious Biddies
The Lashes
The Last Wish
The Last Straw
'The Last Temptation of Superego' (an all-star tribute to The Last Waltz) featuring members of Fastball, Damnations TX, The Stingers, Prescott Curlywolf, Beaver Nelson, Ted Roddy, Golden Arm Trio, Lil' Cap'n Travis, The Conrads, Darin Murphy, Orange Mothers, Alterego and many more playing songs of The Band, Bob Dylan, Neil Young, and Van Morrison!
The Last Town Chorus
The Last Vegas
The Latebirds
The Latin Playerz
The Laughing
The Law
The Lawrence Arms
The Lazy Cowgirls
The League Of Extraordinary G'z
The Lee Boys
The Left
The Legendary K.O.
The Legendary Porch Pounders
The Legendary Shack Shakers
The Legendary Stardust Cowboy
The Lemonheads
The Len Price 3
The Lennings
The Leprechaun featuring Lil' Flip
The Leslie Spit Tree-O
The Letters Organize
The Librarians
The Life and Times
The Lifters
The Lighthouse and the Whaler
The Like
The Like Young
The Lilybandits
The Lilys
The Limes
The Linus Pauling Quartet
The Lisa Marr Experiment
The Little Bicycles
The Little Ones
The Little Rabbits
The Little Willies
The Living Blue
The Living Daylights
The Living End
The Living Legends
The Living Pins
The Living Things
The LK
The Locust
The London Souls
The Lonely Forest
The Lonely H
The Lones
The Long Winters
The Longcut
The Lonnie Brooks Blues Band
The Lord Vishnu
The Lords of Altamont
The Lost Brothers
The Lost Sounds
The Lot Six
The Love Experts
The Love Language
The Love Me Nots
The Love Scene
The Love Squad
The Love Supreme
The Loved Ones
The Lovelies
The Lovely Eggs
The Lovely Feathers
The Lovely Sparrows
The Lovemakers
The Low Anthem
The Low Lows
The Low Road
The Low Standards
The Lucky Bishops
The Lucky Strikes
The Lush Rollers
The Lyndsay Diaries

The Lynne Arriale Trio
The Mad Caddies
The Mad Capsule Markets
The Mad Hannans
The Mades
The Mae Shi
The Magic Kids
the Magic Magicians
The Magic Numbers
The Magic of Television
The Magnificents
The Magnolias
The Main Street Gospel
The Maldives
The Mall
The Mammals
The Mamou Prairie Band
The Manhattan Love Suicides
The Mannish Boys
The Marcia Ball Band
The Marginal Prophets
The Marilyns
The Mark Eitzel Ordeal
The Maroons
The Marshall Ford Swing Band
The Marshmallow Overcoat
The Martinets
The Martini Henry Rifles
The Marvelous 3
The Mary Janes
The Masons
The Matches
The Materialistics
The Mavericks
The Maximus
The Maxxturs
The May Fire
The Mayflies
The Mayflies USA
The Meat Puppets
The Meat Purveyors
The Meatmen
The Mechanical Walking Robotboy
The Meeting Places
The Megaphonic Thrift
The Meices
The Mekons
The Meligrove Band
The Melismatics
The Mellors
The Men of Porn
The Mendoza Line
The Menu
The Mercury Program
The Mercury Stars
The Meredith Miller Band
The Mermen
The Merrymakers
The Mess Hall
The Metrosexuals
The Micranots
The Middle East
The Mighty Blue Kings
The Mighty Stef
The Millions
The Minders
The Miners of Muzo
The Mini-Skirt Mob
The Minni-Thins
The Minstrels
The Mint Chicks
The Minus 5
The Minutes
The Miracle Drug
The Miracle of 86
The Mirrors
The Mirrors (Grey Ashley)
The Miserable Rich
The Miss Alans
The Messies
The Missiles
The Mission District
The Mistreaters
The Mittens
The Mo
The Moaners
The Modey Lemon
The Mohawk Lodge
The Moi Non Plus
The Mojo Filters
The Moldy Peaches
The Monas
The Monets
The Monolith
The Moog
The Moon
The Moondoggies
The Mooney Suzuki
The Mopeds
The Morells
The Morning After Girls
The Morning Benders
The Most Serene Republic
The Motels
The Mother Hips
The Mother Truckers
The Motive
The Mountain Goats
The Movement
The Movie Stars
The Movielife
The Movies
The M's
The Mudville Project
The Muffs

The Mullens
The Murder City Devils
The Music
The Muslims
The Mustangs
The Mutaytor
The Mutton Birds
The Mutts
The Muttz
The Mynabirds
The Mysteries of Life
The Name
The Narrator
The National
The National Pastime
The Natural History
The Naughty Ones
The Navigators
The Naysayer
The Neal Pollack Invasion
The Needles
The Negro Problem
The Neighbors
The Nein
The Nelsons
The Neptunes
The Nervous Exits
The Nervous Wreckords
The Nevers
The New Basics Brass Band
The New Deal
The New Duncan Imperials
The New Familiars
The New Flesh
The New Frontiers
The New Left
The New Orleans Social Club
The New Pornographers
The New Wine
The New Year
The Nice Boys
The Nice Ones
The Nice Outfit
The Nields
The Night Marchers
The Nightcaps
The Nightwatchman
The Nightwatchman (Tom Morello solo acoustic)
The Nimoys
The Niro
The Nitz
The Nixons
The Nomads
The Non
The No-No's
The Norma Zenteno Band
The North Atlantic
The Nothing Bastards
The Novaks
The Novas
The Number Twelve Looks Like You
The Numbers
The Nymphets
The Oaks
The Oblivious
The Observers
The Occasion
The Ocean Blue
The Octopus Project
The Odds
The Offenders
The Oktober People
The Old 97's
The Old Ceremony
The Old Joe Clarks
The Old-Timerz
The Olive Group
The Onlys
The Oohlas
The Optimysticals
The Opus
The Orange Peels
The Oranges Band
The Orbitsuns
The Orchid Highway
The Organ
The Original Brothers and Sisters of Love
The Original Dirty Rapper
The Original Harmony Ridge Creek Dippers
The Original Sins
The O's
The Other 99
The Other Side
The Others
The Outriders
The Owls
The Pack
The Pack A.D.
The Pains of Being Pure at Heart
The Painted Birds
The Paladins
The Pale
The Palladinos
The Pan I Am
The Panda Band
The Pandas
The Panic Choir
The Panics
The Paper Chase
The Paper Raincoat
The Paranoid Critical Revolution
The Paranoids
The Parisians

The Parkas
The Parlor Mob
The Parlotones
The Parties
The Party of Helicopters
The Pasties
The Pastry Heroes
The Pattern
The Paul Q-Pek Band
The Paul White Quintet
The Paybacks
The Peak Show
The Pee Wee Fist
The Peekers
The Peelies
The Peels
The Peenbeets
The Pendletons
The People's Revolutionary Choir
The Pepper Pots
The Perceptionists (Mr. Lif, Akrobatik, Fakts One)
The Perpetrators
The Pete Droge Band
The Phantom Family Halo
The Pharmacy
The Phenomenal Handclap Band
The Phoids
The Photo Atlas
The Physics of Meaning
The Picketts
The Pictish Trail
The Picture
The Pierces
The Pigeon Detectives
The Pillows
The Pilot Ships
The Pine Valley Cosmonauts
The Pines
The Pinholes
The Pink Noise
The Pink Spiders
The Pink Swords
The Pinker Tones
The Pipettes
The Pits
The Pity Party
The Plaid Camels
The Plan
The Planet The
The Plastic Constellations
The Playdoh Squad
The Playing Favorites
The Pleased
The Pleasure Club
The Plimsouls
The Plot to Blow up the Eiffel Tower
The Pocket FishRmen
The Pocket Symphonies
The Poison Arrows (IL)
The Polyphonic Spree
The Ponys (IL)
the Ponys (ME)
The Pope County Bootleggers
The Populist
The Posies
The Possibilities
The Post
The Post Office Gals
The Postelles
The Postman Syndrome
The Postmarks
The Potatoes
The Pragmatic
The Prayer Boat
The Preacher's Kids
The Presets
The President
The Presidents
The Presidents of the United States of America
The Pretenders
The Pretty Please
The Priests
The Procession
The Proclaimers
The Prodigal Sons
The Prom
The Promise Breakers
The Promise Ring
The Protomen
The Psychedelic Kinky Fellows
The Psychic Paramount
The Psychotic Aztecs
The Punkaroos
The Punks
The Pursuit of Happiness
The Push Stars
The Pushbacks
The Pusjkins
The Put-Downs
The Q
The Quails
The Quebe Sisters Band
The Queen Killing Kings
The Queers
The Quinsonics
The Race
The Radio Kings
The Radishes
The Raging Woodies
The Rain
The Rakes
The Rambelins

The Ranch
The Rapture
The Rascals
The Raveonettes
The Reaction
The Ready Set
The Real Heroes
The Realistics
The Rebel
The Rebirth Brass Band
The Recliners
The Red Hot Valentines
The Red King
The Red Light Sting
The Red Romance
The Red Scare
The Red Stick Ramblers
The Red Thread
The Redneck Manifesto
The Redwalls
The Rees Shad Band
The Refreshments
The Refugee All Stars
The Reign
The Reivers
The Remainders
The Renderers
The Rene Saenz Group
The Republic Tigers
The Reputation
The Rescues
The Research
The Resentments
The Resignators
The Reverend Billy C. Wirtz
The Revs
The Rhythm Kings
The Right Ons
The Rinse
The Ripe
The Riptones
The Rise
The Ritchie Whites
The Rite Flyers
The River Phoenix
The River Raid
The Riverboat Gamblers
The Road Kings
The Robert Ealey Band
The Robot Ate Me
The Robustos
The Rocket Summer
The Rocketboys
The Rockin' Highliners
The Rocking Horse Winner
The Rodeo
The Rodeo Carburettor
The Rogers Sisters
The Rosebuds
The Rosenbergs
The Rounders
The Rousers
The Royal Highness
The Rub
The Rub: DJ Ayres & Cosmo Baker
The Rubies (from The Emeralds)
The Ruby Doe
The Ruby Suns
The Rugburns
The Rum Diary
The Rumble Strips
The Rural Alberta Advantage
The Russian Futurists
The Rustlanders
The S.I.G.I.T.
The Sadies
The Saffron Sect
The Saints
The Salads
THE SALINGER
The Salteens
The Sam Brothers Zydeco Band
The Sammies
The Samples
The Sandmen
The Sandwitches
The Saturday Knights
The Satyrs
The Savage Trip
The Saw Doctors
The Scabs
The Scam
The Scheme
The Schramms
The Schramms /Kate Jacobs
The Scooters
The Score
The Scott Laurent Band
The Sea
The Search for Saturnalia
The Second Grace
The Seconds
The Secret Life of Sofia
The Secret Machines
The Section Quartet
The Seedy Seeds
The Senders
The Service
The Service Industry
The Set Up
The Setters
The Sextants
The Sexy Magazines
The Shackeltons
The Shaft
The Shagnastys

The Shakes
The Shakin' Apostles
The Shaky Hands
The Shame Idols
The Shams
The Shanes
The ShapeShifters
The Sharp Things
The Shazam
The She Creatures
The Sheila Divine
The Sheperd Band
The Shindigs
The Shines
The Shins
The Shitsez
The Shivers
The Shook Ones
The Shore
The Show Is The Rainbow
The Showoffs
The Shuffle Demons
The Shys
The Sick
The Sid Hillman Quartet
The Sidehackers
The Sights
The Signalmen
The Sign-Offs
The Silent League
The Silent Years
The Silos
The Silver-Tongued Devils
The Simpletons
The Singles
The Sinking Ships
The Sippy Cups
The Sir Finks
The Six Parts Seven
The SkeeterHawks
The Skeletones
The Skeletons
The Skeletons w/ special guest Dave Alvin
The Skydiggers
The Slants
The Slats
The Sleeping
The Sleepover Disaster
The Sleepwalkers
The Sleepy Jackson
The Slip
The Slits
The Slugs
The Small Stars
The Smith Brothers
The Smugglers
The Smyrk
The Snails
The Snake The Cross The Crown
The Snake Trap
The Sneeze
The Snobs
The So So Glos
The Soft Explosions
The Soft Lightes
The Soft Pack
The Soldier Thread
The Solid Senders
The Sonics
The Soul Of John Black
The Sound of URCHIN
The Sound of URCHIN (featuring Tomato 11 and Barbie Smooth)
The Sounds
The Soundtrack of Our Lives
The Sour Notes
The Southland
The Space Police
The Spades
The Spanic Boys
The Special Goodness
The Spider Bags
The Spiders
The Spies
The Spill Canvas
The Spin
The Spinanes
The Spinns
The Spinto Band
The Spit Brothers
The Spitfires
The Spits
The Spoilers
The Sprague Brothers
The Spring Standards
The Spunks
The Stand Out Selector & DJ Barry
The Standard
The Star Room Boys
The Starkweathers
The Starlight Mints
The Starvations
The Static Age
The Static Jacks
The Stationary Set
The Stems
The Stepbrothers
The Steps
The Stereo
The Sterns
The Stewart-Mayfield Project
The Stills
The Stingers

The Stingers ATX
The Stitches
The Stooges
The Story Of
The Storys
The Strand
The Stranded Lads
The Strange Boys
The Stratford 4
The Strays
The Streetwalkin' Cheetahs
The Stringdusters
The Strokes
The Strugglers
The Studdogs
The Studebakers
The Stylites
The Subdudes
The Subjects
The Submarines
The Subways
The Suede Chain
The Suffragettes
The Summer Set
The Summer Wardrobe
The Sun
The Sun Sawed in 1/2
The Sundogs
The Sundresses
The Sunshine Fix
The Sunshine Underground
The Suntanama
The Supa Brotha Scientists
The Super Friendz
The Superjesus
The Supersuckers
The Supreme Dicks
The Surfing Brides
The Suspects
The Suzan
The Sway Machinery
The Sweethearts
The Swells
The Swiftys
The Sword
The Tailgators
The Takers
The Talk
The Tallest Man On Earth
The Tares
The Tearjerkers
The Teenage Idols
The Teenage Prayers
The Teeners
The Teeth
The Telepathic Butterflies
The Telephone Company
The Temper Trap
The Tenant
The Tenants
The Tender Box
The Tender Idols
The Tennessee Boltsmokers
The Tennessee Three
The Teresa Banks Profiles
The Terns
The Texas Instruments
The Theater Fire
The Therapy Sisters
The Thermals
The Thin Man
The Things
The Third Man
The Thirst
The Thompson Brothers
The Thousand Dollar Playboys
The Thrills
The Thunder Boys
The Ticks
The Tigerlilies
The Time Flys
The Ting Tings
The Tiny
The Tiny Adventurers
The Tiny Tin Hearts
The Tiny White Baptists
The Tinys
The Titanics
The Titz
The Toadies
The Tontons
The Ton-Ups
The Tossers
The Touch Gallery
The Tough Alliance
The Toxic Avenger
The Toxic Avenger & Franki Chan
The Trade w/Leah Alvarez
The Tragically Hip
The Transgressors
The Transmissions
The Trashies
The Travelin' McCourys
The Trees
The Tremolo Beer Gut
The Tremors
The Trews
The Tribulations
The Triggers
The Trishas
The Troll Dolls
The Trophy Wives
The Trucks
The Tuna Helpers
The Turbo A.C.'s
The Turn-Ons

continued on page 253

Navigating The Turbulent Waters Of Change

Wow! Has it really been 25 years? Either the old adage that time flies is actually true, or more likely, I was having way too much fun every March in Austin to notice time slipping by. If memory serves me well, I have attended SXSW every year since 1993, which means when I arrive in town this March, it will have been an unbroken string of 18 years of attendance. Do I get a gold watch?

SXSW MEMORIES

I seem to recall that the first time I attended SXSW it was still a fledgling conference that was held at either the Marriott or the Ramada Inn on Sixth Street. *[Editors' note: '93 was actually the first year in the Convention Center.]* There was a passion amongst the organizers that you couldn't miss. It created an instant camaraderie – "all of us solemnly gathered in this room today ALL LOVE ALTERNATIVE MUSIC AND YOU CAN'T TAKE IT AWAY FROM US!!" Or something like that…

Heady days for sure. Yet as we know, everything in the universe is in constant flux, and so it was for SXSW over the years. With growth comes challenges – a cliché, I know, but very true. As SXSW became more popular over the years its inevitable growth created some discomfort for the cognoscenti. One discomfort for me was when the major labels realized there was a huge captive audience in town every March and began using their bottomless pockets to fund showcases of artists that were more mainstream, and decidedly less alternative, than most of the young bands who'd gotten into the festival on a prayer and a hail mary. "Alternative" music had been co-opted by rock radio and the major labels, and therefore had become a meaningless term.

Still, there was plenty of fun to be had every year. You just had to look for it, and it was often found by avoiding the "buzz bands." Why stand in line for hours waiting to see a band that was crowned the next big thing by the music biz fat cats sitting on their wallets in the Four Seasons lounge, when you could just stumble upon a great show accidentally? That still remains one of my favorite experiences at SXSW, especially with the advent of the all-day parties and shows that can be found on every street corner or vacant lot these days.

It's 2011 and SXSW is all grown up. I was never one for nostalgia, as I understand that all things must pass and that continuity is a hard discipline; yet one has to marvel that SXSW has been able to navigate the turbulent waters

'Take It To The Independent Jungle'

The 2008 SXSW was a burning point as a result of the recording companies having finally burnt all of their bridges with artists, and there now being an obvious future that is not dragged down by the shackles of age and legal larceny. Of course, this has been creeping up on us for a few years and, of course, there remains a sort of artist who may shine through what is left of the machine, but this year at SXSW (in a year, I must add, that the event was written off in more places than usual, the fate that befalls all great movements), the glow was in the air, and that extra bud of I do not know what was blooming on the tree of tomorrow's music. What I experienced was a delight. What was great was the removal of the "might I get signed to a major?" doldrums. The answer is "No, you will not!" The groups and performers can now just get on with it. There is really no need to consider the beast of burden; it would be like smoking grandad's ashes. awful.

So take it to the road. Take it to SXSW. Take it to the independent jungle that belongs to us all. I saw the weight truly removed at this year's SXSW, and the music was the better for it. ■ Andrew Loog Oldham, producer/manager/impresario/author

of change unlike the very industry that it serves – the recording business. I have lost all faith in the recording business, but I'm willing to hold out a lifeline to the music "industry," the one made up of those musicians who experiment with and challenge the status quo, who work hard often under the radar, to bring us the best they can possibly muster in the face of the biggest cultural and societal upheaval in recent memory – the advent of the internet.

Unlike the recording industry, SXSW very smartly embraced the digital revolution by creating a world-class interactive and digital conference. My work in music is pretty much done. I too embraced the digital revolution back in the mid-'90s and never looked back. I believe that when musicians truly understand the music "container" has been replaced by the internet, we will see a renaissance of the entire industry. Until then, after attending to my day job during SXSW Interactive, I will always enjoy my annual spring break vacation in Austin, soaking up as much music as I can possibly hear. And if you see me doing just that, you'll notice an ear-to-ear grin on the face of this old SXSW hand.

Happy 25th, SXSW! I look forward to many more years. ■ Dave Allen, director, Insights & Digital Media (and founding member of Gang Of Four)

The Life And Times Of Quincy Jones

Quincy Jones arrived at SXSW '09 making the word "convivial" inadequate. I got a glimpse of what we were in for just before introducing him for his keynote. He was seated on the side of the stage when I walked over and bent at the waist to speak to him and shake his hand. Instantly, I was in his world as he began telling stories and sharing observations at a very fast clip, not needing to pause for a breath, no doubt because of the wind control from his days as a trumpet player.

After about five minutes, my back was starting to hurt from bending over, and I managed to get a word in saying that it was nearly time for him to speak. He continued his monologue, undeterred, still holding on to my hand, and while what he was saying was fascinating, the time for him to start his speech had come and gone. Finally, someone else came over to speak to him, and he released my hand to shake theirs. I took the opportunity to jump up onstage to introduce him.

Quincy took the stage and began his totally fascinating speech about his amazing career, filled with anecdotes about the most famous people of the past 50 years. By the time Quincy breezed past Michelle Shocked (1992 keynote), then Lucinda Williams (1999), and then shattered the record Robbie Robertson set in 2002 for longest keynote ever, Andy Flynn (SXSW Music Panels Coordinator) was looking pretty pale.

The time to start the panel that was scheduled in the same room after Quincy's keynote had come and gone. Andy quickly found another room and got that panel going. We were approaching the time when the panel after the panel after Quincy's speech was coming up, and Quincy was still on *Off The Wall* and hadn't gotten to *Thriller* yet.

Backstage things were getting wacky, too. I was standing at the intersection of the two main corridors of the back of the house, talking on my phone, trying to calm down Andy, when someone tapped me on the shoulder and said, "Roland, would you like to meet Devo?" I turned and sure enough, there were the members of Devo, standing in a formation, wearing their jumpsuits and Devo helmets.

Just then, someone else tapped me on the shoulder and said, "Roland, meet the Oak Ridge Boys." And there were the Oak Ridge Boys, with their long beards and mustaches.

I stammered, "Uh, Devo, meet the Oak Ridge Boys." Both groups were there to do onstage interviews, and we were running out of green room space and dressing rooms.

I excused myself and went and listened to the rest of Quincy's speech. He was telling an Obama story when I got there, so I knew we were near the end. ■ **Roland Swenson, SXSW Director**

Where Films Meet Politics

For a filmmaker, SXSW brings an incredibly passionate and engaged audience. The festival is completely without pretense but with a lot of organization (the screenings started on time and were run with incredible efficiency), and the audiences are demanding and accepting all at once. The programming was filled with new discoveries from Europe and some of the best regional filmmaking I've seen. The festival also has a place – in a political/academic film-going city – for politics in cinema. I arrived with a film about death in Darfur, and the audiences were not only willing to drive through pounding rain storms to come see it, but they were also eager to get involved. We worked closely with a Sudan divestment group who had initiated a Texas legislative bill, and the combination was powerful. The bill passed unanimously, the Texas divestment vote was covered on local TV during the festival, and the audiences who came to our screenings got the sense that films can make a difference. ■ Annie Sundberg, co-director of *The Devil Came On Horseback*

Rawking SXSW

There's always something magical about seeing a wildly diverse group of smart professionals express themselves both personally and professionally while sipping beers and eating roasted animals. Your head can break when you think about it. I've had the opportunity to discuss Darth Vader as the ultimate representative of lawful evil and then immediately slip into conversations about how companies like Suicide Girls, Threadless, Dogster, and Vampire Freaks are transforming their business models and marketing plans to mimic Starbucks' evolution from coffee beans to a comprehensive media and lifestyle brand. You can't get that experience anywhere else. ■ **Min Jung Kim, writer/ blogger and organizer of the "How to Rawk SXSW" panel**

Elvis Has Entered The Building

Saturday night at the Red Eyed Fly for the Bloodshot showcase and as usual, the Waco Brothers have been chosen for that precious 1am spot. I've spent half the night outside trying to get drunk friends in, but with the line down the street, the guy on the door is unimpressed at the number of "wives" we have with us tonight. Once we get onstage, all is well and things get

pretty lively; it's a bloody long road from a KUT session at 11am to where we are now, but we're still firing on several cylinders. I'm sure we're running overtime, so Deano and I commence the big guitar smashing, string-snapping finale of destruction only to see the stage manager (digits aloft) gesturing 10 more minutes...Oops, disaster! But just at that moment, Danbert Nobacon (late of Chumbawumba) dives onstage in a gleaming white Elvis suit, complete with cape, to save the day and lead us through a rousing annihilation of "Folsom Prison Blues." The next day on South Congress, some bloke asks me how we got Graham Parker to dress up in that Elvis suit... ■ **Jon Langford, Waco Brothers/Mekons/Pine Valley Cosmonauts**

Where's The Large Belt Buckles?

I was born in the Middle East and have lived in London, New York and now Los Angeles. My only exposure to Texas had been through J.R. Ewing on *Dallas* and TV coverage of Mr. Bush's frequent visits to his Crawford resort. It's Texas – didn't they burn Dixie Chicks albums here? "They're going to hate my film," I thought. I expected frosty glares from men in large hats with large belt buckles and Rush Limbaugh bumper stickers on their trucks. As I was sent to the "special" security line at LAX on my outbound journey, I wondered if it would be better or worse if they would mistake me for being Mexican.

Upon arrival, I quickly discovered a textured and cosmopolitan city that I had least expected. From "grand old America" to the flickering fluorescents down Film Noir-esque alleys, I came across a rare combination of the hip, the grungy and the refined stacked right on top of one another. At the SXSW screenings, they served meals in the cinema; instead of previews, they showed 16mm PSAs from the 1970s. The local audience was savvy and diverse. Oddly, I felt right at home; for me, it recalled Soho and Tribeca in New York, the West End in London, and even the warmth and laid-back culture of the Middle East. Austin feels like a compact intersection of places I've known. ■ **Filmmaker Vineet Dewan (*Clear Cut, Simple*)**

Keeping Jeff Buckley Alive

During their rare acoustic performance on the SXSW Day Stage, Scott Rinning and Ramsay Miller, the two frontmen from Glasgow band the Cinematics, had explained that their career began busking on the streets of Glasgow, and that when they were feeling adventurous, they would feature Jeff Buckley's rich and complex music, with Rinning also explaining how Buckley's music had been a great influence on them. As a finale, the pair performed a haunting, pitch-perfect rendition of Buckley's song "Grace."

As the lads stepped off the stage, they were approached by two ladies, one of whom announced that she would like to introduce them to her friend, Mary Guibert, mother of Jeff Buckley. It took just a split second for this to register, and the enormity of what this meant was immediately apparent as both were drawn to tears. Guibert stood calmly, beaming at the two young maestros before saying that their performance had made her shudder and stopped her in her tracks. She had been in the conference hall alongside the Day Stage when her friend overheard the rendition and rushed her into the room to listen.

Rinning was so overwhelmed he had to disappear to the dressing room, unable to contain his emotions, while Miller composed himself and continued chatting. Guibert continued, praising their performance and appreciating how artists and fans are managing to keep Buckley's spirit alive and strong. ■ **Andy Sheppard, London, U.K.**

All Things Are Possible

James Hetfield called it "the worst kept secret in rock & roll history." For the lucky few who witnessed Metallica's creeping death at Stubb's in 2009, it was perhaps the ultimate example of the SXSW Music Conference's promotional magnitude. I'll never forget it: the Four Horsemen of thrash metal, up close and personal, for 80 colossal minutes of apocalyptic bliss.

In a year when even Kanye West and Jane's Addiction unofficially crashed the party, that was hardly the only celebratory moment, though. Looking back at my personal calendar from that four-day stretch, the names, dates and places don't seem to add up: Primal Scream's acid-house dementia at La Zona Rosa and the spirit-folk of Wovenhand at Spiro's Amphitheater (both of those after the Metallica electrocution); Here We Go Magic and J Tillman silencing Mohawk; French diva Yelle and Titus Andronicus at Maggie Mae's; the Dicks scorching the Austin Music Hall with David Yow; and Girls indoors at Emo's.

Japan's heavy-psych Zen masters, Flower Travellin' Band, were in a league of their own. The group's transcendent 1971 LP *Satori*, a five-part, Far Eastern meditation on classic rock mythology, remains one of my favorite albums of all time. Never did I once consider the possibly of seeing it performed live. That's a large part of the reason why I'll always feel indebted to SXSW: It's a place where the impossible, or at least the completely unexpected, becomes reality. ■ Austin Powell, music columnist for *The Austin Chronicle*

Seeking Sustainability At SXSW

A few short minutes into our panel, someone in the back accidentally switched off half the lights. Rather than accept the apology as a disturbance, Perry Farrell, being the artist that he is, embraced the opportunity to start reducing our environmental impact in that moment.

The 50% reduction in light during the presentation not only reduced our footprint by demonstration but also changed the atmosphere, making it more comfortable for everyone in the room. It's amazing how as a society, we deliver what we think is appropriate, and we accept what is provided for us without question. It struck me during this panel how important it is for us to communicate and use creative solutions to reduce our impact...to question the industry standards. Do we really need all that light?

We also talked in detail regarding SXSW's move toward sustainability in 2007. Una Johnston spoke eloquently of the methodology behind going carbon neutral not just as an event but as a global organization. I helped the audience to understand the ever-confusing world of carbon management, renewable energy credits, and carbon offsets. Rick Farman, of Bonnaroo, showed us that we have power with our events to facilitate change by insisting that vendors utilize innovative technologies. It was amazing to see not only representatives from the largest festivals in the country, but the founders, chief operating officers and other leaders, all present and looking to make a difference. ■ **Neil Turley, moderator of 2007's "Greening The Entertainment Industry" panel**

More Magic On The Day Stage

Knowing that I would miss Robyn Hitchcock's main showcase [in 2007], I made a point to catch his set at the Day Stage in the convention center. I've seen him many times before and knew what to expect, so I saw this as just a way to pass a pleasant half-hour. I was wrong, though – instead of his usual acid pop musings, Hitchcock accompanied author/producer Joe Boyd. As Boyd would read excerpts from his autobiography _White Bicycles_, Hitchcock would perform a period-relevant song. Hearing Hitchcock perform songs by Nick Drake, Syd Barrett and the Incredible String Band as enhancement to Boyd's fascinating stories was an unexpected treat. ■ Michael Toland, _High Bias, LiveJournal_ editor

This Land Was Made For You And Me

There was a desire and passion inside me to get out of the situation that our country had trapped us in. I wanted (and still want) only to play music. Before participating in SXSW, we had toured in Europe, but SXSW was something else. Symbolically, it was like a "Freedom" for me!

Rewards include opening new views for us, bringing hope, meeting lots of new people, and media talking about us. More rewards are great energy, positive feedback and appreciations that we get from the world, because of what we went through just for playing music.

Although still my original band members are trapped (back in Iran), we keep this hope alive that SXSW will save them too. ■ **Arash Rahbary, bassist-vocalist, TarantisT (Tehran, Iran)**

"Would You Be An Outlaw For My Love..."

A few weeks ago, my teenage son was in the throes of apocalyptic heartbreak. His girlfriend had broken up with him, and they were having frequent and painful electronic exchanges about it. After a particularly difficult instant-message conversation, he sat in our darkened living room with an anguished look on his face. I was sitting with him, doing what I do – trying to make him feel better with, you know, words – and failing miserably.

So I finally asked: "Want to hear a song that's about exactly how you feel right now?" Sure, he said, and I pulled out Big Star's "Thirteen." For my green, "Thirteen" is the best expression of teenage heartbreak there is. And yet I was hesitant about trotting it out because "Thirteen" is a quiet acoustic ballad and my son's tastes trend toward nasty, aggressive metal. Still...it just melted him (and me, too). He must've played it a dozen times that night, and he sent it to a bunch of friends. The girl, too. Didn't solve anything, of course, and they're still broken up. But it made both of us feel better. One takes redemption where one finds it.

So why am I telling you this now? Because Jody Stephens, Big Star's drummer, was in Austin for South by Southwest this week, I was able to share this story with him – and he was visibly moved. I could tell it made his day, and it kind of made

mine, too. And it's exactly this sort of connection, with music and the people who make it and love it, that keeps me coming back down here after 22 years.

For all the snide complaints you hear about SXSW, there's still no better place to get back in touch with one's inner fan of music and passion and life — for me, anyway. It's a big, sprawling, confusing mess of bands and panel discussions and people on the move and on the make, a bewildering mob scene that's impossible to make sense of. Yet it's still the most fun I have year after year, whether stumbling across something new, flying the hometown flag or reconnecting with old favorites.
■ **David Menconi,** *Raleigh News & Observer,* **2009**

Children By The Million Sing For Alex Chilton

It was a very unusual SXSW for the Memphis Music Foundation team this year [2010]. On one hand, there were our usual amazing events: a sold-out showcase at the Dirty Dog on Thursday featuring some of Memphis' best in 8 Ball + MJG, Hill Country Revue, Lord T + Eloise, Cory Branan, Star & Micey and Harlan T. Bobo. Memphis music was performed daily at our trade show booth, and street teams worked everyday to promote our city's artists.

But on the other hand, there was the devastating news of the death of Alex Chilton on Wednesday night. Big Star had been due at our booth on Friday to promote their Saturday night show. But what an amazing thing this tragedy turned into. Attendees from around the world stopped by the Memphis booth to pay their respects to Alex, and we became the place to check on the latest on the Big Star panel on Saturday or what was happening with the tribute concert on Saturday night. It was inspiring to see the effect that Alex and Big Star had over the years on differnet generations of musicians; the SXSW community wanted to let us know how much they were appreciated, and how much Alex will be missed. It was a SXSW that Memphis Music will always remember. ■ **Dean A. Deyo, Memphis Music Foundation president**

On Austin And Alex

Austin has such a magical feel to it, so it makes sense that something like South by Southwest would happen in a place like Austin, because the city is so supportive of music. Austin is a place where even the cops, and the people who tell the cops where to get off, understand that music is important, and that it's worthwhile to create an environment where people can come and see a lot of music, get loopy and have a good time and be fairly safe.

One of the coolest things that SXSW has allowed to happen was the Alex Chilton tribute show last year [2010]. It was a really beautiful, touching thing that everybody was in one town at the same time and could spontaneously come together like that. Alex reached a lot of people, and to see the outpouring of love and affection for him and his work was really amazing. It spoke of community, in a way that hardly anything does. It was a really neat night, and it was something real that was allowed to happen because of South by Southwest. And that it could happen at a music industry event is a beautiful thing, because it's a reminder that it's an industry based on *music.* ■ **Cris Kirkwood, Meat Puppets**

Big Garage From Texas

In 2010 I attended SXSW for the first time, to host a panel and a showcase concert on English folk music. I generally try and stay away from music industry events, but SXSW was completely different from most: far more friendly, and driven by a passion for interesting music more than business. The highlight was a panel on '60s garage music followed by a showcase of original Texas garage bands that I had grown up listening to, loving and idolizing: Randy Alvey & the Green Fuz, Mouse & the Traps, and best of all, Kenny & the Kasuals. There can surely be no other industry event in the world where you can find sixty-something, Stetson-wearing, former garage dudes playing their hearts out for a small audience of friends, family, and the odd English garage obsessive. The parties, the talks, and the big concerts were fun too, but for me, SXSW was all about music from the fringes being celebrated. ■ **Will Hodgkinson, journalist/ author, London, U.K.**

The Church, The Park, And Other Things

I've had some amazing experiences in the 17 or 18 years I've been going to SXSW, playing with the Continental Drifters and then with my own band. But I think my favorite year was 2008, when the Cowsills came to play SXSW for the first time.

The venue we got — the Central Presbyterian Church — was perfect. The acoustics were awesome, and it was appropriate because my brothers first started singing in church as choirboys. They got a very warm, sweet, gracious reception, and it

was such a special show. I'll never forget looking out and seeing all of our friends sitting in the pews. Then on Saturday morning, my brothers and I got up early to sing with the Allen Oldies Band at the Continental Club, which was a lot of fun.

But the best, best part of the whole week was the softball tournament on Sunday. My brothers Bob and Paul, my husband Russ Broussard, and our bass player Tad Armstrong and Bob's son Ryan all played. My brothers Bob and Paul were both major jocks in their youth, and Paul actually could have had a professional baseball career. And they're both ex-partiers, so unlike most of the musicians in town, they weren't all hung over on Sunday morning.

I think the musicians' team finished in third place, which I believe was a historic achievement. Not only that, but my brother Paul got the Most Valuable Player trophy. So of all of my SXSW adventures, I think my most satisfying achievement may have been to bring my boys to SXSW and have them ring in a victory for the musicians' team. ■ **Susan Cowsill, Continental Drifters/Cowsills**

A Princely Premiere

About 10 years ago, a friend was building an addition on her house in Austin, and she told me that I should meet the contractor who had made movies with Martin Scorsese. I told her he was lying to her. After months of prodding, I agreed to go over there. As soon as the contractor turned around and spoke, I recognized him. It was Steven Prince, a.k.a. Easy Andy, the gun salesman from *Taxi Driver* and the subject of Martin Scorsese's lost documentary *American Boy*. We were both living in Austin at the time, so it was fitting to premiere the film at SXSW. Having Steven there to present both films was great; he said, "Ya, it was a great experience. First of all to see *American Boy* on the big screen and such a very good copy was fantastic. Then *American Prince* put that time period of American film in clear perspective." It was a great return to home for both of us, and we were both very proud to be part of a festival with so many talented filmmakers. ■ **Tommy Pallotta, director of *American Prince* (2009)**

Still Working After All These Years

This SXSW [2007] was another lovely confab of old friends, new acquaintances and great music. I was proud to sit next to Donovan at the BMI songwriters' panel and be regaled by tales of Swinging London. I enjoyed seeing kids playing in the Lego morass at the bottom of the escalators. I cruised through Flatstock, amazed at the phenomenal talent in the poster world today. Mostly, I was thrilled to see that so many of the folks that I 'came up with' in this business are still at work, trying to get good music to unsuspecting ears, be they musicians, writers, publicists or managers. ■ Peter Holsapple, musician

The View From Malta

Performing three times at SXSW in the past six years gave us as a band the amazing opportunity to experience all of the following things at once: Austin, Texas, with its warmth, great bars and venues, margaritas and beers, and its genuine love for music; other music enthusiasts and journalists; musical heroes of ours like Lou Reed and the B-52s; European artists humbled by the grandeur of the States; and crazy Japanese bands and nights which fit in so well with the atmosphere and the mixed sounds of the festival. We also secured a licensing and publishing deal last time round so, all in all, it was a successful venture. ■ **Alison Galea, Beangrowers (Malta)**

He Who Isn't Busy Being Born...

On the last night of SXSW Interactive 2008, my friend Kevin and I made a pilgrimage to the former home of writer Bruce Sterling, whose keynote rants were a highlight of SXSW Interactive for many years, and whose free-for-all house parties were the birthplace of many personal and professional relationships. We drove around for almost half an hour before we found it. After a few minutes, we'd seen all the places where we enjoyed free beer and shared internet memes with some of the luminaries of the web. I hustled Kevin back to the car but he didn't start the ignition. He was still lost in his reverie, lamenting the fact that we haven't had a party in this house since 2004. We're grizzled veterans who met at SXSW in 2002. Between us, we've attended 17 times. I thought of joining Kevin in his melancholy mood, but instead, I reminded him that traditions die all the time, and that many people have come to SXSW for the first time in 2008. They're busy starting traditions of their own. ■ **James McNally, Toronto, Canada**

Going With The Flow

SXSW [2009] was all of the stuff that I didn't plan: the accidental encounters, the random encounters with friends or just someone in a PiL T-shirt. Trying to see photographer Paul Natkin, I ended up listening to the woman who works with Beck describing her side of the creative process with him. I had to leave this to do a book signing at Barnes & Noble and met up with Saul Williams. Walking down Sixth Street, I saw a band playing on the street with their CDs in brown paper bags; each had been meticulously typed all over in the back of their van. Then I met Kimberly from One-Eyed Doll. She was just doing it – not waiting for anyone to give her permission, really fuelling.

Sometimes the background noise (aural and psychic vibrations) of so many bands looking for a chance got to be a bit much (I picked up on all of it), like birds sitting on the telephone wires. Then after hanging out with a couple of Suicide Girls (Selket and Illyria), I accidentally saw the Victorian English Gentlemens Club drop their third show that day...they were amazing and reminded me (again) what music is really all about. I lost myself (as I think they did) in their set for 30 minutes, then was happy to buy their CD. It was all so cool I forgot I had a record label. ■ **Martin Atkins, drummer (Public Image Ltd., Ministry, et al.)**

The Kids Are Alright

If a stranger had walked up to me when I was 16 and told me that I would be playing SXSW in fewer than three years, I would not have believed them. Nor would I have believed that when my best friend and I put together a group and began recording in an old ranch house, we would be on the front end of a youth music movement. In the past year or so, organizations catering to young musicians in Austin have synthesized, coinciding with the development of several strong young Austin bands. 375 people packed Momo's for the first SXSW official underage day party, and nothing can describe the euphoria of taking the stage in front of a packed SXSW venue. ■ **Aaron Miller, El Guapos**

'Breaking Down Borders And Conquering Mountains'

For Systema Solar, SXSW was a first showing of our work outside of Colombia, and a unique opportunity to make it to the U.S.A. For Colombian artists, it is extremely hard, and many times impossible, to be granted a visa into the U.S.A. The fact that SXSW is such an important event at an international scale and because of the relentless work of SXSW, we were able to get visas for the group and performed in two showcases. To us, this felt as though we were breaking down borders and conquering mountains, as we were finally able to perform our art, share our music, our vibes, our aesthetic, our videos, our joy and spirit with a North American public. We are grateful to SXSW for this opportunity and wish the organizers success in their continuous work supporting artists from parts of the world that otherwise would not get an opportunity to perform on U.S. soil. ■ **Pata de Perro, Systema Solar (Taganga, Colombia)**

Runaway – It's Kim Fowley!

My SXSW veered drastically, though positively, from the original plan on the first day of the Music festival [2010]. In a twist of fate, while working the trade show's Canadian Blast booth, I met the infamous Hollywood record producer, Kim

South By South America

This year's SXSW [2009] brought Oxé to the U.S.A. for the first time. As soon we got onto the airplane in Sao Paulo, all of the visa, petition, equipment and money nightmares that plagued us were quickly forgotten. Our Brazilian Night showcase was amazing as the semi-crowded event turned into a huge dance floor. The Brazilians at the show cracked out all the traditional dances next to people from who knows where, who were laughing while tripping over their feet in attempts to follow along. The next day, instead of spending the day parking ourselves on our friend's couch, we got dressed and painted again and took the rhythms of maracatu, samba and frevo to Sixth Street. Armed with our Brazilian drums, we spent hours on the streets dancing and singing with the huge crowds that gathered to watch. What an experience to be in a place where people from all over the world come to watch and play music! ■ Oxé, Sao Paulo, Brazil

A Learning Experience

For me, SXSW is about the intersection of the things I love most, technology and music. This year [2010], I went to panels at both Interactive and Music that really influenced my thinking about how musicians can manage their careers and engage their fans with social media. "How the Internet is Disrupting the Concert Industry" and "Crowdfunding Music: Raising Money from your Fans" both provided data and techniques that I can begin discussing with musicians immediately. I can always count on SXSW to keep me on the cutting edge of trends and ideas. ■ Dr. Cindy Royal, Texas State University

Do Believe The Hype

It's a long way from Leigh-on-Sea, Essex, England, to Austin, Texas.

Sitting at my kitchen table in Leigh-on-Sea at the back end of 2008, I was debating whether to make the trip to SXSW Interactive. I posed the question out loud – via Twitter – and was answered by Melissa Pierce over in Chicago, who invited me to co-present her core conversation on "Living The Unplanned Life" at SXSW Interactive 2009.

Did it live up to the hype? You bet. Ideas and new thinking are at the heart of all I do; whether it's a book I'm writing or a client's business challenge, I need to keep topped up on ideas. SXSW is like one giant espresso where I can drink in all that inspiration, meet some cool people and return home, the obligatory moleskine brimming with new ideas. So it was no surprise I was back in 2010 with a new collaborator to launch our "Unplan Your Business" idea.

SXSW is full of surprises. Walking down a street one afternoon I heard the familiar sound of singer-songwriter Billy Bragg blasting through the open window of Latitude 30. Billy also hails from Essex and I've been a fan ever since I interviewed him on local radio back in the late '80s. He was in the bar sound-checking for a gig; I went in, grabbed a drink and got reacquainted. And of course it's encounters like this where the true value of SXSW lies.

In 2010, I got invited on to Zappos CEO Tony Hsieh's customized school bus for an on-board party that toured the streets and parties of Austin. Tony was the perfect host, grabbing food for us and making sure the vodkas flowed from the on-board bar. The next afternoon I was able to chat with the author Tim Ferriss at cocktail hour on an Austin rooftop, shake hands with Jason Fried, and later that night none other than Wine Guy Gary Vaynerchuk was pouring me a glass of red at another party. Where else on Planet Earth could I have met a singer-songwriter from my home county, a couple of best-selling authors, the CEO of a billion-dollar business – a bunch of people who have inspired and influenced me – all in 24 hours or so?

In my SXSW debut, the word from the festival was "awesome." That's not a word us Brits were using a lot in March 2009, but hey, by the end of my second SXSW experience, "awesome" was the only word for it. ■ Ian Sanders, ideas guy, marketing expert and author

Fowley. The next afternoon, receiving precise instructions, this indie music publicist from western Canada found herself working through red carpet flashbulbs to attend the premiere of The Runaways with Fowley, the man who created the band behind the story. It was a very fruitful year and I am connecting now with many folks who I may never have had the chance to connect with through regular business dealings! ■ Joelle May, ModMay Promotions, Calgary, Canada

'The Rise Of DJ Culture'

The whole Dubspot crew had a blast at SXSW this year [2010], from the Gear Show to our official Funk Aid party. Seeing the rise of DJ culture was especially great for us, as that is our business and why we came. From the Mad Descent carnival, to the Ancient Astronauts, to Glitch Mob, to Daedelus at the AM Only showcase, seeing and hearing about the ever-expanding representation of electronic and non-traditional music at SXSW has made us look forward to the future. We can't wait to come back and bring the Dubspot experience in a bigger way. ■ Adam Sellers, Dubspot, New York City

But Don't Give Yourself Away

Growing up in Wisconsin in the '70s, Cheap Trick were my #1 cruising music of choice, so, fast-forward 30 years later – handling a SXSW press day for them when they played the BMI Stage in 2010 was a nostalgic, near out-of-body experience. I had to really work hard to restrain the stoner high school fan that wanted to come giggling out! ■ Kay Clary, BMI senior director of media relations

What Do I Remember About SXSW?

I remember keynote speakers. In 1994, Johnny Cash – one of the most road-worthy performers of all time – was a bundle of sweaty nerves about having to make a speech to a packed ballroom of music industry hipsters. In 2005, Robert Plant told rock legend stories, like the time Led Zeppelin came off a massive world tour and realized that with too much time on their hands, they would likely piss away all their hard-earned money with the cocaine dealers of Los Angeles and New York. Instead, they hired a boat big enough to carry the band and some friends and a tiny collection of drums and amps and sailed the North Sea coast, stopping at tiny herding and fishing villages. They would dock the boat and play impromptu sets at local pubs. In 2002, Robbie Robertson talked (and talked and talked) about his entire career from A to Z.

I remember tears. In 1994, the first year of SXSW Film, a senior Film Fest staffer was curled up under a table crying. Apparently to save money on expensive film reels, we had rented exactly enough reels to handle one day of screenings. Overnight the Film Fest techs were supposed to break down - unspool and pack for shipping - an entire day of movies and build all the movies for the next day. By day two, all the film techs had called bullshit on the plan, and one lone volunteer in

white cotton gloves was frantically working nonstop trying to catch up. It was a disaster. We finally located a film supply warehouse in Boston that could ship a small supply of reels for delivery that night, and got another batch in San Antonio for the following day.

I remember rain and mud. In 1999, massive downpours had turned the scruffy grass fields at Waterloo Park into muck and mire, threatening our two days of free concerts with the likes of Fastball, Spoon, Guided By Voices and Joe Ely. We decided to try covering the park with hay, but the farmers couldn't tell us how many bales we needed to do the job. So Music Fest Production Manager Leslie Uppinghouse and I paced the park from end to end, randomly deciding that every 10 steps equaled one bale of hay. The shows went on without a hitch, but the bad news is, nobody wants your used wet muddy hay. Our solution to the problem: homeless men with pitchforks. Four words no insurance company wants to hear.

I remember Multimedia. The SXSW Interactive behemoth started as a single track of panels and seminars that launched in 1994 along with Film. It was called SXSW Multimedia – a catch-all description for the budding fields of computer gaming, video entertainment, and a mysterious new thing called the world wide web.

I remember cheap hotels. These days a Four Seasons room costs $420 a night during SXSW, but back in the day that same room was just $99. And you could stay downtown for as little as $40. Those days are long gone.

I remember the craziness of the great internet boom. Startups were loaded down with venture capital that they had to spend to qualify for their next round of funding. We had companies calling to tell us how much money they needed to spend and wondering what they could buy for that. Good times.

I remember Twitter. I laughed in 2007 when I heard a brand-new company was ramping up their service at SXSW Interactive. Multiple computer screens would be posted around the conference, and attendees could post 140-character "tweets" to tell complete strangers where they were and what they were doing. That idea's going nowhere, I thought.

Of 25 South by Southwests, my sweaty fingerprints will be found on 21 of them. It's hard to believe the sheer volume of work produced by the incredibly tiny staffs from the old days. You had to experience firsthand the drop-dead exhaustion of the all-day, all-night, all-week sessions grinding out schedules and directories and badges. The whole massive thing was assembled by hand in the dark

Sweet Tweets From SXSW, In Absentia

Editor's note: Chicago musician Dag Juhlin, a longtime member of Poi Dog Pondering among other bands, sent out more than 100 tweets during SXSW 2009 – though he didn't actually attend. Here's a hand-picked selection, in chronological order...

> **I am going to start Tweeting from South by Southwest! (Warning: I am not attending South by Southwest this year...Please enjoy.)** Wed Mar 18 15:58:11 2009 via web

> **Just got handed the new CD by Punch Me, I'm Wearing A White Belt. Now I need to find some hand sanitizer.** Wed Mar 18 16:16:24 2009 via web

> **DUDES! Just formed a group with Jack White! We're called The Janitors Of The Blues. I kick a crate and sing lead. Showcase gig tonight @9PM.** Wed Mar 18 16:21:36 2009 via web

> **Thought I ordered a pork taco, wound up accidentally proposing to the waiter. Good news: he accepted!** Wed Mar 18 16:30:09 2009 via web

> **Holy Fuck! Surprise reunion gig for the original Harmonicats! Crowd going apeshit! A stampede! Tears! "Sabre Dance" is KILLING!** Wed Mar 18 16:36:09 2009 via web

> **Austin Chronicle says "Dag Juhlin slouches into town toting a vast, well-earned obscurity." Hope that sells tix 4 my showcase 2nite!** Thu Mar 19 12:03:07 2009 via web

> **Good news – I am riding in Chris Cornell's limo! Bad news – I am in the trunk.** Thu Mar 19 12:13:08 2009 via web

> **Getting psyched for my showcase tonight. Also on the bill: The Microtards, GLUNT and Short-Haired Life Partner. V. nervous!** Thu Mar 19 12:45:59 2009 via web

> **Ratio of ironic use of cowboy hats to un-ironic use of cowboy hats: 3 to 1.** Thu Mar 19 15:04:43 2009 via web

> **Hey, anyone know where I can find a determined young band in giant sunglasses handing out their CD? Oh, wait, here are 6,000 of them.** Thu Mar 19 16:01:15 2009 via web

> **Help! Can anyone out there forward me Wavy Gravy's cellphone number. I need to talk to him about a possible show.** Thu Mar 19 17:33:10 2009 via web

> **Hey! Think I might have picked up some VD last night (long story; yes, drinks involved) anyone know a good doctor/v. fast cure? thx.!** Sat Mar 21 17:11:23 2009 via web

> **Things still going strong. No one seems tired whatsoever. Prepared for at least six more nights of this stuff. Let's do it, Austin.** Sun Mar 22 00:36:58 2009 via web

> **You ever hear the rumor that the cops down here in Austin will sell you pot? It's TRUE, and it's GREAT pot. Ask any one of them.** Sun Mar 22 00:43:38 2009 via web

> **Great panels on the last day: That One Record Label Guy Will Never Call You, How To Quit Music, and How To Find The Austin Airport.** Sun Mar 22 09:24:59 2009 via web

> **Didn't get signed? : - (Career options: 1. Blogger 2. Unspecified "green" job 3. Typewriter repair 4. Surly barista 5. Stay-at-home-son** Sun Mar 22 12:28:24 2009 via web ■ **Dag Juhlin, musician**

of night. We were the shoemaker elves of the entertainment world. People don't really understand all the moving parts and nonstop work it takes to put on an event of this magnitude. They'll ask what we do from April to December or if we've started working on next year. But we spend a lot of time looking into the future. I've got contracts signed for 2016. I carry around a calendar that's nothing but March – every March from 1987 to 2030 with the SXSW dates highlighted. That sounds crazy, but it's the world we live in.

Austin itself has been a secret weapon – it's creative and unique and not too big. People have fun here. But I think the two most important elements of SXSW's success are the decision to be an international event from day one, and the practice of producing the best possible event with the smallest possible budget. The former is what brought us good times, and the latter is what got us through the rough times.

Sometimes lack of sleep leaves you punch-drunk during SXSW. It's hard to tell whether you're experiencing a transcendent moment or you're just exhausted. My best SXSW moments: real or hallucinated – who knows? Nick Lowe with an acoustic guitar singing "What's So Funny 'Bout Peace, Love, And Understanding" with heartbreaking sincerity while bad, bad shit was going on in the world outside. Taking my sons Connor and Mason to an Iggy Pop show, or my wife Toni to see World Party. Meeting my heroes like Kris Kristofferson, Little Richard, Elvis Costello, Spike Lee, Pete Townshend and a slew of others.

From Worst To First

From 1995 to 2008, the Mighty Minions had won all of two games in the South by Southwest Softball Tourney. Granted, we mostly fielded a team of overworked, exhausted and hungover SXSW volunteers and staffers who didn't have the fresh legs or clean livers of the "in bed by 11pm" Print Media or Talent Buyer teams. Every year we stunk up the field.

If we somehow managed to beat the hapless Musicians, another team was waiting in the wings to give us a drubbing. After getting sent home in the first round of the 2008 tourney, the Minions turned things around. The core SXSW staffers began practicing and playing city league softball in the summer. The team got better and made it to the finals of the SXSW 2009 softball tourney, only to get crushed by Print Media in the final game.

Print Media gloated all summer of '09, but we kept practicing and playing so we could avenge our loss and rub their ink-stained noses in it. At the 2010 tournament, we came prepared: no booze the night before (well, not much), and a required five hours of sleep. We rolled through the first two games, but still had to overcome the reigning champs and the snarky banter of the commentators in the final match. We prepared for a close game, but it was nothing of the sort: The Mighty Minions dominated from the start and punished Print Media so bad the commissioner claimed she forgot to write down the score. The 2010 softball champs went from worst to first. ■ Darin Klein, SXSW director of special projects and team captain of the Mighty Minions

Maybe the finest moment was standing on the balcony of the Hyatt Presidential Suite at sunrise after the final night of an especially grueling SXSW. The city across the river was lit a brilliant red. We had survived and thrived a week of noisy chaos, and it was just another quiet Sunday morning in Austin, Texas. Roland Swenson, Una Johnston and I took in the spectacle, drank a whiskey toast to a job well done, and started talking about next year. ■ Mike Shea, SXSW executive planner

Lord Of The Key Rings

During SXSW, senior director Nick Barbaro spends most of his time in the little room behind registration that we call "Directors' Hell." Most of the work there is authorizing comps the staff needs to give out to people who didn't fill out their paperwork in time – press, speakers and the like.

One year the lanyards we'd ordered for the badges inexplicably came with small round key rings attached to the clip. The badge-making crew didn't like them, because it made it harder to attach the badges, so they began removing them and tossing them aside. Nick is notorious for not wanting to waste anything, and there are too many stories to count about him rescuing supplies, food, cigarette butts and other refuse he deemed still worthy of use.

So when Nick began connecting the round key rings into long, long chains, no one took much notice. By the second day, he had begun connecting the strips of key rings together to form a chain-mail fabric. By the third day, he had made a chain-mail vest, which he wore proudly. He took measurements, and tailored a few more for staffers who were puzzled, but professed to want one, too.

Sadly, by the fourth day, well into an experiment to add sleeves to the vests, he ran out of key rings. ■ Roland Swenson, SXSW managing director

Ozomatli at Auditorium Shores (2007)

Van Morrison at La Zona Rosa (2008)

R.E.M.'s Michael Stipe at Stubb's (2008)

Isaac Hayes, William Bell, Eddie Floyd at Stax 50 Revue at Antone's (2007)

‹ Pete Townshend at the Convention Center (2007)

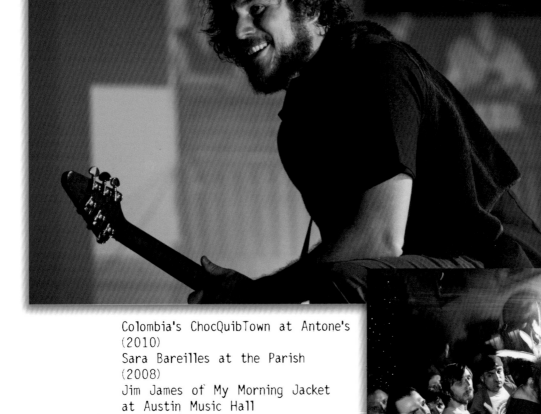

Colombia's ChocQuibTown at Antone's
(2010)
Sara Bareilles at the Parish
(2008)
Jim James of My Morning Jacket
at Austin Music Hall
(2008)
Saul Williams at Vice
(2008)

Spoon's Britt Daniel at Stubb's (2010)

Devo's Mark Mothersbaugh at Austin Music Hall (2009)

‹ The Circle Jerks' Keith Morris at Emo's (2009)

Quincy Jones at the keynote (2009)

continued from page 232

The Twang Dudes
The Twelves
The Twenty Twos
The Twilight Sad
The Twilight Singers
The Twist Offs
The Twistin' Tarantulas
The Two Dollar Pistols
The Tyde
The Ugly Beats
The Uglysuit
The Unband
The Unconscious
The Underbosses
The Unfinished Sympathy
The Unholy Two
The Uninvited
The United Steel Workers of Montreal
The Unsane
The Unseen
The Unthanks
The Upper Crust
The Upsidedown
The Uptown Bums
The Upwelling
The Urge
The Urge
The Urgencies
The Urgency
The Urges
The Used
The Vacancies
The Vacation
The Valentine Killers
The Valley Arena
The Van Buren Wheels
The Van Goghs
The Van Pelt
The Vanguards
The Vanishing
The Veils
The Velour Motel
The Velvet Teen
The Vents
The Venue
The Verve Pipe
The Very Best
The Vexers
The Via Satellites
The Vibro Champs
The Victorian English Gentlemens Club
The Vidalias
The Village Green
The Vines
The Violets
The Virgins
The Von Bondies
The Voom Blooms
The Vulgar Boatmen
The Waco Brothers
The Waifs
The Wailin' Jennys
The Wailin' Yeahs
The Wailing Wall
The Waistcoats
The Waiting Hurt
The Waking Eyes
The Waking Hours
The Walking Dead
The Walk-Ins
The Walkmen
The Wallflowers
The Walls
The Waltons
The Wannabes
The War Against Sleep
The Warlocks
The Warriors ATX
The Washdown
The Watchman
The Watson Twins
The Wave Pictures
The Waxwings
The Way Outs
The Waybacks
The Wayne Kamin Jazz Ensemble
The Way-Outs
The Weakerthans
The Weather Underground
The Webb Brothers
The Webb Sisters
The Weeds
The Week That Was
The Weepies
The Weird Lovemakers
The Weird Weeds
The Weirding
The West Seventies
The West Side Horns
The Westbury Squares
The Western Civilization
The Wet Secrets
The Whigs
The Whip
The Whispertown 2000
The White Stripes
The Whitsundays
The Why Store
The Wichdoctors & the Imperial Monkeys
The Wickers
The Wiggins
The Wild Cards
The Wilders
The Wildhearts
The Willowz
The Windbreakers
The Winks
The Winnerys
The Winter Pageant
The Wishniaks
The Witches
The Witnesses
The Wives
The Woes
The Woggles
The Wombats
The Wonderbreads
The Wong Boys
The Wontons
The Wooden Birds
The Wooden Sky
The Woods
The Wooldridge Brothers
The World Provider
The WPP
The Wrens
The Wrights
The Wronglers
The Wynona Riders
The xx
The XYZ Affair
The Yardbirds
The Yayhoos
The Yellow Dogs
The Yoko Casionos
The Young
The Young Knives
The Young Republic
The Young Veins
The Youngblood Brass Band
The Yo-Yo's
The Yuppie Pricks
The Zebras
The Zeros
The Zico Chain
The Ziggens
The Zimmermans
The Zincs
The Zipper
The Zutons
The50Kaitenz
Thea Gilmore
THEART
thebrotheregg
TheDeathSet
Thee Armada
Thee Fine Lines
Thee Headliners
Thee Misfitz
Thee More Shallows
Thee Oh Sees
Thee Shams
Thee Vicars
Them Wranch
Themselves
Themselves w/ DJ Thanksgiving Brown
Theodore
Theophilus London
Theoretical Girl
Theory of a Deadman
Theresa Andersson
Thermo
Theryl "Houseman" DeClouet
These Are Powers
These Are They
These Arms Are Snakes
These New Puritans
These United States
Thesis
theSTART
They Eat Their Young
They Might Be Giants
They Shoot Horses Don't They
Thieves Like Us
Thighmaster
Thin Lizard Dawn
Thine Eyes Bleed
Things That Go Pop!
Think About Life
Third Eye Blind
Third Eye Reggae Band
Third Language
Third Leg
Third Stone
Thirteen
Thirteen Senses
Thirteen XIII
Thirty Ought Six
Thirty-two Frames

The xx (2010)

This Bike is a Pipe Bomb
This Busy Monster
This Day Forward
This Drama
This Is Me Smiling
This Is My Condition
This Microwave World
This Moment In Black History
This Will Destroy You
Thisway
Thomas & Sampson
Thomas Denver Jonsson
Thomas Dolby
Thomas Dybdahl
Thomas Function
Thomas Hargrove
Thomas Hart
Thomas Jefferson Slave Apartments
Thomas Mapfumo & the Blacks Unlimited with Wadada Leo Smith and N'Da Kulture
Thomas Piper
Thomas Sahs
Thon-gya!
Those Bastard Souls
Those Darlins
Those Darn Accordians!
Those Hombres
Those Magnificent Men
Those Melvins
Those Peabodys
Those Who Dig
Thou
Thoz Hombres
Thrall
Three 4 Tens
Three Blue Teardrops
Three Cent Stomp
Three Merry Widows
Three Mile Pilot
Three On A Hill
Three Walls Down
Thrice
Thrift Store Cowboys
Thrillbilly
Thriving Ivory
Throat
Throttle Back Sparky
Throttlerod
Through the Sparks
Throw
Throw Me The Statue
Throw Rag
Throwdown
Throwing Muses
Thrush Hermit
Thunder Power
Thunderbirds are Now!
Thunderfoot
Thunderheist
Thunderin' Hearts
Thunderlip
Thuringian Alphorns
Thurogood Wordsmith
Thurston Moore
Thurston Moore Instrumental
Thurston Moore w/ Band
Tia Carrera
Tides Of Man
Tierra Tejana
Tiffany & the Gospel Motions
Tiffany Anders
Tift Merritt
Tig Notaro
Tiger
Tiger Lou
Tiger Saw
Tiger! Shit! Tiger! Tiger!
Tiger! Tiger!
TigerBeat
Tigercity
Tigersapien.
Tight Phantomz
Tijuana Hercules
Til We're Blue or Destroy
Tilly and the Wall
Tim Brantley
Tim Carroll
Tim Cohn
Tim Easton
Tim Fite
Tim Garon
Tim Gibbard
Tim Keegan (Departure Lounge)
Tim Lee
Tim Mech's Peep-Show
Tim Miner
Tim O'Brien
Tim O'Reagan
Tim William & The Arcade Stars
Tim Williams
timandEric.com
Timber Timbre
Timbuk 3
Timbuktu & Chords
Timco
Time & A Half
Time Fly's
Times New Viking
Timonium
Timothy "Speed" Levitch
Timothy Mason
Timothy "Speed" Levitch & the Ongoing Wow
Tin Hat Trio
Tina and the B-Side Movement
Tina Dico
Tina Lear
Tina Marsh and CO2
Tina Rae
Tina Schlieske
Tinco
Tinsel Teeth
Tinted Windows
Tiny Animals
Tiny Hat Orchestra
Tiny Lights
Tiny Lights
Tiny Masters of Today
Tiny Steps
Tiny Vipers
Tio Manuel
Tippi
Tish Hinojosa
Tita Lima
Titan Go King's
Title Tracks
Tito & Tarantula
Tito Menchaca
Tittsworth
Titus Andronicus
Tiye Phoenix
Tizzy Bac
T-Minus
T-Minus Band
T-Model Ford
T-Nice
To Live And Die In LA
To My Surprise
To Rococo Rot
Toad the Wet Sprocket
Toast
Tobacco
Tobias Fröberg
Tobias Thomas
Toby Anderson Band
Toby Lightman
Toby Slater
Tocotronic
Today is the Day
Todd
Todd Barry
Todd Deatherage
Todd Snider
Todd Snider & the Nervous Wrecks
Todd Thibaud
Todd Walker
Todd Walker Band
Toddle
Todosantos
Toenut
Toho Ehio
Toki Wright
Tokyo Elektron
Tokyo Nites
Tokyo Police Club
Tokyo Rose
Tokyo Sex Destruction
Tolchock Trio
Tolidos
Tolpuddle Martyrs
Tom Armstrong
Tom Baxter
Tom Brosseau
Tom Cary
Tom Clelland
Tom Daily
Tom Faulkner
Tom Freund
Tom Hickox
Tom House
Tom Kimmel
Tom Leach
Tom McRae
Tom Pacheco
Tom Prasada-Rao
Tom Principato
Tom Russell
Tom Russell and Andrew Hardin
Tom Vek
Tom Waits
Tom Wilson
Tom Wood
Tom Wood
Tomas Ramirez
Tomas Ramirez (Jazzmanian Devils)
Tomas Rivera
TOMBS
Tombstone Trailerpark
Tommie Sunshine
Tommy Eglin
Tommy Eiskes
Tommy Eiskes Band
Tommy Elgin
Tommy Elskes
Tommy Flake
Tommy Floyd Band
Tommy Guerrero
Tommy Jay
Tommy Jay/Mike Rep
Tommy Keene
Tommy M. Gomez
Tommy Pierce
Tommy Pierce & the Personals
Tommy Price & the Personals
Tommy Reilly
Tommy Sands
Tommy Sands with Vedran Smailovic
Tommy Shane Steiner
Tommy Tee
Tommy Tutone
Tommy Womack
Tomorrow's Friend.
Tomovsky
Tone (DC)
Tone (Denmark)
Tongue
Toni Price
Toni Price Band
Toni Ringgold
Tonic
Tony Bell & Kutchie
Tony Bennett
Tony Campise
Tony Carey
Tony Coleman Band
Tony Conrad
Tony Joe White
Tony Moore
Tony Morley
Tony Perez
Tony Scalzo
Tony Scherr
Tony Sly
Tony Teardrop
Too Solid Flesh
Toof
Toots and the Maytals with Special Guests (Rachael Yamagata & Charlie Mars)
Roots Rock Society
Top Notch
Topaz
Toqui Amaru
Tora! Tora! Torrance!
Torch
Torche
Torcher
Tori Amos
Torngat
Toro Y Moi
Torrez
Tosca
Tosca String Quartet
Tosca String Quartet + Lambchop
Toshi Reagon
Tosin & the ScrewShop
Total Abuse
Totally Michael
Totally Radd!!
Totimoshi
Toubab Krewe
Touchcandy
Tow Down
Towed Up
Towers of London
Townes Van Zandt
Townies
Toxic Reasons
Toy Horses
Toy Selectah!
Toyacoyah
Trachtenburg Family Slideshow Players
Tracie Lynn
Tracie Morris' Words & Music
Track 10
Track Star
Trackademicks
Tracker
Tracy & the Hindenburg Ground Crew
Tracy Bonham
Tracy Bonham Group
Tracy Lawrence
Tracy Nelson
Tracy Santa
Tracy Shedd
Trae
Trae & SLAB
Trae Tha Truth
Tragedy, A Metal Tribute to the Bee Gees
Trail of Dead
Trailer Bride
Trailer Hitch
Train
Trainwreck Ghosts
Trainwreck Riders
Tralala
Trampled by Turtles
Trance Farmers
Trances Arc
Trans Am
Transfer
Transfixr
Transformer Lootbag
Transistor Sound & Lighting Co.
Translator
Transmatic
Transportation
Trapeze
Trash Can Sinatras
Trash Fashion
Trash Talk
Travie McCoy and the Lazarus Project
Travis County Pickin'
Travoltas
Tre Hardson
TRE9
Treasure Fingers
Treat Her Right
Treaty Of Paris
Treble Charger
Tree Wave
Treetop Flyers
Trek Life
Trembling Bells
Trembling Blue Stars
Tremor
Tremors
Trendsettin' DJ Knowledge
Trent Dabbs
Trent Durham
Tres
Tres Chicas
Trespassers William
Trevor Hall
Trevor Lissauer and the Glass Plastiks
Trevor Menear
Trey Brown
Trey God
Trey Lopez
Triangle
Tribal Nation
Tribal Opera
Tribe
Tribe 8
Tribe After Tribe
Tribe Nunzio
Tribe of Gypsies
Tribeca
Tribu de Ixchel
Tricia Mitchell
Tricia Walker
Trick Pony
Tricky
Triclops!
Trigger Happy
Trik Trax
Trillbass
Trinidad Pan Masters
Trio Erik Marchand
Trip Shakespeare
Trip the Spring
Triple Cobra
Triple Fast Action
Triple R Threat
TripleWide
Tripping Daisy
Trish Murphy
Trish Murphy Band
Tristan Perich
Tristan Prettyman
Tristan Psionic
Tristeza
Triumph of Gnomes
Trivium
Trmens
T-Roc
Trojan Country Club
Trolley
Trombone Shorty & Orleans Avenue
Trona
Trouble Dolls
Troubled Hubble
Troublemaker
Trout Fishing in America
Troy Campbell
Troy Dillinger
Troy Dillinger & Del Dragons
Troy Olsen
Troy Young Campbell
Truckasauras
True Believers
True Infidels
True Nature
True Widow
Trunk Federation
Truth Decay
Truth Universal
TRUTHLiVE
Tsk Tsk
TSOL
TsuShiMaMiRe
TTC
Tuatara
Tub Ring
TubeTop
Tublatanka
Tucker B's
Tucker Livingston
Tucker Rountree Sound
Tuesday's Child
Tuh-nie
Tuh-nie & Gnaws
Tullycraft
Tulsa (CA)
Tulsa (MA)
Tum Tum
Tummler
Tuner
Tungsten Coil
Tunji
Tunng
Turbo
Turbo A.C.'s
Turbo Fruits
Turbogeist
Turbonegro
Turbowolf
Turing Machine
Turmoil in the Toybox
Turn
Turn Me On Dead Man
Turntable Bay
Turtle
Turtleheads
Turzi
Tutu Jones
TUULI
Tuxedo Killers
TV Carnage
TV Fifty
TV Ghost
Tv On The Radio
TV Smith
TV Torso
TV/TV
Twang Twang Shock-a-Boom
Tweak Bird
Tweaker
Twenty Mondays
Twice Wilted
Twilight Hotel
Twin Atlantic
Twin Crystals
Twin Sister
Twin Tigers
Twin-A
Twine
Twinemen
Twinstar
Twist of Fate
Twist-1
Twisted Hippy Children
Two Cow Garage
Two Dollar Bash
Two Dollar Guitar
Two Fresh
Two Gallants
Two Guy Trio
Two Headed Dog
Two High String Band
Two Hoots & a Holler
Two Hour Parking
Two Hours Traffic
Two Man Advantage
Two Minute Sinatra
Two Minutes Hate
Two Nice Girls
Two Star Symphony
Two Ton Boa
Two Tons of Steel
Two Way Radio
TX TKO
Ty Gavin
Ty Segall
Tyler Hilton
Tyler Keith & the Preacher's Kids
Tyler Mabry
Tyler Ramsey
Tyler Read
Tyrades
Tyrant Swing
Tyrone Bowen
Tyrone Wells
Tyvek

U

U Can Unlearn Guitar
U.S. Christmas
U.S. Girls
U.S.E.
USS Friendship
Uffie
UGK
UGK Records Presents
Ugly Americans
Ugly Americans II
Ugly Casanova
Ugly Duckling
Ugly Mustard
Uh Huh Her
Ukalipthis
Ulali
Ulrich Schnauss
Ultimate Fakebook
Ultimate Force
Ultimate Power Duo
Ultrababyfat
Ultrafix
Ultramagnetic MC's
Ultrasonic
ultrasound
Ultraswiss
Ultraviolet
Ultraviolet Crown
Ultraworld
ulu
Uluteka
Ume
Umekichi
Umphrey's McGee
Unbusted
Uncle Earl
Uncle Lucius
Uncle Monk
Uncle Tupelo
Uncle Walts Band
Uncut
Undaground Assassins
Under Byen
Under the Big Top
Underdog Turntablists
Underground Garage Go Go
Underground Lovers
Underground Orchestra
understatements
Underwater Tea Party
Unexpect
Unfadeable Young Guns
Ungdomskulen
U-N-I
Unicorn Kid
Unida
Unified Tribe
Uninhabitable Mansions
Union 13
Union Youth
United States Three
Universal Honey
Universal Recovered
University
Unleashed
Unloco
Unnatural Helpers
Unni Lovlid
Unsane
Until June
Unwed Sailor
Unwound
Unwritten Law
Up Above DJ Set
Up Syndrome
Upground
Upsilon Acrux
Urinals
Ursa Major
Ursa Minor
Useless ID
Useless Playboys
User
UUVVWWZ
Uvilov
Uz Jsme Doma
Uzbegim Taronasi

V

V Roc of V Roc's Beats Productions
V.I.P.
V.I.P. - Versace Ice Platinum
V.I.P. (Philly)
Vadoinmessico
Vagenius
Vagiant
Vague Angels
Vains of Jenna
Val Emmich
Vale Rodriguez
Valeria Oliveira
Valerio Rinaldi
Valet
Valient Thorr
Valis
Vallejo
Valv
Vampire Weekend
Van Hunt
Van Morrison
Van Stone
Van Wilks
Vance Gilbert
Vancougar
Vandaveer
Vander Lee
Vandex
Vandura
Vanilla C
Vanilla Ice
Vanilla Trainwreck
Vaquero
Varnaline
Varttina
Vasallo Crab 75
Vashti Bunyan
Vaski
Vast Aire
Vaudeville
Vaughan T
Vaux
Vaz
VCR
Vedera
VEGA
Vega 4
Vegas DeMilo
Vehicular
Velella Velella
Velorum
Velouria
Veltpunch
VELVET
Velvet Hammer
Velvethead
Vendetta Red
Venice
Venice Is Sinking
Venison
Venison Whirled
Ventilader
Venus & the Idiots
Venus Flytrap
Venus Hum
Venus in Furs
Veracruz
Verbal Seed
Verbena
Verde3
The Verlaines
Vermont
Verona

continued on page 254

continued from page 253

Wanda Jackson (2010)

SXSW SPOTLIGHT

For My Father

By Brent Grulke

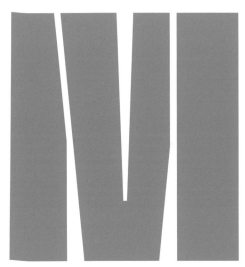 **y father, being a good father and knowing his son well,** worried about my ability to take care of myself in the music business. He casually enjoyed music and listened to commercial country radio, but never bought a record or CD and could never name more than a handful of acts whose music he liked. So I figured he'd never enjoy coming to South by Southwest much, and I didn't encourage him to. And he had never done so. But in 2007 he let me know that he'd like to "come and see what it is you do."

I found a nice hotel for him, and once he and my stepmother, Greta, arrived, I walked him around the convention center and introduced him to my friends and colleagues. I thought that would be that, and I'd catch up with him on Sunday again once the event was over.

But every time I looked up, he and Greta were there. Like all SXSW attendees, they quickly sussed out where the free food and drink was, and expected that I knew where more of it might be. They planned their schedule to see bands. Dad, being an Iowa native and not knowing any of the acts performing, decided they'd go see all the bands from Iowa. Which they did.

By Saturday they were experts, and had roped my wife and 2-year-old son into another romp around the convention center. My wife Kristen arrived after they did. When she found them, they were concerned. "Kristen," Greta worriedly asked, pointing, "Look! There's a transient in here eating pizza out of the trash! He's been going around from bin to bin eating garbage! Is there someone we should let know about this?"

Kristen looked up and burst out laughing. "That's no transient! That's Nick, he's one of the bosses here!"

Late that evening, just minutes before the adrenaline was scheduled to be withdrawn, I got a call. A doorman on Red River had punched a cop, one of the cops working with us. Both the club and the police were pissed off, I was told. I was with Roland, and we both decided we'd better quickly get headed toward the club.

So I'm hustling down the street and I see Greta and my father on Red River. This is about 1 in the morning. I can't really just run past them without saying something, so I stop and say that I'm surprised to see them, it being late and them having a perfectly nice hotel room a couple of blocks away.

"No, no son, we're having a blast. We just stopped in to see this band here." He points to Emo's. I ask him, "Er, what band did you see at Emo's?"

Dad: "Let's see. We liked them, They were really good. Energetic. We picked them because of their name...what was it, Greta?"

Greta: "Hmm. Buzz something?"

Me: "You went to see the Buzzcocks? Because you liked their name? And you enjoyed it?"

Dad: "Yes, very much. But excuse us, we've got to go, there's another band we want to see from Iowa. See you tomorrow!"

I had been thinking the strangest thing I'd encounter that night — and I'd encountered a lot of weirdness that night, as I have every night during SXSW — would be sorting out how, and why, a policeman got hit by a bouncer. Little did I know.

On Sunday, sitting at my house with my family (his grandson being, I suspect, the true bait that lured him to Austin in March), he debriefed me about the best parties he'd attended and the bands he'd seen. He paused for a minute, and quietly told me, "Son, I guess I don't have to worry about your being in the music business anymore."

My father didn't live to see another South by Southwest. ■ **Brent Grulke is SXSW's creative director.**